# CCENT
## Cisco Certified Entry
## Networking Technician
### Study Guide

# CCENT®
## Cisco Certified Entry Networking Technician
### Study Guide

Todd Lammle

SYBEX®
A Wiley Brand

Senior Acquisitions Editor: Jeff Kellum
Development Editor: Pete Gaughan
Technical Editors: John Swartz and Dennis Frye
Production Editor: Christine O'Connor
Copy Editor: Judy Flynn
Editorial Manager: Pete Gaughan
Production Manager: Tim Tate
Vice President and Executive Group Publisher: Richard Swadley
Vice President and Publisher: Neil Edde
Media Project Manager I: Laura Moss-Hollister
Media Associate Producer: Doug Kuhn
Media Quality Assurance: Marilyn Hummel
Book Designers: Judy Fung and Bill Gibson
Compositor: Craig Woods, Happenstance Type-O-Rama
Proofreaders: Sarah Kaikini and Josh Chase, Word One New York
Indexer: Robert Swanson
Project Coordinator, Cover: Katherine Crocker
Cover Designer: Ryan Sneed

Copyright © 2013 by John Wiley & Sons, Inc., Indianapolis, Indiana

Published simultaneously in Canada

ISBN: 978-1-118-74968-5
ISBN: 978-1-118-74950-0 (ebk.)
ISBN: 978-1-118-79158-5 (ebk.)

Dear Reader,

Thank you for choosing *CCENT Study Guide*. This book is part of a family of premium-quality Sybex books, all of which are written by outstanding authors who combine practical experience with a gift for teaching.

Sybex was founded in 1976. More than 30 years later, we're still committed to producing consistently exceptional books. With each of our titles, we're working hard to set a new standard for the industry. From the paper we print on, to the authors we work with, our goal is to bring you the best books available.

I hope you see all that reflected in these pages. I'd be very interested to hear your comments and get your feedback on how we're doing. Feel free to let me know what you think about this or any other Sybex book by sending me an email at nedde@wiley.com. If you think you've found a technical error in this book, please visit http://sybex.custhelp.com. Customer feedback is critical to our efforts at Sybex.

Best regards,

Neil Edde
Vice President and Publisher
Sybex, an Imprint of Wiley

# Acknowledgments

There are many people that work to put a book together, and although as an author I dedicate an enormous amount of time to write the book, it would never be published without the dedicated, hard work of many other people.

Monica Worthy Lammle was crucial to the finished product this book has become, going over every word of every chapter with me to fine tune the language, and grammar. Without Monica's guidance and patience, I'd never have finished writing this book.

Next in line to thank was my new technical editor, John Swartz, who also co-authored the *CCNA Data Center Study Guide* with me. His expertise in the Cisco technical field, and his history of networking in general, is second to none. His detailed analysis of my work helped make this my best *CCENT Study Guide* ever. Thank you, John, for working hard under pressure, with tight deadlines, and for staying the course of delivering high-quality work in a short time frame.

Jeff Kellum, my acquisitions editor, is instrumental to my success in the Cisco world. Jeff, I look forward to our continued progress together in the Cisco certification world.

Christine O'Connor, my production editor, and Judy Flynn, my copy editor, are my rock and foundation for formatting and intense editing of every page in this book. This amazing team gives me the confidence to help me keep moving during the difficult and very long days, week after week. How Christine stays so organized with all my enormous amount of changes as well as making sure every figure is in the right place in the book is still a mystery to me! You're amazing, Christine! Thank you! Judy understands my writing style so well now, after doing at least a dozen books with me, she can tell when I made a technical error that I may have missed when previously going through the material. Thank you, Judy, for doing such a great job! I truly thank you both.

Troy McMillian: Troy has become my de facto writer, technical editor, and researcher, and he always comes through on any unreasonable deadline. I always look forward to working with Troy.

Jim Frye is my admin and student liaison at GlobalNet Training, and he was instrumental in taking my figures that I created and making them a masterpiece. Thank you, Jim!

Finally, a big thanks to Craig Woods at Happenstance-Type-O-Rama, proofreaders Josh Chase and Sarah Kaikini, indexer Robert Swanson, and to the Sybex media-development team.

# About the Author

**Todd Lammle**   is the Authority on Cisco Certification and internetworking. He is a world-renowned author, speaker, trainer, and consultant. Todd has three decades of experience working with LANs, WANs, and large licensed and unlicensed wireless networks, and lately he has been implementing large Cisco data centers worldwide. His three decades of real world experience is prevalent in his writing; he is not just an author but an experienced networking engineer with very practical experience working on the largest networks in the world. Todd has published over 60 books, including the very popular *CCNA: Cisco Certified Network Associate Study Guide, CCNA Wireless Study Guide*, and *CCNA Data Center Study Guide*, all from Sybex. He runs an international training and consulting company based in Colorado, Texas, and San Francisco.

You can reach Todd through his forum and blog at www.lammle.com.

# Contents at a Glance

# Contents

**Chapter   7**      **Managing a Cisco Internetwork**       **281**

**Appendix C      Disabling and Configuring Network Services      655**

**Appendix D      About the Additional Study Tools      667**

# Introduction

Welcome to the exciting world of Cisco certification! If you've picked up this book because you want to improve yourself and your life with a better, more satisfying and secure job, you've done the right thing. Whether you're striving to enter the thriving, dynamic IT sector or seeking to enhance your skillset and advance your position within it, being Cisco certified can seriously stack the odds in your favor to help you attain your goals!

Cisco certifications are powerful instruments of success that also markedly improve your grasp of all things internetworking. As you progress through this book, you'll gain a complete understanding of networking that reaches far beyond Cisco devices. By the end of this course, you'll comprehensively know how disparate network topologies and technologies work together to form the fully operational networks that are vital to today's very way of life in the developed world. The knowledge and expertise you'll gain here is essential for and relevant to every networking job and is why Cisco certifications are in such high demand—even at companies with few Cisco devices!

Although it's now common knowledge that Cisco rules routing and switching, the fact that it also rocks the voice, data center, and service provider world is also well recognized. And Cisco certifications reach way beyond the popular but less extensive certifications like those offered by CompTIA and Microsoft to equip you with indispensable insight into today's vastly complex networking realm. Essentially, by deciding to become Cisco certified, you're proudly announcing that you want to become an unrivaled networking expert—a goal that this book will get you well on your way to achieving. Congratulations in advance to the beginning of your brilliant future!

For up-to-the-minute updates covering additions or modifications to the Cisco certification exams, as well as additional study tools, review questions, and bonus material, be sure to visit the Todd Lammle websites and forum at www.lammle.com, www.lammlesim.com, www.lammle.com/forum, or the book's web page at www.sybex.com/go/ccentsg.

# Cisco's Network Certifications

It used to be that to secure the holy grail of Cisco certifications—the CCIE—you passed only one written test before being faced with a grueling, formidable hands-on lab. This intensely daunting, all-or-nothing approach made it nearly impossible to succeed and predictably didn't work out too well for most people. Cisco responded to this issue by creating a series of new certifications, which not only made it easier to eventually win the highly coveted CCIE prize, it gave employers a way to accurately rate and measure the skill levels of prospective and current employees. This exciting paradigm shift in Cisco's certification path truly opened doors that few were allowed through before!

Beginning in 1998, obtaining the Cisco Certified Network Associate (CCNA) certification was the first milestone in the Cisco certification climb as well as the unofficial prerequisite to each of the more advanced levels. But that changed when Cisco announced the Cisco Certified Entry Network Technician (CCENT) certification. And then in March 2013, Cisco once again proclaimed that all-new tests will be required beginning in October of the same year; now the Cisco certification process looks like Figure I.1.

**FIGURE I.1**    The Cisco Certification Path

Cisco 2013 Certification Path Announcements

 I have included only the most popular tracks in Figure I.1. In addition to the ones in this image, there are also tracks for Design, Service Provider, Service Provider Operations, and Video. Also note that the CCIE Voice certification will retire in February 2014.

The Cisco Routing and Switching (R/S) path is by far the most popular and could very well remain so, but soon you'll see the Data Center path become more and more of a focus as companies migrate to data center technologies. The Voice track also actually does provide a good job opportunity. Still, understanding the foundation of R/S before attempting any other certification track is something I highly recommend.

Even so, and as the figure shows, you only need your CCENT certification to get underway for most of the tracks. Also, note that there are a few other certification tracks you can go down that are not shown in the figure, although they're not as popular as the ones shown. You can find information on all Cisco certification tracks at www.cisco.com.

## Cisco Certified Entry Network Technician (CCENT)

Don't be fooled by the oh-so misleading name of this first certification because it absolutely isn't! Okay—maybe entry level for Cisco's certification path, but definitely not for someone without experience trying to break into the highly lucrative yet challenging IT job market! For the uninitiated, the CompTIA A+ and Network+ certifications aren't official prerequisites, but know that Cisco does expect you to have that type and level of experience before embarking on your Cisco certification journey.

All of this gets us to 2013, when the climb to Cisco supremacy just got much harder again. The innocuous-sounding siren's call of the CCENT can lure you to some serious trouble if you're not prepared, because it's actually much harder than the old CCNA ever was. This will rapidly become apparent once you start studying, but be encouraged! The fact that the certification process is getting harder really works better for you in the long run, because that which is harder to obtain only becomes that much more valuable when you finally do, right? Yes, indeed!

One important factor to keep in mind is that the CCENT requires you to only pass one exam: Interconnecting Cisco Network Devices Part I (number 100-101 exam), which this book was written for. The exam costs $150 per attempt, but is very difficult to pass! The good news is that this book will guide you step-by-step in building a strong foundation in routing and switching technologies. You really need to build on a strong technical foundation and stay away from exam cram type books, suspicious online material, and the like. They can help somewhat, but understand that you'll pass the Cisco certification exams only if you have a strong foundation and that you'll get that solid foundation only by reading as much as you can, performing the written labs and review questions in this book, and practicing lots and lots of hands-on labs. Additional practice exam questions, videos, and labs are offered on my website, and what seems like a million other sites offer additional material that can help you study.

However, there is one way to skip the CCENT exam and still meet the prerequisite required before moving on to any other certification track, and that path is through the CCNA R/S Composite exam.

## Cisco Certified Network Associate Routing and Switching (CCNA R/S)

Once you have achieved your CCENT certification, you can take the ICND2 (200-101) exam in order to achieve your CCNA R/S certification. This is now the most popular certification Cisco has by far because it's the most sought-after certification of all employers.

As with the CCENT, the ICND2 exam is also $150 per attempt—although thinking you can just skim a book and pass any of these exams would probably be a really expensive mistake! The CCENT/CCNA exams are extremely hard and cover a lot of material, so you have to really know your stuff. Taking a Cisco class or spending months with hands-on experience is definitely a requirement to succeed when faced with this monster!

Sybex is also publishing a book for the ICND2 exam. Visit www.sybex.com/go/cccnaicnd2 for details.

And once you have your CCNA, you don't have to stop there—you can choose to continue and achieve an even higher certification, called the Cisco Certified Network Professional (CCNP). There are various ones as shown in Figure I.1. The CCNP R/S is still the most popular, with Voice certifications coming in at a close second. And I've got to tell you that the Data Center certification will be catching up fast. Also good to know is that anyone with a CCNP has all the skills and knowledge needed to attempt the notoriously dreaded but coveted CCIE lab. But just becoming a CCENT/CCNA can land you that job you've dreamed about and that's what this book is all about: helping you to get and keep a great job!

Still, why take two exams to get your CCNA if you don't have to? Cisco still has the Composite exam 200-120 that, if passed, will land you with your CCENT and your CCNA R/S via only one test priced accordingly at $300. Some people like the one test approach, some people like the two-test approach, but this book will help you with either path you choose.

 For details on Sybex's CCNA Routing and Switching Study Guide, visit www.sybex.com/go/cccna_r_ssg.

## Why Become a CCENT and CCNA R/S?

Cisco, like Microsoft and other vendors that provide certification, has created the certification process to give administrators a set of skills and to equip prospective employers with a way to measure those skills or match certain criteria. And as you probably know, becoming a CCENT or CCNA R/S is certainly the initial, key step on a successful journey toward a new, highly rewarding, and sustainable networking career.

The CCENT and CCNA programs are created to provide a solid introduction not only to the Cisco Internetwork Operating System (IOS) and Cisco hardware but also to internetworking in general, making it helpful to you in areas that are not exclusively Cisco's. And regarding today's certification process, it's not unrealistic that network managers—even those without Cisco equipment—require Cisco certifications for their job applicants.

Rest assured that if you make it through the CCENT and CCNA and are still interested in Cisco and internetworking, you're headed down a path to certain success!

## What Skills Do You Need to Become a CCENT?

As stated above, to earn your CCENT, you need to pass the Interconnecting Cisco Network Devices, Part I exam, number 100-101. This exam tests a candidate for the knowledge and skills required to successfully install, operate, and troubleshoot a small branch office network.

The exam includes topics on the operation of IP data networks, LAN switching technologies, IPv6, IP routing technologies, IP services (DHCP, NAT, ACLs), network device security, and basic troubleshooting.

## What Skills Do You Need to Become a CCNA R/S?

If you already have your CCENT and want to become a CCNA in Routing and Switching, you only need to take the Interconnecting Cisco Network Devices Part 2 exam (number 200-101). This exam tests a candidate for the knowledge and skills required to successfully install, operate, and troubleshoot a small to medium-size enterprise branch network. The exam includes topics on LAN switching technologies, IP routing technologies, IP services (FHRP, syslog, SNMP v2 and v3), troubleshooting, and WAN technologies.

## How Do You Become a CCNA R/S with Just One Test?

If you don't want to take two exams and want to earn your CCNA, you have another option: passing the CCNA Composite exam (number 200-120).

The way to become a CCNA R/S is to pass one little test (CCNA Composite exam 200-120) without having to take the CCENT exam. Then—poof!—you're a CCNA R/S. Oh, but don't you wish it were that easy? True, it's just one test, but it's a whopper, and to pass it you must possess enough knowledge to understand what the test writers are saying.

I can't stress this point enough: It's critical that you have some hands-on experience with Cisco routers. If you can get a hold of some basic routers and switches, you're set; but if you can't, I've worked hard to provide hundreds of configuration examples throughout this book to help network administrators, or people who want to become network administrators, learn the skills they need to pass the CCENT and CCNA exams. In addition, a simulator called LammleSim IOS Version is available for free with the purchase of this book. This small simulator will run through all the hands-on labs found in this book—nice huh?

 For Cisco certification hands-on training with Todd Lammle, please see www.lammle.com. Each student will get hands-on experience by configuring at least three routers and two switches—no sharing of equipment!

# What Does This Book Cover?

This book covers everything you need to know to pass the CCENT (ICND1) 100-101 exam. But as I've said, taking plenty of time to study and practice with routers or a router simulator is the real key to success.

You will learn the following information in this book:

**Chapter 1: Internetworking**   You will learn the basics of the Open Systems Interconnection (OSI) model the way Cisco wants you to learn it. There are written labs and plenty of review questions to help you. Do not even think of skipping the fundamental written labs in this chapter!

**Chapter 2: Ethernet Networking and Data Encapsulation**   This chapter will provide you the Ethernet foundation you need in order to pass both the CCENT and CCNA exams. Data encapsulation is discussed in detail in this chapter as well. And as with the other chapters, this chapter includes written labs and review questions to help you.

**Chapter 3: Introduction to TCP/IP**   This chapter provides you with the background necessary for success on the exam as well as in the real world with a thorough presentation of TCP/IP. This in-depth chapter covers the very beginnings of the Internet Protocol stack and goes all the way to IP addressing and understanding the difference between a network address and a broadcast address before finally ending with network troubleshooting.

**Chapter 4: Easy Subnetting**   You'll actually be able to subnet a network in your head after reading this chapter if you really want to! And you'll find plenty of help in this chapter as long as you don't skip the written labs and review questions at the end.

**Chapter 5: VLSMs, Summarization, and Troubleshooting TCP/IP**   Here, you'll find out all about variable length subnet masks (VLSMs) and how to design a network using VLSMs. This chapter will finish with summarization techniques and configurations. As with Chapter 4, plenty of help is there for you if you don't skip the written lab and review questions.

**Chapter 6: Cisco's Internetworking Operating System (IOS)**   This chapter introduces you to the Cisco Internetworking Operating System (IOS) and command-line interface (CLI). In this chapter you'll learn how to turn on a router and configure the basics of the IOS, including setting passwords, banners, and more. Hands-on labs will help you gain a firm grasp of the concepts taught in the chapter. Before you go through the hands-on labs, be sure to complete the written lab and review questions.

**Chapter 7: Managing a Cisco Internetwork**   This chapter provides you with the management skills needed to run a Cisco IOS network. Backing up and restoring the IOS, as well as router configuration, is covered, as are the troubleshooting tools necessary to keep a network up and running. As always, before tackling the hands-on labs in this chapter, complete the written labs and review questions.

**Chapter 8: IP Routing**   This is a fun chapter because we will begin to build our network, add IP addresses, and route data between routers. You will also learn about static, default, and dynamic routing using RIP and RIPv2. Hands-on labs, a written lab, and the review questions will help you fully nail down IP routing.

**Chapter 9: Open Shortest Path First (OSPF)**   Chapter 9 dives into more complex dynamic routing by covering OSPF routing. The written lab, hands-on labs, and review questions will help you master this vital routing protocol.

**Chapter 10: Layer 2 Switching**   This chapter sets you up with the solid background you need on layer 2 switching, how switches perform address learning and make forwarding and filtering decisions. In addition, switch port security with MAC addresses is covered in detail. As always, go through the hands-on labs, written lab, and review questions to make sure you've really got layer 2 switching down!

**Chapter 11: VLANs and InterVLAN Routing**   Here I cover virtual LANs and how to use them in your internetwork. This chapter covers the nitty-gritty of VLANs and the different concepts and protocols used with VLANs. I'll also guide you through troubleshooting techniques in this all-important chapter. The hands-on labs, written lab, and review questions are there to reinforce the VLAN material.

**Chapter 12: Security**   This chapter covers security and access lists, which are created on routers to filter the network. IP standard, extended, and named access lists are covered in detail. Written and hands-on labs, along with review questions, will help you study for the security and access-list portion of the Cisco exams.

**Chapter 13: Network Address Translation (NAT)**   New information, commands, troubleshooting, and detailed hands-on labs will help you nail the NAT CCENT objectives.

**Chapter 14: Internet Protocol Version 6 (IPv6)**   This is a fun chapter chock full of some great information. IPv6 is not the big, bad scary creature that most people think it is, and it's a really important objective on the latest exam, so study this chapter carefully—don't just skim it. And make sure you hit those hands-on labs hard!

**Appendix A: Answers to the Written Labs**   This appendix contains the answers to the book's written labs.

**Appendix B: Answers to the Review Questions**   This appendix provides the answers to the end-of-chapter review questions.

**Appendix C: Disabling and Configuring Network Services**   Appendix C takes a look at the basic services you should disable on your routers to make your network less of a target for denial of service (DoS) attacks and break-in attempts.

**Appendix D: About the Additional Study Tools**   This describes the technical requirements for the digital study tools that come with this book. (Those tools are described further in the following section!)

Be sure to check the announcements section of my forum to find out how to download bonus material I created specifically for this book.

# What's Available Online?

I have worked hard to provide some really great tools to help you with your certification process. All of the following tools, most of them available at www.sybex.com/go/ccentsg, should be loaded on your workstation when you're studying for the test. As a fantastic bonus, I was able to add to the download link a preview section from my CCNA video series! Please understand that these are not the full versions, but they're still a great value for you included free with this book.

**Test Preparation Software**   The test preparation software prepares you to pass the CCENT exam. In the test engine, you'll find all the review and assessment questions from the book *plus* practice exam questions that appear exclusively among the downloadable additional study tools.

**Electronic Flashcards**   The companion study tools include electronic flashcards specifically written to hit you hard, so don't get discouraged if you don't ace your way through them at first! They're there to ensure that you're really ready for the exam. And no worries—armed with the review questions, practice exams, and flashcards, you'll be more than prepared when exam day comes!

**LammleSim IOS Version**   At www.sybex.com/go/ccentsg or www.lammlesim.com, I have provided an IOS simulator that can be used with all of the hands-on labs in this book.

**Glossary**   A complete glossary of CCENT, CCNA, and Cisco routing terms is available at www.sybex.com/go/ccentsg.

**Todd Lammle Bonus Material and Labs**   Be sure to check the announcement section of my forum at www.lammle.com/forum for directions on how to download all the latest bonus material created specifically to help you study for your CCENT exam.

**Todd Lammle Videos**   I have created a full CCNA series of videos that can be purchased in either DVD or downloadable format from www.lammlepress.com. As a bonus included with this book, the first three modules can be downloaded from the book's web page, www.sybex.com/go/ccentsg, as a preview. Although this isn't the full version, the video included with this book is over 1 hour of foundational CCNA information. This is a $99 value, so don't skip this video because it covers the internetworking objectives, TCP/IP, and subnetting, which are integral topics on the CCENT/CCNA exams.

# How to Use This Book

If you want a solid foundation for the serious effort of preparing for the CCENT ICND1 100-101 exam, then look no further. I've spent hundreds of hours putting together this book with the sole intention of helping you to pass the CCENT exam as well as really learn how to correctly configure Cisco routers and switches!

This book is loaded with valuable information, and you will get the most out of your studying time if you understand why the book is organized the way it is.

So to maximize your benefit from this book, I recommend the following study method:

1. Take the Assessment Test that's provided at the end of this introduction. (The answers are at the end of the test.) It's okay if you don't know any of the answers; that's why you bought this book! Carefully read over the explanations for any question you get wrong and note the chapters in which the material relevant to them is covered. This information should help you plan your study strategy.

2. Study each chapter carefully, making sure you fully understand the information and the test objectives listed at the beginning of each one. Pay extra-close attention to any chapter that includes material covered in questions you missed.

3. Complete the written labs at the end of each chapter. (Answers to these appear in Appendix A.) Do *not* skip these written exercises because they directly relate to the CCENT exam and what you must glean from the chapters in which they appear. Do not just skim these labs! Make sure you completely understand the reason for each correct answer.

4. Complete all hands-on labs in the chapter, referring to the text of the chapter so that you understand the reason for each step you take. Try to get your hands on some real equipment, but if you don't have Cisco equipment available, try the LammleSim IOS Version, which you can use for the hands-on labs found only in this book. Together, these will equip you with everything you need for all your Cisco certification goals.

5. Answer all of the review questions related to each chapter. (The answers appear in Appendix B.) Note the questions that confuse you, and study the topics they cover again, until the concepts are crystal clear. And again—do not just skim these questions! Make sure you fully comprehend the reason for each correct answer. Remember that these will not be the exact questions you find on the exam, but they're written to help you understand the chapter material and ultimately pass it!

6. Try your hand at the practice exam that is exclusive to this book. The questions in this exam can be found only at www.sybex.com/go/ccentsg. And be sure to check out www.lammle.com for more Cisco exam prep questions, videos, Todd Lammle bootcamps, and more.

7. Also on the download link is the first three modules from my complete CCNA video series, which covers internetworking, TCP/IP, and subnetting. This is critical information for the CCENT exam, so make sure you don't miss out on the video preview edition!

Please understand that these are preview versions found at www.lammlepress.com. The videos on the free download link are not the full versions, but they're still a great value loaded with information.

8. Test yourself using all the flashcards, which are also found on the download link. These are brand-new and updated flashcard programs to help you prepare for the CCENT exam and a wonderful study tool!

To learn every bit of the material covered in this book, you'll have to apply yourself regularly, and with discipline. Try to set aside the same time period every day to study, and select a comfortable and quiet place to do so. I'm confident that if you work hard, you'll be surprised at how quickly you learn this material!

If you follow these steps and really study—*doing hands-on labs every single day*—in addition to using the review questions, the practice exams, the Todd Lammle video sections, and the flashcards as well as all the written labs—it would actually be hard to fail the CCENT exam. But understand that studying for the CCENT exam is a lot like getting in shape—if you do not go to the gym every day, it's not going to happen!

# Where Do You Take the Exams?

You may take the CCENT or any Cisco exam at any of the Pearson VUE authorized testing centers (www.vue.com) or call 877-404-EXAM (3926).

To register for a Cisco exam, follow these steps:

1. Determine the number of the exam you want to take. (The CCENT exam number is 100-101.)

2. Register with the nearest Pearson VUE testing center. At this point, you will be asked to pay in advance for the exam. At the time of this writing, the exam is $125 and must be taken within one year of payment. You can schedule exams up to six weeks in advance or as late as the day you want to take it—but if you fail a Cisco exam, you must wait five days before you will be allowed to retake it. If something comes up and you need to cancel or reschedule your exam appointment, contact Pearson VUE at least 24 hours in advance.

3. When you schedule the exam, you'll get instructions regarding all appointment and cancellation procedures, the ID requirements, and information about the testing-center location.

## Tips for Taking Your CCENT Exam

The CCENT exam contains about 40 to 50 questions and must be completed in 90 minutes or less. This information can change per exam. You must get a score of about 85 percent to pass this exam, but again, each exam can be different.

Many questions on the exam have answer choices that at first glance look identical—especially the syntax questions! So remember to read through the choices carefully because close just doesn't cut it. If you get commands in the wrong order or forget one measly character, you'll get the question wrong. So, to practice, do the hands-on exercises at the end of this book's chapters over and over again until they feel natural to you.

Also, never forget that the right answer is the Cisco answer. In many cases, more than one appropriate answer is presented, but the *correct* answer is the one that Cisco recommends. On the exam, you will always be told to pick one, two, or three options, never "choose all that apply." The CCENT exam may include the following test formats:

- Multiple-choice single answer
- Multiple-choice multiple answer

- Drag-and-drop
- Router simulations

Cisco proctored exams will not show the steps to follow in completing a router interface configuration, but they do allow partial command responses. For example, show config or sho config or sh conf would be acceptable. Router#show ip protocol or router#show ip prot would also be acceptable.

Here are some general tips for exam success:

- Arrive early at the exam center so you can relax and review your study materials.

- Read the questions *carefully*. Don't jump to conclusions. Make sure you're clear about *exactly* what each question asks. "Read twice, answer once" is what I always tell my students.

- When answering multiple-choice questions that you're not sure about, use the process of elimination to get rid of the obviously incorrect answers first. Doing this greatly improves your odds if you need to make an educated guess.

- You can no longer move forward and backward through the Cisco exams, so double-check your answer before clicking Next since you can't change your mind.

After you complete an exam, you'll get immediate, online notification of your pass or fail status, a printed examination score report that indicates your pass or fail status, and your exam results by section. (The test administrator will give you the printed score report.) Test scores are automatically forwarded to Cisco within five working days after you take the test, so you don't need to send your score to them. If you pass the exam, you'll receive confirmation from Cisco, typically within two to four weeks, sometimes a bit longer.

# CCENT Exam Objectives

Exam objectives are subject to change at any time without prior notice and at Cisco's sole discretion. Please visit Cisco's certification website (www.cisco.com/web/learning) for the latest information on the CCENT exam.

| Objectives | Chapter(s) |
|---|---|
| **Operation of IP Data Networks** | |
| Recognize the purpose and functions of various network devices such as Routers, Switches, Bridges and Hubs. | 1, 2 |
| Select the components required to meet a given network specification. | 1, 2 |
| Identify common applications and their impact on the network. | 1, 3 |
| Describe the purpose and basic operation of the protocols in the OSI and TCP/IP models. | 1, 3 |
| Predict the data flow between two hosts across a network. | 1, 2, 13 |
| Identify the appropriate media, cables, ports, and connectors to connect Cisco network devices to other network devices and hosts in a LAN. | 2 |
| **LAN Switching Technologies** | |
| Determine the technology and media access control method for Ethernet networks. | 2 |
| Identify basic switching concepts and the operation of Cisco switches. | 2, 10 |
| ■  Collision Domains | |
| ■  Broadcast Domains | |
| ■  Types of switching | |
| ■  CAM Table | |
| Configure and verify initial switch configuration including remote access management. | 6, 10 |
| ■  Cisco IOS commands to perform basic switch setup | |
| Verify network status and switch operation using basic utilities such as ping, telnet and ssh. | 7, 10 |
| Describe how VLANs create logically separate networks and the need for routing between them. | 11 |
| ■  Explain network segmentation and basic traffic management concepts | |

| Objectives | Chapter(s) |
|---|---|
| Configure and verify VLANs | 11 |
| Configure and verify trunking on Cisco switches | 11 |
| ▪ DTP | |
| ▪ Auto negotiation | |

**IP addressing (IPv4 / IPv6)**

| Objectives | Chapter(s) |
|---|---|
| Describe the operation and necessity of using private and public IP addresses for IPv4 addressing. | 3, 4 |
| Identify the appropriate IPv6 addressing scheme to satisfy addressing requirements in a LAN/WAN environment. | 14 |
| Identify the appropriate IPv4 addressing scheme using VLSM and summarization to satisfy addressing requirements in a LAN/WAN environment. | 5 |
| Describe the technological requirements for running IPv6 in conjunction with IPv4 such as dual stack. | 14 |
| Describe IPv6 addresses | 14 |
| ▪ Global unicast | |
| ▪ Multicast | |
| ▪ Link local | |
| ▪ Unique local | |
| ▪ eui 64 | |
| ▪ autoconfiguration | |

**IP Routing Technologies**

| Objectives | Chapter(s) |
|---|---|
| Describe basic routing concepts | 8 |
| ▪ CEF | |
| ▪ Packet forwarding | |
| ▪ Router lookup process | |
| Configure and verify utilizing the CLI to set basic Router configuration | 6, 7 |
| ▪ Cisco IOS commands to perform basic router setup | |
| Configure and verify operation status of an ethernet interface | 6 |
| Verify router configuration and network connectivity | 6, 7 |
| ▪ Cisco IOS commands to review basic router information and network connectivity | |

| Objectives | Chapter(s) |
|---|---|
| Configure and verify routing configuration for a static or default route given specific routing requirements | 8 |
| Differentiate methods of routing and routing protocols | 8 |

- Static vs. Dynamic
- Link state vs. Distance Vector
- next hop
- ip routing table
- Passive interfaces

| | |
|---|---|
| Configure and verify OSPF (single area) | 9, 14 |

- Benefit of single area
- Configure OSPF v2
- Configure OSPF v3
- Router ID
- Passive interface

| | |
|---|---|
| Configure and verify interVLAN routing (Router on a stick) | 11 |

- sub interfaces
- upstream routing
- encapsulation

| | |
|---|---|
| Configure SVI interfaces | 11 |

**IP Services**

| | |
|---|---|
| Configure and verify DHCP (IOS Router) | 7 |

- configuring router interfaces to use DHCP
- DHCP options
- excluded addresses
- lease time

| | |
|---|---|
| Describe the types, features, and applications of ACLs | 12 |

- Standard
  - Sequence numbers
  - Editing
- Extended
- Named
- Numbered
- Log option

**Network Device Security**

- Device password security
- Enable secret vs. enable
- Transport
- Disable telnet
- SSH
- VTYs
- Physical security
- Service password
- Describe external authentication methods

| Objectives | Chapter(s) |
|---|---|
| Configure and verify Switch Port Security features such as | 10 |

- Sticky MAC
- MAC address limitation
- Static / dynamic
- Violation modes
  - Err disable
  - Shutdown
  - Protect restrict
- Shutdown unused ports
- Err disable recovery
- Assign unused ports to an unused VLAN
- Setting native VLAN to other than VLAN 1

| | |
|---|---|
| Configure and verify ACLs to filter network traffic | 12 |
| Configure and verify ACLs to limit telnet and SSH access to the router | 12 |

**Troubleshooting**

| | |
|---|---|
| Troubleshoot and correct common problems associated with IP addressing and host configurations. | 5 |
| Troubleshoot and Resolve VLAN problems | 11 |

- identify that VLANs are configured
- port membership correct
- IP address configured

| | |
|---|---|
| Troubleshoot and Resolve trunking problems on Cisco switches | 11 |

- correct trunk states
- correct encapsulation configured
- correct VLANs allowed

| | |
|---|---|
| Troubleshoot and Resolve ACL issues | 12 |

- Statistics
- Permitted networks
- Direction
  - Interface

| Objectives | Chapter(s) |
|---|---|
| Troubleshoot and Resolve Layer 1 problems | 6 |

- Framing
- CRC
- Runts
- Giants
- Dropped packets
- Late collision
- Input / Output errors

# Assessment Test

1. IPv6 unicast routing is running on the Corp router. Which of the following addresses would show up with the show ipv6 int brief command?

   ```
   Corp#sh int f0/0
   FastEthernet0/0 is up, line protocol is up
     Hardware is AmdFE, address is 000d.bd3b.0d80 (bia 000d.bd3b.0d80)
   [output cut]
   ```

   A. FF02::3c3d:0d:bdff:fe3b:0d80
   B. FE80::3c3d:2d:bdff:fe3b:0d80
   C. FE80::3c3d:0d:bdff:fe3b:0d80
   D. FE80::3c3d:2d:ffbd:3bfe:0d80

2. A host sends a type of NDP message providing the MAC address that was requested. Which type of NDP was sent?

   A. NA
   B. RS
   C. RA
   D. NS

3. Each field in an IPv6 address is how many bits long?

   A. 4
   B. 16
   C. 32
   D. 128

4. To enable OSPFv3, which of the following would you use?

   A. Router(config-if)#ipv6 ospf 10 area 0.0.0.0
   B. Router(config-if)#ipv6 router rip 1
   C. Router(config)#ipv6 router eigrp 10
   D. Router(config-rtr)#no shutdown
   E. Router(config-if)#ospf ipv6 10 area 0

5. What does the command routerA(config)#line cons 0 allow you to perform next?

   A. Set the Telnet password.
   B. Shut down the router.
   C. Set your console password.
   D. Disable console connections.

**6.** Which two statements describe the IP address 10.16.3.65/23? (Choose two.)

    **A.** The subnet address is 10.16.3.0 255.255.254.0.

    **B.** The lowest host address in the subnet is 10.16.2.1 255.255.254.0.

    **C.** The last valid host address in the subnet is 10.16.2.254 255.255.254.0.

    **D.** The broadcast address of the subnet is 10.16.3.255 255.255.254.0.

    **E.** The network is not subnetted.

**7.** On which interface do you configure an IP address for a switch?

    **A.** `int fa0/0`

    **B.** `int vty 0 15`

    **C.** `int vlan 1`

    **D.** `int s/0/0`

**8.** Which of the following is the valid host range for the subnet on which the IP address 192.168.168.188 255.255.255.192 resides?

    **A.** 192.168.168.129–190

    **B.** 192.168.168.129–191

    **C.** 192.168.168.128–190

    **D.** 192.168.168.128–192

**9.** Which of the following is considered to be the inside host's address after translation?

    **A.** Inside local

    **B.** Outside local

    **C.** Inside global

    **D.** Outside global

**10.** Your inside locals are not being translated to the inside global addresses. Which of the following commands will show you if your inside globals are allowed to use the NAT pool?

```
ip nat pool Corp 198.18.41.129 198.18.41.134 netmask 255.255.255.248
ip nat inside source list 100 int pool Corp overload
```

    **A.** `debug ip nat`

    **B.** `show access-list`

    **C.** `show ip nat translation`

    **D.** `show ip nat statistics`

**11.** How many collision domains are created when you segment a network with a 12-port switch?

   **A.** 1

   **B.** 2

   **C.** 5

   **D.** 12

**12.** Which of the following commands will allow you to set your Telnet password on a Cisco router?

   **A.** `line telnet 0 4`

   **B.** `line aux 0 4`

   **C.** `line vty 0 4`

   **D.** `line con 0`

**13.** Which router command allows you to view the entire contents of all access lists?

   **A.** `show all access-lists`

   **B.** `show access-lists`

   **C.** `show ip interface`

   **D.** `show interface`

**14.** What does a VLAN do?

   **A.** Acts as the fastest port to all servers

   **B.** Provides multiple collision domains on one switch port

   **C.** Breaks up broadcast domains in a layer 2 switch internetwork

   **D.** Provides multiple broadcast domains within a single collision domain

**15.** If you wanted to delete the configuration stored in NVRAM, what would you type?

   **A.** `erase startup`

   **B.** `erase nvram`

   **C.** `delete nvram`

   **D.** `erase running`

**16.** Which protocol is used to send a destination network unknown message back to originating hosts?

   **A.** TCP

   **B.** ARP

   **C.** ICMP

   **D.** BootP

**17.** Which class of IP address provides 15 bits available for subnetting?

   **A.** A

   **B.** B

   **C.** C

   **D.** D

**18.** There are three possible routes for a router to reach a destination network. The first route is from OSPF with a metric of 782. The second route is from RIPv2 with a metric of 4. The third is from EIGRP with a composite metric of 20514560. Which route will be installed by the router in its routing table?

   **A.** RIPv2

   **B.** EIGRP

   **C.** OSPF

   **D.** All three

**19.** Which one of the following is true regarding VLANs?

   **A.** Two VLANs are configured by default on all Cisco switches.

   **B.** VLANs only work if you have a complete Cisco switched internetwork. No off-brand switches are allowed.

   **C.** You should not have more than 10 switches in the same VTP domain.

   **D.** VTP is used to send VLAN information to switches in a configured VTP domain.

**20.** Which two of the following commands will place network 10.2.3.0/24 into area 0? (Choose two.)

   **A.** `router eigrp 10`

   **B.** `router ospf 10`

   **C.** `router rip`

   **D.** `network 10.0.0.0`

   **E.** `network 10.2.3.0 255.255.255.0 area 0`

   **F.** `network 10.2.3.0 0.0.0.255 area0`

   **G.** `network 10.2.3.0 0.0.0.255 area 0`

**21.** How many broadcast domains are created when you segment a network with a 12-port switch?

   **A.** 1

   **B.** 2

   **C.** 5

   **D.** 12

**22.** If routers in a single area are configured with the same priority value, what value does a router use for the OSPF router ID in the absence of a loopback interface?

   **A.** The lowest IP address of any physical interface

   **B.** The highest IP address of any physical interface

   **C.** The lowest IP address of any logical interface

   **D.** The highest IP address of any logical interface

**23.** What protocols are used to configure trunking on a switch? (Choose two.)

   **A.** VLAN Trunking Protocol

   **B.** VLAN

   **C.** 802.1Q

   **D.** ISL

**24.** What is a stub network?

   **A.** A network with more than one exit point

   **B.** A network with more than one exit and entry point

   **C.** A network with only one entry and no exit point

   **D.** A network that has only one entry and exit point

**25.** Where is a hub specified in the OSI model?

   **A.** Session layer

   **B.** Physical layer

   **C.** Data Link layer

   **D.** Application layer

**26.** What are the two main types of access control lists (ACLs)? (Choose two.)

   **A.** Standard

   **B.** IEEE

   **C.** Extended

   **D.** Specialized

**27.** Which of the following is the best summarization of the following networks: 192.168.128.0 through 192.168.159.0?

   **A.** 192.168.0.0/24

   **B.** 192.168.128.0/16

   **C.** 192.168.128.0/19

   **D.** 192.168.128.0/20

**28.** What command is used to create a backup configuration?

    **A.** copy running backup

    **B.** copy running-config startup-config

    **C.** config mem

    **D.** wr net

**29.** 1000Base-T is which IEEE standard?

    **A.** 802.3F

    **B.** 802.3z

    **C.** 802.3ab

    **D.** 802.3ae

**30.** Which protocol does DHCP use at the Transport layer?

    **A.** IP

    **B.** TCP

    **C.** UDP

    **D.** ARP

**31.** If your router is facilitating a CSU/DSU, which of the following commands do you need to use to provide the router with a 64000 bps serial link?

    **A.** RouterA(config)#**bandwidth 64**

    **B.** RouterA(config-if)#**bandwidth 64000**

    **C.** RouterA(config)#**clockrate 64000**

    **D.** RouterA(config-if)#**clock rate 64**

    **E.** RouterA(config-if)#**clock rate 64000**

**32.** Which command is used to determine if an access list is enabled on a particular interface?

    **A.** show access-lists

    **B.** show interface

    **C.** show ip interface

    **D.** show interface access-lists

**33.** Which of the following statements is true with regard to ISL and 802.1q?

    **A.** 802.1q encapsulates the frame with control information; ISL inserts an ISL field along with tag control information.

    **B.** 802.1q is Cisco proprietary.

    **C.** ISL encapsulates the frame with control information; 802.1q inserts an 802.1q field along with tag control information.

    **D.** ISL is a standard.

**34.** The protocol data unit (PDU) encapsulation is completed in which order?

    **A.** Bits, frames, packets, segments, data

    **B.** Data, bits, segments, frames, packets

    **C.** Data, segments, packets, frames, bits

    **D.** Packets, frames, bits, segments, data

**35.** Based on the configuration shown below, what statement is true?

```
S1(config)#ip routing
S1(config)#int vlan 10
S1(config-if)#ip address 192.168.10.1 255.255.255.0
S1(config-if)#int vlan 20
S1(config-if)#ip address 192.168.20.1 255.255.255.0
```

    **A.** This is a multilayer switch.

    **B.** The two VLANs are in the same subnet.

    **C.** Encapsulation must be configured.

    **D.** VLAN 10 is the management VLAN.

# Answers to Assessment Test

1. **B.** This can be a hard question if you don't remember to invert the 7th bit of the first octet in the MAC address! Always look for the 7th bit when studying for the CCENT/CCNA and when using EUI-64, invert it. The EUI-64 autoconfiguration then inserts an FF:FE in the middle of the 48-bit MAC address to create a unique IPv6 address. See Chapter 14 for more information.

2. **A.** The NDP neighbor advertisement (NA) contains the MAC address. A neighbor solicitation (NS) was initially sent asking for the MAC address. See Chapter 14 for more information.

3. **B.** Each field in an IPv6 address is 16 bits long. An IPv6 address is a total of 128 bits. See Chapter 14 for more information.

4. **A.** To enable OSPFv3, you enable the protocol at the interface level, as with RIPng. The command string is ipv6 ospf *process-id* area *area-id*. See Chapter 14 for more information.

5. **C.** The command line console 0 places you at a prompt where you can then set your console user-mode password. See Chapter 6 for more information.

6. **B, D.** The mask 255.255.254.0 (/23) used with a Class A address means that there are 15 subnet bits and 9 host bits. The block size in the third octet is 2 (256 − 254). So this makes the subnets in the interesting octet 0, 2, 4, 6, etc., all the way to 254. The host 10.16.3.65 is in the 2.0 subnet. The next subnet is 4.0, so the broadcast address for the 2.0 subnet is 3.255. The valid host addresses are 2.1 through 3.254. See Chapter 4 for more information.

7. **C.** The IP address is configured under a logical interface, called a management domain or VLAN 1. See Chapter 10 for more information.

8. **A.** 256 − 192 = 64, so 64 is our block size. Just count in increments of 64 to find our subnet: 64 + 64 = 128. 128 + 64 = 192. The subnet is 128, the broadcast address is 191, and the valid host range is the numbers in between, or 129–190. See Chapter 4 for more information.

9. **C.** An inside global address is considered to be the IP address of the host on the private network after translation. See Chapter 13 for more information.

10. **B.** Once you create your pool, the command ip nat inside source must be used to say which inside locals are allowed to use the pool. In this question, we need to see if access list 100 is configured correctly, if at all, so show access-list is the best answer. See Chapter 13 for more information.

**11.** D. Layer 2 switching creates individual collision domains per port. See Chapter 1 for more information.

**12.** C. The command line vty 0 4 places you in a prompt that will allow you to set or change your Telnet password. See Chapter 6 for more information.

**13.** B. To see the contents of all access lists, use the show access-lists command. See Chapter 12 for more information.

**14.** C. VLANs break up broadcast domains at layer 2. See Chapter 11 for more information.

**15.** A. The command erase startup-config deletes the configuration stored in NVRAM. See Chapter 6 for more information.

**16.** C. ICMP is the protocol at the Network layer that is used to send messages back to an originating router. See Chapter 3 for more information.

**17.** A. Class A addressing provides 22 bits for host addressing, Class B provides 16 bits, but only 14 are available for subnetting, Class C provides only 6 bits for subnetting. See Chapter 3 for more information.

**18.** B. Only the EIGRP route will be placed in the routing table because EIGRP has the lowest administrative distance (AD), and that is always used before metrics. See Chapter 8 for more information.

**19.** D. Switches do not propagate VLAN information by default; you must configure the VTP domain for this to occur. VLAN Trunking Protocol (VTP) is used to propagate VLAN information across a trunk link. See Chapter 11 for more information.

**20.** B, G. To enable OSPF, you must first start OSPF using a process ID. The number is irrelevant; just choose a number from 1 to 65,535 and you're good to go. After you start the OSPF process, you must configure interfaces on which to activate OSPF using the network command with wildcards and specification of an area. Option F is wrong because there must be a space after the parameter area and before you list the area number. See Chapter 9 for more information.

**21.** A. By default, switches break up collision domains on a per-port basis but are one large broadcast domain. See Chapter 1 for more information.

**22.** B. At the moment of OSPF process startup, the highest IP address on any active interface will be the router ID (RID) of the router. If you have a loopback interface configured (logical interface), then that will override the interface IP address and become the RID of the router automatically. See Chapter 9 for more information.

**23.** C, D. VTP is not right because it has nothing to do with trunking except that it sends VLAN information across a trunk link. 802.1q and ISL encapsulations are used to configure trunking on a port. See Chapter 11 for more information.

**24.** D. Stub networks have only one connection to an internetwork. Default routes should be set on a stub network or network loops may occur; however, there are exceptions to this rule. See Chapter 8 for more information.

**25.** B. Hubs regenerate electrical signals, which are specified at the Physical layer. See Chapter 1 for more information.

**26.** A, C. Standard and extended access control lists (ACLs) are used to configure security on a router. See Chapter 12 for more information.

**27.** C. If you start at 192.168.128.0 and go through 192.168.159.0, you can see this is a block of 32 in the third octet. Since the network address is always the first one in the range, the summary address is 192.168.128.0. What mask provides a block of 32 in the third octet? The answer is 255.255.224.0, or /19. See Chapter 5 for more information.

**28.** B. The command to back up the configuration on a router is copy running-config startup-config. See Chapter 7 for more information.

**29.** C. IEEE 802.3ab is the standard for 1 Gbps on twisted-pair. See Chapter 2 for more information.

**30.** C. User Datagram Protocol is a connection network service at the Transport layer, and DHCP uses this connectionless service. See Chapter 3 for more information.

**31.** E. The clock rate command is two words, and the speed of the line is in bits per second (bps). See Chapter 6 for more information.

**32.** C. The show ip interface command will show you if any interfaces have an outbound or inbound access list set. See Chapter 12 for more information.

**33.** C. Unlike ISL, which encapsulates the frame with control information, 802.1q inserts an 802.1q field along with tag control information. See Chapter 11 for more information.

**34.** C. The PDU encapsulation method defines how data is encoded as it goes through each layer of the TCP/IP model. Data is segmented at the Transport later, packets created at the Network layer, frames at the Data Link layer, and finally, the Physical layer encodes the 1s and 0s into a digital signal. See Chapter 2 for more information.

**35.** A. With a multilayer switch, enable IP routing and create one logical interface for each VLAN using the interface vlan number command and you're now doing inter-VLAN routing on the backplane of the switch! See Chapter 11 for more information.

# Chapter

# 1

# Internetworking

## THE FOLLOWING ICND1 EXAM TOPICS ARE COVERED IN THIS CHAPTER:

✓ **Operation of IP Data Networks**

- Recognize the purpose and functions of various network devices such as Routers, Switches, Bridges and Hubs.

- Select the components required to meet a given network specification.

- Identify common applications and their impact on the network.

- Describe the purpose and basic operation of the protocols in the OSI and TCP/IP models.

Welcome to the exciting world of internetworking. This first chapter will serve as an internetworking review by focusing on how to connect networks together using Cisco routers and switches, and I've written it with the assumption that you have some simple basic networking knowledge. The emphasis of this review will be on the Cisco CCENT and/or CCNA Routing and Switching (CCNA R/S) objectives you'll need a solid grasp on in order to succeed in getting your certifications.

Let's start by defining exactly what an internetwork is: You create an internetwork when you connect two or more networks via a router and configure a logical network addressing scheme with a protocol such as IP or IPv6.

We'll also dissect the Open Systems Interconnection (OSI) model, and I'll describe each part of it to you in detail because you really need complete, reliable knowledge of it. Understanding the OSI model is key for the solid foundation you'll need to build upon with the more advanced Cisco networking knowledge gained as you become increasingly skilled.

The OSI model has seven hierarchical layers that were developed to enable different networks to communicate reliably between disparate systems. Since this book is centering upon all things CCNA, it's crucial for you to understand the OSI model as Cisco sees it, so that's how I'll be presenting the seven layers to you.

After you finish reading this chapter, you'll encounter review questions and written labs. These are given to you to really lock the information from this chapter into your memory. So don't skip them!

**To find up-to-the-minute updates for this chapter, please see** www.lammle.com/forum **or the book's web page at** www.sybex.com.

# Internetworking Basics

Before exploring internetworking models and the OSI model's specifications, you need to grasp the big picture and the answer to this burning question: Why is it so important to learn Cisco internetworking anyway?

Networks and networking have grown exponentially over the past 20 years, and understandably so. They've had to evolve at light speed just to keep up with huge increases in basic, mission-critical user needs, (e.g. simple sharing data and printers), as well as greater burdens like multimedia remote presentations and conferencing. Unless everyone who needs to share network resources is located in the same office space—an increasingly uncommon situation—the challenge is to connect relevant networks so all users can share the wealth of whatever services and resources are required.

Figure 1.1 shows a basic *local area network (LAN)* that's connected using a *hub*, which is basically just an antiquated device that connects wires together. Keep in mind that a simple network like this would be considered one collision domain and one broadcast domain. No worries if you have no idea what I mean by that because coming up soon, I'm going to talk about collision and broadcast domains enough to make you dream about them!

**FIGURE 1.1**   A very basic network

Okay, things really can't get much simpler than this. And yes, though you can still find this configuration in some home networks, even many of those as well as the smallest business networks are more complicated today. As we move through this book, I'll just keep building upon this tiny network a bit at a time until we arrive at some really nice, robust and current network designs—the types that will help you get your certification and a job!

But as I said, we'll get there one step at a time, so let's get back to the network shown in Figure 1.1 with this scenario: Bob wants to send Sally a file, and to complete that goal in this kind of network, he'll simply broadcast that he's looking for her, which is basically just shouting out over the network. Think of it like this, Bob walking out of his house and yelling down a street called Chaos Court in order to contact Sally. This might work if Bob and Sally were the only ones living there, but not so much if it's crammed with homes and all the others living there are always hollering up and down the street to their neighbors just like Bob. Nope, Chaos Court would absolutely live up to its name, with all those residents going off whenever they felt like it—and believe it or not, our networks actually still work this way to a degree! So, given a choice, would you stay in Chaos, or would you pull up stakes and move on over to a nice new modern community called Broadway Lanes, which offers plenty of amenities and room for your home plus future additions all on nice, wide streets that can easily handle all present and future traffic? Good choice... so did Sally, who now lives a much quieter life, getting letters (packets) from Bob instead of a headache!

The scenario I just described brings me to the basic point of what this book and the Cisco certification objectives are really all about. My goal of showing you how to create efficient networks and segment them correctly in order to minimize all the chaotic yelling and screaming going on in them is a universal theme throughout my CCENT and CCNA series books. It's just inevitable that you'll have to break up a large network into a bunch of smaller ones at some point to match a network's equally inevitable growth, and as that expansion occurs, user response time simultaneously dwindles to a frustrating crawl. But if you master the vital technology and skills I have in store for you in this series, you'll be well equipped to rescue your network and its users by creating an efficient new network neighborhood to give them key amenities like the bandwidth they need to meet their evolving demands.

And this is no joke; most of us think of growth as good—and it can be—but as many of us experience daily when commuting to work, school, etc., it can also mean your LAN's traffic congestion can reach critical mass and grind to a complete halt! Again, the solution to this problem begins with breaking up a massive network into a number of smaller ones—something called *network segmentation*. This concept is a lot like planning a new community or modernizing an existing one. More streets are added, complete with new intersections and traffic signals, plus post offices with official maps documenting all those street names and directions on how to get to each are built. You'll need to effect new laws to keep order to it all and provide a police station to protect this nice new neighborhood as well. In a networking neighborhood environment, all of this is carried out using devices like *routers*, *switches*, and *bridges*.

So let's take a look at our new neighborhood now, because the word has gotten out; many more hosts have moved into it, so it's time to upgrade that new high-capacity infrastructure that we promised to handle the increase in population. Figure 1.2 shows a network that's been segmented with a switch, making each network segment that connects to the switch its own separate collision domain. Doing this results in a lot less yelling!

**FIGURE 1.2**   A switch can break up collision domains.

This is a great start, but I really want you to make note of the fact that this network is still one, single broadcast domain, meaning that we've really only decreased our screaming and yelling, not eliminated it. For example, if there's some sort of vital announcement that everyone in our neighborhood needs to hear about, it will definitely still get loud! You can see that the hub used in Figure 1.2 just extended the one collision domain from the switch port. The result is that John received the data from Bob but, happily, Sally did not. This is good because Bob intended to talk with John directly, and if he had needed to send a broadcast instead, everyone, including Sally, would have received it, possibly causing unnecessary congestion.

Here's a list of some of the things that commonly cause LAN traffic congestion:

- Too many hosts in a collision or broadcast domain
- Broadcast storms
- Too much multicast traffic
- Low bandwidth
- Adding hubs for connectivity to the network
- A bunch of ARP broadcasts

Take another look at Figure 1.2 and make sure you see that I extended the main hub from Figure 1.1 to a switch in Figure 1.2. I did that because hubs don't segment a network; they just connect network segments. Basically, it's an inexpensive way to connect a couple of PCs, and again, that's great for home use and troubleshooting, but that's about it!

As our planned community starts to grow, we'll need to add more streets with traffic control, and even some basic security. We'll achieve this by adding routers because these convenient devices are used to connect networks and route packets of data from one network to another. Cisco became the de facto standard for routers because of its unparalleled selection of high-quality router products and fantastic service. So never forget that by default, routers are basically employed to efficiently break up a *broadcast domain*—the set of all devices on a network segment, which are allowed to "hear" all broadcasts sent out on that specific segment.

Figure 1.3 depicts a router in our growing network, creating an internetwork and breaking up broadcast domains.

**FIGURE 1.3**   Routers create an internetwork.

I LOVE SHOUTING!
... HEY EVERYONE!                          Sure is nice and quiet here.

The network in Figure 1.3 is actually a pretty cool little network. Each host is connected to its own collision domain because of the switch, and the router has created two broadcast domains. So now our Sally is happily living in peace in a completely different neighborhood, no longer subjected to Bob's incessant shouting! If Bob wants to talk with Sally, he has to send a packet with a destination address using her IP address—he cannot broadcast for her!

But there's more... routers provide connections to *wide area network (WAN)* services as well via a serial interface for WAN connections—specifically, a V.35 physical interface on a Cisco router.

Let me make sure you understand why breaking up a broadcast domain is so important. When a host or server sends a network broadcast, every device on the network must read and process that broadcast—unless you have a router. When the router's interface receives this broadcast, it can respond by basically saying, "Thanks, but no thanks," and discard the broadcast without forwarding it on to other networks. Even though routers are known for breaking up broadcast domains by default, it's important to remember that they break up collision domains as well.

There are two advantages to using routers in your network:

- They don't forward broadcasts by default.
- They can filter the network based on layer 3, Network layer, information such as an IP address.

Here are four ways a router functions in your network:

- Packet switching
- Packet filtering
- Internetwork communication
- Path selection

I'll tell you all about the various layers later in this chapter, but for now, it's helpful to think of routers as layer 3 switches. Unlike plain-vanilla layer 2 switches, which forward or filter frames, routers (layer 3 switches) use logical addressing and provide an important capacity called *packet switching*. Routers can also provide packet filtering via access lists, and when routers connect two or more networks together and use logical addressing (IP or IPv6), you then have an *internetwork*. Finally, routers use a routing table, which is essentially a map of the internetwork, to make best path selections for getting data to its proper destination and properly forward packets to remote networks.

Conversely, we don't use layer 2 switches to create internetworks because they don't break up broadcast domains by default. Instead, they're employed to add functionality to a network LAN. The main purpose of these switches is to make a LAN work better—to optimize its performance—providing more bandwidth for the LAN's users. Also, these switches don't forward packets to other networks like routers do. Instead, they only "switch" frames from one port to another within the switched network. And don't worry, even though you're probably thinking, "Wait—what are frames and packets?" I promise to completely fill you in later in this chapter. For now, think of a packet as a package containing data.

Okay, so by default, switches break up collision domains, but what are these things? *Collision domain* is an Ethernet term used to describe a network scenario in which one device sends a packet out on a network segment and every other device on that same segment is forced to pay attention no matter what. This isn't very efficient because if a different device tries to transmit at the same time, a collision will occur, requiring both devices to retransmit, one at a time—not good! This happens a lot in a hub environment, where each host segment connects to a hub that represents only one collision domain and a single broadcast domain. By contrast, each and every port on a switch represents its own collision domain, allowing network traffic to flow much more smoothly.

Switches create separate collision domains within a single broadcast domain. Routers provide a separate broadcast domain for each interface. Don't let this ever confuse you!

The term *bridging* was introduced before routers and switches were implemented, so it's pretty common to hear people referring to switches as bridges. That's because bridges and switches basically do the same thing—break up collision domains on a LAN. Note to self that you cannot buy a physical bridge these days, only LAN switches, which use bridging technologies. This does mean that you'll still hear Cisco and others refer to LAN switches as multiport bridges now and then.

But does it mean that a switch is just a multiple-port bridge with more brainpower? Well, pretty much, only there are still some key differences. Switches do provide a bridging function, but they do that with greatly enhanced management ability and features. Plus, most bridges had only 2 or 4 ports, which is severely limiting. Of course, it was possible to get your hands on a bridge with up to 16 ports, but that's nothing compared to the hundreds of ports available on some switches!

You would use a bridge in a network to reduce collisions within broadcast domains and to increase the number of collision domains in your network. Doing this provides more bandwidth for users. And never forget that using hubs in your Ethernet network can contribute to congestion. As always, plan your network design carefully!

Figure 1.4 shows how a network would look with all these internetwork devices in place. Remember, a router doesn't just break up broadcast domains for every LAN interface, it breaks up collision domains too.

Looking at Figure 1.4, did you notice that the router has the center stage position and connects each physical network together? I'm stuck with using this layout because of the ancient bridges and hubs involved. I really hope you don't run across a network like this, but it's still really important to understand the strategic ideas that this figure represents!

See that bridge up at the top of our internetwork shown in Figure 1.4? It's there to connect the hubs to a router. The bridge breaks up collision domains, but all the hosts connected to both hubs are still crammed into the same broadcast domain. That bridge also created only three collision domains, one for each port, which means that each device connected to a hub is in the same collision domain as every other device connected to that same hub. This is really lame and to be avoided if possible, but it's still better than having one collision domain for all hosts! So don't do this at home; it's a great museum piece and a wonderful example of what not to do, but this inefficient design would be terrible for use in today's networks! It does show us how far we've come though, and again, the foundational concepts it illustrates are really important for you to get.

**FIGURE 1.4**    Internetworking devices

And I want you to notice something else: The three interconnected hubs at the bottom of the figure also connect to the router. This setup creates one collision domain and one broadcast domain and makes that bridged network, with its two collision domains, look majorly better by contrast!

> Don't misunderstand... bridges/switches are used to segment networks, but they will not isolate broadcast or multicast packets.

The best network connected to the router is the LAN switched network on the left. Why? Because each port on that switch breaks up collision domains. But it's not all good—all devices are still in the same broadcast domain. Do you remember why this can be really bad? Because all devices must listen to all broadcasts transmitted, that's why! And if your broadcast domains are too large, the users have less bandwidth and are required to process more broadcasts. Network response time eventually will slow to a level that could cause riots and strikes, so it's important to keep your broadcast domains small in the vast majority of networks today.

Once there are only switches in our example network, things really change a lot! Figure 1.5 demonstrates a network you'll typically stumble upon today.

Here I've placed the LAN switches at the center of this network world, with the routers connecting the logical networks. If I went ahead and implemented this design, I've created something called virtual LANs, or VLANs, which are used when you logically break up broadcast domains in a layer 2, switched network. It's really important to understand that even in a switched network environment, you still need a router to provide communication between VLANs. Don't forget that!

**FIGURE 1.5**   Switched networks creating an internetwork

Still, clearly the best network design is the one that's perfectly configured to meet the business requirements of the specific company or client it serves, and it's usually one in which LAN switches exist in harmony with routers strategically placed in the network. It's my hope that this book will help you understand the basics of routers and switches so you can make solid, informed decisions on a case-by-case basis and be able to achieve that goal! But I digress...

So let's go back to Figure 1.4 now for a minute and really scrutinize it because I want to ask you this question: How many collision domains and broadcast domains are really there in this internetwork? I hope you answered nine collision domains and three broadcast domains! The broadcast domains are definitely the easiest to spot because only routers break up broadcast domains by default, and since there are three interface connections, that gives you three broadcast domains. But do you see the nine collision domains? Just in case that's a no, I'll explain. The all-hub network at the bottom is one collision domain; the bridge network on top equals three collision domains. Add in the switch network of five collision domains—one for each switch port—and you get a total of nine!

While we're at this, in Figure 1.5, each port on the switch is a separate collision domain, and each VLAN would be a separate broadcast domain. So how many collision domains do you see here? I'm counting 12—remember that connections between the switches are considered a collision domain! Since the figure doesn't show any VLAN information, we can assume the default of one broadcast domain is in place.

---

**Real World Scenario**

### Should I Replace My Existing 10/100 Mbps Switches?

Let's say you're a network administrator at a large company. The boss comes to you and says that he got your requisition to buy a bunch of new switches but he's really freaking out about the price tag! Should you push it—do you really need to go this far?

If you can, absolutely! Make your case and go for it because the newest switches add really huge capacity to a network that older 10/100 Mbps switches just can't touch. And yes, five-year-old switches are considered pretty Pleistocene these days. But in reality, most of us just don't have an unlimited budget to buy all new gigabit switches and 10/100 Mbps switches can still create a nice network—if you design and implement that network correctly! Still, plan and budget accordingly because you'll have to replace those 10/100 switches eventually.

Another good question: Do you really need 1 Gbps or better switch ports for all your users, servers, and other devices? Yes, you *absolutely* need new higher-end switches! This is because servers and hosts are no longer the bottlenecks of our internetworks, our routers and switches are—especially legacy ones. We now need gigabit on the desktop and on every router interface; 10 Gbps would be better, and go even higher if you can afford it.

So, go ahead. Put that requisition for all new switches. You'll be a hero before long!

---

Okay, so now that you've gotten a pretty thorough introduction to internetworking and the various devices that populate an internetwork, it's time to head into exploring the internetworking models.

# Internetworking Models

First a little history: When networks first came into being, computers could typically communicate only with computers from the same manufacturer. For example, companies ran either a complete DECnet solution or an IBM solution, never both together. In the late 1970s, the *Open Systems Interconnection (OSI) reference model* was created by the International Organization for Standardization (ISO) to break through this barrier.

The OSI model was meant to help vendors create interoperable network devices and software in the form of protocols so that different vendor networks could work in peaceable accord with each other. Like world peace, it'll probably never happen completely, but it's still a great goal!

Anyway the OSI model is the primary architectural model for networks. It describes how data and network information are communicated from an application on one computer through the network media to an application on another computer. The OSI reference model breaks this approach into layers.

Coming up, I'll explain the layered approach to you plus how we can use it to help us troubleshoot our internetworks.

Goodness! ISO, OSI, and soon you'll hear about IOS! Just remember that the ISO created the OSI and that Cisco created the Internetworking Operating System (IOS), which is what this book is all-so-about.

## The Layered Approach

Understand that a *reference model* is a conceptual blueprint of how communications should take place. It addresses all the processes required for effective communication and divides them into logical groupings called *layers*. When a communication system is designed in this manner, it's known as a hierarchical or *layered architecture*.

Think of it like this: You and some friends want to start a company. One of the first things you'll do is sort out every task that must be done and decide who will do what. You would move on to determine the order in which you would like everything to be done with careful consideration of how all your specific operations relate to each other. You would then organize everything into departments (e.g., sales, inventory, and shipping), with each department dealing with its specific responsibilities and keeping its own staff busy enough to focus on their own particular area of the enterprise.

In this scenario, departments are a metaphor for the layers in a communication system. For things to run smoothly, the staff of each department has to trust in and rely heavily upon those in the others to do their jobs well. During planning sessions, you would take notes, recording the entire process to guide later discussions and clarify standards of operation, thereby creating your business blueprint—your own reference model.

And once your business is launched, your department heads, each armed with the part of the blueprint relevant to their own department, will develop practical ways to implement their distinct tasks. These practical methods, or protocols, will then be compiled into a standard operating procedures manual and followed closely because each procedure will have been included for different reasons, delimiting their various degrees of importance and implementation. All of this will become vital if you form a partnership or acquire another company because then it will be really important that the new company's business model is compatible with yours!

Models happen to be really important to software developers too. They often use a reference model to understand computer communication processes so they can determine which functions should be accomplished on a given layer. This means that if someone is creating a protocol for a certain layer, they only need to be concerned with their target layer's function. Software that maps to another layers' protocols and is specifically designed to be deployed there will handle additional functions. The technical term for this idea is *binding*. The communication processes that are related to each other are bound, or grouped together, at a particular layer.

## Advantages of Reference Models

The OSI model is hierarchical, and there are many advantages that can be applied to any layered model, but as I said, the OSI model's primary purpose is to allow different vendors' networks to interoperate.

Here's a list of some of the more important benefits for using the OSI layered model:

- It divides the network communication process into smaller and simpler components, facilitating component development, design, and troubleshooting.

- It allows multiple-vendor development through the standardization of network components.

- It encourages industry standardization by clearly defining what functions occur at each layer of the model.

- It allows various types of network hardware and software to communicate.

- It prevents changes in one layer from affecting other layers to expedite development.

# The OSI Reference Model

One of best gifts the OSI specifications gives us is paving the way for the data transfer between disparate hosts running different operating systems, like Unix hosts, Windows machines, Macs, smartphones, and so on.

And remember, the OSI is a logical model, not a physical one. It's essentially a set of guidelines that developers can use to create and implement applications to run on a network. It also provides a framework for creating and implementing networking standards, devices, and internetworking schemes.

The OSI has seven different layers, divided into two groups. The top three layers define how the applications within the end stations will communicate with each other as well as with users. The bottom four layers define how data is transmitted end to end.

Figure 1.6 shows the three upper layers and their functions.

**FIGURE 1.6**   The upper layers

| Application | • Provides a user interface |
|---|---|
| Presentation | • Presents data<br>• Handles processing such as encryption |
| Session | • Keeps different applications' data separate |

When looking at Figure 1.6, understand that users interact with the computer at the Application layer and also that the upper layers are responsible for applications communicating between hosts. None of the upper layers knows anything about networking or network addresses because that's the responsibility of the four bottom layers.

In Figure 1.7, which shows the four lower layers and their functions, you can see that it's these four bottom layers that define how data is transferred through physical media like wire, cable, fiber optics, switches, and routers. These bottom layers also determine how to rebuild a data stream from a transmitting host to a destination host's application.

**FIGURE 1.7**   The lower layers

| Transport | • Provides reliable or unreliable delivery<br>• Performs error correction before retransmit |
|-----------|---------------------------------------------|
| Network | • Provides logical addressing, which routers use for path determination |
| Data Link | • Combines packets into bytes and bytes into frames<br>• Provides access to media using MAC address<br>• Performs error detection not correction |
| Physical | • Moves bits between devices<br>• Specifies voltage, wire speed, and pinout of cables |

The following network devices operate at all seven layers of the OSI model:

- *Network management stations (NMSs)*
- Web and application servers
- Gateways (not default gateways)
- Servers
- Network hosts

Basically, the ISO is pretty much the Emily Post of the network protocol world. Just as Ms. Post wrote the book setting the standards—or protocols—for human social interaction, the ISO developed the OSI reference model as the precedent and guide for an open network protocol set. Defining the etiquette of communication models, it remains the most popular means of comparison for protocol suites today.

The OSI reference model has the following seven layers:

- Application layer (layer 7)
- Presentation layer (layer 6)
- Session layer (layer 5)
- Transport layer (layer 4)
- Network layer (layer 3)
- Data Link layer (layer 2)
- Physical layer (layer 1)

Some people like to use a mnemonic to remember the seven layers, such as **All People Seem To Need Data Processing**. Figure 1.8 shows a summary of the functions defined at each layer of the OSI model.

**FIGURE 1.8**   OSI layer functions

| Application | • File, print, message, database, and application services |
|---|---|
| Presentation | • Data encryption, compression, and translation services |
| Session | • Dialog control |

| Transport | • End-to-end connection |
|---|---|
| Network | • Routing |

| Data Link | • Framing |
|---|---|
| Physical | • Physical topology |

I've separated the 7-layer model into three different functions: the upper layers, the middle layers and the bottom layers. The upper layers communicate with the user interface and application, the middle layers do reliable communication and routing to a remote network, and the bottom layers communicate to the local network.

With this in hand, you're now ready to explore each layer's function in detail!

## The Application Layer

The *Application layer* of the OSI model marks the spot where users actually communicate to the computer and comes into play only when it's clear that access to the network will be needed soon. Take the case of Internet Explorer (IE). You could actually uninstall every trace of networking components like TCP/IP, the NIC card, and so on and still use IE to view a local HTML document. But things would get ugly if you tried to do things like view a remote HTML document that must be retrieved because IE and other browsers act on these types of requests by attempting to access the Application layer. So basically, the Application layer is working as the interface between the actual application program and the next layer down by providing ways for the application to send information down through the protocol stack. This isn't actually part of the layered structure, because browsers don't live in the Application layer, but they interface with it as well as the relevant protocols when asked to access remote resources.

Identifying and confirming the communication partner's availability and verifying the required resources to permit the specified type of communication to take place also occurs at the Application layer. This is important because, like the lion's share of browser functions, computer applications sometimes need more than desktop resources. It's more typical than you would think for the communicating components of several network applications to come together to carry out a requested function. Here are a few good examples of these kinds of events:

- File transfers
- Email
- Enabling remote access
- Network management activities
- Client/server processes
- Information location

Many network applications provide services for communication over enterprise networks, but for present and future internetworking, the need is fast developing to reach beyond the limits of current physical networking.

The Application layer works as the interface between actual application programs. This means end-user programs like Microsoft Word don't reside at the Application layer, they interface with the Application layer protocols. Later, in Chapter 3, "TCP/IP," I'll talk in detail about a few important programs that actually reside at the Application layer, like Telnet, FTP and TFTP.

## The Presentation Layer

The *Presentation layer* gets its name from its purpose: It presents data to the Application layer and is responsible for data translation and code formatting. Think of it as the OSI model's translator, providing coding and conversion services. One very effective way of ensuring a successful data transfer is to convert the data into a standard format before transmission. Computers are configured to receive this generically formatted data and then reformat it back into its native state to read it. An example of this type of translation service occurs when translating old Extended Binary Coded Decimal Interchange Code (EBCDIC) data to ASCII, the American Standard Code for Information Interchange (often pronounced "askee"). So just remember that by providing translation services, the Presentation layer ensures that data transferred from the Application layer of one system can be read by the Application layer of another one.

With this in mind, it follows that the OSI would include protocols that define how standard data should be formatted, so key functions like data compression, decompression, encryption, and decryption are also associated with this layer. Some Presentation layer standards are involved in multimedia operations as well.

## The Session Layer

The *Session layer* is responsible for setting up, managing, and dismantling sessions between Presentation layer entities and keeping user data separate. Dialog control between devices also occurs at this layer.

Communication between hosts' various applications at the Session layer, as from a client to a server, is coordinated and organized via three different modes: *simplex, half-duplex,* and *full-duplex.* Simplex is simple one-way communication, kind of like saying something and not getting a reply. Half-duplex is actual two-way communication, but it can take place in only one direction at a time, preventing the interruption of the transmitting device. It's like when pilots and ship captains communicate over their radios, or even a walkie-talkie. But full-duplex is exactly like a real conversation where devices can transmit and receive at the same time, much like two people arguing or interrupting each other during a telephone conversation.

## The Transport Layer

The *Transport layer* segments and reassembles data into a single data stream. Services located at this layer take all the various data received from upper-layer applications, then combine it into the same, concise data stream. These protocols provide end-to-end data transport services and can establish a logical connection between the sending host and destination host on an internetwork.

A pair of well-known protocols called TCP and UDP are integral to this layer, but no worries if you're not already familiar with them because I'll bring you up to speed later, in Chapter 3. For now, understand that although both work at the Transport layer, TCP known as a reliable service but UDP is not. This distinction gives application developers more options because they have a choice between the two protocols when they are designing products for this layer.

The Transport layer is responsible for providing mechanisms for multiplexing upper-layer applications, establishing sessions, and tearing down virtual circuits. It can also hide the details of network-dependent information from the higher layers as well as provide transparent data transfer.

 The term *reliable networking* can be used at the Transport layer. Reliable networking requires that acknowledgments, sequencing, and flow control will all be used.

The Transport layer can either be connectionless or connection-oriented, but because Cisco really wants you to understand the connection-oriented function of the Transport layer, I'm going to go into that in more detail here.

### Connection-Oriented Communication

For reliable transport to occur, a device that wants to transmit must first establish a connection-oriented communication session with a remote device—its peer system—known as a *call setup* or a *three-way handshake.* Once this process is complete, the data transfer occurs, and when it's finished, a call termination takes place to tear down the virtual circuit.

Figure 1.9 depicts a typical reliable session taking place between sending and receiving systems. In it, you can see that both hosts' application programs begin by notifying their individual operating systems that a connection is about to be initiated. The two operating systems communicate by sending messages over the network confirming that the transfer is approved and that both sides are ready for it to take place. After all of this required synchronization takes place, a connection is fully established and the data transfer begins. And by the way, it's really helpful to understand that this virtual circuit setup is often referred to as overhead!

**FIGURE 1.9**    Establishing a connection-oriented session

Okay, now while the information is being transferred between hosts, the two machines periodically check in with each other, communicating through their protocol software to ensure that all is going well and that the data is being received properly.

Here's a summary of the steps in the connection-oriented session—that three-way handshake—pictured in Figure 1.9:

- The first "connection agreement" segment is a request for *synchronization (SYN)*.

- The next segments *acknowledge (ACK)* the request and establish connection parameters—the rules—between hosts. These segments request that the receiver's sequencing is synchronized here as well so that a bidirectional connection can be formed.

- The final segment is also an acknowledgment, which notifies the destination host that the connection agreement has been accepted and that the actual connection has been established. Data transfer can now begin.

Sounds pretty simple, but things don't always flow so smoothly. Sometimes during a transfer, congestion can occur because a high-speed computer is generating data traffic a lot faster than the network itself can process it! And a whole bunch of computers simultaneously sending datagrams through a single gateway or destination can also jam things up pretty badly. In the latter case, a gateway or destination can become congested even though no single source caused the problem. Either way, the problem is basically akin to a freeway bottleneck—too much traffic for too small a capacity. It's not usually one car that's the problem; it's just that there are way too many cars on that freeway at once!

But what actually happens when a machine receives a flood of datagrams too quickly for it to process? It stores them in a memory section called a *buffer*. Sounds great; it's just that this buffering action can solve the problem only if the datagrams are part of a small burst. If the datagram deluge continues, eventually exhausting the device's memory, its flood capacity will be exceeded and it will dump any and all additional datagrams it receives just like an inundated overflowing bucket!

## Flow Control

Since floods and losing data can both be tragic, we have a fail-safe solution in place known as *flow control*. Its job is to ensure data integrity at the Transport layer by allowing applications to request reliable data transport between systems. Flow control prevents a sending host on one side of the connection from overflowing the buffers in the receiving host. Reliable data transport employs a connection-oriented communications session between systems, and the protocols involved ensure that the following will be achieved:

- The segments delivered are acknowledged back to the sender upon their reception.

- Any segments not acknowledged are retransmitted.

- Segments are sequenced back into their proper order upon arrival at their destination.

- A manageable data flow is maintained in order to avoid congestion, overloading, or worse, data loss.

 The purpose of flow control is to provide a way for the receiving device to control the amount of data sent by the sender.

Because of the transport function, network flood control systems really work well. Instead of dumping and losing data, the Transport layer can issue a "not ready" indicator to the sender, or potential source of the flood. This mechanism works kind of like a stoplight, signaling the sending device to stop transmitting segment traffic to its overwhelmed peer. After the peer receiver processes the segments already in its memory reservoir—its buffer—it sends out a "ready" transport indicator. When the machine waiting to transmit the rest of its datagrams receives this "go" indicator, it resumes its transmission. The process is pictured in Figure 1.10.

In a reliable, connection-oriented data transfer, datagrams are delivered to the receiving host hopefully in the same sequence they're transmitted. A failure will occur if any data segments are lost, duplicated, or damaged along the way—a problem solved by having the receiving host acknowledge that it has received each and every data segment.

A service is considered connection-oriented if it has the following characteristics:

- A virtual circuit, or "three-way handshake" is set up.

- It uses sequencing.

- It uses acknowledgments.

- It uses flow control.

**FIGURE 1.10** Transmitting segments with flow control

The types of flow control are buffering, windowing, and congestion avoidance.

## Windowing

Ideally, data throughput happens quickly and efficiently. And as you can imagine, it would be painfully slow if the transmitting machine had to actually wait for an acknowledgment after sending each and every segment! The quantity of data segments, measured in bytes, that the transmitting machine is allowed to send without receiving an acknowledgment is called a *window*.

Windows are used to control the amount of outstanding, unacknowledged data segments.

The size of the window controls how much information is transferred from one end to the other before an acknowledgement is required. While some protocols quantify information depending on the number of packets, TCP/IP measures it by counting the number of bytes.

As you can see in Figure 1.11, there are two window sizes—one set to 1 and one set to 3.

If you've configured a window size of 1, the sending machine will wait for an acknowledgment for each data segment it transmits before transmitting another one but will allow three to be transmitted before receiving an acknowledgement if the window size is set to 3.

In this simplified example, both the sending and receiving machines are workstations. Remember that in reality, the transmission isn't based on simple numbers but in the amount of bytes that can be sent!

**FIGURE 1.11**   Windowing

If a receiving host fails to receive all the bytes that it should acknowledge, the host can improve the communication session by decreasing
the window size.

## Acknowledgments

Reliable data delivery ensures the integrity of a stream of data sent from one machine to the
other through a fully functional data link. It guarantees that the data won't be duplicated or
lost. This is achieved through something called *positive acknowledgment with retransmission*—a technique that requires a receiving machine to communicate with the transmitting
source by sending an acknowledgment message back to the sender when it receives data. The
sender documents each segment measured in bytes, then sends and waits for this acknowledgment before sending the next segment. Also important is that when it sends a segment, the
transmitting machine starts a timer and will retransmit if it expires before it gets an acknowledgment back from the receiving end. Figure 1.12 shows the process I just described.

In the figure, the sending machine transmits segments 1, 2, and 3. The receiving node
acknowledges that it has received them by requesting segment 4 (what it is expecting next).
When it receives the acknowledgment, the sender then transmits segments 4, 5, and 6. If
segment 5 doesn't make it to the destination, the receiving node acknowledges that event
with a request for the segment to be re-sent. The sending machine will then resend the lost
segment and wait for an acknowledgment, which it must receive in order to move on to the
transmission of segment 7.

The Transport layer, working in tandem with the Session layer, also separates the data from
different applications, an activity known as *session multiplexing*, and it happens when a client
connects to a server with multiple browser sessions open. This is exactly what's taking place

when you go someplace online like Amazon and click multiple links, opening them simultaneously to get information when comparison shopping. The client data from each browser session must be separate when the server application receives it, which is pretty slick technologically speaking, and it's the Transport layer to the rescue for that juggling act!

**FIGURE 1.12**   Transport layer reliable delivery

## The Network Layer

The *Network layer*, or layer 3, manages device addressing, tracks the location of devices on the network, and determines the best way to move data. This means that it's up to the Network layer to transport traffic between devices that aren't locally attached. Routers, which are layer 3 devices, are specified at this layer and provide the routing services within an internetwork.

Here's how that works: first, when a packet is received on a router interface, the destination IP address is checked. If the packet isn't destined for that particular router, it will look up the destination network address in the routing table. Once the router chooses an exit interface, the packet will be sent to that interface to be framed and sent out on the local network. If the router can't find an entry for the packet's destination network in the routing table, the router drops the packet.

Data and route update packets are the two types of packets used at the Network layer:

**Data packets**   These are used to transport user data through the internetwork. Protocols used to support data traffic are called routed protocols, and IP and IPv6 are key examples. I'll cover IP addressing in Chapter 3, "TCP/IP," and Chapter 4, "Easy Subnetting," and I'll cover IPv6 in Chapter 14, "Internet Protocol Version 6 (IPV6)".

**Route update packets**   These packets are used to update neighboring routers about the networks connected to all routers within the internetwork. Protocols that send route update packets are called routing protocols; the most critical ones for CCNA are RIP, RIPv2, EIGRP, and OSPF. Route update packets are used to help build and maintain routing tables.

Figure 1.13 shows an example of a routing table. The routing table each router keeps and refers to includes the following information:

**FIGURE 1.13**   Routing table used in a router

**Network addresses**   Protocol-specific network addresses. A router must maintain a routing table for individual routing protocols because each routed protocol keeps track of a network with a different addressing scheme. For example, the routing tables for IP, IPv6, and IPX are completely different, so the router keeps a table for each one. Think of it as a street sign in each of the different languages spoken by the American, Spanish, and French people living on a street; the street sign would read, Cat/Gato/Chat.

**Interface**   The exit interface a packet will take when destined for a specific network.

**Metric**   The distance to the remote network. Different routing protocols use different ways of computing this distance. I'm going to cover routing protocols thoroughly in Chapter 8, "IP Routing," and Chapter 9, "Open Shortest Path First." For now, know that some routing protocols like the Routing Information Protocol, or RIP, use hop count, which refers to the number of routers a packet passes through en route to a remote network. Others use bandwidth, delay of the line, or even tick count ($\frac{1}{18}$ of a second) to determine the best path for data to get to a given destination.

And as I mentioned earlier, routers break up broadcast domains, which means that by default, broadcasts aren't forwarded through a router. Do you remember why this is a good thing? Routers also break up collision domains, but you can also do that using layer 2, Data Link layer, switches. Because each interface in a router represents a separate network, it must be assigned unique network identification numbers, and each host on the network connected to that router must use the same network number. Figure 1.14 shows how a router works in an internetwork.

**FIGURE 1.14**   A router in an internetwork. Each router LAN interface is a broadcast domain. Routers break up broadcast domains by default and provide WAN services.

Here are some router characteristics that you should never forget:

- Routers, by default, will not forward any broadcast or multicast packets.

- Routers use the logical address in a Network layer header to determine the next-hop router to forward the packet to.

- Routers can use access lists, created by an administrator, to control security based on the types of packets allowed to enter or exit an interface.

- Routers can provide layer 2 bridging functions if needed and can simultaneously route through the same interface.

- Layer 3 devices—in this case, routers—provide connections between *virtual LANs (VLANs)*.

- Routers can provide *quality of service (QoS)* for specific types of network traffic.

## The Data Link Layer

The *Data Link layer* provides for the physical transmission of data and handles error notification, network topology, and flow control. This means that the Data Link layer will ensure that messages are delivered to the proper device on a LAN using hardware addresses and will translate messages from the Network layer into bits for the Physical layer to transmit.

The Data Link layer formats the message, each called a *data frame*, and adds a customized header containing the hardware destination and source address. This added information forms a sort of capsule that surrounds the original message in much the same way that engines, navigational devices, and other tools were attached to the lunar modules of the Apollo project. These various pieces of equipment were useful only during certain stages of space flight and were stripped off the module and discarded when their designated stage was completed. The process of data traveling through networks is similar.

Figure 1.15 shows the Data Link layer with the Ethernet and IEEE specifications. When you check it out, notice that the IEEE 802.2 standard is used in conjunction with and adds functionality to the other IEEE standards. (You'll read more about the important IEEE 802 standards used with the Cisco objectives in Chapter 2 "Ethernet Networking and Data Encapsulation.")

It's important for you to understand that routers, which work at the Network layer, don't care at all about where a particular host is located. They're only concerned about where networks are located and the best way to reach them—including remote ones. Routers are totally obsessive when it comes to networks, which in this case is a good thing! It's the Data Link layer that's responsible for the actual unique identification of each device that resides on a local network.

**FIGURE 1.15** Data Link layer

802.11     802.3     802.2

For a host to send packets to individual hosts on a local network as well as transmit packets between routers, the Data Link layer uses hardware addressing. Each time a packet is sent between routers, it's framed with control information at the Data Link layer, but that information is stripped off at the receiving router and only the original packet is left completely intact. This framing of the packet continues for each hop until the packet is finally delivered to the correct receiving host. It's really important to understand that the packet itself is never altered along the route; it's only encapsulated with the type of control information required for it to be properly passed on to the different media types.

The IEEE Ethernet Data Link layer has two sublayers:

**Media Access Control (MAC)** Defines how packets are placed on the media. Contention media access is "first come/first served" access where everyone shares the same bandwidth—hence the name. Physical addressing is defined here as well as logical topologies. What's a logical topology? It's the signal path through a physical topology. Line discipline, error notification (but not correction), the ordered delivery of frames, and optional flow control can also be used at this sublayer.

**Logical Link Control (LLC)** Responsible for identifying Network layer protocols and then encapsulating them. An LLC header tells the Data Link layer what to do with a packet once a frame is received. It works like this: a host receives a frame and looks in the LLC header to find out where the packet is destined—for instance, the IP protocol at the Network layer. The LLC can also provide flow control and sequencing of control bits.

The switches and bridges I talked about near the beginning of the chapter both work at the Data Link layer and filter the network using hardware (MAC) addresses. I'll talk about these next.

As data is encoded with control information at each layer of the OSI model, the data is named with something called a Protocol Data Unit (PDU). At the Transport layer the PDU is called a Segment, Network layer is Packet, Data Link is Frame, and Physical layer is Bits. This method of naming the data at each layer is covered thoroughly in Chapter 2.

## Switches and Bridges at the Data Link Layer

Layer 2 switching is considered hardware-based bridging because it uses specialized hardware called an *application-specific integrated circuit (ASIC)*. ASICs can run up to high gigabit speeds with very low latency rates.

> *Latency* is the time measured from when a frame enters a port to when it exits a port.

Bridges and switches read each frame as it passes through the network. The layer 2 device then puts the source hardware address in a filter table and keeps track of which port the frame was received on. This information (logged in the bridge's or switch's filter table) is what helps the machine determine the location of the specific sending device. Figure 1.16 shows a switch in an internetwork and how John is sending packets to the Internet and Sally doesn't hear his frames because she is in a different collision domain. The destination frame goes directly to the default gateway router, and Sally doesn't see John's traffic, much to her relief.

**FIGURE 1.16**    A switch in an internetwork

**Mac Address—Table**
F0/1: 00c0.1234.2211
F0/2: 00c0.1234.2212
F0/3: 00c0.1234.2213
F0/4: 00c0.1234.2214

The real estate business is all about location, location, location, and it's the same way for both layer 2 and layer 3 devices. Though both need to be able to negotiate the network, it's crucial to remember that they're concerned with very different parts of it. Primarily, layer 3 machines (such as routers) need to locate specific networks, whereas layer 2 machines (switches and bridges) need to eventually locate specific devices. So, networks are to routers as individual devices are to switches and bridges. And routing tables that "map" the internetwork are for routers, as filter tables that "map" individual devices are for switches and bridges.

After a filter table is built on the layer 2 device, it will forward frames only to the segment where the destination hardware address is located. If the destination device is on the same segment as the frame, the layer 2 device will block the frame from going to any other segments. If the destination is on a different segment, the frame can be transmitted only to that segment. This is called *transparent bridging.*

When a switch interface receives a frame with a destination hardware address that isn't found in the device's filter table, it will forward the frame to all connected segments. If the unknown device that was sent the "mystery frame" replies to this forwarding action, the switch updates its filter table regarding that device's location. But in the event the destination address of the transmitting frame is a broadcast address, the switch will forward all broadcasts to every connected segment by default.

All devices that the broadcast is forwarded to are considered to be in the same broadcast domain. This can be a problem because layer 2 devices propagate layer 2 broadcast storms that can seriously choke performance, and the only way to stop a broadcast storm from propagating through an internetwork is with a layer 3 device—a router!

The biggest benefit of using switches instead of hubs in your internetwork is that each switch port is actually its own collision domain. Remember that a hub creates one large collision domain, which is not a good thing! But even armed with a switch, you still don't get to just break up broadcast domains by default because neither switches nor bridges will do that. They'll simply forward all broadcasts instead.

Another benefit of LAN switching over hub-centered implementations is that each device on every segment plugged into a switch can transmit simultaneously. Well, at least they can as long as there's only one host on each port and there isn't a hub plugged into a switch port! As you might have guessed, this is because hubs allow only one device per network segment to communicate at a time.

## The Physical Layer

Finally arriving at the bottom, we find that the *Physical layer* does two things: it sends bits and receives bits. Bits come only in values of 1 or 0—a Morse code with numerical values. The Physical layer communicates directly with the various types of actual communication media. Different kinds of media represent these bit values in different ways. Some use audio tones, while others employ *state transitions*—changes in voltage from high to low and low to high. Specific protocols are needed for each type of media to describe the proper bit patterns to be used, how data is encoded into media signals, and the various qualities of the physical media's attachment interface.

The Physical layer specifies the electrical, mechanical, procedural, and functional requirements for activating, maintaining, and deactivating a physical link between end systems. This layer is also where you identify the interface between the *data terminal equipment (DTE)* and the *data communication equipment (DCE)*. (Some old phone-company employees still call DCE "data circuit-terminating equipment.") The DCE is usually located at the service provider, while the DTE is the attached device. The services available to the DTE are most often accessed via a modem or *channel service unit/data service unit (CSU/DSU)*.

The Physical layer's connectors and different physical topologies are defined by the OSI as standards, allowing disparate systems to communicate. The Cisco exam objectives are interested only in the IEEE Ethernet standards.

## Hubs at the Physical Layer

A hub is really a multiple-port repeater. A repeater receives a digital signal, reamplifies or regenerates that signal, then forwards the signal out the other port without looking at any data. A hub does the same thing across all active ports: any digital signal received from a segment on a hub port is regenerated or reamplified and transmitted out all other ports on the hub. This means all devices plugged into a hub are in the same collision domain as well as in the same broadcast domain. Figure 1.17 shows a hub in a network, and how when one host transmits, all other hosts must stop and listen.

**FIGURE 1.17**   A hub in a network

I love it when everyone has to listen to everything I say!

Hubs, like repeaters, don't examine any of the traffic as it enters or before it's transmitted out to the other parts of the physical media. And every device connected to the hub, or hubs, must listen if a device transmits. A physical star network, where the hub is a central device and cables extend in all directions out from it, is the type of topology a hub creates. Visually, the design really does resemble a star, whereas Ethernet networks run a logical bus topology, meaning that the signal has to run through the network from end to end.

> **NOTE**   Hubs and repeaters can be used to enlarge the area covered by a single LAN segment, but I really do not recommend going with this configuration! LAN switches are affordable for almost every situation and will make you much happier.

# Summary

Whew! I know this seemed like the chapter that wouldn't end, but it did—and you made it through! You're now armed with a ton of fundamental information; you're ready to build upon it and are well on your way to certification.

I started by discussing simple, basic networking and the differences between collision and broadcast domains.

I then discussed the OSI model—the seven-layer model used to help application developers design applications that can run on any type of system or network. Each layer has its special jobs and select responsibilities within the model to ensure that solid, effective communications do, in fact, occur. I provided you with complete details of each layer and discussed how Cisco views the specifications of the OSI model.

In addition, each layer in the OSI model specifies different types of devices, and I described the different devices used at each layer.

Remember that hubs are Physical layer devices and repeat the digital signal to all segments except the one from which it was received. Switches segment the network using hardware addresses and break up collision domains. Routers break up broadcast domains as well as collision domains and use logical addressing to send packets through an internetwork.

# Exam Essentials

**Identify the possible causes of LAN traffic congestion.**    Too many hosts in a broadcast domain, broadcast storms, multicasting, and low bandwidth are all possible causes of LAN traffic congestion.

**Describe the difference between a collision domain and a broadcast domain.**    Collision domain is an Ethernet term used to describe a network collection of devices in which one particular device sends a packet on a network segment, forcing every other device on that same segment to pay attention to it. With a broadcast domain, a set of all devices on a network hear all broadcasts sent on all segments.

**Differentiate a MAC address and an IP address and describe how and when each address type is used in a network.**    A MAC address is a hexadecimal number identifying the physical connection of a host. MAC addresses are said to operate on layer 2 of the OSI model. IP addresses, which can be expressed in binary or decimal format, are logical identifiers that are said to be on layer 3 of the OSI model. Hosts on the same physical segment locate one another with MAC addresses, while IP addresses are used when they reside on different LAN segments or subnets.

**Understand the difference between a hub, a bridge, a switch, and a router.**    A hub creates one collision domain and one broadcast domain. A bridge breaks up collision domains but creates one large broadcast domain. They use hardware addresses to filter the network. Switches are really just multiple-port bridges with more intelligence; they break up collision domains but creates one large broadcast domain by default. Bridges and switches use hardware addresses to filter the network. Routers break up broadcast domains (and collision domains) and use logical addressing to filter the network.

**Identify the functions and advantages of routers.**    Routers perform packet switching, filtering, and path selection, and they facilitate internetwork communication. One advantage of routers is that they reduce broadcast traffic.

**Differentiate connection-oriented and connectionless network services and describe how each is handled during network communications.** Connection-oriented services use acknowledgments and flow control to create a reliable session. More overhead is used than in a connectionless network service. Connectionless services are used to send data with no acknowledgments or flow control. This is considered unreliable.

**Define the OSI layers, understand the function of each, and describe how devices and networking protocols can be mapped to each layer.** You must remember the seven layers of the OSI model and what function each layer provides. The Application, Presentation, and Session layers are upper layers and are responsible for communicating from a user interface to an application. The Transport layer provides segmentation, sequencing, and virtual circuits. The Network layer provides logical network addressing and routing through an internetwork. The Data Link layer provides framing and placing of data on the network medium. The Physical layer is responsible for taking 1s and 0s and encoding them into a digital signal for transmission on the network segment.

# Written Labs

In this section, you'll complete the following labs to make sure you've got the information and concepts contained within them fully dialed in:

Lab 1.1: OSI Questions

Lab 1.2: Defining the OSI Layers and Devices

Lab 1.3: Identifying Collision and Broadcast Domains

The answers to these labs can be found in Appendix A, "Answers to Written Labs."

## Written Lab 1.1: OSI Questions

Answer the following questions about the OSI model:

1. Which layer chooses and determines the availability of communicating partners along with the resources necessary to make the connection; coordinates partnering applications; and forms a consensus on procedures for controlling data integrity and error recovery?

2. Which layer is responsible for converting data packets from the Data Link layer into electrical signals?

3. At which layer is routing implemented, enabling connections and path selection between two end systems?

4. Which layer defines how data is formatted, presented, encoded, and converted for use on the network?

5. Which layer is responsible for creating, managing, and terminating sessions between applications?

6. Which layer ensures the trustworthy transmission of data across a physical link and is primarily concerned with physical addressing, line discipline, network topology, error notification, ordered delivery of frames, and flow control?

7. Which layer is used for reliable communication between end nodes over the network and provides mechanisms for establishing, maintaining, and terminating virtual circuits; transport-fault detection and recovery; and controlling the flow of information?

8. Which layer provides logical addressing that routers will use for path determination?

9. Which layer specifies voltage, wire speed, and cable pinouts and moves bits between devices?

10. Which layer combines bits into bytes and bytes into frames, uses MAC addressing, and provides error detection?

**11.** Which layer is responsible for keeping the data from different applications separate on the network?

**12.** Which layer is represented by frames?

**13.** Which layer is represented by segments?

**14.** Which layer is represented by packets?

**15.** Which layer is represented by bits?

**16.** Put the following in order of encapsulation:

Packets

Frames

Bits

Segments

**17.** Which layer segments and reassembles data into a data stream?

**18.** Which layer provides the physical transmission of the data and handles error notification, network topology, and flow control?

**19.** Which layer manages logical device addressing, tracks the location of devices on the internetwork, and determines the best way to move data?

**20.** What is the bit length and expression form of a MAC address?

# Written Lab 1.2: Defining the OSI Layers and Devices

Fill in the blanks with the appropriate layer of the OSI or hub, switch, or router device.

| Description | Device or OSI Layer |
| --- | --- |
| This device sends and receives information about the Network layer. | |
| This layer creates a virtual circuit before transmitting between two end stations. | |
| This device uses hardware addresses to filter a network. | |
| Ethernet is defined at these layers. | |
| This layer supports flow control, sequencing, and acknowledgments. | |

| Description | Device or OSI Layer |
|---|---|
| This device can measure the distance to a remote network. | |
| Logical addressing is used at this layer. | |
| Hardware addresses are defined at this layer. | |
| This device creates one big collision domain and one large broadcast domain. | |
| This device creates many smaller collision domains, but the network is still one large broadcast domain. | |
| This device can never run full-duplex. | |
| This device breaks up collision domains and broadcast domains. | |

# Written Lab 1.3: Identifying Collision and Broadcast Domains

1. In the following exhibit, identify the number of collision domains and broadcast domains in each specified device. Each device is represented by a letter:

   **A.** Hub

   **B.** Bridge

   **C.** Switch

   **D.** Router

# Review Questions

The answers to these questions can be found in Appendix B, "Answers to Chapter Review Questions."

1. Which of the following statements is/are true with regard to the device shown below? (Choose all that apply.)

   A. It includes one collision domain and one broadcast domain

   B. It includes one collision domain and 10 broadcast domains

   C. It includes 10 collision domains and one broadcast domain

   D. It includes one collision domain and 10 broadcast domains

   E. It includes 10 collision domains and 10 broadcast domains

2. With respect to the OSI model, which of the following are correct statements about PDUs?

   A. A segment contains IP addresses.

   B. A packet contains IP addresses.

   C. A segment contains MAC addresses.

   D. A packet contains MAC addresses.

3. You are the Cisco administrator for your company. A new branch office is opening and you are selecting the necessary hardware to support the network. There will be two groups of computers, each organized by department. The Sales group computers will be assigned IP addresses ranging from 192.168.1.2 to 192.168.1.50. The Accounting group will be assigned IP addresses ranging from 10.0.0.2 to 10.0.0.50. What type of device should you select to connect the two groups of computers so that data communication can occur?

   A. Hub

   B. Switch

   C. Router

   D. Bridge

4. The most effective way to mitigate congestion on a LAN would be to_____?

   **A.** Upgrade the network cards

   **B.** Change the cabling to CAT 6

   **C.** Replace the hubs with switches

   **D.** Upgrade the CPUs in the routers

5. In the work area below draw a line from the OSI model layer to its PDU.

| Layer | Description |
|-------|-------------|
| Transport | Bits |
| Data Link | Segment |
| Physical | Packet |
| Network | Frame |

6. In the diagram below what procedure is shown?

   **A.** flow control

   **B.** windowing

   **C.** TCP handshake

   **D.** reliable delivery

**7.** You need to provide network connectivity to 150 client computers that will reside in the same sub network, and each client computer must be allocated dedicated bandwidth. Which device should you use to accomplish the task?

   **A.** Hub

   **B.** Switch

   **C.** Router

   **D.** Bridge

**8.** In the work area below, drag the OSI model layer on the left to its description on the right.

*left list:*

**Layer**

**Transport**

**Physical**

**Data Link**

**Network**

*right list:*

**Description**

**Framing**

**End-to-end connection**

**Routing**

**Conversion to bits**

**9.** What feature of TCP is illustrated below?

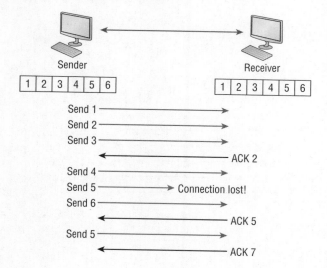

   **A.** flow control

   **B.** UDP handshake

   **C.** TCP handshake

   **D.** reliable delivery

**10.** Which of the following is an example of a routed protocol?

    **A.** EIGRP

    **B.** IP

    **C.** OSPF

    **D.** BGP

**11.** Which of the following is NOT a function carried out on the Application layer of the OSI model?

    **A.** email

    **B.** data translation and code formatting

    **C.** file transfers

    **D.** client/server processes

**12.** Which of the following layers of the OSI model was later subdivided into two layers?

    **A.** Presentation

    **B.** Transport

    **C.** Data Link

    **D.** Physical

**13.** What feature of TCP is illustrated below?

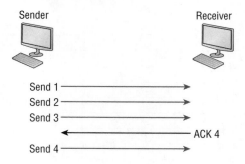

    **A.** flow control

    **B.** windowing

    **C.** TCP handshake

    **D.** reliable delivery

14. An example of a device that operates on the physical layer is a _____.
    A. Hub
    B. Switch
    C. Router
    D. Bridge

15. Which of the following is NOT a benefit of using a reference model?
    A. divides the network communication process into smaller and simpler components
    B. encourages industry standardization
    C. enforces consistency across vendors
    D. allows various types of network hardware and software to communicate

16. Which of the following statements is not true with regard to routers?
    A. They forward broadcasts by default
    B. They can filter the network based on Network layer information
    C. They perform path selection
    D. They perform packet switching

17. Switches break up _____ domains and routers break up _____ domains.
    A. broadcast, broadcast
    B. collision, collision
    C. collision, broadcast
    D. broadcast, collision

**18.** How many collision domains are present in the diagram below?

    **A.** eight

    **B.** nine

    **C.** ten

    **D.** eleven

**19.** Which of the following layers of the OSI model is not involved in defining how the applications within the end stations will communicate with each other as well as with users?

    **A.** Transport

    **B.** Application

    **C.** Presentation

    **D.** Session

**20.** Which if the following is the ONLY device that operates at all layers of the OSI model?

    **A.** Network host

    **B.** Switch

    **C.** Router

    **D.** Bridge

# Chapter

# 2

# Ethernet Networking and Data Encapsulation

## THE FOLLOWING ICND1 EXAM TOPICS ARE COVERED IN THIS CHAPTER:

✓ **Operation of IP Data Networks**

- Recognize the purpose and functions of various network devices such as Routers, Switches, Bridges and Hubs.

- Select the components required to meet a given network specification.

- Predict the data flow between two hosts across a network.

- Identify the appropriate media, cables, ports, and connectors to connect Cisco network devices to other network devices and hosts in a LAN

✓ **LAN Switching Technologies**

- Determine the technology and media access control method for Ethernet networks

- Identify basic switching concepts and the operation of Cisco switches.

  - Collision Domains

  - Broadcast Domains

Before we begin exploring a set of key foundational topics like the TCP/IP DoD model, IP addressing, subnetting, and routing in the upcoming chapters, I really want you to grasp the big picture of LANs conceptually. The role Ethernet plays in today's networks as well as what Media Access Control (MAC) addresses are and how they are used are two more critical networking basics you'll want a solid understanding of as well.

We'll cover these important subjects and more in this chapter, beginning with Ethernet basics and the way MAC addresses are used on an Ethernet LAN, and then we'll focus in on the actual protocols used with Ethernet at the Data Link layer. To round out this discussion, you'll also learn about some very important Ethernet specifications.

You know by now that there are a whole bunch of different devices specified at the various layers of the OSI model and that it's essential to be really familiar with the many types of cables and connectors employed to hook them up to the network correctly. I'll review the types of cabling used with Cisco devices in this chapter, demonstrate how to connect to a router or switch, plus show you how to connect a router or switch via a console connection.

I'll also introduce you to a vital process of encoding data as it makes its way down the OSI stack known as encapsulation.

I'm not nagging at all here—okay, maybe just a little, but promise that you'll actually work through the four written labs and 20 review questions I added to the end of this chapter just for you. You'll be so happy you did because they're written strategically to make sure that all the important material covered in this chapter gets locked in, vault-tight into your memory. So don't skip them!

To find up-to-the minute updates for this chapter, please see www.lammle.com/forum or the book's web page at www.sybex.com.

# Ethernet Networks in Review

*Ethernet* is a contention-based media access method that allows all hosts on a network to share the same link's bandwidth. Some reasons it's so popular are that Ethernet is really pretty simple to implement and it makes troubleshooting fairly straightforward as well. Ethernet is so readily scalable, meaning that it eases the process of integrating new technologies into an existing network infrastructure, like upgrading from Fast Ethernet to Gigabit Ethernet.

Ethernet uses both Data Link and Physical layer specifications, so you'll be presented with information relative to both layers, which you'll need to effectively implement, troubleshoot, and maintain an Ethernet network.

## Collision Domain

In Chapter 1, "Internetworking," you learned that the Ethernet term *collision domain* refers to a network scenario wherein one device sends a frame out on a physical network segment forcing every other device on the same segment to pay attention to it. This is bad because if two devices on a single physical segment just happen to transmit simultaneously, it will cause a collision and require these devices to retransmit. Think of a collision event as a situation where each device's digital signals totally interfere with one another on the wire. Figure 2.1 shows an old, legacy network that's a single collision domain where only one host can transmit at a time.

**FIGURE 2.1**   Legacy collision domain design

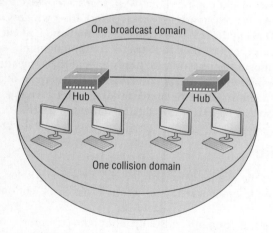

The hosts connected to each hub are in the same collision domain, so if one of them transmits, all the others must take the time to listen for and read the digital signal. It is easy to see how collisions can be a serious drag on network performance, so I'll show you how to strategically avoid them soon!

Okay—take another look at the network pictured in Figure 2.1. True, it has only one collision domain, but worse, it's also a single broadcast domain—what a mess! Let's check out an example, in Figure 2.2, of a typical network design still used today and see if it's any better.

**FIGURE 2.2**    A typical network you'd see today

Because each port off a switch is a single collision domain, we gain more bandwidth for users, which is a great start. But switches don't break up broadcast domains by default, so this is still only one broadcast domain, which is not so good. This can work in a really small network, but to expand it at all, we would need to break up the network into smaller broadcast domains or our users won't get enough bandwidth! And you're probably wondering about that device in the lower-right corner, right? Well, that's a *wireless access point*, which is sometimes referred as an AP (which stands for access point). It's a wireless device that allows hosts to connect wirelessly using the IEEE 802.11 specification and I added it to the figure to demonstrate how these devices can be used to extend a collision domain. But still, understand that APs don't actually segment the network, they only extend them, meaning our LAN just got a lot bigger, with an unknown amount of hosts that are all still part of one measly broadcast domain! This clearly demonstrates why understanding exactly what a broadcast domain is, is so important, and now is a great time to talk about them in detail.

## Broadcast Domain

Let me start by giving you the formal definition: *broadcast domain* refers to a group of devices on a specific network segment that hear all the broadcasts sent out on that specific network segment.

But even though a broadcast domain is usually a boundary delimited by physical media like switches and routers, it can also refer to a logical division of a network segment, where all hosts can communicate via a Data Link layer, hardware address broadcast.

Figure 2.3 shows how a router would create a broadcast domain boundary.

Here you can see there are two router interfaces giving us two broadcast domains, and I count 10 switch segments, meaning we've got 10 collision domains.

The design depicted in Figure 2.3 is still in use today, and routers will be around for a long time, but in the latest, modern switched networks, it's important to create small broadcast domains. We achieve this by building virtual LANs (VLANs) within our switched networks, which I'll demonstrate shortly. Without employing VLANs in today's switched environments, there wouldn't be much bandwidth available to individual users. Switches break up collision domains with each port, which is awesome, but they're still only one broadcast domain by default! It's also one more reason why it's extremely important to design our networks very carefully.

**FIGURE 2.3**   A router creates broadcast domain boundaries.

Two broadcast domains. How many collision domains do you see?

And key to carefully planning your network design is never to allow broadcast domains to grow too large and get out of control. Both collision and broadcast domains can easily be controlled with routers and VLANs, so there's just no excuse to allow user bandwidth to slow to a painful crawl when there are plenty of tools in your arsenal to prevent the suffering!

An important reason for this book's existence is to ensure that you really get the foundational basics of Cisco networks nailed down so you can affectively design, implement, configure, troubleshoot, and even dazzle colleagues and superiors with elegant designs that lavish your users with all the bandwidth their hearts could possibly desire.

To make it to the top of that mountain, you need more than just the basic story, so let's move on to explore the collision detection mechanism used in half-duplex Ethernet.

# CSMA/CD

Ethernet networking uses a protocol called *Carrier Sense Multiple Access with Collision Detection (CSMA/CD)*, which helps devices share the bandwidth evenly while preventing two devices from transmitting simultaneously on the same network medium. CSMA/CD was actually created to overcome the problem of the collisions that occur when packets are transmitted from different nodes at the same time. And trust me—good collision management is crucial, because when a node transmits in a CSMA/CD network, all the other nodes on the network receive and examine that transmission. Only switches and routers can affectively prevent a transmission from propagating throughout the entire network!

So, how does the CSMA/CD protocol work? Let's start by taking a look at Figure 2.4.

**FIGURE 2.4**   CSMA/CD

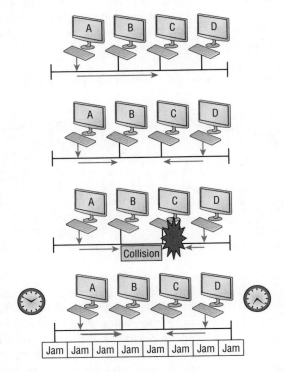

When a host wants to transmit over the network, it first checks for the presence of a digital signal on the wire. If all is clear and no other host is transmitting, the host will then proceed with its transmission.

But it doesn't stop there. The transmitting host constantly monitors the wire to make sure no other hosts begin transmitting. If the host detects another signal on the wire, it sends out an extended jam signal that causes all nodes on the segment to stop sending data—think busy signal.

The nodes respond to that jam signal by waiting a bit before attempting to transmit again. Backoff algorithms determine when the colliding stations can retransmit. If collisions keep occurring after 15 tries, the nodes attempting to transmit will then time out. Half-duplex can be pretty messy!

When a collision occurs on an Ethernet LAN, the following happens:

1. A jam signal informs all devices that a collision occurred.

2. The collision invokes a random backoff algorithm.

3. Each device on the Ethernet segment stops transmitting for a short time until its backoff timer expires.

4. All hosts have equal priority to transmit after the timers have expired.

The ugly effects of having a CSMA/CD network sustain heavy collisions are delay, low throughput, and congestion.

> Backoff on an Ethernet network is the retransmission delay that's enforced when a collision occurs. When that happens, a host will resume transmission only after the forced time delay has expired. Keep in mind that after the backoff has elapsed, all stations have equal priority to transmit data.

At this point, let's take a minute to talk about Ethernet in detail at both the Data Link layer (layer 2) and the Physical layer (layer 1).

## Half- and Full-Duplex Ethernet

Half-duplex Ethernet is defined in the original IEEE 802.3 Ethernet specification, which differs a bit from how Cisco describes things. Cisco says Ethernet uses only one wire pair with a digital signal running in both directions on the wire. Even though the IEEE specifications discuss the half-duplex process somewhat differently, it's not actually a full-blown technical disagreement. Cisco is really just talking about a general sense of what's happening with Ethernet.

Half-duplex also uses the CSMA/CD protocol I just discussed to help prevent collisions and to permit retransmitting if one occurs. If a hub is attached to a switch, it must operate in half-duplex mode because the end stations must be able to detect collisions. Figure 2.5 shows a network with four hosts connected to a hub.

**FIGURE 2.5**   Half-duplex example

The problem here is that we can only run half-duplex, and if two hosts communicate at the same time there will be a collision. Also, half-duplex Ethernet is only about 30 to 40 percent efficient because a large 100Base-T network will usually only give you 30 to 40 Mbps, at most, due to overhead.

But full-duplex Ethernet uses two pairs of wires at the same time instead of a single wire pair like half-duplex. And full-duplex uses a point-to-point connection between the transmitter of the transmitting device and the receiver of the receiving device. This means that full-duplex data transfers happen a lot faster when compared to half-duplex transfers.

Also, because the transmitted data is sent on a different set of wires than the received data, collisions won't happen. Figure 2.6 shows four hosts connected to a switch, plus a hub, and definitely try not to use hubs if you can help it!

**FIGURE 2.6**  Full-duplex example

Theoretically all hosts connected to the switch in Figure 2.6 can communicate at the same time because they can run full-duplex. Just keep in mind that the switch port connecting to the hub as well as the hosts connecting to that hub must run at half-duplex.

The reason you don't need to worry about collisions is because now it's like a freeway with multiple lanes instead of the single-lane road provided by half-duplex. Full-duplex Ethernet is supposed to offer 100-percent efficiency in both directions—for example, you can get 20 Mbps with a 10 Mbps Ethernet running full-duplex, or 200 Mbps for Fast Ethernet. But this rate is known as an aggregate rate, which translates as "you're supposed to get" 100 percent efficiency. No guarantees, in networking as in life!

You can use full-duplex Ethernet in at least the following six situations:

- With a connection from a switch to a host
- With a connection from a switch to a switch
- With a connection from a host to a host
- With a connection from a switch to a router
- With a connection from a router to a router
- With a connection from a router to a host

**NOTE**  Full-duplex Ethernet requires a point-to-point connection when only two nodes are present. You can run full-duplex with just about any device except a hub.

Now this may be a little confusing because this begs the question that if it's capable of all that speed, why wouldn't it actually deliver? Well, when a full-duplex Ethernet port is powered on, it first connects to the remote end and then negotiates with the other end of the Fast Ethernet link. This is called an *auto-detect mechanism*. This mechanism first decides on the exchange capability, which means it checks to see if it can run at 10, 100, or even 1000 Mbps. It then checks to see if it can run full-duplex, and if it can't, it will run half-duplex.

Remember that half-duplex Ethernet shares a collision domain and provides a lower effective throughput than full-duplex Ethernet, which typically has a private per-port collision domain plus a higher effective throughput.

Last, remember these important points:

- There are no collisions in full-duplex mode.
- A dedicated switch port is required for each full-duplex node.
- The host network card and the switch port must be capable of operating in full-duplex mode.
- The default behavior of 10Base-T and 100Base-T hosts is 10 Mbps half-duplex if the autodetect mechanism fails, so it is always good practice to set the speed and duplex of each port on a switch if you can.

Now let's take a look at how Ethernet works at the Data Link layer.

# Ethernet at the Data Link Layer

Ethernet at the Data Link layer is responsible for Ethernet addressing, commonly referred to as MAC or hardware addressing. Ethernet is also responsible for framing packets received from the Network layer and preparing them for transmission on the local network through the Ethernet contention-based media access method.

## Ethernet Addressing

Here's where we get into how Ethernet addressing works. It uses the *Media Access Control (MAC)* address burned into each and every Ethernet network interface card (NIC). The MAC, or hardware, address is a 48-bit (6-byte) address written in a hexadecimal format.

Figure 2.7 shows the 48-bit MAC addresses and how the bits are divided.

**FIGURE 2.7**   Ethernet addressing using MAC addresses

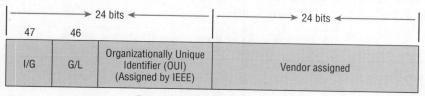

Example: 0000.0c12.3456

The *organizationally unique identifier (OUI)* is assigned by the IEEE to an organization. It's composed of 24 bits, or 3 bytes, and it in turn assigns a globally administered address also made up of 24 bits, or 3 bytes, that's supposedly unique to each and every adapter an organization manufactures. Surprisingly, there's no guarantee when it comes to that unique claim! Okay, now look closely at the figure. The high-order bit is the Individual/Group (I/G) bit. When it has a value of 0, we can assume that the address is the MAC address of a device and that it may well appear in the source portion of the MAC header. When it's a 1, we can assume that the address represents either a broadcast or multicast address in Ethernet.

The next bit is the global/local bit, sometimes called the G/L bit or U/L bit, where *U* means *universal*. When set to 0, this bit represents a globally administered address, as assigned by the IEEE, but when it's a 1, it represents a locally governed and administered address. The low-order 24 bits of an Ethernet address represent a locally administered or manufacturer-assigned code. This portion commonly starts with 24 0s for the first card made and continues in order until there are 24 1s for the last (16,777,216th) card made. You'll find that many manufacturers use these same six hex digits as the last six characters of their serial number on the same card.

Let's stop for a minute and go over some addressing schemes important in the Ethernet world.

## Binary to Decimal and Hexadecimal Conversion

Before we get into working with the TCP/IP protocol and IP addressing, which we'll do in Chapter 3, "TCP/IP," it's really important for you to truly grasp the differences between binary, decimal, and hexadecimal numbers and how to convert one format into the other.

We'll start with binary numbering, which is really pretty simple. The digits used are limited to either a 1 or a 0, and each digit is called a *bit*, which is short for *binary digit*. Typically, you group either 4 or 8 bits together, with these being referred to as a nibble and a byte, respectively.

The interesting thing about binary numbering is how the value is represented in a decimal format—the typical decimal format being the base-10 number scheme that we've all used since kindergarten. The binary numbers are placed in a value spot, starting at the right and moving left, with each spot having double the value of the previous spot.

Table 2.1 shows the decimal values of each bit location in a nibble and a byte. Remember, a nibble is 4 bits and a byte is 8 bits.

**TABLE 2.1**   Binary values

| Nibble Values | Byte Values |
| --- | --- |
| 8 4 2 1 | 128 64 32 16 8 4 2 1 |

What all this means is that if a one digit (1) is placed in a value spot, then the nibble or byte takes on that decimal value and adds it to any other value spots that have a 1. If a zero (0) is placed in a bit spot, you don't count that value.

Let me clarify this a little. If we have a 1 placed in each spot of our nibble, we would then add up 8 + 4 + 2 + 1 to give us a maximum value of 15. Another example for our nibble values would be 1001, meaning that the 8 bit and the 1 bit are turned on, which equals a decimal value of 9. If we have a nibble binary value of 0110, then our decimal value would be 6, because the 4 and 2 bits are turned on.

But the *byte* decimal values can add up to a number that's significantly higher than 15. This is how: If we counted every bit as a one (1), then the byte binary value would look like the following example because, remember, 8 bits equal a byte:

11111111

We would then count up every bit spot because each is turned on. It would look like this, which demonstrates the maximum value of a byte:

128 + 64 + 32 + 16 + 8 + 4 + 2 + 1 = 255

There are plenty of other decimal values that a binary number can equal. Let's work through a few examples:

10010110

Which bits are on? The 128, 16, 4, and 2 bits are on, so we'll just add them up: 128 + 16 + 4 + 2 = 150.

01101100

Which bits are on? The 64, 32, 8, and 4 bits are on, so we just need to add them up: 64 + 32 + 8 + 4 = 108.

11101000

Which bits are on? The 128, 64, 32, and 8 bits are on, so just add the values up: 128 + 64 + 32 + 8 = 232.

I highly recommend that you memorize Table 2.2 before braving the IP sections in Chapter 3, "TCP/IP," and Chapter 4, "Easy Subnetting"!

**TABLE 2.2**   Binary to decimal memorization chart

| Binary Value | Decimal Value |
| --- | --- |
| 10000000 | 128 |
| 11000000 | 192 |
| 11100000 | 224 |
| 11110000 | 240 |
| 11111000 | 248 |
| 11111100 | 252 |
| 11111110 | 254 |
| 11111111 | 255 |

Hexadecimal addressing is completely different than binary or decimal—it's converted by reading nibbles, not bytes. By using a nibble, we can convert these bits to hex pretty simply. First, understand that the hexadecimal addressing scheme uses only the characters 0 through 9. Because the numbers 10, 11, 12, and so on can't be used (because they are two-digit numbers), the letters *A*, *B*, *C*, *D*, *E*, and *F* are used instead to represent 10, 11, 12, 13, 14, and 15, respectively.

*Hex* is short for *hexadecimal*, which is a numbering system that uses the first six letters of the alphabet, *A* through *F*, to extend beyond the available 10 characters in the decimal system. These values are not case sensitive.

Table 2.3 shows both the binary value and the decimal value for each hexadecimal digit.

**TABLE 2.3** Hex to binary to decimal chart

| Hexadecimal Value | Binary Value | Decimal Value |
| --- | --- | --- |
| 0 | 0000 | 0 |
| 1 | 0001 | 1 |
| 2 | 0010 | 2 |
| 3 | 0011 | 3 |
| 4 | 0100 | 4 |
| 5 | 0101 | 5 |
| 6 | 0110 | 6 |
| 7 | 0111 | 7 |
| 8 | 1000 | 8 |
| 9 | 1001 | 9 |
| A | 1010 | 10 |
| B | 1011 | 11 |
| C | 1100 | 12 |
| D | 1101 | 13 |

| Hexadecimal Value | Binary Value | Decimal Value |
| --- | --- | --- |
| E | 1110 | 14 |
| F | 1111 | 15 |

Did you notice that the first 10 hexadecimal digits (0–9) are the same value as the decimal values? If not, look again because this handy fact makes those values super easy to convert!

Okay, now suppose you have something like this: 0x6A. This is important because sometimes Cisco likes to put *0x* in front of characters so you know that they are a hex value. It doesn't have any other special meaning. So what are the binary and decimal values? All you have to remember is that each hex character is one nibble and that two hex characters joined together make a byte. To figure out the binary value, put the hex characters into two nibbles and then join them together into a byte. 6 = 0110; A, which is 10 in hex = 1010; so the complete byte would be 01101010.

To convert from binary to hex, just take the byte and break it into nibbles. Let me clarify this.

Say you have the binary number 01010101. First, break it into nibbles—0101 and 0101—with the value of each nibble being 5 since the 1 and 4 bits are on. This makes the hex answer 0x55. And in decimal format, the binary number is 01010101, which converts to 64 + 16 + 4 + 1 = 85.

Here's another binary number:

11001100

Your answer would be 1100 = 12 and 1100 = 12, so therefore, it's converted to CC in hex. The decimal conversion answer would be 128 + 64 + 8 + 4 = 204.

One more example, then we need to get working on the Physical layer. Suppose you had the following binary number:

10110101

The hex answer would be 0xB5, since 1011 converts to B and 0101 converts to 5 in hex value. The decimal equivalent is 128 + 32 + 16 + 4 + 1 = 181.

Make sure you check out Written Lab 2.1 for more practice with binary/decimal/hex conversion!

## Ethernet Frames

The Data Link layer is responsible for combining bits into bytes and bytes into frames. Frames are used at the Data Link layer to encapsulate packets handed down from the Network layer for transmission on a type of media access.

The function of Ethernet stations is to pass data frames between each other using a group of bits known as a MAC frame format. This provides error detection from a *cyclic redundancy check (CRC)*. But remember—this is error detection, not error correction. An example of a typical Ethernet frame used today is shown in Figure 2.8.

**FIGURE 2.8**  Typical Ethernet frame format

**Ethernet_II**

| Preamble<br>7 bytes | SFD<br>1 byte | Destination<br>6 bytes | Source<br>6 bytes | Type<br>2 bytes | Data and Pad<br>46 – 1500 bytes | FCS<br>4 bytes |
|---|---|---|---|---|---|---|

Packet

Encapsulating a frame within a different type of frame is called *tunneling*.

Following are the details of the various fields in the typical Ethernet frame type:

**Preamble**   An alternating 1,0 pattern provides a 5 MHz clock at the start of each packet, which allows the receiving devices to lock the incoming bit stream.

**Start Frame Delimiter (SFD)/Synch**   The preamble is seven octets and the SFD is one octet (synch). The SFD is 10101011, where the last pair of 1s allows the receiver to come into the alternating 1,0 pattern somewhere in the middle and still sync up to detect the beginning of the data.

**Destination Address (DA)**   This transmits a 48-bit value using the least significant bit (LSB) first. The DA is used by receiving stations to determine whether an incoming packet is addressed to a particular node. The destination address can be an individual address or a broadcast or multicast MAC address. Remember that a broadcast is all 1s—all Fs in hex— and is sent to all devices. A multicast is sent only to a similar subset of nodes on a network.

**Source Address (SA)**   The SA is a 48-bit MAC address used to identify the transmitting device, and it uses the least significant bit first. Broadcast and multicast address formats are illegal within the SA field.

**Length or Type**   802.3 uses a Length field, but the Ethernet_II frame uses a Type field to identify the Network layer protocol. The old, original 802.3 cannot identify the upper-layer protocol and must be used with a proprietary LAN—IPX, for example.

**Data**   This is a packet sent down to the Data Link layer from the Network layer. The size can vary from 46 to 1,500 bytes.

**Frame Check Sequence (FCS)**    FCS is a field at the end of the frame that's used to store the cyclic redundancy check (CRC) answer. The CRC is a mathematical algorithm that's run when each frame is built based on the data in the frame. When a receiving host receives the frame and runs the CRC, the answer should be the same. If not, the frame is discarded, assuming errors have occurred.

Let's pause here for a minute and take a look at some frames caught on my trusty network analyzer. You can see that the frame below has only three fields: Destination, Source, and Type, which is shown as Protocol Type on this particular analyzer:

```
Destination:    00:60:f5:00:1f:27
Source:         00:60:f5:00:1f:2c
Protocol Type: 08-00 IP
```

This is an Ethernet_II frame. Notice that the Type field is IP, or 08-00, mostly just referred to as 0x800 in hexadecimal.

The next frame has the same fields, so it must be an Ethernet_II frame as well:

```
Destination:    ff:ff:ff:ff:ff:ff Ethernet Broadcast
Source:         02:07:01:22:de:a4
Protocol Type: 08-00 IP
```

Did you notice that this frame was a broadcast? You can tell because the destination hardware address is all 1s in binary, or all *F*s in hexadecimal.

Let's take a look at one more Ethernet_II frame. I'll talk about this next example again when we use IPv6 in Chapter 14, "IPv6 Routing," but you can see that the Ethernet frame is the same Ethernet_II frame used with the IPv4 routed protocol. The Type field has 0x86dd when the frame is carrying IPv6 data, and when we have IPv4 data, the frame uses 0x0800 in the protocol field:

```
Destination: IPv6-Neighbor-Discovery_00:01:00:03 (33:33:00:01:00:03)
Source: Aopen_3e:7f:dd (00:01:80:3e:7f:dd)
Type: IPv6 (0x86dd)
```

This is the beauty of the Ethernet_II frame. Because of the Type field, we can run any Network layer routed protocol and the frame will carry the data because it can identify the Network layer protocol!

## Ethernet at the Physical Layer

Ethernet was first implemented by a group called DIX, which stands for Digital, Intel, and Xerox. They created and implemented the first Ethernet LAN specification, which the IEEE used to create the IEEE 802.3 committee. This was a 10 Mbps network that ran on coax and then eventually twisted-pair and fiber physical media.

The IEEE extended the 802.3 committee to three new committees known as 802.3u (Fast Ethernet), 802.3ab (Gigabit Ethernet on category 5) and then finally one more, 802.3ae (10 Gbps over fiber and coax). There are more standards evolving almost daily, such as the new 100 Gbps Ethernet (802.3ba)!

When designing your LAN, it's really important to understand the different types of Ethernet media available to you. Sure, it would be great to run Gigabit Ethernet to each desktop and 10 Gbps between switches, but you would need to figure out how to justify the cost of that network today! However, if you mix and match the different types of Ethernet media methods currently available, you can come up with a cost-effective network solution that works really great.

The *EIA/TIA* (Electronic Industries Alliance and the newer Telecommunications Industry Association) is the standards body that creates the Physical layer specifications for Ethernet. The EIA/TIA specifies that Ethernet use a *registered jack (RJ) connector* on *unshielded twisted-pair (UTP)* cabling (RJ45). But the industry is moving toward simply calling this an 8-pin modular connector.

Every Ethernet cable type that's specified by the EIA/TIA has inherent attenuation, which is defined as the loss of signal strength as it travels the length of a cable and is measured in decibels (dB). The cabling used in corporate and home markets is measured in categories. A higher-quality cable will have a higher-rated category and lower attenuation. For example, category 5 is better than category 3 because category 5 cables have more wire twists per foot and therefore less crosstalk. Crosstalk is the unwanted signal interference from adjacent pairs in the cable.

Here is a list of some of the most common IEEE Ethernet standards, starting with 10 Mbps Ethernet:

**10Base-T (IEEE 802.3)**   10 Mbps using category 3 unshielded twisted pair (UTP) wiring for runs up to 100 meters. Unlike with the 10Base-2 and 10Base-5 networks, each device must connect into a hub or switch, and you can have only one host per segment or wire. It uses an RJ45 connector (8-pin modular connector) with a physical star topology and a logical bus.

**100Base-TX (IEEE 802.3u)**   100Base-TX, most commonly known as Fast Ethernet, uses EIA/TIA category 5, 5E, or 6 UTP two-pair wiring. One user per segment; up to 100 meters long. It uses an RJ45 connector with a physical star topology and a logical bus.

**100Base-FX (IEEE 802.3u)**   Uses fiber cabling 62.5/125-micron multimode fiber. Point-to-point topology; up to 412 meters long. It uses ST and SC connectors, which are media-interface connectors.

**1000Base-CX (IEEE 802.3z)**   Copper twisted-pair, called twinax, is a balanced coaxial pair that can run only up to 25 meters and uses a special 9-pin connector known as the High Speed Serial Data Connector (HSSDC). This is used in Cisco's new Data Center technologies.

**1000Base-T (IEEE 802.3ab)**   Category 5, four-pair UTP wiring up to 100 meters long and up to 1 Gbps.

**1000Base-SX (IEEE 802.3z)**   The implementation of 1 Gigabit Ethernet running over multimode fiber-optic cable instead of copper twisted-pair cable, using short wavelength laser. Multimode fiber (MMF) using 62.5- and 50-micron core; uses an 850 nanometer (nm) laser and can go up to 220 meters with 62.5-micron, 550 meters with 50-micron.

**1000Base-LX (IEEE 802.3z)**   Single-mode fiber that uses a 9-micron core and 1300 nm laser and can go from 3 kilometers up to 10 kilometers.

**1000Base-ZX (Cisco standard)**   1000BaseZX, or 1000Base-ZX, is a Cisco specified standard for Gigabit Ethernet communication. 1000BaseZX operates on ordinary single-mode fiber-optic links with spans up to 43.5 miles (70 km).

**10GBase-T (802.3.an)**   10GBase-T is a standard proposed by the IEEE 802.3an committee to provide 10 Gbps connections over conventional UTP cables, (category 5e, 6, or 7 cables). 10GBase-T allows the conventional RJ45 used for Ethernet LANs and can support signal transmission at the full 100-meter distance specified for LAN wiring.

If you want to implement a network medium that is not susceptible to electromagnetic interference (EMI), fiber-optic cable provides a more secure, long-distance cable that is not susceptible to EMI at high speeds.

Armed with the basics covered so far in this chapter, you're equipped to go to the next level and put Ethernet to work using various Ethernet cabling.

 **Real World Scenario**

### Interference or Host Distance Issue?

Quite a few years ago, I was consulting at a very large aerospace company in the Los Angeles area. In the very busy warehouse, they had hundreds of hosts provide many different services to the various departments working in that area.

However, a small group of hosts have been experiencing intermittent outages that no one could explain since most hosts in the same area have no problems whatsoever. So I decided to take a crack at this problem and see what I could find.

First, I traced the backbone connection from the main switch to multiple switches in the warehouse area. Assuming that the hosts with the issues were connected to the same switch, I traced each cable, and much to my surprise they were connected to various switches! Now my interest really peaked because the simplest issue had been eliminated right off the bat. It wasn't a simple switch problem!

I continued to trace each cable one-by-one, and this is what I found:

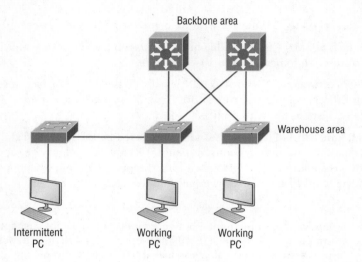

As I drew this network out, I noticed that they had many repeaters in place, which isn't a cause for immediate suspicion since bandwidth was not their biggest requirement here. So I looked deeper still. At this point, I decided to measure the distance of one of the intermittent hosts connecting to their hub/repeater.

This is what I measured. Can you see the problem?

Having a hub or repeater in your network isn't a problem, unless you need better bandwidth (which they didn't in this case), but the distance was! It's not always easy to tell how far away a host is from their connection in an extremely large area, so these hosts ended up having a connection past the 100-meter Ethernet specification which created a problem for the hosts not cabled correctly. Understand that this didn't stop the hosts from completely working, but the workers felt the hosts stopped working when they were at their most stressful point of the day. Sure, that makes sense, because whenever my host stops working, that becomes my most stressful part of the day!

# Ethernet Cabling

A discussion about Ethernet cabling is an important one, especially if you are planning on taking the Cisco exams. You need to really understand the following three types of cables:

- Straight-through cable
- Crossover cable
- Rolled cable

We will look at each in the following sections, but first, let's take a look at the most common Ethernet cable used today, the category 5 Enhanced Unshielded Twisted Pair (UTP), shown in Figure 2.9.

**FIGURE 2.9**   Category 5 Enhanced UTP cable

The category 5 Enhanced UTP cable can handle speeds up to a gigabit with a distance of up to 100 meters. Typically we'd use this cable for 100 Mbps and category 6 for a gigabit, but the category 5 Enhanced is rated for gigabit speeds and category 6 is rated for 10 Gbps!

## Straight-Through Cable

The *straight-through cable* is used to connect the following devices:

- Host to switch or hub
- Router to switch or hub

Four wires are used in straight-through cable to connect Ethernet devices. It's relatively simple to create this type, and Figure 2.10 shows the four wires used in a straight-through Ethernet cable.

**FIGURE 2.10**    Straight-through Ethernet cable

Transmit on pins 1 & 2
Receive on pins 3 & 6

Receive on pins 1 & 2
Transmit on pins 3 & 6

Notice that only pins 1, 2, 3, and 6 are used. Just connect 1 to 1, 2 to 2, 3 to 3, and 6 to 6 and you'll be up and networking in no time. However, remember that this would be a 10/100 Mbps Ethernet-only cable and wouldn't work with gigabit, voice, or other LAN or WAN technology.

## Crossover Cable

The *crossover cable* can be used to connect the following devices:

- Switch to switch
- Hub to hub
- Host to host
- Hub to switch
- Router direct to host
- Router to router

The same four wires used in the straight-through cable are used in this cable—we just connect different pins together. Figure 2.11 shows how the four wires are used in a crossover Ethernet cable.

**FIGURE 2.11**  Crossover Ethernet cable

Receive on pins 1 & 2          Transmit on pins 3 & 6

Notice that instead of connecting 1 to 1, 2 to 2, and so on, here we connect pins 1 to 3 and 2 to 6 on each side of the cable. Figure 2.12 shows some typical uses of straight-through and crossover cables.

**FIGURE 2.12**  Typical uses for straight-through and cross-over Ethernet cables

The crossover examples in Figure 2.12 are switch port to switch port, router Ethernet port to router Ethernet port, and PC Ethernet to router Ethernet port. For the straight-through examples I used PC Ethernet to switch port and router Ethernet port to switch port.

> It's very possible to connect a straight-through cable between two switches, and it will start working because of autodetect mechanisms called auto-mdix. But be advised that the CCNA objectives do not typically consider autodetect mechanisms valid between devices!

## UTP Gigabit Wiring (1000Base-T)

In the previous examples of 10Base-T and 100Base-T UTP wiring, only two wire pairs were used, but that is not good enough for Gigabit UTP transmission.

1000Base-T UTP wiring (Figure 2.13) requires four wire pairs and uses more advanced electronics so that each and every pair in the cable can transmit simultaneously. Even so, gigabit wiring is almost identical to my earlier 10/100 example, except that we'll use the other two pairs in the cable.

**FIGURE 2.13**    UTP Gigabit crossover Ethernet cable

For a straight-through cable it's still 1 to 1, 2 to 2, and so on up to pin 8. And in creating the gigabit crossover cable, you'd still cross 1 to 3 and 2 to 6, but you would add 4 to 7 and 5 to 8—pretty straightforward!

# Rolled Cable

Although *rolled cable* isn't used to connect any Ethernet connections together, you can use a rolled Ethernet cable to connect a host EIA-TIA 232 interface to a router console serial communication (COM) port.

If you have a Cisco router or switch, you would use this cable to connect your PC, Mac, or a device like an iPad to the Cisco hardware. Eight wires are used in this cable to connect serial devices, although not all eight are used to send information, just as in Ethernet networking. Figure 2.14 shows the eight wires used in a rolled cable.

**FIGURE 2.14**    Rolled Ethernet cable

These are probably the easiest cables to make because you just cut the end off on one side of a straight-through cable, turn it over, and put it back on—with a new connector, of course!

Okay, once you have the correct cable connected from your PC to the Cisco router or switch console port, you can start your emulation program such as putty or SecureCRT to create a console connection and configure the device. Set the configuration as shown in Figure 2.15.

**FIGURE 2.15**    Configuring your console emulation program

Notice that Bit Rate is set to 9600, Data Bits to 8, Parity to None, and Flow Control is set to None. At this point, you can click Connect and press the Enter key and you should be connected to your Cisco device console port.

Figure 2.16 shows a nice new 2960 switch with two console ports.

**FIGURE 2.16**    A Cisco 2960 console connections

Notice there are two console connections on this new switch—a typical original RJ45 connection, and the newer mini type-B USB console. Remember that the new USB port supersedes the RJ45 port if you just happen to plug into both at the same time, and the USB port can have speeds up to 115,200 Kbps, which is awesome if you have to use Xmodem to update an IOS. I've even seen some cables that work on iPhones and iPads and allow them to connect to these mini USB ports!

Now that you've seen the various RJ45 unshielded twisted-pair (UTP) cables, what type of cable is used between the switches in Figure 2.17?

**FIGURE 2.17**    RJ45 UTP cable question #1

In order for host A to ping host B, you need a crossover cable to connect the two switches together. But what types of cables are used in the network shown in Figure 2.18?

**FIGURE 2.18**    RJ45 UTP cable question #2

In Figure 2.18, there's a whole menu of cables in use. For the connection between the switches, we'd obviously use a crossover cable like we saw in Figure 2.13. The trouble is that you must understand that we have a console connection that uses a rolled cable. Plus, the connection from the router to the switch is a straight-through cable, as is true for the hosts to the switches. Keep in mind that if we had a serial connection, which we don't, we would use a V.35 to connect us to a WAN.

## Fiber Optic

Fiber-optic cabling has been around for a long time and has some solid standards. The cable allows for very fast transmission of data, is made of glass (or even plastic!), is very thin, and works as a waveguide to transmit light between two ends of the fiber. Fiber optics has been used to go very long distances, as in intercontinental connections, but it is becoming more and more popular in Ethernet LAN networks due to the fast speeds available and because, unlike UTP, it's immune to interference like cross-talk.

Some main components of this cable are the core and the cladding. The core will hold the light and the cladding confines the light in the core. The tighter the cladding, the smaller the core, and when the core is small, less light will be sent, but it can go faster and farther!

In Figure 2.19 you can see that there is a 9-micron core, which is very small and can be measured against a human hair, which is 50 microns.

**FIGURE 2.19**  Typical fiber cable

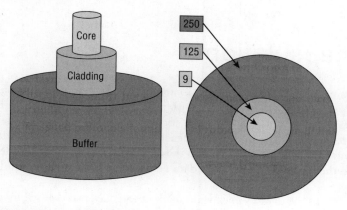

Dimensions are in um ($10^{-6}$ meters). Not to scale.

The cladding is 125 microns, which is actually a fiber standard that allows manufacturers to make connectors for all fiber cables. The last piece of this cable is the buffer, which is there to protect the delicate glass.

There are two major types of fiber optics: single-mode and multimode. Figure 2.20 shows the differences between multimode and single-mode fibers.

**FIGURE 2.20**  Multimode and single-mode fibers

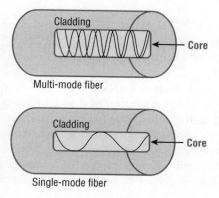

Single-mode is more expensive, has a tighter cladding, and can go much farther distances than multimode. The difference comes in the tightness of the cladding, which makes a smaller core, meaning that only one mode of light will propagate down the fiber. Multimode is looser and has a larger core so it allows multiple light particles to travel down the glass. These particles have to be put back together at the receiving end, so distance is less than that with single-mode fiber, which allows only very few light particles to travel down the fiber.

There are about 70 different connectors for fiber, and Cisco uses a few different types. Looking back at Figure 2.16, the two bottom ports are referred to as Small Form-Factor Pluggable, or SFPs.

# Data Encapsulation

When a host transmits data across a network to another device, the data goes through a process called *encapsulation* and is wrapped with protocol information at each layer of the OSI model. Each layer communicates only with its peer layer on the receiving device.

To communicate and exchange information, each layer uses *protocol data units (PDUs)*. These hold the control information attached to the data at each layer of the model. They are usually attached to the header in front of the data field but can also be at the trailer, or end, of it.

Each PDU attaches to the data by encapsulating it at each layer of the OSI model, and each has a specific name depending on the information provided in each header. This PDU information is read-only by the peer layer on the receiving device. After its read, it's stripped off and the data is then handed to the next layer up.

Figure 2.21 shows the PDUs and how they attach control information to each layer. This figure demonstrates how the upper-layer user data is converted for transmission on the network. The data stream is then handed down to the Transport layer, which sets up a virtual circuit to the receiving device by sending over a synch packet. Next, the data stream is broken up into smaller pieces, and a Transport layer header is created and attached to the header of the data field; now the piece of data is called a *segment* (a PDU). Each segment can be sequenced so the data stream can be put back together on the receiving side exactly as it was transmitted.

Each segment is then handed to the Network layer for network addressing and routing through the internetwork. Logical addressing (for example, IP and IPv6) is used to get each segment to the correct network. The Network layer protocol adds a control header to the segment handed down from the Transport layer, and what we have now is called a *packet* or *datagram*. Remember that the Transport and Network layers work together to rebuild a data stream on a receiving host, but it's not part of their work to place their PDUs on a local network segment—which is the only way to get the information to a router or host.

It's the Data Link layer that's responsible for taking packets from the Network layer and placing them on the network medium (cable or wireless). The Data Link layer encapsulates each packet in a *frame*, and the frame's header carries the hardware addresses of the source and destination hosts. If the destination device is on a remote network, then the frame is sent to a router to be routed through an internetwork. Once it gets to the destination network, a new frame is used to get the packet to the destination host.

**FIGURE 2.21**    Data encapsulation

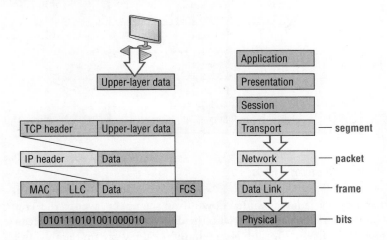

To put this frame on the network, it must first be put into a digital signal. Since a frame is really a logical group of 1s and 0s, the physical layer is responsible for encoding these digits into a digital signal, which is read by devices on the same local network. The receiving devices will synchronize on the digital signal and extract (decode) the 1s and 0s from the digital signal. At this point, the devices reconstruct the frames, run a CRC, and then check their answer against the answer in the frame's FCS field. If it matches, the packet is pulled from the frame and what's left of the frame is discarded. This process is called *de-encapsulation*. The packet is handed to the Network layer, where the address is checked. If the address matches, the segment is pulled from the packet and what's left of the packet is discarded. The segment is processed at the Transport layer, which rebuilds the data stream and acknowledges to the transmitting station that it received each piece. It then happily hands the data stream to the upper-layer application.

At a transmitting device, the data encapsulation method works like this:

1. User information is converted to data for transmission on the network.

2. Data is converted to segments, and a reliable connection is set up between the transmitting and receiving hosts.

3. Segments are converted to packets or datagrams, and a logical address is placed in the header so each packet can be routed through an internetwork.

4. Packets or datagrams are converted to frames for transmission on the local network. Hardware (Ethernet) addresses are used to uniquely identify hosts on a local network segment.

5. Frames are converted to bits, and a digital encoding and clocking scheme is used.

To explain this in more detail using the layer addressing, I'll use Figure 2.22.

**FIGURE 2.22** PDU and layer addressing

Remember that a data stream is handed down from the upper layer to the Transport layer. As technicians, we really don't care who the data stream comes from because that's really a programmer's problem. Our job is to rebuild the data stream reliably and hand it to the upper layers on the receiving device.

Before we go further in our discussion of Figure 2.22, let's discuss port numbers and make sure you understand them. The Transport layer uses port numbers to define both the virtual circuit and the upper-layer processes, as you can see from Figure 2.23.

**FIGURE 2.23** Port numbers at the Transport layer

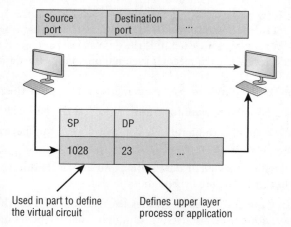

When using a connection-oriented protocol like TCP, the Transport layer takes the data stream, makes segments out of it, and establishes a reliable session by creating a virtual circuit. It then sequences (numbers) each segment and uses acknowledgments and flow control. If you're using TCP, the virtual circuit is defined by the source and destination port number plus the source and destination IP address and called a socket. Understand that the host just makes this up, starting at port number 1024 because 0 through 1023 are reserved for well-known port numbers. The destination port number defines the upper-layer process or application that the data stream is handed to when the data stream is reliably rebuilt on the receiving host.

Now that you understand port numbers and how they are used at the Transport layer, let's go back to Figure 2.22. Once the Transport layer header information is added to the piece of data, it becomes a segment that's handed down to the Network layer along with the destination IP address. As you know, the destination IP address was handed down from the upper layers to the Transport layer with the data stream and was identified via name resolution at the upper layers—probably with DNS.

The Network layer adds a header and adds the logical addressing such as IP addresses to the front of each segment. Once the header is added to the segment, the PDU is called a packet. The packet has a protocol field that describes where the segment came from (either UDP or TCP) so it can hand the segment to the correct protocol at the Transport layer when it reaches the receiving host.

The Network layer is responsible for finding the destination hardware address that dictates where the packet should be sent on the local network. It does this by using the Address Resolution Protocol (ARP)—something I'll talk about more in Chapter 3. IP at the Network layer looks at the destination IP address and compares that address to its own source IP address and subnet mask. If it turns out to be a local network request, the hardware address of the local host is requested via an ARP request. If the packet is destined for a remote host, IP will look for the IP address of the default gateway (router) instead.

The packet, along with the destination hardware address of either the local host or default gateway, is then handed down to the Data Link layer. The Data Link layer will add a header to the front of the packet and the piece of data then becomes a frame. It's called a frame because both a header and a trailer are added to the packet, which makes it look like it's within bookends—a frame—as shown in Figure 2.22. The frame uses an Ether-Type field to describe which protocol the packet came from at the Network layer. Now a cyclic redundancy check is run on the frame, and the answer to the CRC is placed in the Frame Check Sequence field found in the trailer of the frame.

The frame is now ready to be handed down, one bit at a time, to the Physical layer, which will use bit-timing rules to encode the data in a digital signal. Every device on the network segment will receive the digital signal and synchronize with the clock and extract the 1s and 0s from the digital signal to build a frame. After the frame is rebuilt, a CRC is run to make sure the frame is in proper order. If everything turns out to be all good, the hosts will check the destination MAC and IP addresses to see if the frame is for them.

If all this is making your eyes cross and your brain freeze, don't freak. I'll be going over exactly how data is encapsulated and routed through an internetwork later, in Chapter 8, "IP Routing."

# The Cisco Three-Layer Hierarchical Model

Most of us were exposed to hierarchy early in life. Anyone with older siblings learned what it was like to be at the bottom of the hierarchy. Regardless of where you first discovered the concept of hierarchy, most of us experience it in many aspects of our lives. It's *hierarchy* that helps us understand where things belong, how things fit together, and what functions go where. It brings order to otherwise complex models. If you want a pay raise, for instance, hierarchy dictates that you ask your boss, not your subordinate, because that's the person whose role it is to grant or deny your request. So basically, understanding hierarchy helps us discern where we should go to get what we need.

Hierarchy has many of the same benefits in network design that it does in other areas of life. When used properly, it makes networks more predictable and helps us define which areas should perform certain functions. Likewise, you can use tools such as access lists at certain levels in hierarchical networks and avoid them at others.

Let's face it: Large networks can be extremely complicated, with multiple protocols, detailed configurations, and diverse technologies. Hierarchy helps us summarize a complex collection of details into an understandable model, bringing order from the chaos. Then, as specific configurations are needed, the model dictates the appropriate manner in which to apply them.

The Cisco hierarchical model can help you design, implement, and maintain a scalable, reliable, cost-effective hierarchical internetwork. Cisco defines three layers of hierarchy, as shown in Figure 2.24, each with specific functions.

Each layer has specific responsibilities. Keep in mind that the three layers are logical and are not necessarily physical devices. Consider the OSI model, another logical hierarchy. Its seven layers describe functions but not necessarily protocols, right? Sometimes a protocol maps to more than one layer of the OSI model, and sometimes multiple protocols communicate within a single layer. In the same way, when we build physical implementations of hierarchical networks, we may have many devices in a single layer, or there may be a single device performing functions at two layers. Just remember that the definition of the layers is logical, not physical!

So let's take a closer look at each of the layers now.

## The Core Layer

The *core layer* is literally the core of the network. At the top of the hierarchy, the core layer is responsible for transporting large amounts of traffic both reliably and quickly. The only purpose of the network's core layer is to switch traffic as fast as possible. The traffic transported across the core is common to a majority of users. But remember that user data is processed at the distribution layer, which forwards the requests to the core if needed.

**FIGURE 2.24**   The Cisco hierarchical model

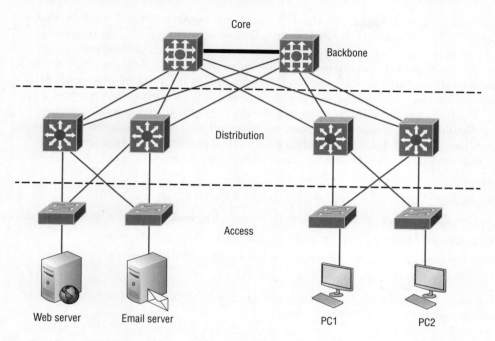

If there's a failure in the core, *every single user* can be affected! This is why fault toler-ance at this layer is so important. The core is likely to see large volumes of traffic, so speed and latency are driving concerns here. Given the function of the core, we can now consider some design specifics. Let's start with some things we don't want to do:

- Never do anything to slow down traffic. This includes using access lists, routing between virtual local area networks and implementing packet filtering.

- Don't support workgroup access here.

- Avoid expanding the core (e.g., adding routers when the internetwork grows). If perfor-mance becomes an issue in the core, give preference to upgrades over expansion.

Here's a list of things that we want to achieve as we design the core:

- Design the core for high reliability. Consider data-link technologies that facilitate both speed and redundancy, like Gigabit Ethernet with redundant links or even 10 Gigabit Ethernet.

- Design with speed in mind. The core should have very little latency.

- Select routing protocols with lower convergence times. Fast and redundant data-link connectivity is no help if your routing tables are shot!

## The Distribution Layer

The *distribution layer* is sometimes referred to as the *workgroup layer* and is the communication point between the access layer and the core. The primary functions of the distribution layer are to provide routing, filtering, and WAN access and to determine how packets can access the core, if needed. The distribution layer must determine the fastest way that network service requests are handled—for example, how a file request is forwarded to a server. After the distribution layer determines the best path, it forwards the request to the core layer if necessary. The core layer then quickly transports the request to the correct service.

The distribution layer is where we want to implement policies for the network because we are allowed a lot of flexibility in defining network operation here. There are several things that should generally be handled at the distribution layer:

- Routing
- Implementing tools (such as access lists), packet filtering, and queuing
- Implementing security and network policies, including address translation and firewalls
- Redistributing between routing protocols, including static routing
- Routing between VLANs and other workgroup support functions
- Defining broadcast and multicast domains

Key things to avoid at the distribution layer are those that are limited to functions that exclusively belong to one of the other layers!

## The Access Layer

The *access layer* controls user and workgroup access to internetwork resources. The access layer is sometimes referred to as the *desktop layer*. The network resources most users need will be available locally because the distribution layer handles any traffic for remote services. The following are some of the functions to be included at the access layer:

- Continued (from distribution layer) use of access control and policies
- Creation of separate collision domains (segmentation)
- Workgroup connectivity into the distribution layer

Technologies like Gigabit or Fast Ethernet switching are frequently seen in the access layer.

I can't stress this enough—just because there are three separate levels does not imply three separate devices! There could be fewer or there could be more. After all, this is a *layered* approach.

# Summary

In this chapter, you learned the fundamentals of Ethernet networking, how hosts communicate on a network. You discovered how CSMA/CD works in an Ethernet half-duplex network.

I also talked about the differences between half- and full-duplex modes, and we discussed the collision detection mechanism called CSMA/CD.

I described the common Ethernet cable types used in today's networks in this chapter as well, and by the way, you'd be wise to study that section really well!

Important enough to not gloss over, this chapter provided an introduction to encapsulation. Encapsulation is the process of encoding data as it goes down the OSI stack.

Last, I covered the Cisco three-layer hierarchical model. I described in detail the three layers and how each is used to help design and implement a Cisco internetwork.

# Exam Essentials

**Describe the operation of Carrier Sense Multiple Access with Collision Detection (CSMA/CD).** CSMA/CD is a protocol that helps devices share the bandwidth evenly without having two devices transmit at the same time on the network medium. Although it does not eliminate collisions, it helps to greatly reduce them, which reduces retransmissions, resulting in a more efficient transmission of data for all devices.

**Differentiate half-duplex and full-duplex communication and define the requirements to utilize each method.** Full-duplex Ethernet uses two pairs of wires at the same time instead of one wire pair like half-duplex. Full-duplex allows for sending and receiving at the same time, using different wires to eliminate collisions, while half-duplex can send or receive but not at the same time and still can suffer collisions. To use full-duplex, the devices at both ends of the cable must be capable of and configured to perform full-duplex.

**Describe the sections of a MAC address and the information contained in each section.** The MAC, or hardware, address is a 48-bit (6-byte) address written in a hexadecimal format. The first 24 bits, or 3 bytes, are called the organizationally unique identifier (OUI), which is assigned by the IEEE to the manufacturer of the NIC. The balance of the number uniquely identifies the NIC.

**Identify the binary and hexadecimal equivalent of a decimal number.** Any number expressed in one format can also be expressed in the other two. The ability to perform this conversion is critical to understanding IP addressing and subnetting. Be sure to go through the written labs covering binary to decimal to hexadecimal conversion.

**Identify the fields in the Data Link portion of an Ethernet frame.** The fields in the Data Link portion of a frame include the preamble, Start Frame Delimiter, destination MAC address, source MAC address, Length or Type, Data, and Frame Check Sequence.

**Identify the IEEE physical standards for Ethernet cabling.**   These standards describe the capabilities and physical characteristics of various cable types and include but are not limited to 10Base-2, 10Base-5, and 10Base-T.

**Differentiate types of Ethernet cabling and identify their proper application.**   The three types of cables that can be created from an Ethernet cable are straight-through (to connect a PC's or router's Ethernet interface to a hub or switch), crossover (to connect hub to hub, hub to switch, switch to switch, or PC to PC), and rolled (for a console connection from a PC to a router or switch).

**Describe the data encapsulation process and the role it plays in packet creation.**   Data encapsulation is a process whereby information is added to the frame from each layer of the OSI model. This is also called packet creation. Each layer communicates only with its peer layer on the receiving device.

**Understand how to connect a console cable from a PC to a router and switch.**   Take a rolled cable and connect it from the COM port of the host to the console port of a router. Start your emulations program such as putty or SecureCRT and set the bits per second to 9600 and flow control to None.

**Identify the layers in the Cisco three-layer model and describe the ideal function of each layer.** The three layers in the Cisco hierarchical model are the core (responsible for transporting large amounts of traffic both reliably and quickly), distribution (provides routing, filtering, and WAN access), and access (workgroup connectivity into the distribution layer).

# Written Labs

In this section, you'll complete the following labs to make sure you've got the information and concepts contained within them fully dialed in:

   Lab 2.1: Binary/Decimal/Hexadecimal Conversion

   Lab 2.2: CSMA/CD Operations

   Lab 2.3: Cabling

   Lab 2.4: Encapsulation

   The answers to these labs can be found in Appendix A, "Answers to Written Labs."

# Written Lab 2.1: Binary/Decimal/Hexadecimal Conversion

1. Convert from decimal IP address to binary format.

   Complete the following table to express 192.168.10.15 in binary format.

| 128 | 64 | 32 | 16 | 8 | 4 | 2 | 1 | Binary |
|-----|-----|-----|-----|-----|-----|-----|-----|--------|
|     |     |     |     |     |     |     |     |        |

Complete the following table to express 172.16.20.55 in binary format.

| 128 | 64 | 32 | 16 | 8 | 4 | 2 | 1 | Binary |
|-----|-----|-----|-----|-----|-----|-----|-----|--------|
|     |     |     |     |     |     |     |     |        |

Complete the following table to express 10.11.12.99 in binary format.

| 128 | 64 | 32 | 16 | 8 | 4 | 2 | 1 | Binary |
| --- | --- | --- | --- | --- | --- | --- | --- | --- |
| | | | | | | | | |

**2.** Convert the following from binary format to decimal IP address.

Complete the following table to express 11001100.00110011.10101010.01010101 in decimal IP address format.

| 128 | 64 | 32 | 16 | 8 | 4 | 2 | 1 | Decimal |
| --- | --- | --- | --- | --- | --- | --- | --- | --- |
| | | | | | | | | |

Complete the following table to express 11000110.11010011.00111001.11010001 in decimal IP address format.

| 128 | 64 | 32 | 16 | 8 | 4 | 2 | 1 | Decimal |
| --- | --- | --- | --- | --- | --- | --- | --- | --- |
|  |  |  |  |  |  |  |  |  |

Complete the following table to express 10000100.11010010.10111000.10100110 in decimal IP address format.

| 128 | 64 | 32 | 16 | 8 | 4 | 2 | 1 | Decimal |
| --- | --- | --- | --- | --- | --- | --- | --- | --- |
|  |  |  |  |  |  |  |  |  |

**3.** Convert the following from binary format to hexadecimal.

Complete the following table to express 11011000.00011011.00111101.01110110 in hexadecimal.

| 128 | 64 | 32 | 16 | 8 | 4 | 2 | 1 | Hexadecimal |
|-----|----|----|----|----|----|----|----|-------------|
|     |    |    |    |    |    |    |    |             |

Complete the following table to express 11001010.11110101.10000011.11101011 in hexadecimal.

| 128 | 64 | 32 | 16 | 8 | 4 | 2 | 1 | Hexadecimal |
|-----|----|----|----|----|----|----|----|-------------|
|     |    |    |    |    |    |    |    |             |

Complete the following table to express 10000100.11010010.01000011.10110011 in hexadecimal.

| 128 | 64 | 32 | 16 | 8 | 4 | 2 | 1 | Hexadecimal |
|-----|----|----|----|----|----|----|----|----|

## Written Lab 2.2: CSMA/CD Operations

Carrier Sense Multiple Access with Collision Detection (CSMA/CD) helps to minimize collisions in the network, thereby increasing data transmission efficiency. Place the following steps of its operation in the order in which they occur.

- All hosts have equal priority to transmit after the timers have expired.
- Each device on the Ethernet segment stops transmitting for a short time until the timers expire.
- The collision invokes a random backoff algorithm.
- A jam signal informs all devices that a collision occurred.

## Written Lab 2.3: Cabling

For each of the following situations, determine whether a straight-through, crossover, or rolled cable would be used.

1. Host to host
2. Host to switch or hub
3. Router direct to host
4. Switch to switch
5. Router to switch or hub

6. Hub to hub

7. Hub to switch

8. Host to a router console serial communication (COM) port

## Written Lab 2.4: Encapsulation

Place the following steps of the encapsulation process in the proper order.

▪ Packets or datagrams are converted to frames for transmission on the local network. Hardware (Ethernet) addresses are used to uniquely identify hosts on a local network segment.

▪ Segments are converted to packets or datagrams, and a logical address is placed in the header so each packet can be routed through an internetwork.

▪ User information is converted to data for transmission on the network.

▪ Frames are converted to bits, and a digital encoding and clocking scheme is used.

▪ Data is converted to segments, and a reliable connection is set up between the transmitting and receiving hosts.

# Review Questions

The following questions are designed to test your understanding of this chapter's material. For more information on how to get additional questions, please see this book's introduction.

The answers to these questions can be found in Appendix B, "Answers to Chapter Review Questions."

1. In the accompanying graphic, what is the name for the section of the MAC address marked as unknown?

Example: 0000.0c12.3456

   **A.** IOS

   **B.** OSI

   **C.** ISO

   **D.** OUI

2. _____on an Ethernet network is the retransmission delay that's enforced when a collision occurs.

   **A.** Backoff

   **B.** Carrier sense

   **C.** Forward delay

   **D.** Jamming

**3.** On which type of device could the situation shown in the diagram occur?

  **A.** Hub

  **B.** Switch

  **C.** Router

  **D.** Bridge

**4.** In the Ethernet II frame shown here, what is the function of the section labeled "FCS"?

**Ethernet_II**

| Preamble 7 bytes | SFD 1 byte | Destination 6 bytes | Source 6 bytes | Type 2 bytes | Data and Pad 46 – 1500 bytes | FCS 4 bytes |
|---|---|---|---|---|---|---|

  **A.** Allows the receiving devices to lock the incoming bit stream.

  **B.** Error detection

  **C.** Identifies the upper-layer protocol

  **D.** Identifies the transmitting device

**5.** The contention method used by Ethernet is called _____.

  **A.** Token passing

  **B.** CSMA/CD

  **C.** Polling

  **D.** CSMA/CA

**6.** In which if the following situations can you *not* use full-duplex?

  **A.** With a connection from a switch to a switch

  **B.** With a connection from a router to a router

  **C.** With a connection from a host to a host

  **D.** With a connection from a host to a hub

**7.** Between which systems could you use a cable that uses the pinout pattern shown below?

   **A.** With a connection from a switch to a switch

   **B.** With a connection from a router to a router

   **C.** With a connection from a host to a host

   **D.** With a connection from a host to a switch

**8.** When the I/G bit in a MAC address is set to 1 the transmission is _____. (Choose all that apply.)

   **A.** Unicast

   **B.** Broadcast

   **C.** Multicast

   **D.** Anycast

**9.** What type of cable uses the pinout shown here?

   **A.** Fiber optic

   **B.** Crossover Gigabit Ethernet cable

   **C.** Straight-through FastEthernet

   **D.** Coaxial

**10.** When configuring a terminal emulation program which of the following is an incorrect setting?

   **A.** Bit rate: 9600

   **B.** Parity: None

   **C.** Flow control: None

   **D.** Data bits: 1

11. Which part of a MAC address indicates whether the address is a locally or globally administered address?

   A. FCS

   B. I/G bit

   C. OUI

   D. U/L bit

12. What cable type uses the pinout arrangement shown below?

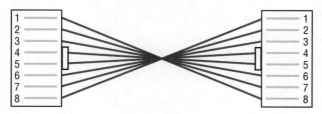

   A. Fiber optic

   B. Rolled

   C. Straight through

   D. Crossover

13. Which of the following is *not* one of the actions taken in the operation of CSMA/CD when a collision occurs?

   A. A jam signal informs all devices that a collision occurred.

   B. The collision invokes a random backoff algorithm on the systems involved in the collision.

   C. Each device on the Ethernet segment stops transmitting for a short time until their backoff timers expire.

   D. All hosts have equal priority to transmit after the timers have expired.

14. Which of the following statements is *false* with regard to Ethernet?

   A. There are very few collisions in full-duplex mode.

   B. A dedicated switch port is required for each full-duplex node.

   C. The host network card and the switch port must be capable of operating in full-duplex mode to use full-duplex.

   D. The default behavior of 10Base-T and 100Base-T hosts is 10 Mbps half-duplex if the autodetect mechanism fails.

**15.** In the diagram below, identify the cable types required for connections A and B.

    **A.** A crossover, B crossover

    **B.** A crossover, B straight through

    **C.** A straight through, B straight through

    **D.** A straight through, B crossover

**16.** In the work area below match the cable type to the standard with which it goes.

| | |
|---|---|
| 1000Base-T | IEEE 802.3u |
| 1000Base-CX | IEEE 802.3 |
| 10Base-T | IEEE 802.3ab |
| 100Base-TX | IEEE 802.3z |

**17.** The cable used to connect to the console port on a router or switch is called a _____ cable.

    **A.** Crossover

    **B.** Rollover

    **C.** Straight-through

    **D.** Full-duplex

**18.** Which of the following items comprise a socket?

    **A.** IP address and MAC address

    **B.** IP address and port number

    **C.** Port number and MAC address

    **D.** MAC address and DLCI

**19.** Which of the following hexadecimal numbers converts to 28 in decimal?

　　**A.** 1c

　　**B.** 12

　　**C.** 15

　　**D.** ab

**20.** What cable type is shown in the below graphic?

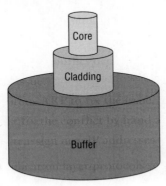

　　**A.** Fiber optic

　　**B.** Rollover

　　**C.** Coaxial

　　**D.** Full-duplex

# Chapter

# 3

# Introduction to TCP/IP

## THE FOLLOWING ICND1 EXAM TOPICS ARE COVERED IN THIS CHAPTER:

✓ **Operation of IP Data Networks**

- Identify common applications and their impact on the network

- Describe the purpose and basic operation of the protocols in the OSI and TCP/IP models.

✓ **IP addressing (IPv4 / IPv6)**

- Describe the operation and necessity of using private and public IP addresses for IPv4 addressing

The *Transmission Control Protocol/Internet Protocol (TCP/IP)* suite was designed and implemented by the Department of Defense (DoD) to ensure and preserve data integrity as well as maintain communications in the event of catastrophic war. So it follows that if designed and implemented correctly, a TCP/IP network can be a secure, dependable and resilient one. In this chapter, I'll cover the protocols of TCP/IP, and throughout this book, you'll learn how to create a solid TCP/IP network with Cisco routers and switches.

We'll begin by exploring the DoD's version of TCP/IP, then compare that version and its protocols with the OSI reference model that we discussed earlier.

Once you understand the protocols and processes used at the various levels of the DoD model, we'll take the next logical step by delving into the world of IP addressing and the different classes of IP addresses used in networks today.

 Subnetting is so vital, it will be covered in its own Chapter 4, "Easy Subnetting."

Because having a good grasp of the various IPv4 address types is critical to understanding IP addressing, subnetting and variable length subnet masks (VLSMs), we'll explore these key topics in detail, ending this chapter by discussing the various types of IPv4 addresses that you'll need to have down for the exam.

I'm not going to cover Internet Protocol version 6 in this chapter because we'll get into that later, in Chapter 14, "Internet Protocol Version 6 (IPv6)." And just so you know, you'll simply see Internet Protocol version 4 written as just IP, rarely as IPv4.

 To find up-to-the minute updates for this chapter, please see www.lammle.com/forum or the book's web page at www.sybex.com.

# Introducing TCP/IP

TCP/IP is at the very core of all things networking, so I really want to ensure that you have a comprehensive and functional command of it. I'll start by giving you the whole TCP/IP backstory, including its inception, and then move on to describe the important technical goals as defined by its original architects. And of course I'll include how TCP/IP compares to the theoretical OSI model.

## A Brief History of TCP/IP

TCP first came on the scene way back in 1973, and in 1978, it was divided into two distinct protocols: TCP and IP. Later, in 1983, TCP/IP replaced the Network Control Protocol (NCP) and was authorized as the official means of data transport for anything connecting to ARPAnet, the Internet's ancestor. The DoD's Advanced Research Projects Agency (ARPA) created this ancient network way back in 1957 in a cold war reaction to the Soviet's launching of *Sputnik*. Also in 1983, ARPA was redubbed DARPA and divided into ARPAnet and MILNET until both were finally dissolved in 1990.

It may be counterintuitive, but most of the development work on TCP/IP happened at UC Berkeley in Northern California, where a group of scientists were simultaneously working on the Berkeley version of UNIX, which soon became known as the Berkeley Software Distribution (BSD) series of UNIX versions. Of course, because TCP/IP worked so well, it was packaged into subsequent releases of BSD Unix and offered to other universities and institutions if they bought the distribution tape. So basically, BSD Unix bundled with TCP/IP began as shareware in the world of academia. As a result, it became the foundation for the tremendous success and unprecedented growth of today's Internet as well as smaller, private and corporate intranets.

As usual, what started as a small group of TCP/IP aficionados evolved, and as it did, the US government created a program to test any new published standards and make sure they passed certain criteria. This was to protect TCP/IP's integrity and to ensure that no developer changed anything too dramatically or added any proprietary features. It's this very quality—this open-systems approach to the TCP/IP family of protocols—that sealed its popularity because this quality guarantees a solid connection between myriad hardware and software platforms with no strings attached.

# TCP/IP and the DoD Model

The DoD model is basically a condensed version of the OSI model that comprises four instead of seven layers:

- Process/Application layer
- Host-to-Host layer/or Transport
- Internet layer
- Network Access layer/or Link

Figure 3.1 offers a comparison of the DoD model and the OSI reference model. As you can see, the two are similar in concept, but each has a different number of layers with different names. Cisco may at times use different names for the same layer, such as both "Network Access" and "Link" used to describe the bottom layer.

**FIGURE 3.1**    The DoD and OSI models

When the different protocols in the IP stack are discussed, the layers of the OSI and DoD models are interchangeable. In other words, be prepared for the exam objectives to call the Host-to-Host layer the Transport layer!

A vast array of protocols join forces at the DoD model's *Process/Application layer*. These processes integrate the various activities and duties spanning the focus of the OSI's corresponding top three layers (Application, Presentation, and Session). We'll focus on a few of the most important applications found in the CCNA objectives. In short, the Process/Application layer defines protocols for node-to-node application communication and controls user-interface specifications.

The *Host-to-Host layer* parallels the functions of the OSI's Transport layer, defining protocols for setting up the level of transmission service for applications. It tackles issues like creating reliable end-to-end communication and ensuring the error-free delivery of data. It handles packet sequencing and maintains data integrity.

The *Internet layer* corresponds to the OSI's Network layer, designating the protocols relating to the logical transmission of packets over the entire network. It takes care of the addressing of hosts by giving them an IP (Internet Protocol) address and handles the routing of packets among multiple networks.

At the bottom of the DoD model, the *Network Access layer* implements the data exchange between the host and the network. The equivalent of the Data Link and Physical layers of the OSI model, the Network Access layer oversees hardware addressing and defines protocols for the physical transmission of data. The reason TCP/IP became so popular is because there were no set physical layer specifications, so it could run on any existing or future physical network!

The DoD and OSI models are alike in design and concept and have similar functions in similar layers. Figure 3.2 shows the TCP/IP protocol suite and how its protocols relate to the DoD model layers.

In the following sections, we will look at the different protocols in more detail, beginning with those found at the Process/Application layer.

**FIGURE 3.2** The TCP/IP protocol suite

**DoD Model**

| | | | | |
|---|---|---|---|---|
| Process/Application | Telnet | FTP | LPD | SNMP |
| | TFTP | SMTP | NFS | X Window |

| | | |
|---|---|---|
| Host-to-Host | TCP | UDP |

| | | | |
|---|---|---|---|
| Internet | ICMP | ARP | RARP |
| | IP | | |

| | | | | |
|---|---|---|---|---|
| Network Access | Ethernet | Fast Ethernet | Gigabit Ethernet | 10 Gig Ethernet |

# The Process/Application Layer Protocols

Coming up, I'll describe the different applications and services typically used in IP networks, and although there are many more protocols defined here, we'll focus in on the protocols most relevant to the CCNA objectives. Here's a list of the protocols and applications we'll cover in this section:

- Telnet
- SSH
- FTP
- TFTP
- SNMP
- HTTP
- HTTPS
- NTP
- DNS
- DHCP/BootP

## Telnet

*Telnet* was one of the first Internet standards, developed in 1969, and is the chameleon of protocols—its specialty is terminal emulation. It allows a user on a remote client machine, called the Telnet client, to access the resources of another machine, the Telnet server, in order to access a command-line interface. Telnet achieves this by pulling a fast one on the Telnet server and making the client machine appear as though it were a terminal directly attached to the local network. This projection is actually a software image—a virtual terminal that can interact with the chosen remote host. A drawback is that there are no encryption techniques available within the Telnet protocol, so everything must be sent in clear text, including passwords! Figure 3.3 shows an example of a Telnet client trying to connect to a Telnet server.

**FIGURE 3.3**   Telnet

These emulated terminals are of the text-mode type and can execute defined procedures such as displaying menus that give users the opportunity to choose options and access the applications on the duped server. Users begin a Telnet session by running the Telnet client software and then logging into the Telnet server. Telnet uses an 8-bit, byte-oriented data connection over TCP, which makes it very thorough. It's still in use today because it is so simple and easy to use, with very low overhead, but again, with everything sent in clear text, it's not recommended in production.

## Secure Shell (SSH)

*Secure Shell (SSH)* protocol sets up a secure session that's similar to Telnet over a standard TCP/IP connection and is employed for doing things like logging into systems, running programs on remote systems, and moving files from one system to another. And it does all of this while maintaining an encrypted connection. Figure 3.4 shows a SSH client trying to connect to a SSH server. The client must send the data encrypted!

You can think of it as the new-generation protocol that's now used in place of the antiquated and very unused `rsh` and `rlogin`—even Telnet.

## File Transfer Protocol (FTP)

*File Transfer Protocol (FTP)* actually lets us transfer files, and it can accomplish this between any two machines using it. But FTP isn't just a protocol; it's also a program. Operating as a protocol, FTP is used by applications. As a program, it's employed by users to perform file tasks by hand. FTP also allows for access to both directories and files and can accomplish certain types of directory operations, such as relocating into different ones (Figure 3.5).

But accessing a host through FTP is only the first step. Users must then be subjected to an authentication login that's usually secured with passwords and usernames implemented by system administrators to restrict access. You can get around this somewhat by adopting the username *anonymous*, but you'll be limited in what you'll be able to access.

**FIGURE 3.4** Secure Shell

**FIGURE 3.5** FTP

Even when employed by users manually as a program, FTP's functions are limited to listing and manipulating directories, typing file contents, and copying files between hosts. It can't execute remote files as programs.

## Trivial File Transfer Protocol (TFTP)

*Trivial File Transfer Protocol (TFTP)* is the stripped-down, stock version of FTP, but it's the protocol of choice if you know exactly what you want and where to find it because it's fast and so easy to use!

But TFTP doesn't offer the abundance of functions that FTP does because it has no directory-browsing abilities, meaning that it can only send and receive files (Figure 3.6). Still, it's heavily used for managing file systems on Cisco devices, as I'll show you in Chapter 7, "Managing and Troubleshooting a Cisco Internetwork."

**FIGURE 3.6**   TFTP

This compact little protocol also skimps in the data department, sending much smaller blocks of data than FTP. Also, there's no authentication as with FTP, so it's even more insecure, and few sites support it because of the inherent security risks.

---

 **Real World Scenario**

### When Should You Use FTP?

Let's say everyone at your San Francisco office needs a 50 GB file emailed to them right away. What do you do? Many email servers would reject that email due to size limits (a lot of ISPs don't allow files larger than 5 MB or 10 MB to be emailed) and, even if there are no size limits on the server, it would still take a while to send this huge file. FTP to the rescue!

If you need to give someone a large file or you need to get a large file from someone, FTP is a nice choice. To use FTP, you would need to set up an FTP server on the Internet so that the files can be shared.

Besides resolving size issues, FTP is faster than email. In addition, because it uses TCP and is connection-oriented, if the session dies, FTP can sometimes start up where it left off. Try that with your email client!

---

## Simple Network Management Protocol (SNMP)

*Simple Network Management Protocol (SNMP)* collects and manipulates valuable network information, as you can see in Figure 3.7. It gathers data by polling the devices on the network from a network management station (NMS) at fixed or random intervals, requiring them to disclose certain information, or even asking for certain information from the device. In addition, network devices can inform the NMS station about problems as they occur so the network administrator is alerted.

**FIGURE 3.7**    SNMP

When all is well, SNMP receives something called a *baseline*—a report delimiting the operational traits of a healthy network. This protocol can also stand as a watchdog over the network, quickly notifying managers of any sudden turn of events. These network watchdogs are called *agents*, and when aberrations occur, agents send an alert called a *trap* to the management station.

---

### SNMP Versions 1, 2, and 3

SNMP versions 1 and 2 are pretty much obsolete. This doesn't mean you won't see them in a network now and then, but you'll only come across v1 rarely, if ever. SNMPv2 provided improvements, especially in performance. But one of the best additions was called GETBULK, which allowed a host to retrieve a large amount of data at once. Even so, v2 never really caught on in the networking world and SNMPv3 is now the standard. Unlike v1, which used only UDP, v3 uses both TCP and UDP and added even more security, message integrity, authentication, and encryption.

---

## Hypertext Transfer Protocol (HTTP)

All those snappy websites comprising a mélange of graphics, text, links, ads and so on rely on the *Hypertext Transfer Protocol (HTTP)* to make it all possible (Figure 3.8). It's used to manage communications between web browsers and web servers and opens the right resource when you click a link, wherever that resource may actually reside.

In order for a browser to display a web page, it must find the exact server that has the right web page, plus the exact details that identify the information requested. This information must be then be sent back to the browser. Nowadays, it's highly doubtful that a web server would have only one page to display!

**FIGURE 3.8**   HTTP

Your browser can understand what you need when you enter a Uniform Resource Locator (URL), which we usually refer to as a web address, e.g. `http://www.lammle.com/forum` and `http://www.lammle.com/blog`.

So basically, each URL defines the protocol used to transfer data, the name of the server, and the particular web page on that server.

## Hypertext Transfer Protocol Secure (HTTPS)

*Hypertext Transfer Protocol Secure (HTTPS)* is also known as Secure Hypertext Transfer Protocol. It uses Secure Sockets Layer (SSL). Sometimes you'll see it referred to as SHTTP or S-HTTP, which were slightly different protocols, but since Microsoft supported HTTPS, it became the de facto standard for securing web communication. But no matter—as indicated, it's a secure version of HTTP that arms you with a whole bunch of security tools for keeping transactions between a web browser and a server secure.

It's what your browser needs to fill out forms, sign in, authenticate, and encrypt an HTTP message when you do things online like make a reservation, access your bank, or buy something.

## Network Time Protocol (NTP)

Kudos to Professor David Mills of the University of Delaware for coming up with this handy protocol that's used to synchronize the clocks on our computers to one standard time source (typically, an atomic clock). *Network Time Protocol (NTP)* works by synchronizing devices to ensure that all computers on a given network agree on the time (Figure 3.9).

This may sound pretty simple, but it's very important because so many of the transactions done today are time and date stamped. Think about databases—a server can get messed up pretty badly and even crash if it's out of sync with the machines connected to it by even mere seconds! You can't have a transaction entered by a machine at, say, 1:50 a.m. when the server records that transaction as having occurred at 1:45 a.m. So basically, NTP works to prevent a "back to the future *sans* DeLorean" scenario from bringing down the network—very important indeed!

I'll tell you a lot more about NTP in Chapter 7, including how to configure this protocol in a Cisco environment.

**FIGURE 3.9**    NTP

## Domain Name Service (DNS)

*Domain Name Service (DNS)* resolves hostnames—specifically, Internet names, such as www
.lammle.com. But you don't have to actually use DNS. You just type in the IP address of any
device you want to communicate with and find the IP address of a URL by using the Ping
program. For example, >ping www.cisco.com will return the IP address resolved by DNS.

An IP address identifies hosts on a network and the Internet as well, but DNS was designed
to make our lives easier. Think about this: What would happen if you wanted to move your
web page to a different service provider? The IP address would change and no one would
know what the new one was. DNS allows you to use a domain name to specify an IP address.
You can change the IP address as often as you want and no one will know the difference.

To resolve a DNS address from a host, you'd typically type in the URL from your favorite browser, which would hand the data to the Application layer interface to be transmitted
on the network. The application would look up the DNS address and send a UDP request
to your DNS server to resolve the name (Figure 3.10).

**FIGURE 3.10**    DNS

If your first DNS server doesn't know the answer to the query, then the DNS server forwards a TCP request to its root DNS server. Once the query is resolved, the answer is transmitted back to the originating host, which means the host can now request the information from the correct web server.

DNS is used to resolve a *fully qualified domain name (FQDN)*—for example, www.lammle .com or todd.lammle.com. An FQDN is a hierarchy that can logically locate a system based on its domain identifier.

If you want to resolve the name *todd*, you either must type in the FQDN of todd.lammle .com or have a device such as a PC or router add the suffix for you. For example, on a Cisco router, you can use the command ip domain-name lammle.com to append each request with the lammle.com domain. If you don't do that, you'll have to type in the FQDN to get DNS to resolve the name.

> An important thing to remember about DNS is that if you can ping a device with an IP address but cannot use its FQDN, then you might have some type of DNS configuration failure.

## Dynamic Host Configuration Protocol (DHCP)/Bootstrap Protocol (BootP)

*Dynamic Host Configuration Protocol (DHCP)* assigns IP addresses to hosts. It allows for easier administration and works well in small to very large network environments. Many types of hardware can be used as a DHCP server, including a Cisco router.

DHCP differs from BootP in that BootP assigns an IP address to a host but the host's hardware address must be entered manually in a BootP table. You can think of DHCP as a dynamic BootP. But remember that BootP is also used to send an operating system that a host can boot from. DHCP can't do that.

But there's still a lot of information a DHCP server can provide to a host when the host is requesting an IP address from the DHCP server. Here's a list of the most common types of information a DHCP server can provide:

- IP address
- Subnet mask
- Domain name
- Default gateway (routers)
- DNS server address
- WINS server address

A client that sends out a DHCP Discover message in order to receive an IP address sends out a broadcast at both layer 2 and layer 3.

- The layer 2 broadcast is all *F*s in hex, which looks like this: ff:ff:ff:ff:ff:ff.
- The layer 3 broadcast is 255.255.255.255, which means all networks and all hosts.

DHCP is connectionless, which means it uses User Datagram Protocol (UDP) at the Transport layer, also known as the Host-to-Host layer, which we'll talk about later.

Seeing is believing, so here's an example of output from my analyzer showing the layer 2 and layer 3 broadcasts:

```
Ethernet II, Src: 0.0.0.0 (00:0b:db:99:d3:5e),Dst: Broadcast(ff:ff:ff:ff:ff:ff)
Internet Protocol, Src: 0.0.0.0 (0.0.0.0),Dst: 255.255.255.255(255.255.255.255)
```

The Data Link and Network layers are both sending out "all hands" broadcasts saying, "Help—I don't know my IP address!"

DHCP will be discussed in more detail, including configuration on a Cisco router and switch, in Chapter 7 and Chapter 8, "IP Routing."

Figure 3.11 shows the process of a client-server relationship using a DHCP connection.

**FIGURE 3.11** DHCP client four-step process

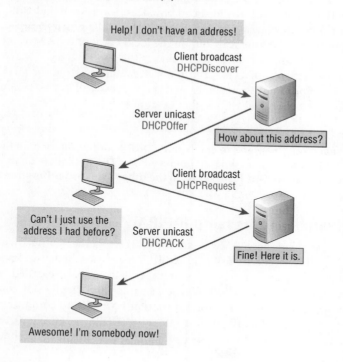

This is the four-step process a client takes to receive an IP address from a DHCP server:

1. The DHCP client broadcasts a DHCP Discover message looking for a DHCP server (Port 67).

2. The DHCP server that received the DHCP Discover message sends a layer 2 unicast DHCP Offer message back to the host.

3. The client then broadcasts to the server a DHCP Request message asking for the offered IP address and possibly other information.

4. The server finalizes the exchange with a unicast DHCP Acknowledgment message.

### DHCP Conflicts

A DHCP address conflict occurs when two hosts use the same IP address. This sounds bad, and it is! We'll never even have to discuss this problem once we get to the chapter on IPv6!

During IP address assignment, a DHCP server checks for conflicts using the Ping program to test the availability of the address before it's assigned from the pool. If no host replies, then the DHCP server assumes that the IP address is not already allocated. This helps the server know that it's providing a good address, but what about the host? To provide extra protection against that terrible IP conflict issue, the host can broadcast for its own address!

A host uses something called a gratuitous ARP to help avoid a possible duplicate address. The DHCP client sends an ARP broadcast out on the local LAN or VLAN using its newly assigned address to solve conflicts before they occur.

So, if an IP address conflict is detected, the address is removed from the DHCP pool (scope), and it's really important to remember that the address will not be assigned to a host until the administrator resolves the conflict by hand!

 Please see Chapter 8 to check out a DHCP configuration on a Cisco router and also to find out what happens when a DHCP client is on one side of a router but the DHCP server is on the other side on a different network!

## Automatic Private IP Addressing (APIPA)

Okay, so what happens if you have a few hosts connected together with a switch or hub and you don't have a DHCP server? You can add IP information by hand, known as *static IP addressing*, but later Windows operating systems provide a feature called Automatic Private IP Addressing (APIPA). With APIPA, clients can automatically self-configure an IP address and subnet mask—basic IP information that hosts use to communicate—when a DHCP server isn't available. The IP address range for APIPA is 169.254.0.1 through 169.254.255.254. The client also configures itself with a default Class B subnet mask of 255.255.0.0.

But when you're in your corporate network working and you have a DHCP server running, and your host shows that it's using this IP address range, it means that either your DHCP client on the host is not working or the server is down or can't be reached due to some network issue. Believe me—I don't know anyone who's seen a host in this address range and has been happy about it!

Now, let's take a look at the Transport layer, or what the DoD calls the Host-to-Host layer.

# The Host-to-Host Layer Protocols

The main purpose of the Host-to-Host layer is to shield the upper-layer applications from the complexities of the network. This layer says to the upper layer, "Just give me your data stream, with any instructions, and I'll begin the process of getting your information ready to send."

Coming up, I'll introduce you to the two protocols at this layer:

- Transmission Control Protocol (TCP)
- User Datagram Protocol (UDP)

In addition, we'll look at some of the key host-to-host protocol concepts, as well as the port numbers.

Remember, this is still considered layer 4, and Cisco really likes the way layer 4 can use acknowledgments, sequencing, and flow control.

## Transmission Control Protocol (TCP)

*Transmission Control Protocol (TCP)* takes large blocks of information from an application and breaks them into segments. It numbers and sequences each segment so that the destination's TCP stack can put the segments back into the order the application intended. After these segments are sent on the transmitting host, TCP waits for an acknowledgment of the receiving end's TCP virtual circuit session, retransmitting any segments that aren't acknowledged.

Before a transmitting host starts to send segments down the model, the sender's TCP stack contacts the destination's TCP stack to establish a connection. This creates a *virtual circuit*, and this type of communication is known as *connection-oriented*. During this initial handshake, the two TCP layers also agree on the amount of information that's going to be sent before the recipient's TCP sends back an acknowledgment. With everything agreed upon in advance, the path is paved for reliable communication to take place.

TCP is a full-duplex, connection-oriented, reliable, and accurate protocol, but establishing all these terms and conditions, in addition to error checking, is no small task. TCP is very complicated, and so not surprisingly, it's costly in terms of network overhead. And since today's networks are much more reliable than those of yore, this added reliability is often unnecessary. Most programmers use TCP because it removes a lot of programming work, but for real-time video and VoIP, *User Datagram Protocol (UDP)* is often better because using it results in less overhead.

## TCP Segment Format

Since the upper layers just send a data stream to the protocols in the Transport layers, I'll use Figure 3.12 to demonstrate how TCP segments a data stream and prepares it for the Internet layer. When the Internet layer receives the data stream, it routes the segments as packets through an internetwork. The segments are handed to the receiving host's Host-to-Host layer protocol, which rebuilds the data stream for the upper-layer applications or protocols.

**FIGURE 3.12**   TCP segment format

| 16-bit source port | | | 16-bit destination port | |
|---|---|---|---|---|
| 32-bit sequence number | | | | |
| 32-Bit Acknowledgment Number | | | | |
| 4-bit header length | Reserved | Flags | 16-bit window size | |
| 16-bit TCP checksum | | | 16-bit urgent pointer | |
| Options | | | | |
| Data | | | | |

Figure 3.12 shows the TCP segment format and shows the different fields within the TCP header. This isn't important to memorize for the Cisco exam objectives, but you need to understand it well because it's really good foundational information.

The TCP header is 20 bytes long, or up to 24 bytes with options. You need to understand what each field in the TCP segment is in order to build a strong educational foundation:

**Source port**   This is the port number of the application on the host sending the data, which I'll talk about more thoroughly a little later in this chapter.

**Destination port**   This is the port number of the application requested on the destination host.

**Sequence number**   A number used by TCP that puts the data back in the correct order or retransmits missing or damaged data during a process called sequencing.

**Acknowledgment number**   The value is the TCP octet that is expected next.

**Header length**   The number of 32-bit words in the TCP header, which indicates where the data begins. The TCP header (even one including options) is an integral number of 32 bits in length.

**Reserved**   Always set to zero.

**Code bits/flags**   Controls functions used to set up and terminate a session.

**Window**   The window size the sender is willing to accept, in octets.

**Checksum**   The cyclic redundancy check (CRC), used because TCP doesn't trust the lower layers and checks everything. The CRC checks the header and data fields.

**Urgent**  A valid field only if the Urgent pointer in the code bits is set. If so, this value indicates the offset from the current sequence number, in octets, where the segment of non-urgent data begins.

**Options**  May be 0, meaning that no options have to be present, or a multiple of 32 bits. However, if any options are used that do not cause the option field to total a multiple of 32 bits, padding of 0s must be used to make sure the data begins on a 32-bit boundary. These boundaries are known as words.

**Data**  Handed down to the TCP protocol at the Transport layer, which includes the upper-layer headers.

Let's take a look at a TCP segment copied from a network analyzer:

```
TCP - Transport Control Protocol
 Source Port:        5973
 Destination Port: 23
 Sequence Number:  1456389907
 Ack Number:       1242056456
 Offset:           5
 Reserved:         %000000
 Code:             %011000
       Ack is valid
       Push Request
Window:             61320
Checksum:           0x61a6
Urgent Pointer:     0
No TCP Options
TCP Data Area:
vL.5.+.5.+.5.+.5  76 4c 19 35 11 2b 19 35 11 2b 19 35 11
 2b 19 35 +. 11 2b 19
Frame Check Sequence: 0x0d00000f
```

Did you notice that everything I talked about earlier is in the segment? As you can see from the number of fields in the header, TCP creates a lot of overhead. Again, this is why application developers may opt for efficiency over reliability to save overhead and go with UDP instead. It's also defined at the Transport layer as an alternative to TCP.

## User Datagram Protocol (UDP)

*User Datagram Protocol (UDP)* is basically the scaled-down economy model of TCP, which is why UDP is sometimes referred to as a thin protocol. Like a thin person on a park bench, a thin protocol doesn't take up a lot of room—or in this case, require much bandwidth on a network.

UDP doesn't offer all the bells and whistles of TCP either, but it does do a fabulous job of transporting information that doesn't require reliable delivery, using far less network resources. (UDP is covered thoroughly in Request for Comments 768.)

So clearly, there are times that it's wise for developers to opt for UDP rather than TCP, one of them being when reliability is already taken care of at the Process/Application layer. Network File System (NFS) handles its own reliability issues, making the use of TCP both impractical and redundant. But ultimately, it's up to the application developer to opt for using UDP or TCP, not the user who wants to transfer data faster!

UDP does *not* sequence the segments and does not care about the order in which the segments arrive at the destination. UDP just sends the segments off and forgets about them. It doesn't follow through, check up on them, or even allow for an acknowledgment of safe arrival—complete abandonment. Because of this, it's referred to as an unreliable protocol. This does not mean that UDP is ineffective, only that it doesn't deal with reliability issues at all.

Furthermore, UDP doesn't create a virtual circuit, nor does it contact the destination before delivering information to it. Because of this, it's also considered a *connectionless* protocol. Since UDP assumes that the application will use its own reliability method, it doesn't use any itself. This presents an application developer with a choice when running the Internet Protocol stack: TCP for reliability or UDP for faster transfers.

It's important to know how this process works because if the segments arrive out of order, which is commonplace in IP networks, they'll simply be passed up to the next layer in whatever order they were received. This can result in some seriously garbled data! On the other hand, TCP sequences the segments so they get put back together in exactly the right order, which is something UDP just can't do.

## UDP Segment Format

Figure 3.13 clearly illustrates UDP's markedly lean overhead as compared to TCP's hungry requirements. Look at the figure carefully—can you see that UDP doesn't use windowing or provide for acknowledgments in the UDP header?

**FIGURE 3.13**   UDP segment

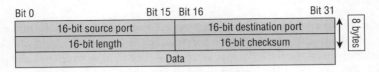

It's important for you to understand what each field in the UDP segment is:

**Source port**   Port number of the application on the host sending the data

**Destination port**   Port number of the application requested on the destination host

**Length**   Length of UDP header and UDP data

**Checksum**   Checksum of both the UDP header and UDP data fields

**Data**   Upper-layer data

UDP, like TCP, doesn't trust the lower layers and runs its own CRC. Remember that the Frame Check Sequence (FCS) is the field that houses the CRC, which is why you can see the FCS information.

The following shows a UDP segment caught on a network analyzer:

```
UDP - User Datagram Protocol
 Source Port:        1085
 Destination Port: 5136
 Length:             41
 Checksum:          0x7a3c
 UDP Data Area:
 ..Z......00 01 5a 96 00 01 00 00 00 00 00 11 0000 00
 ...C..2._C._C  2e 03 00 43 02 1e 32 0a 00 0a 00 80 43 00 80
Frame Check Sequence: 0x00000000
```

Notice that low overhead! Try to find the sequence number, ack number, and window size in the UDP segment. You can't because they just aren't there!

## Key Concepts of Host-to-Host Protocols

Since you've now seen both a connection-oriented (TCP) and connectionless (UDP) protocol in action, it's a good time to summarize the two here. Table 3.1 highlights some of the key concepts about these two protocols for you to memorize.

**TABLE 3.1**  Key features of TCP and UDP

| TCP | UDP |
|---|---|
| Sequenced | Unsequenced |
| Reliable | Unreliable |
| Connection-oriented | Connectionless |
| Virtual circuit | Low overhead |
| Acknowledgments | No acknowledgment |
| Windowing flow control | No windowing or flow control of any type |

And if all this isn't quite clear yet, a telephone analogy will really help you understand how TCP works. Most of us know that before you speak to someone on a phone, you must first establish a connection with that other person no matter where they are. This is akin to establishing a virtual circuit with the TCP protocol. If you were giving someone important information during your conversation, you might say things like, "You know? or "Did you get that?" Saying things like this is a lot like a TCP acknowledgment—it's designed to get you verification. From time to time, especially on mobile phones, people ask, "Are you still there?" People end their conversations with a "Goodbye" of some kind, putting closure on the phone call, which you can think of as tearing down the virtual circuit that was created for your communication session. TCP performs these types of functions.

Conversely, using UDP is more like sending a postcard. To do that, you don't need to contact the other party first, you simply write your message, address the postcard, and send it off. This is analogous to UDP's connectionless orientation. Since the message on the postcard is probably not a matter of life or death, you don't need an acknowledgment of its receipt. Similarly, UDP does not involve acknowledgments.

Let's take a look at another figure, one that includes TCP, UDP, and the applications associated to each protocol: Figure 3.14 (discussed in the next section).

**FIGURE 3.14**    Port numbers for TCP and UDP

## Port Numbers

TCP and UDP must use *port numbers* to communicate with the upper layers because these are what keep track of different conversations crossing the network simultaneously. Originating-source port numbers are dynamically assigned by the source host and will equal some number starting at 1024. Port number 1023 and below are defined in RFC 3232 (or just see www.iana.org), which discusses what we call well-known port numbers.

Virtual circuits that don't use an application with a well-known port number are assigned port numbers randomly from a specific range instead. These port numbers identify the source and destination application or process in the TCP segment.

The Requests for Comments (RFCs) form a series of notes about the Internet (originally the ARPAnet) began in 1969. These notes discuss many aspects of computer communication, focusing on networking protocols, procedures, programs, and concepts; but they also include meeting notes, opinions, and sometimes even humor. You can find the RFCs by visiting www.iana.org.

Figure 3.14 illustrates how both TCP and UDP use port numbers. I'll cover the different port numbers that can be used next:

- Numbers below 1024 are considered well-known port numbers and are defined in RFC 3232.

- Numbers 1024 and above are used by the upper layers to set up sessions with other hosts and by TCP and UDP to use as source and destination addresses in the segment.

## TCP Session: Source Port

Let's take a minute to check out analyzer output showing a TCP session I captured with my analyzer software session now:

```
TCP - Transport Control Protocol
 Source Port:      5973
 Destination Port: 23
 Sequence Number:  1456389907
 Ack Number:       1242056456
 Offset:           5
 Reserved:         %000000
 Code:             %011000
      Ack is valid
      Push Request
 Window:           61320
 Checksum:         0x61a6
 Urgent Pointer:   0
 No TCP Options
 TCP Data Area:
 vL.5.+.5.+.5.+.5   76 4c 19 35 11 2b 19 35 11 2b 19 35 11
  2b 19 35 +. 11 2b 19
Frame Check Sequence: 0x0d00000f
```

Notice that the source host makes up the source port, which in this case is 5973. The destination port is 23, which is used to tell the receiving host the purpose of the intended connection (Telnet).

By looking at this session, you can see that the source host makes up the source port by using numbers from 1024 to 65535. But why does the source make up a port number? To differentiate between sessions with different hosts because how would a server know where information is coming from if it didn't have a different number from a sending host? TCP and the upper layers don't use hardware and logical addresses to understand the sending host's address as the Data Link and Network layer protocols do. Instead, they use port numbers.

## TCP Session: Destination Port

You'll sometimes look at an analyzer and see that only the source port is above 1024 and the destination port is a well-known port, as shown in the following trace:

```
TCP - Transport Control Protocol
 Source Port:        1144
 Destination Port: 80 World Wide Web HTTP
 Sequence Number:   9356570
 Ack Number:        0
 Offset:            7
 Reserved:          %000000
 Code:              %000010
       Synch Sequence
 Window:            8192
 Checksum:          0x57E7
 Urgent Pointer:    0
 TCP Options:
  Option Type: 2 Maximum Segment Size
    Length:    4
    MSS:       536
  Option Type: 1 No Operation
  Option Type: 1 No Operation
  Option Type: 4
    Length:    2
    Opt Value:
  No More HTTP Data
Frame Check Sequence: 0x43697363
```

And sure enough, the source port is over 1024, but the destination port is 80, indicating an HTTP service. The server, or receiving host, will change the destination port if it needs to.

In the preceding trace, a "SYN" packet is sent to the destination device. This Synch (as shown in the output) sequence is what's used to inform the remote destination device that it wants to create a session.

## TCP Session: Syn Packet Acknowledgment

The next trace shows an acknowledgment to the syn packet:

```
TCP - Transport Control Protocol
 Source Port:       80 World Wide Web HTTP
 Destination Port: 1144
 Sequence Number:   2873580788
 Ack Number:        9356571
 Offset:            6
```

```
    Reserved:        %000000
    Code:            %010010
        Ack is valid
        Synch Sequence
    Window:          8576
    Checksum:        0x5F85
    Urgent Pointer:  0
    TCP Options:
     Option Type: 2 Maximum Segment Size
       Length:    4
       MSS:       1460
    No More HTTP Data
Frame Check Sequence: 0x6E203132
```

Notice the *Ack is valid*, which means that the source port was accepted and the device agreed to create a virtual circuit with the originating host.

And here again, you can see that the response from the server shows that the source is 80 and the destination is the 1144 sent from the originating host—all's well!

Table 3.2 gives you a list of the typical applications used in the TCP/IP suite by showing their well-known port numbers, and the Transport layer protocols used by each application or process. It's really key to memorize this table.

**TABLE 3.2**   Key protocols that use TCP and UDP

| TCP | UDP |
| --- | --- |
| Telnet 23 | SNMP 161 |
| SMTP 25 | TFTP 69 |
| HTTP 80 | DNS 53 |
| FTP 20, 21 | BooTPS/DHCP 67 |
| DNS 53 | |
| HTTPS 443 | |
| SSH 22 | |
| POP3 110 | |
| NTP 123 | |
| IMAP4 143 | |

Notice that DNS uses both TCP and UDP. Whether it opts for one or the other depends on what it's trying to do. Even though it's not the only application that can use both protocols, it's certainly one that you should make sure to remember in your studies.

 What makes TCP reliable is sequencing, acknowledgments, and flow control (windowing). UDP does not have reliability.

Okay—I want to discuss one more item before we move down to the Internet layer—session multiplexing. Session multiplexing is used by both TCP and UDP and basically allows a single computer, with a single IP address, to have multiple sessions occurring simultaneously. Say you go to www.lammle.com and are browsing and then you click a link to another page. Doing this opens another session to your host. Now you go to www.lammle.com/forum from another window and that site opens a window as well. Now you have three sessions open using one IP address because the Session layer is sorting the separate request based on the Transport layer port number. This is the job of the Session layer: to keep application layer data separate!

## The Internet Layer Protocols

In the DoD model, there are two main reasons for the Internet layer's existence: routing and providing a single network interface to the upper layers.

None of the other upper- or lower-layer protocols have any functions relating to routing—that complex and important task belongs entirely to the Internet layer. The Internet layer's second duty is to provide a single network interface to the upper-layer protocols. Without this layer, application programmers would need to write "hooks" into every one of their applications for each different Network Access protocol. This would not only be a pain in the neck, but it would lead to different versions of each application—one for Ethernet, another one for wireless, and so on. To prevent this, IP provides one single network interface for the upper-layer protocols. With that mission accomplished, it's then the job of IP and the various Network Access protocols to get along and work together.

All network roads don't lead to Rome—they lead to IP. And all the other protocols at this layer, as well as all those at the upper layers, use it. Never forget that. All paths through the DoD model go through IP. Here's a list of the important protocols at the Internet layer that I'll cover individually in detail coming up:

- Internet Protocol (IP)
- Internet Control Message Protocol (ICMP)
- Address Resolution Protocol (ARP)

### Internet Protocol (IP)

*Internet Protocol (IP)* essentially is the Internet layer. The other protocols found here merely exist to support it. IP holds the big picture and could be said to "see all," because it's aware of all the interconnected networks. It can do this because all the machines on the network have a software, or logical, address called an IP address, which we'll explore more thoroughly later in this chapter.

For now, understand that IP looks at each packet's address. Then, using a routing table, it decides where a packet is to be sent next, choosing the best path to send it upon. The protocols of the Network Access layer at the bottom of the DoD model don't possess IP's enlightened scope of the entire network; they deal only with physical links (local networks).

Identifying devices on networks requires answering these two questions: Which network is it on? And what is its ID on that network? The first answer is the *software address*, or *logical address*. You can think of this as the part of the address that specifies the correct street. The second answer is the hardware address, which goes a step further to specify the correct mailbox. All hosts on a network have a logical ID called an IP address. This is the software, or logical, address and contains valuable encoded information, greatly simplifying the complex task of routing. (IP is discussed in RFC 791.)

IP receives segments from the Host-to-Host layer and fragments them into datagrams (packets) if necessary. IP then reassembles datagrams back into segments on the receiving side. Each datagram is assigned the IP address of the sender and that of the recipient. Each router or switch (layer 3 device) that receives a datagram makes routing decisions based on the packet's destination IP address.

Figure 3.15 shows an IP header. This will give you a picture of what the IP protocol has to go through every time user data that is destined for a remote network is sent from the upper layers.

**FIGURE 3.15**    IP header

The following fields make up the IP header:

**Version**    IP version number.

**Header length**    Header length (HLEN) in 32-bit words.

**Priority and Type of Service**    Type of Service tells how the datagram should be handled. The first 3 bits are the priority bits, now called the differentiated services bits.

**Total length**    Length of the packet, including header and data.

**Identification**    Unique IP-packet value used to differentiate fragmented packets from different datagrams.

**Flags**   Specifies whether fragmentation should occur.

**Fragment offset**   Provides fragmentation and reassembly if the packet is too large to put in a frame. It also allows different maximum transmission units (MTUs) on the Internet.

**Time To Live**   The time to live (TTL) is set into a packet when it is originally generated. If it doesn't get to where it's supposed to go before the TTL expires, boom—it's gone. This stops IP packets from continuously circling the network looking for a home.

**Protocol**   Port of upper-layer protocol; for example, TCP is port 6 or UDP is port 17. Also supports Network layer protocols, like ARP and ICMP, and can referred to as the Type field in some analyzers. We'll talk about this field more in a minute.

**Header checksum**   Cyclic redundancy check (CRC) on header only.

**Source IP address**   32-bit IP address of sending station.

**Destination IP address**   32-bit IP address of the station this packet is destined for.

**Options**   Used for network testing, debugging, security, and more.

**Data**   After the IP option field, will be the upper-layer data.

Here's a snapshot of an IP packet caught on a network analyzer. Notice that all the header information discussed previously appears here:

```
IP Header - Internet Protocol Datagram
 Version:               4
 Header Length:         5
 Precedence:            0
 Type of Service:       %000
 Unused:                %00
 Total Length:          187
 Identifier:            22486
 Fragmentation Flags:   %010 Do Not Fragment
 Fragment Offset:       0
 Time To Live:          60
 IP Type:               0x06 TCP
 Header Checksum:       0xd031
 Source IP Address:     10.7.1.30
 Dest. IP Address:      10.7.1.10
 No Internet Datagram Options
```

The Type field is typically a Protocol field, but this analyzer sees it as an IP Type field. This is important. If the header didn't carry the protocol information for the next layer, IP wouldn't know what to do with the data carried in the packet. The preceding example clearly tells IP to hand the segment to TCP.

Figure 3.16 demonstrates how the Network layer sees the protocols at the Transport layer when it needs to hand a packet up to the upper-layer protocols.

**FIGURE 3.16**   The Protocol field in an IP header

In this example, the Protocol field tells IP to send the data to either TCP port 6 or UDP port 17. But it will be UDP or TCP only if the data is part of a data stream headed for an upper-layer service or application. It could just as easily be destined for Internet Control Message Protocol (ICMP), Address Resolution Protocol (ARP), or some other type of Network layer protocol.

Table 3.3 is a list of some other popular protocols that can be specified in the Protocol field.

**TABLE 3.3**   Possible protocols found in the Protocol field of an IP header

| Protocol | Protocol Number |
|----------|-----------------|
| ICMP | 1 |
| IP in IP (tunneling) | 4 |
| TCP | 6 |
| UDP | 17 |
| EIGRP | 88 |
| OSPF | 89 |
| IPv6 | 41 |
| GRE | 47 |
| Layer 2 tunnel (L2TP) | 115 |

You can find a complete list of Protocol field numbers at www.iana.org/ assignments/protocol-numbers.

## Internet Control Message Protocol (ICMP)

*Internet Control Message Protocol (ICMP)* works at the Network layer and is used by IP for many different services. ICMP is basically a management protocol and messaging service provider for IP. Its messages are carried as IP datagrams. RFC 1256 is an annex to ICMP, which gives hosts extended capability in discovering routes to gateways.

ICMP packets have the following characteristics:

* They can provide hosts with information about network problems.

* They are encapsulated within IP datagrams.

The following are some common events and messages that ICMP relates to:

**Destination unreachable**   If a router can't send an IP datagram any further, it uses ICMP to send a message back to the sender, advising it of the situation. For example, take a look at Figure 3.17, which shows that interface E0 of the Lab_B router is down.

**FIGURE 3.17**    ICMP error message is sent to the sending host from the remote router.

When Host A sends a packet destined for Host B, the Lab_B router will send an ICMP destination unreachable message back to the sending device, which is Host A in this example.

**Buffer full/source quench**   If a router's memory buffer for receiving incoming datagrams is full, it will use ICMP to send out this message alert until the congestion abates.

**Hops/time exceeded**   Each IP datagram is allotted a certain number of routers, called hops, to pass through. If it reaches its limit of hops before arriving at its destination, the last router to receive that datagram deletes it. The executioner router then uses ICMP to send an obituary message, informing the sending machine of the demise of its datagram.

**Ping**   Packet Internet Groper (Ping) uses ICMP echo request and reply messages to check the physical and logical connectivity of machines on an internetwork.

**Traceroute**   Using ICMP time-outs, Traceroute is used to discover the path a packet takes as it traverses an internetwork.

Both Ping and Traceroute are usually just called Trace. Microsoft Windows uses tracert to allow you to verify address configurations in your internetwork.

The following data is from a network analyzer catching an ICMP echo request:

```
Flags:        0x00
 Status:       0x00
 Packet Length: 78
 Timestamp:     14:04:25.967000 12/20/03
Ethernet Header
 Destination: 00:a0:24:6e:0f:a8
 Source:       00:80:c7:a8:f0:3d
 Ether-Type:   08-00 IP
IP Header - Internet Protocol Datagram
 Version:          4
 Header Length:    5
 Precedence:       0
 Type of Service:  %000
 Unused:           %00
 Total Length:     60
 Identifier:       56325
 Fragmentation Flags: %000
 Fragment Offset:  0
 Time To Live:     32
 IP Type:          0x01 ICMP
 Header Checksum:  0x2df0
 Source IP Address:  100.100.100.2
 Dest. IP Address:   100.100.100.1
 No Internet Datagram Options
ICMP - Internet Control Messages Protocol
 ICMP Type:    8 Echo Request
 Code:         0
 Checksum:     0x395c
 Identifier:   0x0300
 Sequence Number: 4352
 ICMP Data Area:
 abcdefghijklmnop  61 62 63 64 65 66 67 68 69 6a 6b 6c 6d 6e 6f 70
 qrstuvwabcdefghi  71 72 73 74 75 76 77 61 62 63 64 65 66 67 68 69
Frame Check Sequence: 0x00000000
```

Notice anything unusual? Did you catch the fact that even though ICMP works at the Internet (Network) layer, it still uses IP to do the Ping request? The Type field in the IP header is 0x01, which specifies that the data we're carrying is owned by the ICMP protocol. Remember, just as all roads lead to Rome, all segments or data *must* go through IP!

> The Ping program uses the alphabet in the data portion of the packet as a payload, typically around 100 bytes by default, unless, of course, you are pinging from a Windows device, which thinks the alphabet stops at the letter *W* (and doesn't include *X*, *Y*, or *Z*) and then starts at *A* again. Go figure!

If you remember reading about the Data Link layer and the different frame types in Chapter 2, "Ethernet Technologies and Data Encapsulation," you should be able to look at the preceding trace and tell what type of Ethernet frame this is. The only fields are destination hardware address, source hardware address, and Ether-Type. The only frame that uses an Ether-Type field exclusively is an Ethernet_II frame.

We'll move on soon, but before we get into the ARP protocol, let's take another look at ICMP in action. Figure 3.18 shows an internetwork—it has a router, so it's an internetwork, right?

**FIGURE 3.18** ICMP in action

Server1 (10.1.2.2) telnets to 10.1.1.5 from a DOS prompt. What do you think Server1 will receive as a response? Server1 will send the Telnet data to the default gateway, which is the router, and the router will drop the packet because there isn't a network 10.1.1.0 in the routing table. Because of this, Server1 will receive an ICMP destination unreachable back from the router.

## Address Resolution Protocol (ARP)

*Address Resolution Protocol (ARP)* finds the hardware address of a host from a known IP address. Here's how it works: When IP has a datagram to send, it must inform a Network Access protocol, such as Ethernet or wireless, of the destination's hardware address on the local network. Remember that it has already been informed by upper-layer protocols of the destination's IP address. If IP doesn't find the destination host's hardware address in the ARP cache, it uses ARP to find this information.

As IP's detective, ARP interrogates the local network by sending out a broadcast asking the machine with the specified IP address to reply with its hardware address. So basically, ARP translates the software (IP) address into a hardware address—for example, the destination machine's Ethernet adapter address—and from it, deduces its whereabouts on the LAN by broadcasting for this address. Figure 3.19 shows how an ARP broadcast looks to a local network.

**FIGURE 3.19** Local ARP broadcast

 ARP resolves IP addresses to Ethernet (MAC) addresses.

The following trace shows an ARP broadcast—notice that the destination hardware address is unknown and is all *F*s in hex (all 1s in binary)—and is a hardware address broadcast:

```
Flags:         0x00
Status:        0x00
Packet Length: 64
Timestamp:     09:17:29.574000 12/06/03
```

```
Ethernet Header
 Destination:    FF:FF:FF:FF:FF:FF Ethernet Broadcast
 Source:         00:A0:24:48:60:A5
 Protocol Type: 0x0806 IP ARP
ARP - Address Resolution Protocol
 Hardware:                 1 Ethernet (10Mb)
 Protocol:                 0x0800 IP
 Hardware Address Length: 6
 Protocol Address Length: 4
 Operation:                1 ARP Request
 Sender Hardware Address: 00:A0:24:48:60:A5
 Sender Internet Address: 172.16.10.3
 Target Hardware Address: 00:00:00:00:00:00 (ignored)
 Target Internet Address: 172.16.10.10
Extra bytes (Padding):
 ................ 0A 0A 0A 0A 0A 0A 0A 0A 0A 0A 0A 0A 0A
  0A 0A 0A 0A 0A
Frame Check Sequence: 0x00000000
```

# IP Addressing

One of the most important topics in any discussion of TCP/IP is IP addressing. An *IP address* is a numeric identifier assigned to each machine on an IP network. It designates the specific location of a device on the network.

An IP address is a software address, not a hardware address—the latter is hard-coded on a network interface card (NIC) and used for finding hosts on a local network. IP addressing was designed to allow hosts on one network to communicate with a host on a different network regardless of the type of LANs the hosts are participating in.

Before we get into the more complicated aspects of IP addressing, you need to understand some of the basics. First I'm going to explain some of the fundamentals of IP addressing and its terminology. Then you'll learn about the hierarchical IP addressing scheme and private IP addresses.

## IP Terminology

Throughout this chapter you're being introduced to several important terms that are vital to understanding the Internet Protocol. Here are a few to get you started:

**Bit**   A bit is one digit, either a 1 or a 0.

**Byte**   A byte is 7 or 8 bits, depending on whether parity is used. For the rest of this chapter, always assume a byte is 8 bits.

**Octet**    An octet, made up of 8 bits, is just an ordinary 8-bit binary number. In this chapter, the terms byte and octet are completely interchangeable.

**Network address**    This is the designation used in routing to send packets to a remote network—for example, 10.0.0.0, 172.16.0.0, and 192.168.10.0.

**Broadcast address**    The address used by applications and hosts to send information to all nodes on a network is called the broadcast address. Examples of layer 3 broadcasts include 255.255.255.255, which is any network, all nodes; 172.16.255.255, which is all subnets and hosts on network 172.16.0.0; and 10.255.255.255, which broadcasts to all subnets and hosts on network 10.0.0.0.

# The Hierarchical IP Addressing Scheme

An IP address consists of 32 bits of information. These bits are divided into four sections, referred to as octets or bytes, with each containing 1 byte (8 bits). You can depict an IP address using one of three methods:

- Dotted-decimal, as in 172.16.30.56
- Binary, as in 10101100.00010000.00011110.00111000
- Hexadecimal, as in AC.10.1E.38

All these examples represent the same IP address. Pertaining to IP addressing, hexadecimal isn't used as often as dotted-decimal or binary, but you still might find an IP address stored in hexadecimal in some programs.

The 32-bit IP address is a structured or hierarchical address, as opposed to a flat or nonhierarchical address. Although either type of addressing scheme could have been used, *hierarchical addressing* was chosen for a good reason. The advantage of this scheme is that it can handle a large number of addresses, namely 4.3 billion (a 32-bit address space with two possible values for each position—either 0 or 1—gives you $2^{32}$, or 4,294,967,296). The disadvantage of the flat addressing scheme, and the reason it's not used for IP addressing, relates to routing. If every address were unique, all routers on the Internet would need to store the address of each and every machine on the Internet. This would make efficient routing impossible, even if only a fraction of the possible addresses were used!

The solution to this problem is to use a two- or three-level hierarchical addressing scheme that is structured by network and host or by network, subnet, and host.

This two- or three-level scheme can also be compared to a telephone number. The first section, the area code, designates a very large area. The second section, the prefix, narrows the scope to a local calling area. The final segment, the customer number, zooms in on the specific connection. IP addresses use the same type of layered structure. Rather than all 32 bits being treated as a unique identifier, as in flat addressing, a part of the address is designated as the network address and the other part is designated as either the subnet and host or just the node address.

Next, we'll cover IP network addressing and the different classes of address we can use to address our networks.

## Network Addressing

The *network address* (which can also be called the network number) uniquely identifies each network. Every machine on the same network shares that network address as part of its IP address. For example, in the IP address 172.16.30.56, 172.16 is the network address.

The *node address* is assigned to, and uniquely identifies, each machine on a network. This part of the address must be unique because it identifies a particular machine—an individual—as opposed to a network, which is a group. This number can also be referred to as a *host address*. In the sample IP address 172.16.30.56, the 30.56 specifies the node address.

The designers of the Internet decided to create classes of networks based on network size. For the small number of networks possessing a very large number of nodes, they created the rank *Class A network*. At the other extreme is the *Class C network*, which is reserved for the numerous networks with a small number of nodes. The class distinction for networks between very large and very small is predictably called the *Class B network*.

Subdividing an IP address into a network and node address is determined by the class designation of one's network. Figure 3.20 summarizes the three classes of networks used to address hosts—a subject I'll explain in much greater detail throughout this chapter.

**FIGURE 3.20**   Summary of the three classes of networks

To ensure efficient routing, Internet designers defined a mandate for the leading-bits section of the address for each different network class. For example, since a router knows that a Class A network address always starts with a 0, the router might be able to speed a packet on its way after reading only the first bit of its address. This is where the address schemes define the difference between a Class A, a Class B, and a Class C address. Coming up, I'll discuss the differences between these three classes, followed by a discussion of the Class D and Class E addresses. Classes A, B, and C are the only ranges that are used to address hosts in our networks.

### Network Address Range: Class A

The designers of the IP address scheme decided that the first bit of the first byte in a Class A network address must always be off, or 0. This means a Class A address must be between 0 and 127 in the first byte, inclusive.

Consider the following network address:

`0xxxxxxx`

If we turn the other 7 bits all off and then turn them all on, we'll find the Class A range of network addresses:

`00000000 = 0`
`01111111 = 127`

So, a Class A network is defined in the first octet between 0 and 127, and it can't be less or more. Understand that 0 and 127 are not valid in a Class A network because they're reserved addresses, which I'll explain soon.

## Network Address Range: Class B

In a Class B network, the RFCs state that the first bit of the first byte must always be turned on but the second bit must always be turned off. If you turn the other 6 bits all off and then all on, you will find the range for a Class B network:

`10000000 = 128`
`10111111 = 191`

As you can see, a Class B network is defined when the first byte is configured from 128 to 191.

## Network Address Range: Class C

For Class C networks, the RFCs define the first 2 bits of the first octet as always turned on, but the third bit can never be on. Following the same process as the previous classes, convert from binary to decimal to find the range. Here's the range for a Class C network:

`11000000 = 192`
`11011111 = 223`

So, if you see an IP address that starts at 192 and goes to 223, you'll know it is a Class C IP address.

## Network Address Ranges: Classes D and E

The addresses between 224 to 255 are reserved for Class D and E networks. Class D (224–239) is used for multicast addresses and Class E (240–255) for scientific purposes, but I'm not going into these types of addresses because they are beyond the scope of knowledge you need to gain from this book.

## Network Addresses: Special Purpose

Some IP addresses are reserved for special purposes, so network administrators can't ever assign these addresses to nodes. Table 3.4 lists the members of this exclusive little club and the reasons why they're included in it.

**TABLE 3.4**   Reserved IP addresses

| Address | Function |
|---|---|
| Network address of all 0s | Interpreted to mean "this network or segment." |
| Network address of all 1s | Interpreted to mean "all networks." |
| Network 127.0.0.1 | Reserved for loopback tests. Designates the local node and allows that node to send a test packet to itself without generating network traffic. |
| Node address of all 0s | Interpreted to mean "network address" or any host on a specified network. |
| Node address of all 1s | Interpreted to mean "all nodes" on the specified network; for example, 128.2.255.255 means "all nodes" on network 128.2 (Class B address). |
| Entire IP address set to all 0s | Used by Cisco routers to designate the default route. Could also mean "any network." |
| Entire IP address set to all 1s (same as 255.255.255.255) | Broadcast to all nodes on the current network; sometimes called an "all 1s broadcast" or local broadcast. |

## Class A Addresses

In a Class A network address, the first byte is assigned to the network address and the three remaining bytes are used for the node addresses. The Class A format is as follows:

*network.node.node.node*

For example, in the IP address 49.22.102.70, the 49 is the network address and 22.102.70 is the node address. Every machine on this particular network would have the distinctive network address of 49.

Class A network addresses are 1 byte long, with the first bit of that byte reserved and the 7 remaining bits available for manipulation (addressing). As a result, the maximum number of Class A networks that can be created is 128. Why? Because each of the 7 bit positions can be either a 0 or a 1, thus $2^7$, or 128.

To complicate matters further, the network address of all 0s (0000 0000) is reserved to designate the default route (see Table 3.4 in the previous section). Additionally, the address 127, which is reserved for diagnostics, can't be used either, which means that you can really only use the numbers 1 to 126 to designate Class A network addresses. This means the actual number of usable Class A network addresses is 128 minus 2, or 126.

The IP address 127.0.0.1 is used to test the IP stack on an individual node and cannot be used as a valid host address. However, the loopback address creates a shortcut method for TCP/IP applications and services that run on the same device to communicate with each other.

Each Class A address has 3 bytes (24-bit positions) for the node address of a machine. This means there are $2^{24}$—or 16,777,216—unique combinations and, therefore, precisely that many possible unique node addresses for each Class A network. Because node addresses with the two patterns of all 0s and all 1s are reserved, the actual maximum usable number of nodes for a Class A network is $2^{24}$ minus 2, which equals 16,777,214. Either way, that's a huge number of hosts on a single network segment!

### Class A Valid Host IDs

Here's an example of how to figure out the valid host IDs in a Class A network address:

- All host bits off is the network address: 10.0.0.0.
- All host bits on is the broadcast address: 10.255.255.255.

The valid hosts are the numbers in between the network address and the broadcast address: 10.0.0.1 through 10.255.255.254. Notice that 0s and 255s can be valid host IDs. All you need to remember when trying to find valid host addresses is that the host bits can't all be turned off or on at the same time.

## Class B Addresses

In a Class B network address, the first 2 bytes are assigned to the network address and the remaining 2 bytes are used for node addresses. The format is as follows:

network.network.node.node

For example, in the IP address 172.16.30.56, the network address is 172.16 and the node address is 30.56.

With a network address being 2 bytes (8 bits each), you get $2^{16}$ unique combinations. But the Internet designers decided that all Class B network addresses should start with the binary digit 1, then 0. This leaves 14 bit positions to manipulate, therefore 16,384, or $2^{14}$ unique Class B network addresses.

A Class B address uses 2 bytes for node addresses. This is $2^{16}$ minus the two reserved patterns of all 0s and all 1s for a total of 65,534 possible node addresses for each Class B network.

### Class B Valid Host IDs

Here's an example of how to find the valid hosts in a Class B network:

- All host bits turned off is the network address: 172.16.0.0.
- All host bits turned on is the broadcast address: 172.16.255.255.

The valid hosts would be the numbers in between the network address and the broadcast address: 172.16.0.1 through 172.16.255.254.

## Class C Addresses

The first 3 bytes of a Class C network address are dedicated to the network portion of the address, with only 1 measly byte remaining for the node address. Here's the format:

`network.network.network.node`

Using the example IP address 192.168.100.102, the network address is 192.168.100 and the node address is 102.

In a Class C network address, the first three bit positions are always the binary 110. The calculation is as follows: 3 bytes, or 24 bits, minus 3 reserved positions leaves 21 positions. Hence, there are $2^{21}$, or 2,097,152, possible Class C networks.

Each unique Class C network has 1 byte to use for node addresses. This leads to $2^8$, or 256, minus the two reserved patterns of all 0s and all 1s, for a total of 254 node addresses for each Class C network.

### Class C Valid Host IDs

Here's an example of how to find a valid host ID in a Class C network:

- All host bits turned off is the network ID: 192.168.100.0.
- All host bits turned on is the broadcast address: 192.168.100.255.

The valid hosts would be the numbers in between the network address and the broadcast address: 192.168.100.1 through 192.168.100.254.

# Private IP Addresses (RFC 1918)

The people who created the IP addressing scheme also created private IP addresses. These addresses can be used on a private network, but they're not routable through the Internet. This is designed for the purpose of creating a measure of well-needed security, but it also conveniently saves valuable IP address space.

If every host on every network was required to have real routable IP addresses, we would have run out of IP addresses to hand out years ago. But by using private IP addresses, ISPs, corporations, and home users only need a relatively tiny group of bona fide IP addresses to connect their networks to the Internet. This is economical because they can use private IP addresses on their inside networks and get along just fine.

To accomplish this task, the ISP and the corporation—the end user, no matter who they are—need to use something called *Network Address Translation (NAT)*, which basically takes a private IP address and converts it for use on the Internet. (NAT is covered in Chapter 13, "Network Address Translation.") Many people can use the same real IP address to transmit out onto the Internet. Doing things this way saves megatons of address space—good for us all!

The reserved private addresses are listed in Table 3.5.

**TABLE 3.5** Reserved IP address space

| Address Class | Reserved Address Space |
| --- | --- |
| Class A | 10.0.0.0 through 10.255.255.255 |
| Class B | 172.16.0.0 through 172.31.255.255 |
| Class C | 192.168.0.0 through 192.168.255.255 |

You must know your private address space to become Cisco certified!

---

### So, What Private IP Address Should I Use?

That's a really great question: Should you use Class A, Class B, or even Class C private addressing when setting up your network? Let's take Acme Corporation in SF as an example. This company is moving into a new building and needs a whole new network. It has 14 departments, with about 70 users in each. You could probably squeeze one or two Class C addresses to use, or maybe you could use a Class B, or even a Class A just for fun.

The rule of thumb in the consulting world is, when you're setting up a corporate network—regardless of how small it is—you should use a Class A network address because it gives you the most flexibility and growth options. For example, if you used the 10.0.0.0 network address with a /24 mask, then you'd have 65,536 networks, each with 254 hosts. Lots of room for growth with that network!

But if you're setting up a home network, you'd opt for a Class C address because it is the easiest for people to understand and configure. Using the default Class C mask gives you one network with 254 hosts—plenty for a home network.

With the Acme Corporation, a nice 10.1.*x*.0 with a /24 mask (the *x* is the subnet for each department) makes this easy to design, install, and troubleshoot.

# IPv4 Address Types

Most people use the term *broadcast* as a generic term, and most of the time, we understand what they mean—but not always! For example, you might say, "The host broadcasted through a router to a DHCP server," but, well, it's pretty unlikely that this would ever really happen. What you probably mean—using the correct technical jargon—is, "The DHCP client broad- casted for an IP address and a router then forwarded this as a unicast packet to the DHCP server." Oh, and remember that with IPv4, broadcasts are pretty important, but with IPv6, there aren't any broadcasts sent at all—now there's something to look forward to reading about in Chapter 14!

Okay, I've referred to IP addresses throughout the preceding chapters and now all throughout this chapter, and even showed you some examples. But I really haven't gone into the different terms and uses associated with them yet, and it's about time I did. So here are the address types that I'd like to define for you:

**Loopback (localhost)**   Used to test the IP stack on the local computer. Can be any address from 127.0.0.1 through 127.255.255.254.

**Layer 2 broadcasts**   These are sent to all nodes on a LAN.

**Broadcasts (layer 3)**   These are sent to all nodes on the network.

**Unicast**   This is an address for a single interface, and these are used to send packets to a single destination host.

**Multicast**   These are packets sent from a single source and transmitted to many devices on different networks. Referred to as "one-to-many."

## Layer 2 Broadcasts

First, understand that layer 2 broadcasts are also known as hardware broadcasts—they only go out on a LAN, but they don't go past the LAN boundary (router).

The typical hardware address is 6 bytes (48 bits) and looks something like 45:AC:24:E3:60:A5. The broadcast would be all 1s in binary, which would be all *F*s in hexadecimal, as in ff:ff:ff:ff:ff:ff and shown in Figure 3.21.

Every network interface card (NIC) will receive and read the frame, including the router, since this was a layer 2 broadcast, but the router would never, ever forward this!

## Layer 3 Broadcasts

Then there are the plain old broadcast addresses at layer 3. Broadcast messages are meant to reach all hosts on a broadcast domain. These are the network broadcasts that have all host bits on.

Here's an example that you're already familiar with: The network address of 172.16.0.0 255.255.0.0 would have a broadcast address of 172.16.255.255—all host bits on. Broadcasts can also be "any network and all hosts," as indicated by 255.255.255.255, and shown in Figure 3.22.

**FIGURE 3.21**    Local layer 2 broadcasts

**FIGURE 3.22**    Layer 3 broadcasts

In Figure 3.22, all hosts on the LAN will get this broadcast on their NIC, including the router, but by default the router would never forward this packet.

## Unicast Address

A unicast is defined as a single IP address that's assigned to a network interface card and is the destination IP address in a packet—in other words, it's used for directing packets to a specific host.

In Figure 3.23 both the MAC address and the destination IP address are for a single NIC on the network. All hosts on the broadcast domain would receive this frame and accept it. Only the destination NIC of 10.1.1.2 would accept the packet; the other NICs would discard the packet.

**FIGURE 3.23**   Unicast address

## Multicast Address

Multicast is a different beast entirely. At first glance, it appears to be a hybrid of unicast and broadcast communication, but that isn't quite the case. Multicast does allow point-to-multipoint communication, which is similar to broadcasts, but it happens in a different manner. The crux of *multicast* is that it enables multiple recipients to receive messages without flooding the messages to all hosts on a broadcast domain. However, this is not the default behavior—it's what we *can* do with multicasting if it's configured correctly!

Multicast works by sending messages or data to IP *multicast group* addresses. Unlike with broadcasts, which aren't forwarded, routers then forward copies of the packet out to every interface that has hosts *subscribed* to that group address. This is where multicast differs from broadcast messages—with multicast communication, copies of packets, in theory, are sent only to subscribed hosts. For example, when I say in theory, I mean that the hosts will receive a multicast packet destined for 224.0.0.10. This is an EIGRP packet, and only a router running the EIGRP protocol will read these. All hosts on the broadcast LAN, and Ethernet is a broadcast multi-access LAN technology, will pick up the frame, read the destination address, then immediately discard the frame unless they're in the multicast group. This saves PC processing, not LAN bandwidth. Be warned though—multicasting can cause some serious LAN congestion if it's not implemented carefully! Figure 3.24 shows a Cisco router sending an EIGRP multicast packet on the local LAN and only the other Cisco router will accept and read this packet.

**FIGURE 3.24**    EIGRP multicast example

There are several different groups that users or applications can subscribe to. The range of multicast addresses starts with 224.0.0.0 and goes through 239.255.255.255. As you can see, this range of addresses falls within IP Class D address space based on classful IP assignment.

# Summary

If you made it this far and understood everything the first time through, you should be extremely proud of yourself! We really covered a lot of ground in this chapter, but understand that the information in it is critical to being able to navigate well through the rest of this book.

If you didn't get a complete understanding the first time around, don't stress. It really wouldn't hurt you to read this chapter more than once. There is still a lot of ground to cover, so make sure you've got this material all nailed down. That way, you'll be ready for more, and just so you know, there's a lot more! What we're doing up to this point is building a solid foundation to build upon as you advance.

With that in mind, after you learned about the DoD model, the layers, and associated protocols, you learned about the oh-so-important topic of IP addressing. I discussed in detail the difference between each address class, how to find a network address and broadcast address, and what denotes a valid host address range. I can't stress enough how important it is for you to have this critical information unshakably understood before moving on to Chapter 4!

Since you've already come this far, there's no reason to stop now and waste all those brainwaves and new neural connections. So don't stop—go through the written lab and review questions at the end of this chapter and make sure you understand each answer's explanation. The best is yet to come!

# Exam Essentials

**Differentiate the DoD and the OSI network models.**   The DoD model is a condensed version of the OSI model, composed of four layers instead of seven, but is nonetheless like the OSI model in that it can be used to describe packet creation and devices and protocols can be mapped to its layers.

**Identify Process/Application layer protocols.**   Telnet is a terminal emulation program that allows you to log into a remote host and run programs. File Transfer Protocol (FTP) is a connection-oriented service that allows you to transfer files. Trivial FTP (TFTP) is a connectionless file transfer program. Simple Mail Transfer Protocol (SMTP) is a sendmail program.

**Identify Host-to-Host layer protocols.**   Transmission Control Protocol (TCP) is a connection-oriented protocol that provides reliable network service by using acknowledgments and flow control. User Datagram Protocol (UDP) is a connectionless protocol that provides low overhead and is considered unreliable.

**Identify Internet layer protocols.**   Internet Protocol (IP) is a connectionless protocol that provides network address and routing through an internetwork. Address Resolution Protocol (ARP) finds a hardware address from a known IP address. Reverse ARP (RARP) finds an IP address from a known hardware address. Internet Control Message Protocol (ICMP) provides diagnostics and destination unreachable messages.

**Describe the functions of DNS and DHCP in the network.**   Dynamic Host Configuration Protocol (DHCP) provides network configuration information (including IP addresses) to hosts, eliminating the need to perform the configurations manually. Domain Name Service (DNS) resolves hostnames—both Internet names such as www.lammle.com and device names such as Workstation 2—to IP addresses, eliminating the need to know the IP address of a device for connection purposes.

**Identify what is contained in the TCP header of a connection-oriented transmission.**   The fields in the TCP header include the source port, destination port, sequence number, acknowledgment number, header length, a field reserved for future use, code bits, window size, checksum, urgent pointer, options field, and finally, the data field.

**Identify what is contained in the UDP header of a connectionless transmission.**   The fields in the UDP header include only the source port, destination port, length, checksum, and data. The smaller number of fields as compared to the TCP header comes at the expense of providing none of the more advanced functions of the TCP frame.

**Identify what is contained in the IP header.**   The fields of an IP header include version, header length, priority or type of service, total length, identification, flags, fragment offset, time to live, protocol, header checksum, source IP address, destination IP address, options, and finally, data.

**Compare and contrast UDP and TCP characteristics and features.**   TCP is connection-oriented, acknowledged, and sequenced and has flow and error control, while UDP is connectionless, unacknowledged, and not sequenced and provides no error or flow control.

**Understand the role of port numbers.** Port numbers are used to identify the protocol or service that is to be used in the transmission.

**Identify the role of ICMP.** Internet Control Message Protocol (ICMP) works at the Network layer and is used by IP for many different services. ICMP is a management protocol and messaging service provider for IP.

**Define the Class A IP address range.** The IP range for a Class A network is 1–126. This provides 8 bits of network addressing and 24 bits of host addressing by default.

**Define the Class B IP address range.** The IP range for a Class B network is 128–191. Class B addressing provides 16 bits of network addressing and 16 bits of host addressing by default.

**Define the Class C IP address range.** The IP range for a Class C network is 192 through 223. Class C addressing provides 24 bits of network addressing and 8 bits of host addressing by default.

**Identify the private IP ranges.** The Class A private address range is 10.0.0.0 through 10.255.255.255. The Class B private address range is 172.16.0.0 through 172.31.255.255. The Class C private address range is 192.168.0.0 through 192.168.255.255.

**Understand the difference between a broadcast, unicast, and multicast address.** A broadcast is to all devices in a subnet, a unicast is to one device, and a multicast is to some but not all devices.

# Written Labs

In this section, you'll complete the following labs to make sure you've got the information and concepts contained within them fully dialed in:

Lab 3.1: TCP/IP

Lab 3.2: Mapping Applications to the DoD Model

The answers to these labs can be found in Appendix A, "Answers to Written Labs."

## Written Lab 3.1: TCP/IP

Answer the following questions about TCP/IP:

1. What is the Class C address range in decimal and in binary?
2. What layer of the DoD model is equivalent to the Transport layer of the OSI model?
3. What is the valid range of a Class A network address?
4. What is the 127.0.0.1 address used for?
5. How do you find the network address from a listed IP address?
6. How do you find the broadcast address from a listed IP address?
7. What is the Class A private IP address space?
8. What is the Class B private IP address space?
9. What is the Class C private IP address space?
10. What are all the available characters that you can use in hexadecimal addressing?

## Written Lab 3.2: Mapping Applications to the DoD Model

The four layers of the DoD model are Process/Application, Host-to-Host, Internet, and Network Access. Identify the layer of the DoD model on which each of these protocols operates.

1. Internet Protocol (IP)
2. Telnet
3. FTP
4. SNMP
5. DNS
6. Address Resolution Protocol (ARP)
7. DHCP/BootP
8. Transmission Control Protocol (TCP)

9. X Window
10. User Datagram Protocol (UDP)
11. NFS
12. Internet Control Message Protocol (ICMP)
13. Reverse Address Resolution Protocol (RARP)
14. Proxy ARP
15. TFTP
16. SMTP
17. LPD

# Review Questions

The following questions are designed to test your understanding of this chapter's material. For more information on how to get additional questions, please see this book's introduction.

The answers to these questions can be found in Appendix B, "Answers to Chapter Review Questions."

1.  What must happen if a DHCP IP conflict occurs?

    **A.** Proxy ARP will fix the issue.

    **B.** The client uses a gratuitous ARP to fix the issue.

    **C.** The administrator must fix the conflict by hand at the DHCP server.

    **D.** The DHCP server will reassign new IP addresses to both computers.

2.  Which of the following Application layer protocols sets up a secure session that's similar to Telnet?

    **A.** FTP

    **B.** SSH

    **C.** DNS

    **D.** DHCP

3.  Which of the following mechanisms is used by the client to avoid a duplicate IP address during the DHCP process?

    **A.** ping

    **B.** traceroute

    **C.** gratuitous arp

    **D.** pathping

4.  What protocol is used to find the hardware address of a local device?

    **A.** RARP

    **B.** ARP

    **C.** IP

    **D.** ICMP

    **E.** BootP

**5.** Which of the following are layers in the TCP/IP model? (Choose three.)

    **A.** Application

    **B.** Session

    **C.** Transport

    **D.** Internet

    **E.** Data Link

    **F.** Physical

**6.** Which class of IP address provides a maximum of only 254 host addresses per network ID?

    **A.** Class A

    **B.** Class B

    **C.** Class C

    **D.** Class D

    **E.** Class E

**7.** Which of the following describe the DHCP Discover message? (Choose two.)

    **A.** It uses FF:FF:FF:FF:FF:FF as a layer 2 broadcast.

    **B.** It uses UDP as the Transport layer protocol.

    **C.** It uses TCP as the Transport layer protocol.

    **D.** It does not use a layer 2 destination address.

**8.** Which layer 4 protocol is used for a Telnet connection?

    **A.** IP

    **B.** TCP

    **C.** TCP/IP

    **D.** UDP

    **E.** ICMP

**9.** Private IP addressing was specified in RFC _____.

**10.** Which of the following services use TCP? (Choose three.)

    **A.** DHCP

    **B.** SMTP

    **C.** SNMP

    **D.** FTP

    **E.** HTTP

    **F.** TFTP

**11.** Which Class of IP addresses uses the pattern shown below?

| Network | Network | Network | Host |
|---------|---------|---------|------|

    **A.** Class A

    **B.** Class B

    **C.** Class C

    **D.** Class D

**12.** Which of the following is an example of a multicast address?

    **A.** 10.6.9.1

    **B.** 192.168.10.6

    **C.** 224.0.0.10

    **D.** 172.16.9.5

**13.** The following illustration shows a data structure header. What protocol is this header from?

| 16-Bit Source Port | | 16-Bit Destination Port | |
|---|---|---|---|
| 32-Bit Sequence Number | | | |
| 32-Bit Acknowledgement Number | | | |
| 4-Bit Header Length | Reserved | Flags | 16-Bit Window Size |
| 16-bit TCP Checksum | | 16-bit Urgent Pointer | |
| Options | | | |
| Data | | | |

    **A.** IP

    **B.** ICMP

    **C.** TCP

    **D.** UDP

    **E.** ARP

    **F.** RARP

**14.** If you use either Telnet or FTP, what layer are you using to generate the data?

    **A.** Application

    **B.** Presentation

    **C.** Session

    **D.** Transport

**15.** The DoD model (also called the TCP/IP stack) has four layers. Which layer of the DoD model is equivalent to the Network layer of the OSI model?

   **A.** Application

   **B.** Host-to-Host

   **C.** Internet

   **D.** Network Access

**16.** Which two of the following are private IP addresses?

   **A.** 12.0.0.1

   **B.** 168.172.19.39

   **C.** 172.20.14.36

   **D.** 172.33.194.30

   **E.** 192.168.24.43

**17.** What layer in the TCP/IP stack is equivalent to the Transport layer of the OSI model?

   **A.** Application

   **B.** Host-to-Host

   **C.** Internet

   **D.** Network Access

**18.** Which statements are true regarding ICMP packets? (Choose two).

   **A.** ICMP guarantees datagram delivery.

   **B.** ICMP can provide hosts with information about network problems.

   **C.** ICMP is encapsulated within IP datagrams.

   **D.** ICMP is encapsulated within UDP datagrams.

**19.** What is the address range of a Class B network address in binary?

   **A.** 01*xxxxxx*

   **B.** 0*xxxxxxx*

   **C.** 10*xxxxxx*

   **D.** 110*xxxxx*

**20.** Drag the steps in the DHCP process and place them in the correct order on the right.

| *left list:* | *right list:* |
| --- | --- |
| **DHCPOffer** | **Drop Target A** |
| **DHCPDiscover** | **Drop Target B** |
| **DHCPAck** | **Drop Target C** |
| **DHCPRequest** | **Drop Target D** |

# Chapter

# 4

# Easy Subnetting

## THE FOLLOWING ICND1 EXAM TOPICS ARE COVERED IN THIS CHAPTER:

✓ **IP addressing (IPv4 / IPv6)**

- Describe the operation and necessity of using private and public IP addresses for IPv4 addressing

We'll pick up right where we left off in the last chapter and continue to explore the world of IP addressing. I'll open this chapter by telling you how to subnet an IP network—an indispensably crucial skill that's central to mastering networking in general! Forewarned is forearmed, so prepare yourself because being able to subnet quickly and accurately is pretty challenging and you'll need time to practice what you've learned to really nail it. So be patient and don't give up on this key aspect of networking until your skills are seriously sharp. I'm not kidding—this chapter is so important you should really just graft it into your brain!

So be ready because we're going to hit the ground running and thoroughly cover IP subnetting from the very start. And though I know this will sound weird to you, you'll be much better off if you just try to forget everything you've learned about subnetting before reading this chapter—especially if you've been to an official Cisco or Microsoft class! I think these forms of special torture often do more harm than good and sometimes even scare people away from networking completely. Those that survive and persevere usually at least question the sanity of continuing to study in this field. If this is you, relax, breathe, and know that you'll find that the way I tackle the issue of subnetting is relatively painless because I'm going to show you a whole new, much easier method to conquer this monster!

After working through this chapter, and I can't say this enough, after working through the extra study material at the end as well, you'll be able to tame the IP addressing/subnetting beast—just don't give up! I promise that you'll be really glad you didn't. It's one of those things that once you get it down, you'll wonder why you used to think it was so hard!

To find up-to-the minute updates for this chapter, please see www.lammle.com/forum or the book's web page at www.sybex.com.

# Subnetting Basics

In Chapter 3, "TCP/IP," you learned how to define and find the valid host ranges used in a Class A, Class B, and Class C network address by turning the host bits all off and then all on. This is very good, but here's the catch: you were defining only one network, as shown in Figure 4.1.

**FIGURE 4.1**    One network

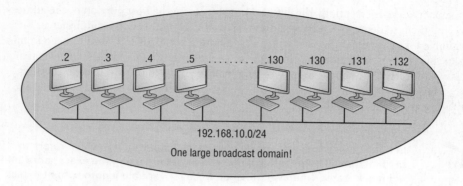

.2    .3    .4    .5    . . . . . . . . .    .130    .130    .131    .132

192.168.10.0/24

One large broadcast domain!

By now you know that having one large network is not a good thing because the first three chapters you just read were veritably peppered with me incessantly telling you that! But how would you fix the out of control problem that Figure 4.1 illustrates? Wouldn't it be nice to be able to break up that one, huge network address and create four manageable networks from it? You betcha it would, but to make that happen, you would need to apply the infamous trick of *subnetting* because it's the best way to break up a giant network into a bunch of smaller ones. Take a look at Figure 4.2 and see how this might look.

**FIGURE 4.2**    Multiple networks connected together

192.168.10.0

192.168.10.32

192.168.10.64        192.168.10.96

What are those 192.168.10.x addresses shown in the figure? Well that is what this chapter will explain! How to make one network into many networks!

Let's take off from where we left in Chapter 3 and start working in the host section (host bits) of a network address, where we can borrow bits to create subnets.

## How to Create Subnets

Creating subnetworks is essentially the act of taking bits from the host portion of the address and reserving them to define the subnet address instead. Clearly this will result in fewer bits being available for defining your hosts, which is something you'll always want to keep in mind.

Later in this chapter, I'll guide you through the entire process of creating subnets starting with Class C addresses. As always in networking, before you actually implement anything, including subnetting, you must first determine your current requirements and make sure to plan for future conditions as well.

In this first section, we'll be discussing classful routing, which refers to the fact that all hosts (nodes) in the network are using the exact same subnet mask. Later, when we move on to cover variable length subnet masks (VLSMs), I'll tell you all about classless routing, which is an environment wherein each network segment *can* use a different subnet mask.

Okay—to create a subnet, we'll start by fulfilling these three steps:

1. Determine the number of required network IDs:
   - One for each LAN subnet
   - One for each wide area network connection

2. Determine the number of required host IDs per subnet:
   - One for each TCP/IP host
   - One for each router interface

3. Based on the above requirements, create the following:
   - A unique subnet mask for your entire network
   - A unique subnet ID for each physical segment
   - A range of host IDs for each subnet

## Subnet Masks

For the subnet address scheme to work, every machine on the network must know which part of the host address will be used as the subnet address. This condition is met by assigning a *subnet mask* to each machine. A subnet mask is a 32-bit value that allows the device that's receiving IP packets to distinguish the network ID portion of the IP address from the host ID portion of the IP address. This 32-bit subnet mask is composed of 1s and 0s, where the 1s represent the positions that refer to the network subnet addresses.

Not all networks need subnets, and if not, it really means that they're using the default subnet mask, which is basically the same as saying that a network doesn't have a subnet address. Table 4.1 shows the default subnet masks for Classes A, B, and C.

**TABLE 4.1**   Default subnet mask

| Class | Format | Default Subnet Mask |
|-------|--------|---------------------|
| A | network.node.node.node | 255.0.0.0 |
| B | network.network.node.node | 255.255.0.0 |
| C | network.network.network.node | 255.255.255.0 |

Although you can use any mask in any way on an interface, typically it's not usually good to mess with the default masks. In other words, you don't want to make a Class B subnet mask read 255.0.0.0, and some hosts won't even let you type it in. But these days, most devices will. For a Class A network, you wouldn't change the first byte in a subnet mask because it should read 255.0.0.0 at a minimum. Similarly, you wouldn't assign 255.255.255.255 because this is all 1s, which is a broadcast address. A Class B address starts with 255.255.0.0, and a Class C starts with 255.255.255.0, and for the CCNA especially, there is no reason to change the defaults!

### Understanding the Powers of 2

Powers of 2 are important to understand and memorize for use with IP subnetting. Reviewing powers of 2, remember that when you see a number noted with an exponent, it means you should multiply the number by itself as many times as the upper number specifies. For example, $2^3$ is 2 x 2 x 2, which equals 8. Here's a list of powers of 2 to commit to memory:

| | |
|---|---|
| $2^1 = 2$ | $2^8 = 256$ |
| $2^2 = 4$ | $2^9 = 512$ |
| $2^3 = 8$ | $2^{10} = 1,024$ |
| $2^4 = 16$ | $2^{11} = 2,048$ |
| $2^5 = 32$ | $2^{12} = 4,096$ |
| $2^6 = 64$ | $2^{13} = 8,192$ |
| $2^7 = 128$ | $2^{14} = 16,384$ |

Memorizing these powers of 2 is a good idea, but it's not absolutely necessary. Just remember that since you're working with powers of 2, each successive power of 2 is double the previous one.

It works like this—all you have to do to remember the value of $2^9$ is to first know that $2^8 = 256$. Why? Because when you double 2 to the eighth power (256), you get $2^9$ (or 512). To determine the value of $2^{10}$, simply start at $2^8 = 256$, and then double it twice.

You can go the other way as well. If you needed to know what $2^6$ is, for example, you just cut 256 in half two times: once to reach $2^7$ and then one more time to reach $2^6$.

## Classless Inter-Domain Routing (CIDR)

Another term you need to familiarize yourself with is *Classless Inter-Domain Routing (CIDR)*. It's basically the method that Internet service providers (ISPs) use to allocate a number of addresses to a company, a home—their customers. They provide addresses in a certain block size, something I'll talk about in greater detail soon.

When you receive a block of addresses from an ISP, what you get will look something like this: 192.168.10.32/28. This is telling you what your subnet mask is. The slash notation (/) means how many bits are turned on (1s). Obviously, the maximum could only be /32 because a byte is 8 bits and there are 4 bytes in an IP address: (4 × 8 = 32). But keep in mind that regardless of the class of address, the largest subnet mask available relevant to the Cisco exam objectives can only be a /30 because you've got to keep at least 2 bits for host bits.

Take, for example, a Class A default subnet mask, which is 255.0.0.0. This tells us that the first byte of the subnet mask is all ones (1s), or 11111111. When referring to a slash notation, you need to count all the 1-bits to figure out your mask. The 255.0.0.0 is considered a /8 because it has 8 bits that are 1s—that is, 8 bits that are turned on.

A Class B default mask would be 255.255.0.0, which is a /16 because 16 bits are ones (1s): 11111111.11111111.00000000.00000000.

Table 4.2 has a listing of every available subnet mask and its equivalent CIDR slash notation.

**TABLE 4.2**   CIDR values

| Subnet Mask | CIDR Value |
| --- | --- |
| 255.0.0.0 | /8 |
| 255.128.0.0 | /9 |
| 255.192.0.0 | /10 |
| 255.224.0.0 | /11 |

| Subnet Mask | CIDR Value |
|---|---|
| 255.240.0.0 | /12 |
| 255.248.0.0 | /13 |
| 255.252.0.0 | /14 |
| 255.254.0.0 | /15 |
| 255.255.0.0 | /16 |
| 255.255.128.0 | /17 |
| 255.255.192.0 | /18 |
| 255.255.224.0 | /19 |
| 255.255.240.0 | /20 |
| 255.255.248.0 | /21 |
| 255.255.252.0 | /22 |
| 255.255.254.0 | /23 |
| 255.255.255.0 | /24 |
| 255.255.255.128 | /25 |
| 255.255.255.192 | /26 |
| 255.255.255.224 | /27 |
| 255.255.255.240 | /28 |
| 255.255.255.248 | /29 |
| 255.255.255.252 | /30 |

The /8 through /15 can only be used with Class A network addresses. /16 through /23 can be used by Class A and B network addresses. /24 through /30 can be used by Class A, B, and C network addresses. This is a big reason why most companies use Class A network addresses. Since they can use all subnet masks, they get the maximum flexibility in network design.

No, you cannot configure a Cisco router using this slash format. But wouldn't that be nice? Nevertheless, it's *really* important for you to know subnet masks in the slash notation (CIDR).

## IP Subnet-Zero

Even though IP subnet-zero is not a new command, Cisco courseware and Cisco exam objectives didn't used to cover it. Know that Cisco certainly covers it now! This command allows you to use the first and last subnet in your network design. For instance, the Class C mask of 255.255.255.192 provides subnets 64 and 128, another facet of subnetting that we'll discuss more thoroughly later in this chapter. But with the ip subnet-zero command, you now get to use subnets 0, 64, 128, and 192. It may not seem like a lot, but this provides two more subnets for every subnet mask we use.

Even though we don't discuss the command-line interface (CLI) until Chapter 6, "Cisco's Internetworking Operating System (IOS)," it's important for you to be at least a little familiar with this command at this point:

```
Router#sh running-config
Building configuration...
Current configuration : 827 bytes
!
hostname Pod1R1
!
ip subnet-zero
!
```

This router output shows that the command ip subnet-zero is enabled on the router. Cisco has turned this command on by default starting with Cisco IOS version 12.*x* and now we're running 15.*x* code.

When taking your Cisco exams, make sure you read very carefully to see if Cisco is asking you *not* to use ip subnet-zero. There are actually instances where this may happen.

## Subnetting Class C Addresses

There are many different ways to subnet a network. The right way is the way that works best for you. In a Class C address, only 8 bits are available for defining the hosts. Remember that subnet bits start at the left and move to the right, without skipping bits. This means that the only Class C subnet masks can be the following:

```
Binary      Decimal     CIDR
-----------------------------------------------------------
00000000 = 255.255.255.0        /24
```

```
10000000 = 255.255.255.128     /25
11000000 = 255.255.255.192     /26
11100000 = 255.255.255.224     /27
11110000 = 255.255.255.240     /28
11111000 = 255.255.255.248     /29
11111100 = 255.255.255.252     /30
```

We can't use a /31 or /32 because, as I've said, we must have at least 2 host bits for assigning IP addresses to hosts. But this is only mostly true. Certainly we can never use a /32 because that would mean zero host bits available, yet Cisco has various forms of the IOS, as well as the new Cisco Nexus switches operating system, that support the /31 mask. The /31 is above the scope of the CCENT and CCNA objectives, so we won't be covering it in this book.

Coming up, I'm going to teach you that significantly less painful method of subnetting I promised you at the beginning of this chapter, which makes it ever so much easier to subnet larger numbers in a flash. Excited—good! Because I'm not kidding when I tell you that you absolutely need to be able to subnet quickly and accurately to succeed in the networking real world and on the exam too!

## Subnetting a Class C Address—The Fast Way!

When you've chosen a possible subnet mask for your network and need to determine the number of subnets, valid hosts, and the broadcast addresses of a subnet that mask will provide, all you need to do is answer five simple questions:

- How many subnets does the chosen subnet mask produce?
- How many valid hosts per subnet are available?
- What are the valid subnets?
- What's the broadcast address of each subnet?
- What are the valid hosts in each subnet?

This is where you'll be really glad you followed my advice and took the time to memorize your powers of 2. If you didn't, now would be a good time… Just refer back to the sidebar, "Understanding the Powers of 2," earlier if you need to brush up. Here's how you arrive at the answers to those five big questions:

- *How many subnets?* $2^x$ = number of subnets. $x$ is the number of masked bits, or the 1s. For example, in 11000000, the number of 1s gives us $2^2$ subnets. So in this example, there are 4 subnets.

- *How many hosts per subnet?* $2^y - 2$ = number of hosts per subnet. $y$ is the number of unmasked bits, or the 0s. For example, in 11000000, the number of 0s gives us $2^6 - 2$ hosts, or 62 hosts per subnet. You need to subtract 2 for the subnet address and the broadcast address, which are not valid hosts.

- *What are the valid subnets?* 256 − subnet mask = block size, or increment number. An example would be the 255.255.255.192 mask, where the interesting octet is the fourth octet (interesting because that is where our subnet numbers are). Just use this math: 256 – 192 = 64. The block size of a 192 mask is always 64. Start counting at zero in blocks of 64 until you reach the subnet mask value and these are your subnets in the fourth octet: 0, 64, 128, 192. Easy, huh?

- *What's the broadcast address for each subnet?* Now here's the really easy part. Since we counted our subnets in the last section as 0, 64, 128, and 192, the broadcast address is always the number right before the next subnet. For example, the 0 subnet has a broadcast address of 63 because the next subnet is 64. The 64 subnet has a broadcast address of 127 because the next subnet is 128, and so on. Remember, the broadcast address of the last subnet is always 255.

- *What are the valid hosts?* Valid hosts are the numbers between the subnets, omitting the all-0s and all-1s. For example, if 64 is the subnet number and 127 is the broadcast address, then 65–126 is the valid host range. Your valid range is *always* the group of numbers between the subnet address and the broadcast address.

If you're still confused, don't worry because it really isn't as hard as it seems to be at first—just hang in there! To help lift any mental fog, try a few of the practice examples next.

## Subnetting Practice Examples: Class C Addresses

Here's your opportunity to practice subnetting Class C addresses using the method I just described. This is so cool. We're going to start with the first Class C subnet mask and work through every subnet that we can, using a Class C address. When we're done, I'll show you how easy this is with Class A and B networks too!

### Practice Example #1C: 255.255.255.128 (/25)

Since 128 is 10000000 in binary, there is only 1 bit for subnetting and 7 bits for hosts. We're going to subnet the Class C network address 192.168.10.0.

192.168.10.0 = Network address

255.255.255.128 = Subnet mask

Now, let's answer our big five:

- *How many subnets?* Since 128 is 1 bit on (**10000000**), the answer would be $2^1 = 2$.

- *How many hosts per subnet?* We have 7 host bits off (**10000000**), so the equation would be $2^7 - 2 = 126$ hosts. Once you figure out the block size of a mask, the amount of hosts is always the block size minus 2. No need to do extra math if you don't need to!

- *What are the valid subnets?* 256 – 128 = 128. Remember, we'll start at zero and count in our block size, so our subnets are 0, 128. By just counting your subnets when counting in your block size, you really don't need to do steps 1 and 2. We can see we have two subnets, and in the step before this one, just remember that the amount of hosts is always the block size minus 2, and in this example, that gives us 2 subnets, each with 126 hosts.

- *What's the broadcast address for each subnet?* The number right before the value of the next subnet is all host bits turned on and equals the broadcast address. For the zero subnet, the next subnet is 128, so the broadcast of the 0 subnet is 127.

- *What are the valid hosts?* These are the numbers between the subnet and broadcast address. The easiest way to find the hosts is to write out the subnet address and the broadcast address, which makes valid hosts completely obvious. The following table shows the 0 and 128 subnets, the valid host ranges of each, and the broadcast address of both subnets:

| Subnet | 0 | 128 |
|---|---|---|
| First host | 1 | 129 |
| Last host | 126 | 254 |
| Broadcast | 127 | 255 |

Okay, looking at a Class C /25, it's pretty clear that there are two subnets. But so what—why is this significant? Well actually, it's not because that's not the right question. What you really want to know is what you would do with this information!

I know this isn't exactly everyone's favorite pastime, but what we're about to do is really important, so bear with me; we're going to talk about subnetting—period. The key to understanding subnetting is to understand the very reason you need to do it, and I'm going to demonstrate this by going through the process of building a physical network.

Okay—because we added that router shown in Figure 4.3, in order for the hosts on our internetwork to communicate, they must now have a logical network addressing scheme. We could use IPv6, but IPv4 is still the most popular for now. It's also what we're studying at the moment, so that's what we're going with.

**FIGURE 4.3**   Implementing a Class C /25 logical network

```
Router#show ip route
[output cut]
C 192.168.10.0 is directly connected to Ethernet 0
C 192.168.10.128 is directly connected to Ethernet 1
```

Looking at Figure 4.3, you can see that there are two physical networks, so we're going to implement a logical addressing scheme that allows for two logical networks. As always, it's a really good idea to look ahead and consider likely short- and long-term growth scenarios, but for this example in this book, a /25 gets it done.

Figure 4.3 shows us that both subnets have been assigned to a router interface, which creates our broadcast domains and assigns our subnets. Use the command show ip route to see the routing table on a router. Notice that instead of one large broadcast domain, there are now two smaller broadcast domains, providing for up to 126 hosts in each. The C in the router output translates to "directly connected network," and we can see we have two of those with two broadcast domains and that we created and implemented them. So congratulations—you did it! You have successfully subnetted a network and applied it to a network design. Nice! Let's do it again.

## Practice Example #2C: 255.255.255.192 (/26)

This time, we're going to subnet the network address 192.168.10.0 using the subnet mask 255.255.255.192.

192.168.10.0 = Network address

255.255.255.192 = Subnet mask

Now, let's answer the big five:

- *How many subnets?* Since 192 is 2 bits on (**11000000**), the answer would be $2^2 = 4$ subnets.

- *How many hosts per subnet?* We have 6 host bits off (**11000000**), giving us $2^6 - 2 = 62$ hosts. The amount of hosts is always the block-size minus 2.

- *What are the valid subnets?* $256 - 192 = 64$. Remember, to start at zero and count in our block size. This means our subnets are 0, 64, 128, and 192. We can see we have a block size of 64, so we have 4 subnets, each with 62 hosts.

- *What's the broadcast address for each subnet?* The number right before the value of the next subnet is all host bits turned on and equals the broadcast address. For the zero subnet, the next subnet is 64, so the broadcast address for the zero subnet is 63.

- *What are the valid hosts?* These are the numbers between the subnet and broadcast address. As I said, the easiest way to find the hosts is to write out the subnet address and the broadcast address, which clearly delimits our valid hosts. The following table shows the 0, 64, 128, and 192 subnets, the valid host ranges of each, and the broadcast address of each subnet:

| | | | | |
|---|---|---|---|---|
| **The subnets (do this first)** | 0 | 64 | 128 | 192 |
| Our first host (perform host addressing last) | 1 | 65 | 129 | 193 |
| Our last host | 62 | 126 | 190 | 254 |
| The broadcast address (do this second) | 63 | 127 | 191 | 255 |

Okay, again, before getting into the next example, you can see that we can now subnet a /26 as long as we can count in increments of 64. And what are you going to do with this fascinating information? Implement it! We'll use Figure 4.4 to practice a /26 network implementation.

**FIGURE 4.4**    Implementing a class C /26 (with three networks)

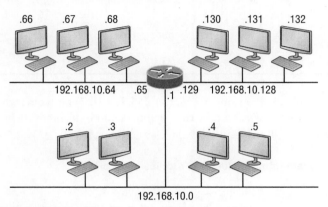

```
Router#show ip route
 [output cut]
C 192.168.10.0 is directly connected to Ethernet 0
C 192.168.10.64 is directly connected to Ethernet 1
C 192.168.10.128 is directly connected to Ethernet 2
```

The /26 mask provides four subnetworks, and we need a subnet for each router interface. With this mask, in this example, we actually have room with a spare subnet to add to another router interface in the future. Always plan for growth if possible!

### Practice Example #3C: 255.255.255.224 (/27)

This time, we'll subnet the network address 192.168.10.0 and subnet mask 255.255.255.224.

192.168.10.0 = Network address

255.255.255.224 = Subnet mask

- *How many subnets?* 224 is 11100000, so our equation would be $2^3 = 8$.

- *How many hosts?* $2^5 - 2 = 30$.

- *What are the valid subnets?* 256 − 224 = 32. We just start at zero and count to the subnet mask value in blocks (increments) of 32: 0, 32, 64, 96, 128, 160, 192, and 224.

- *What's the broadcast address for each subnet (always the number right before the next subnet)?*

- *What are the valid hosts (the numbers between the subnet number and the broadcast address)?*

To answer the last two questions, first just write out the subnets, then write out the broadcast addresses—the number right before the next subnet. Last, fill in the host addresses. The following table gives you all the subnets for the 255.255.255.224 Class C subnet mask:

| The subnet address | 0 | 32 | 64 | 96 | 128 | 160 | 192 | 224 |
|---|---|---|---|---|---|---|---|---|
| The first valid host | 1 | 33 | 65 | 97 | 129 | 161 | 193 | 225 |
| The last valid host | 30 | 62 | 94 | 126 | 158 | 190 | 222 | 254 |
| The broadcast address | 31 | 63 | 95 | 127 | 159 | 191 | 223 | 255 |

In practice example #3C, we're using a 255.255.255.224 (/27) network, which provides eight subnets as shown above. We can take these subnets and implement them as shown in Figure 4.5 using any of the subnets available.

**FIGURE 4.5**   Implementing a Class C /27 logical network

```
Router#show ip route
 [output cut]
C 192.168.10.0 is directly connected to Ethernet 0
C 192.168.10.32 is directly connected to Ethernet 1
C 192.168.10.64 is directly connected to Ethernet 2
C 192.168.10.96 is directly connected to Serial 0
```

Noticed I used six of the eight subnets available for my network design. The lightning bolt symbol in the figure represents a wide area network (WAN) such as a T1 or other serial connection through an ISP or telco. In other words, something you don't own, but it's still a subnet just like any LAN connection on a router. As usual, I used the first valid host in each subnet as the router's interface address. This is just a rule of thumb; you can use any address in the valid host range as long as you remember what address you configured so you can set the default gateways on your hosts to the router address.

### Practice Example #4C: 255.255.255.240 (/28)

Let's practice another one:

> 192.168.10.0 = Network address
>
> 255.255.255.240 = Subnet mask

- *Subnets?* 240 is 11110000 in binary. $2^4 = 16$.
- *Hosts?* 4 host bits, or $2^4 - 2 = 14$.
- *Valid subnets?* 256 – 240 = 16. Start at 0: 0 + 16 = 16. 16 + 16 = 32. 32 + 16 = 48. 48 + 16 = 64. 64 + 16 = 80. 80 + 16 = 96. 96 + 16 = 112. 112 + 16 = 128. 128 + 16 = 144. 144 + 16 = 160. 160 + 16 = 176. 176 + 16 = 192. 192 + 16 = 208. 208 + 16 = 224. 224 + 16 = 240.
- *Broadcast address for each subnet?*
- *Valid hosts?*

To answer the last two questions, check out the following table. It gives you the subnets, valid hosts, and broadcast addresses for each subnet. First, find the address of each subnet using the block size (increment). Second, find the broadcast address of each subnet increment, which is always the number right before the next valid subnet, and then just fill in the host addresses. The following table shows the available subnets, hosts, and broadcast addresses provided from a Class C 255.255.255.240 mask.

| Subnet | 0 | 16 | 32 | 48 | 64 | 80 | 96 | 112 | 128 | 144 | 160 | 176 | 192 | 208 | 224 | 240 |
|---|---|---|---|---|---|---|---|---|---|---|---|---|---|---|---|---|
| First host | 1 | 17 | 33 | 49 | 65 | 81 | 97 | 113 | 129 | 145 | 161 | 177 | 193 | 209 | 225 | 241 |
| Last host | 14 | 30 | 46 | 62 | 78 | 94 | 110 | 126 | 142 | 158 | 174 | 190 | 206 | 222 | 238 | 254 |
| Broadcast | 15 | 31 | 47 | 63 | 79 | 95 | 111 | 127 | 143 | 159 | 175 | 191 | 207 | 223 | 239 | 255 |

**TIP** Cisco has figured out that most people cannot count in 16s and therefore have a hard time finding valid subnets, hosts, and broadcast addresses with the Class C 255.255.255.240 mask. You'd be wise to study this mask.

### Practice Example #5C: 255.255.255.248 (/29)

Let's keep practicing:

> 192.168.10.0 = Network address
>
> 255.255.255.248 = Subnet mask

- *Subnets?* 248 in binary = 11111000. $2^5 = 32$.
- *Hosts?* $2^3 - 2 = 6$.
- *Valid subnets?* 256 – 248 = 0, 8, 16, 24, 32, 40, 48, 56, 64, 72, 80, 88, 96, 104, 112, 120, 128, 136, 144, 152, 160, 168, 176, 184, 192, 200, 208, 216, 224, 232, 240, and 248.

▪ *Broadcast address for each subnet?*

▪ *Valid hosts?*

Take a look at the following table. It shows some of the subnets (first four and last four only), valid hosts, and broadcast addresses for the Class C 255.255.255.248 mask:

| Subnet | 0 | 8 | 16 | 24 | ... | 224 | 232 | 240 | 248 |
|---|---|---|---|---|---|---|---|---|---|
| First host | 1 | 9 | 17 | 25 | ... | 225 | 233 | 241 | 249 |
| Last host | 6 | 14 | 22 | 30 | ... | 230 | 238 | 246 | 254 |
| Broadcast | 7 | 15 | 23 | 31 | ... | 231 | 239 | 247 | 255 |

If you try to configure a router interface with the address 192.168.10.6 255.255.255.248 and receive this error:

```
Bad mask /29 for address 192.168.10.6
```

It means that ip subnet-zero is not enabled. You must be able to subnet to see that the address used in this example is in the zero subnet!

## Practice Example #6C: 255.255.255.252 (/30)

Okay—just one more:

192.168.10.0 = Network address

255.255.255.252 = Subnet mask

▪ *Subnets?* 64.

▪ *Hosts?* 2.

▪ *Valid subnets?* 0, 4, 8, 12, etc., all the way to 252.

▪ *Broadcast address for each subnet?* (always the number right before the next subnet)

▪ *Valid hosts?* (the numbers between the subnet number and the broadcast address)

The following table shows you the subnet, valid host, and broadcast address of the first four and last four subnets in the 255.255.255.252 Class C subnet:

| Subnet | 0 | 4 | 8 | 12 | ... | 240 | 244 | 248 | 252 |
|---|---|---|---|---|---|---|---|---|---|
| First host | 1 | 5 | 9 | 13 | ... | 241 | 245 | 249 | 253 |
| Last host | 2 | 6 | 10 | 14 | ... | 242 | 246 | 250 | 254 |
| Broadcast | 3 | 7 | 11 | 15 | ... | 243 | 247 | 251 | 255 |

---

**⊕ Real World Scenario**

**Should We Really Use This Mask That Provides Only Two Hosts?**

You are the network administrator for Acme Corporation in San Francisco, with dozens of WAN links connecting to your corporate office. Right now your network is a classful network, which means that the same subnet mask is on each host and router interface. You've read about classless routing, where you can have different sized masks, but don't know what to use on your point-to-point WAN links. Is the 255.255.255.252 (/30) a helpful mask in this situation?

Yes, this is a very helpful mask in wide area networks!

If you were to use the 255.255.255.0 mask in this situation, then each network would have 254 hosts. But you use only 2 addresses with a WAN link, which is a waste of 252 hosts per subnet! If you use the 255.255.255.252 mask, then each subnet has only 2 hosts, and you don't want to waste precious addresses. This is a really important subject, one that we'll address in a lot more detail in the section on VLSM network design in the next chapter!

---

## Subnetting in Your Head: Class C Addresses

It really is possible to subnet in your head? Yes, and it's not all that hard either—take the following example:

192.168.10.50 = Node address

255.255.255.224 = Subnet mask

First, determine the subnet and broadcast address of the network in which the above IP address resides. You can do this by answering question 3 of the big 5 questions: 256 − 224 = 32. 0, 32, 64, and so on. The address of 33 falls between the two subnets of 32 and 64 and must be part of the 192.168.10.32 subnet. The next subnet is 64, so the broadcast address of the 32 subnet is 63. Don't forget that the broadcast address of a subnet is always the number right before the next subnet. The valid host range equals the numbers between the subnet and broadcast address, or 33–62. This is too easy!

Okay, let's try another one. We'll subnet another Class C address:

192.168.10.50 = Node address

255.255.255.240 = Subnet mask

What is the subnet and broadcast address of the network of which the above IP address is a member? 256 − 240 = 16. Now just count by our increments of 16 until we pass the host address: 0, 16, 32, 48, 64. Bingo—the host address is between the 48 and 64 subnets. The subnet is 192.168.10.48, and the broadcast address is 63 because the next subnet is 64. The valid host range equals the numbers between the subnet number and the broadcast address, or 49–62.

Let's do a couple more to make sure you have this down.

You have a node address of 192.168.10.174 with a mask of 255.255.255.240. What is the valid host range?

The mask is 240, so we'd do a 256 – 240 = 16. This is our block size. Just keep adding 16 until we pass the host address of 174, starting at zero, of course: 0, 16, 32, 48, 64, 80, 96, 112, 128, 144, 160, 176. The host address of 174 is between 160 and 176, so the subnet is 160. The broadcast address is 175; the valid host range is 161–174. That was a tough one!

One more—just for fun. This one is the easiest of all Class C subnetting:

192.168.10.17 = Node address

255.255.255.252 = Subnet mask

What is the subnet and broadcast address of the subnet in which the above IP address resides? 256 – 252 = 0 (always start at zero unless told otherwise). 0, 4, 8, 12, 16, 20, etc. You've got it! The host address is between the 16 and 20 subnets. The subnet is 192.168.10.16, and the broadcast address is 19. The valid host range is 17–18.

Now that you're all over Class C subnetting, let's move on to Class B subnetting. But before we do, let's go through a quick review.

## What Do We Know?

Okay—here's where you can really apply what you've learned so far and begin committing it all to memory. This is a very cool section that I've been using in my classes for years. It will really help you nail down subnetting for good!

When you see a subnet mask or slash notation (CIDR), you should know the following:

**/25**    What do we know about a /25?

- 128 mask
- 1 bit on and 7 bits off (10000000)
- Block size of 128
- Subnets 0 and 128
- 2 subnets, each with 126 hosts

**/26**    What do we know about a /26?

- 192 mask
- 2 bits on and 6 bits off (11000000)
- Block size of 64
- Subnet 0, 64, 128, 192
- 4 subnets, each with 62 hosts

**/27**    What do we know about a /27?

- 224 mask
- 3 bits on and 5 bits off (11100000)

- Block size of 32
- Subnets 0, 32, 64, 96, 128, 160, 192, 224
- 8 subnets, each with 30 hosts

**/28**  What do we know about a /28?

- 240 mask
- 4 bits on and 4 bits off
- Block size of 16
- Subnets 0, 16, 32, 48, 64, 80, 96, 112, 128, 144, 160, 176, 192, 208, 224, 240
- 16 subnets, each with 14 hosts

**/29**  What do we know about a /29?

- 248 mask
- 5 bits on and 3 bits off
- Block size of 8
- Subnets 0, 8, 16, 24, 32, 40, 48, etc.
- 32 subnets, each with 6 hosts

**/30**  What do we know about a /30?

- 252 mask
- 6 bits on and 2 bits off
- Block size of 4
- Subnets 0, 4, 8, 12, 16, 20, 24, etc.
- 64 subnets, each with 2 hosts

The below table 4.3 puts all of the above information into one compact little table. You should practice writing this table out on scratch paper, and if you can do it, write it down before you start your exam!

**TABLE 4.3**  What do you know?

| CIDR Notation | Mask | Bits | Block Size | Subnets | Hosts |
| --- | --- | --- | --- | --- | --- |
| /25 | 128 | 1 bit on and 7 bits off | 128 | 0 and 128 | 2 subnets, each with 126 hosts |
| /26 | 192 | 2 bits on and 6 bits off | 64 | 0, 64, 128, 192 | 4 subnets, each with 62 hosts |
| /27 | 224 | 3 bits on and 5 bits off | 32 | 0, 32, 64, 96, 128, 160, 192, 224 | 8 subnets, each with 30 hosts |

**TABLE 4.3**   What do you know? *(continued)*

| CIDR Notation | Mask | Bits | Block Size | Subnets | Hosts |
|---|---|---|---|---|---|
| /28 | 240 | 4 bits on and 4 bits off | 16 | 0, 16, 32, 48, 64, 80, 96, 112, 128, 144, 160, 176, 192, 208, 224, 240 | 16 subnets, each with 14 hosts |
| /29 | 248 | 5 bits on and 3 bits off | 8 | 0, 8, 16, 24, 32, 40, 48, etc. | 32 subnets, each with 6 hosts |
| /30 | 252 | 6 bits on and 2 bits off | 4 | 0, 4, 8, 12, 16, 20, 24, etc. | 64 subnets, each with 2 hosts |

Regardless of whether you have a Class A, Class B, or Class C address, the /30 mask will provide you with only two hosts, ever. As suggested by Cisco, this mask is suited almost exclusively for use on point-to-point links.

If you can memorize this "What Do We Know?" section, you'll be much better off in your day-to-day job and in your studies. Try saying it out loud, which helps you memorize things—yes, your significant other and/or coworkers will think you've lost it, but they probably already do if you're in the networking field anyway. And if you're not yet in the networking field but are studying all this to break into it, get used to it!

It's also helpful to write these on some type of flashcards and have people test your skill. You'd be amazed at how fast you can get subnetting down if you memorize block sizes as well as this "What Do We Know?" section.

## Subnetting Class B Addresses

Before we dive into this, let's look at all the possible Class B subnet masks first. Notice that we have a lot more possible subnet masks than we do with a Class C network address:

```
255.255.0.0      (/16)
255.255.128.0    (/17)      255.255.255.0     (/24)
255.255.192.0    (/18)      255.255.255.128   (/25)
255.255.224.0    (/19)      255.255.255.192   (/26)
255.255.240.0    (/20)      255.255.255.224   (/27)
255.255.248.0    (/21)      255.255.255.240   (/28)
255.255.252.0    (/22)      255.255.255.248   (/29)
255.255.254.0    (/23)      255.255.255.252   (/30)
```

We know the Class B network address has 16 bits available for host addressing. This means we can use up to 14 bits for subnetting because we need to leave at least 2 bits for host addressing. Using a /16 means you are not subnetting with Class B, but it *is* a mask you can use!

By the way, do you notice anything interesting about that list of subnet values—a pattern, maybe? Ah ha! That's exactly why I had you memorize the binary-to-decimal numbers earlier in Chapter 2. Since subnet mask bits start on the left and move to the right and bits can't be skipped, the numbers are always the same regardless of the class of address. If you haven't already, memorize this pattern!

The process of subnetting a Class B network is pretty much the same as it is for a Class C, except that you have more host bits and you start in the third octet.

Use the same subnet numbers for the third octet with Class B that you used for the fourth octet with Class C, but add a zero to the network portion and a 255 to the broadcast section in the fourth octet. The following table shows you an example host range of two subnets used in a Class B 240 (/20) subnet mask:

| Subnet address | 16.0 | 32.0 |
|---|---|---|
| Broadcast address | 31.255 | 47.255 |

Just add the valid hosts between the numbers and you're set!

The preceding example is true only until you get up to /24. After that, it's numerically exactly like Class C.

## Subnetting Practice Examples: Class B Addresses

The following sections will give you an opportunity to practice subnetting Class B addresses. Again, I have to mention that this is the same as subnetting with Class C, except we start in the third octet—with the exact same numbers!

### Practice Example #1B: 255.255.128.0 (/17)

172.16.0.0 = Network address

255.255.128.0 = Subnet mask

- *Subnets?* $2^1 = 2$ (same amount as Class C).
- *Hosts?* $2^{15} - 2 = 32,766$ (7 bits in the third octet, and 8 in the fourth).
- *Valid subnets?* 256 – 128 = 128. 0, 128. Remember that subnetting is performed in the third octet, so the subnet numbers are really 0.0 and 128.0, as shown in the next table. These are the exact numbers we used with Class C; we use them in the third octet and add a 0 in the fourth octet for the network address.
- *Broadcast address for each subnet?*
- *Valid hosts?*

The following table shows the two subnets available, the valid host range, and the broadcast address of each:

| Subnet | 0.0 | 128.0 |
|---|---|---|
| First host | 0.1 | 128.1 |
| Last host | 127.254 | 255.254 |
| Broadcast | 127.255 | 255.255 |

Okay, notice that we just added the fourth octet's lowest and highest values and came up with the answers. And again, it's done exactly the same way as for a Class C subnet. We just used the same numbers in the third octet and added 0 and 255 in the fourth octet—pretty simple, huh? I really can't say this enough: it's just not that hard. The numbers never change; we just use them in different octets!

Question: Using the above subnet mask, do you think 172.16.10.0 is a valid host address? What about 172.16.10.255? Can 0 and 255 in the fourth octet ever be a valid host address? The answer is absolutely, yes, those are valid hosts! Any number between the subnet number and the broadcast address is always a valid host.

### Practice Example #2B: 255.255.192.0 (/18)

172.16.0.0 = Network address

255.255.192.0 = Subnet mask

- *Subnets?* $2^2 = 4$.
- *Hosts?* $2^{14} - 2 = 16,382$ (6 bits in the third octet, and 8 in the fourth).
- *Valid subnets?* $256 - 192 = 64$. 0, 64, 128, 192. Remember that the subnetting is performed in the third octet, so the subnet numbers are really 0.0, 64.0, 128.0, and 192.0, as shown in the next table.
- *Broadcast address for each subnet?*
- *Valid hosts?*

The following table shows the four subnets available, the valid host range, and the broadcast address of each:

| Subnet | 0.0 | 64.0 | 128.0 | 192.0 |
|---|---|---|---|---|
| First host | 0.1 | 64.1 | 128.1 | 192.1 |
| Last host | 63.254 | 127.254 | 191.254 | 255.254 |
| Broadcast | 63.255 | 127.255 | 191.255 | 255.255 |

Again, it's pretty much the same as it is for a Class C subnet—we just added 0 and 255 in the fourth octet for each subnet in the third octet.

### Practice Example #3B: 255.255.240.0 (/20)

172.16.0.0 = Network address

255.255.240.0 = Subnet mask

- *Subnets?* $2^4 = 16$.
- *Hosts?* $2^{12} - 2 = 4094$.
- *Valid subnets?* $256 - 240 = 0, 16, 32, 48$, etc., up to 240. Notice that these are the same numbers as a Class C 240 mask—we just put them in the third octet and add a 0 and 255 in the fourth octet.
- *Broadcast address for each subnet?*
- *Valid hosts?*

The following table shows the first four subnets, valid hosts, and broadcast addresses in a Class B 255.255.240.0 mask:

| Subnet | 0.0 | 16.0 | 32.0 | 48.0 |
|---|---|---|---|---|
| First host | 0.1 | 16.1 | 32.1 | 48.1 |
| Last host | 15.254 | 31.254 | 47.254 | 63.254 |
| Broadcast | 15.255 | 31.255 | 47.255 | 63.255 |

### Practice Example #4B: 255.255.248.0 (/21)

172.16.0.0 = Network address

255.255.248.0 = Subnet mask

- *Subnets?* $2^5 = 32$.
- *Hosts?* $2^{11} - 2 = 2046$.
- *Valid subnets?* $256 - 248 = 0, 8, 16, 24, 32$, etc., up to 248.
- *Broadcast address for each subnet?*
- *Valid hosts?*

The following table shows the first five subnets, valid hosts, and broadcast addresses in a Class B 255.255.248.0 mask:

| Subnet | 0.0 | 8.0 | 16.0 | 24.0 | 32.0 |
|---|---|---|---|---|---|
| First host | 0.1 | 8.1 | 16.1 | 24.1 | 32.1 |
| Last host | 7.254 | 15.254 | 23.254 | 31.254 | 39.254 |
| Broadcast | 7.255 | 15.255 | 23.255 | 31.255 | 39.255 |

## Practice Example #5B: 255.255.252.0 (/22)

172.16.0.0 = Network address

255.255.252.0 = Subnet mask

- *Subnets?* $2^6 = 64$.
- *Hosts?* $2^{10} - 2 = 1022$.
- *Valid subnets?* 256 − 252 = 0, 4, 8, 12, 16, etc., up to 252.
- *Broadcast address for each subnet?*
- *Valid hosts?*

The following table shows the first five subnets, valid hosts, and broadcast addresses in a Class B 255.255.252.0 mask:

| Subnet | 0.0 | 4.0 | 8.0 | 12.0 | 16.0 |
|---|---|---|---|---|---|
| First host | 0.1 | 4.1 | 8.1 | 12.1 | 16.1 |
| Last host | 1.254 | 7.254 | 11.254 | 15.254 | 19.254 |
| Broadcast | 3.255 | 7.255 | 11.255 | 15.255 | 19.255 |

## Practice Example #6B: 255.255.254.0 (/23)

172.16.0.0 = Network address

255.255.254.0 = Subnet mask

- *Subnets?* $2^7 = 128$.
- *Hosts?* $2^9 - 2 = 510$.
- *Valid subnets?* 256 − 254 = 0, 2, 4, 6, 8, etc., up to 254.

- *Broadcast address for each subnet?*
- *Valid hosts?*

The following table shows the first five subnets, valid hosts, and broadcast addresses in a Class B 255.255.254.0 mask:

| Subnet | 0.0 | 2.0 | 4.0 | 6.0 | 8.0 |
|---|---|---|---|---|---|
| First host | 0.1 | 2.1 | 4.1 | 6.1 | 8.1 |
| Last host | 1.254 | 3.254 | 5.254 | 7.254 | 9.254 |
| Broadcast | 1.255 | 3.255 | 5.255 | 7.255 | 9.255 |

## Practice Example #7B: 255.255.255.0 (/24)

Contrary to popular belief, 255.255.255.0 used with a Class B network address is not called a Class B network with a Class C subnet mask. It's amazing how many people see this mask used in a Class B network and think it's a Class C subnet mask. This is a Class B subnet mask with 8 bits of subnetting—it's logically different from a Class C mask. Subnetting this address is fairly simple:

172.16.0.0 = Network address

255.255.255.0 = Subnet mask

- *Subnets?* $2^8 = 256$.
- *Hosts?* $2^8 - 2 = 254$.
- *Valid subnets?* 256 − 255 = 1. 0, 1, 2, 3, etc., all the way to 255.
- *Broadcast address for each subnet?*
- *Valid hosts?*

The following table shows the first four and last two subnets, the valid hosts, and the broadcast addresses in a Class B 255.255.255.0 mask:

| Subnet | 0.0 | 1.0 | 2.0 | 3.0 | ... | 254.0 | 255.0 |
|---|---|---|---|---|---|---|---|
| First host | 0.1 | 1.1 | 2.1 | 3.1 | ... | 254.1 | 255.1 |
| Last host | 0.254 | 1.254 | 2.254 | 3.254 | ... | 254.254 | 255.254 |
| Broadcast | 0.255 | 1.255 | 2.255 | 3.255 | ... | 254.255 | 255.255 |

## Practice Example #8B: 255.255.255.128 (/25)

This is actually one of the hardest subnet masks you can play with. And worse, it actually is a really good subnet to use in production because it creates over 500 subnets with 126 hosts for each subnet—a nice mixture. So, don't skip over it!

  172.16.0.0 = Network address

  255.255.255.128 = Subnet mask

- *Subnets?* $2^9$ = 512.

- *Hosts?* $2^7 - 2$ = 126.

- *Valid subnets?* Okay, now for the tricky part. 256 − 255 = 1. 0, 1, 2, 3, etc., for the third octet. But you can't forget the one subnet bit used in the fourth octet. Remember when I showed you how to figure one subnet bit with a Class C mask? You figure this the same way. You actually get two subnets for each third octet value, hence the 512 subnets. For example, if the third octet is showing subnet 3, the two subnets would actually be 3.0 and 3.128.

- *Broadcast address for each subnet?* The numbers right before the next subnet.

- *Valid hosts?* The numbers between the subnet numbers and the broadcast address.

The following graphic shows how you can create subnets, valid hosts, and broadcast addresses using the Class B 255.255.255.128 subnet mask. The first eight subnets are shown, followed by the last two subnets:

| Subnet | 0.0 | 0.128 | 1.0 | 1.128 | 2.0 | 2.128 | 3.0 | 3.128 | ... | 255.0 | 255.128 |
|---|---|---|---|---|---|---|---|---|---|---|---|
| First host | 0.1 | 0.129 | 1.1 | 1.129 | 2.1 | 2.129 | 3.1 | 3.129 | ... | 255.1 | 255.129 |
| Last host | 0.126 | 0.254 | 1.126 | 1.254 | 2.126 | 2.254 | 3.126 | 3.254 | ... | 255.126 | 255.254 |
| Broadcast | 0.127 | 0.255 | 1.127 | 1.255 | 2.127 | 2.255 | 3.127 | 3.255 | ... | 255.127 | 255.255 |

## Practice Example #9B: 255.255.255.192 (/26)

Now, this is where Class B subnetting gets easy. Since the third octet has a 255 in the mask section, whatever number is listed in the third octet is a subnet number. And now that we have a subnet number in the fourth octet, we can subnet this octet just as we did with Class C subnetting. Let's try it out:

  172.16.0.0 = Network address

  255.255.255.192 = Subnet mask

- *Subnets?* $2^{10}$ = 1024.

- *Hosts?* $2^6 - 2$ = 62.

- *Valid subnets?* 256 − 192 = 64. The subnets are shown in the following table. Do these numbers look familiar?

- *Broadcast address for each subnet?*
- *Valid hosts?*

The following table shows the first eight subnet ranges, valid hosts, and broadcast addresses:

| Subnet | 0.0 | 0.64 | 0.128 | 0.192 | 1.0 | 1.64 | 1.128 | 1.192 |
| --- | --- | --- | --- | --- | --- | --- | --- | --- |
| First host | 0.1 | 0.65 | 0.129 | 0.193 | 1.1 | 1.65 | 1.129 | 1.193 |
| Last host | 0.62 | 0.126 | 0.190 | 0.254 | 1.62 | 1.126 | 1.190 | 1.254 |
| Broadcast | 0.63 | 0.127 | 0.191 | 0.255 | 1.63 | 1.127 | 1.191 | 1.255 |

Notice that for each subnet value in the third octet, you get subnets 0, 64, 128, and 192 in the fourth octet.

## Practice Example #10B: 255.255.255.224 (/27)

This one is done the same way as the preceding subnet mask, except that we just have more subnets and fewer hosts per subnet available.

172.16.0.0 = Network address

255.255.255.224 = Subnet mask

- *Subnets?* $2^{11}$ = 2048.
- *Hosts?* $2^5 - 2$ = 30.
- *Valid subnets?* 256 – 224 = 32. 0, 32, 64, 96, 128, 160, 192, 224.
- *Broadcast address for each subnet?*
- *Valid hosts?*

The following table shows the first eight subnets:

| Subnet | 0.0 | 0.32 | 0.64 | 0.96 | 0.128 | 0.160 | 0.192 | 0.224 |
| --- | --- | --- | --- | --- | --- | --- | --- | --- |
| First host | 0.1 | 0.33 | 0.65 | 0.97 | 0.129 | 0.161 | 0.193 | 0.225 |
| Last host | 0.30 | 0.62 | 0.94 | 0.126 | 0.158 | 0.190 | 0.222 | 0.254 |
| Broadcast | 0.31 | 0.63 | 0.95 | 0.127 | 0.159 | 0.191 | 0.223 | 0.255 |

This next table shows the last eight subnets:

| Subnet | 255.0 | 255.32 | 255.64 | 255.96 | 255.128 | 255.160 | 255.192 | 255.224 |
|---|---|---|---|---|---|---|---|---|
| First host | 255.1 | 255.33 | 255.65 | 255.97 | 255.129 | 255.161 | 255.193 | 255.225 |
| Last host | 255.30 | 255.62 | 255.94 | 255.126 | 255.158 | 255.190 | 255.222 | 255.254 |
| Broadcast | 255.31 | 255.63 | 255.95 | 255.127 | 255.159 | 255.191 | 255.223 | 255.255 |

## Subnetting in Your Head: Class B Addresses

Are you nuts? Subnet Class B addresses in our heads? It's actually easier than writing it out—I'm not kidding! Let me show you how:

*Question:* What is the subnet and broadcast address of the subnet in which 172.16.10.33 /27 resides?

*Answer:* The interesting octet is the fourth one. 256 – 224 = 32. 32 + 32 = 64. You've got it: 33 is between 32 and 64. But remember that the third octet is considered part of the subnet, so the answer would be the 10.32 subnet. The broadcast is 10.63, since 10.64 is the next subnet. That was a pretty easy one.

*Question:* What subnet and broadcast address is the IP address 172.16.66.10 255.255.192.0 (/18) a member of?

*Answer:* The interesting octet here is the third octet instead of the fourth one. 256 – 192 = 64. 0, 64, 128. The subnet is 172.16.64.0. The broadcast must be 172.16.127.255 since 128.0 is the next subnet.

*Question:* What subnet and broadcast address is the IP address 172.16.50.10 255.255.224.0 (/19) a member of?

*Answer:* 256 – 224 = 0, 32, 64 (remember, we always start counting at 0). The subnet is 172.16.32.0, and the broadcast must be 172.16.63.255 since 64.0 is the next subnet.

*Question:* What subnet and broadcast address is the IP address 172.16.46.255 255.255.240.0 (/20) a member of?

*Answer:* 256 – 240 = 16. The third octet is important here: 0, 16, 32, 48. This subnet address must be in the 172.16.32.0 subnet, and the broadcast must be 172.16.47.255 since 48.0 is the next subnet. So, yes, 172.16.46.255 is a valid host.

*Question:* What subnet and broadcast address is the IP address 172.16.45.14 255.255.255.252 (/30) a member of?

*Answer:* Where is our interesting octet? 256 – 252 = 0, 4, 8, 12, 16—the fourth. The subnet is 172.16.45.12, with a broadcast of 172.16.45.15 because the next subnet is 172.16.45.16.

*Question:* What is the subnet and broadcast address of the host 172.16.88.255/20?

*Answer:* What is a /20 written out in dotted decimal? If you can't answer this, you can't answer this question, can you? A /20 is 255.255.240.0, gives us a block size of 16 in the third octet, and since no subnet bits are on in the fourth octet, the answer is always 0 and 255 in the fourth octet: 0, 16, 32, 48, 64, 80, 96. Because 88 is between 80 and 96, the subnet is 80.0 and the broadcast address is 95.255.

*Question:* A router receives a packet on an interface with a destination address of 172.16.46.191/26. What will the router do with this packet?

*Answer:* Discard it. Do you know why? 172.16.46.191/26 is a 255.255.255.192 mask, which gives us a block size of 64. Our subnets are then 0, 64, 128 and 192. 191 is the broadcast address of the 128 subnet, and by default, a router will discard any broadcast packets.

# Subnetting Class A Addresses

You don't go about Class A subnetting any differently than Classes B and C, but there are 24 bits to play with instead of the 16 in a Class B address and the 8 in a Class C address.
Let's start by listing all the Class A masks:

```
255.0.0.0        (/8)
255.128.0.0      (/9)        255.255.240.0    (/20)
255.192.0.0      (/10)       255.255.248.0    (/21)
255.224.0.0      (/11)       255.255.252.0    (/22)
255.240.0.0      (/12)       255.255.254.0    (/23)
255.248.0.0      (/13)       255.255.255.0    (/24)
255.252.0.0      (/14)       255.255.255.128  (/25)
255.254.0.0      (/15)       255.255.255.192  (/26)
255.255.0.0      (/16)       255.255.255.224  (/27)
255.255.128.0    (/17)       255.255.255.240  (/28)
255.255.192.0    (/18)       255.255.255.248  (/29)
255.255.224.0    (/19)       255.255.255.252  (/30)
```

That's it. You must leave at least 2 bits for defining hosts. I hope you can see the pattern by now. Remember, we're going to do this the same way as a Class B or C subnet. It's just that, again, we simply have more host bits and we just use the same subnet numbers we used with Class B and C, but we start using these numbers in the second octet. However, the reason class A addresses are so popular to implement is because they give the most flexibility. You can subnet in the 2nd, 3rd or 4th octet. I'll show you this in the next examples.

## Subnetting Practice Examples: Class A Addresses

When you look at an IP address and a subnet mask, you must be able to distinguish the bits used for subnets from the bits used for determining hosts. This is imperative. If you're still struggling with this concept, please reread the section, "IP Addressing" in Chapter 3. It shows you how to determine the difference between the subnet and host bits and should help clear things up.

### Practice Example #1A: 255.255.0.0 (/16)

Class A addresses use a default mask of 255.0.0.0, which leaves 22 bits for subnetting because you must leave 2 bits for host addressing. The 255.255.0.0 mask with a Class A address is using 8 subnet bits:

- *Subnets?* $2^8$ = 256.
- *Hosts?* $2^{16} - 2$ = 65,534.
- *Valid subnets?* What is the interesting octet? 256 − 255 = 1. 0, 1, 2, 3, etc. (all in the second octet). The subnets would be 10.0.0.0, 10.1.0.0, 10.2.0.0, 10.3.0.0, etc., up to 10.255.0.0.
- *Broadcast address for each subnet?*
- *Valid hosts?*

The following table shows the first two and the last two subnets, the valid host range and the broadcast addresses for the private Class A 10.0.0.0 network:

| Subnet | 10.0.0.0 | 10.1.0.0 | ... | 10.254.0.0 | 10.255.0.0 |
|---|---|---|---|---|---|
| First host | 10.0.0.1 | 10.1.0.1 | ... | 10.254.0.1 | 10.255.0.1 |
| Last host | 10.0.255.254 | 10.1.255.254 | ... | 10.254.255.254 | 10.255.255.254 |
| Broadcast | 10.0.255.255 | 10.1.255.255 | ... | 10.254.255.255 | 10.255.255.255 |

### Practice Example #2A: 255.255.240.0 (/20)

255.255.240.0 gives us 12 bits of subnetting and leaves us 12 bits for host addressing.

- *Subnets?* $2^{12}$ = 4096.
- *Hosts?* $2^{12} - 2$ = 4094.
- *Valid subnets?* What is your interesting octet? 256 − 240 = 16. The subnets in the second octet are a block size of 1 and the subnets in the third octet are 0, 16, 32, etc.
- *Broadcast address for each subnet?*
- *Valid hosts?*

The following table shows some examples of the host ranges—the first three subnets and the last subnet:

| Subnet | 10.0.0.0 | 10.0.16.0 | 10.0.32.0 | ... | 10.255.240.0 |
|---|---|---|---|---|---|
| First host | 10.0.0.1 | 10.0.16.1 | 10.0.32.1 | ... | 10.255.240.1 |
| Last host | 10.0.15.254 | 10.0.31.254 | 10.0.47.254 | ... | 10.255.255.254 |

| Subnet | 10.0.0.0 | 10.0.16.0 | 10.0.32.0 | ... | 10.255.240.0 |
|---|---|---|---|---|---|
| Broadcast | 10.0.15.255 | 10.0.31.255 | 10.0.47.255 | ... | 10.255.255.255 |

### Practice Example #3A: 255.255.255.192 (/26)

Let's do one more example using the second, third, and fourth octets for subnetting:

- *Subnets?* $2^{18} = 262{,}144$.
- *Hosts?* $2^6 - 2 = 62$.
- *Valid subnets?* In the second and third octet, the block size is 1, and in the fourth octet, the block size is 64.
- *Broadcast address for each subnet?*
- *Valid hosts?*

The following table shows the first four subnets and their valid hosts and broadcast addresses in the Class A 255.255.255.192 mask:

| Subnet | 10.0.0.0 | 10.0.0.64 | 10.0.0.128 | 10.0.0.192 |
|---|---|---|---|---|
| First host | 10.0.0.1 | 10.0.0.65 | 10.0.0.129 | 10.0.0.193 |
| Last host | 10.0.0.62 | 10.0.0.126 | 10.0.0.190 | 10.0.0.254 |
| Broadcast | 10.0.0.63 | 10.0.0.127 | 10.0.0.191 | 10.0.0.255 |

This table shows the last four subnets and their valid hosts and broadcast addresses:

| Subnet | 10.255.255.0 | 10.255.255.64 | 10.255.255.128 | 10.255.255.192 |
|---|---|---|---|---|
| First host | 10.255.255.1 | 10.255.255.65 | 10.255.255.129 | 10.255.255.193 |
| Last host | 10.255.255.62 | 10.255.255.126 | 10.255.255.190 | 10.255.255.254 |
| Broadcast | 10.255.255.63 | 10.255.255.127 | 10.255.255.191 | 10.255.255.255 |

## Subnetting in Your Head: Class A Addresses

Again, I know this sounds hard, but as with Class C and Class B, the numbers are the same; we just start in the second octet. What makes this easy? You only need to worry about the octet that has the largest block size, which is typically called the interesting octet, and one that is something other than 0 or 255, such as, for example, 255.255.240.0 (/20) with a Class

A network. The second octet has a block size of 1, so any number listed in that octet is a subnet. The third octet is a 240 mask, which means we have a block size of 16 in the third octet. If your host ID is 10.20.80.30, what is your subnet, broadcast address, and valid host range?

The subnet in the second octet is 20 with a block size of 1, but the third octet is in block sizes of 16, so we'll just count them out: 0, 16, 32, 48, 64, 80, 96... voilà! By the way, you can count by 16s by now, right? Good! This makes our subnet 10.20.80.0, with a broadcast of 10.20.95.255 because the next subnet is 10.20.96.0. The valid host range is 10.20.80.1 through 10.20.95.254. And yes, no lie! You really can do this in your head if you just get your block sizes nailed!

Okay, let's practice on one more, just for fun!

Host IP: 10.1.3.65/23

First, you can't answer this question if you don't know what a /23 is. It's 255.255.254.0. The interesting octet here is the third one: 256 − 254 = 2. Our subnets in the third octet are 0, 2, 4, 6, etc. The host in this question is in subnet 2.0, and the next subnet is 4.0, so that makes the broadcast address 3.255. And any address between 10.1.2.1 and 10.1.3.254 is considered a valid host.

# Summary

Did you read Chapters 3 and 4 and understand everything on the first pass? If so, that is fantastic—congratulations! However, you probably really did get lost a couple of times. No worries because as I told you, that's what usually happens. Don't waste time feeling bad if you have to read each chapter more than once, or even 10 times, before you're truly good to go. If you do have to read the chapters more than once, you'll be seriously better off in the long run even if you were pretty comfortable the first time through!

This chapter provided you with an important understanding of IP subnetting—the painless way! And when you've got the key material presented in this chapter really nailed down, you should be able to subnet IP addresses in your head.

This chapter is extremely essential to your Cisco certification process, so if you just skimmed it, please go back, read it thoroughly, and don't forget to do all the written labs too!

# Exam Essentials

**Identify the advantages of subnetting.**   Benefits of subnetting a physical network include reduced network traffic, optimized network performance, simplified management, and facilitated spanning of large geographical distances.

**Describe the effect of the `ip subnet-zero` command.**   This command allows you to use the first and last subnet in your network design.

**Identify the steps to subnet a classful network.**   Understand how IP addressing and subnetting work. First, determine your block size by using the 256-subnet mask math. Then count your subnets and determine the broadcast address of each subnet—it is always the number right before the next subnet. Your valid hosts are the numbers between the subnet address and the broadcast address.

**Determine possible block sizes.**   This is an important part of understanding IP addressing and subnetting. The valid block sizes are always 2, 4, 8, 16, 32, 64, 128, etc. You can determine your block size by using the 256-subnet mask math.

**Describe the role of a subnet mask in IP addressing.**   A subnet mask is a 32-bit value that allows the recipient of IP packets to distinguish the network ID portion of the IP address from the host ID portion of the IP address.

**Understand and apply the $2^x - 2$ formula.**   Use this formula to determine the proper subnet mask for a particular size network given the application of that subnet mask to a particular classful network.

**Explain the impact of Classless Inter-Domain Routing (CIDR).**   CIDR allows the creation of networks of a size other than those allowed with the classful subnetting by allowing more than the three classful subnet masks.

# Written Labs

In this section, you'll complete the following labs to make sure you've got the information and concepts contained within them fully dialed in:

   Lab 4.1: Written Subnet Practice #1

   Lab 4.2: Written Subnet Practice #2

   Lab 4.3: Written Subnet Practice #3

   The answers to these labs can be found in Appendix A, "Answers to Written Labs."

## Written Lab 4.1: Written Subnet Practice #1

Write the subnet, broadcast address, and a valid host range for question 1 through question 6. Then answer the remaining questions.

   **1.** 192.168.100.25/30

   **2.** 192.168.100.37/28

   **3.** 192.168.100.66/27

   **4.** 192.168.100.17/29

   **5.** 192.168.100.99/26

6. 192.168.100.99/25
7. You have a Class B network and need 29 subnets. What is your mask?
8. What is the broadcast address of 192.168.192.10/29?
9. How many hosts are available with a Class C /29 mask?
10. What is the subnet for host ID 10.16.3.65/23?

# Written Lab 4.2: Written Subnet Practice #2

Given a Class B network and the net bits identified (CIDR), complete the following table to identify the subnet mask and the number of host addresses possible for each mask.

| Classful Address | Subnet Mask | Number of Hosts per Subnet ($2^x - 2$) |
| --- | --- | --- |
| /16 | | |
| /17 | | |
| /18 | | |
| /19 | | |
| /20 | | |
| /21 | | |
| /22 | | |
| /23 | | |
| /24 | | |
| /25 | | |
| /26 | | |
| /27 | | |
| /28 | | |
| /29 | | |
| /30 | | |

# Written Lab 4.3: Written Subnet Practice #3

Complete the following based on the decimal IP address.

| Decimal IP Address | Address Class | Number of Subnet and Host Bits | Number of Subnets ($2^x$) | Number of Hosts ($2^x - 2$) |
|---|---|---|---|---|
| 10.25.66.154/23 | | | | |
| 172.31.254.12/24 | | | | |
| 192.168.20.123/28 | | | | |
| 63.24.89.21/18 | | | | |
| 128.1.1.254/20 | | | | |
| 208.100.54.209/30 | | | | |

# Review Questions

The following questions are designed to test your understanding of this chapter's material. For more information on how to get additional questions, please see this book's introduction.

The answers to these questions can be found in Appendix B, "Answers to Chapter Review Questions."

1. What is the maximum number of IP addresses that can be assigned to hosts on a local subnet that uses the 255.255.255.224 subnet mask?

   A. 14

   B. 15

   C. 16

   D. 30

   E. 31

   F. 62

2. You have a network that needs 29 subnets while maximizing the number of host addresses available on each subnet. How many bits must you borrow from the host field to provide the correct subnet mask?

   A. 2

   B. 3

   C. 4

   D. 5

   E. 6

   F. 7

3. What is the subnetwork address for a host with the IP address 200.10.5.68/28?

   A. 200.10.5.56

   B. 200.10.5.32

   C. 200.10.5.64

   D. 200.10.5.0

**4.** The network address of 172.16.0.0/19 provides how many subnets and hosts?

   **A.** 7 subnets, 30 hosts each

   **B.** 7 subnets, 2,046 hosts each

   **C.** 7 subnets, 8,190 hosts each

   **D.** 8 subnets, 30 hosts each

   **E.** 8 subnets, 2,046 hosts each

   **F.** 8 subnets, 8,190 hosts each

**5.** Which two statements describe the IP address 10.16.3.65/23? (Choose two.)

   **A.** The subnet address is 10.16.3.0 255.255.254.0.

   **B.** The lowest host address in the subnet is 10.16.2.1 255.255.254.0.

   **C.** The last valid host address in the subnet is 10.16.2.254 255.255.254.0.

   **D.** The broadcast address of the subnet is 10.16.3.255 255.255.254.0.

   **E.** The network is not subnetted.

**6.** If a host on a network has the address 172.16.45.14/30, what is the subnetwork this host belongs to?

   **A.** 172.16.45.0

   **B.** 172.16.45.4

   **C.** 172.16.45.8

   **D.** 172.16.45.12

   **E.** 172.16.45.16

**7.** Which mask should you use on point-to-point WAN links in order to reduce the waste of IP addresses?

   **A.** /27

   **B.** /28

   **C.** /29

   **D.** /30

   **E.** /31

**8.** What is the subnetwork number of a host with an IP address of 172.16.66.0/21?

   **A.** 172.16.36.0

   **B.** 172.16.48.0

   **C.** 172.16.64.0

   **D.** 172.16.0.0

9. You have an interface on a router with the IP address of 192.168.192.10/29. Including the router interface, how many hosts can have IP addresses on the LAN attached to the router interface?

   A. 6

   B. 8

   C. 30

   D. 62

   E. 126

10. You need to configure a server that is on the subnet 192.168.19.24/29. The router has the first available host address. Which of the following should you assign to the server?

    A. 192.168.19.0 255.255.255.0

    B. 192.168.19.33 255.255.255.240

    C. 192.168.19.26 255.255.255.248

    D. 192.168.19.31 255.255.255.248

    E. 192.168.19.34 255.255.255.240

11. You have an interface on a router with the IP address of 192.168.192.10/29. What is the broadcast address the hosts will use on this LAN?

    A. 192.168.192.15

    B. 192.168.192.31

    C. 192.168.192.63

    D. 192.168.192.127

    E. 192.168.192.255

12. You need to subnet a network that has 5 subnets, each with at least 16 hosts. Which classful subnet mask would you use?

    A. 255.255.255.192

    B. 255.255.255.224

    C. 255.255.255.240

    D. 255.255.255.248

**13.** You configure a router interface with the IP address 192.168.10.62 255.255.255.192 and receive the following error:

```
Bad mask /26 for address 192.168.10.62
```

Why did you receive this error?

A. You typed this mask on a WAN link and that is not allowed.

B. This is not a valid host and subnet mask combination.

C. `ip subnet-zero` is not enabled on the router.

D. The router does not support IP.

**14.** If an Ethernet port on a router were assigned an IP address of 172.16.112.1/25, what would be the valid subnet address of this interface?

A. 172.16.112.0

B. 172.16.0.0

C. 172.16.96.0

D. 172.16.255.0

E. 172.16.128.0

**15.** Using the following illustration, what would be the IP address of E0 if you were using the eighth subnet? The network ID is 192.168.10.0/28 and you need to use the last available IP address in the range. The zero subnet should not be considered valid for this question.

192.168.10.0/28

A. 192.168.10.142

B. 192.168.10.66

C. 192.168.100.254

D. 192.168.10.143

E. 192.168.10.126

**16.** Using the illustration from the previous question, what would be the IP address of S0 if you were using the first subnet? The network ID is 192.168.10.0/28 and you need to use the last available IP address in the range. Again, the zero subnet should not be considered valid for this question.

    **A.** 192.168.10.24

    **B.** 192.168.10.62

    **C.** 192.168.10.30

    **D.** 192.168.10.127

**17.** Which configuration command must be in effect to allow the use of 8 subnets if the Class C subnet mask is 255.255.255.224?

    **A.** Router(config)#`ip classless`

    **B.** Router(config)#`ip version 6`

    **C.** Router(config)#`no ip classful`

    **D.** Router(config)#`ip unnumbered`

    **E.** Router(config)#`ip subnet-zero`

    **F.** Router(config)#`ip all-nets`

**18.** You have a network with a subnet of 172.16.17.0/22. Which is the valid host address?

    **A.** 172.16.17.1 255.255.255.252

    **B.** 172.16.0.1 255.255.240.0

    **C.** 172.16.20.1 255.255.254.0

    **D.** 172.16.16.1 255.255.255.240

    **E.** 172.16.18.255 255.255.252.0

    **F.** 172.16.0.1 255.255.255.0

**19.** Your router has the following IP address on Ethernet0: 172.16.2.1/23. Which of the following can be valid host IDs on the LAN interface attached to the router? (Choose two.)

    **A.** 172.16.0.5

    **B.** 172.16.1.100

    **C.** 172.16.1.198

    **D.** 172.16.2.255

    **E.** 172.16.3.0

    **F.** 172.16.3.255

**20.** To test the IP stack on your local host, which IP address would you ping?

    **A.** 172.0.0.1

    **B.** 1.0.0.127

    **C.** 127.0.0.1

    **D.** 127.255.255.255

    **E.** 255.255.255.255

# Chapter

# 5

# VLSMs, Summarization, and Troubleshooting TCP/IP

## THE FOLLOWING ICND1 EXAM TOPICS ARE COVERED IN THIS CHAPTER:

✓ **IP addressing (IPv4 / IPv6)**

- Identify the appropriate IPv4 addressing scheme using VLSM and summarization to satisfy addressing requirements in a LAN/WAN environment.

✓ **Troubleshooting**

- Troubleshoot and correct common problems associated with IP addressing and host configurations.

Now that IP addressing and subnetting have been thoroughly covered in the last two chapters, you're now fully prepared and ready to learn all about variable length subnet masks (VLSMs). I'll also show you how to design and implement a network using VLSM in this chapter. After ensuring you've mastered VLSM design and implementation, I'll demonstrate how to summarize classful boundaries.

We'll wrap up the chapter by going over IP address troubleshooting, focusing on the steps Cisco recommends to follow when troubleshooting an IP network.

So get psyched because this chapter will give you powerful tools to hone your knowledge of IP addressing and networking and seriously refine the important skills you've gained so far. So stay with me—I guarantee that your hard work will pay off! Ready? Let's go!

 To find up-to-the minute updates for this chapter, please see www.lammle.com/forum or the book's web page at www.sybex.com.

# Variable Length Subnet Masks (VLSMs)

Teaching you a simple way to create many networks from a large single network using subnet masks of different lengths in various kinds of network designs is what my primary focus will be in this chapter. Doing this is called VLSM networking, and it brings up another important subject I mentioned in Chapter 4, "Easy Subnetting," classful and classless networking.

Older routing protocols like Routing Information Protocol version 1 (RIPv1) do not have a field for subnet information, so the subnet information gets dropped. This means that if a router running RIP has a subnet mask of a certain value, it assumes that *all* interfaces within the classful address space have the same subnet mask. This is called classful routing, and RIP is considered a classful routing protocol. We'll cover RIP and the difference between classful and classless networks later on in Chapter 8, "IP Routing," but for now, just remember that if you try to mix and match subnet mask lengths in a network that's running an old routing protocol, such as RIP, it just won't work!

However, classless routing protocols do support the advertisement of subnet information, which means you can use VLSM with routing protocols such as RIPv2, Enhanced Interior Gateway Protocol (EIGRP), and Open Shortest Path First (OSPF). The benefit of this type of network is that it saves a bunch of IP address space.

As the name suggests, VLSMs can use subnet masks with different lengths for different router interfaces. Check out Figure 5.1 to see an example of why classful network designs are inefficient.

**FIGURE 5.1**  Typical classful network

Looking at Figure 5.1, you can see that there are two routers, each with two LANs and connected together with a WAN serial link. In a typical classful network design that's running RIP, you could subnet a network like this:

192.168.10.0 = Network

255.255.255.240 (/28) = Mask

Our subnets would be—you know this part, right?— 0, 16, 32, 48, 64, 80, etc., which allows us to assign 16 subnets to our internetwork. But how many hosts would be available on each network? Well, as you know by now, each subnet provides only 14 hosts, so each LAN has only 14 valid hosts available (don't forget that the router interface needs an address too and is included in the amount of needed valid hosts). This means that one LAN doesn't even have enough addresses needed for all the hosts, and this network as it is shown would not work as addressed in the figure! Since the point-to-point WAN link also has 14 valid hosts, it would be great to be able to nick a few valid hosts from that WAN link to give to our LANs!

All hosts and router interfaces have the same subnet mask—again, known as classful routing—and if we want this network to be efficient, we would definitely need to add different masks to each router interface.

But that's not our only problem—the link between the two routers will never use more than two valid hosts! This wastes valuable IP address space, and it's the big reason you need to learn about VLSM network design.

# VLSM Design

Let's take Figure 5.1 and use a classless design instead, which will become the new network shown in Figure 5.2. In the previous example, we wasted address space—one LAN didn't have enough addresses because every router interface and host used the same subnet mask. Not so good. A better solution would be to provide for only the needed number of hosts on each router interface, and we're going to use VLSMs to achieve that goal.

**FIGURE 5.2**    Classless network design

Now remember that we can use different size masks on each router interface. If we use a /30 on our WAN links and a /27, /28, and /29 on our LANs, we'll get 2 hosts per WAN interface and 30, 14, and 6 hosts per LAN interface—nice! This makes a huge difference—not only can we get just the right amount of hosts on each LAN, we still have room to add more WANs and LANs using this same network!

To implement a VLSM design on your network, you need to have a routing protocol that sends subnet mask information with the route updates. The protocols that do that are RIPv2, EIGRP, and OSPF. Remember, RIPv1 will not work in classless networks, so it's considered a classful routing protocol.

# Implementing VLSM Networks

To create VLSMs quickly and efficiently, you need to understand how block sizes and charts work together to create the VLSM masks. Table 5.1 shows you the block sizes used when creating VLSMs with Class C networks. For example, if you need 25 hosts, then you'll need a block size of 32. If you need 11 hosts, you'll use a block size of 16. Need 40 hosts? Then you'll need a block of 64. You cannot just make up block sizes—they've got to be the block sizes shown in Table 5.1. So memorize the block sizes in this table—it's easy. They're the same numbers we used with subnetting!

**TABLE 5.1**   Block sizes

| Prefix | Mask | Hosts | Block Size |
|--------|------|-------|------------|
| /25 | 128 | 126 | 128 |
| /26 | 192 | 62 | 64 |
| /27 | 224 | 30 | 32 |
| /28 | 240 | 14 | 16 |
| /29 | 248 | 6 | 8 |
| /30 | 252 | 2 | 4 |

The next step is to create a VLSM table. Figure 5.3 shows you the table used in creating a VLSM network. The reason we use this table is so we don't accidentally overlap networks.

You'll find the sheet shown in Figure 5.3 very valuable because it lists every block size you can use for a network address. Notice that the block sizes start at 4 and advance all the way up to a block size of 128. If you have two networks with block sizes of 128, you can have only 2 networks. With a block size of 64, you can have only 4, and so on, all the way to 64 networks using a block size of 4. Of course, this is assuming you're using the ip subnet-zero command in your network design.

So now all you need to do is fill in the chart in the lower-left corner, then add the subnets to the worksheet and you're good to go!

Based on what you've learned so far about block sizes and the VLSM table, let's create a VLSM network using a Class C network address 192.168.10.0 for the network in Figure 5.4, then fill out the VLSM table, as shown in Figure 5.5.

In Figure 5.4, we have four WAN links and four LANs connected together, so we need to create a VLSM network that will save address space. Looks like we have two block sizes of 32, a block size of 16, and a block size of 8, and our WANs each have a block size of 4. Take a look and see how I filled out our VLSM chart in Figure 5.5.

There are two important things to note here, the first is that we still have plenty of room for growth with this VLSM network design. The second point is that we could never achieve this goal with one subnet mask using classful routing.

**FIGURE 5.3**    The VLSM table

| Subnet | Mask | Subnets | Hosts | Block |
|--------|------|---------|-------|-------|
| /25 | 128 | 2 | 126 | 128 |
| /26 | 192 | 4 | 62 | 64 |
| /27 | 224 | 8 | 30 | 32 |
| /28 | 240 | 16 | 14 | 16 |
| /29 | 248 | 32 | 6 | 8 |
| /30 | 252 | 64 | 2 | 4 |

| Network | Hosts | Block | Subnet | Mask |
|---------|-------|-------|--------|------|
| A | | | | |
| B | | | | |
| C | | | | |
| D | | | | |
| E | | | | |
| F | | | | |
| G | | | | |
| H | | | | |
| I | | | | |
| J | | | | |
| K | | | | |
| L | | | | |

**FIGURE 5.4** VLSM network example 1

Let's do another one. Figure 5.6 shows a network with 11 networks, two block sizes of 64, one of 32, five of 16, and three of 4.

First, create your VLSM table and use your block size chart to fill in the table with the subnets you need. Figure 5.7 shows a possible solution.

Notice that I filled in this entire chart and only have room for one more block size of 4. You can only gain that amount of address space savings with a VLSM network!

Keep in mind that it doesn't matter where you start your block sizes as long as you always begin counting from zero. For example, if you had a block size of 16, you must start at 0 and incrementally progress from there—0, 16, 32, 48, and so on. You can't start with a block size of 16 or some value like 40, and you can't progress using anything but increments of 16.

Here's another example. If you had block sizes of 32, start at zero like this: 0, 32, 64, 96, etc. Again, you don't get to start wherever you want; you must always start counting from zero. In the example in Figure 5.7, I started at 64 and 128, with my two block sizes of 64. I didn't have much choice because my options are 0, 64, 128, and 192. However, I added the block size of 32, 16, 8, and 4 elsewhere, but they were always in the correct increments required of the specific block size. Remember that if you always start with the largest blocks first, then make your way to the smaller blocks sizes, you will automatically fall on an increment boundary. It also guarantees that you are using your address space in the most effective way.

Okay—you have three locations you need to address, and the IP network you have received is 192.168.55.0 to use as the addressing for the entire network. You'll use `ip subnet-zero` and RIPv2 as the routing protocol because RIPv2 supports VLSM networks but RIPv1 does not. Figure 5.8 shows the network diagram and the IP address of the RouterA S0/0 interface.

**FIGURE 5.5**    VLSM table example 1

| Subnet | Mask | Subnets | Hosts | Block |
|--------|------|---------|-------|-------|
| /25 | 128 | 2 | 126 | 128 |
| /26 | 192 | 4 | 62 | 64 |
| /27 | 224 | 8 | 30 | 32 |
| /28 | 240 | 16 | 14 | 16 |
| /29 | 248 | 32 | 6 | 8 |
| /30 | 252 | 64 | 2 | 4 |

| Network | Hosts | Block | Subnet | Mask |
|---------|-------|-------|--------|------|
| A | 12 | 16 | /28 | 240 |
| B | 20 | 32 | /27 | 224 |
| C | 25 | 32 | /27 | 224 |
| D | 4 | 8 | /29 | 248 |
| E | 2 | 4 | /30 | 252 |
| F | 2 | 4 | /30 | 252 |
| G | 2 | 4 | /30 | 252 |
| H | 2 | 4 | /30 | 252 |

**FIGURE 5.6**    VLSM network example 2

From the list of IP addresses on the right of the figure, which IP address do you think will be placed in each router's FastEthernet 0/0 interface and serial 0/1 of RouterB?

To answer this, look for clues in Figure 5.8. The first is that interface S0/0 on RouterA has IP address 192.168.55.2/30 assigned, which makes for an easy answer because A /30 is 255.255.255.252, which gives you a block size of 4. Your subnets are 0, 4, 8, etc. Since the known host has an IP address of 2, the only other valid host in the zero subnet is 1, so the third answer down is the right one for the S0/1 interface of RouterB.

The next clues are the listed number of hosts for each of the LANs. RouterA needs 7 hosts—a block size of 16 (/28). RouterB needs 90 hosts—a block size of 128 (/25). And RouterC needs 23 hosts—a block size of 32 (/27).

Figure 5.9 illustrates this solution.

This is actually pretty simple because once you've figured out the block size needed for each LAN, all you need to get to the right solution is to identify proper clues and, of course, know your block sizes well!

One last example of VLSM design before we move on to summarization. Figure 5.10 shows three routers, all running RIPv2. Which Class C addressing scheme would you use to maintain the needs of this network while saving as much address space as possible?

This is actually a pretty clean network design that's just waiting for you to fill out the chart. There are block sizes of 64, 32, and 16 and two block sizes of 4. Coming up with the right solution should be a slam dunk! Take a look at my answer in Figure 5.11.

My solution began at subnet 0, and I used the block size of 64. Clearly, I didn't have to go with a block size of 64 because I could've chosen a block size of 4 instead. But I didn't because I usually like to start with the largest block size and move to the smallest. With that done, I added the block sizes of 32 and 16 as well as the two block sizes of 4. This solution is optimal because it still leaves lots of room to add subnets to this network!

**FIGURE 5.7**    VLSM table example 2

| Subnet | Mask | Subnets | Hosts | Block |
|--------|------|---------|-------|-------|
| /25 | 128 | 2 | 126 | 128 |
| /26 | 192 | 4 | 62 | 64 |
| /27 | 224 | 8 | 30 | 32 |
| /28 | 240 | 16 | 14 | 16 |
| /29 | 248 | 32 | 6 | 8 |
| /30 | 252 | 64 | 2 | 4 |

| Network | Hosts | Block | Subnet | Mask |
|---------|-------|-------|--------|------|
| A | | | | |
| B | | | | |
| C | | | | |
| D | | | | |
| E | | | | |
| F | | | | |
| G | | | | |
| H | | | | |
| I | | | | |
| J | | | | |
| K | | | | |

**FIGURE 5.8**  VLSM design example 1

**FIGURE 5.9**  Solution to VLSM design example 1

**FIGURE 5.10**  VLSM design example 2

**FIGURE 5.11**  Solution to VLSM design example 2

---

**Why Bother with VLSM Design?**

You have just been hired by a new company and need to add on to their existing network. There are no restrictions to prevent you from starting over with a completely new IP address scheme. Should you use a VLSM classless network or opt for a classful network?

Let's say you happen to have plenty of address space because you're using the Class A 10.0.0.0 private network address, so you really can't imagine that you'd ever run out of IP addresses. So why would you want to bother with the VLSM design process in this environment?

Good question! Here's your answer...

By creating contiguous blocks of addresses to specific areas of your network, you can then easily summarize the network and keep route updates with a routing protocol to a minimum. Why would anyone want to advertise hundreds of networks between buildings when you can just send one summary route between buildings and achieve the same result? This approach will optimize the network's performance dramatically!

To make sure this is clear, let me take a second to explain summary routes. Summarization, also called supernetting, provides route updates in the most efficient way possible by advertising many routes in one advertisement instead of individually. This saves a ton of bandwidth and minimizes router processing. As always, you need to use blocks of addresses to configure your summary routes and watch your network's performance hum along efficiently! And remember, block sizes are used in all sorts of networks anyway.

Still, it's important to understand that summarization works only if you design your network properly. If you carelessly hand out IP subnets to any location on the network, you'll quickly notice that you no longer have any summary boundaries. And you won't get very far creating summary routes without those, so watch your step!

# Summarization

Summarization, also called route aggregation, allows routing protocols to advertise many networks as one address. The purpose of this is to reduce the size of routing tables on routers to save memory, which also shortens the amount of time IP requires to parse the routing table when determining the best path to a remote network.

Figure 5.12 shows how a summary address would be used in an internetwork.

**FIGURE 5.12**   Summary address used in an internetwork

Summarization is pretty straightforward because all you really need to have down is a solid understanding of the block sizes we've been using for subnetting and VLSM design. For example, if you wanted to summarize the following networks into one network advertisement, you just have to find the block size first, which will make it easy to find your answer:

192.168.16.0 through network 192.168.31.0

Okay—so what's the block size? Well, there are exactly 16 Class C networks, which fit neatly into a block size of 16.

Now that we've determined the block size, we just need to find the network address and mask used to summarize these networks into one advertisement. The network address used to advertise the summary address is always the first network address in the block—in this example, 192.168.16.0. To figure out a summary mask, we just need to figure out which mask will get us a block size of 16. If you came up with 240, you got it right! 240 would be placed in the third octet, which is exactly the octet where we're summarizing, so the mask would be 255.255.240.0.

Here's another example:

Networks 172.16.32.0 through 172.16.50.0

This isn't as clean as the previous example because there are two possible answers. Here's why: Since you're starting at network 32, your options for block sizes are 4, 8, 16, 32, 64, etc., and block sizes of 16 and 32 could work as this summary address. Let's explore your two options:

- If you went with a block size of 16, then the network address would be 172.16.32.0 with a mask of 255.255.240.0 (240 provides a block of 16). The problem is that this only summarizes from 32 to 47, which means that networks 48 through 50 would be advertised as single networks. Even so, this could still be a good solution depending on your network design.

- If you decided to go with a block size of 32 instead, then your summary address would still be 172.16.32.0, but the mask would be 255.255.224.0 (224 provides a block of 32). The possible problem with this answer is that it will summarize networks 32 through 63 and we only have networks 32 to 50. No worries if you're planning on adding networks 51 to 63 later into the same network, but you could have serious problems in your inter-network if somehow networks 51 to 63 were to show up and be advertised from somewhere else in your network! So even though this option does allow for growth, it's a lot safer to go with option #1.

Let's take a look at another example: Your summary address is 192.168.144.0/20, so what's the range of host addresses that would be forwarded according to this summary? The /20 provides a summary address of 192.168.144.0 and mask of 255.255.240.0.

The third octet has a block size of 16, and starting at summary address 144, the next block of 16 is 160, so your network summary range is 144 to 159 in the third octet. This is why it comes in handy to be able to count in 16s!

A router with this summary address in the routing table will forward any packet having destination IP addresses of 192.168.144.1 through 192.168.159.254.

Only two more summarization examples, then we'll move on to troubleshooting.

In summarization example 4, Figure 5.13, the Ethernet networks connected to router R1 are being summarized to R2 as 192.168.144.0/20. Which range of IP addresses will R2 forward to R1 according to this summary?

**FIGURE 5.13**  Summarization example 4. The Ethernet networks connected to router R1 are being summarized to R2 as 192.168.144.0/20. Which IP addresses will R2 forward to R1 according to this summary?

No worries—solving this is easier than it looks initially. The question actually has the summary address listed in it: 192.168.144.0/20. You already know that /20 is 255.255.240.0, which means you've got a block size of 16 in the third octet. Starting at 144, which is also right there in the question, makes the next block size of 16 equal 160. You can't go above 159 in the third octet, so the IP addresses that will be forwarded are 192.168.144.1 through 192.168.159.254.

Okay, last one. In Figure 5.14, there are five networks connected to router R1. What's the best summary address to R2?

**FIGURE 5.14**   Summarization example 5

I'll be honest with you—this is a much harder question than the one in Figure 5.13, so you're going to have to look carefully to see the answer.  A good approach here would be to write down all the networks and see if you can find anything in common with all of them:

- 172.1.4.128/25
- 172.1.7.0/24
- 172.1.6.0/24
- 172.1.5.0/24
- 172.1.4.0/25

Do you see an octet that looks interesting to you? I do. It's the third octet. 4, 5, 6, 7, and yes, it's a block size of 4. So you can summarize 172.1.4.0 using a mask of 255.255.252.0, meaning you would use a block size of 4 in the third octet. The IP addresses forwarded with this summary would be 172.1.4.1 through 172.1.7.255.

To summarize the summarization section, if you've nailed down your block sizes, then finding and applying summary addresses and masks is a relatively straightforward task. But you're going to get bogged down pretty quickly if you don't know what a /20 is or if you can't count by 16s!

# Troubleshooting IP Addressing

Because running into trouble now and then in networking is a given, being able to trouble-shoot IP addressing is clearly a vital skill. I'm not being negative here—just realistic. The positive side to this is that if you're the one equipped with the tools to diagnose and clear up the inevitable trouble, you get to be the hero when you save the day! Even better? You can usually fix an IP network regardless of whether you're on site or at home!

So this is where I'm going to show you the "Cisco way" of troubleshooting IP addressing. Let's use Figure 5.15 as an example of your basic IP trouble—poor Sally can't log in to the Windows server. Do you deal with this by calling the Microsoft team to tell them their server is a pile of junk and causing all your problems? Though tempting, a better approach is to first double-check and verify your network instead.

**FIGURE 5.15**    Basic IP troubleshooting

EO
172.16.10.1

Sally
172.16.10.2

Server
172.16.20.2

Okay, let's get started by going through the troubleshooting steps that Cisco recommends. They're pretty simple, but important nonetheless. Pretend you're at a customer host and they're complaining that they can't communicate to a server that just happens to be on a remote net-work. Here are the four troubleshooting steps Cisco recommends:

1. Open a Command window and ping 127.0.0.1. This is the diagnostic, or loopback, address, and if you get a successful ping, your IP stack is considered initialized. If it fails, then you have an IP stack failure and need to reinstall TCP/IP on the host.

```
C:\>ping 127.0.0.1
Pinging 127.0.0.1 with 32 bytes of data:
Reply from 127.0.0.1: bytes=32 time<1ms TTL=128
Reply from 127.0.0.1: bytes=32 time<1ms TTL=128
Reply from 127.0.0.1: bytes=32 time<1ms TTL=128
Reply from 127.0.0.1: bytes=32 time<1ms TTL=128
Ping statistics for 127.0.0.1:
```

```
Packets: Sent = 4, Received = 4, Lost = 0 (0% loss),
Approximate round trip times in milli-seconds:
    Minimum = 0ms, Maximum = 0ms, Average = 0ms
```

**2.** From the Command window, ping the IP address of the local host (we'll assume correct configuration here, but always check the IP configuration too!). If that's successful, your network interface card (NIC) is functioning. If it fails, there is a problem with the NIC. Success here doesn't just mean that a cable is plugged into the NIC, only that the IP protocol stack on the host can communicate to the NIC via the LAN driver.

```
C:\>ping 172.16.10.2
Pinging 172.16.10.2 with 32 bytes of data:
Reply from 172.16.10.2: bytes=32 time<1ms TTL=128
Reply from 172.16.10.2: bytes=32 time<1ms TTL=128
Reply from 172.16.10.2: bytes=32 time<1ms TTL=128
Reply from 172.16.10.2: bytes=32 time<1ms TTL=128
Ping statistics for 172.16.10.2:
    Packets: Sent = 4, Received = 4, Lost = 0 (0% loss),
Approximate round trip times in milli-seconds:
    Minimum = 0ms, Maximum = 0ms, Average = 0ms
```

**3.** From the CMD window, ping the default gateway (router). If the ping works, it means that the NIC is plugged into the network and can communicate on the local network. If it fails, you have a local physical network problem that could be anywhere from the NIC to the router.

```
C:\>ping 172.16.10.1
Pinging 172.16.10.1 with 32 bytes of data:
Reply from 172.16.10.1: bytes=32 time<1ms TTL=128
Reply from 172.16.10.1: bytes=32 time<1ms TTL=128
Reply from 172.16.10.1: bytes=32 time<1ms TTL=128
Reply from 172.16.10.1: bytes=32 time<1ms TTL=128
Ping statistics for 172.16.10.1:
    Packets: Sent = 4, Received = 4, Lost = 0 (0% loss),
Approximate round trip times in milli-seconds:
    Minimum = 0ms, Maximum = 0ms, Average = 0ms
```

**4.** If steps 1 through 3 were successful, try to ping the remote server. If that works, then you know that you have IP communication between the local host and the remote server. You also know that the remote physical network is working.

```
C:\>ping 172.16.20.2
Pinging 172.16.20.2 with 32 bytes of data:
```

```
Reply from 172.16.20.2: bytes=32 time<1ms TTL=128
Reply from 172.16.20.2: bytes=32 time<1ms TTL=128
Reply from 172.16.20.2: bytes=32 time<1ms TTL=128
Reply from 172.16.20.2: bytes=32 time<1ms TTL=128
Ping statistics for 172.16.20.2:
    Packets: Sent = 4, Received = 4, Lost = 0 (0% loss),
Approximate round trip times in milli-seconds:
    Minimum = 0ms, Maximum = 0ms, Average = 0ms
```

If the user still can't communicate with the server after steps 1 through 4 have been completed successfully, you probably have some type of name resolution problem and need to check your Domain Name System (DNS) settings. But if the ping to the remote server fails, then you know you have some type of remote physical network problem and need to go to the server and work through steps 1 through 3 until you find the snag.

Before we move on to determining IP address problems and how to fix them, I just want to mention some basic commands that you can use to help troubleshoot your network from both a PC and a Cisco router. Keep in mind that though these commands may do the same thing, they're implemented differently.

**ping**   Uses ICMP echo request and replies to test if a node IP stack is initialized and alive on the network.

**traceroute**   Displays the list of routers on a path to a network destination by using TTL time-outs and ICMP error messages. This command will not work from a command prompt.

**tracert**   Same function as `traceroute`, but it's a Microsoft Windows command and will not work on a Cisco router.

**arp -a**   Displays IP-to-MAC-address mappings on a Windows PC.

**show ip arp**   Same function as `arp -a`, but displays the ARP table on a Cisco router. Like the commands `traceroute` and `tracert`, `arp -a` and `show ip arp` are not interchangeable through DOS and Cisco.

**ipconfig /all**   Used only from a Windows command prompt; shows you the PC network configuration.

Once you've gone through all these steps and, if necessary, used the appropriate commands, what do you do when you find a problem? How do you go about fixing an IP address configuration error? Time to cover the next step—determining and fixing the issue at hand!

## Determining IP Address Problems

It's common for a host, router, or other network device to be configured with the wrong IP address, subnet mask, or default gateway. Because this happens way too often, you must know how to find and fix IP address configuration errors.

A good way to start is to draw out the network and IP addressing scheme. If that's already been done, consider yourself lucky because though sensible, it's rarely done. Even if it is, it's usually outdated or inaccurate anyway. So either way, it's a good idea to bite the bullet and start from scratch.

 I'll show you how a great way to draw out your network using the Cisco Discovery Protocol (CDP) soon, in Chapter 7, "Managing and Troubleshooting a Cisco Internetwork."

Once you have your network accurately drawn out, including the IP addressing scheme, you need to verify each host's IP address, mask, and default gateway address to establish the problem. Of course, this is assuming that you don't have a physical layer problem, or if you did, that you've already fixed it.

Let's check out the example illustrated in Figure 5.16. A user in the sales department calls and tells you that she can't get to ServerA in the marketing department. You ask her if she can get to ServerB in the marketing department, but she doesn't know because she doesn't have rights to log on to that server. What do you do?

First, guide your user through the four troubleshooting steps you learned in the preceding section. Okay—let's say steps 1 through 3 work but step 4 fails. By looking at the figure, can you determine the problem? Look for clues in the network drawing. First, the WAN link between the Lab_A router and the Lab_B router shows the mask as a /27. You should already know that this mask is 255.255.255.224 and determine that all networks are using this mask. The network address is 192.168.1.0. What are our valid subnets and hosts? 256 − 224 = 32, so this makes our subnets 0, 32, 64, 96, 128, etc. So, by looking at the figure, you can see that subnet 32 is being used by the sales department. The WAN link is using subnet 96, and the marketing department is using subnet 64.

**FIGURE 5.16**    IP address problem 1

Now you've got to establish what the valid host ranges are for each subnet. From what you learned at the beginning of this chapter, you should now be able to easily determine the subnet address, broadcast addresses, and valid host ranges. The valid hosts for the Sales LAN are 33 through 62, and the broadcast address is 63 because the next subnet is 64, right? For the Marketing LAN, the valid hosts are 65 through 94 (broadcast 95), and for the WAN link, 97 through 126 (broadcast 127). By closely examining the figure, you can determine that the default gateway on the Lab_B router is incorrect. That address is the broadcast address for subnet 64, so there's no way it could be a valid host!

If you tried to configure that address on the Lab_B router interface, you'd receive a "bad mask error." Cisco routers don't let you type in subnet and broadcast addresses as valid hosts!

Did you get all that? Let's try another one to make sure. Figure 5.17 shows a network problem. A user in the Sales LAN can't get to ServerB. You have the user run through the four basic troubleshooting steps and find that the host can communicate to the local network but not to the remote network. Find and define the IP addressing problem.

If you went through the same steps used to solve the last problem, you can see that first, the WAN link again provides the subnet mask to use— /29, or 255.255.255.248. Assuming classful addressing, you need to determine what the valid subnets, broadcast addresses, and valid host ranges are to solve this problem.

**FIGURE 5.17**    IP address problem 2

The 248 mask is a block size of 8 (256 – 248 = 8, as discussed in Chapter 4), so the subnets both start and increment in multiples of 8. By looking at the figure, you see that the Sales LAN is in the 24 subnet, the WAN is in the 40 subnet, and the Marketing LAN is in the 80 subnet. Can you see the problem yet? The valid host range for the Sales LAN is 25–30, and the configuration appears correct. The valid host range for the WAN link is 41–46, and this also appears correct. The valid host range for the 80 subnet is 81–86, with a broadcast address of 87 because the next subnet is 88. ServerB has been configured with the broadcast address of the subnet.

Okay, now that you can figure out misconfigured IP addresses on hosts, what do you do if a host doesn't have an IP address and you need to assign one? What you need to do is scrutinize the other hosts on the LAN and figure out the network, mask, and default gateway. Let's take a look at a couple of examples of how to find and apply valid IP addresses to hosts.

You need to assign a server and router IP addresses on a LAN. The subnet assigned on that segment is 192.168.20.24/29. The router needs to be assigned the first usable address and the server needs the last valid host ID. What is the IP address, mask, and default gateway assigned to the server?

To answer this, you must know that a /29 is a 255.255.255.248 mask, which provides a block size of 8. The subnet is known as 24, the next subnet in a block of 8 is 32, so the broadcast address of the 24 subnet is 31 and the valid host range is 25–30.

Server IP address: 192.168.20.30

Server mask: 255.255.255.248

Default gateway: 192.168.20.25 (router's IP address)

Take a look at Figure 5.18 and solve this problem.

**FIGURE 5.18**   Find the valid host #1

Router A

E0: 192.168.10.33/27

Look at the router's IP address on Ethernet0. What IP address, subnet mask, and valid host range could be assigned to the host?

The IP address of the router's Ethernet0 is 192.168.10.33/27. As you already know, a /27 is a 224 mask with a block size of 32. The router's interface is in the 32 subnet. The next subnet is 64, so that makes the broadcast address of the 32 subnet 63 and the valid host range 33–62.

Host IP address: 192.168.10.34–62 (any address in the range except for 33, which is assigned to the router)

Mask: 255.255.255.224

Default gateway: 192.168.10.33

Figure 5.19 shows two routers with Ethernet configurations already assigned. What are the host addresses and subnet masks of HostA and HostB?

**FIGURE 5.19**  Find the valid host #2

RouterA has an IP address of 192.168.10.65/26 and RouterB has an IP address of 192.168.10.33/28. What are the host configurations? RouterA Ethernet0 is in the 192.168.10.64 subnet and RouterB Ethernet0 is in the 192.168.10.32 network.

Host A IP address: 192.168.10.66–126

Host A mask: 255.255.255.192

Host A default gateway: 192.168.10.65

Host B IP address: 192.168.10.34–46

Host B mask: 255.255.255.240

Host B default gateway: 192.168.10.33

Just a couple more examples before you can put this chapter behind you—hang in there! Figure 5.20 shows two routers. You need to configure the S0/0 interface on RouterA. The network assigned to the serial link is 172.16.17.0/22. What IP address can be assigned?

**FIGURE 5.20**  Find the valid host address #3

First, know that a /22 CIDR is 255.255.252.0, which makes a block size of 4 in the third octet. Since 17 is listed, the available range is 16.1 through 19.254, so in this example, the IP address S0/0 could be 172.16.18.255 since that's within the range.

Okay, last one! You need to find a classful network add that has one Class C network ID and you need to provide one usable subnet per city while allowing enough usable host addresses for each city specified in Figure 5.21. What is your mask?

**FIGURE 5.21**    Find the valid subnet mask.

Actually, this is probably the easiest thing you've done all day! I count 5 subnets needed, and the Wyoming office needs 16 users—always look for the network that needs the most hosts! What block size is needed for the Wyoming office? Your answer is 32. You can't use a block size of 16 because you always have to subtract 2. What mask provides you with a block size of 32? 224 is your answer because this provides 8 subnets, each with 30 hosts.

You're done—the diva has sung and the chicken has safely crossed the road…whew! Time to take a break, but skip the shot and the beer if that's what you had in mind because you need to have your head straight to go through the written lab and review questions next!

# Summary

Again, if you got to this point without getting lost along the way a few times, you're awesome, but if you did get lost, don't stress because most people do! Just be patient with yourself and go back over the material that tripped you up until it's all crystal clear. You'll get there!

This chapter provided you with keys to understanding the oh-so-very-important topic of variable length subnet masks. You should also know how to design and implement simple VLSM networks and be clear on summarization as well.

And make sure you understand and memorize Cisco's troubleshooting methods. You must remember the four steps that Cisco recommends to take when trying to narrow down exactly where a network and/or IP addressing problem is and then know how to proceed systematically to fix it. In addition, you should be able to find valid IP addresses and subnet masks by looking at a network diagram.

# Exam Essentials

**Describe the benefits of variable length subnet masks (VLSMs).** VLSMs enable the creation of subnets of specific sizes and allow the division of a classless network into smaller networks that do not need to be equal in size. This makes use of the address space more efficient because many times IP addresses are wasted with classful subnetting.

**Understand the relationship between the subnet mask value and the resulting block size and the allowable IP addresses in each resulting subnet.** The relationship between the classful network being subdivided and the subnet mask used determines the number of possible hosts or the block size. It also determines where each subnet begins and ends and which IP addresses cannot be assigned to a host within each subnet.

**Describe the process of summarization or route aggregation and its relationship to subnetting.** Summarization is the combining of subnets derived from a classful network for the purpose of advertising a single route to neighboring routers instead of multiple routes, reducing the size of routing tables and speeding the route process.

**Calculate the summary mask that will advertise a single network representing all subnets.** The network address used to advertise the summary address is always the first network address in the block of subnets. The mask is the subnet mask value that yields the same block size.

**Remember the four diagnostic steps.** The four simple steps that Cisco recommends for troubleshooting are ping the loopback address, ping the NIC, ping the default gateway, and ping the remote device.

**Identify and mitigate an IP addressing problem.** Once you go through the four trouble-shooting steps that Cisco recommends, you must be able to determine the IP addressing problem by drawing out the network and finding the valid and invalid hosts addressed in your network.

**Understand the troubleshooting tools that you can use from your host and a Cisco router.** The ping 127.0.0.1 command tests your local IP stack, and tracert is a Windows command to track the path a packet takes through an internetwork to a destination. Cisco routers use the command traceroute, or just trace for short. Don't confuse the Windows and Cisco commands. Although they produce the same output, they don't work from the same prompts. The command ipconfig /all will display your PC network configuration from a DOS prompt, and arp -a (again from a DOS prompt) will display IP-to-MAC-address mapping on a Windows PC.

# Written Lab 5

The answers to this lab can be found in Appendix A, "Answers to Written Labs."

For each of the following sets of networks, determine the summary address and the mask to be used that will summarize the subnets.

1. 192.168.1.0/24 through 192.168.12.0/24
2. 172.144.0.0 through 172.159.0.0
3. 192.168.32.0 through 192.168.63.0
4. 192.168.96.0 through 192.168.111.0
5. 66.66.0.0 through 66.66.15.0
6. 192.168.1.0 through 192.168.120.0
7. 172.16.1.0 through 172.16.7.0
8. 192.168.128.0 through 192.168.190.0
9. 53.60.96.0 through 53.60.127.0
10. 172.16.10.0 through 172.16.63.0

# Review Questions

The following questions are designed to test your understanding of this chapter's material. For more information on how to get additional questions, please see this book's introduction.

The answers to these questions can be found in Appendix B, "Answers to Chapter Review Questions."

1. On a VLSM network, which mask should you use on point-to-point WAN links in order to reduce the waste of IP addresses?

   A. /27

   B. /28

   C. /29

   D. /30

   E. /31

2. In the network shown in the diagram, how many computers could be in subnet B?

   A. 6

   B. 12

   C. 14

   D. 30

**3.** In the diagram below, in order to have as efficient IP addressing as possible, which network should use a /29 mask?

**A.** A

**B.** B

**C.** C

**D.** D

**4.** To use VLSM, what capability must the routing protocols in use possess?

**A.** Support for multicast

**B.** Multiprotocol support

**C.** Transmission of subnet mask information

**D.** Support for unequal load balancing

**5.** What summary address would cover all the networks shown and advertise a single, efficient route to Router B that won't advertise more networks than needed?

172.16.1.0/24
172.16.10.0/24
172.16.5.0/24
172.16.15.0/24
172.16.7.0/24
172.16.11.0/24
172.16.6.0/24

**A.** 172.16.0.0/24

**B.** 172.16.1.0/24

**C.** 172.16.0.0/24

**D.** 172.16.0.0/20

**E.** 172.16.16.0/28

**F.** 172.16.0.0/27

**6.** In the diagram below what is the most likely reason the station cannot ping outside of its network?

RouterA

E0: 192.168.10.33/27

IP 192.168.10.28/27
Default gateway 192.168.10.33/27

  **A.** The IP address is incorrect on E0 of the router.

  **B.** The default gateway address is incorrect on the station.

  **C.** The IP address on the station is incorrect.

  **D.** The router is malfunctioning.

**7.** If Host A is configured with an incorrect default gateway and all other computers and the router are known to be configured correctly, which of the following statements is TRUE?

  **A.** Host A cannot communicate with the router.

  **B.** Host A can communicate with other hosts in the same subnet.

  **C.** Host A can communicate with hosts in other subnets.

  **D.** Host A can communicate with no other systems.

**8.** Which of the following troubleshooting steps, if completed successfully, also confirms the other steps will succeed as well?

  **A.** ping a remote computer

  **B.** ping the loopback address

  **C.** ping the NIC

  **D.** ping the default gateway

**9.** When a ping to the local host IP address fails, what can you assume?

  **A.** The IP address of the local host is incorrect.

  **B.** The IP address of the remote host is incorrect.

  **C.** The NIC is not functional.

  **D.** The IP stack has failed to initialize.

**10.** When a ping to the local host IP address succeeds but a ping to the default gateway IP address fails, what can you rule out? (Choose all that apply.)

    **A.** The IP address of the local host is incorrect.

    **B.** The IP address of the gateway is incorrect.

    **C.** The NIC is not functional.

    **D.** The IP stack has failed to initialize.

**11.** Which of the networks in the diagram could use a /29 mask?

    **A.** Corporate

    **B.** LA

    **C.** SF

    **D.** NY

    **E.** none

**12.** What network service is the most likely problem if you can ping a computer by IP address but not by name?

    **A.** DNS

    **B.** DHCP

    **C.** ARP

    **D.** ICMP

**13.** When you issue the ping command, what protocol are you using?

    **A.** DNS

    **B.** DHCP

    **C.** ARP

    **D.** ICMP

**14.** Which of the following commands displays the networks traversed on a path to a network destination?

    **A.** ping

    **B.** traceroute

    **C.** pingroute

    **D.** pathroute

**15.** What command generated the output shown below?

```
Reply from 172.16.10.2: bytes=32 time<1ms TTL=128
Reply from 172.16.10.2: bytes=32 time<1ms TTL=128
Reply from 172.16.10.2: bytes=32 time<1ms TTL=128
Reply from 172.16.10.2: bytes=32 time<1ms TTL=128
```

    **A.** traceroute

    **B.** show ip route

    **C.** ping

    **D.** pathping

**16.** In the work area, match the command to its function on the right.

| | |
|---|---|
| traceroute | Displays the ARP table on a Cisco router |
| arp -a | Displays the list of routers on a path to a network destination |
| show ip arp | Shows you the PC network configuration |
| ipconfig /all | Displays IP-to-MAC-address mappings on a Windows PC |

**17.** Which of the following network addresses correctly summarizes the three networks shown below efficiently?

10.0.0.0/16

10.1.0.0/16

10.2.0.0/16

    **A.** 10.0.0.0/15

    **B.** 10.1.0.0/8

    **C.** 10.0.0.0/14

    **D.** 10.0.0.8/16

**18.** What command displays the ARP table on a Cisco router?

   **A.** show ip arp

   **B.** traceroute

   **C.** arp -a

   **D.** tracert

**19.** What switch must be added to the ipconfig command on a PC to verify DNS configuration?

   **A.** /dns

   **B.** -dns

   **C.** /all

   **D.** showall

**20.** Which of the following is the best summarization of the following networks: 192.168.128.0 through 192.168.159.0

   **A.** 192.168.0.0/24

   **B.** 192.168.128.0/16

   **C.** 192.168.128.0/19

   **D.** 192.168.128.0/20

# Chapter

# 6

# Cisco's Internetworking Operating System (IOS)

## THE FOLLOWING ICND1 EXAM TOPICS ARE COVERED IN THIS CHAPTER:

✓ **LAN Switching Technologies**

- Configure and verify initial switch configuration including remote access management.
  - Cisco IOS commands to perform basic switch setup

✓ **IP Routing Technologies**

- Configure and verify utilizing the CLI to set basic Router configuration
  - Cisco IOS commands to perform basic router setup
- Configure and verify operation status of an ethernet interface
- Verify router configuration and network connectivity
  - Cisco IOS commands to review basic router information and network connectivity

✓ **Network Device Security**

- Configure and verify network device security features such as
  - Device password security
  - Enable secret vs enable
  - Transport
  - Disable telnet
  - SSH
  - VTYs

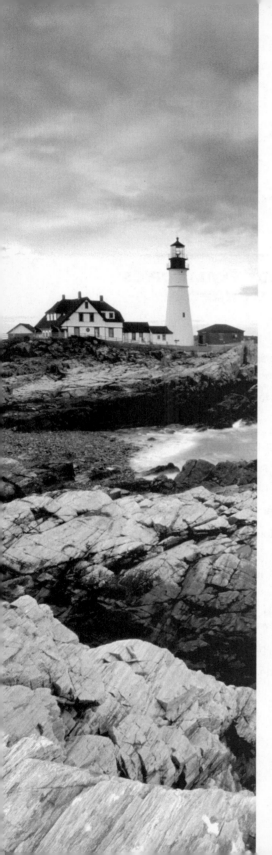

- Physical security
- Service password
- Describe external authentication methods

✓ **Troubleshooting**

- Troubleshoot and resolve Layer 1 problems
  - Framing
  - CRC
  - Runts
  - Giants
  - Dropped packets
  - Late collision
  - Input / Output errors

It's time to introduce you to the Cisco Internetwork Operating System (IOS). The IOS is what runs Cisco routers as well as Cisco's switches, and it's also what we use to configure these devices.

So that's what you're going to learn about in this chapter. I'm going to show you how to configure a Cisco IOS device using the Cisco IOS command-line interface (CLI). Once proficient with this interface, you'll be able to configure hostnames, banners, passwords, and more as well as troubleshoot skillfully using the Cisco IOS.

We'll also begin the journey to mastering the basics of router and switch configurations plus command verifications in this chapter.

I'll start with a basic IOS switch to begin building the network we'll use throughout this book for configuration examples. Don't forget—I'll be using both switches and routers throughout this chapter, and we configure these devices pretty much the same way. Things diverge when we get to the interfaces where the differences between the two become key, so pay attention closely when we get to that point!

Just as it was with preceding chapters, the fundamentals presented in this chapter are important building blocks to have solidly in place before moving on to the more advanced material coming up in the next ones.

To find up-to-the minute updates for this chapter, please see www.lammle.com/forum or the book's web page at www.sybex.com.

# The IOS User Interface

The *Cisco Internetwork Operating System (IOS)* is the kernel of Cisco routers as well as all current Catalyst switches. In case you didn't know, a kernel is the elemental, indispensable part of an operating system that allocates resources and manages tasks like low-level hardware interfaces and security.

Coming up, I'll show you the Cisco IOS and how to configure a Cisco switch using the *command-line interface (CLI)*. The configurations you'll see in this chapter are exactly the same as they are on a Cisco router.

# Cisco IOS

The Cisco IOS is a proprietary kernel that provides routing, switching, internetworking, and telecommunications features. The first IOS was written by William Yeager in 1986 and enabled networked applications. It runs on most Cisco routers as well as a growing number of Cisco Catalyst switches, like the Catalyst 2960 and 3560 series switches used in this book. And it's an essential for the Cisco exam objectives!

Here's a short list of some important things that the Cisco router IOS software is responsible for:

▪ Carrying network protocols and functions

▪ Connecting high-speed traffic between devices

▪ Adding security to control access and stop unauthorized network use

▪ Providing scalability for ease of network growth and redundancy

▪ Supplying network reliability for connecting to network resources

You can access the Cisco IOS through the console port of a router or switch, from a modem into the auxiliary (or aux) port on a router, or even through Telnet and Secure Shell (SSH). Access to the IOS command line is called an *EXEC session*.

# Connecting to a Cisco IOS Device

We connect to a Cisco device to configure it, verify its configuration, and check statistics, and although there are different approaches to this, the first place you would usually connect to is the console port. The *console port* is usually an RJ-45, 8-pin modular connection located at the back of the device, and there may or may not be a password set on it by default.

> Look back into Chapter 2, "Ethernet Networking and Data Encapsulation," to review how to configure a PC and enable it to connect to a router console port.

You can also connect to a Cisco router through an *auxiliary port*, which is really the same thing as a console port, so it follows that you can use it as one. The main difference with an auxiliary port is that it also allows you to configure modem commands so that a modem can be connected to the router. This is a cool feature because it lets you dial up a remote router and attach to the auxiliary port if the router is down and you need to configure it remotely, *out-of-band*. One of the differences between Cisco routers and switches is that switches do not have an auxiliary port.

The third way to connect to a Cisco device is *in-band*, through the program *Telnet* or *Secure Shell (SSH)*. In-band means configuring the device via the network, the opposite of *out-of-band*. We covered Telnet and SSH back in Chapter 3, and in this chapter, I'll show you how to configure access to both of these protocols on a Cisco device.

Figure 6.1 shows an illustration of a Cisco 2960 switch. Really focus in on all the different kinds of interfaces and connections! On the right side is the 10/100/1000 uplink. You can use either the UTP port or the fiber port, but not both at the same time.

**FIGURE 6.1**    A Cisco 2960 switch

The 3560 switch I'll be using in this book looks a lot like the 2960, but it can perform layer 3 switching, unlike the 2960, which is limited to only layer 2 functions.

I also want to take a moment and tell you about the 2800 series router because that's the router series I'll be using in this book. This router is known as an Integrated Services Router (ISR) and Cisco has updated this to the 2900 series but I still have plenty of 2800 series routers in my production networks. Figure 6.2 shows a new 1900 series router. The new ISR series of routers are nice; they get their name because many services, like security, are built into it. It's a modular device, much faster and a lot sleeker than the older 2600 series routers, and it's elegantly designed to support a broad new range of interface options. The new ISR series router can offer multiple serial interfaces, which can be used for connecting a T1 using a serial V.35 WAN connection. And multiple Fast Ethernet or Gigabit Ethernet ports can be used on the router, depending on the model. This router also has one console via an RJ-45 connector and another through the USB port. There is also an auxiliary connection to allow a console connection via a remote modem.

**FIGURE 6.2**    A new Cisco 1900 router

You need to keep in mind that for the most part, you get some serious bang for your buck with the 2800/2900—unless you start adding a bunch of interfaces to it. You've got to pony up for each one of those little beauties, so this can really start to add up and fast!

A couple of other series of routers that will set you back a lot less than the 2800 series are the 1800/1900s, so look into these routers if you want a less-expensive alternative to the 2800/2900 but still want to run the same IOS.

So even though I'm going to be using mostly 2800 series routers and 2960/3560 switches throughout this book to demonstrate examples of IOS configurations, I want to point out that the particular *router* model you use to practice for the Cisco exam isn't really important. The *switch* types are, though—you definitely need 2950 or 2960 switches, as well as a 3560 switch if you want to measure up to the exam objectives!

You can find more information about all Cisco routers at www.cisco.com/
en/US/products/hw/routers/index.html.

## Bringing Up a Switch

When you first bring up a Cisco IOS device, it will run a power-on self-test—a POST. Upon passing that, the machine will look for and then load the Cisco IOS from flash memory if an IOS file is present, then expand it into RAM. As you probably know, flash memory is electronically erasable programmable read-only memory—an EEPROM. The next step is for the IOS to locate and load a valid configuration known as the startup-config that will be stored in *nonvolatile RAM (NVRAM)*.

Once the IOS is loaded and up and running, the startup-config will be copied from NVRAM into RAM and from then on referred to as the running-config.

But if a valid startup-config isn't found in NVRAM, your switch will enter setup mode, giving you a step-by-step dialog to help configure some basic parameters on it.

You can also enter setup mode at any time from the command line by typing the command **setup** from privileged mode, which I'll get to in a minute. Setup mode only covers some basic commands and generally isn't really all that helpful. Here's an example:

```
Would you like to enter the initial configuration dialog? [yes/no]: y

At any point you may enter a question mark '?' for help.
Use ctrl-c to abort configuration dialog at any prompt.
Default settings are in square brackets '[]'.

Basic management setup configures only enough connectivity
for management of the system, extended setup will ask you
to configure each interface on the system

Would you like to enter basic management setup? [yes/no]: y
Configuring global parameters:

  Enter host name [Switch]: Ctrl+C
Configuration aborted, no changes made.
```

You can exit setup mode at any time by pressing Ctrl+C.

I highly recommend going through setup mode once, then never again because you should always use the CLI instead!

# Command-Line Interface (CLI)

I sometimes refer to the CLI as "cash line interface" because the ability to create advanced configurations on Cisco routers and switches using the CLI will earn you some decent cash!

## Entering the CLI

After the interface status messages appear and you press Enter, the `Switch>` prompt will pop up. This is called *user exec mode,* or user mode for short, and although it's mostly used to view statistics, it is also a stepping stone along the way to logging in to *privileged exec mode*, called privileged mode for short.

You can view and change the configuration of a Cisco router only while in privileged mode, and you enter it via the `enable` command like this:

```
Switch>enable
Switch#
```

The `Switch#` prompt signals you're in privileged mode where you can both view and change the switch configuration. You can go back from privileged mode into user mode by using the `disable` command:

```
Switch#disable
Switch>
```

You can type **logout** from either mode to exit the console:

```
Switch>logout


Switch con0 is now available
Press RETURN to get started.
```

Next, I'll show how to perform some basic administrative configurations.

## Overview of Router Modes

To configure from a CLI, you can make global changes to the router by typing **configure terminal** or just **config t**. This will get you into global configuration mode where you can make changes to the running-config. Commands run from global configuration mode are predictably referred to as global commands, and they are typically set only once and affect the entire router.

Type **config** from the privileged-mode prompt and then press Enter to opt for the default of terminal like this:

```
Switch#config
Configuring from terminal, memory, or network [terminal]? [press enter]
Enter configuration commands, one per line.  End with CNTL/Z.
Switch(config)#
```

At this point, you make changes that affect the router as a whole (globally), hence the term *global configuration mode*. For instance, to change the running-config—the current configuration running in dynamic RAM (DRAM)—use the configure terminal command, as I just demonstrated.

## CLI Prompts

Let's explore the different prompts you'll encounter when configuring a switch or router now, because knowing them well will really help you orient yourself and recognize exactly where you are at any given time while in configuration mode. I'm going to demonstrate some of the prompts used on a Cisco switch and cover the various terms used along the way. Make sure you're very familiar with them, and always check your prompts before making any changes to a router's configuration!

We're not going to venture into every last obscure command prompt you could potentially come across in the configuration mode world because that would get us deep into territory that's beyond the scope of this book. Instead, I'm going to focus on the prompts you absolutely must know to pass the exam plus the very handy and seriously vital ones you'll need and use the most in real-life networking—the cream of the crop.

Don't freak! It's not important that you understand exactly what each of these command prompts accomplishes just yet because I'm going to completely fill you in on all of them really soon. For now, relax and focus on just becoming familiar with the different prompts available and all will be well!

### Interfaces

To make changes to an interface, you use the interface command from global configuration mode:

```
Switch(config)#interface ?
  Async           Async interface
  BVI             Bridge-Group Virtual Interface
  CTunnel         CTunnel interface
  Dialer          Dialer interface
```

```
FastEthernet        FastEthernet IEEE 802.3
Filter              Filter interface
Filtergroup         Filter Group interface
GigabitEthernet     GigabitEthernet IEEE 802.3z
Group-Async         Async Group interface
Lex                 Lex interface
Loopback            Loopback interface
Null                Null interface
Port-channel        Ethernet Channel of interfaces
Portgroup           Portgroup interface
Pos-channel         POS Channel of interfaces
Tunnel              Tunnel interface
Vif                 PGM Multicast Host interface
Virtual-Template    Virtual Template interface
Virtual-TokenRing   Virtual TokenRing
Vlan                Catalyst Vlans
fcpa                Fiber Channel
range               interface range command
Switch(config)#interface fastEthernet 0/1
Switch(config-if)#)
```

Did you notice that the prompt changed to Switch(config-if)#? This tells you that you're in *interface configuration mode*. And wouldn't it be nice if the prompt also gave you an indication of what interface you were configuring? Well, at least for now we'll have to live without the prompt information, because it doesn't. But it should already be clear to you that you really need to pay attention when configuring an IOS device!

## Line Commands

To configure user-mode passwords, use the line command. The prompt then becomes Switch(config-line)#:

```
Switch(config)#line ?
  <0-16>   First Line number
  console  Primary terminal line
  vty      Virtual terminal
Switch(config)#line console 0
Switch(config-line)#
```

The line console 0 command is a global command, and sometimes you'll also hear people refer to global commands as major commands. In this example, any command typed from the (config-line) prompt is known as a subcommand.

## Access List Configurations

To configure a standard named access list, you'll need to get to the prompt
`Switch(config-std-nacl)#`:

```
Switch#config t
Switch(config)#ip access-list standard Todd
Switch(config-std-nacl)#
```

What you see here is a typical basic standard ACL prompt. There are various ways to configure access lists, and the prompts are only slightly different from this particular example.

## Routing Protocol Configurations

I need to point out that we don't use routing or router protocols on 2960 switches, but we can and will use them on my 3560 switches. Here is an example of configuring routing on a layer 3 switch:

```
Switch(config)#router rip
IP routing not enabled
Switch(config)#ip routing
Switch(config)#router rip
Switch(config-router)#
```

Did you notice that the prompt changed to `Switch(config-router)#`? To make sure you achieve the objectives specific to the Cisco exam and this book, I'll configure RIPv2, OSPF, RIPng, and OSPFv3. And don't worry—I'll explain all of these in detail soon, in Chapter 8, "IP Routing," and Chapter 14, "Internet Protocol Version 6 (IPv6)"!

## Defining Router Terms

Table 6.1 defines some of the terms I've used so far.

**TABLE 6.1**   Router terms

| Mode | Definition |
| --- | --- |
| User exec mode | Limited to basic monitoring commands |
| Privileged exec mode | Provides access to all other router commands |
| Global configuration mode | Commands that affect the entire system |
| Specific configuration modes | Commands that affect interfaces/processes only |
| Setup mode | Interactive configuration dialog |

# Editing and Help Features

The Cisco advanced editing features can also help you configure your router. If you type in a question mark (?) at any prompt, you'll be given a list of all the commands available from that prompt:

```
Switch#?
Exec commands:
  access-enable     Create a temporary Access-List entry
  access-template   Create a temporary Access-List entry
  archive           manage archive files
  cd                Change current directory
  clear             Reset functions
  clock             Manage the system clock
  cns               CNS agents
  configure         Enter configuration mode
  connect           Open a terminal connection
  copy              Copy from one file to another
  debug             Debugging functions (see also 'undebug')
  delete            Delete a file
  diagnostic        Diagnostic commands
  dir               List files on a filesystem
  disable           Turn off privileged commands
  disconnect        Disconnect an existing network connection
  dot1x             IEEE 802.1X Exec Commands
  enable            Turn on privileged commands
  eou               EAPoUDP
  erase             Erase a filesystem
  exit              Exit from the EXEC
 --More-- ?
Press RETURN for another line, SPACE for another page, anything else to quit
```

And if this is not enough information for you, you can press the spacebar to get another whole page of information, or you can press Enter to go one command at a time. You can also press Q, or any other key for that matter, to quit and return to the prompt. Notice that I typed a question mark (?) at the more prompt and it told me what my options were from that prompt.

Here's a shortcut: To find commands that start with a certain letter, use the letter and the question mark with no space between them, like this:

```
Switch#c?
cd      clear  clock  cns  configure
```

```
connect   copy
Switch#c
```

Okay, see that? By typing **c?**, I got a response listing all the commands that start with *c*. Also notice that the Switch#**c** prompt reappears after the list of commands is displayed. This can be really helpful when you happen to be working with long commands but you're short on patience and still need the next possible one. It would get old fast if you actually had to retype the entire command every time you used a question mark!

So with that, let's find the next command in a string by typing the first command and then a question mark:

```
Switch#clock ?
  set  Set the time and date
```

```
Switch#clock set ?
  hh:mm:ss  Current Time
```

```
Switch#clock set 2:34 ?
% Unrecognized command
Switch#clock set 2:34:01 ?
  <1-31>  Day of the month
  MONTH   Month of the year
```

```
Switch#clock set 2:34:01 21 july ?
  <1993-2035>  Year
```

```
Switch#clock set 2:34:01 21 august 2013
Switch#
00:19:45: %SYS-6-CLOCKUPDATE: System clock has been updated from 00:19:45 UTC Mon
Mar 1 1993 to 02:34:01 UTC Wed Aug 21 2013, configured from console by console.
```

I entered the **clock ?** command and got a list of the next possible parameters plus what they do. Make note of the fact that you can just keep typing a command, a space, and then a question mark until <cr> (carriage return) is your only option left.

And if you're typing commands and receive

```
Switch#clock set 11:15:11
% Incomplete command.
```

no worries—that's only telling you that the command string simply isn't complete quite yet. All you need to do is to press the up arrow key to redisplay the last command entered and then continue with the command by using your question mark.

But if you get the error

```
Switch(config)#access-list 100 permit host 1.1.1.1 host 2.2.2.2
                                       ^
% Invalid input detected at '^' marker.
```

all is not well because it means you actually have entered a command incorrectly. See that little caret—the ^? It's a very helpful tool that marks the exact point where you blew it and made a mess.

Here's another example of when you'll see that caret:

```
Switch#sh fastethernet 0/0
          ^
% Invalid input detected at '^' marker.
```

This command looks right, but be careful! The problem is that the full command is show interface fastethernet 0/0.

Now if you receive the error

```
Switch#sh cl
% Ambiguous command:  "sh cl"
```

you're being told that there are multiple commands that begin with the string you entered and it's not unique. Use the question mark to find the exact command you need:

```
Switch#sh cl?
class-map  clock  cluster
```

Case in point: There are three commands that start with show cl.

Table 6.2 lists the enhanced editing commands available on a Cisco router.

**TABLE 6.2**  Enhanced editing commands

| Command | Meaning |
| --- | --- |
| Ctrl+A | Moves your cursor to the beginning of the line |
| Ctrl+E | Moves your cursor to the end of the line |
| Esc+B | Moves back one word |
| Ctrl+B | Moves back one character |
| Ctrl+F | Moves forward one character |
| Esc+F | Moves forward one word |

**TABLE 6.2** Enhanced editing commands *(continued)*

| Command | Meaning |
|---|---|
| Ctrl+D | Deletes a single character |
| Backspace | Deletes a single character |
| Ctrl+R | Redisplays a line |
| Ctrl+U | Erases a line |
| Ctrl+W | Erases a word |
| Ctrl+Z | Ends configuration mode and returns to EXEC |
| Tab | Finishes typing a command for you |

Another really cool editing feature you need to know about is the automatic scrolling of long lines. In the following example, the command I typed reached the right margin and automatically moved 11 spaces to the left. How do I know this? Because the dollar sign [$] is telling me that the line has been scrolled to the left:

```
Switch#config t
Switch(config)#$ 100 permit ip host 192.168.10.1 192.168.10.0 0.0.0.255
```

You can review the router-command history with the commands shown in Table 6.3.

**TABLE 6.3** Router-command history

| Command | Meaning |
|---|---|
| Ctrl+P or up arrow | Shows last command entered |
| Ctrl+N or down arrow | Shows previous commands entered |
| show history | Shows last 20 commands entered by default |
| show terminal | Shows terminal configurations and history buffer size |
| terminal history size | Changes buffer size (max 256) |

The following example demonstrates the show history command as well as how to change the history's size. It also shows how to verify the history with the show terminal command. First, use the show history command, which will allow you to see the last 20 commands that were entered on the router (even though my particular router reveals only 10 commands because that's all I've entered since rebooting it). Check it out:

```
Switch#sh history
  sh fastethernet 0/0
  sh ru
  sh cl
  config t
  sh history
  sh flash
  sh running-config
  sh startup-config
  sh ver
  sh history
```

Okay—now, we'll use the show terminal command to verify the terminal history size:

```
Switch#sh terminal
Line 0, Location: "", Type: ""
Length: 24 lines, Width: 80 columns
Baud rate (TX/RX) is 9600/9600, no parity, 2 stopbits, 8 databits
Status: PSI Enabled, Ready, Active, Ctrl-c Enabled, Automore On
  0x40000
Capabilities: none
Modem state: Ready
[output cut]
Modem type is unknown.
Session limit is not set.
Time since activation: 00:17:22
Editing is enabled.
History is enabled, history size is 10.
DNS resolution in show commands is enabled
Full user help is disabled
Allowed input transports are none.
Allowed output transports are telnet.
Preferred transport is telnet.
No output characters are padded
No special data dispatching characters
```

---

**When Should I Use the Cisco Editing Features?**

You'll find yourself using a couple of editing features quite often and some not so much, if at all. Understand that Cisco didn't make these up; these are just old Unix commands! Even so, Ctrl+A is still a really helpful way to negate a command.

For example, if you were to put in a long command and then decide you didn't want to use that command in your configuration after all, or if it didn't work, then you could just press your up arrow key to show the last command entered, press Ctrl+A, type **no** and then a space, press Enter—and poof! The command is negated. This doesn't work on every command, but it works on a lot of them and saves some serious time!

---

# Administrative Configurations

Even though the following sections aren't critical to making a router or switch *work* on a network, they're still really important. I'm going to guide you through configuring specific commands that are particularly helpful when administering your network.

You can configure the following administrative functions on a router and switch:

- Hostnames
- Banners
- Passwords
- Interface descriptions

Remember, none of these will make your routers or switches work better or faster, but trust me, your life will be a whole lot better if you just take the time to set these configurations on each of your network devices. This is because doing so makes troubleshooting and maintaining your network a great deal easier—seriously! In this next section, I'll be demonstrating commands on a Cisco switch, but understand that these commands are used in the exact same way on a Cisco router.

## Hostnames

We use the hostname command to set the identity of the router. This is only locally significant, meaning it doesn't affect how the router performs name lookups or how the device actually works on the internetwork. But the hostname is still important because it's often used for authentication in many wide area networks (WANs). Here's an example:

```
Switch#config t
Switch(config)#hostname Todd
```

```
Todd(config)#hostname Chicago
Chicago(config)#hostname Todd
Todd(config)#
```

I know it's pretty tempting to configure the hostname after your own name, but it's usually a much better idea to name the router something that relates to its physical location. A name that maps to where the device lives will make finding it a whole lot easier, which among other things, confirms that you're actually configuring the correct device. Even though it seems like I'm completely ditching my own advice by naming mine *Todd*, I'm not, because this particular device really does live in "Todd's" office. Its name perfectly maps to where it is, so it won't be confused with those in the other networks I work with!

# Banners

A very good reason for having a *banner* is to give any and all who dare attempt to telnet or sneak into your internetwork a little security notice. And they're very cool because you can create and customize them so that they'll greet anyone who shows up on the router with exactly the information you want them to have!

Here are the three types of banners you need to be sure you're familiar with:

- Exec process creation banner
- Login banner
- Message of the day banner

And you can see them all illustrated in the following code:

```
Todd(config)#banner ?
  LINE            c banner-text c, where 'c' is a delimiting character
  exec            Set EXEC process creation banner
  incoming        Set incoming terminal line banner
  login           Set login banner
  motd            Set Message of the Day banner
  prompt-timeout  Set Message for login authentication timeout
  slip-ppp        Set Message for SLIP/PPP
```

Message of the day (MOTD) banners are the most widely used banners because they give a message to anyone connecting to the router via Telnet or an auxiliary port or even through a console port as seen here:

```
Todd(config)#banner motd ?
LINE c banner-text c, where 'c' is a delimiting character
Todd(config)#banner motd #
Enter TEXT message. End with the character '#'.
$ Acme.com network, then you must disconnect immediately.
```

```
#
Todd(config)#^Z (Press the control key + z keys to return to privileged mode)
Todd#exit

Router con0 is now available

Press RETURN to get started.

If you are not authorized to be in Acme.com network, then you
must disconnect immediately.
Todd#
```

This MOTD banner essentially tells anyone connecting to the router to get lost if they're not on the guest list. The part to focus upon here is the delimiting character, which is what informs the router the message is done. Clearly, you can use any character you want for it except for the delimiting character in the message itself. Once the message is complete, press Enter, then the delimiting character, and then press Enter again. Everything will still work if you don't follow this routine unless you have more than one banner. If that's the case, make sure you do follow it or your banners will all be combined into one message and put on a single line!

You can set a banner on one line like this:

```
Todd(config)#banner motd x Unauthorized access prohibited! x
```

Let's take a minute to go into more detail about the other two types of banners I mentioned:

**Exec banner**   You can configure a line-activation (exec) banner to be displayed when EXEC processes such as a line activation or an incoming connection to a VTY line have been created. Simply initiating a user exec session through a console port will activate the exec banner.

**Login banner**   You can configure a login banner for display on all connected terminals. It will show up after the MOTD banner but before the login prompts. This login banner can't be disabled on a per-line basis, so to globally disable it you've got to delete it with the no banner login command.

Here's what a login banner output looks like:

```
!
banner login ^C
-----------------------------------------------------------------
Cisco Router and Security Device Manager (SDM) is installed on this device.
This feature requires the one-time use of the username "cisco"
with the password "cisco". The default username and password
have a privilege level of 15.
Please change these publicly known initial credentials using
```

```
SDM or the IOS CLI.
Here are the Cisco IOS commands.
username <myuser>  privilege 15 secret 0 <mypassword>
no username cisco
Replace <myuser> and <mypassword> with the username and
password you want to use.
For more information about SDM please follow the instructions
in the QUICK START GUIDE for your router or go to http://www.cisco.com/go/sdm
----------------------------------------------------------------
^C
!
```

The above login banner should look pretty familiar to anyone who's ever logged into an ISR router because it's the banner Cisco has in the default configuration for its ISR routers.

 Remember that the login banner is displayed before the login prompts and after the MOTD banner.

## Setting Passwords

There are five passwords you'll need to secure your Cisco routers: console, auxiliary, telnet (VTY), enable password, and enable secret. The enable secret and enable password are the ones used to set the password for securing privileged mode. Once the enable commands are set, users will be prompted for a password. The other three are used to configure a password when user mode is accessed through the console port, through the auxiliary port, or via Telnet.

Let's take a look at each of these now.

### Enable Passwords

You set the enable passwords from global configuration mode like this:

```
Todd(config)#enable ?
 last-resort Define enable action if no TACACS servers
            respond
 password   Assign the privileged level password
 secret     Assign the privileged level secret
 use-tacacs Use TACACS to check enable passwords
```

The following list describes the enable password parameters:

**last-resort**    This allows you to still enter the router if you set up authentication through a TACACS server and it's not available. It won't be used if the TACACS server is working.

**password**    This sets the enable password on older, pre-10.3 systems, and isn't ever used if an enable secret is set.

**secret**    The newer, encrypted password that overrides the enable password if it has been set.

**use-tacacs**    This tells the router to authenticate through a TACACS server. It comes in really handy when you have lots of routers because changing the password on a multitude of them can be insanely tedious. It's much easier to simply go through the TACACS server and change the password only once!

Here's an example that shows how to set the enable passwords:

```
Todd(config)#enable secret todd
Todd(config)#enable password todd
The enable password you have chosen is the same as your
   enable secret. This is not recommended. Re-enter the
   enable password.
```

If you try to set the enable secret and enable passwords the same, the router will give you a polite warning to change the second password. Make a note to yourself that if there aren't any old legacy routers involved, you don't even bother to use the enable password!

User-mode passwords are assigned via the line command like this:

```
Todd(config)#line ?
   <0-16>   First Line number
   console  Primary terminal line
   vty      Virtual terminal
```

And these two lines are especially important for the exam objectives:

**console**    Sets a console user-mode password.

**vty**    Sets a Telnet password on the router. If this password isn't set, then by default, Telnet can't be used.

To configure user-mode passwords, choose the line you want and configure it using the login command to make the switch prompt for authentication. Let's focus in on the configuration of individual lines now.

## Console Password

We set the console password with the line console 0 command, but look at what happened when I tried to type **line console ?** from the (config-line)# prompt—I received an error! Here's the example:

```
Todd(config-line)#line console ?
% Unrecognized command
```

```
Todd(config-line)#exit
Todd(config)#line console ?
  <0-0>  First Line number
Todd(config-line)#password console
Todd(config-line)#login
```

You can still type **line console 0** and that will be accepted, but the help screens just don't work from that prompt. Type **exit** to go back one level, and you'll find that your help screens now work. This is a "feature." Really.

Because there's only one console port, I can only choose line console 0. You can set all your line passwords to the same password, but doing this isn't exactly a brilliant security move!

And it's also important to remember to apply the login command or the console port won't prompt for authentication. The way Cisco has this process set up means you can't set the login command before a password is set on a line because if you set it but don't then set a password, that line won't be usable. You'll actually get prompted for a password that doesn't exist, so Cisco's method isn't just a hassle; it makes sense and is a feature after all!

Definitely remember that although Cisco has this "password feature" on its routers starting with IOS 12.2 and above, it's not in included in older IOSs.

Okay, there are a few other important commands you need to know regarding the console port.

For one, the exec-timeout 0 0 command sets the time-out for the console EXEC session to zero, ensuring that it never times out. The default time-out is 10 minutes.

If you're feeling mischievous, try this on people at work: Set the exec-timeout command to 0 1. This will make the console time out in 1 second, and to fix it, you have to continually press the down arrow key while changing the time-out time with your free hand!

Logging synchronous is such a cool command that it should be a default, but it's not. It's great because it's the antidote for those annoying console messages that disrupt the input you're trying to type. The messages will still pop up, but at least you get returned to your router prompt without your input being interrupted! This makes your input messages oh-so-much easier to read!

Here's an example of how to configure both commands:

```
Todd(config-line)#line con 0
Todd(config-line)#exec-timeout ?
  <0-35791>  Timeout in minutes
Todd(config-line)#exec-timeout 0 ?
  <0-2147483>  Timeout in seconds
  <cr>
```

```
Todd(config-line)#exec-timeout 0 0
Todd(config-line)#logging synchronous
```

 You can set the console to go from never timing out (0 0) to timing out in 35,791 minutes and 2,147,483 seconds. Remember that the default is 10 minutes.

## Telnet Password

To set the user-mode password for Telnet access into the router or switch, use the line vty command. IOS switches typically have 16 lines, but routers running the Enterprise edition have considerably more. The best way to find out how many lines you have is to use that handy question mark like this:

```
Todd(config-line)#line vty 0 ?
% Unrecognized command
Todd(config-line)#exit
Todd(config)#line vty 0 ?
  <1-15>  Last Line number
  <cr>
Todd(config)#line vty 0 15
Todd(config-line)#password telnet
Todd(config-line)#login
```

This output clearly shows that you cannot get help from your (config-line)# prompt. You must go back to global config mode in order to use the question mark (?).

So what will happen if you try to telnet into a device that doesn't have a VTY password set? You'll receive an error saying the connection has been refused because the password isn't set. So, if you telnet into a switch and receive a message like this one that I got from Switch B

```
Todd#telnet SwitchB
Trying SwitchB (10.0.0.1)…Open


Password required, but none set
[Connection to SwitchB closed by foreign host]
Todd#
```

it means the switch doesn't have the VTY password set. But you can still get around this and tell the switch to allow Telnet connections without a password by using the no login command:

```
SwitchB(config-line)#line vty 0 15
SwitchB(config-line)#no login
```

**WARNING**  I definitely do not recommend using the no login command to allow Telnet connections without a password, unless you're in a testing or classroom environment. In a production network, always set your VTY password!

After your IOS devices are configured with an IP address, you can use the Telnet program to configure and check your routers instead of having to use a console cable. You can use the Telnet program by typing **telnet** from any command prompt (DOS or Cisco). I'll cover all things Telnet more thoroughly in Chapter 7, "Managing a Cisco Internetwork."

## Auxiliary Password

To configure the auxiliary password on a router, go into global configuration mode and type **line aux ?**. And by the way, you won't find these ports on a switch. This output shows that you only get a choice of 0–0, which is because there's only one port:

```
Todd#config t
Todd(config)#line aux ?
  <0-0>  First Line number
Todd(config)#line aux 0
Todd(config-line)#login
% Login disabled on line 1, until 'password' is set
Todd(config-line)#password aux
Todd(config-line)#login
```

## Setting Up Secure Shell (SSH)

I strongly recommend using Secure Shell (SSH) instead of Telnet because it creates a more secure session. The Telnet application uses an unencrypted data stream, but SSH uses encryption keys to send data so your username and password aren't sent in the clear, vulnerable to anyone lurking around!

Here are the steps for setting up SSH:

**1.** Set your hostname:

```
Router(config)#hostname Todd
```

**2.** Set the domain name—both the hostname and domain name are required for the encryption keys to be generated:

```
Todd(config)#ip domain-name Lammle.com
```

**3.** Set the username to allow SSH client access:

```
Todd(config)#username Todd password Lammle
```

**4.** Generate the encryption keys for securing the session:

```
Todd(config)#crypto key generate rsa
The name for the keys will be: Todd.Lammle.com
Choose the size of the key modulus in the range of 360 to
4096 for your General Purpose Keys. Choosing a key modulus
Greater than 512 may take a few minutes.


How many bits in the modulus [512]: 1024
% Generating 1024 bit RSA keys, keys will be non-exportable...
[OK] (elapsed time was 6 seconds)


Todd(config)#
1d14h: %SSH-5-ENABLED: SSH 1.99 has been enabled*June 24
19:25:30.035: %SSH-5-ENABLED: SSH 1.99 has been enabled
```

**5.** Enable SSH version 2 on the router—not mandatory, but strongly suggested:

```
Todd(config)#ip ssh version 2
```

**6.** Connect to the VTY lines of the switch:

```
Todd(config)#line vty 0 15
```

**7.** Configure your access protocols:

```
Todd(config-line)#transport input ?
  all    All protocols
  none   No protocols
  ssh    TCP/IP SSH protocol
  telnet TCP/IP Telnet protocol
```

Beware of this next line, and make sure you never use it in production because it's a horrendous security risk:

```
Todd(config-line)#transport input all
```

I recommend using the next line to secure your VTY lines with SSH:

```
Todd(config-line)#transport input ssh ?
  telnet  TCP/IP Telnet protocol
  <cr>
```

I actually do use Telnet once in a while when a situation arises that specifically calls for it. It just doesn't happen very often. But if you want to go with Telnet, here's how you do that:

```
Todd(config-line)#transport input ssh telnet
```

Know that if you don't use the keyword telnet at the end of the command string, then only SSH will work on the device. You can go with either, just so long as you understand that SSH is way more secure than Telnet.

## Encrypting Your Passwords

Because only the enable secret password is encrypted by default, you'll need to manually configure the user-mode and enable passwords for encryption.

Notice that you can see all the passwords except the enable secret when performing a show running-config on a switch:

```
Todd#sh running-config
Building configuration...


Current configuration : 1020 bytes
!
! Last configuration change at 00:03:11 UTC Mon Mar 1 1993
!
version 15.0
no service pad
service timestamps debug datetime msec
service timestamps log datetime msec
no service password-encryption
!
hostname Todd
!
enable secret 4 ykw.3/tgsOuy9.6qmgG/EeYOYgBvfX4v.S8UNA9Rddg
enable password todd
!
[output cut]
!
line con 0
 password console
 login
line vty 0 4
```

```
 password telnet
 login
line vty 5 15
 password telnet
 login
!
end
```

To manually encrypt your passwords, use the service password-encryption command. Here's how:

```
Todd#config t
Todd(config)#service password-encryption
Todd(config)#exit
Todd#show run
Building configuration...
!
!
enable secret 4 ykw.3/tgsOuy9.6qmgG/EeYOYgBvfX4v.S8UNA9Rddg
enable password 7 1506040800
!
[output cut]
!
!
line con 0
 password 7 050809013243420C
 login
line vty 0 4
 password 7 06120A2D424B1D
 login
line vty 5 15
 password 7 06120A2D424B1D
 login
!
end
Todd#config t
Todd(config)#no service password-encryption
Todd(config)#^Z
Todd#
```

Nicely done—the passwords will now be encrypted. All you need to do is encrypt the passwords, perform a show run, then turn off the command if you want. This output clearly shows us that the enable password and the line passwords are all encrypted.

Before we move on to find out how to set descriptions on your interfaces, I want to stress some points about password encryption. As I said, if you set your passwords and then turn on the service password-encryption command, you have to perform a show running-config before you turn off the encryption service or your passwords won't be encrypted. You don't have to turn off the encryption service at all—you'd only do that if your switch is running low on processes. And if you turn on the service before you set your passwords, then you don't even have to view them to have them encrypted.

## Descriptions

Setting descriptions on an interface is another administratively helpful thing, and like the hostname, it's also only locally significant. One case where the description command comes in really handy is when you want to keep track of circuit numbers on a switch or a router's serial WAN port.

Here's an example on my switch:

```
Todd#config t
Todd(config)#int fa0/1
Todd(config-if)#description Sales VLAN Trunk Link
Todd(config-if)#^Z
Todd#
```

And on a router serial WAN:

```
Router#config t
Router(config)#int s0/0/0
Router(config-if)#description WAN to Miami
Router(config-if)#^Z
```

You can view an interface's description with either the show running-config command or the show interface—even with the show interface description command:

```
Todd#sh run
Building configuration...


Current configuration : 855 bytes
!
interface FastEthernet0/1
 description Sales VLAN Trunk Link
!
 [output cut]
```

```
Todd#sh int f0/1
FastEthernet0/1 is up, line protocol is up (connected)
  Hardware is Fast Ethernet, address is ecc8.8202.8282 (bia ecc8.8202.8282)
  Description: Sales VLAN Trunk Link
  MTU 1500 bytes, BW 100000 Kbit/sec, DLY 100 usec,
 [output cut]


Todd#sh int description
Interface                   Status          Protocol Description
Vl1                         up              up
Fa0/1                       up              up       Sales VLAN Trunk Link
Fa0/2                       up              up
```

**Real World Scenario**

**description: A Helpful Command**

Bob, a senior network admin at Acme Corporation in San Francisco, has over 50 WAN links to branches throughout the United States and Canada. Whenever an interface goes down, Bob wastes lots of time trying to figure out the circuit number and the phone number of the provider of his ailing WAN link.

This kind of scenario shows just how helpful the interface description command can be. It would save Bob a lot of work because he could use it on his most important switch LAN links to find out exactly where every interface is connected. Bob's life would also be made a lot easier by adding circuit numbers to each and every WAN interface on his routers, along with the phone number of the responsible provider.

So if Bob had just taken time in advance to preventively add this information to his interfaces, he would have saved himself an ocean of stress and a ton of precious time when his WAN links inevitably go down!

## Doing the *do* Command

In every previous example so far, we've had to run all show from privileged mode. But I've got great news—beginning with IOS version 12.3, Cisco has finally added a command to the IOS that allows you to view the configuration and statistics from within configuration mode!

In fact, with any IOS, you'd get the following error if you tried to view the configuration from global config:

```
Todd(config)#sh run
                ^
% Invalid input detected at '^' marker.
```

Compare that to the output I get from entering that same command on my router that's running the 15.0 IOS using the "do" syntax:

```
Todd(config)#do show run
Building configuration...


Current configuration : 759 bytes
!
version 15.0
no service pad
service timestamps debug datetime msec
service timestamps log datetime msec
no service password-encryption
!
hostname Todd
!
boot-start-marker
boot-end-marker
!
[output cut]
```

So now you can pretty much run any command from any configuration prompt—nice, huh? Looking back through all those examples for encrypting our passwords, you can see that the do command would definitely have gotten the party started sooner, making this innovation one to celebrate for sure!

# Router and Switch Interfaces

Interface configuration is arguably the most important router configuration because without interfaces, a router is a pretty useless object. Furthermore, interface configurations must be totally precise to enable communication with other devices. Network layer addresses, media type, bandwidth, and other administrator commands are all used to configure an interface.

On a layer 2 switch, interface configurations typically involve a lot less work than router interface configuration. Check out the output from the powerful verification command show ip interface brief, which reveals all the interfaces on my 3560 switch:

```
Todd#sh ip interface brief
Interface              IP-Address        OK? Method Status          Protocol
Vlan1                  192.168.255.8     YES DHCP   up                up
FastEthernet0/1        unassigned        YES unset  up                up
FastEthernet0/2        unassigned        YES unset  up                up
FastEthernet0/3        unassigned        YES unset  down              down
FastEthernet0/4        unassigned        YES unset  down              down
FastEthernet0/5        unassigned        YES unset  up                up
FastEthernet0/6        unassigned        YES unset  up                up
FastEthernet0/7        unassigned        YES unset  down              down
FastEthernet0/8        unassigned        YES unset  down              down
GigabitEthernet0/1     unassigned        YES unset  down              down
```

The above output shows the default routed port found on all Cisco switches (VLAN 1), plus nine switch FastEthernet interface ports, with one port being a Gigabit Ethernet port used for uplinks to other switches.

Different routers use different methods to choose the interfaces used on them. For instance, the following command shows one of my 2800 ISR Cisco routers with two FastEthernet interfaces along with two serial WAN interfaces:

```
Router>sh ip int brief
Interface        IP-Address      OK? Method Status               Protocol
FastEthernet0/0  192.168.255.11  YES DHCP   up                     up
FastEthernet0/1  unassigned      YES unset  administratively down down
Serial0/0/0      unassigned      YES unset  administratively down down
Serial0/1/0      unassigned      YES unset  administratively down down
Router>
```

Previously, we always used the interface type number sequence to configure an interface, but the newer routers come with an actual physical slot and include a port number on the module plugged into it. So on a modular router, the configuration would be interface type slot/port, as demonstrated here:

```
Todd#config t
Todd(config)#interface GigabitEthernet 0/1
Todd(config-if)#
```

You can see that we are now at the Gigabit Ethernet slot 0, port 1 prompt, and from here we can make configuration changes to the interface. Make note of the fact that you can't just type int gigabitethernet 0. No shortcuts on the slot/port—you've got to type the slot/port variables in the command: type slot/port or, for example, int gigabitethernet 0/1 (or just int g0/1).

Once in interface configuration mode, we can configure various options. Keep in mind that speed and duplex are the two factors to be concerned with for the LAN:

```
Todd#config t
Todd(config)#interface GigabitEthernet 0/1
Todd(config-if)#speed 1000
Todd(config-if)#duplex full
```

So what's happened here? Well basically, this has shut off the auto-detect mechanism on the port, forcing it to only run gigabit speeds at full duplex. For the ISR series router, it's basically the same, but you get even more options! The LAN interfaces are the same, but the rest of the modules are different—they use three numbers instead of two. The three numbers used here can represent slot/subslot/port, but this depends on the card used in the ISR router. For the objectives you just need to remember this: The first 0 is the router itself. You then choose the slot and then the port. Here's an example of a serial interface on my 2811:

```
Todd(config)#interface serial ?
  <0-2>  Serial interface number
Todd(config)#interface serial 0/0/?
  <0-1>  Serial interface number
Todd(config)#interface serial 0/0/0
Todd(config-if)#
```

This might look a little dicey to you, but I promise it's really not that hard! It helps to remember that you should always view the output of the show ip interface brief command or a show running-config output first so you know the exact interfaces you have to deal with. Here's one of my 2811's output that has even more serial interfaces installed:

```
Todd(config-if)#do show run
Building configuration...
[output cut]
!
interface FastEthernet0/0
 no ip address
 shutdown
 duplex auto
 speed auto
!
interface FastEthernet0/1
 no ip address
 shutdown
 duplex auto
 speed auto
!
interface Serial0/0/0
```

```
 no ip address
 shutdown
 no fair-queue
!
interface Serial0/0/1
 no ip address
 shutdown
!
interface Serial0/1/0
 no ip address
 shutdown
!
interface Serial0/2/0
 no ip address
 shutdown
 clock rate 2000000
!
 [output cut]
```

For the sake of brevity, I didn't include my complete running-config, but I've displayed all you really need. You can see the two built-in FastEthernet interfaces, the two serial interfaces in slot 0 (0/0/0 and 0/0/1), the serial interface in slot 1 (0/1/0), and the serial interface in slot 2 (0/2/0). And once you see the interfaces like this, it makes it a lot easier to understand how the modules are inserted into the router.

Just understand that if you type **interface e0** on an old 2500 series router, **interface fastethernet 0/0** on a modular router (such as the 2800 series router), or **interface serial 0/1/0** on a ISR router, all you're actually doing is choosing an interface to configure. Essentially, they're all configured the same way after that.

Let's delve deeper into our router interface discussion by exploring how to bring up the interface and set an IP address on it next.

## Bringing Up an Interface

You can disable an interface with the interface command shutdown and enable it with the no shutdown command. Just to remind you, all switch ports are enabled by default and all router ports are disabled by default, so we're going to talk more about router ports than switch ports in the next few sections.

If an interface is shut down, it'll display as administratively down when you use the show interfaces command (sh int for short):

```
Router#sh int f0/0
FastEthernet0/1 is administratively down, line protocol is down
[output cut]
```

Another way to check an interface's status is via the show running-config command. You can bring up the router interface with the no shutdown command (no shut for short):

```
Router(config)#int f0/0
Router(config-if)#no shutdown
*August 21 13:45:08.455: %LINK-3-UPDOWN: Interface FastEthernet0/0,
    changed state to up
Router(config-if)#do show int f0/0
FastEthernet0/0 is up, line protocol is up
[output cut]
```

## Configuring an IP Address on an Interface

Even though you don't have to use IP on your routers, it's usually what everyone uses. To configure IP addresses on an interface, use the ip address command from interface configuration mode and remember that you do not set an IP address on a layer 2 switch port!

```
Todd(config)#int f0/1
Todd(config-if)#ip address 172.16.10.2 255.255.255.0
```

Also, don't forget to enable the interface with the no shutdown command. Remember to look at the command show interface *int* output to see if the interface is administratively shut down or not. Show ip int brief and show running-config will also give you this information.

The ip address *address mask* command starts the IP processing on the router interface. Again, you do not configure an IP address on a layer 2 switch interface!

Okay—now if you want to add a second subnet address to an interface, you have to use the secondary parameter. If you type another IP address and press Enter, it will replace the existing primary IP address and mask. This is definitely one of the Cisco IOS's coolest features!

So let's try it. To add a secondary IP address, just use the secondary parameter:

```
Todd(config-if)#ip address 172.16.20.2 255.255.255.0 ?
  secondary  Make this IP address a secondary address
  <cr>
Todd(config-if)#ip address 172.16.20.2 255.255.255.0 secondary
Todd(config-if)#^Z
Todd(config-if)#do sh run
Building configuration...
[output cut]
```

```
interface FastEthernet0/1
 ip address 172.16.20.2 255.255.255.0 secondary
 ip address 172.16.10.2 255.255.255.0
 duplex auto
 speed auto
!
```

But I've got to stop here to tell you that I really wouldn't recommend having multiple IP addresses on an interface because it's really inefficient. I showed you how anyway just in case you someday find yourself dealing with an MIS manager who's in love with really bad network design and makes you administer it! And who knows? Maybe someone will ask you about it someday and you'll get to seem really smart because you know this.

## Using the Pipe

No, not that pipe. I mean the output modifier. Although, I've got to say that some of the router configurations I've seen in my career make me wonder! Anyway, this pipe ( | ) allows us to wade through all the configurations or other long outputs and get straight to our goods fast. Here's an example:

```
Router#sh run | ?
  append    Append redirected output to URL (URLs supporting append
            operation only)
  begin     Begin with the line that matches
  exclude   Exclude lines that match
  include   Include lines that match
  redirect  Redirect output to URL
  section   Filter a section of output
  tee       Copy output to URL


Router#sh run | begin interface
interface FastEthernet0/0
 description Sales VLAN
 ip address 10.10.10.1 255.255.255.248
 duplex auto
 speed auto
!
interface FastEthernet0/1
 ip address 172.16.20.2 255.255.255.0 secondary
 ip address 172.16.10.2 255.255.255.0
 duplex auto
 speed auto
!
```

```
interface Serial0/0/0
 description Wan to SF circuit number 6fdda 12345678
 no ip address
!
```

So basically, the pipe symbol—the output modifier—is what you need to help you get where you want to go light years faster than mucking around in a router's entire configuration. I use it a lot when scrutinizing a large routing table to find out whether a certain route is in the routing table. Here's an example:

```
Todd#sh ip route | include 192.168.3.32
R       192.168.3.32 [120/2] via 10.10.10.8, 00:00:25, FastEthernet0/0
Todd#
```

First, you need to know that this routing table had over 100 entries, so without my trusty pipe, I'd probably still be looking through that output! It's a powerfully efficient tool that saves you major time and effort by quickly finding a line in a configuration—or as the preceding example shows, a single route within a huge routing table.

Give yourself a little time to play around with the pipe command to get the hang of it and you'll be naturally high on your newfound ability to quickly parse through router output!

## Serial Interface Commands

But wait! Before you just jump in and configure a serial interface, you need some key information, like knowing the interface will usually be attached to a CSU/DSU type of device that provides clocking for the line to the router. Check out Figure 6.3 for an example.

**FIGURE 6.3**  A typical WAN connection. Clocking is typically provided by a DCE network to routers. In nonproduction environments, a DCE network is not always present.

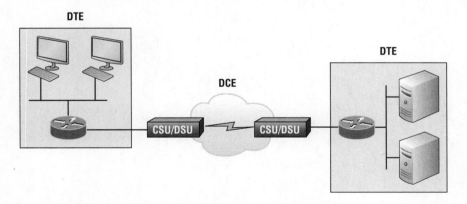

Here you can see that the serial interface is used to connect to a DCE network via a CSU/DSU that provides the clocking to the router interface. But if you have a back-to-back configuration, such as one that's used in a lab environment like the one in Figure 6.4, one end—the data communication equipment (DCE) end of the cable—must provide clocking!

**FIGURE 6.4**    Providing clocking on a nonproduction network

Set clock rate if needed

Todd# config t
Todd(config)# interface serial 0
Todd(config-if)#clock rate 1000000    DCE

DTE

DCE side determined by the cable.
Add clocking to DCE side only.

>**show controllers** *int* will show the cable connection type

By default, Cisco router serial interfaces are all data terminal equipment (DTE) devices, which means that you must configure an interface to provide clocking if you need it to act like a DCE device. Again, you would not provide clocking on a production T1 connection because you would have a CSU/DSU connected to your serial interface, as shown in Figure 6.3.

You configure a DCE serial interface with the clock rate command:

```
Router#config t
Enter configuration commands, one per line.  End with CNTL/Z.
Router(config)#int s0/0/0
Router(config-if)#clock rate ?
      Speed (bits per second)
  1200
  2400
  4800
  9600
  14400
  19200
  28800
  32000
  38400
  48000
  56000
  57600
  64000
  72000
  115200
```

```
125000
128000
148000
192000
250000
256000
384000
500000
512000
768000
800000
1000000
2000000
4000000
5300000
8000000


<300-8000000>     Choose clockrate from list above
```

Router(config-if)#**clock rate 1000000**

The clock rate command is set in bits per second. Besides looking at the cable end to check for a label of DCE or DTE, you can see if a router's serial interface has a DCE cable connected with the show controllers *int* command:

```
Router#sh controllers s0/0/0
Interface Serial0/0/0
Hardware is GT96K
DTE V.35idb at 0x4342FCB0, driver data structure at 0x434373D4
```

Here is an example of an output depicting a DCE connection:

```
Router#sh controllers s0/2/0
Interface Serial0/2/0
Hardware is GT96K
DCE V.35, clock rate 1000000
```

The next command you need to get acquainted with is the bandwidth command. Every Cisco router ships with a default serial link bandwidth of T1 (1.544 Mbps). But this has nothing to do with how data is transferred over a link. The bandwidth of a serial link is used by routing protocols like EIGRP and OSPF to calculate the best cost path to a remote network. So if you're using RIP routing, the bandwidth setting of a serial link is irrelevant since RIP uses only hop count to determine this.

You may be rereading this part and thinking, "Huh? What? Routing protocols? Metrics?" But don't freak! I'm going over all of that soon in Chapter 8,
"IP Routing."

Here's an example of using the **bandwidth** command:

```
Router#config t
Router(config)#int s0/0/0
Router(config-if)#bandwidth ?
  <1-10000000>  Bandwidth in kilobits
  inherit       Specify that bandwidth is inherited
  receive       Specify receive-side bandwidth
Router(config-if)#bandwidth 1000
```

Did you notice that, unlike the clock rate command, the bandwidth command is configured in kilobits per second?

After going through all these configuration examples regarding the clock
rate command, understand that the new ISR routers automatically detect
DCE connections and set clock rate to 2000000. But know that you still
need to understand the clock rate command for the Cisco objectives,
even though the new routers set it for you automatically!

# Viewing, Saving, and Erasing Configurations

If you run through setup mode, you'll be asked if you want to use the configuration you just
created. If you say yes, the configuration running in DRAM that's known as the running-
config will be copied into NVRAM, and the file will be named startup-config. Hopefully,
you'll be smart and always use the CLI, not setup mode!

You can manually save the file from DRAM, which is usually just called RAM, to
NVRAM by using the copy running-config startup-config command. You can use
the shortcut copy run start as well:

```
Todd#copy running-config startup-config
Destination filename [startup-config]? [press enter]
Building configuration...
[OK]
```

```
Todd#
Building configuration...
```

When you see a question with an answer in [], it means that if you just press Enter, you're choosing the default answer.

Also, when the command asks for the destination filename, the default answer is startup-config. The reason it asks is because you can copy the configuration to pretty much anywhere you want. Take a look at the output from my switch:

```
Todd#copy running-config ?
```

```
  flash:          Copy to flash: file system
  ftp:            Copy to ftp: file system
  http:           Copy to http: file system
  https:          Copy to https: file system
  null:           Copy to null: file system
  nvram:          Copy to nvram: file system
  rcp:            Copy to rcp: file system
  running-config  Update (merge with) current system configuration
  scp:            Copy to scp: file system
  startup-config  Copy to startup configuration
  syslog:         Copy to syslog: file system
  system:         Copy to system: file system
  tftp:           Copy to tftp: file system
  tmpsys:         Copy to tmpsys: file system
  vb:             Copy to vb: file system
```

To reassure you, we'll get deeper into how and where to copy files in Chapter 7.

For now, you can view the files by typing **show running-config** or **show startup-config** from privileged mode. The sh run command, which is a shortcut for show running-config, tells us that we're viewing the current configuration:

```
Todd#sh run
Building configuration...


Current configuration : 855 bytes
!
! Last configuration change at 23:20:06 UTC Mon Mar 1 1993
!
version 15.0
[output cut]
```

The sh start command—one of the shortcuts for the show startup-config command— shows us the configuration that will be used the next time the router is reloaded. It also tells us how much NVRAM is being used to store the startup-config file. Here's an example:

```
Todd#sh start
Using 855 out of 524288 bytes
!
! Last configuration change at 23:20:06 UTC Mon Mar 1 1993
!
version 15.0
[output cut]
```

But beware—if you try and view the configuration and see

```
Todd#sh start
startup-config is not present
```

you have not saved your running-config to NVRAM, or you've deleted the backup configuration! Let me talk about just how you would do that now.

## Deleting the Configuration and Reloading the Device

You can delete the startup-config file by using the erase startup-config command:

```
Todd#erase start
% Incomplete command.
```

First, notice that you can no longer use the shortcut commands for erasing the backup configuration. This started in IOS 12.4 with the ISR routers.

```
Todd#erase startup-config
Erasing the nvram filesystem will remove all configuration files! Continue? [confirm]
[OK]
Erase of nvram: complete
Todd#
*Mar  5 01:59:45.206: %SYS-7-NV_BLOCK_INIT: Initialized the geometry of nvram
Todd#reload
Proceed with reload? [confirm]
```

Now if you reload or power the router down after using the erase startup-config command, you'll be offered setup mode because there's no configuration saved in NVRAM. You can press Ctrl+C to exit setup mode at any time, but the reload command can only be used from privileged mode.

At this point, you shouldn't use setup mode to configure your router. So just say **no** to setup mode, because it's there to help people who don't know how to use the cash line interface (CLI), and this no longer applies to you. Be strong—you can do it!

## Verifying Your Configuration

Obviously, `show running-config` would be the best way to verify your configuration and `show startup-config` would be the best way to verify the configuration that'll be used the next time the router is reloaded—right?

Well, once you take a look at the running-config, if all appears well, you can verify your configuration with utilities like Ping and Telnet. Ping is a program that uses ICMP echo requests and replies, which we covered in Chapter 3, "TCP/IP." For review, Ping sends a packet to a remote host, and if that host responds, you know that it's alive. But you don't know if it's alive and also *well*; just because you can ping a Microsoft server does not mean you can log in! Even so, Ping is an awesome starting point for troubleshooting an internetwork.

Did you know that you can ping with different protocols? You can, and you can test this by typing **ping ?** at either the router user-mode or privileged-mode prompt:

```
Todd#ping ?
  WORD  Ping destination address or hostname
  clns  CLNS echo
  ip    IP echo
  ipv6  IPv6 echo
  tag   Tag encapsulated IP echo
  <cr>
```

If you want to find a neighbor's Network layer address, either you go straight to the router or switch itself or you can type **show cdp entry * protocol** to get the Network layer addresses you need for pinging.

You can also use an extended ping to change the default variables, as shown here:

```
Todd#ping
Protocol [ip]:
Target IP address: 10.1.1.1
Repeat count [5]:
% A decimal number between 1 and 2147483647.
Repeat count [5]: 5000
Datagram size [100]:
% A decimal number between 36 and 18024.
Datagram size [100]: 1500
Timeout in seconds [2]:
```

```
Extended commands [n]: y
Source address or interface: FastEthernet 0/1
Source address or interface: Vlan 1
Type of service [0]:
Set DF bit in IP header? [no]:
Validate reply data? [no]:
Data pattern [0xABCD]:
Loose, Strict, Record, Timestamp, Verbose[none]:
Sweep range of sizes [n]:
Type escape sequence to abort.
Sending 5000, 1500-byte ICMP Echos to 10.1.1.1, timeout is 2 seconds:
Packet sent with a source address of 10.10.10.1
```

Notice that by using the question mark, I was able to determine that extended ping allows you to set the repeat count higher than the default of 5 and the datagram size larger. This raises the MTU and allows for a more accurate testing of throughput. The source interface is one last important piece of information I'll pull out of the output. You can choose which interface the ping is sourced from, which is really helpful in certain diagnostic situations. Using my switch to display the extended ping capabilities, I had to use my only routed port, which is named VLAN 1, by default.

    Cisco Discovery Protocol (CDP) is covered in Chapter 7.

Traceroute uses ICMP with IP time to live (TTL) time-outs to track the path a given packet takes through an internetwork. This is in contrast to Ping, which just finds the host and responds. Traceroute can also be used with multiple protocols. Check out this output:

```
Todd#traceroute ?
  WORD       Trace route to destination address or hostname
  aaa        Define trace options for AAA events/actions/errors
  appletalk  AppleTalk Trace
  clns       ISO CLNS Trace
  ip         IP Trace
  ipv6       IPv6 Trace
  ipx        IPX Trace
  mac        Trace Layer2 path between 2 endpoints
  oldvines   Vines Trace (Cisco)
  vines      Vines Trace (Banyan)
  <cr>
```

Telnet, FTP, and HTTP are really the best tools because they use IP at the Network layer and TCP at the Transport layer to create a session with a remote host. If you can telnet, ftp, or http into a device, you know that your IP connectivity just has to be solid!

```
Todd#telnet ?
 WORD  IP address or hostname of a remote system
 <cr>
```

From the switch or router prompt, you just type a hostname or IP address and it will assume you want to telnet—you don't need to type the actual command, telnet.

Coming up, I'll show you how to verify the interface statistics.

## Verifying with the *show interface* Command

Another way to verify your configuration is by typing show interface commands, the first of which is the show interface ? command. Doing this will reveal all the available interfaces to verify and configure.

> The show interfaces command, with an *s*, displays the configurable parameters and statistics of all interfaces on a router.

This command comes in really handy when you're verifying and troubleshooting router and network issues.

The following output is from my freshly erased and rebooted 2811 router:

```
Router#sh int ?
  Async             Async interface
  BVI               Bridge-Group Virtual Interface
  CDMA-Ix           CDMA Ix interface
  CTunnel           CTunnel interface
  Dialer            Dialer interface
  FastEthernet      FastEthernet IEEE 802.3
  Loopback          Loopback interface
  MFR               Multilink Frame Relay bundle interface
  Multilink         Multilink-group interface
  Null              Null interface
  Port-channel      Ethernet Channel of interfaces
  Serial            Serial
  Tunnel            Tunnel interface
  Vif               PGM Multicast Host interface
  Virtual-PPP       Virtual PPP interface
  Virtual-Template  Virtual Template interface
  Virtual-TokenRing Virtual TokenRing
```

```
accounting        Show interface accounting
counters          Show interface counters
crb               Show interface routing/bridging info
dampening         Show interface dampening info
description       Show interface description
etherchannel      Show interface etherchannel information
irb               Show interface routing/bridging info
mac-accounting    Show interface MAC accounting info
mpls-exp          Show interface MPLS experimental accounting info
precedence        Show interface precedence accounting info
pruning           Show interface trunk VTP pruning information
rate-limit        Show interface rate-limit info
stats             Show interface packets & octets, in & out, by switching path
status            Show interface line status
summary           Show interface summary
switching         Show interface switching
switchport        Show interface switchport information
trunk             Show interface trunk information
|                 Output modifiers
<cr>
```

The only "real" physical interfaces are FastEthernet, Serial, and Async—the rest are all logical interfaces or commands you can use to verify with.

The next command is show interface fastethernet 0/0. It reveals the hardware address, logical address, and encapsulation method as well as statistics on collisions, as seen here:

```
Router#sh int f0/0
FastEthernet0/0 is up, line protocol is up
  Hardware is MV96340 Ethernet, address is 001a.2f55.c9e8 (bia 001a.2f55.c9e8)
  Internet address is 192.168.1.33/27
MTU 1500 bytes, BW 100000 Kbit, DLY 100 usec,
    reliability 255/255, txload 1/255, rxload 1/255
  Encapsulation ARPA, loopback not set
  Keepalive set (10 sec)
  Auto-duplex, Auto Speed, 100BaseTX/FX
  ARP type: ARPA, ARP Timeout 04:00:00
  Last input never, output 00:02:07, output hang never
  Last clearing of "show interface" counters never
  Input queue: 0/75/0/0 (size/max/drops/flushes); Total output drops: 0
  Queueing strategy: fifo
  Output queue: 0/40 (size/max)
```

```
 5 minute input rate 0 bits/sec, 0 packets/sec
 5 minute output rate 0 bits/sec, 0 packets/sec
    0 packets input, 0 bytes
    Received 0 broadcasts, 0 runts, 0 giants, 0 throttles
    0 input errors, 0 CRC, 0 frame, 0 overrun, 0 ignored
    0 watchdog
    0 input packets with dribble condition detected
    16 packets output, 960 bytes, 0 underruns
    0 output errors, 0 collisions, 0 interface resets
    0 babbles, 0 late collision, 0 deferred
    0 lost carrier, 0 no carrier
    0 output buffer failures, 0 output buffers swapped out
Router#
```

You probably guessed that we're going to go over the important statistics from this output, but first, just for fun, I've got to ask you, which subnet is FastEthernet 0/0 a member of and what's the broadcast address and valid host range?

I'm serious—you really have to be able to nail these things NASCAR-fast! Just in case you didn't, the address is 192.168.1.33/27. And I've gotta be honest—if you don't know what a /27 is at this point, you'll need a miracle to pass the exam! That or you need to actually read this book. (As a quick reminder, a /27 is 255.255.255.224.) The fourth octet is a block size of 32. The subnets are 0, 32, 64, etc.; the FastEthernet interface is in the 32 subnet; the broadcast address is 63; and the valid hosts are 33–62. All good now?

 If you struggled with any of this, please save yourself from certain doom and get yourself back into Chapter 4, "Easy Subnetting," now! Read and reread it until you've got it dialed in!

Okay—back to the output. The preceding interface is working and looks to be in good shape. The show interfaces command will show you if you're receiving errors on the interface, and it will also show you the maximum transmission unit (MTU). MTU is the maximum packet size allowed to transmit on that interface, bandwidth (BW) is for use with routing protocols, and 255/255 means that reliability is perfect! The load is 1/255, meaning no load.

Continuing through the output, can you figure out the bandwidth of the interface? Well, other than the easy giveaway of the interface being called a "FastEthernet" interface, we can see that the bandwidth is 100000 Kbit, which is 100,000,000. Kbit means to add three zeros, which is 100 Mbits per second, or FastEthernet. Gigabit would be 1000000 Kbits per second.

Be sure you don't miss the output errors and collisions, which show 0 in my output. If these numbers are increasing, then you have some sort of Physical or Data Link layer issue. Check your duplex! If you have one side as half-duplex and one at full-duplex, your interface will work, albeit really slow and those numbers will be increasing fast!

The most important statistic of the show interface command is the output of the line and Data Link protocol status. If the output reveals that FastEthernet 0/0 is up and the line protocol is up, then the interface is up and running:

```
Router#sh int fa0/0
FastEthernet0/0 is up, line protocol is up
```

The first parameter refers to the Physical layer, and it's up when it receives carrier detect. The second parameter refers to the Data Link layer, and it looks for keepalives from the connecting end. Keepalives are important because they're used between devices to make sure connectivity hasn't been dropped.

Here's an example of where your problem will often be found—on serial interfaces:

```
Router#sh int s0/0/0
Serial0/0 is up, line protocol is down
```

If you see that the line is up but the protocol is down, as displayed here, you're experiencing a clocking (keepalive) or framing problem—possibly an encapsulation mismatch. Check the keepalives on both ends to make sure they match. Make sure that the clock rate is set, if needed, and that the encapsulation type is equal on both ends. The preceding output tells us that there's a Data Link layer problem.

If you discover that both the line interface and the protocol are down, it's a cable or interface problem. The following output would indicate a Physical layer problem:

```
Router#sh int s0/0/0
Serial0/0 is down, line protocol is down
```

As you'll see next, if one end is administratively shut down, the remote end would present as down and down:

```
Router#sh int s0/0/0
Serial0/0 is administratively down, line protocol is down
```

To enable the interface, use the command no shutdown from interface configuration mode.

The next show interface serial 0/0/0 command demonstrates the serial line and the maximum transmission unit (MTU)—1,500 bytes by default. It also shows the default bandwidth (BW) on all Cisco serial links, which is 1.544 Kbps. This is used to determine the bandwidth of the line for routing protocols like EIGRP and OSPF. Another important configuration to notice is the keepalive, which is 10 seconds by default. Each router sends a keepalive message to its neighbor every 10 seconds, and if both routers aren't configured for the same keepalive time, it won't work! Check out this output:

```
Router#sh int s0/0/0
Serial0/0 is up, line protocol is up
 Hardware is HD64570
 MTU 1500 bytes, BW 1544 Kbit, DLY 20000 usec,
   reliability 255/255, txload 1/255, rxload 1/255
```

```
Encapsulation HDLC, loopback not set, keepalive set
 (10 sec)
Last input never, output never, output hang never
Last clearing of "show interface" counters never
Queueing strategy: fifo
Output queue 0/40, 0 drops; input queue 0/75, 0 drops
5 minute input rate 0 bits/sec, 0 packets/sec
5 minute output rate 0 bits/sec, 0 packets/sec
  0 packets input, 0 bytes, 0 no buffer
  Received 0 broadcasts, 0 runts, 0 giants, 0 throttles
  0 input errors, 0 CRC, 0 frame, 0 overrun, 0 ignored,
  0 abort
  0 packets output, 0 bytes, 0 underruns
  0 output errors, 0 collisions, 16 interface resets
  0 output buffer failures, 0 output buffers swapped out
  0 carrier transitions
  DCD=down DSR=down DTR=down RTS=down CTS=down
```

You can clear the counters on the interface by typing the command **clear counters**:

```
Router#clear counters ?
  Async             Async interface
  BVI               Bridge-Group Virtual Interface
  CTunnel           CTunnel interface
  Dialer            Dialer interface
  FastEthernet      FastEthernet IEEE 802.3
  Group-Async       Async Group interface
  Line              Terminal line
  Loopback          Loopback interface
  MFR               Multilink Frame Relay bundle interface
  Multilink         Multilink-group interface
  Null              Null interface
  Serial            Serial
  Tunnel            Tunnel interface
  Vif               PGM Multicast Host interface
  Virtual-Template  Virtual Template interface
  Virtual-TokenRing Virtual TokenRing
  <cr>
```

```
Router#clear counters s0/0/0
Clear "show interface" counters on this interface
  [confirm][enter]
```

```
Router#
00:17:35: %CLEAR-5-COUNTERS: Clear counter on interface
  Serial0/0/0 by console
Router#
```

## Troubleshooting with the *show interfaces* command

Let's take a look at the output of the show interfaces command one more time before I move on. There are some important statistics in this output that are important for the Cisco objectives.

```
275496 packets input, 35226811 bytes, 0 no buffer
   Received 69748 broadcasts (58822 multicasts)
   0 runts, 0 giants, 0 throttles
   0 input errors, 0 CRC, 0 frame, 0 overrun, 0 ignored
   0 watchdog, 58822 multicast, 0 pause input
   0 input packets with dribble condition detected
   2392529 packets output, 337933522 bytes, 0 underruns
   0 output errors, 0 collisions, 1 interface resets
   0 babbles, 0 late collision, 0 deferred
   0 lost carrier, 0 no carrier, 0 PAUSE output
   0 output buffer failures, 0 output buffers swapped out
```

Finding where to start when troubleshooting an interface can be the difficult part, but certainly we'll look for the number of input errors and CRCs right away. Typically we'd see those statistics increase with a duplex error, but it could be another Physical layer issue such as the cable might be receiving excessive interference or the network interface cards might have a failure. Typically you can tell if it is interference when the CRC and input errors output grow but the collision counters do not.

Let's take a look at some of the output:

**No buffer**   This isn't a number you want to see incrementing. This means you don't have any buffer room left for incoming packets. Any packets received once the buffers are full are discarded. You can see how many packets are dropped with the ignored output.

**Ignored**   If the packet buffers are full, packets will be dropped. You see this increment along with the no buffer output. Typically if the no buffer and ignored outputs are incrementing, you have some sort of broadcast storm on your LAN. This can be caused by a bad NIC or even a bad network design.

**Runts**   Frames that did not meet the minimum frame size requirement of 64 bytes. Typically caused by collisions.

**Giants**   Frames received that are larger than 1518 bytes

**Input Errors**   This is the total of many counters: runts, giants, no buffer, CRC, frame, overrun, and ignored counts.

**CRC**   At the end of each frame is a Frame Check Sequence (FCS) field that holds the answer to a cyclic redundancy check (CRC). If the receiving host's answer to the CRC does not match the sending host's answer, then a CRC error will occur.

**Frame**   This output increments when frames received are of an illegal format, or not complete, which is typically incremented when a collision occurs.

**Packets Output**   Total number of packets (frames) forwarded out to the interface.

**Output Errors**   Total number of packets (frames) that the switch port tried to transmit but for which some problem occurred.

**Collisions**   When transmitting a frame in half-duplex, the NIC listens on the receiving pair of the cable for another signal. If a signal is transmitted from another host, a collision has occurred. This output should not increment if you are running full-duplex.

**Late Collisions**   If all Ethernet specifications are followed during the cable install, all collisions should occur by the 64th byte of the frame. If a collision occurs after 64 bytes, the late collisions counter increments. This counter will increment on a duplex mismatched interface, or if cable length exceeds specifications.

## Verifying with the *show ip interface* Command

The show ip interface command will provide you with information regarding the layer 3 configurations of a router's interfaces:

```
Router#sh ip interface
FastEthernet0/0 is up, line protocol is up
  Internet address is 1.1.1.1/24
  Broadcast address is 255.255.255.255
  Address determined by setup command
  MTU is 1500 bytes
  Helper address is not set
  Directed broadcast forwarding is disabled
  Outgoing access list is not set
  Inbound  access list is not set
  Proxy ARP is enabled
  Security level is default
  Split horizon is enabled
[output cut]
```

The status of the interface, the IP address and mask, information on whether an access list is set on the interface, and basic IP information are all included in this output.

## Using the *show ip interface brief* Command

The show ip interface brief command is probably one of the best commands that you can ever use on a Cisco router. This command provides a quick overview of the router's interfaces, including the logical address and status:

```
Router#sh ip int brief
Interface          IP-Address      OK? Method Status                Protocol
FastEthernet0/0    unassigned      YES unset  up                    up
FastEthernet0/1    unassigned      YES unset  up                    up
Serial0/0/0        unassigned      YES unset  up                    down
Serial0/0/1        unassigned      YES unset  administratively down down
Serial0/1/0        unassigned      YES unset  administratively down down
Serial0/2/0        unassigned      YES unset  administratively down down
```

Remember, administratively down means that you need to type no shutdown in order to enable the interface. Notice that Serial0/0/0 is up/down, which means that the Physical layer is good and carrier detect is sensed but no keepalives are being received from the remote end. In a nonproduction network, like the one I am working with, this tells us the clock rate hasn't been set.

## Verifying with the *show protocols* Command

The show protocols command is also a really helpful command that you'd use in order to quickly see the status of layers 1 and 2 of each interface as well as the IP addresses used.

Here's a look at one of my production routers:

```
Router#sh protocols
Global values:
  Internet Protocol routing is enabled
Ethernet0/0 is administratively down, line protocol is down
Serial0/0 is up, line protocol is up
  Internet address is 100.30.31.5/24
Serial0/1 is administratively down, line protocol is down
Serial0/2 is up, line protocol is up
  Internet address is 100.50.31.2/24
Loopback0 is up, line protocol is up
  Internet address is 100.20.31.1/24
```

The show ip interface brief and show protocols command provides the layer 1 and layer 2 statistics of an interface as well as the IP addresses. The next command, show controllers, only provides layer 1 information. Let's take a look.

## Using the *show controllers* Command

The show controllers command displays information about the physical interface itself. It'll also give you the type of serial cable plugged into a serial port. Usually, this will only be a DTE cable that plugs into a type of data service unit (DSU).

```
Router#sh controllers serial 0/0
HD unit 0, idb = 0x1229E4, driver structure at 0x127E70
buffer size 1524 HD unit 0, V.35 DTE cable
```

```
Router#sh controllers serial 0/1
HD unit 1, idb = 0x12C174, driver structure at 0x131600
buffer size 1524 HD unit 1, V.35 DCE cable
```

Notice that serial 0/0 has a DTE cable, whereas the serial 0/1 connection has a DCE cable. Serial 0/1 would have to provide clocking with the clock rate command. Serial 0/0 would get its clocking from the DSU.

Let's look at this command again. In Figure 6.5, see the DTE/DCE cable between the two routers? Know that you will not see this in production networks!

**FIGURE 6.5**    Where do you configure clocking? Use the show controllers command on each router's serial interface to find out.

Router R1 has a DTE connection, which is typically the default for all Cisco routers. Routers R1 and R2 can't communicate. Check out the output of the show controllers s0/0 command here:

```
R1#sh controllers serial 0/0
HD unit 0, idb = 0x1229E4, driver structure at 0x127E70
buffer size 1524 HD unit 0, V.35 DCE cable
```

The show controllers s0/0 command reveals that the interface is a V.35 DCE cable. This means that R1 needs to provide clocking of the line to router R2. Basically, the interface has the wrong label on the cable on the R1 router's serial interface. But if you add clocking on the R1 router's serial interface, the network should come right up.

Let's check out another issue in Figure 6.6 that you can solve by using the show controllers command. Again, routers R1 and R2 can't communicate.

**FIGURE 6.6**   By looking at R1, the show controllers command reveals that R1 and R2 can't communicate.

Here's the output of R1's show controllers s0/0 command and show ip interface s0/0:

```
R1#sh controllers s0/0
HD unit 0, idb = 0x1229E4, driver structure at 0x127E70
buffer size 1524 HD unit 0,
DTE V.35 clocks stopped
cpb = 0xE2, eda = 0x4140, cda = 0x4000


R1#sh ip interface s0/0
Serial0/0 is up, line protocol is down
  Internet address is 192.168.10.2/24
  Broadcast address is 255.255.255.255
```

If you use the show controllers command and the show ip interface command, you'll see that router R1 isn't receiving the clocking of the line. This network is a nonproduction network, so no CSU/DSU is connected to provide clocking for it. This means the DCE end of the cable will be providing the clock rate—in this case, the R2 router. The show ip interface indicates that the interface is up but the protocol is down, which means that no keepalives are being received from the far end. In this example, the likely culprit is the result of bad cable, or simply the lack of clocking.

# Summary

This was a fun chapter! I showed you a lot about the Cisco IOS, and I really hope you gained a lot of insight into the Cisco router world. I started off by explaining the Cisco Internetwork Operating System (IOS) and how you can use the IOS to run and configure Cisco routers. You learned how to bring a router up and what setup mode does. Oh, and by the way, since you can now basically configure Cisco routers, you should never use setup mode, right?

After I discussed how to connect to a router with a console and LAN connection, I covered the Cisco help features and how to use the CLI to find commands and command parameters. In addition, I discussed some basic show commands to help you verify your configurations.

Administrative functions on a router help you administer your network and verify that you are configuring the correct device. Setting router passwords is one of the most important configurations you can perform on your routers. I showed you the five passwords you must set, plus I introduced you to the hostname, interface description, and banners as tools to help you administer your router.

Well, that concludes your introduction to the Cisco IOS. And, as usual, it's super-important for you to have the basics that we went over in this chapter down rock-solid before you move on to the following chapters!

# Exam Essentials

**Describe the responsibilities of the IOS.**   The Cisco router IOS software is responsible for network protocols and providing supporting functions, connecting high-speed traffic between devices, adding security to control access and preventing unauthorized network use, providing scalability for ease of network growth and redundancy, and supplying network reliability for connecting to network resources.

**List the options available to connect to a Cisco device for management purposes.**   The three options available are the console port, auxiliary port, and in-band communication, such as Telnet, SSH and HTTP. Don't forget, a Telnet connection is not possible until an IP address has been configured and a Telnet password has been configured.

**Understand the boot sequence of a router.**   When you first bring up a Cisco router, it will run a power-on self-test (POST), and if that passes, it will look for and load the Cisco IOS from flash memory, if a file is present. The IOS then proceeds to load and looks for a valid configuration in NVRAM called the startup-config. If no file is present in NVRAM, the router will go into setup mode.

**Describe the use of setup mode.**   Setup mode is automatically started if a router boots and no startup-config is in NVRAM. You can also bring up setup mode by typing setup from privileged mode. Setup provides a minimum amount of configuration in an easy format for someone who does not understand how to configure a Cisco router from the command line.

**Differentiate user, privileged, and global configuration modes, both visually and from a command capabilities perspective.**   User mode, indicated by the **routername>** prompt, provides a command-line interface with very few available commands by default. User mode does not allow the configuration to be viewed or changed. Privileged mode, indicated by the **routername#** prompt, allows a user to both view and change the configuration of a router. You can enter privileged mode by typing the command **enable** and entering the enable password or enable secret password, if set. Global configuration mode, indicated by the **routername(config)#** prompt, allows configuration changes to be made that apply to the entire router (as opposed to a configuration change that might affect only one interface, for example).

**Recognize additional prompts available in other modes and describe their use.**   Additional modes are reached via the global configuration prompt, **routername(config)#**, and their prompts include interface, **router(config-if)#**, for making interface settings; line configuration mode, **router(config-line)#**, used to set passwords and make other settings to various connection methods; and routing protocol modes for various routing protocols, **router(config-router)#**, used to enable and configure routing protocols.

**Access and utilize editing and help features.**  Make use of typing a question mark at the end of commands for help in using the commands. Additionally, understand how to filter command help with the same question mark and letters. Use the command history to retrieve commands previously utilized without retyping. Understand the meaning of the caret when an incorrect command is rejected. Finally, identify useful hot key combinations.

**Identify the information provided by the show version command.**  The show version command will provide basic configuration for the system hardware as well as the software version, the names and sources of configuration files, the configuration register setting, and the boot images.

**Set the hostname of a router.**  The command sequence to set the hostname of a router is as follows:

```
enable
config t
hostname Todd
```

**Differentiate the enable password and enable secret password.**  Both of these passwords are used to gain access into privileged mode. However, the enable secret password is newer and is always encrypted by default. Also, if you set the enable password and then set the enable secret, only the enable secret will be used.

**Describe the configuration and use of banners.**  Banners provide information to users accessing the device and can be displayed at various login prompts. They are configured with the banner command and a keyword describing the specific type of banner.

**Set the enable secret on a router.**  To set the enable secret, you use the global config command enable secret. Do not use enable secret password password or you will set your password to password password. Here is an example:

```
enable
config t
enable secret todd
```

**Set the console password on a router.**  To set the console password, use the following sequence:

```
enable
config t
line console 0
password todd
login
```

**Set the Telnet password on a router.** To set the Telnet password, the sequence is as follows:

```
enable
config t
line vty 0 4
password todd
login
```

**Describe the advantages of using Secure Shell and list its requirements.** Secure Shell (SSH) uses encrypted keys to send data so that usernames and passwords are not sent in the clear. It requires that a hostname and domain name be configured and that encryption keys be generated.

**Describe the process of preparing an interface for use.** To use an interface, you must configure it with an IP address and subnet mask in the same subnet of the hosts that will be connecting to the switch that is connected to that interface. It also must be enabled with the no shutdown command. A serial interface that is connected back to back with another router serial interface must also be configured with a clock rate on the DCE end of the serial cable.

**Understand how to troubleshoot a serial link problem.** If you type **show interface serial 0/0** and see down, **line protocol** is down, this will be considered a Physical layer problem. If you see it as up, **line protocol** is down, then you have a Data Link layer problem.

**Understand how to verify your router with the show interfaces command.** If you type **show interfaces**, you can view the statistics for the interfaces on the router, verify whether the interfaces are shut down, and see the IP address of each interface.

**Describe how to view, edit, delete, and save a configuration.** The show running-config command is used to view the current configuration being used by the router. The show startup-config command displays the last configuration that was saved and is the one that will be used at next startup. The copy running-config startup-config command is used to save changes made to the running configuration in NVRAM. The erase startup-config command deletes the saved configuration and will result in the invocation of the setup menu when the router is rebooted because there will be no configuration present.

# Written Lab 6

The answers to this lab can be found in Appendix A, "Answers to Written Labs."
   Write out the command or commands for the following questions:

1. What command is used to set a serial interface to provide clocking to another router at 1000 Kb?

2. If you telnet into a switch and get the response connection refused, password not set, what commands would you execute on the destination device to stop receiving this message and not be prompted for a password?

3. If you type show int fastethernet 0/1 and notice the port is administratively down, what commands would you execute to enable the interface?

4. If you wanted to delete the configuration stored in NVRAM, what command(s) would you type?

5. If you wanted to set the user-mode password to *todd* for the console port, what command(s) would you type?

6. If you wanted to set the enable secret password to *cisco*, what command(s) would you type?

7. If you wanted to determine if serial interface 0/2 on your router should provide clocking, what command would you use?

8. What command would you use to see the terminal history size?

9. You want to reinitialize the switch and totally replace the running-config with the current startup-config. What command will you use?

10. How would you set the name of a switch to *Sales*?

# Hands-on Labs

In this section, you will perform commands on a Cisco switch (or you can use a router) that will help you understand what you learned in this chapter.

You'll need at least one Cisco device—two would be better, three would be outstanding. The hands-on labs in this section are included for use with real Cisco routers, but all of these labs work with the LammleSim IOS Version or Cisco Packet Tracer router simulator. Last, for the Cisco exam it doesn't matter what model of switch or router you use with these labs, as long as you're running IOS 12.2 or newer. Yes, I know the objectives are 15 code, but that is not important for any of these labs.

It is assumed that the device you're going to use has no current configuration present. If necessary, erase any existing configuration with Hands-on Lab 6.1; otherwise, proceed to Hands-on Lab 6.2:

Lab 6.1: Erasing an Existing Configuration

Lab 6.2: Exploring User, Privileged, and Configuration Modes

Lab 6.3: Using the Help and Editing Features

Lab 6.4: Saving a Configuration

Lab 6.5: Setting Passwords

Lab 6.6: Setting the Hostname, Descriptions, IP Address, and Clock Rate

## Hands-on Lab 6.1: Erasing an Existing Configuration

The following lab may require the knowledge of a username and password to enter privileged mode. If the router has a configuration with an unknown username and password for privileged mode, this procedure will not be possible. It is possible to erase a configuration without a privileged mode password, but the exact steps depend on the model and will not be covered until Chapter 7.

1. Start the switch up and when prompted, press Enter.

2. At the Switch> prompt, type **enable**.

3. If prompted, enter the username and press Enter. Then enter the correct password and press Enter.

4. At the privileged mode prompt, type **erase startup-config**.

5. At the privileged mode prompt, type **reload**, and when prompted to save the configuration, type **n** for no.

## Hands-on Lab 6.2: Exploring User, Privileged, and Configuration Modes

In the following lab, you'll explore user, privileged, and configuration modes:

1. Plug the switch in, or turn the router on. If you just erased the configuration as in Hands-on Lab 6.1, when prompted to continue with the configuration dialog, enter **n** for no and press Enter. When prompted, press Enter to connect to your router. This will put you into user mode.

2. At the Switch> prompt, type a question mark (**?**).

3. Notice the -more- at the bottom of the screen.

4. Press the Enter key to view the commands line by line. Press the spacebar to view the commands a full screen at a time. You can type **q** at any time to quit.

5. Type **enable** or **en** and press Enter. This will put you into privileged mode where you can change and view the router configuration.

6. At the Switch# prompt, type a question mark (**?**). Notice how many options are available to you in privileged mode.

7. Type **q** to quit.

8. Type **config** and press Enter.

9. When prompted for a method, press Enter to configure your router using your terminal (which is the default).

10. At the Switch(config)# prompt, type a question mark (**?**), then **q** to quit, or press the spacebar to view the commands.

11. Type **interface f0/1** or **int f0/1** (or even **int gig0/1**) and press Enter. This will allow you to configure interface FastEthernet 0/1 or Gigabit 0/1.

12. At the Switch(config-if)# prompt, type a question mark (**?**).

13. If using a router, type **int s0/0**, **interface s0/0** or even **interface s0/0/0** and press Enter. This will allow you to configure interface serial 0/0. Notice that you can go from interface to interface easily.

14. Type **encapsulation ?**.

15. Type **exit**. Notice how this brings you back one level.

16. Press Ctrl+Z. Notice how this brings you out of configuration mode and places you back into privileged mode.

17. Type **disable**. This will put you into user mode.

18. Type **exit**, which will log you out of the router or switch.

## Hands-on Lab 6.3: Using the Help and Editing Features

This lab will provide hands-on experience with Cisco's help and editing features.

1. Log into your device and go to privileged mode by typing **en** or **enable**.

2. Type a question mark (**?**).

3. Type **cl?** and then press Enter. Notice that you can see all the commands that start with *cl*.

4. Type **clock ?** and press Enter.

Notice the difference between steps 3 and 4. Step 3 has you type letters with no space and a question mark, which will give you all the commands that start with *cl*. Step 4 has you type a command, space, and question mark. By doing this, you will see the next available parameter.

5. Set the clock by typing **clock ?** and, following the help screens, setting the time and date. The following steps walk you through setting the date and time:

6. Type **clock ?**.

7. Type **clock set ?**.

8. Type **clock set 10:30:30 ?**.

9. Type **clock set 10:30:30 14 May ?**.

10. Type **clock set 10:30:30 14 May 2011**.

11. Press Enter.

12. Type **show clock** to see the time and date.

13. From privileged mode, type **show access-list 10**. Don't press Enter.

14. Press Ctrl+A. This takes you to the beginning of the line.

15. Press Ctrl+E. This should take you back to the end of the line.

16. The Ctrl+A takes your cursor back to the beginning of the line, and then the Ctrl+F moves your cursor forward one character.

17. Press Ctrl+B, which will move you back one character.

18. Press Enter, then press Ctrl+P. This will repeat the last command.

19. Press the up arrow key on your keyboard. This will also repeat the last command.

20. Type **sh history**. This shows you the last 10 commands entered.

21. Type **terminal history size ?**. This changes the history entry size. The ? is the number of allowed lines.

22. Type **show terminal** to gather terminal statistics and history size.

23. Type **terminal no editing**. This turns off advanced editing. Repeat steps 14 through 18 to see that the shortcut editing keys have no effect until you type **terminal editing**.

24. Type **terminal editing** and press Enter to re-enable advanced editing.

25. Type **sh run**, then press your Tab key. This will finish typing the command for you.

26. Type **sh start**, then press your Tab key. This will finish typing the command for you.

## Hands-on Lab 6.4: Saving a Configuration

In this lab, you will get hands-on experience saving a configuration:

1. Log into your device and go into privileged mode by typing **en** or **enable**, then press Enter.

2. To see the configuration stored in NVRAM, type **sh start** and press Tab and Enter, or type **show startup-config** and press Enter. However, if no configuration has been saved, you will get an error message.

3. To save a configuration to NVRAM, which is known as startup-config, you can do one of the following:

   ■ Type **copy run start** and press Enter.

   ■ Type **copy running**, press Tab, type **start**, press Tab, and press Enter.

   ■ Type **copy running-config startup-config** and press Enter.

4. Type **sh start**, press Tab, then press Enter.

5. Type **sh run**, press Tab, then press Enter.

6. Type **erase startup-config**, press Tab, then press Enter.

7. Type **sh start**, press Tab, then press Enter. The router will either tell you that NVRAM is not present or display some other type of message, depending on the IOS and hardware.

8. Type **reload**, then press Enter. Acknowledge the reload by pressing Enter. Wait for the device to reload.

9. Say no to entering setup mode, or just press Ctrl+C.

## Hands-on Lab 6.5: Setting Passwords

This hands-on lab will have you set your passwords.

1. Log into the router and go into privileged mode by typing **en** or **enable**.

2. Type **config t** and press Enter.

3. Type **enable ?**.

4. Set your enable secret password by typing **enable secret** *password* (the third word should be your own personalized password) and pressing Enter. Do not add the parameter password after the parameter secret (this would make your password the word *password*). An example would be enable secret todd.

5. Now let's see what happens when you log all the way out of the router and then log in. Log out by pressing Ctrl+Z, and then type **exit** and press Enter. Go to privileged mode. Before you are allowed to enter privileged mode, you will be asked for a password. If you successfully enter the secret password, you can proceed.

6. Remove the secret password. Go to privileged mode, type **config t**, and press Enter. Type **no enable secret** and press Enter. Log out and then log back in again; now you should not be asked for a password.

7. One more password used to enter privileged mode is called the enable password. It is an older, less secure password and is not used if an enable secret password is set. Here is an example of how to set it:

```
config t
enable password todd1
```

8. Notice that the enable secret and enable passwords are different. They should never be set the same. Actually, you should never use the enable password, only enable secret.

9. Type **config t** to be at the right level to set your console and auxiliary passwords, then type **line ?**.

10. Notice that the parameters for the line commands are auxiliary, vty, and console. You will set all three if you're on a router; if you're on a switch, only the console and VTY lines are available.

11. To set the Telnet or VTY password, type **line vty 0 4** and then press Enter. The 0 4 is the range of the five available virtual lines used to connect with Telnet. If you have an enterprise IOS, the number of lines may vary. Use the question mark to determine the last line number available on your router.

12. The next command is used to set the authentication on or off. Type **login** and press Enter to prompt for a user-mode password when telnetting into the device. You will not be able to telnet into a Cisco device if the password is not set.

> **NOTE**    You can use the no login command to disable the user-mode password prompt when using Telnet. Do not do this in production!

13. One more command you need to set for your VTY password is password. Type **password** *password* to set the password. (*password* is your password.)

14. Here is an example of how to set the VTY password:

```
config t
line vty 0 4
password todd
login
```

15. Set your auxiliary password by first typing **line auxiliary 0** or **line aux 0** (if you are using a router).

16. Type **login**.

17. Type **password** *password*.

18. Set your console password by first typing **line console 0** or **line con 0**.

19. Type **login**.

20. Type **password** *password*. Here is an example of the last two command sequences:

```
config t
line con 0
password todd1
login
line aux 0
```

```
password todd
login
```

21. You can add the Exec-timeout 0 0 command to the console 0 line. This will stop the console from timing out and logging you out. The command sequence will now look like this:

```
config t
line con 0
password todd2
login
exec-timeout 0 0
```

22. Set the console prompt to not overwrite the command you're typing with console messages by using the command logging synchronous.

```
config t
line con 0
logging synchronous
```

## Hands-on Lab 6.6: Setting the Hostname, Descriptions, IP Address, and Clock Rate

This lab will have you set your administrative functions on each device.

1. Log into the switch or router and go into privileged mode by typing **en** or **enable**. If required, enter a username and password.

2. Set your hostname by using the hostname command. Notice that it is one word. Here is an example of setting your hostname on your router, but the switch uses the exact same command:

```
Router#config t
Router(config)#hostname RouterA
RouterA(config)#
```

Notice that the hostname of the router changed in the prompt as soon as you pressed Enter.

3. Set a banner that the network administrators will see by using the banner command, as shown in the following steps.

4. Type **config t**, then **banner ?**.

5. Notice that you can set at least four different banners. For this lab we are only interested in the login and message of the day (MOTD) banners.

6. Set your MOTD banner, which will be displayed when a console, auxiliary, or Telnet connection is made to the router, by typing this:

```
config t
banner motd #
This is an motd banner
#
```

7. The preceding example used a # sign as a delimiting character. This tells the router when the message is done. You cannot use the delimiting character in the message itself.

8. You can remove the MOTD banner by typing the following command:

```
config t
no banner motd
```

9. Set the login banner by typing this:

```
config t
banner login #
This is a login banner
#
```

10. The login banner will display immediately after the MOTD but before the user-mode password prompt. Remember that you set your user-mode passwords by setting the console, auxiliary, and VTY line passwords.

11. You can remove the login banner by typing this:

```
config t
no banner login
```

12. You can add an IP address to an interface with the ip address command if you are using a router. You need to get into interface configuration mode first; here is an example of how you do that:

```
config t
int f0/1
ip address 1.1.1.1 255.255.0.0
no shutdown
```

Notice that the IP address (1.1.1.1) and subnet mask (255.255.0.0) are configured on one line. The no shutdown (or no shut for short) command is used to enable the interface. All interfaces are shut down by default on a router. If you are on a layer 2 switch, you can set an IP address only on the VLAN 1 interface.

**13.** You can add identification to an interface by using the description command. This is useful for adding information about the connection. Here is an example:

```
config t
int f0/1
ip address 2.2.2.1 255.255.0.0
no shut
description LAN link to Finance
```

**14.** You can add the bandwidth of a serial link as well as the clock rate when simulating a DCE WAN link on a router. Here is an example:

```
config t
int s0/0
bandwidth 1000
clock rate 1000000
```

# Review Questions

The following questions are designed to test your understanding of this chapter's material. For more information on how to get additional questions, please see this book's introduction.

The answers to these questions can be found in Appendix B, "Answers to Chapter Review Questions."

1. You type **show interfaces fa0/1** and get this output:

```
275496 packets input, 35226811 bytes, 0 no buffer
   Received 69748 broadcasts (58822 multicasts)
   0 runts, 0 giants, 0 throttles
   111395 input errors, 511987 CRC, 0 frame, 0 overrun, 0 ignored
   0 watchdog, 58822 multicast, 0 pause input
   0 input packets with dribble condition detected
   2392529 packets output, 337933522 bytes, 0 underruns
   0 output errors, 0 collisions, 1 interface resets
   0 babbles, 0 late collision, 0 deferred
   0 lost carrier, 0 no carrier, 0 PAUSE output
   0 output buffer failures, 0 output buffers swapped out
```

   What could the problem possibly be with this interface?

   **A.** Speed mismatch on directly connected interfaces

   **B.** Collisions causing CRC errors

   **C.** Frames received are too large

   **D.** Interference on the Ethernet cable

2. The output of the show running-config command comes from _____.

   **A.** NVRAM

   **B.** Flash

   **C.** RAM

   **D.** Firmware

**3.** Which two of the following commands are required when configuring SSH on your router? (Choose two.)

   **A.** `enable secret password`

   **B.** `exec-timeout 0 0`

   **C.** `ip domain-name name`

   **D.** `username name password password`

   **E.** `ip ssh version 2`

**4.** Which command will show you whether a DTE or a DCE cable is plugged into serial 0/0 on your router's WAN port?

   **A.** `sh int s0/0`

   **B.** `sh int serial 0/0`

   **C.** `show controllers s 0/0`

   **D.** `show serial 0/0 controllers`

**5.** In the work area, drag the router term to its definition on the right.

| Mode | Definition |
| --- | --- |
| User EXEC mode | Commands that affect the entire system |
| Privileged EXEC mode | Commands that affect interfaces/processes only |
| Global configuration mode | Interactive configuration dialog |
| Specific configuration modes | Provides access to all other router commands |
| Setup mode | Limited to basic monitoring commands |

**6.** Using the given output, what type of interface is f0/0?

```
[output cut]
Hardware is MV96340 Ethernet, address is 001a.2f55.c9e8 (bia 001a.2f55.c9e8)
Internet address is 192.168.1.33/27
MTU 1500 bytes, BW 100000 Kbit, DLY 100 usec,
    reliability 255/255, txload 1/255, rxload 1/255
```

   **A.** 10 MB

   **B.** 100 MB

   **C.** 1000 MB

   **D.** 1000 MB

**7.** Which of the following commands will configure all the default VTY ports on a switch?

   **A.** Switch#`line vty 0 4`

   **B.** Switch(config)#`line vty 0 4`

   **C.** Switch(config-if)#`line console 0`

   **D.** Switch(config)#`line vty all`

**8.** Which of the following commands sets the privileged mode password to Cisco and encrypts the password?

   **A.** enable secret password Cisco

   **B.** enable secret cisco

   **C.** enable secret Cisco

   **D.** enable password Cisco

**9.** If you wanted administrators to see a message when logging into the switch, which command would you use?

   **A.** message banner motd

   **B.** banner message motd

   **C.** banner motd

   **D.** message motd

**10.** Which of the following prompts indicates that the switch is currently in privileged mode?

   **A.** Switch(config)#

   **B.** Switch>

   **C.** Switch#

   **D.** Switch(config-if)

**11.** What command do you type to save the configuration stored in RAM to NVRAM?

   **A.** Switch(config)#`copy current to starting`

   **B.** Switch#`copy starting to running`

   **C.** Switch(config)#`copy running-config startup-config`

   **D.** Switch#`copy run start`

**12.** You try to telnet into SF from router Corp and receive this message:

```
Corp#telnet SF
Trying SF (10.0.0.1)…Open


Password required, but none set
[Connection to SF closed by foreign host]
Corp#
```

Which of the following sequences will address this problem correctly?

**A.** Corp(config)#line console 0

  Corp (config-line)#password *password*

  Corp (config-line)#login

**B.** SF (config)#line console 0

  SF(config-line)#enable secret *password*

  SF(config-line)#login

**C.** Corp(config)#line vty 0 4

  Corp (config-line)#password *password*

  Corp (config-line)#login

**D.** SF (config)#line vty 0 4

  SF(config-line)#password *password*

  SF(config-line)#login

**13.** Which command will delete the contents of NVRAM on a switch?

**A.** delete NVRAM

**B.** delete startup-config

**C.** erase flash

**D.** erase startup-config

**E.** erase start

**14.** What is the problem with an interface if you type **show interface g0/1** and receive the following message?

Gigabit 0/1 is administratively down, line protocol is down

**A.** The keepalives are different times.

**B.** The administrator has the interface shut down.

**C.** The administrator is pinging from the interface.

**D.** No cable is attached.

**15.** Which of the following commands displays the configurable parameters and statistics of all interfaces on a switch?

    **A.** `show running-config`

    **B.** `show startup-config`

    **C.** `show interfaces`

    **D.** `show versions`

**16.** If you delete the contents of NVRAM and reboot the switch, what mode will you be in?

    **A.** Privileged mode

    **B.** Global mode

    **C.** Setup mode

    **D.** NVRAM loaded mode

**17.** You type the following command into the switch and receive the following output:

```
Switch#show fastethernet 0/1
          ^
% Invalid input detected at '^' marker.
```

Why was this error message displayed?

    **A.** You need to be in privileged mode.

    **B.** You cannot have a space between `fastethernet` and `0/1`.

    **C.** The switch does not have a Fastethernet 0/1 interface.

    **D.** Part of the command is missing.

**18.** You type **Switch#sh r** and receive a `% ambiguous command` error. Why did you receive this message?

    **A.** The command requires additional options or parameters.

    **B.** There is more than one show command that starts with the letter *r*.

    **C.** There is no show command that starts with *r*.

    **D.** The command is being executed from the wrong mode.

**19.** Which of the following commands will display the current IP addressing and the layer 1 and 2 status of an interface? (Choose two.)

    **A.** `show version`

    **B.** `show interfaces`

    **C.** `show controllers`

    **D.** `show ip interface`

    **E.** `show running-config`

**20.** At which layer of the OSI model would you assume the problem is if you type **show interface serial 1** and receive the following message?

Serial1 is down, line protocol is down

  **A.** Physical layer

  **B.** Data Link layer

  **C.** Network layer

  **D.** None; it is a router problem.

# Chapter

# 7

# Managing a Cisco Internetwork

## THE FOLLOWING ICND1 EXAM TOPICS ARE COVERED IN THIS CHAPTER:

✓ **LAN Switching Technologies**

- Verify network status and switch operation using basic utilities such as ping, telnet, and ssh

✓ **IP Routing Technologies**

- Configure and verify utilizing the CLI to set basic Router configuration
  - Cisco IOS commands to perform basic router setup
- Verify router configuration and network connectivity
  - Cisco IOS commands to review basic router information and network connectivity

✓ **IP Services**

- Configure and verify DHCP (IOS Router)
  - configuring router interfaces to use DHCP
  - DHCP options
  - excluded addresses
  - lease time
- Configure and verify NTP as a client

Here in Chapter 7, I'm going to show you how to manage Cisco routers and switches on an internetwork. You'll find out how to manage Cisco devices by using the copy command with a TFTP host and how to configure DHCP and NTP, plus you'll get a survey of the Cisco Discovery Protocol (CDP). I'll also show you how to resolve hostnames.

I'll wrap up the chapter by guiding you through some important Cisco IOS troubleshooting techniques to ensure that you're well equipped with these key skills.

To find up-to-the minute updates for this chapter, please see www.lammle.com/forum or the book's web page at www.sybex.com.

# The Internal Components of a Cisco Router and Switch

Unless you happen to be really savvy about the inner and outer workings of all your car's systems and its machinery and how all of that technology works together, you'll take it to someone who *does* know how to keep it maintained, figure out what's wrong when it stops running, and get it up and running again. It's the same deal with Cisco networking devices—you need to know all about their major components, pieces, and parts as well as what they all do and why and how they all work together to make a network work. The more solid your knowledge, the more expert you are about these things and the better equipped you'll be to configure and troubleshoot a Cisco internetwork. Toward that goal, study Table 7.1 for an introductory description of a Cisco router's major components.

**TABLE 7.1**   Cisco router components

| Component | Description |
| --- | --- |
| Bootstrap | Stored in the microcode of the ROM, the bootstrap is used to bring a router up during initialization. It boots the router up and then loads the IOS. |

| Component | Description |
|---|---|
| POST (power-on self-test) | Also stored in the microcode of the ROM, the POST is used to check the basic functionality of the router hardware and determines which interfaces are present. |
| ROM monitor | Again, stored in the microcode of the ROM, the ROM monitor is used for manufacturing, testing, and troubleshooting, as well as running a mini-IOS when the IOS in flash fails to load. |
| Mini-IOS | Called the RXBOOT or bootloader by Cisco, the mini-IOS is a small IOS in ROM that can be used to bring up an interface and load a Cisco IOS into flash memory. The mini-IOS can also perform a few other maintenance operations. |
| RAM (random access memory) | Used to hold packet buffers, ARP cache, routing tables, and also the software and data structures that allow the router to function. Running-config is stored in RAM, and most routers expand the IOS from flash into RAM upon boot. |
| *ROM (read-only memory)* | Used to start and maintain the router. Holds the POST and the bootstrap program as well as the mini-IOS. |
| *Flash memory* | Stores the Cisco IOS by default. Flash memory is not erased when the router is reloaded. It is EEPROM (electronically erasable programmable read-only memory) created by Intel. |
| NVRAM (nonvolatile RAM) | Used to hold the router and switch configuration. NVRAM is not erased when the router or switch is reloaded. Does not store an IOS. The configuration register is stored in NVRAM. |
| *Configuration register* | Used to control how the router boots up. This value can be found as the last line of the show version command output and by default is set to 0x2102, which tells the router to load the IOS from flash memory as well as to load the configuration from NVRAM. |

## The Router and Switch Boot Sequence

When a Cisco device boots up, it performs a series of steps, called the *boot sequence*, to test the hardware and load the necessary software. The boot sequence comprises the following steps:

1. The IOS device performs a POST, which tests the hardware to verify that all components of the device are present and operational. The post takes stock of the different interfaces on the switch or router, and it's stored in and runs from read-only memory (ROM).

2. The bootstrap in ROM then locates and loads the Cisco IOS software by executing programs responsible for finding where each IOS program is located. Once they are found, it then loads the proper files. By default, the IOS software is loaded from flash memory in all Cisco devices.

 The default order of an IOS loading from a Cisco device begins with flash, then TFTP server, and finally, ROM.

3. The IOS software then looks for a valid configuration file stored in NVRAM. This file is called startup-config and will be present only if an administrator has copied the running-config file into NVRAM.

4. If a startup-config file is found in NVRAM, the router or switch will copy it, place it in RAM, and name the file the running-config. The device will use this file to run, and the router/switch should now be operational. If no startup-config file is found in NVRAM, the router/switch reacts by broadcasting out any interface that detects carrier detect (CD) to locate a TFTP host in its search for a configuration. When that fails, which it typically does, the device will begin the setup mode configuration process. Most people don't even realize the device has attempted this process!

# Backing Up and Restoring the Cisco Configuration

Any changes that you make to the configuration are stored in the running-config file. And if you don't enter a copy run start command after you make a change to running-config, that change will totally disappear if the device reboots or gets powered down. As always, backups are good, so you'll want to make another backup of the configuration information just in case the router or switch completely dies on you. Even if your machine is healthy and happy, it's good to have a backup for reference and documentation reasons!

Next, I'll cover how to copy the configuration of a router to a TFTP server as well as how to restore that configuration.

## Backing Up the Cisco Configuration

To copy the configuration from an IOS device to a TFTP server, you can use either the copy running-config tftp or the copy startup-config tftp command. Either one will back up the router configuration that's currently running in DRAM or one that's stored in NVRAM.

## Verifying the Current Configuration

To verify the configuration in DRAM, use the show running-config command (sh run for short) like this:

```
Router#show running-config
Building configuration...


Current configuration : 855 bytes
!
version 15.0
```

The current configuration information indicates that the router is running version 15.0 of the IOS.

## Verifying the Stored Configuration

Next, you should check the configuration stored in NVRAM. To see this, use the show startup-config command (sh start for short) like this:

```
Router#sh start
Using 855 out of 524288 bytes
!
! Last configuration change at 04:49:14 UTC Fri Mar 5 1993
!
version 15.0
```

The first line shows you how much room your backup configuration is taking up. Here, we can see that NVRAM is about 524 KB and that only 855 bytes of it are being used. But memory is easier to reveal via the show version command when you're using an ISR router.

If you're not sure that the files are the same and the running-config file is what you want to go with, then use the copy running-config startup-config command. This will help you ensure that both files are in fact the same. I'll guide you through this in the next section.

## Copying the Current Configuration to NVRAM

By copying running-config to NVRAM as a backup, as shown in the following output, you ensure that your running-config will always be reloaded if the router gets rebooted. Starting in the 12.0 IOS, you'll be prompted for the filename you want to use:

```
Router#copy running-config startup-config
Destination filename [startup-config]?[enter]
Building configuration...
[OK]
```

The reason the filename prompt appears is that there are now so many options you can use when using the copy command—check it out:

```
Router#copy running-config ?
  flash:          Copy to flash: file system
  ftp:            Copy to ftp: file system
  http:           Copy to http: file system
  https:          Copy to https: file system
  null:           Copy to null: file system
  nvram:          Copy to nvram: file system
  rcp:            Copy to rcp: file system
  running-config  Update (merge with) current system configuration
  scp:            Copy to scp: file system
  startup-config  Copy to startup configuration
  syslog:         Copy to syslog: file system
  system:         Copy to system: file system
  tftp:           Copy to tftp: file system
  tmpsys:         Copy to tmpsys: file system
```

We'll go over the copy command in more detail in the Sybex ICND2 Study Guide.

## Copying the Configuration to a TFTP Server

Once the file is copied to NVRAM, you can make a second backup to a TFTP server by using the copy running-config tftp command, or copy run tftp for short. I'm going to set the hostname to Todd before I run this command:

```
Todd#copy running-config tftp
Address or name of remote host []? 10.10.10.254
Destination filename [todd-confg]?
!!
776 bytes copied in 0.800 secs (970 bytes/sec)
```

If you have a hostname already configured, the command will automatically use the hostname plus the extension -confg as the name of the file.

# Restoring the Cisco Configuration

What do you do if you've changed your running-config file and want to restore the configuration to the version in the startup-config file? The easiest way to get this done is to use the copy startup-config running-config command, or copy start run for short, but this will work only if you copied running-config into NVRAM before you made any changes! Of course, a reload of the device will work too!

If you did copy the configuration to a TFTP server as a second backup, you can restore the configuration using the copy tftp running-config command (copy tftp run for short), or the copy tftp startup-config command (copy tftp start for short), as shown in the output below. Just so you know, the old command we used to use for this is config net:

```
Todd#copy tftp running-config
Address or name of remote host []?10.10.10.254
Source filename []?todd-confg
Destination filename[running-config]?[enter]
Accessing tftp://10.10.10.254/todd-confg...
Loading todd-confg from 10.10.10.254 (via FastEthernet0/0):
!!
[OK - 776 bytes]
776 bytes copied in 9.212 secs (84 bytes/sec)
Todd#
*Mar  7 17:53:34.071: %SYS-5-CONFIG_I: Configured from
    tftp://10.10.10.254/todd-confg by console
```

Okay, here we can see that the configuration file is an ASCII text file, meaning that before you copy the configuration stored on a TFTP server back to a router, you can make changes to the file with any text editor.

Remember that when you copy or merge a configuration from a TFTP server to a freshly erased and rebooted router's RAM, the interfaces are shut down by default and you must manually enable each interface with the no shutdown command.

## Erasing the Configuration

To delete the startup-config file on a Cisco router or switch, use the command erase startup-config, like this:

```
Todd#erase startup-config
Erasing the nvram filesystem will remove all configuration files!
    Continue? [confirm][enter]
[OK]
Erase of nvram: complete
*Mar  7 17:56:20.407: %SYS-7-NV_BLOCK_INIT: Initialized the geometry of nvram
Todd#reload
System configuration has been modified. Save? [yes/no]:n
Proceed with reload? [confirm][enter]
 *Mar  7 17:56:31.059: %SYS-5-RELOAD: Reload requested by console.
    Reload Reason: Reload Command.
```

This command deletes the contents of NVRAM on the switch and router. If you type **reload** while in privileged mode and say no to saving changes, the switch or router will reload and come up into setup mode.

# Configuring DHCP

We went over DHCP in Chapter 3, "Introduction to TCP/IP", where I described how it works and what happens when there's a conflict. At this point, you're ready to learn how to configure DHCP on Cisco's IOS as well as how to configure a DHCP forwarder for when your hosts don't live on the same LAN as the DHCP server. Do you remember the four-way handshake hosts used to get an address from a server? If not, now would be a really great time to head back to Chapter 3 and thoroughly review that before moving on with this!

To configure a DHCP server for your hosts, you need the following information at minimum:

**Network and mask for each LAN**   Network ID, also called a scope. All addresses in a subnet can be leased to hosts by default.

**Reserved/excluded addresses**   Reserved addresses for printers, servers, routers, etc. These addresses will not be handed out to hosts. I usually reserve the first address of each subnet for the router, but you don't have to do this.

**Default router**   This is the router's address for each LAN.

**DNS address**   A list of DNS server addresses provided to hosts so they can resolve names.

Here are your configuration steps:

1. Exclude the addresses you want to reserve. The reason you do this step first is because as soon as you set a network ID, the DHCP service will start responding to client requests.

2. Create your pool for each LAN using a unique name.

3. Choose the network ID and subnet mask for the DHCP pool that the server will use to provide addresses to hosts.

4. Add the address used for the default gateway of the subnet.

5. Provide the DNS server address(es).

6. If you don't want to use the default lease time of 24 hours, you need to set the lease time in days, hours, and minutes.

I'll configure the switch in Figure 7.1 to be the DHCP server for the Sales Wireless LAN.

**FIGURE 7.1**    DHCP Configuration example on a switch

Understand that this configuration could just have easily been placed on the router in Figure 7.1. Here's how we'll configure DHCP using the 192.168.10.0/24 network ID:

```
Switch(config)#ip dhcp excluded-address 192.168.10.1 192.168.10.10
Switch(config)#ip dhcp pool Sales_Wireless
Switch(dhcp-config)#network 192.168.10.0 255.255.255.0
Switch(dhcp-config)#default-router 192.168.10.1
Switch(dhcp-config)#dns-server 4.4.4.4
Switch(dhcp-config)#lease 3 12 15
```

First, you can see that I reserved 10 addresses in the range for the router, servers, and printers, etc. I then created the pool named Sales_Wireless, added the default gateway and DNS server, and set the lease to 3 days, 12 hours, and 15 minutes (which isn't really significant because I just set it that way for demonstration purposes). Pretty straightforward, right? The switch will now respond to DHCP client requests. But what happens if we need to provide an IP address from a DHCP server to a host that's not in our broadcast domain, or if we want to receive a DHCP address for a client from a remote server?

## DHCP Relay

If you need to provide addresses from a DHCP server to hosts that aren't on the same LAN as the DHCP server, you can configure your router interface to relay or forward the DHCP client requests, as shown in Figure 7.2. If we don't provide this service, our router would receive the DHCP client broadcast, promptly discard it, and the remote host would never receive an address—unless we added a DHCP server on every broadcast domain! Let's take a look at how we would typically configure DHCP service in today's networks.

So we know that because the hosts off the router don't have access to a DHCP server, the router will simply drop their client request broadcast messages by default. To solve this problem, we can configure the F0/0 interface of the router to accept the DHCP client requests and forward them to the DHCP server like this:

```
Router#config t
Router(config)#interface fa0/0
Router(config-if)#ip helper-address 10.10.10.254
```

**FIGURE 7.2**   Configuring a DHCP relay

Now I know that was a pretty simple example, and there are definitely other ways to configure the relay, but rest assured that I've covered the objectives for you. Also, I want you to know that ip helper-address forwards more than just DHCP client requests, so be sure to research this command before you implement it! Now that I've demonstrated how to create the DHCP service, let's take a minute to verify DHCP before moving on to NTP.

## Verifying DHCP on Cisco IOS

There are some really useful verification commands to use on a Cisco IOS device for monitoring and verifying a DHCP service. You'll get to see the output for these commands when I build the network in Chapter 8, "IP Routing," and add DHCP to the two remote LANs. I just want you to begin getting familiar with them, so here's a list of four very important ones and what they do:

**show ip dhcp binding**   Lists state information about each IP address currently leased to a client.

**show ip dhcp pool [poolname]**   Lists the configured range of IP addresses, plus statistics for the number of currently leased addresses and the high watermark for leases from each pool.

**show ip dhcp server statistics**   Lists DHCP server statistics—a lot of them!

**show ip dhcp conflict**   If someone statically configures an IP address on a LAN and the DHCP server hands out that same address, you'll end up with a duplicate address. This isn't good, which is why this command is so helpful!

Again, no worries because we'll cover these vital commands thoroughly in the next chapter.

# Network Time Protocol (NTP)

Network Time Protocol provides pretty much what it describes: time to all your network devices. To be more precise, NTP synchronizes clocks of computer systems over packet-switched, variable-latency data networks.

Typically you'll have an NTP server that connects through the Internet to an atomic clock. This time can then be synchronized through the network to keep all routers, switches, servers, etc. receiving the same time information.

Correct network time within the network is important:

- Correct time allows the tracking of events in the network in the correct order.
- Clock synchronization is critical for the correct interpretation of events within the syslog data.
- Clock synchronization is critical for digital certificates.

Making sure all your devices have the correct time is especially helpful for your routers and switches for looking at logs regarding security issues or other maintenance issues. Routers and switches issue log messages when different events take place—for example, when an interface goes down and then back up. As you already know, all messages generated by the IOS go only to the console port by default. However, as shown in Figure 7.3, those console messages can be directed to a syslog server.

**FIGURE 7.3**   Sending console messages to a syslog server

A syslog server saves copies of console messages and can time-stamp them so you can view them at a later time. This is actually rather easy to do. Here would be your configuration on the SF router:

```
SF(config)#logging host 172.16.10.1
SF(config)#service timestamps log datetime msec
```

Now all the console messages will be stored in one location that you can view at your convenience. However, even though I had the messages time-stamped in Figure 7.3 with the command service timestamps log datetime msec, this doesn't mean that we'll know the exact time if using default clock sources. To make sure all devices are synchronized with the same time information, we'll configure our devices to receive the accurate time information from a centralized server, as shown in Figure 7.4:

```
SF(config)#ntp server 172.16.10.1 version 4
```

**FIGURE 7.4**   Synchronizing time information

Just use that one simple command on all your devices and each network device on your network will then have the same exact time and date information. You can then rest assured that your time stamps are accurate. You can also make your router or switch be an NTP server with the ntp master command.

To verify our VTP client is receiving clocking information, we use the following commands:

```
SF#sh ntp ?
  associations  NTP associations
  status        NTP status  status     VTP domain status


SF#sh ntp status
Clock is unsynchronized, stratum 16, no reference clock
nominal freq is 119.2092 Hz, actual freq is 119.2092 Hz, precision is 2**18
reference time is 00000000.00000000 (00:00:00.000 UTC Mon Jan 1 1900)
clock offset is 0.0000 msec, root delay is 0.00 msec

S1#sh ntp associations

address     ref clock     st  when  poll reach  delay  offset    disp
~172.16.10.1  0.0.0.0           16    -    64    0     0.0    0.00  16000.
 * master (synced), # master (unsynced), + selected, - candidate, ~ configured
```

You can see in the example that the NTP client in SF is not synchronized with the server by using the show ntp status command. The stratum value is a number from 1 to 15, and a lower stratum value indicates a higher NTP priority; 16 means there is no clocking received.

There are many other configurations of an NTP client that are available, such as authentication of NTP so a router or switch isn't fooled into changing the time of an attack, for example.

# Using Cisco Discovery Protocol (CDP)

Cisco Discovery Protocol (CDP) is a proprietary protocol designed by Cisco to help administrators collect information about locally attached devices. Armed with CDP, you can gather hardware and protocol information about neighbor devices, which is crucial information to have when troubleshooting and documenting the network.

Let's start by exploring the CDP timer and CDP commands we'll need to verify our network.

## Getting CDP Timers and Holdtime Information

The show cdp command (sh cdp for short) gives you information about two CDP global parameters that can be configured on Cisco devices:

- *CDP timer* delimits how often CDP packets are transmitted out all active interfaces.

- *CDP holdtime* delimits the amount of time that the device will hold packets received from neighbor devices.

Both Cisco routers and switches use the same parameters. Check out Figure 7.5 to see how CDP works within a switched network that I set up for my switching labs in this book.

**FIGURE 7.5**   Cisco Discovery Protocol

The output on my 3560 SW-3 looks like this:

```
SW-3#sh cdp
Global CDP information:
```

```
            Sending CDP packets every 60 seconds
            Sending a holdtime value of 180 seconds
            Sending CDPv2 advertisements is enabled
```

This output tells us that the default transmits every 60 seconds and will hold packets from a neighbor in the CDP table for 180 seconds. I can use the global commands cdp holdtime and cdp timer to configure the CDP holdtime and timer on a router if necessary like this:

```
SW-3(config)#cdp ?
  advertise-v2  CDP sends version-2 advertisements
  holdtime      Specify the holdtime (in sec) to be sent in packets
  run           Enable CDP
  timer         Specify the rate at which CDP packets are sent (in sec)
  tlv           Enable exchange of specific tlv information


SW-3(config)#cdp holdtime ?
  <10-255>  Length of time  (in sec) that receiver must keep this packet


SW-3(config)#cdp timer ?
  <5-254>  Rate at which CDP packets are sent (in  sec)
```

You can turn off CDP completely with the no cdp run command from global configuration mode of a router and enable it with the cdp run command:

```
SW-3(config)#no cdp run
SW-3(config)#cdp run
```

To turn CDP off or on for an interface, use the no cdp enable and cdp enable commands.

## Gathering Neighbor Information

The show cdp neighbor command (sh cdp nei for short) delivers information about directly connected devices. It's important to remember that CDP packets aren't passed through a Cisco switch and that you only see what's directly attached. So this means that if your router is connected to a switch, you won't see any of the Cisco devices connected to that switch!

The following output shows the show cdp neighbor command I used on my SW-3:

```
SW-3#sh cdp neighbors
Capability Codes: R - Router, T - Trans Bridge, B - Source Route Bridge
                  S - Switch, H - Host, I - IGMP, r - Repeater, P - Phone,
                  D - Remote, C - CVTA, M - Two-port Mac Relay Device ID
Local Intrfce    Holdtme    Capability  Platform   Port ID
SW-1    Fas 0/1     170          S I      WS-C3560-  Fas 0/15
```

```
SW-1    Fas 0/2     170         S I    WS-C3560- Fas 0/16
SW-2    Fas 0/5     162         S I    WS-C3560- Fas 0/5
SW-2    Fas 0/6     162         S I    WS-C3560- Fas 0/6
```

Okay—we can see that I'm directly connected with a console cable to the SW-3 switch and also that SW-3 is directly connected to two other switches. However, do we really need the figure to draw out our network? We don't! CDP allows me to see who my directly connected neighbors are and gather information about them. From the SW-3 switch, we can see that there are two connections to SW-1 and two connections to SW-2. SW-3 connects to SW-1 with ports Fas 0/1 and Fas 0/2, and we have connections to SW-2 with local interfaces Fas 0/5 and Fas 0/6. Both the SW-1 and SW-2 switches are 3650 switches, and SW-1 is using ports Fas 0/15 and Fas 0/16 to connect to SW-3. SW-2 is using ports Fas 0/5 and Fas 0/6.

To sum this up, the device ID shows the configured hostname of the connected device, that the local interface is our interface, and the port ID is the remote devices' directly connected interface. Remember that all you get to view are directly connected devices!

Table 7.2 summarizes the information displayed by the show cdp neighbor command for each device.

**TABLE 7.2**  Output of the show cdp neighbors command

| Field | Description |
|---|---|
| Device ID | The hostname of the device directly connected. |
| Local Interface | The port or interface on which you are receiving the CDP packet. |
| Holdtime | The remaining amount of time the router will hold the information before discarding it if no more CDP packets are received. |
| Capability | The capability of the neighbor—the router, switch, or repeater. The capability codes are listed at the top of the command output. |
| Platform | The type of Cisco device directly connected. In the previous output, the SW-3 shows it's directly connected to two 3560 switches. |
| Port ID | The neighbor device's port or interface on which the CDP packets are multicast. |

It's imperative that you can look at the output of a show cdp neighbors command and decipher the information gained about the neighbor device's capability, whether it's a router or switch, the model number (platform), your port connecting to that device (local interface), and the port of the neighbor connecting to you (port ID).

Another command that will deliver the goods on neighbor information is the show cdp neighbors detail command (show cdp nei de for short). This command can be run on both routers and switches, and it displays detailed information about each device connected to the device you're running the command on. Check out the router output in Listing 7.1.

**Listing 7.1:** Showing CDP Neighbors

```
SW-3#sh cdp neighbors detail
-------------------------
Device ID: SW-1
Entry address(es):
  IP address: 10.100.128.10
Platform: cisco WS-C3560-24TS,  Capabilities: Switch IGMP
Interface: FastEthernet0/1,  Port ID (outgoing port): FastEthernet0/15
Holdtime : 137 sec


Version :
Cisco IOS Software, C3560 Software (C3560-IPSERVICESK9-M), Version 12.2(55)SE7,
RELEASE SOFTWARE (fc1)
Technical Support: http://www.cisco.com/techsupport
Copyright (c) 1986-2013 by Cisco Systems, Inc.
Compiled Mon 28-Jan-13 10:10 by prod_rel_team


advertisement version: 2
Protocol Hello:  OUI=0x00000C, Protocol ID=0x0112; payload len=27, value=00000000
FFFFFFFF010221FF000000000000001C575EC880FF0000
VTP Management Domain: 'NULL'
Native VLAN: 1
Duplex: full
Power Available TLV:


    Power request id: 0, Power management id: 1, Power available: 0, Power
management level: -1
Management address(es):
  IP address: 10.100.128.10
-------------------------
```

```
[ouput cut]


------------------------
Device ID: SW-2
Entry address(es):
  IP address: 10.100.128.9
Platform: cisco WS-C3560-8PC,  Capabilities: Switch IGMP
Interface: FastEthernet0/5,  Port ID (outgoing port): FastEthernet0/5
Holdtime : 129 sec


Version :
Cisco IOS Software, C3560 Software (C3560-IPBASE-M), Version 12.2(35)SE5, RELEASE
SOFTWARE (fc1)
Copyright (c) 1986-2007 by Cisco Systems, Inc.
Compiled Thu 19-Jul-07 18:15 by nachen


advertisement version: 2
Protocol Hello:  OUI=0x00000C, Protocol ID=0x0112; payload len=27, value=00000000
FFFFFFFF010221FF000000000000B41489D91880FF0000
VTP Management Domain: 'NULL'
Native VLAN: 1
Duplex: full
Power Available TLV:


    Power request id: 0, Power management id: 1, Power available: 0, Power
management level: -1
Management address(es):
  IP address: 10.100.128.9
[output cut]
```

So what's revealed here? First, we've been given the hostname and IP address of all directly connected devices. And in addition to the same information displayed by the show cdp neighbor command (see Table 7.2), the show cdp neighbor detail command tells us about the IOS version and IP address of the neighbor device—that's quite a bit!

The show cdp entry * command displays the same information as the show cdp neighbors detail command. There isn't any difference between these commands.

## Real World Scenario

### CDP Can Save Lives!

Karen has just been hired as a senior network consultant at a large hospital in Dallas, Texas, so she's expected to be able to take care of any problem that rears its ugly head. As if that weren't enough pressure, she also has to worry about the horrid possibility that people won't receive correct health care solutions—even the correct medications—if the network goes down. Talk about a potential life-or-death situation!

But Karen is confident and begins her job optimistically. Of course, it's not long before the network reveals that it has a few problems. Unfazed, she asks one of the junior administrators for a network map so she can troubleshoot the network. This person tells her that the old senior administrator, who she replaced, had them with him and now no one can find them. The sky begins to darken!

Doctors are calling every couple of minutes because they can't get the necessary information they need to take care of their patients. What should she do?

It's CDP to the rescue! And it's a gift that this hospital happens to be running Cisco routers and switches exclusively, because CDP is enabled by default on all Cisco devices. Karen is also in luck because the disgruntled former administrator didn't turn off CDP on any devices before he left!

So all Karen has to do now is to use the show cdp neighbor detail command to find all the information she needs about each device to help draw out the hospital network, bringing it back up to speed so the personnel who rely upon it can get on to the important business of saving lives!

The only snag for you nailing this in your own network is if you don't know the passwords of all those devices. Your only hope then is to somehow find out the access passwords or to perform password recovery on them.

So, use CDP—you never know when you may end up saving someone's life.

By the way, this is a true story!

# Documenting a Network Topology Using CDP

With that moving real-life scenario in mind, I'm now going to show you how to document a sample network by using CDP. You'll learn to determine the appropriate router types, interface types, and IP addresses of various interfaces using only CDP commands and the show running-config command. And you can only console into the Lab_A router to document the network. You'll have to assign any remote routers the next IP address in each range. We'll use a different figure for this example—Figure 7.6— to help us to complete the necessary documentation.

**FIGURE 7.6**    Documenting a network topology using CDP

In this output, you can see that you have a router with four interfaces: two Fast Ethernet and two serial. First, determine the IP addresses of each interface by using the show running-config command like this:

```
Lab_A#sh running-config
Building configuration...


Current configuration : 960 bytes
!
version 12.2
service timestamps debug uptime
service timestamps log uptime
no service password-encryption
!
hostname Lab_A
!
ip subnet-zero
!
!
interface FastEthernet0/0
 ip address 192.168.21.1 255.255.255.0
 duplex auto
!
```

```
interface FastEthernet0/1
 ip address 192.168.18.1 255.255.255.0
 duplex auto
!
interface Serial0/0
ip address 192.168.23.1 255.255.255.0
!
interface Serial0/1
ip address 192.168.28.1 255.255.255.0
!
ip classless
!
line con 0
line aux 0
line vty 0 4
!
end
```

With this step completed, you can now write down the IP addresses of the Lab_A router's four interfaces. Next, you must determine the type of device on the other end of each of these interfaces. It's easy—just use the show cdp neighbors command:

```
Lab_A#sh cdp neighbors
Capability Codes: R - Router, T - Trans Bridge, B - Source Route Bridge
S - Switch, H - Host, I - IGMP, r - Repeater
Device ID    Local Intrfce    Holdtme    Capability Platform  Port ID
Lab_B        Fas 0/0          178        R          2501      E0
Lab_C        Fas 0/1          137        R          2621      Fa0/0
Lab_D        Ser 0/0          178        R          2514      S1
Lab_E        Ser 0/1          137        R          2620      S0/1
```

Wow—looks like we're connected to some old routers! But it's not our job to judge. Our mission is to draw out our network, so it's good that we've got some nice information to meet the challenge with now. By using both the show running-config and show cdp neighbors commands, we know about all the IP addresses of the Lab_A router, the types of routers connected to each of the Lab_A router's links, and all the interfaces of the remote routers.

Now that we're equipped with all the information gathered via show running-config and show cdp neighbors, we can accurately create the topology in Figure 7.7.

If we needed to, we could've also used the show cdp neighbors detail command to view the neighbor's IP addresses. But since we know the IP addresses of each link on the Lab_A router, we already know what the next available IP address is going to be.

**FIGURE 7.7**   Network topology documented

## Link Layer Discovery Protocol (LLDP)

Before moving on from CDP, I want to tell you about a nonproprietary discovery protocol that provides pretty much the same information as CDP but works in multi-vendor networks.

The IEEE created a new standardized discovery protocol called 802.1AB for Station and Media Access Control Connectivity Discovery. We'll just call it *Link Layer Discovery Protocol (LLDP)*.

LLDP defines basic discovery capabilities, but it was also enhanced to specifically address the voice application, and this version is called LLDP-MED (Media Endpoint Discovery). It's good to remember that LLDP and LLDP-MED are not compatible.

You can find out more about these protocols at these two locations:

`www.cisco.com/en/US/docs/ios/cether/configuration/guide/ce_lldp-med.html`

`www.cisco.com/en/US/technologies/tk652/tk701/technologies_white_`
`paper0900aecd804cd46d.html`

But it's probably easier to go to `www.cisco.com` and search on LLDP than type in the URLs above.

# Using Telnet

As part of the TCP/IP protocol suite, *Telnet* is a virtual terminal protocol that allows you to make connections to remote devices, gather information, and run programs.

After your routers and switches are configured, you can use the Telnet program to reconfigure and/or check up on them without using a console cable. You run the Telnet program by typing **telnet** from any command prompt (Windows or Cisco), but you need to have VTY passwords set on the IOS devices for this to work.

Remember, you can't use CDP to gather information about routers and switches that aren't directly connected to your device. But you can use the Telnet application to connect to your neighbor devices and then run CDP on those remote devices to get information on them.

You can issue the `telnet` command from any router or switch prompt. Below, I'm trying to telnet from switch 1 to switch 3:

```
SW-1#telnet 10.100.128.8
Trying 10.100.128.8 ... Open


Password required, but none set


[Connection to 10.100.128.8 closed by foreign host]
```

Oops—clearly, I didn't set my passwords—how embarrassing! Remember that the VTY ports are default configured as `login`, meaning that we have to either set the VTY passwords or use the no `login` command. If you need to review the process of setting passwords, take a quick look back in Chapter 6, "Cisco's Internetworking Operating System (IOS)."

If you can't telnet into a device, it could be that the password on the remote device hasn't been set. It's also quite possible that an access control list is filtering the Telnet session.

On a Cisco device, you don't need to use the `telnet` command; you can just type in an IP address from a command prompt and the router will assume that you want to telnet to the device. Here's how that looks using just the IP address:

```
SW-1#10.100.128.8
Trying 10.100.128.8... Open


Password required, but none set


[Connection to 10.100.128.8 closed by foreign host]
SW-1#
```

Now would be a great time to set those VTY passwords on the SW-3 that I want to telnet into. Here's what I did on the switch named SW-3:

```
SW-3(config)#line vty 0 15
SW-3(config-line)#login
SW-3(config-line)#password telnet
SW-3(config-line)#login
SW-3(config-line)#^Z
```

Now let's try this again. This time, I'm connecting to SW-3 from the SW-1 console:

```
SW-1#10.100.128.8
Trying 10.100.128.8 ... Open


User Access Verification


Password:
SW-3>
```

Remember that the VTY password is the user-mode password, not the enable-mode password. Watch what happens when I try to go into privileged mode after telnetting into the switch:

```
SW-3>en
% No password set
SW-3>
```

It's totally slamming the door in my face, which happens to be a really nice security feature! After all, you don't want just anyone telnetting into your device and typing the enable command to get into privileged mode now, do you? You've got to set your enable-mode password or enable secret password to use Telnet to configure remote devices.

 When you telnet into a remote device, you won't see console messages by default. For example, you will not see debugging output. To allow console messages to be sent to your Telnet session, use the `terminal monitor` command.

Using the next group of examples, I'll show you how to telnet into multiple devices simultaneously as well as how to use hostnames instead of IP addresses.

## Telnetting into Multiple Devices Simultaneously

If you telnet to a router or switch, you can end the connection by typing **exit** at any time. But what if you want to keep your connection to a remote device going while still coming back to your original router console? To do that, you can press the Ctrl+Shift+6 key combination, release it, and then press X.

Here's an example of connecting to multiple devices from my SW-1 console:

```
SW-1#10.100.128.8
Trying 10.100.128.8... Open
```

```
User Access Verification


Password:
SW-3>Ctrl+Shift+6
SW-1#
```

Here you can see that I telnetted to SW-1 and then typed the password to enter user mode. Next, I pressed Ctrl+Shift+6, then X, but you won't see any of that because it doesn't show on the screen output. Notice that my command prompt now has me back at the SW-1 switch.

Now let's run through some verification commands.

## Checking Telnet Connections

If you want to view the connections from your router or switch to a remote device, just use the show sessions command. In this case, I've telnetted into both the SW-3 and SW-2 switches from SW1:

```
SW-1#sh sessions
Conn Host          Address         Byte  Idle Conn Name
   1 10.100.128.9  10.100.128.9    0          10.100.128.9
*  2 10.100.128.8  10.100.128.8    0          10.100.128.8
SW-1#
```

See that asterisk (*) next to connection 2? It means that session 2 was the last session I connected to. You can return to your last session by pressing Enter twice. You can also return to any session by typing the number of the connection and then Enter.

## Checking Telnet Users

You can reveal all active consoles and VTY ports in use on your router with the show users command:

```
SW-1#sh users
    Line        User        Host(s)         Idle      Location
*   0 con 0                 10.100.128.9    00:00:01
                            10.100.128.8    00:01:06
```

In the command's output, con represents the local console, and we can see that the console session is connected to two remote IP addresses—in other words, two devices.

## Closing Telnet Sessions

You can end Telnet sessions a few different ways. Typing exit or disconnect are probably the two quickest and easiest.

To end a session from a remote device, use the `exit` command:

```
SW-3>exit
[Connection to 10.100.128.8 closed by foreign host]
SW-1#
```

To end a session from a local device, use the `disconnect` command:

```
SW-1#sh session
Conn Host                Address          Byte  Idle Conn Name
   *2 10.100.128.9    10.100.128.9      0            10.100.128.9
SW-1#disconnect ?
   <2-2>  The number of an active network connection
   qdm    Disconnect QDM web-based clients
   ssh    Disconnect an active SSH connection
SW-1#disconnect 2
Closing connection to 10.100.128.9 [confirm][enter]
```

In this example, I used session number 2 because that was the connection I wanted to conclude. As demonstrated, you can use the `show sessions` command to see the connection number.

# Resolving Hostnames

If you want to use a hostname instead of an IP address to connect to a remote device, the device that you're using to make the connection must be able to translate the hostname to an IP address.

There are two ways to resolve hostnames to IP addresses. The first is by building a host table on each router, and the second is to build a Domain Name System (DNS) server. The latter method is similar to creating a dynamic host table assuming that you're dealing with dynamic DNS.

## Building a Host Table

An important factor to remember is that although a host table provides name resolution, it does that only on the specific router that it was built upon. The command you use to build a host table on a router looks this:

```
ip host host_name [tcp_port_number] ip_address
```

The default is TCP port number 23, but you can create a session using Telnet with a different TCP port number if you want. You can also assign up to eight IP addresses to a hostname.

Here's how I configured a host table on the SW-1 switch with two entries to resolve the names for the SW-2 and SW-3:

```
SW-1#config t
SW-1(config)#ip host SW-2 ?
  <0-65535>   Default telnet port number
  A.B.C.D     Host IP address
  additional  Append addresses


SW-1(config)#ip host SW-2 10.100.128.9
SW-1(config)#ip host SW-3 10.100.128.8
```

Notice that I can just keep adding IP addresses to reference a unique host, one after another. To view our newly built host table, I'll just use the show hosts command:

```
SW-1(config)#do sho hosts
Default domain is not set
Name/address lookup uses domain service
Name servers are 255.255.255.255


Codes: u - unknown, e - expired, * - OK, ? - revalidate
       t - temporary, p - permanent


Host              Port  Flags      Age Type  Address(es)
SW-3              None  (perm, OK)  0   IP    10.100.128.8
SW-2              None  (perm, OK)  0   IP    10.100.128.9
```

In this output, you can see the two hostnames plus their associated IP addresses. The perm in the Flags column means that the entry has been manually configured. If it read temp, it would be an entry that was resolved by DNS.

The show hosts command provides information on temporary DNS entries and permanent name-to-address mappings created using the ip host command.

To verify that the host table resolves names, try typing the hostnames at a router prompt. Remember that if you don't specify the command, the router will assume you want to telnet.

In the following example, I'll use the hostnames to telnet into the remote devices and press Ctrl+Shift+6 and then X to return to the main console of the SW-1 router:

```
SW-1#sw-3
Trying SW-3 (10.100.128.8)... Open
```

```
User Access Verification
```

```
Password:
SW-3> Ctrl+Shift+6
SW-1#
```

It worked—I successfully used entries in the host table to create a session to the SW-3 device by using the name to telnet into it. And just so you know, names in the host table are not case-sensitive.

Notice that the entries in the following show sessions output now display the hostnames and IP addresses instead of just the IP addresses:

```
SW-1#sh sessions
Conn Host              Address        Byte  Idle Conn Name
   1 SW-3              10.100.128.8   0     1    SW-3
*  2 SW-2              10.100.128.9   0     1    SW-2
SW-1#
```

If you want to remove a hostname from the table, all you need to do is use the no ip host command like this:

```
SW-1(config)#no ip host SW-3
```

The drawback to going with this host table method is that you must create a host table on each router in order to be able to resolve names. So clearly, if you have a whole bunch of routers and want to resolve names, using DNS is a much better option!

## Using DNS to Resolve Names

If you have a lot of devices, you don't want to create a host table in each one of them unless you've also got a lot of time to waste. Since most of us don't, I highly recommend using a DNS server to resolve hostnames instead!

Anytime a Cisco device receives a command it doesn't understand, it will try to resolve it through DNS by default. Watch what happens when I type the special command todd at a Cisco router prompt:

```
SW-1#todd
Translating "todd"...domain server (255.255.255.255)
% Unknown command or computer name, or unable to find
  computer address
SW-1#
```

Because it doesn't know my name or the command I'm trying to type, it tries to resolve this through DNS. This is really annoying for two reasons: first, because it doesn't know my name <grin>, and second, because I need to hang out and wait for the name lookup to time out. You can get around this and prevent a time-consuming DNS lookup by using the no ip domain-lookup command on your router from global configuration mode.

So if you have a DNS server on your network, you'll need to add a few commands to make DNS name resolution work well for you:

- The first command is ip domain-lookup, which is turned on by default. It needs to be entered only if you previously turned it off with the no ip domain-lookup command. The command can be used without the hyphen as well with the syntax ip domain lookup.

- The second command is ip name-server. This sets the IP address of the DNS server. You can enter the IP addresses of up to six servers.

- The last command is ip domain-name. Although this command is optional, you really set it because it appends the domain name to the hostname you type in. Since DNS uses a fully qualified domain name (FQDN) system, you must have a second-level DNS name, in the form *domain.com*.

Here's an example of using these three commands:

```
SW-1#config t
SW-1(config)#ip domain-lookup
SW-1(config)#ip name-server ?
  A.B.C.D  Domain server IP address (maximum of 6)
SW-1(config)#ip name-server 4.4.4.4
SW-1(config)#ip domain-name lammle.com
SW-1(config)#^Z
```

After the DNS configurations have been set, you can test the DNS server by using a hostname to ping or telnet into a device like this:

```
SW-1#ping SW-3
Translating "SW-3"...domain server (4.4.4.4) [OK]
Type escape sequence to abort.
Sending 5, 100-byte ICMP Echos to 10.100.128.8, timeout is
  2 seconds:
!!!!!
Success rate is 100 percent (5/5), round-trip min/avg/max
  = 28/31/32 ms
```

Notice that the router uses the DNS server to resolve the name.

After a name is resolved using DNS, use the show hosts command to verify that the device cached this information in the host table. If I hadn't used the ip domain-name lammle.com command, I would have needed to type in ping sw-3.lammle.com, which is kind of a hassle.

## Real World Scenario

### Should You Use a Host Table or a DNS Server?

Karen has finally finished mapping her network via CDP and the hospital's staff is now much happier. But Karen is still having a difficult time administering the network because she has to look at the network drawing to find an IP address every time she needs to telnet to a remote router.

Karen was thinking about putting host tables on each router, but with literally hundreds of routers, this is a daunting task and not the best solution. What should she do?

Most networks have a DNS server now anyway, so adding a hundred or so hostnames into it would be much easier—certainly better than adding these hostnames to each and every router! She can just add the three commands on each router and voilà—she's resolving names!

Using a DNS server makes it easy to update any old entries too. Remember, for even one little change, her alternative would be to go to each and every router to manually update its table if she's using static host tables.

Keep in mind that this has nothing to do with name resolution on the network and nothing to do with what a host on the network is trying to accomplish. You only use this method when you're trying to resolve names from the router console.

# Checking Network Connectivity and Troubleshooting

You can use the ping and traceroute commands to test connectivity to remote devices, and both of them can be used with many protocols, not just IP. But don't forget that the show ip route command is a great troubleshooting command for verifying your routing table and the show interfaces command will reveal the status of each interface to you.

I'm not going to get into the show interfaces commands here because we've already been over that in Chapter 6. But I am going to go over both the debug command and the show processes command that come in very handy when you need to troubleshoot a router.

## Using the *ping* Command

So far, you've seen lots of examples of pinging devices to test IP connectivity and name resolution using the DNS server. To see all the different protocols that you can use with the *Ping* program, type **ping ?**:

```
SW-1#ping ?
  WORD  Ping destination address or hostname
  clns  CLNS echo
  ip    IP echo
  ipv6  IPv6 echo
  tag   Tag encapsulated IP echo
  <cr>
```

The ping output displays the minimum, average, and maximum times it takes for a ping packet to find a specified system and return. Here's an example:

```
SW-1#ping SW-3
Translating "SW-3"...domain server (4.4.4.4) [OK]
Type escape sequence to abort.
Sending 5, 100-byte ICMP Echos to 10.100.128.8, timeout is
  2 seconds:
!!!!!
Success rate is 100 percent (5/5), round-trip min/avg/max
  = 28/31/32 ms
```

This output tells us that the DNS server was used to resolve the name, and the device was pinged in a minimum of 28 ms (milliseconds), an average of 31 ms, and up to 32 ms. This network has some latency!

**NOTE**    The ping command can be used in user and privileged mode but not configuration mode!

## Using the *traceroute* Command

*Traceroute*—the traceroute command, or trace for short—shows the path a packet takes to get to a remote device. It uses time to live (TTL), time-outs, and ICMP error messages to outline the path a packet takes through an internetwork to arrive at a remote host.

The trace command, which you can deploy from either user mode or privileged mode, allows you to figure out which router in the path to an unreachable network host should be examined more closely as the probable cause of your network's failure.

To see the protocols that you can use with the traceroute command, type **traceroute ?**:

```
SW-1#traceroute ?
  WORD       Trace route to destination address or hostname
  appletalk  AppleTalk Trace
  clns       ISO CLNS Trace
  ip         IP Trace
  ipv6       IPv6 Trace
  ipx        IPX Trace
  mac        Trace Layer2 path between 2 endpoints
  oldvines   Vines Trace (Cisco)
  vines      Vines Trace (Banyan)
  <cr>
```

The traceroute command shows the hop or hops that a packet traverses on its way to a remote device.

Do not get confused! You can't use the tracert command; that's a Windows command. For a router, use the traceroute command!

Here's an example of using tracert on a Windows prompt—notice that the command is tracert, not traceroute:

```
C:\>tracert www.whitehouse.gov


Tracing route to a1289.g.akamai.net [69.8.201.107]
over a maximum of 30 hops:


  1     *        *        *       Request timed out.
  2    53 ms    61 ms    53 ms   hlrn-dsl-gw15-207.hlrn.qwest.net [207.225.112.207]
  3    53 ms    55 ms    54 ms   hlrn-agw1.inet.qwest.net [71.217.188.113]
  4    54 ms    53 ms    54 ms   hlr-core-01.inet.qwest.net [205.171.253.97]
  5    54 ms    53 ms    54 ms   apa-cntr-01.inet.qwest.net [205.171.253.26]
  6    54 ms    53 ms    53 ms   63.150.160.34
  7    54 ms    54 ms    53 ms   www.whitehouse.gov [69.8.201.107]


Trace complete.
```

Okay, let's move on now and talk about how to troubleshoot your network using the debug command.

# Debugging

Debug is a useful troubleshooting command that's available from the privileged exec mode of Cisco IOS. It's used to display information about various router operations and the related traffic generated or received by the router, plus any error messages.

Even though it's a helpful, informative tool, there are a few important facts that you need to know about it. Debug is regarded as a very high-overhead task because it can consume a huge amount of resources and the router is forced to process-switch the packets being debugged. So you don't just use debug as a monitoring tool—it's meant to be used for a short period of time and only as a troubleshooting tool. It's highly useful for discovering some truly significant facts about both working and faulty software and/or hardware components, but remember to limit its use as the beneficial troubleshooting tool it's designed to be.

Because debugging output takes priority over other network traffic, and because the debug all command generates more output than any other debug command, it can severely diminish the router's performance—even render it unusable! Because of this, it's nearly always best to use more specific debug commands.

As you can see from the following output, you can't enable debugging from user mode, only privileged mode:

```
SW-1>debug ?
% Unrecognized command
SW-1>en
SW-1#debug ?
  aaa                 AAA Authentication, Authorization and Accounting
  access-expression   Boolean access expression
  adjacency           adjacency
  aim                 Attachment Information Manager
  all                 Enable all debugging
  archive             debug archive commands
  arp                 IP ARP and HP Probe transactions
  authentication      Auth Manager debugging
  auto                Debug Automation
  beep                BEEP debugging
  bgp                 BGP information
  bing                Bing(d) debugging
  call-admission      Call admission control
  cca                 CCA activity
  cdp                 CDP information
  cef                 CEF address family independent operations
  cfgdiff             debug cfgdiff commands
  cisp                CISP debugging
  clns                CLNS information
```

```
cluster              Cluster information
cmdhd                Command Handler
cns                  CNS agents
condition            Condition
configuration        Debug Configuration behavior
[output cut]
```

If you've got the freedom to pretty much take out a router or switch and you really want to have some fun with debugging, use the debug all command:

```
Sw-1#debug all
```

```
This may severely impact network performance. Continue? (yes/[no]):yes
All possible debugging has been turned on
```

At this point my switch overloaded and crashed and I had to reboot it. Try this on your switch at work and see if you get the same results. Just kidding!

To disable debugging on a router, just use the command no in front of the debug command:

```
SW-1#no debug all
```

I typically just use the undebug all command since it is so easy when using the shortcut:

```
SW-1#un all
```

Remember that instead of using the debug all command, it's usually a much better idea to use specific commands—and only for short periods of time. Here's an example:

```
S1#debug ip icmp
ICMP packet debugging is on
S1#ping 192.168.10.17
```

```
Type escape sequence to abort.
Sending 5, 100-byte ICMP Echos to 192.168.10.17, timeout is 2 seconds:
!!!!!
Success rate is 100 percent (5/5), round-trip min/avg/max = 1/1/1 ms
S1#
1w4d: ICMP: echo reply sent, src 192.168.10.17, dst 192.168.10.17
1w4d: ICMP: echo reply rcvd, src 192.168.10.17, dst 192.168.10.17
1w4d: ICMP: echo reply sent, src 192.168.10.17, dst 192.168.10.17
1w4d: ICMP: echo reply rcvd, src 192.168.10.17, dst 192.168.10.17
1w4d: ICMP: echo reply sent, src 192.168.10.17, dst 192.168.10.17
1w4d: ICMP: echo reply rcvd, src 192.168.10.17, dst 192.168.10.17
```

```
1w4d: ICMP: echo reply sent, src 192.168.10.17, dst 192.168.10.17
1w4d: ICMP: echo reply rcvd, src 192.168.10.17, dst 192.168.10.17
1w4d: ICMP: echo reply sent, src 192.168.10.17, dst 192.168.10.17
1w4d: ICMP: echo reply rcvd, src 192.168.10.17, dst 192.168.10.17
SW-1#un all
```

I'm sure you can see that the debug command is one powerful command. And because of this, I'm also sure you realize that before you use any of the debugging commands, you should make sure you check the CPU utilization capacity of your router. This is important because in most cases, you don't want to negatively impact the device's ability to process the packets on your internetwork. You can determine a specific router's CPU utilization information by using the show processes command.

Remember, when you telnet into a remote device, you will not see console messages by default! For example, you will not see debugging output. To allow console messages to be sent to your Telnet session, use the terminal monitor command.

## Using the *show processes* Command

As I've said, you've really got to be careful when using the debug command on your devices. If your router's CPU utilization is consistently at 50 percent or more, it's probably not a good idea to type in the debug all command unless you want to see what a router looks like when it crashes!

So what other approaches can you use? Well, the show processes (or show processes cpu) is a good tool for determining a given router's CPU utilization. Plus, it'll give you a list of active processes along with their corresponding process ID, priority, scheduler test (status), CPU time used, number of times invoked, and so on. Lots of great stuff! Plus, this command is super handy when you want to evaluate your router's performance and CPU utilization and are otherwise tempted to reach for the debug command!

Okay—what do you see in the following output? The first line shows the CPU utilization output for the last 5 seconds, 1 minute, and 5 minutes. The output provides 5%/0% in front of the CPU utilization for the last 5 seconds: The first number equals the total utilization, and the second one indicates the utilization due to interrupt routines. Take a look:

```
SW-1#sh processes
CPU utilization for five seconds: 5%/0%; one minute: 7%; five minutes: 8%
 PID QTy       PC Runtime(ms)   Invoked   uSecs    Stacks   TTY Process
   1 Cwe  29EBC58      0           22        0   5236/6000     0 Chunk Manager
   2 Csp  1B9CF10    241       206881        1   2516/3000     0 Load Meter
   3 Hwe  1F108D0      0            1        0   8768/9000     0 Connection Mgr
   4 Lst  29FA5C4 9437909     454026    20787   5540/6000     0 Check heaps
```

| | | | | | | | | |
|---|---|---|---|---|---|---|---|---|
| 5 | Cwe | 2A02468 | 0 | 2 | 0 | 5476/6000 | 0 | Pool Manager |
| 6 | Mst | 1E98F04 | 0 | 2 | 0 | 5488/6000 | 0 | Timers |
| 7 | Hwe | 13EB1B4 | 3686 | 101399 | 36 | 5740/6000 | 0 | Net Input |
| 8 | Mwe | 13BCD84 | 0 | 1 | 0 | 23668/24000 | 0 | Crash writer |
| 9 | Mwe | 1C591B4 | 4346 | 53691 | 80 | 4896/6000 | 0 | ARP Input |
| 10 | Lwe | 1DA1504 | 0 | 1 | 0 | 5760/6000 | 0 | CEF MIB API |
| 11 | Lwe | 1E76ACC | 0 | 1 | 0 | 5764/6000 | 0 | AAA_SERVER_DEADT |
| 12 | Mwe | 1E6F980 | 0 | 2 | 0 | 5476/6000 | 0 | AAA high-capacit |
| 13 | Mwe | 1F56F24 | 0 | 1 | 0 | 11732/12000 | 0 | Policy Manager [output |

cut]

So basically, the output from the show processes command reveals that our router is happily able to process debugging commands without being overloaded—nice!

# Summary

In this chapter, you learned how Cisco routers are configured and how to manage those configurations.

We covered the internal components of a router, including ROM, RAM, NVRAM, and flash.

Next, you found out how to back up and restore the configuration of a Cisco router and switch.

You also learned how to use CDP and Telnet to gather information about remote devices. Finally, you discovered how to resolve hostnames and use the ping and trace commands to test network connectivity as well as how to use the debug and show processes commands—well done!

# Exam Essentials

**Define the Cisco Router components.**   Describe the functions of the bootstrap, POST, ROM monitor, mini-IOS, RAM, ROM, flash memory, NVRAM, and the configuration register.

**Identify the steps in the router boot sequence.**   The steps in the boot sequence are POST, loading the IOS, and copying the startup configuration from NVRAM to RAM.

**Save the configuration of a router or switch.**   There are a couple of ways to do this, but the most common, as well as the most tested, method is copy running-config startup-config.

**Erase the configuration of a router or switch.**   Type the privileged-mode command erase startup-config and reload the router.

**Describe the value of CDP.**   Cisco Discovery Protocol can be used to help you document as well as troubleshoot your network.

**List the information provided by the output of the show cdp neighbors command.**   The show cdp neighbors command provides the following information: device ID, local interface, holdtime, capability, platform, and port ID (remote interface).

**Understand how to establish a Telnet session with multiple routers simultaneously.**   If you telnet to a router or switch, you can end the connection by typing exit at any time. However, if you want to keep your connection to a remote device but still come back to your original router console, you can press the Ctrl+Shift+6 key combination, release it, and then press X.

**Identify current Telnet sessions.**   The command show sessions will provide you with information about all the currently active sessions your router has with other routers.

**Build a static host table on a router.**   By using the global configuration command *ip host host_name ip_address*, you can build a static host table on your router. You can apply multiple IP addresses against the same host entry.

**Verify the host table on a router.**   You can verify the host table with the show hosts command.

**Describe the function of the ping command.**   Packet Internet Groper (ping) uses ICMP echo requests and ICMP echo replies to verify an active IP address on a network.

**Ping a valid host ID from the correct prompt.**   You can ping an IP address from a router's user mode or privileged mode but not from configuration mode, unless you use the do command. You must ping a valid address, such as 1.1.1.1.

# Written Lab 7

In this section, you'll complete the following labs to make sure you've got the information and concepts contained within them fully dialed in:

Lab 7.1: IOS Management

Lab 7.2: Router Memory

The answers to these labs can be found in Appendix A, "Answers to Written Labs."

## Written Lab 7.1: IOS Management

Write the answers to the following questions:

1. What is the command to copy the startup-config file to DRAM?

2. What command can you use to see the neighbor router's IP address from your router prompt?

3. What command can you use to see the hostname, local interface, platform, and remote port of a neighbor router?

4. What keystrokes can you use to telnet into multiple devices simultaneously?

5. What command will show you your active Telnet connections to neighbor and remote devices?

6. What command can you use to merge a backup configuration with the configuration in RAM?

7. What protocol can be used on a network to synchronize clock and date information?

8. What command is used by a router to forward a DHCP client request to a remote DHCP server?

9. What command enables your switch or router to receive clock and date information and synchronize with the NTP server?

10. Which NTP verification command will show the reference master for the client?

## Written Lab 7.2: Router Memory

Identify the location in a router where each of the following files is stored by default.

1. Cisco IOS

2. Bootstrap

3. Startup configuration

4. POST routine

5. Running configuration

**6.** ARP cache

**7.** Mini IOS

**8.** ROM Monitor

**9.** Routing tables

**10.** Packet buffers

# Hands-on Labs

To complete the labs in this section, you need at least one router or switch (three would be best) and at least one PC running as a TFTP server. TFTP server software must be installed and running on the PC. For this lab, it is also assumed that your PC and the Cisco devices are connected together with a switch and that all interfaces (PC NIC and router interfaces) are in the same subnet. You can alternately connect the PC directly to the router or connect the routers directly to one another (use a crossover cable in that case). Remember that the labs listed here were created for use with real routers but can easily be used with LammleSim IOS Version or Cisco's Packet Tracer program. Last, although it doesn't matter if you are using a switch or router in these labs, I'm just going to use my routers, but feel free to use your switch to go through these labs!

Here is a list of the labs in this chapter:

Lab 7.1: Backing Up the Router Configuration

Lab 7.2: Using the Cisco Discovery Protocol (CDP)

Lab 7.3: Using Telnet

Lab 7.4: Resolving Hostnames

## Hands-on Lab 7.1: Backing Up the Router Configuration

In this lab, you'll back up the router configuration:

**1.** Log into your router and go into privileged mode by typing **en** or **enable**.

**2.** Ping the TFTP server to make sure you have IP connectivity.

**3.** From RouterB, type **copy run tftp**.

**4.** When prompted, type the IP address of the TFTP server (for example, 172.16.30.2) and press Enter.

**5.** By default, the router will prompt you for a filename. The hostname of the router is followed by the suffix -confg (yes, I spelled that correctly). You can use any name you want.

```
Name of configuration file to write [RouterB-confg]?
```

Press Enter to accept the default name.

```
Write file RouterB-confg on host 172.16.30.2? [confirm]
```

Press Enter to confirm.

## Hands-on Lab 7.2: Using the Cisco Discovery Protocol (CDP)

CDP is an important objective for the Cisco exams. Please go through this lab and use CDP as much as possible during your studies.

1. Log into your router and go into privileged mode by typing **en** or **enable**.

2. From the router, type **sh cdp** and press Enter. You should see that CDP packets are being sent out to all active interfaces every 60 seconds and the holdtime is 180 seconds (these are the defaults).

3. To change the CDP update frequency to 90 seconds, type **cdp timer 90** in global configuration mode.

   ```
   Router#config t
   Enter configuration commands, one per line.  End with
     CNTL/Z.
   Router(config)#cdp timer ?
     <5-900>  Rate at which CDP packets are sent (in sec)
   Router(config)#cdp timer 90
   ```

4. Verify that your CDP timer frequency has changed by using the command **show cdp** in privileged mode.

   ```
   Router#sh cdp
   Global CDP information:
   Sending CDP packets every 90 seconds
   Sending a holdtime value of 180 seconds
   ```

5. Now use CDP to gather information about neighbor routers. You can get the list of available commands by typing **sh cdp ?**.

   ```
   Router#sh cdp ?
     entry     Information for specific neighbor entry
     interface CDP interface status and configuration
     neighbors CDP neighbor entries
   ```

```
traffic    CDP statistics
<cr>
```

6. Type **sh cdp int** to see the interface information plus the default encapsulation used by the interface. It also shows the CDP timer information.

7. Type **sh cdp entry *** to see complete CDP information received from all devices.

8. Type **show cdp neighbors** to gather information about all connected neighbors. (You should know the specific information output by this command.)

9. Type **show cdp neighbors detail**. Notice that it produces the same output as show cdp entry *.

## Hands-on Lab 7.3: Using Telnet

Secure Shell was covered in Chapter 6, which is what you should use for remote access into a Cisco device. However, the Cisco objectives cover telnet configuration, so let's do a lab on telnet!

1. Log into your router and go into privileged mode by typing **en** or **enable**.

2. From RouterA, telnet into your remote router (RouterB) by typing **telnet *ip_address*** from the command prompt. Type **exit** to disconnect.

3. Now type in RouterB's IP address from RouterA's command prompt. Notice that the router automatically tries to telnet to the IP address you specified. You can use the telnet command or just type in the IP address.

4. From RouterB, press Ctrl+Shift+6 and then X to return to RouterA's command prompt. Now telnet into your third router, RouterC. Press Ctrl+Shift+6 and then X to return to RouterA.

5. From RouterA, type **show sessions**. Notice your two sessions. You can press the number displayed to the left of the session and press Enter twice to return to that session. The asterisk shows the default session. You can press Enter twice to return to that session.

6. Go to the session for your RouterB. Type **show users**. This shows the console connection and the remote connection. You can use the disconnect command to clear the session or just type **exit** from the prompt to close your session with RouterB.

7. Go to RouterC's console port by typing **show sessions** on the first router and using the connection number to return to RouterC. Type **show user** and notice the connection to your first router, RouterA.

8. Type **clear line *line_number*** to disconnect the Telnet session.

# Hands-on Lab 7.4: Resolving Hostnames

It's best to use a DNS server for name resolution, but you can also create a local hosts table to resolve names. Let's take a look.

1. Log into your router and go into privileged mode by typing **en** or **enable**.

2. From RouterA, type **todd** and press Enter at the command prompt. Notice the error you receive and the delay. The router is trying to resolve the hostname to an IP address by looking for a DNS server. You can turn this feature off by using the no ip domain-lookup command from global configuration mode.

3. To build a host table, you use the ip host command. From RouterA, add a host table entry for RouterB and RouterC by entering the following commands:

```
ip host routerb ip_address
ip host routerc ip_address
```

Here is an example:

```
ip host routerb 172.16.20.2
ip host routerc 172.16.40.2
```

4. Test your host table by typing **ping routerb** from the privileged mode prompt (not the config prompt).

```
RouterA#ping routerb
Type escape sequence to abort.
Sending 5, 100-byte ICMP Echos to 172.16.20.2, timeout
  is 2 seconds:
!!!!!
Success rate is 100 percent (5/5), round-trip
  min/avg/max = 4/4/4 ms
```

5. Test your host table by typing **ping routerc**.

```
RouterA#ping routerc
Type escape sequence to abort.
Sending 5, 100-byte ICMP Echos to 172.16.40.2, timeout
  is 2 seconds:
!!!!!
Success rate is 100 percent (5/5), round-trip
  min/avg/max = 4/6/8 ms
```

6. Telnet to RouterB and keep your session to RouterB open to RouterA by pressing Ctrl+Shift+6, then X.

7. Telnet to RouterC by typing **routerc** at the command prompt.

8. Return to RouterA and keep the session to RouterC open by pressing Ctrl+Shift+6, then X.

9. View the host table by typing **show hosts** and pressing Enter.

```
Default domain is not set
Name/address lookup uses domain service
Name servers are 255.255.255.255
Host              Flags      Age Type  Address(es)
routerb           (perm, OK) 0   IP    172.16.20.2
routerc           (perm, OK) 0   IP    172.16.40.2
```

# Review Questions

The following questions are designed to test your understanding of this chapter's material. For more information on how to get additional questions, please see this book's introduction.

The answers to these questions can be found in Appendix B, "Answers to Chapter Review Questions."

1. Which of the following is a standards-based protocol that works much like CDP?

   **A.** DHCP

   **B.** LLDP

   **C.** DDNS

   **D.** SSTP

2. Which command can be used to determine a router's capacity to generate debug output?

   **A.** `show version`

   **B.** `show controllers`

   **C.** `show processes cpu`

   **D.** `show memory`

3. You are troubleshooting a connectivity problem in your corporate network and want to isolate the problem. You suspect that a router on the route to an unreachable network is at fault. What IOS user exec command should you issue?

   **A.** `Router>ping`

   **B.** `Router>trace`

   **C.** `Router>show ip route`

   **D.** `Router>show interface`

   **E.** `Router>show cdp neighbors`

4. You copy a configuration from a network host to a router's RAM. The configuration looks correct, yet it is not working at all. What could the problem be?

   **A.** You copied the wrong configuration into RAM.

   **B.** You copied the configuration into flash memory instead.

   **C.** The copy did not override the `shutdown` command in running-config.

   **D.** The IOS became corrupted after the copy command was initiated.

**5.** In the following command, what does the IP address 10.10.10.254 refer to?

```
Router#config t
Router(config)#interface fa0/0
Router(config-if)#ip helper-address 10.10.10.254
```

   **A.** IP address of the ingress interface on the router

   **B.** IP address of the egress interface on the router

   **C.** IP address of the next hop on the path to the DHCP server

   **D.** IP address of the DHCP server

**6.** The corporate office sends you a new router to connect, but upon connecting the console cable, you see that there is already a configuration on the router. What should be done before a new configuration is entered in the router?

   **A.** RAM should be erased and the router restarted.

   **B.** Flash should be erased and the router restarted.

   **C.** NVRAM should be erased and the router restarted.

   **D.** The new configuration should be entered and saved.

**7.** What command can you use to determine the IP address of a directly connected neighbor?

   **A.** show cdp

   **B.** show cdp neighbors

   **C.** show cdp neighbors detail

   **D.** show neighbor detail

**8.** According to the output, what interface does SW-2 use to connect to SW-3?

```
SW-3#sh cdp neighbors
Capability Codes: R - Router, T - Trans Bridge, B - Source Route BridgeS -
Switch, H - Host, I - IGMP, r - Repeater, P - Phone, D - Remote, C - CVTA, M
- Two-port Mac Relay Device ID
Local Intrfce     Holdtme    Capability  Platform   Port ID
SW-1   Fas 0/1      170          S I      WS-C3560- Fas 0/15
SW-1   Fas 0/2      170          S I      WS-C3560- Fas 0/16
SW-2   Fas 0/5      162          S I      WS-C3560- Fas 0/2
```

   **A.** Fas 0/1

   **B.** Fas 0/16

   **C.** Fas 0/2

   **D.** Fas 0/5

**9.** What command can you use to determine the IP address of a directly connected neighbor?

   **A.** show cdp

   **B.** show cdp neighbors

   **C.** show cdp neighbors detail

   **D.** show neighbor detail

**10.** You save the configuration on a router with the copy running-config startup-config command and reboot the router. The router, however, comes up with a blank configuration. What can the problem be?

   **A.** You didn't boot the router with the correct command.

   **B.** NVRAM is corrupted.

   **C.** The configuration register setting is incorrect.

   **D.** The newly upgraded IOS is not compatible with the hardware of the router.

   **E.** The configuration you saved is not compatible with the hardware.

**11.** If you want to have more than one Telnet session open at the same time, what keystroke combination would you use?

   **A.** Tab+spacebar

   **B.** Ctrl+X, then 6

   **C.** Ctrl+Shift+X, then 6

   **D.** Ctrl+Shift+6, then X

**12.** You are unsuccessful in telnetting into a remote device from your switch, but you could telnet to the router earlier. However, you can still ping the remote device. What could the problem be? (Choose two.)

   **A.** IP addresses are incorrect.

   **B.** Access control list is filtering Telnet.

   **C.** There is a defective serial cable.

   **D.** The VTY password is missing.

**13.** What information is displayed by the show hosts command? (Choose two.)

   **A.** Temporary DNS entries

   **B.** The names of the routers created using the hostname command

   **C.** The IP addresses of workstations allowed to access the router

   **D.** Permanent name-to-address mappings created using the ip host command

   **E.** The length of time a host has been connected to the router via Telnet

**14.** Which three commands can be used to check LAN connectivity problems on a switch? (Choose three.)

    **A.** show interfaces

    **B.** show ip route

    **C.** tracert

    **D.** ping

    **E.** dns lookups

**15.** You telnet to a router and make your necessary changes; now you want to end the Telnet session. What command do you type in?

    **A.** close

    **B.** disable

    **C.** disconnect

    **D.** exit

**16.** You telnet into a remote device and type debug ip icmp, but no output from the debug command is seen. What could the problem be?

    **A.** You must type the show ip icmp command first.

    **B.** IP addressing on the network is incorrect.

    **C.** You must use the terminal monitor command.

    **D.** Debug output is sent only to the console.

**17.** You need to view console messages on a device to which you have connected through telnet. The command you need to execute to see these is _____.

**18.** You need to gather the IP address of a remote switch that is located in Hawaii. What can you do to find the address?

    **A.** Fly to Hawaii, console into the switch, then relax and have a drink with an umbrella in it.

    **B.** Issue the show ip route command on the router connected to the switch.

    **C.** Issue the show cdp neighbor command on the router connected to the switch.

    **D.** Issue the show ip arp command on the router connected to the switch.

    **E.** Issue the show cdp neighbors detail command on the router connected to the switch.

**19.** You need to configure all your routers and switches so they synchronize their clocks from one time source. What command will you type for each device?

    **A.** `clock synchronization` *ip_address*

    **B.** `ntp master` *ip_address*

    **C.** `sync ntp` *ip_address*

    **D.** `ntp server` *ip_address* `version` *number*

**20.** What two commands can you use to verify your NTP client?

    **A.** `show ntp server`

    **B.** `show ntp status`

    **C.** `show vtp status`

    **D.** `show ntp associations`

    **E.** `show clock source`

# Chapter

# 8

# IP Routing

## THE FOLLOWING ICND1 EXAM TOPICS ARE COVERED IN THIS CHAPTER:

✓ **IP Routing Technologies**

- Describe basic routing concepts
  - CEF
  - Packet forwarding
  - Router lookup process
- Configure and verify routing configuration for a static or default route given specific routing requirements
- Differentiate methods of routing and routing protocols
  - Static vs. Dynamic
  - Link State vs. Distance Vector
  - next hop
  - ip routing table
  - Passive interfaces

It's time now to turn our focus toward the core topic of the ubiquitous IP routing process. It's integral to networking because it pertains to all routers and configurations that use it, which is easily the lion's share. IP routing is basically the process of moving packets from one network to another network using routers. And by routers I mean Cisco routers, of course! However, the terms *router* and *layer 3 device* are interchangeable, and throughout this chapter when I use the term *router*, I am referring to any layer 3 device.

Before jumping into this chapter, I want to make sure you understand the difference between a *routing protocol* and a *routed protocol*. Routers use routing protocols to dynamically find all networks within the greater internetwork and to ensure that all routers have the same routing table. Routing protocols are also employed to determine the best path a packet should take through an internetwork to get to its destination most efficiently. RIP, RIPv2, EIGRP, and OSPF are great examples of the most common routing protocols.

Once all routers know about all networks, a routed protocol can be used to send user data (packets) through the established enterprise. Routed protocols are assigned to an interface and determine the method of packet delivery. Examples of routed protocols are IP and IPv6.

I'm going to discuss the RIP routing protocol in this chapter even though I know that it isn't included in any objective. We'll cover it anyway because it will help you gain a solid understanding of the routing process before we get into a study on the much more complex OSPF protocol in the next chapter. We'll also discuss RIP because you just never know when Cisco will toss in exam questions that include topics they haven't bothered to list as a bona fide objective either! So even though I want you to be prepared just in case, I'll promise to keep the RIP section reasonably short.

I'm pretty confident I don't have to underscore how crucial it is for you have this chapter's material down to a near instinctive level. IP routing is innately what Cisco routers do, and they do it very well, so having a firm grasp of the fundamentals and basics of this topic are vital if you want to excel during the exam and in a real-world networking environment as well!

In this chapter, I'm going to show you how to configure and verify IP routing with Cisco routers and guide you through these five key subjects:

- Routing basics
- The IP routing process
- Static routing
- Default routing
- Dynamic routing

We'll get into more the advanced aspects of dynamic routing next in Chapter 9, "Open Shortest Path First (OSPF)." But first, I want to nail down the basics of how packets actually move through an internetwork, so let's get started!

To find up-to-the-minute updates for this chapter, please see www.lammle.com/forum or the book's web page at www.sybex.com.

# Routing Basics

Once you create an internetwork by connecting your WANs and LANs to a router, you'll need to configure logical network addresses, like IP addresses, to all hosts on that internetwork for them to communicate successfully throughout it.

The term *routing* refers to taking a packet from one device and sending it through the network to another device on a different network. Routers don't really care about hosts—they only care about networks and the best path to each one of them. The logical network address of the destination host is key to get packets through a routed network. It's the hardware address of the host that's used to deliver the packet from a router and ensure it arrives at the correct destination host.

Routing is irrelevant if your network has no routers because their job is to route traffic to all the networks in your internetwork, but this is rarely the case! So here's an important list of the minimum factors a router must know to be able to affectively route packets:

- Destination address
- Neighbor routers from which it can learn about remote networks
- Possible routes to all remote networks
- The best route to each remote network
- How to maintain and verify routing information

The router learns about remote networks from neighboring routers or from an administrator. The router then builds a routing table, which is basically a map of the internetwork, and it describes how to find remote networks. If a network is directly connected, then the router already knows how to get to it.

But if a network isn't directly connected to the router, the router must use one of two ways to learn how to get to the remote network. The *static routing* method requires someone to hand-type all network locations into the routing table, which can be a pretty daunting task when used on all but the smallest of networks!

Conversely, when *dynamic routing* is used, a protocol on one router communicates with the same protocol running on neighboring routers. The routers then update each other about all the networks they know about and place this information into the routing table. If a change occurs in the network, the dynamic routing protocols automatically inform all routers about the event. If static routing is used, the administrator is responsible for updating all changes by hand onto all routers. Most people usually use a combination of dynamic and static routing to administer a large network.

Before we jump into the IP routing process, let's take a look at a very simple example that demonstrates how a router uses the routing table to route packets out of an interface. We'll be going into a more detailed study of the process soon, but I want to show you something called the "longest match rule" first. With it, IP will scan a routing table to find the longest match as compared to the destination address of a packet. Let's take a look at Figure 8.1 to get a picture of this process.

**FIGURE 8.1**   A simple routing example

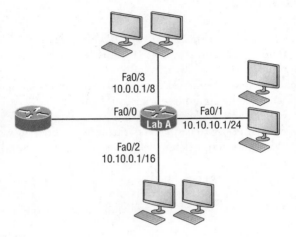

Figure 8.1 shows a simple network. Lab_A has four interfaces. Can you see which interface will be used to forward an IP datagram to a host with a destination IP address of 10.10.10.30?

By using the command show ip route on a router, we can see the routing table (map of the internetwork) that Lab_A has used to make its forwarding decisions:

```
Lab_A#sh ip route
Codes: L - local, C - connected, S - static,
[output cut]
        10.0.0.0/8 is variably subnetted, 6 subnets, 4 masks
C       10.0.0.0/8 is directly connected, FastEthernet0/3
L       10.0.0.1/32 is directly connected, FastEthernet0/3
C       10.10.0.0/16 is directly connected, FastEthernet0/2
L       10.10.0.1/32 is directly connected, FastEthernet0/2
C       10.10.10.0/24 is directly connected, FastEthernet0/1
L       10.10.10.1/32 is directly connected, FastEthernet0/1
S*      0.0.0.0/0 is directly connected, FastEthernet0/0
```

The C in the routing table output means that the networks listed are "directly connected," and until we add a routing protocol like RIPv2, OSPF, etc. to the routers in our internetwork, or enter static routes, only directly connected networks will show up in our routing table. But wait—what about that L in the routing table—that's new, isn't it? Yes it is, because in the new Cisco IOS 15 code, Cisco defines a different route, called a local route. Each has a /32 prefix defining a route just for the one address. So in this example, the router has relied upon these routes that list their own local IP addresses to more efficiently forward packets to the router itself.

So let's get back to the original question: By looking at the figure and the output of the routing table, can you determine what IP will do with a received packet that has a destination IP address of 10.10.10.30? The answer is that the router will packet-switch the packet to interface FastEthernet 0/1, which will frame the packet and then send it out on the network segment. Based upon the longest match rule, IP would look for 10.10.10.30, and if that isn't found in the table, then IP would search for 10.10.10.0, then 10.10.0.0, and so on until a route is discovered.

Here's another example: Based on the output of the next routing table, which interface will a packet with a destination address of 10.10.10.14 be forwarded from?

```
Lab_A#sh ip route
[output cut]
Gateway of last resort is not set
C    10.10.10.16/28 is directly connected, FastEthernet0/0
L    10.10.10.17/32 is directly connected, FastEthernet0/0
C    10.10.10.8/29 is directly connected, FastEthernet0/1
L    10.10.10.9/32 is directly connected, FastEthernet0/1
C    10.10.10.4/30 is directly connected, FastEthernet0/2
L    10.10.10.5/32 is directly connected, FastEthernet0/2
C    10.10.10.0/30 is directly connected, Serial 0/0
L    10.10.10.1/32 is directly connected, Serial0/0
```

To figure this out, look closely at the output until you see that the network is subnetted and each interface has a different mask. And I have to tell you—you just can't answer this question if you can't subnet! 10.10.10.14 would be a host in the 10.10.10.8/29 subnet that's connected to the FastEthernet0/1 interface. Don't freak if you're struggling and don't get this! Instead, just go back and reread Chapter 4, "Easy Subnetting," until it becomes clear to you.

# The IP Routing Process

The IP routing process is fairly simple and doesn't change, regardless of the size of your network. For a good example of this fact, I'll use Figure 8.2 to describe step-by-step what happens when Host_A wants to communicate with Host_B on a different network.

**FIGURE 8.2**   IP routing example using two hosts and one router

In Figure 8.2 a user on Host_A pinged Host_B's IP address. Routing doesn't get any simpler than this, but it still involves a lot of steps, so let's work through them now:

1. Internet Control Message Protocol (ICMP) creates an echo request payload, which is simply the alphabet in the data field.

2. ICMP hands that payload to Internet Protocol (IP), which then creates a packet. At a minimum, this packet contains an IP source address, an IP destination address, and a Protocol field with 01h. Don't forget that Cisco likes to use *0x* in front of hex characters, so this could also look like 0x01. This tells the receiving host to whom it should hand the payload when the destination is reached—in this example, ICMP.

3. Once the packet is created, IP determines whether the destination IP address is on the local network or a remote one.

4. Since IP has determined that this is a remote request, the packet must be sent to the default gateway so it can be routed to the remote network. The Registry in Windows is parsed to find the configured default gateway.

5. The default gateway of Host_A is configured to 172.16.10.1. For this packet to be sent to the default gateway, the hardware address of the router's interface Ethernet 0, which is configured with the IP address of 172.16.10.1, must be known. Why? So the packet can be handed down to the Data Link layer, framed, and sent to the router's interface that's connected to the 172.16.10.0 network. Because hosts communicate only via hardware addresses on the local LAN, it's important to recognize that for Host_A to communicate to Host_B, it has to send packets to the Media Access Control (MAC) address of the default gateway on the local network.

 MAC addresses are always local on the LAN and never go through and past a router.

6. Next, the Address Resolution Protocol (ARP) cache of the host is checked to see if the IP address of the default gateway has already been resolved to a hardware address.

   If it has, the packet is then free to be handed to the Data Link layer for framing. Remember that the hardware destination address is also handed down with that packet. To view the ARP cache on your host, use the following command:

```
C:\>arp -a
Interface: 172.16.10.2 --- 0x3
```

```
Internet Address        Physical Address      Type
172.16.10.1             00-15-05-06-31-b0     dynamic
```

If the hardware address isn't already in the ARP cache of the host, an ARP broadcast will be sent out onto the local network to search for the 172.16.10.1 hardware address. The router then responds to the request and provides the hardware address of Ethernet 0, and the host caches this address.

7. Once the packet and destination hardware address are handed to the Data Link layer, the LAN driver is used to provide media access via the type of LAN being used, which is Ethernet in this case. A frame is then generated, encapsulating the packet with control information. Within that frame are the hardware destination and source addresses plus, in this case, an Ether-Type field, which identifies the specific Network layer protocol that handed the packet to the Data Link layer. In this instance, it's IP. At the end of the frame is something called a Frame Check Sequence (FCS) field that houses the result of the cyclic redundancy check (CRC). The frame would look something like what I've detailed in Figure 8.3. It contains Host_A's hardware (MAC) address and the destination hardware address of the default gateway. It does not include the remote host's MAC address—remember that!

**FIGURE 8.3**   Frame used from Host_A to the Lab_A router when Host_B is pinged

| Destination MAC (router's E0 MAC address) | Source MAC (Host A MAC address) | Ether-Type field | Packet | FCS CRC |
|---|---|---|---|---|

8. Once the frame is completed, it's handed down to the Physical layer to be put on the physical medium (in this example, twisted-pair wire) one bit at a time.

9. Every device in the collision domain receives these bits and builds the frame. They each run a CRC and check the answer in the FCS field. If the answers don't match, the frame is discarded.

   ▪ If the CRC matches, then the hardware destination address is checked to see if it matches (which, in this example, is the router's interface Ethernet 0).

   ▪ If it's a match, then the Ether-Type field is checked to find the protocol used at the Network layer.

10. The packet is pulled from the frame, and what is left of the frame is discarded. The packet is handed to the protocol listed in the Ether-Type field—it's given to IP.

11. IP receives the packet and checks the IP destination address. Since the packet's destination address doesn't match any of the addresses configured on the receiving router itself, the router will look up the destination IP network address in its routing table.

12. The routing table must have an entry for the network 172.16.20.0 or the packet will be discarded immediately and an ICMP message will be sent back to the originating device with a destination network unreachable message.

**13.** If the router does find an entry for the destination network in its table, the packet is switched to the exit interface—in this example, interface Ethernet 1. The output below displays the Lab_A router's routing table. The C means "directly connected." No routing protocols are needed in this network since all networks (all two of them) are directly connected.

```
Lab_A>sh ip route
C       172.16.10.0 is directly connected,    Ethernet0
L       172.16.10.1/32 is directly connected, Ethernet0
C       172.16.20.0 is directly connected,    Ethernet1
L       172.16.20.1/32 is directly connected, Ethernet1
```

**14.** The router packet-switches the packet to the Ethernet 1 buffer.

**15.** The Ethernet 1 buffer needs to know the hardware address of the destination host and first checks the ARP cache.

- If the hardware address of Host_B has already been resolved and is in the router's ARP cache, then the packet and the hardware address will be handed down to the Data Link layer to be framed. Let's take a look at the ARP cache on the Lab_A router by using the show ip arp command:

```
Lab_A#sh ip arp
Protocol  Address      Age(min)  Hardware Addr   Type   Interface
Internet  172.16.20.1  -         00d0.58ad.05f4  ARPA   Ethernet1
Internet  172.16.20.2  3         0030.9492.a5dd  ARPA   Ethernet1
Internet  172.16.10.1  -         00d0.58ad.06aa  ARPA   Ethernet0
Internet  172.16.10.2  12        0030.9492.a4ac  ARPA   Ethernet0
```

  The dash (-) signifies that this is the physical interface on the router. This output shows us that the router knows the 172.16.10.2 (Host_A) and 172.16.20.2 (Host_B) hardware addresses. Cisco routers will keep an entry in the ARP table for 4 hours.

- Now if the hardware address hasn't already been resolved, the router will send an ARP request out E1 looking for the 172.16.20.2 hardware address. Host_B responds with its hardware address, and the packet and destination hardware addresses are then both sent to the Data Link layer for framing.

**16.** The Data Link layer creates a frame with the destination and source hardware addresses, Ether-Type field, and FCS field at the end. The frame is then handed to the Physical layer to be sent out on the physical medium one bit at a time.

**17.** Host_B receives the frame and immediately runs a CRC. If the result matches the information in the FCS field, the hardware destination address will be then checked next. If the host finds a match, the Ether-Type field is then checked to determine the protocol that the packet should be handed to at the Network layer—IP in this example.

18. At the Network layer, IP receives the packet and runs a CRC on the IP header. If that passes, IP then checks the destination address. Since a match has finally been made, the Protocol field is checked to find out to whom the payload should be given.

19. The payload is handed to ICMP, which understands that this is an echo request. ICMP responds to this by immediately discarding the packet and generating a new payload as an echo reply.

20. A packet is then created including the source and destination addresses, Protocol field, and payload. The destination device is now Host_A.

21. IP then checks to see whether the destination IP address is a device on the local LAN or on a remote network. Since the destination device is on a remote network, the packet needs to be sent to the default gateway.

22. The default gateway IP address is found in the Registry of the Windows device, and the ARP cache is checked to see if the hardware address has already been resolved from an IP address.

23. Once the hardware address of the default gateway is found, the packet and destination hardware addresses are handed down to the Data Link layer for framing.

24. The Data Link layer frames the packet of information and includes the following in the header:

   ▪ The destination and source hardware addresses

   ▪ The Ether-Type field with 0x0800 (IP) in it

   ▪ The FCS field with the CRC result in tow

25. The frame is now handed down to the Physical layer to be sent out over the network medium one bit at a time.

26. The router's Ethernet 1 interface receives the bits and builds a frame. The CRC is run, and the FCS field is checked to make sure the answers match.

27. Once the CRC is found to be okay, the hardware destination address is checked. Since the router's interface is a match, the packet is pulled from the frame and the Ether-Type field is checked to determine which protocol the packet should be delivered to at the Network layer.

28. The protocol is determined to be IP, so it gets the packet. IP runs a CRC check on the IP header first and then checks the destination IP address.

**NOTE**   IP does not run a complete CRC as the Data Link layer does—it only checks the header for errors.

Since the IP destination address doesn't match any of the router's interfaces, the routing table is checked to see whether it has a route to 172.16.10.0. If it doesn't have a route over to the destination network, the packet will be discarded immediately. I want to take a minute to point out that this is exactly where the source of confusion begins for a lot of administrators because when a ping fails, most people think the packet never reached the destination host. But as we see here, that's not *always* the case. All it takes for this to happen is for even just one of the remote routers to lack a route back to the originating host's network and—*poof!*—the packet is dropped on the *return trip*, not on its way to the host!

Just a quick note to mention that when (and if) the packet is lost on the way back to the originating host, you will typically see a request timed-out message because it is an unknown error. If the error occurs because of a known issue, such as if a route is not in the routing table on the way to the destination device, you will see a destination unreachable message. This should help you determine if the problem occurred on the way to the destination or on the way back.

29. In this case, the router happens to know how to get to network 172.16.10.0—the exit interface is Ethernet 0—so the packet is switched to interface Ethernet 0.

30. The router then checks the ARP cache to determine whether the hardware address for 172.16.10.2 has already been resolved.

31. Since the hardware address to 172.16.10.2 is already cached from the originating trip to Host_B, the hardware address and packet are then handed to the Data Link layer.

32. The Data Link layer builds a frame with the destination hardware address and source hardware address and then puts IP in the Ether-Type field. A CRC is run on the frame and the result is placed in the FCS field.

33. The frame is then handed to the Physical layer to be sent out onto the local network one bit at a time.

34. The destination host receives the frame, runs a CRC, checks the destination hardware address, then looks into the Ether-Type field to find out to whom to hand the packet.

35. IP is the designated receiver, and after the packet is handed to IP at the Network layer, it checks the Protocol field for further direction. IP finds instructions to give the payload to ICMP, and ICMP determines the packet to be an ICMP echo reply.

36. ICMP acknowledges that it has received the reply by sending an exclamation point (!) to the user interface. ICMP then attempts to send four more echo requests to the destination host.

You've just experienced Todd's 36 easy steps to understanding IP routing. The key point here is that if you had a much larger network, the process would be the *same*. It's just that the larger the internetwork, the more hops the packet goes through before it finds the destination host.

It's super-important to remember that when Host_A sends a packet to Host_B, the destination hardware address used is the default gateway's Ethernet interface. Why? Because frames can't be placed on remote networks—only local networks. So packets destined for remote networks must go through the default gateway.

Let's take a look at Host_A's ARP cache now:

```
C:\ >arp -a
Interface: 172.16.10.2 --- 0x3
  Internet Address     Physical Address        Type
  172.16.10.1          00-15-05-06-31-b0       dynamic
  172.16.20.1          00-15-05-06-31-b0       dynamic
```

Did you notice that the hardware (MAC) address that Host_A uses to get to Host_B is the Lab_A E0 interface? Hardware addresses are *always* local, and they never pass through a router's interface. Understanding this process is as important as air to you, so carve this into your memory!

## The Cisco Router Internal Process

One more thing before we get to testing your understanding of my 36 steps of IP routing. I think it's important to explain how a router forwards packets internally. For IP to look up a destination address in a routing table on a router, processing in the router must take place, and if there are tens of thousands of routes in that table, the amount of CPU time would be enormous. It results in a potentially overwhelming amount of overhead—think about a router at your ISP that has to calculate millions of packets per second and even subnet to find the correct exit interface! Even with the little network I'm using in this book, lots of processing would need to be done if there were actual hosts connected and sending data.

Cisco uses three types of packet-forwarding techniques.

**Process Switching**   This is actually how many people see routers to this day, because it's true that routers actually did perform this type of bare-bones packet switching back in 1990 when Cisco released their very first router. But those days when traffic demands were unimaginably light are long gone—not in today's networks! This process is now extremely complex and involves looking up every destination in the routing table and finding the exit interface for every packet. This is pretty much how I just explained the process in my 36 steps. But even though what I wrote was absolutely true in concept, the internal process requires much more than packet-switching technology today because of the millions of packets per second that must now be processed. So Cisco came up with some other technologies to help with the "big process problem."

**Fast Switching**   This solution was created to make the slow performance of process switching faster and more efficient. Fast-switching uses a cache to store the most recently used destinations so that lookups are not required for every packet. By caching the exit interface of the destination device, as well as the layer 2 header, performance was dramatically improved, but as our networks evolved with the need for even more speed, Cisco created yet another technology!

**Cisco Express Forwarding (CEF)**   This is Cisco's newer creation, and it's the default packet-forwarding method used on all the latest Cisco routers. CEF makes many different cache tables to help improve performance and is change triggered, not packet triggered. Translated, this means that when the network topology changes, the cache changes along with it.

## Testing Your IP Routing Understanding

Since understanding IP routing is super-important, it's time for that little test I talked about earlier on how well you've got the IP routing process down so far. I'm going to do that by having you look at a couple of figures and answer some very basic IP routing questions based upon them.

Figure 8.4 shows a LAN connected to RouterA that's connected via a WAN link to RouterB. RouterB has a LAN connected with an HTTP server attached.

**FIGURE 8.4**   IP routing example 1

The critical information you want to obtain by looking at this figure is exactly how IP routing will occur in this example. Let's determine the characteristics of a frame as it leaves HostA. Okay—we'll cheat a bit. I'll give you the answer, but then you should go back over the figure and see if you can answer example 2 without looking at my three-step answer!

1. The destination address of a frame from HostA would be the MAC address of Router A's Fa0/0 interface.

2. The destination address of a packet would be the IP address of the HTTP server's network interface card (NIC).

3. The destination port number in the segment header would be 80.

That was a pretty simple, straightforward scenario. One thing to remember is that when multiple hosts are communicating to a server using HTTP, they must all use a different source port number. The source and destination IP addresses and port numbers are how the server keeps the data separated at the Transport layer.

Okay—let's complicate matters by adding another device into the network and then see if you can find the answers. Figure 8.5 shows a network with only one router but two switches.

**FIGURE 8.5** IP routing example 2

The key thing to understand about the IP routing process in this scenario is what happens when HostA sends data to the HTTPS server? Here's your answer:

1. The destination address of a frame from HostA would be the MAC address of RouterA's Fa0/0 interface.

2. The destination address of a packet is the IP address of the HTTPS server's network interface card (NIC).

3. The destination port number in the segment header will have a value of 443.

Did you notice that the switches weren't used as either a default gateway or any other destination? That's because switches have nothing to do with routing. I wonder how many of you chose the switch as the default gateway (destination) MAC address for HostA? If you did, don't feel bad—just take another look to see where you went wrong and why. It's very important to remember that the destination MAC address will always be the router's interface—if your packets are destined for outside the LAN, as they were in these last two examples!

Before moving on into some of the more advanced aspects of IP routing, let's look at another issue. Take a look at the output of this router's routing table:

```
Corp#sh ip route
[output cut]
R    192.168.215.0 [120/2] via 192.168.20.2, 00:00:23, Serial0/0
R    192.168.115.0 [120/1] via 192.168.20.2, 00:00:23, Serial0/0
R    192.168.30.0 [120/1] via 192.168.20.2, 00:00:23, Serial0/0
C    192.168.20.0 is directly connected, Serial0/0
L    192.168.20.1/32 is directly connected, Serial0/0
C    192.168.214.0 is directly connected, FastEthernet0/0
L    192.168.214.1/32 is directly connected, FastEthernet0/0
```

What do we see here? If I were to tell you that the corporate router received an IP packet with a source IP address of 192.168.214.20 and a destination address of 192.168.22.3, what do you think the Corp router will do with this packet?

If you said, "The packet came in on the FastEthernet 0/0 interface, but because the routing table doesn't show a route to network 192.168.22.0 (or a default route), the router will discard the packet and send an ICMP destination unreachable message back out to interface FastEthernet 0/0," you're a genius! The reason that's the correct answer is because that's the source LAN where the packet originated from.

Now, let's check out the next figure and talk about the frames and packets in detail. We're not really going over anything new here; I'm just making sure you totally, completely, thoroughly, fully understand basic IP routing! It is the crux of this book, and the topic the exam objectives are geared toward. It's all about IP routing, which means you need to be all over this stuff! We'll use Figure 8.6 for the next few scenarios.

**FIGURE 8.6**   Basic IP routing using MAC and IP addresses

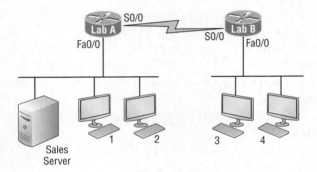

Referring to Figure 8.6, here's a list of all the answers to questions you need inscribed in your brain:

1. In order to begin communicating with the Sales server, Host 4 sends out an ARP request. How will the devices exhibited in the topology respond to this request?

2. Host 4 has received an ARP reply. Host 4 will now build a packet, then place this packet in the frame. What information will be placed in the header of the packet that leaves Host 4 if Host 4 is going to communicate to the Sales server?

3. The Lab_A router has received the packet and will send it out Fa0/0 onto the LAN toward the server. What will the frame have in the header as the source and destination addresses?

4. Host 4 is displaying two web documents from the Sales server in two browser windows at the same time. How did the data find its way to the correct browser windows?

The following should probably be written in a teensy font and put upside down in another part of the book so it would be really hard for you to cheat and peek, but since I'm not that mean and you really need to have this down, here are your answers in the same order that the scenarios were just presented:

1. In order to begin communicating with the server, Host 4 sends out an ARP request. How will the devices exhibited in the topology respond to this request? Since MAC addresses must stay on the local network, the Lab_B router will respond with the MAC address of the Fa0/0 interface and Host 4 will send all frames to the MAC address of the Lab_B Fa0/0 interface when sending packets to the Sales server.

2. Host 4 has received an ARP reply. Host 4 will now build a packet, then place this packet in the frame. What information will be placed in the header of the packet that leaves Host 4 if Host 4 is going to communicate to the Sales server? Since we're now talking about packets, not frames, the source address will be the IP address of Host 4 and the destination address will be the IP address of the Sales server.

3. Finally, the Lab_A router has received the packet and will send it out Fa0/0 onto the LAN toward the server. What will the frame have in the header as the source and destination addresses? The source MAC address will be the Lab_A router's Fa0/0 interface, and the destination MAC address will be the Sales server's MAC address because all MAC addresses must be local on the LAN.

4. Host 4 is displaying two web documents from the Sales server in two different browser windows at the same time. How did the data find its way to the correct browser windows? TCP port numbers are used to direct the data to the correct application window.

Okay—great! But we're not quite done yet. I've got a few more questions for you before you actually get to configure routing in a real network. Ready? Figure 8.7 shows a basic network, and Host 4 needs to get email. Which address will be placed in the destination address field of the frame when it leaves Host 4?

**FIGURE 8.7**   Testing basic routing knowledge

The answer is that Host 4 will use the destination MAC address of the Fa0/0 interface on the Lab_B router—you knew that, right? Look at Figure 8.7 again: What if Host 4 needs to communicate with Host 1—not the server, but with Host 1. Which OSI layer 3 source address will be found in the packet header when it reaches Host 1?

Hopefully you've got this: At layer 3, the source IP address will be Host 4 and the destination address in the packet will be the IP address of Host 1. Of course, the destination MAC address from Host 4 will always be the Fa0/0 address of the Lab_B router, right? And since we have more than one router, we'll need a routing protocol that communicates between both of them so that traffic can be forwarded in the right direction to reach the network that Host 1 is connected to.

Okay—one more scenario and you're on your way to being an IP routing machine! Again, using Figure 8.7, Host 4 is transferring a file to the email server connected to the Lab_A router. What would be the layer 2 destination address leaving Host 4? Yes, I've asked this question more than once. But not this one: What will be the source MAC address when the frame is received at the email server?

Hopefully, you answered that the layer 2 destination address leaving Host 4 is the MAC address of the Fa0/0 interface on the Lab_B router and that the source layer 2 address that the email server will receive is the Fa0/0 interface of the Lab_A router.

If you did, you're ready to discover how IP routing is handled in a larger network environment!

# Configuring IP Routing

It's time to get serious and configure a real network. Figure 8.8 shows three routers: Corp, SF, and LA. Remember that, by default, these routers only know about networks that are directly connected to them. I'll continue to use this figure and network throughout the rest of the chapters in this book. As I progress through this book, I'll add more routers and switches as needed.

As you might guess, I've got quite a nice collection of routers for us to play with. But you don't need a closet full of devices to perform most, if not all, of the commands we'll use in this book. You can get by nicely with pretty much any router or even with a good router simulator.

Getting back to business, the Corp router has two serial interfaces, which will provide a WAN connection to the SF and LA router and two Fast Ethernet interfaces as well. The two remote routers have two serial interfaces and two Fast Ethernet interfaces.

The first step for this project is to correctly configure each router with an IP address on each interface. The following list shows the IP address scheme I'm going to use to configure the network. After we go over how the network is configured, I'll cover how to configure IP routing. Pay attention to the subnet masks—they're important! The LANs all use a /24 mask, but the WANs are using a /30.

**FIGURE 8.8**    Configuring IP routing

## Corp

- Serial 0/0: 172.16.10.1/30
- Serial 0/1: 172.16.10.5/30
- Fa0/0: 10.10.10.1/24

## SF

- S0/0/0: 172.16.10.2/30
- Fa0/0: 192.168.10.1/24

## LA

- S0/0/0: 172.16.10.6/30
- Fa0/0: 192.168.20.1/24

The router configuration is really a pretty straightforward process since you just need to add IP addresses to your interfaces and then perform a no shutdown on those same interfaces. It gets a tad more complex later on, but for right now, let's configure the IP addresses in the network.

## Corp Configuration

We need to configure three interfaces to configure the Corp router. And configuring the hostnames of each router will make identification much easier. While we're at it, let's set the interface descriptions, banner, and router passwords too because it's a really good idea to make a habit of configuring these commands on every router!

To get started, I performed an erase startup-config on the router and reloaded, so we'll start in setup mode. I chose no when prompted to enter setup mode, which will get us straight to the username prompt of the console. I'm going to configure all my routers this same way.

Here's how what I just did looks:

```
      --- System Configuration Dialog ---


Would you like to enter the initial configuration dialog? [yes/no]: n


Press RETURN to get started!
Router>en
Router#config t
Router(config)#hostname Corp
Corp(config)#enable secret GlobalNet
Corp(config)#no ip domain-lookup
Corp(config)#int f0/0
Corp(config-if)#desc Connection to LAN BackBone
Corp(config-if)#ip address 10.10.10.1 255.255.255.0
Corp(config-if)#no shut
Corp(config-if)#int s0/0
Corp(config-if)#desc WAN connection to SF
Corp(config-if)#ip address 172.16.10.1 255.255.255.252
Corp(config-if)#no shut
Corp(config-if)#int s0/1
Corp(config-if)#desc WAN connection to LA
Corp(config-if)#ip address 172.16.10.5 255.255.255.252
Corp(config-if)#no shut
Corp(config-if)#line con 0
Corp(config-line)#password console
Corp(config-line)#login
Corp(config-line)#loggin sync
Corp(config-line)#exit
Corp(config)#line vty 0 ?
  <1-181>  Last Line number
  <cr>
Corp(config)#line vty 0 181
Corp(config-line)#password telnet
Corp(config-line)#login
Corp(config-line)#exit
```

```
Corp(config)#banner motd # This is my Corp Router #
Corp(config)#^Z
Corp#copy run start
Destination filename [startup-config]?
Building configuration...
[OK]
Corp# [OK]
```

Let's talk about the configuration of the Corp router. First, I set the hostname and enable secret, but what is that no ip domain-lookup command? That command stops the router from trying to resolve hostnames, which is an annoying feature unless you've configured a host table or DNS. Next, I configured the three interfaces with descriptions and IP addresses and enabled them with the no shutdown command. The console and VTY passwords came next, but what is that logging sync command under the console line? The logging synchronous command stops console messages from writing over what you are typing in, meaning it's a sanity-saving command that you'll come to love! Last, I set my banner and then saved my configs.

If you're having a hard time understanding this configuration process, refer back to Chapter 6, "Cisco's Internetworking Operating System (IOS)."

To view the IP routing tables created on a Cisco router, use the command show ip route. Here's the command's output:

```
Corp#sh ip route
Codes: L - local, C - connected, S - static, R - RIP, M - mobile, B - BGP
   D - EIGRP, EX - EIGRP external, O - OSPF, IA - OSPF inter area
   N1 - OSPF NSSA external type 1, N2 - OSPF NSSA external type 2
   E1 - OSPF external type 1, E2 - OSPF external type 2
   i - IS-IS, su - IS-IS summary, L1 - IS-IS level-1, L2 - IS-IS level-2
   ia - IS-IS inter area, * - candidate default, U - per-user static route
   o - ODR, P - periodic downloaded static route, H - NHRP, l - LISP
   + - replicated route, % - next hop override
Gateway of last resort is not set


     10.0.0.0/24 is subnetted, 1 subnets
C       10.10.10.0 is directly connected, FastEthernet0/0
L       10.10.10.1/32 is directly connected, FastEthernet0/0
Corp#
```

It's important to remember that only configured, directly connected networks are going to show up in the routing table. So why is it that only the FastEthernet 0/0 interface shows up in the table? No worries—that's just because you won't see the serial interfaces come up until the other side of the links are operational. As soon as we configure our SF and NY routers, those interfaces should pop right up!

But did you notice the C on the left side of the output of the routing table? When you see that there, it means that the network is directly connected. The codes for each type of connection are listed at the top of the show ip route command, along with their descriptions.

For brevity, the codes at the top of the output will be cut in the rest of this chapter.

## SF Configuration

Now we're ready to configure the next router—SF. To make that happen correctly, keep in mind that we have two interfaces to deal with: serial 0/0/0 and FastEthernet 0/0. So let's make sure we don't forget to add the hostname, passwords, interface descriptions, and banners to the router configuration. As I did with the Corp router, I erased the configuration and reloaded since this router had already been configured before.

Here's the configuration I used:

```
R1#erase start
% Incomplete command.
R1#erase startup-config
Erasing the nvram filesystem will remove all configuration files!
  Continue? [confirm][enter]
[OK]
Erase of nvram: complete
R1#reload
Proceed with reload? [confirm][enter]
[output cut]
%Error opening tftp://255.255.255.255/network-confg (Timed out)
%Error opening tftp://255.255.255.255/cisconet.cfg (Timed out)


        --- System Configuration Dialog ---


Would you like to enter the initial configuration dialog? [yes/no]: n
```

Before we move on, let's talk about this output for a second. First, notice that beginning with IOS 12.4, ISR routers will no longer take the command erase start. The router has only one command after erase that starts with s, as shown here:

```
Router#erase s?
startup-config
```

I know, you'd think that the IOS would continue to accept the command, but nope—sorry! The second thing I want to point out is that the output tells us the router is looking for a TFTP host to see if it can download a configuration. When that fails, it goes straight into setup mode. This gives you a great picture of the Cisco router default boot sequence we talked about in Chapter 7, "Managing and Troubleshooting a Cisco Internetwork."

Okay, let's get back to configuring our router:

```
Press RETURN to get started!
Router#config t
Router(config)#hostname SF
SF(config)#enable secret GlobalNet
SF(config)#no ip domain-lookup
SF(config)#int s0/0/0
SF(config-if)#desc WAN Connection to Corp
SF(config-if)#ip address 172.16.10.2 255.255.255.252
SF(config-if)#no shut
SF(config-if)#clock rate 1000000
SF(config-if)#int f0/0
SF(config-if)#desc SF LAN
SF(config-if)#ip address 192.168.10.1 255.255.255.0
SF(config-if)#no shut
SF(config-if)#line con 0
SF(config-line)#password console
SF(config-line)#login
SF(config-line)#logging sync
SF(config-line)#exit
SF(config)#line vty 0 ?
  <1-1180>  Last Line number
  <cr>
SF(config)#line vty 0 1180
SF(config-line)#password telnet
SF(config-line)#login
SF(config-line)#banner motd #This is the SF Branch router#
SF(config)#exit
SF#copy run start
Destination filename [startup-config]?
Building configuration...
 [OK]
```

Let's take a look at our configuration of the interfaces with the following two commands:

```
SF#sh run | begin int
interface FastEthernet0/0
```

```
 description SF LAN
 ip address 192.168.10.1 255.255.255.0
 duplex auto
 speed auto
!
interface FastEthernet0/1
 no ip address
 shutdown
 duplex auto
 speed auto
!
interface Serial0/0/0
 description WAN Connection to Corp
 ip address 172.16.10.2 255.255.255.252
 clock rate 1000000
!
```

```
SF#sh ip int brief
Interface          IP-Address      OK? Method Status                Protocol
FastEthernet0/0    192.168.10.1    YES manual up                    up
FastEthernet0/1    unassigned      YES unset  administratively down down
Serial0/0/0        172.16.10.2     YES manual up                    up
Serial0/0/1        unassigned      YES unset  administratively down down
SF#
```

Now that both ends of the serial link are configured, the link comes up. Remember, the up/up status for the interfaces are Physical/Data Link layer status indicators that don't reflect the layer 3 status! I ask students in my classes, "If the link shows up/up, can you ping the directly connected network?" And they say, "Yes!" The correct answer is, "I don't know," because we can't see the layer 3 status with this command. We only see layers 1 and 2 and verify that the IP addresses don't have a typo. This is really important to understand!

The show ip route command for the SF router reveals the following:

```
SF#sh ip route
C    192.168.10.0/24 is directly connected, FastEthernet0/0
L    192.168.10.1/32 is directly connected, FastEthernet0/0
     172.16.0.0/30 is subnetted, 1 subnets
C       172.16.10.0 is directly connected, Serial0/0/0
L       172.16.10.2/32 is directly connected, Serial0/0/0
```

Notice that router SF knows how to get to networks 172.16.10.0/30 and 192.168.10.0/24; we can now ping to the Corp router from SF:

```
SF#ping 172.16.10.1


Type escape sequence to abort.
Sending 5, 100-byte ICMP Echos to 172.16.10.1, timeout is 2 seconds:
!!!!!
Success rate is 100 percent (5/5), round-trip min/avg/max = 1/3/4 ms
```

Okay—now let's head back to the Corp router and check out the routing table:

```
Corp>sh ip route
     172.16.0.0/30 is subnetted, 1 subnets
C       172.16.10.0 is directly connected, Serial0/0
L       172.16.10.1/32 is directly connected, Serial0/0
     10.0.0.0/24 is subnetted, 1 subnets
C       10.10.10.0 is directly connected, FastEthernet0/0
L       10.10.10.1/32 is directly connected, FastEthernet0/0
```

On the SF router's serial interface 0/0/0 is a DCE connection, which means a clock rate needs to be set on the interface. Remember that you don't need to use the clock rate command in production. While true, it's still imperative that you know how/when you can use it and that you understand it really well when studying for your CCNA exam!

We can see our clocking with the show controllers command:

```
SF#sh controllers s0/0/0
Interface Serial0/0/0
Hardware is GT96K
DCE V.35, clock rate 1000000


Corp>sh controllers s0/0
Interface Serial0/0
Hardware is PowerQUICC MPC860
DTE V.35 TX and RX clocks detected.
```

Since the SF router has a DCE cable connection, I needed to add clock rate to this interface because DTE receives clock. Keep in mind that the new ISR routers will autodetect this and set the clock rate to 2000000. And you still need to make sure you're able to find an interface that is DCE and set clocking to meet the objectives.

Since the serial links are showing up, we can now see both networks in the Corp routing table. And once we configure LA, we'll see one more network in the routing table of the Corp router. The Corp router can't see the 192.168.10.0 network because we don't have any routing configured yet—routers see only directly connected networks by default.

## LA Configuration

To configure LA, we're going to do pretty much the same thing we did with the other two routers. There are two interfaces to deal with, serial 0/0/1 and FastEthernet 0/0, and again, we'll be sure to add the hostname, passwords, interface descriptions, and a banner to the router configuration:

```
Router(config)#hostname LA
LA(config)#enable secret GlobalNet
LA(config)#no ip domain-lookup
LA(config)#int s0/0/1
LA(config-if)#ip address 172.16.10.6 255.255.255.252
LA(config-if)#no shut
LA(config-if)#clock rate 1000000
LA(config-if)#description WAN To Corporate
LA(config-if)#int f0/0
LA(config-if)#ip address 192.168.20.1 255.255.255.0
LA(config-if)#no shut
LA(config-if)#description LA LAN
LA(config-if)#line con 0
LA(config-line)#password console
LA(config-line)#login
LA(config-line)#loggin sync
LA(config-line)#exit
LA(config)#line vty 0 ?
  <1-1180>  Last Line number
  <cr>
LA(config)#line vty 0 1180
LA(config-line)#password telnet
LA(config-line)#login
LA(config-line)#exit
LA(config)#banner motd #This is my LA Router#
LA(config)#exit
LA#copy run start
Destination filename [startup-config]?
Building configuration...
[OK]
```

Nice—everything was pretty straightforward. The output below, which I gained via the show ip route command, displays the directly connected networks of 192.168.20.0 and 172.16.10.0:

```
LA#sh ip route
    172.16.0.0/30 is subnetted, 1 subnets
```

```
C        172.16.10.4 is directly connected, Serial0/0/1
L        172.16.10.6/32 is directly connected, Serial0/0/1
C     192.168.20.0/24 is directly connected, FastEthernet0/0
L     192.168.20.1/32 is directly connected, FastEthernet0/0
```

Okay, so now that we've configured all three routers with IP addresses and administrative functions, we can move on to deal with routing. But I want to do one more thing on the SF and LA routers—since this is a very small network, let's build a DHCP server on the Corp router for each LAN.

## Configuring DHCP on Our Corp Router

While it's true that I could approach this task by going to each remote router and creating a pool, why bother with all that when I can easily create two pools on the Corp router and have the remote routers forward requests to the Corp router? Of course, you remember how to do this from Chapter 7!

Let's give it a shot:

```
Corp#config t
Corp(config)#ip dhcp excluded-address 192.168.10.1
Corp(config)#ip dhcp excluded-address 192.168.20.1
Corp(config)#ip dhcp pool SF_LAN
Corp(dhcp-config)#network 192.168.10.0 255.255.255.0
Corp(dhcp-config)#default-router 192.168.10.1
Corp(dhcp-config)#dns-server 4.4.4.4
Corp(dhcp-config)#exit
Corp(config)#ip dhcp pool LA_LAN
Corp(dhcp-config)#network 192.168.20.0 255.255.255.0
Corp(dhcp-config)#default-router 192.168.20.1
Corp(dhcp-config)#dns-server 4.4.4.4
Corp(dhcp-config)#exit
Corp(config)#exit
Corp#copy run start
Destination filename [startup-config]?
Building configuration...
```

Creating DHCP pools on a router is actually a simple process, and you would go about the configuration the same way on any router you wish to add a DHCP pool to. To designate a router as a DHCP server, you just create the pool name, add the network/subnet and the default gateway, and then exclude any addresses that you don't want handed out. You definitely want to make sure you've excluded the default gateway address, and you'd usually add a DNS server as well. I always add any exclusions first, and remember that you can conveniently exclude a range of addresses on a single line. Soon, I'll demonstrate those verification commands I promised I'd show you back in Chapter 7, but first, we need to figure out why the Corp router still can't get to the remote networks by default!

Now I'm pretty sure I configured DHCP correctly, but I just have this nagging feeling I forgot something important. What could that be? Well, the hosts are remote across a router, so what would I need to do that would allow them to get an address from a DHCP server? If you concluded that I've got to configure the SF and LA F0/0 interfaces to forward the DHCP client requests to the server, you got it!

Here's how we'd go about doing that:

```
LA#config t
LA(config)#int f0/0
LA(config-if)#ip helper-address 172.16.10.5


SF#config t
SF(config)#int f0/0
SF(config-if)#ip helper-address 172.16.10.1
```

I'm pretty sure I did this correctly, but we won't know until I have some type of routing configured and working. So let's get to that next!

# Configuring IP Routing in Our Network

So is our network really good to go? After all, I've configured it with IP addressing, administrative functions, and even clocking that will automatically occur with the ISR routers. But how will our routers send packets to remote networks when they get their destination information by looking into their tables that only include directions about directly connected networks? And you know routers promptly discard packets they receive with addresses for networks that aren't listed in their routing table!

So we're not exactly ready to rock after all. But we will be soon because there are several ways to configure the routing tables to include all the networks in our little internetwork so that packets will be properly forwarded. As usual, one size fits all rarely fits at all, and what's best for one network isn't necessarily what's best for another. That's why understanding the different types of routing will be really helpful when choosing the best solution for your specific environment and business requirements.

These are the three routing methods I'm going to cover with you:

- Static routing
- Default routing
- Dynamic routing

We're going to start with the first way and implement static routing on our network, because if you can implement static routing *and* make it work, you've demonstrated that you definitely have a solid understanding of the internetwork. So let's get started.

# Static Routing

Static routing is the process that ensues when you manually add routes in each router's routing table. Predictably, there are pros and cons to static routing, but that's true for all routing approaches.

Here are the pros:

- There is no overhead on the router CPU, which means you could probably make do with a cheaper router than you would need for dynamic routing.

- There is no bandwidth usage between routers, saving you money on WAN links as well as minimizing overhead on the router since you're not using a routing protocol.

- It adds security because you, the administrator, can be very exclusive and choose to allow routing access to certain networks only.

And here are the cons:

- Whoever the administrator is must have a vault-tight knowledge of the internetwork and how each router is connected in order to configure routes correctly. If you don't have a good, accurate map of your internetwork, things will get very messy quickly!

- If you add a network to the internetwork, you have to tediously add a route to it on all routers by hand, which only gets increasingly insane as the network grows.

- Due to the last point, it's just not feasible to use it in most large networks because maintaining it would be a full-time job in itself.

But that list of cons doesn't mean you get to skip learning all about it mainly because of that first disadvantage I listed—the fact that you must have such a solid understanding of a network to configure it properly and that your administrative knowledge has to practically verge on the supernatural! So let's dive in and develop those skills. Starting at the beginning, here's the command syntax you use to add a static route to a routing table from global config:

```
ip route [destination_network] [mask] [next-hop_address or
  exitinterface] [administrative_distance] [permanent]
```

This list describes each command in the string:

*ip route*   The command used to create the static route.

*destination_network*   The network you're placing in the routing table.

*mask*   The subnet mask being used on the network.

*next-hop_address*   This is the IP address of the next-hop router that will receive packets and forward them to the remote network, which must signify a router interface that's on a directly connected network. You must be able to successfully ping the router interface before you can add the route. Important note to self is that if you type in the wrong next-hop address or the interface to the correct router is down, the static route will show up in the router's configuration but not in the routing table.

*exitinterface*    Used in place of the next-hop address if you want, and shows up as a directly connected route.

*administrative_distance*    By default, static routes have an administrative distance of 1 or 0 if you use an exit interface instead of a next-hop address. You can change the default value by adding an administrative weight at the end of the command. I'll talk a lot more about this later in the chapter when we get to the section on dynamic routing.

permanent    If the interface is shut down or the router can't communicate to the next-hop router, the route will automatically be discarded from the routing table by default. Choosing the permanent option keeps the entry in the routing table no matter what happens.

Before I guide you through configuring static routes, let's take a look at a sample static route to see what we can find out about it:

```
Router(config)#ip route 172.16.3.0 255.255.255.0 192.168.2.4
```

- The ip route command tells us simply that it's a static route.
- 172.16.3.0 is the remote network we want to send packets to.
- 255.255.255.0 is the mask of the remote network.
- 192.168.2.4 is the next hop, or router, that packets will be sent to.

But what if the static route looked like this instead?

```
Router(config)#ip route 172.16.3.0 255.255.255.0 192.168.2.4 150
```

That 150 at the end changes the default administrative distance (AD) of 1 to 150. As said, I'll talk much more about AD when we get into dynamic routing, but for now, just remember that the AD is the trustworthiness of a route, where 0 is best and 255 is worst.

One more example, then we'll start configuring:

```
Router(config)#ip route 172.16.3.0 255.255.255.0 s0/0/0
```

Instead of using a next-hop address, we can use an exit interface that will make the route show up as a directly connected network. Functionally, the next hop and exit interface work exactly the same.

To help you understand how static routes work, I'll demonstrate the configuration on the internetwork shown previously in Figure 8.8. Here it is again in Figure 8.9 to save you the trouble of having to go back and forth to view the same figure.

## Corp

Each routing table automatically includes directly connected networks. To be able to route to all indirectly connected networks within the internetwork, the routing table must include information that describes where these other networks are located and how to get to them.

The Corp router is connected to three networks. For the Corp router to be able to route to all networks, the following networks have to be configured into its routing table:

- 192.168.10.0
- 192.168.20.0

**FIGURE 8.9**   Our internetwork

The following router output shows the static routes on the Corp router and the routing table after the configuration. For the Corp router to find the remote networks, I had to place an entry into the routing table describing the remote network, the remote mask, and where to send the packets. I am going to add a 150 at the end of each line to raise the administrative distance. You'll see why soon when we get to dynamic routing. Here's the output:

```
Corp#config t
Corp(config)#ip route 192.168.10.0 255.255.255.0 172.16.10.2 150
Corp(config)#ip route 192.168.20.0 255.255.255.0 s0/1 150
Corp(config)#do show run | begin ip route
ip route 192.168.10.0 255.255.255.0 172.16.10.2 150
ip route 192.168.20.0 255.255.255.0 Serial0/1 150
```

I needed to use different paths for networks 192.168.10.0 and 192.168.20.0, so I used a next-hop address for the SF router and an exit interface for the LA router. After the router has been configured, you can just type **show ip route** to see the static routes:

```
Corp(config)#do show ip route
S    192.168.10.0/24 [150/0] via 172.16.10.2
     172.16.0.0/30 is subnetted, 2 subnets
C       172.16.10.4 is directly connected, Serial0/1
L       172.16.10.5/32 is directly connected, Serial0/1
C       172.16.10.0 is directly connected, Serial0/0
L       172.16.10.1/32 is directly connected, Serial0/0
S    192.168.20.0/24 is directly connected, Serial0/1
```

```
      10.0.0.0/24 is subnetted, 1 subnets
C        10.10.10.0 is directly connected, FastEthernet0/0
L        10.10.10.1/32 is directly connected, FastEthernet0/0
```

The Corp router is configured to route and know all routes to all networks. But can you see a difference in the routing table for the routes to SF and LA? That's right! The next-hop configuration showed up as via, and the route configured with an exit interface configuration shows up as static but also as directly connected! This demonstrates how they are functionally the same but will display differently in the routing table.

Understand that if the routes don't appear in the routing table, it's because the router can't communicate with the next-hop address you've configured. But you can still use the permanent parameter to keep the route in the routing table even if the next-hop device can't be contacted.

The S in the first routing table entry means that the route is a static entry. The [150/0] stands for the administrative distance and metric to the remote network, respectively.

Okay—we're good. The Corp router now has all the information it needs to communicate with the other remote networks. Still, keep in mind that if the SF and LA routers aren't configured with all the same information, the packets will be discarded. We can fix this by configuring static routes.

Don't stress about the 150 at the end of the static route configuration at all, because I promise to get to it really soon in *this* chapter, not a later one! You really don't need to worry about it at this point.

## SF

The SF router is directly connected to networks 172.16.10.0/30 and 192.168.10.0/24, which means I've got to configure the following static routes on the SF router:

- 10.10.10.0/24
- 192.168.20.0/24
- 172.16.10.4/30

The configuration for the SF router is revealed in the output below. Remember that we'll never create a static route to any network we're directly connected to as well as the fact that we must use the next hop of 172.16.10.1 since that's our only router connection. Let's check out the commands:

```
SF(config)#ip route 10.10.10.0 255.255.255.0 172.16.10.1 150
SF(config)#ip route 172.16.10.4 255.255.255.252 172.16.10.1 150
SF(config)#ip route 192.168.20.0 255.255.255.0 172.16.10.1 150
SF(config)#do show run | begin ip route
ip route 10.10.10.0 255.255.255.0 172.16.10.1 150
ip route 172.16.10.4 255.255.255.252 172.16.10.1 150
ip route 192.168.20.0 255.255.255.0 172.16.10.1 150
```

By looking at the routing table, you can see that the SF router now understands how to find each network:

```
SF(config)#do show ip route
C    192.168.10.0/24 is directly connected, FastEthernet0/0
L    192.168.10.1/32 is directly connected, FastEthernet0/0
     172.16.0.0/30 is subnetted, 3 subnets
S       172.16.10.4 [150/0] via 172.16.10.1
C       172.16.10.0 is directly connected, Serial0/0/0
L       172.16.10.2/32 is directly connected, Serial0/0
S    192.168.20.0/24 [150/0] via 172.16.10.1
     10.0.0.0/24 is subnetted, 1 subnets
S       10.10.10.0 [150/0] via 172.16.10.1
```

And we now can rest assured that the SF router has a complete routing table as well. As soon as the LA router has all the networks in its routing table, SF will be able to communicate with all remote networks!

## LA

The LA router is directly connected to 192.168.20.0/24 and 172.16.10.4/30, so these are the routes that must be added:

- 10.10.10.0/24
- 172.16.10.0/30
- 192.168.10.0/24

And here's the LA router's configuration:

```
LA#config t
LA(config)#ip route 10.10.10.0 255.255.255.0 172.16.10.5 150
LA(config)#ip route 172.16.10.0 255.255.255.252 172.16.10.5 150
LA(config)#ip route 192.168.10.0 255.255.255.0 172.16.10.5 150
LA(config)#do show run | begin ip route
ip route 10.10.10.0 255.255.255.0 172.16.10.5 150
ip route 172.16.10.0 255.255.255.252 172.16.10.5 150
ip route 192.168.10.0 255.255.255.0 172.16.10.5 150
```

This output displays the routing table on the LA router:

```
LA(config)#do sho ip route
S    192.168.10.0/24 [150/0] via 172.16.10.5
     172.16.0.0/30 is subnetted, 3 subnets
C       172.16.10.4 is directly connected, Serial0/0/1
L       172.16.10.6/32 is directly connected, Serial0/0/1
```

```
S        172.16.10.0 [150/0] via 172.16.10.5
C     192.168.20.0/24 is directly connected, FastEthernet0/0
L     192.168.20.1/32 is directly connected, FastEthernet0/0
      10.0.0.0/24 is subnetted, 1 subnets
S        10.10.10.0 [150/0] via 172.16.10.5
```

LA now shows all five networks in the internetwork, so it too can now communicate with all routers and networks. But before we test our little network, as well as our DHCP server, let's cover one more topic.

## Default Routing

The SF and LA routers that I've connected to the Corp router are considered stub routers. A *stub* indicates that the networks in this design have only one way out to reach all other networks, which means that instead of creating multiple static routes, we can just use a single default route. This default route is used by IP to forward any packet with a destination not found in the routing table, which is why it is also called a gateway of last resort. Here's the configuration I could have done on the LA router instead of typing in the static routes due to its stub status:

```
LA#config t
LA(config)#no ip route 10.10.10.0 255.255.255.0 172.16.10.5 150
LA(config)#no ip route 172.16.10.0 255.255.255.252 172.16.10.5 150
LA(config)#no ip route 192.168.10.0 255.255.255.0 172.16.10.5 150
LA(config)#ip route 0.0.0.0 0.0.0.0 172.16.10.5
LA(config)#do sho ip route
[output cut]
Gateway of last resort is 172.16.10.5 to network 0.0.0.0
172.16.0.0/30 is subnetted, 1 subnets
C       172.16.10.4 is directly connected, Serial0/0/1
L       172.16.10.6/32 is directly connected, Serial0/0/1
C    192.168.20.0/24 is directly connected, FastEthernet0/0
L    192.168.20.0/32 is directly connected, FastEthernet0/0
S*   0.0.0.0/0 [1/0] via 172.16.10.5
```

Okay—I've removed all the initial static routes I had configured and adding a default route is a lot easier than typing a bunch of static routes! Can you see the default route listed last in the routing table? The S* shows that as a candidate for the default route. And I really want you to notice that the gateway of last resort is now set too. Everything the router receives with a destination not found in the routing table will be forwarded to 172.16.10.5. You need to be careful where you place default routes because you can easily create a network loop!

So we're there—we've configured all our routing tables! All the routers have the correct routing table, so all routers and hosts should be able to communicate without a hitch—for now. But if you add even one more network or another router to the internetwork, you'll have to update each and every router's routing tables by hand—ugh! Not really a problem at all if you've got a small network like we do, but it would be a time-consuming monster if you're dealing with a large internetwork!

## Verifying Your Configuration

We're still not done yet—once all the routers' routing tables are configured, they must be verified. The best way to do this, besides using the show ip route command, is via Ping. I'll start by pinging from the Corp router to the SF router.

Here's the output I got:

```
Corp#ping 192.168.10.1

Type escape sequence to abort.
Sending 5, 100-byte ICMP Echos to 192.168.10.1, timeout is 2 seconds:
!!!!!
Success rate is 100 percent (5/5), round-trip min/avg/max = 4/4/4 ms
Corp#
```

Here you can see that I pinged from the Corp router to the remote interface of the SF router. Now let's ping the remote network on the LA router, and after that, we'll test our DHCP server and see if that is working too!

```
Corp#ping 192.168.20.1


Type escape sequence to abort.
Sending 5, 100-byte ICMP Echos to 192.168.20.1, timeout is 2 seconds:
!!!!!
Success rate is 100 percent (5/5), round-trip min/avg/max = 1/2/4 ms
Corp#
```

And why not test my configuration of the DHCP server on the Corp router while we're at it? I'm going to go to each host on the SF and LA routers and make them DHCP clients. By the way, I'm using an old router to represent "hosts," which just happens to work great for studying purposes. Here's how I did that:

```
SF_PC(config)#int e0
SF_PC(config-if)#ip address dhcp
SF_PC(config-if)#no shut
Interface Ethernet0 assigned DHCP address 192.168.10.8, mask 255.255.255.0
LA_PC(config)#int e0
LA_PC(config-if)#ip addr dhcp
LA_PC(config-if)#no shut
Interface Ethernet0 assigned DHCP address 192.168.20.4, mask 255.255.255.0
```

Nice! Don't you love it when things just work the first time? Sadly, this just isn't exactly a realistic expectation in the networking world, so we must be able to troubleshoot and verify our networks. Let's verify our DHCP server with a few of the commands you learned back in Chapter 7:

```
Corp#sh ip dhcp binding
Bindings from all pools not associated with VRF:
IP address          Client-ID/            Lease expiration       Type
                    Hardware address/
                    User name
192.168.10.8        0063.6973.636f.2d30.   Sept 16 2013 10:34 AM   Automatic
                    3035.302e.3062.6330.
                    2e30.3063.632d.4574.
                    30
192.168.20.4        0063.6973.636f.2d30.   Sept 16 2013 10:46 AM   Automatic
                    3030.322e.3137.3632.
                    2e64.3032.372d.4574.
                    30
```

We can see from above that our little DHCP server is working! Let's try another couple of commands:

```
Corp#sh ip dhcp pool SF_LAN

Pool SF_LAN :
 Utilization mark (high/low)    : 100 / 0
 Subnet size (first/next)       : 0 / 0
 Total addresses                : 254
 Leased addresses               : 3
 Pending event                  : none
 1 subnet is currently in the pool :
 Current index       IP address range                       Leased addresses
 192.168.10.9        192.168.10.1    - 192.168.10.254        3


Corp#sh ip dhcp conflict
IP address          Detection method   Detection time         VRF
```

The last command would tell us if we had two hosts with the same IP address, so it's good news because there are no conflicts reported! Two detection methods are used to confirm this:

- Ping from the DHCP server to make sure no other host responds before handing out an address.
- A gratuitous ARP from a host that receives a DHCP address from the server.

The DHCP client will send an ARP request with its new IP address looking to see if anyone responds, and if so, it will report the conflict to the server.

Okay, since we can communicate from end to end and to each host without a problem while receiving DHCP addresses from our server, I'd say our static and default route configurations have been a success—cheers!

# Dynamic Routing

Dynamic routing is when protocols are used to find networks and update routing tables on routers. This is whole lot easier than using static or default routing, but it will cost you in terms of router CPU processing and bandwidth on network links. A routing protocol defines the set of rules used by a router when it communicates routing information between neighboring routers.

The routing protocol I'm going to talk about in this chapter is Routing Information Protocol (RIP) versions 1 and 2.

Two types of routing protocols are used in internetworks: *interior gateway protocols (IGPs)* and *exterior gateway protocols (EGPs)*. IGPs are used to exchange routing information with routers in the same *autonomous system (AS)*. An AS is either a single network or a collection of networks under a common administrative domain, which basically means that all routers sharing the same routing-table information are in the same AS. EGPs are used to communicate between ASs. An example of an EGP is Border Gateway Protocol (BGP), which we're not going to bother with because it's beyond the scope of this book.

Since routing protocols are so essential to dynamic routing, I'm going to give you the basic information you need to know about them next. Later on in this chapter, we'll focus on configuration.

## Routing Protocol Basics

There are some important things you should know about routing protocols before we get deeper into them. Being familiar with administrative distances, the three different kinds of routing protocols, and routing loops are three of the most important.

### Administrative Distances

The *administrative distance (AD)* is used to rate the trustworthiness of routing information received on a router from a neighbor router. An administrative distance is an integer from 0 to 255, where 0 is the most trusted and 255 means no traffic will be passed via this route.

If a router receives two updates listing the same remote network, the first thing the router checks is the AD. If one of the advertised routes has a lower AD than the other, then the route with the lowest AD will be chosen and placed in the routing table.

If both advertised routes to the same network have the same AD, then routing protocol metrics like *hop count* and/or the bandwidth of the lines will be used to find the best path to the remote network. The advertised route with the lowest metric will be placed in the routing table, but if both advertised routes have the same AD as well as the same metrics, then the routing protocol will load-balance to the remote network, meaning the protocol will send data down each link.

Table 8.1 shows the default administrative distances that a Cisco router uses to decide which route to take to a remote network.

**TABLE 8.1**   Default administrative distances

| Route Source | Default AD |
| --- | --- |
| Connected interface | 0 |
| Static route | 1 |
| EIGRP | 90 |
| OSPF | 110 |
| RIP | 120 |
| External EIGRP | 170 |
| Unknown | 255 (This route will never be used.) |

If a network is directly connected, the router will always use the interface connected to the network. If you configure a static route, the router will then believe that route over any other ones it learns about. You can change the administrative distance of static routes, but by default, they have an AD of 1. In our previous static route configuration, the AD of each route is set at 150. This AD allows us to configure routing protocols without having to remove the static routes because it's nice to have them there for backup in case the routing protocol experiences some kind of failure.

If you have a static route, an RIP-advertised route, and an EIGRP-advertised route listing the same network, which route will the router go with? That's right—by default, the router will always use the static route unless you change its AD—which we did!

## Routing Protocols

There are three classes of routing protocols:

**Distance vector**   The distance-vector protocols in use today find the best path to a remote network by judging distance. In RIP routing, each instance where a packet goes through a router is called a hop, and the route with the least number of hops to the network will be chosen as the best one. The vector indicates the direction to the remote network. RIP is a distance-vector routing protocol and periodically sends out the entire routing table to directly connected neighbors.

**Link state**   In link-state protocols, also called shortest-path-first protocols, the routers each create three separate tables. One of these tables keeps track of directly attached neighbors, one determines the topology of the entire internetwork, and one is used as the routing table. Link-state routers know more about the internetwork than any distance-vector routing protocol ever could. OSPF is an IP routing protocol that's completely link-state. Link-state protocols send updates containing the state of their own links to all other directly connected routers on the network. This is then propagated to their neighbors.

**Hybrid**   Hybrid protocols use aspects of both distance-vector and link-state protocols, and EIGRP is a great example—even though Cisco typically just calls EIGRP an advanced distance-vector routing protocol!

There's no set of rules to follow that dictate exactly how to broadly configure routing protocols for every situation. It's a task that really must be undertaken on a case-by-case basis, with an eye on specific requirements of each one. If you understand how the different routing protocols work, you can make good, solid decisions that will solidly meet the individual needs of any business!

# Routing Information Protocol (RIP)

Routing Information Protocol (RIP) is a true distance-vector routing protocol. RIP sends the complete routing table out of all active interfaces every 30 seconds. It relies on hop count to determine the best way to a remote network, but it has a maximum allowable hop count of 15 by default, so a destination of 16 would be considered unreachable. RIP works okay in very small networks, but it's super inefficient on large networks with slow WAN links or on networks with a large number of routers installed and completely useless on networks that have links with variable bandwidths!

RIP version 1 uses only *classful routing*, which means that all devices in the network must use the same subnet mask. This is because RIP version 1 doesn't send updates with subnet mask information in tow. RIP version 2 provides something called *prefix routing* and does send subnet mask information with its route updates. This is called *classless routing*. You'll rarely see RIPv1 used in today's networks, and it's not considered in any CCENT and CCNA objective. Even RIPv2 doesn't get much attention in the objectives. So why am I even telling you about them? Because it helps me explain routing protocols a little better before we get into the much more advanced, and very much focused upon, OSPF protocol.

So, with that let's configure our current network with RIPv2, before we move onto OSPF in the next chapter.

## Configuring RIP Routing

To configure RIP routing, just turn on the protocol with the router rip command and tell the RIP routing protocol the networks to advertise. Remember that with static routing, we always configured remote networks and never typed a route to our directly connected networks? Well, dynamic routing is carried out the complete opposite way. You would never type a *remote* network under your routing protocol—only enter your directly connected networks! Let's configure our three-router internetwork, revisited in Figure 8.9, with RIP routing.

## Corp

RIP has an administrative distance of 120. Static routes have an administrative distance of 1 by default, and since we currently have static routes configured, the routing tables won't be populated with RIP information. We're still good though because I added the 150 to the end of each static route!

You can add the RIP routing protocol by using the router rip command and the network command. The network command tells the routing protocol which classful network to advertise. By doing this, you're activating the RIP routing process on the interfaces whose addressing falls within the specified classful networks configured with the network command under the RIP routing process.

Look at the Corp router configuration to see how easy this is. Oh wait—first, I want to verify my directly connected networks so I know what to configure RIP with:

```
Corp#sh ip int brief
Interface       IP-Address     OK? Method Status                 Protocol
FastEthernet0/0 10.10.10.1     YES manual up                     up
Serial0/0       172.16.10.1    YES manual up                     up
FastEthernet0/1 unassigned     YES unset  administratively down  down
Serial0/1       172.16.10.5    YES manual up                     up
Corp#config t
Corp(config)#router rip
Corp(config-router)#network 10.0.0.0
Corp(config-router)#network 172.16.0.0
Corp(config-router)#version 2
Corp(config-router)#no auto-summary
```

That's it—really! Typically just two or three commands and you're done, which sure makes your job a lot easier than dealing with static routes, doesn't it? Be sure to keep in mind the extra router CPU process and bandwidth that you're consuming.

Anyway, so what exactly did I do here? I enabled the RIP routing protocol, added my directly connected networks, made sure I was only running RIPv2, which is a classless routing protocol, and then I disabled auto-summary. We typically don't want our routing protocols summarizing for us because it's better to do that manually and both RIP and EIGRP auto-summarize by default. So a general rule of thumb is to disable auto-summary, which allows them to advertise subnets.

Notice I didn't type in subnets, only the classful network address, which is betrayed by the fact that all subnet bits and host bits are off! That's because with dynamic routing, it's not my job and it's up to the routing protocol to find the subnets and populate the routing tables. And since we have no router buddies running RIP, we won't see any RIP routes in the routing table yet.

Remember that RIP uses the classful address when configuring the network address. To clarify this, refer to the example in our network with an address of 172.16.0.0/24 using subnets 172.16.10.0 and 172.16.20.0. You would only type in the classful network address of 172.16.0.0 and let RIP find the subnets and place them in the routing table. This doesn't mean you are running a classful routing protocol; this is just the way that both RIP and EIGRP are configured.

## SF

Okay, let's configure our SF router now, which is connected to two networks. We need to configure both directly connected classful networks, not subnets:

```
SF#sh ip int brief
Interface         IP-Address     OK? Method Status                Protocol
FastEthernet0/0   192.168.10.1   YES manual up                    up
FastEthernet0/1   unassigned     YES unset  administratively down down
Serial0/0/0       172.16.10.2    YES manual up                    up
Serial0/0/1       unassigned     YES unset  administratively down down
SF#config
SF(config)#router rip
SF(config-router)#network 192.168.10.0
SF(config-router)#network 172.16.0.0
SF(config-router)#version 2
SF(config-router)#no auto-summary
SF(config-router)#do show ip route
C    192.168.10.0/24 is directly connected, FastEthernet0/0
L    192.168.10.1/32 is directly connected, FastEthernet0/0
     172.16.0.0/30 is subnetted, 3 subnets
R       172.16.10.4 [120/1] via 172.16.10.1, 00:00:08, Serial0/0/0
C       172.16.10.0 is directly connected, Serial0/0/0
L       172.16.10.2/32 is directly connected, Serial0/0
S    192.168.20.0/24 [150/0] via 172.16.10.1
     10.0.0.0/24 is subnetted, 1 subnets
R       10.10.10.0 [120/1] via 172.16.10.1, 00:00:08, Serial0/0/0
```

That was pretty straightforward. Let's talk about this routing table. Since we have one RIP buddy out there whom we are exchanging routing tables with, we can see the RIP networks coming from the Corp router. All the other routes still show up as static and local. RIP also found both connections through the Corp router to networks 10.10.10.0 and 172.16.10.4. But we're not done yet!

## LA

Let's configure our LA router with RIP, only I'm going to remove the default route first, even though I don't have to. You'll see why soon:

```
LA#config t
LA(config)#no ip route 0.0.0.0 0.0.0.0
LA(config)#router rip
LA(config-router)#network 192.168.20.0
LA(config-router)#network 172.16.0.0
LA(config-router)#no auto
LA(config-router)#vers 2
LA(config-router)#do show ip route
R    192.168.10.0/24 [120/2] via 172.16.10.5, 00:00:10, Serial0/0/1
     172.16.0.0/30 is subnetted, 3 subnets
C       172.16.10.4 is directly connected, Serial0/0/1
L       172.16.10.6/32 is directly connected, Serial0/0/1
R       172.16.10.0 [120/1] via 172.16.10.5, 00:00:10, Serial0/0/1
C    192.168.20.0/24 is directly connected, FastEthernet0/0
L    192.168.20.1/32 is directly connected, FastEthernet0/0
     10.0.0.0/24 is subnetted, 1 subnets
R       10.10.10.0 [120/1] via 172.16.10.5, 00:00:10, Serial0/0/1
```

The routing table is sprouting new Rs as we add RIP buddies! We can still see that all routes are in the routing table.

This output shows us basically the same routing table and the same entries that it had when we were using static routes—except for those Rs. An R indicates that the networks were added dynamically using the RIP routing protocol. The [120/1] is the administrative distance of the route (120) along with the metric, which for RIP is the number of hops to that remote network (1). From the Corp router, all networks are one hop away.

So, while yes, it's true that RIP has worked in our little internetwork, it's just not a great solution for most enterprises. Its maximum hop count of only 15 is a highly limiting factor. And it performs full routing-table updates every 30 seconds, which would bring a larger internetwork to a painful crawl in no time!

There's still one more thing I want to show you about RIP routing tables and the parameters used to advertise remote networks. Using a different router on a different network as an example for a second, look into the output below. Can you spot where the following routing table shows [120/15] in the 10.1.3.0 network metric? This means that the administrative distance is 120, the default for RIP, but the hop count is 15. Remember that each time a router sends out an update to a neighbor router, the hop count goes up by one incrementally for each route! Here's that output now:

```
Router#sh ip route
     10.0.0.0/24 is subnetted, 12 subnets
```

```
C    10.1.11.0 is directly connected, FastEthernet0/1
L    10.1.11.1/32 is directly connected, FastEthernet0/1
C    10.1.10.0 is directly connected, FastEthernet0/0
L    10.1.10.1/32 is directly connected, FastEthernet/0/0
R    10.1.9.0 [120/2] via 10.1.5.1, 00:00:15, Serial0/0/1
R    10.1.8.0 [120/2] via 10.1.5.1, 00:00:15, Serial0/0/1
R    10.1.12.0 [120/1] via 10.1.11.2, 00:00:00, FastEthernet0/1
R    10.1.3.0 [120/15] via 10.1.5.1, 00:00:15, Serial0/0/1
R    10.1.2.0 [120/1] via 10.1.5.1, 00:00:15, Serial0/0/1
R    10.1.1.0 [120/1] via 10.1.5.1, 00:00:15, Serial0/0/1
R    10.1.7.0 [120/2] via 10.1.5.1, 00:00:15, Serial0/0/1
R    10.1.6.0 [120/2] via 10.1.5.1, 00:00:15, Serial0/0/1
C    10.1.5.0 is directly connected, Serial0/0/1
L    10.1.5.1/32 is directly connected, Serial0/0/1
R    10.1.4.0 [120/1] via 10.1.5.1, 00:00:15, Serial0/0/1
```

So this [120/15] is really bad. We're basically doomed because the next router that receives the table from this router will just discard the route to network 10.1.3.0 since the hop count would rise to 16, which is invalid!

 If a router receives a routing update that contains a higher-cost path to a network that's already in its routing table, the update will be ignored.

## Holding Down RIP Propagations

You probably don't want your RIP network advertised everywhere on your LAN and WAN. There's enough stress in networking already and not a whole lot to be gained by advertising your RIP network to the Internet!

There are a few different ways to stop unwanted RIP updates from propagating across your LANs and WANs, and the easiest one is through the passive-interface command. This command prevents RIP update broadcasts from being sent out of a specified interface but still allows that same interface to receive RIP updates.

Here's an example of how to configure a passive-interface on the Corp routers Fa0/1 interface, which we will pretend is connected to a LAN that we don't want RIP on:

```
Corp#config t
Corp(config)#router rip
Corp(config-router)#passive-interface FastEthernet 0/1
```

This command will stop RIP updates from being propagated out of FastEthernet interface 0/0, but this can still receive RIP updates.

## Advertising a Default Route Using RIP

Okay, now I'm going to guide you through how to advertise a way out of your autonomous system to other routers, and you'll see this is completed the same way with OSPF. Imagine that our Corp router's Fa0/0 interface is connected to some type of Metro-Ethernet as a connection to the Internet. This is a pretty common configuration today that uses a LAN interface to connect to the ISP instead of a serial interface.

If we do add an Internet connection to Corp, all routers in our AS (SF and LA) must know where to send packets destined for networks on the Internet or they'll just drop the packets when they get a remote request. One solution to this little hitch would be to place a default route on every router and funnel the information to Corp, which in turn would have a default route to the ISP. Most people do this type of configuration in small- to medium-size networks because it actually works pretty well!

But since I'm running RIPv2 on all routers, I'll just add a default route on the Corp router to our ISP, as I would normally. I'll then add another command to advertise my network to the other routers in the AS as the default route to show them where to send packets destined for the Internet.

Here's my new Corp configuration:

```
Corp(config)#ip route 0.0.0.0 0.0.0.0 fa0/0
Corp(config)#router rip
Corp(config-router)#default-information originate
```

Now, let's take a look at the last entry found in the Corp routing table:

```
S*   0.0.0.0/0 is directly connected, FastEthernet0/0
```

Let's see if the LA router can see this same entry:

```
LA#sh ip route
Gateway of last resort is 172.16.10.5 to network 0.0.0.0


R    192.168.10.0/24 [120/2] via 172.16.10.5, 00:00:04, Serial0/0/1
     172.16.0.0/30 is subnetted, 2 subnets
C       172.16.10.4 is directly connected, Serial0/0/1
L       172.16.10.5/32 is directly connected, Serial0/0/1
R       172.16.10.0 [120/1] via 172.16.10.5, 00:00:04, Serial0/0/1
C    192.168.20.0/24 is directly connected, FastEthernet0/0
L    192.168.20.1/32 is directly connected, FastEthernet0/0
     10.0.0.0/24 is subnetted, 1 subnets
R       10.10.10.0 [120/1] via 172.16.10.5, 00:00:04, Serial0/0/1
R    192.168.218.0/24 [120/3] via 172.16.10.5, 00:00:04, Serial0/0/1
R    192.168.118.0/24 [120/2] via 172.16.10.5, 00:00:05, Serial0/0/1
R*   0.0.0.0/0 [120/1] via 172.16.10.5, 00:00:05, Serial0/0/1R2#
```

Can you see that last entry? It screams that it's an RIP injected route, but it's also a default route so our default-information originate command is working! Last, notice that the gateway of last resort is now set as well.

If all of what you've learned is clear and understood, congratulations—you're ready to move on to the next chapter right after you go through the written and hands-on labs, and while you're at it, don't forget the review questions!

# Summary

This chapter covered IP routing in detail. Again, it's extremely important to fully understand the basics we covered in this chapter because everything that's done on a Cisco router will typically have some kind of IP routing configured and running.

You learned how IP routing uses frames to transport packets between routers and to the destination host. From there, we configured static routing on our routers and discussed the administrative distance used by IP to determine the best route to a destination network. You found out that if you have a stub network, you can configure default routing, which sets the gateway of last resort on a router.

We then discussed dynamic routing, specifically RIP and how it works on an internetwork, which is not very well!

# Exam Essentials

**Describe the basic IP routing process.**   You need to remember that the frame changes at each hop but that the packet is never changed or manipulated in any way until it reaches the destination device (the TTL field in the IP header is decremented for each hop, but that's it!).

**List the information required by a router to successfully route packets.**   To be able to route packets, a router must know, at a minimum, the destination address, the location of neighboring routers through which it can reach remote networks, possible routes to all remote networks, the best route to each remote network, and how to maintain and verify routing information.

**Describe how MAC addresses are used during the routing process.**   A MAC (hardware) address will only be used on a local LAN. It will never pass a router's interface. A frame uses MAC (hardware) addresses to send a packet on a LAN. The frame will take the packet to either a host on the LAN or a router's interface (if the packet is destined for a remote network). As packets move from one router to another, the MAC addresses used will change, but normally the original source and destination IP addresses within the packet will not.

**View and interpret the routing table of a router.**   Use the show ip route command to view the routing table. Each route will be listed along with the source of the routing information. A C to the left of the route will indicate directly connected routes, and other letters next to the route can also indicate a particular routing protocol that provided the information, such as, for example, R for RIP.

**Differentiate the three types of routing.**   The three types of routing are static (in which routes are manually configured at the CLI), dynamic (in which the routers share routing information via a routing protocol), and default routing (in which a special route is configured for all traffic without a more specific destination network found in the table).

**Compare and contrast static and dynamic routing.**   Static routing creates no routing update traffic and creates less overhead on the router and network links, but it must be configured manually and does not have the ability to react to link outages. Dynamic routing creates routing update traffic and uses more overhead on the router and network links.

**Configure static routes at the CLI.**   The command syntax to add a route is ip route [destination_network] [mask] [next-hop_address or  exitinterface] [administrative_distance] [permanent].

**Create a default route.**   To add a default route, use the command syntax ip route 0.0.0.0 0.0.0.0 *ip-address* or exit interface type and number.

**Understand administrative distance and its role in the selection of the best route.** Administrative distance (AD) is used to rate the trustworthiness of routing information received on a router from a neighbor router. Administrative distance is an integer from 0 to 255, where 0 is the most trusted and 255 means no traffic will be passed via this route. All routing protocols are assigned a default AD, but it can be changed at the CLI.

**Differentiate distance-vector, link-state and hybrid routing protocols.**   Distance-vector routing protocols make routing decisions based on hop count (think RIP), while link-state routing protocols are able to consider multiple factors such as bandwidth available and building a topology table. Hybrid routing protocols exhibit characteristics of both types.

**Configure RIP routing.**   To configure RIP routing, first you must be in global configuration mode and then you type the command router rip. Then you add all directly connected networks, making sure to use the classful address and the version 2 command and to disable auto-summarization.

# Written Lab 8

The answers to this lab can be found in Appendix A, "Answers to Written Labs."
   Write the answers to the following questions:

1. At the appropriate command prompt, create a static route to network 172.16.10.0/24 with a next-hop gateway of 172.16.20.1 and an administrative distance of 150.

2. When a PC sends a packet to another PC in a remote network, what destination addresses will be in the frame that it sends to its default gateway?

3. At the appropriate command prompt, create a default route to 172.16.40.1.

4. On which type of network is a default route most beneficial?

5. At the appropriate command prompt, display the routing table on your router.

6. When creating a static or default route, you don't have to use the next-hop IP address; you can use the _____.

7. True/False: To reach a remote host, you must know the MAC address of the remote host.

8. True/False: To reach a remote host, you must know the IP address of the remote host.

9. At the appropriate command prompt(s), prevent a router from propagating RIP information out serial 1.

10. True/False: RIPv2 is considered classless.

# Hands-on Labs

In the following hands-on labs, you will configure a network with three routers. These exercises assume all the same setup requirements as the labs found in earlier chapters.
   This chapter includes the following labs:

   Lab 8.1: Creating Static Routes

   Lab 8.2: Configuring RIP Routing

The internetwork shown in the following graphic will be used to configure all routers.

Table 8.2 shows our IP addresses for each router (each interface uses a /24 mask).

**TABLE 8.2**  Our IP addresses

| Router | Interface | IP Address |
|--------|-----------|------------|
| Lab_A | Fa0/0 | 172.16.10.1 |
| Lab_A | S0/0 | 172.16.20.1 |
| Lab_B | S0/0 | 172.16.20.2 |
| Lab_B | S0/1 | 172.16.30.1 |
| Lab_C | S0/0 | 172.16.30.2 |
| Lab_C | Fa0/0 | 172.16.40.1 |

These labs were written without using the LAN interface on the Lab_B router. You can choose to add that LAN into the labs if necessary. Also, if you have enough LAN interfaces, then you don't need to add the serial interfaces into this lab. Using all LAN interfaces is fine.

## Hands-on Lab 8.1: Creating Static Routes

In this lab, you will create a static route in all three routers so that the routers see all networks. Verify with the Ping program when complete.

**1.** The Lab_A router is connected to two networks, 172.16.10.0 and 172.16.20.0. You need to add routes to networks 172.16.30.0 and 172.16.40.0. Use the following commands to add the static routes:

```
Lab_A#config t
Lab_A(config)#ip route 172.16.30.0 255.255.255.0
  172.16.20.2
Lab_A(config)#ip route 172.16.40.0 255.255.255.0
  172.16.20.2
```

**2.** Save the current configuration for the Lab_A router by going to privileged mode, typing **copy run start**, and pressing Enter.

3. On the Lab_B router, you have direct connections to networks 172.16.20.0 and 172.16.30.0. You need to add routes to networks 172.16.10.0 and 172.16.40.0. Use the following commands to add the static routes:

```
Lab_B#config t
Lab_B(config)#ip route 172.16.10.0 255.255.255.0
   172.16.20.1
Lab_B(config)#ip route 172.16.40.0 255.255.255.0
   172.16.30.2
```

4. Save the current configuration for router Lab_B by going to the enabled mode, typing **copy run start**, and pressing Enter.

5. On router Lab_C, create a static route to networks 172.16.10.0 and 172.16.20.0, which are not directly connected. Create static routes so that router Lab_C can see all networks, using the commands shown here:

```
Lab_C#config t
Lab_C(config)#ip route 172.16.10.0 255.255.255.0
   172.16.30.1
Lab_C(config)#ip route 172.16.20.0 255.255.255.0
   172.16.30.1
```

6. Save the current configuration for router Lab_C by going to the enable mode, typing **copy run start**, and pressing Enter.

7. Check your routing tables to make sure all four networks show up by executing the **show ip route** command.

8. Now ping from each router to your hosts and from each router to each router. If it is set up correctly, it will work.

## Hands-on Lab 8.2: Configuring RIP Routing

In this lab, we will use the dynamic routing protocol RIP instead of static routing.

1. Remove any static routes or default routes configured on your routers by using the no ip route command. For example, here is how you would remove the static routes on the Lab_A router:

```
Lab_A#config t
Lab_A(config)#no ip route 172.16.30.0 255.255.255.0
   172.16.20.2
Lab_A(config)#no ip route 172.16.40.0 255.255.255.0
   172.16.20.2
```

Do the same thing for routers Lab_B and Lab_C. Verify that only your directly connected networks are in the routing tables.

**2.** After your static and default routes are clear, go into configuration mode on router Lab_A by typing **config t**.

**3.** Tell your router to use RIP routing by typing **router rip** and pressing Enter, as shown here:

```
config t
router rip
```

**4.** Add the network number for the networks you want to advertise. Since router Lab_A has two interfaces that are in two different networks, you must enter a network statement using the network ID of the network in which each interface resides. Alternately, you could use a summarization of these networks and use a single statement, minimizing the size of the routing table. Since the two networks are 172.16.10.0/24 and 172.16.20.0/24, the network summarization 172.16.0.0 would include both subnets. Do this by typing **network 172.16.0.0** and pressing Enter.

**5.** Press Ctrl+Z to get out of configuration mode.

**6.** The interfaces on Lab_B and Lab_C are in the 172.16.20.0/24 and 172.16.30.0/24 networks; therefore, the same summarized network statement will work there as well. Type the same commands, as shown here:

```
Config t
Router rip
network 172.16.0.0
```

**7.** Verify that RIP is running at each router by typing the following commands at each router:

```
show ip protocols
```

(Should indicate to you that RIP is present on the router.)

```
show ip route
```

(Should have routes present with an R to the left of them.)

```
show running-config or show run
```

(Should indicate that RIP is present and the networks are being advertised.)

**8.** Save your configurations by typing **copy run start** or **copy running-config startup-config** and pressing Enter at each router.

**9.** Verify the network by pinging all remote networks and hosts.

# Review Questions

The following questions are designed to test your understanding of this chapter's material. For more information on how to get additional questions, please see this book's introduction.

The answers to these questions can be found in Appendix B, "Answers to Chapter Review Questions."

1. What command was used to generate the following output?

```
Codes: L - local, C - connected, S - static,
[output cut]
        10.0.0.0/8 is variably subnetted, 6 subnets, 4 masks
C       10.0.0.0/8 is directly connected, FastEthernet0/3
L       10.0.0.1/32 is directly connected, FastEthernet0/3
C       10.10.0.0/16 is directly connected, FastEthernet0/2
L       10.10.0.1/32 is directly connected, FastEthernet0/2
C       10.10.10.0/24 is directly connected, FastEthernet0/1
L       10.10.10.1/32 is directly connected, FastEthernet0/1
S*      0.0.0.0/0 is directly connected, FastEthernet0/0
```

2. You are viewing the routing table and you see an entry 10.1.1.1/32. What legend code would you expect to see next to this route?

   A. C

   B. L

   C. S

   D. D

3. Which of the following statements are true regarding the command `ip route 172.16.4.0 255.255.255.0 192.168.4.2`? (Choose two.)

   A. The command is used to establish a static route.

   B. The default administrative distance is used.

   C. The command is used to configure the default route.

   D. The subnet mask for the source address is 255.255.255.0.

   E. The command is used to establish a stub network.

**4.** What destination addresses will be used by HostA to send data to the HTTPS server as shown in the following network? (Choose two.)

**A.** The IP address of the switch

**B.** The MAC address of the remote switch

**C.** The IP address of the HTTPS server

**D.** The MAC address of the HTTPS server

**E.** The IP address of RouterA's Fa0/0 interface

**F.** The MAC address of RouterA's Fa0/0 interface

**5.** Using the output shown, what protocol was used to learn the MAC address for 172.16.10.1?

```
Interface: 172.16.10.2 --- 0x3
  Internet Address      Physical Address      Type
  172.16.10.1           00-15-05-06-31-b0     dynamic
```

**A.** ICMP

**B.** ARP

**C.** TCP

**D.** UDP

**6.** Which of the following is called an advanced distance-vector routing protocol?

**A.** OSPF

**B.** EIGRP

**C.** BGP

**D.** RIP

**7.** When a packet is routed across a network, the _____ in the packet changes at every hop while the ____ does not.

   **A.** MAC address, IP address

   **B.** IP address, MAC address

   **C.** Port number, IP address

   **D.** IP address, port number

**8.** Which statement is true regarding classless routing protocols? (Choose two.)

   **A.** The use of discontiguous networks is not allowed.

   **B.** The use of variable length subnet masks is permitted.

   **C.** RIPv1 is a classless routing protocol.

   **D.** IGRP supports classless routing within the same autonomous system.

   **E.** RIPv2 supports classless routing.

**9.** Which two of the following are true regarding the distance-vector and link-state routing protocols? (Choose two.)

   **A.** Link state sends its complete routing table out of all active interfaces at periodic time intervals.

   **B.** Distance vector sends its complete routing table out of all active interfaces at periodic time intervals.

   **C.** Link state sends updates containing the state of its own links to all routers in the internetwork.

   **D.** Distance vector sends updates containing the state of its own links to all routers in the internetwork.

**10.** When a router looks up the destination in the routing table for every single packet it is called _____ .

   **A.** dynamic switching

   **B.** fast switching

   **C.** process switching

   **D.** Cisco Express Forwarding

**11.** What type(s) of route is the following? Choose all that apply.

```
S*   0.0.0.0/0 [1/0] via 172.16.10.5
```

   **A.** Default

   **B.** Subnetted

   **C.** Static

   **D.** Local

**12.** A network administrator views the output from the show ip route command. A network that is advertised by both RIP and EIGRP appears in the routing table flagged as an EIGRP route. Why is the RIP route to this network not used in the routing table?

    **A.** EIGRP has a faster update timer.

    **B.** EIGRP has a lower administrative distance.

    **C.** RIP has a higher metric value for that route.

    **D.** The EIGRP route has fewer hops.

    **E.** The RIP path has a routing loop.

**13.** Which of the following is NOT an advantage of static routing?

    **A.** Less overhead on the router CPU

    **B.** No bandwidth usage between routers

    **C.** Adds security

    **D.** Recovers automatically from lost routes

**14.** What metric does RIPv2 use to find the best path to a remote network?

    **A.** Hop count

    **B.** MTU

    **C.** Cumulative interface delay

    **D.** Load

    **E.** Path bandwidth value

**15.** The Corporate router receives an IP packet with a source IP address of 192.168.214.20 and a destination address of 192.168.22.3. Looking at the output from the Corp router, what will the router do with this packet?

```
Corp#sh ip route
[output cut]
R    192.168.215.0 [120/2] via 192.168.20.2, 00:00:23, Serial0/0
R    192.168.115.0 [120/1] via 192.168.20.2, 00:00:23, Serial0/0
R    192.168.30.0 [120/1] via 192.168.20.2, 00:00:23, Serial0/0
C    192.168.20.0 is directly connected, Serial0/0
C    192.168.214.0 is directly connected, FastEthernet0/0
```

    **A.** The packet will be discarded.

    **B.** The packet will be routed out of the S0/0 interface.

    **C.** The router will broadcast looking for the destination.

    **D.** The packet will be routed out of the Fa0/0 interface.

**16.** If your routing table has a static, an RIP, and an EIGRP route to the same network, which route will be used to route packets by default?

    **A.** Any available route

    **B.** RIP route

    **C.** Static route

    **D.** EIGRP route

    **E.** They will all load-balance.

**17.** Which of the following is an EGP?

    **A.** RIPv2

    **B.** EIGRP

    **C.** BGP

    **D.** RIP

**18.** Which of the following is an advantage of static routing?

    **A.** Less overhead on the router CPU

    **B.** No bandwidth usage between routers

    **C.** Adds security

    **D.** Recovers automatically from lost routes

**19.** What command produced the following output?

```
Interface         IP-Address      OK? Method Status              Protocol
FastEthernet0/0   192.168.10.1    YES manual up                      up
FastEthernet0/1   unassigned      YES unset  administratively down down
Serial0/0/0       172.16.10.2     YES manual up                      up
Serial0/0/1       unassigned      YES unset  administratively down down
```

    **A.** show ip route

    **B.** show interfaces

    **C.** show ip interface brief

    **D.** show ip arp

**20.** In the following command what does the 150 at the end of the command mean?

```
Router(config)#ip route 172.16.3.0 255.255.255.0 192.168.2.4 150
```

    **A.** Metric

    **B.** Administrative distance

    **C.** Hop count

    **D.** Cost

# Chapter

# 9

# Open Shortest Path First (OSPF)

## THE FOLLOWING ICND1 EXAM TOPICS ARE COVERED IN THIS CHAPTER:

✓ **IP Routing Technologies**

- Configure and verify OSPF (single area)

  - Benefit of single area

  - Configure OSPF v2

  - Router ID

  - Passive interface

Open Shortest Path First (OSPF) is by far the most popular and important routing protocol in use today—so important, I'm devoting this entire chapter to it! Sticking with the same approach we've adhered to throughout this book, we'll begin with the basics by completely familiarizing you with key OSPF terminology. Once we've covered that thoroughly, I'll guide you through OSPF's internal operation and then move on to tell you all about OSPF's many advantages over RIP.

This chapter is going to be more than chock full of vitally important information and it's also going to be really exciting because together, we'll explore some seriously critical factors and issues innate to implementing OSPF! I'll walk you through exactly how to implement single-area OSPF in a variety of networking environments and then demonstrate some great techniques you'll need to verify that everything is configured correctly and running smoothly.

To find up-to-the-minute updates for this chapter, please see www.lammle.com/forum or the book's web page at www.sybex.com.

# Open Shortest Path First (OSPF) Basics

*Open Shortest Path First* is an open standard routing protocol that's been implemented by a wide variety of network vendors, including Cisco. And it's that open standard characteristic that's the key to OSPF's flexibility and popularity.

Most people opt for OSPF, which works by using the Dijkstra algorithm to initially construct a shortest path tree and follows that by populating the routing table with the resulting best paths. EIGRP's convergence time may be blindingly fast, but OSPF isn't that far behind, and its quick convergence is another reason it's a favorite. Another two great advantages OSPF offers are that it supports multiple, equal-cost routes to the same destination, and like EIGRP, it also supports both IP and IPv6 routed protocols.

Here's a list that summarizes some of OSPF's best features:

- Allows for the creation of areas and autonomous systems
- Minimizes routing update traffic

- Is highly flexible, versatile, and scalable
- Supports VLSM/CIDR
- Offers an unlimited hop count
- Is open standard and supports multi-vendor deployment

Because OSPF is the first link-state routing protocol that most people run into, it's a good idea to size it up against more traditional distance-vector protocols like RIPv2 and RIPv1. Table 9.1 presents a nice comparison of all three of these common protocols.

**TABLE 9.1**   OSPF and RIP comparison

| Characteristic | OSPF | RIPv2 | RIPv1 |
| --- | --- | --- | --- |
| Type of protocol | Link state | Distance vector | Distance vector |
| Classless support | Yes | Yes | No |
| VLSM support | Yes | Yes | No |
| Auto-summarization | No | Yes | Yes |
| Manual summarization | Yes | Yes | No |
| Noncontiguous support | Yes | Yes | No |
| Route propagation | Multicast on change | Periodic multicast | Periodic broadcast |
| Path metric | Bandwidth | Hops | Hops |
| Hop count limit | None | 15 | 15 |
| Convergence | Fast | Slow | Slow |
| Peer authentication | Yes | Yes | No |
| Hierarchical network requirement | Yes (using areas) | No (flat only) | No (flat only) |
| Updates | Event triggered | Periodic | Periodic |
| Route computation | Dijkstra | Bellman-Ford | Bellman-Ford |

I want you know that OSPF has many features beyond the few I've listed in Table 9.1 and all of them combine to produce a fast, scalable, robust protocol that's also flexible enough to be actively deployed in a vast array of production networks!

One of OSPF's most useful traits is that its design is intended to be hierarchical in use, meaning that it allows us to subdivide the larger internetwork into smaller internetworks called areas. It's a really powerful feature that I recommend using, and I promise to show you how to do that later in the chapter.

Here are three of the biggest reasons to implement OSPF in a way that makes full use of its intentional, hierarchical design:

- To decrease routing overhead
- To speed up convergence
- To confine network instability to single areas of the network

Because free lunches are invariably hard to come by, all this wonderful functionality predictably comes at a price and doesn't exactly make configuring OSPF any easier. But no worries—we'll crush it!

Let's start by checking out Figure 9.1, which shows a very typical, yet simple OSPF design. I really want to point out the fact that some routers connect to the backbone—called area 0— the backbone area. OSPF absolutely must have an area 0, and all other areas should connect to it except for those connected via virtual links, which are beyond the scope of this book. A router that connects other areas to the backbone area within an AS is called an *area border router (ABR)*, and even these must have at least one of their interfaces connected to area 0.

**FIGURE 9.1** OSPF design example. An OSPF hierarchical design minimizes routing table entries and keeps the impact of any topology changes contained within a specific area.

OSPF runs great inside an autonomous system, but it can also connect multiple autonomous systems together. The router that connects these ASs is called an *autonomous system boundary router (ASBR)*. Ideally, your aim is to create other areas of networks to help keep route updates to a minimum, especially in larger networks. Doing this also keeps problems from propagating throughout the network, affectively isolating them to a single area.

But let's pause here to cover some key OSPF terms that are really essential for you to nail down before we move on any further.

## OSPF Terminology

Imagine being given a map and compass with no prior concept of east, west, north or south— not even what rivers, mountains, lakes, or deserts are. I'm guessing that without any ability to orient yourself in a basic way, your cool, new tools wouldn't help you get anywhere but completely lost, right? This is exactly why we're going to begin exploring OSPF by getting you solidly acquainted with a fairly long list of terms before setting out from base camp into the great unknown! Here are those vital terms to commit to memory now:

**Link**  A *link* is a network or router interface assigned to any given network. When an interface is added to the OSPF process, it's considered to be a link. This link, or interface, will have up or down state information associated with it as well as one or more IP addresses.

**Router ID**  The *router ID (RID)* is an IP address used to identify the router. Cisco chooses the router ID by using the highest IP address of all configured loopback interfaces. If no loopback interfaces are configured with addresses, OSPF will choose the highest IP address out of all active physical interfaces. To OSPF, this is basically the "name" of each router.

**Neighbor**  *Neighbors* are two or more routers that have an interface on a common network, such as two routers connected on a point-to-point serial link. OSPF neighbors must have a number of common configuration options to be able to successfully establish a neighbor relationship, and all of these options must be configured exactly the same way:

- Area ID
- Stub area flag
- Authentication password (if using one)
- Hello and Dead intervals

**Adjacency**  An *adjacency* is a relationship between two OSPF routers that permits the direct exchange of route updates. Unlike EIGRP, which directly shares routes with all of its neighbors, OSPF is really picky about sharing routing information and will directly share routes only with neighbors that have also established adjacencies. And not all neighbors will become adjacent—this depends upon both the type of network and the configuration of the routers. In multi-access networks, routers form adjacencies with designated and backup designated routers. In point-to-point and point-to-multipoint networks, routers form adjacencies with the router on the opposite side of the connection.

**Designated router**  A *designated router (DR)* is elected whenever OSPF routers are connected to the same broadcast network to minimize the number of adjacencies formed and to publicize received routing information to and from the remaining routers on the broadcast network or link. Elections are won based upon a router's priority level, with the one having the highest priority becoming the winner. If there's a tie, the router ID will be used to break it. All routers on the shared network will establish adjacencies with the DR and the BDR, which ensures that all routers' topology tables are synchronized.

**Backup designated router**   A *backup designated router (BDR)* is a hot standby for the DR on broadcast, or multi-access, links. The BDR receives all routing updates from OSPF adjacent routers but does not disperse LSA updates.

**Hello protocol**   The OSPF Hello protocol provides dynamic neighbor discovery and maintains neighbor relationships. Hello packets and Link State Advertisements (LSAs) build and maintain the topological database. Hello packets are addressed to multicast address 224.0.0.5.

**Neighborship database**   The *neighborship database* is a list of all OSPF routers for which Hello packets have been seen. A variety of details, including the router ID and state, are maintained on each router in the neighborship database.

**Topological database**   The *topological database* contains information from all of the Link State Advertisement packets that have been received for an area. The router uses the information from the topology database as input into the Dijkstra algorithm that computes the shortest path to every network.

   LSA packets are used to update and maintain the topological database.

**Link State Advertisement**   A *Link State Advertisement (LSA)* is an OSPF data packet containing link-state and routing information that's shared among OSPF routers. There are different types of LSA packets, and I'll cover these in the ICND2 book. An OSPF router will exchange LSA packets only with routers to which it has established adjacencies.

**OSPF areas**   An *OSPF area* is a grouping of contiguous networks and routers. All routers in the same area share a common area ID. Because a router can be a member of more than one area at a time, the area ID is associated with specific interfaces on the router. This would allow some interfaces to belong to area 1 while the remaining interfaces can belong to area 0. All of the routers within the same area have the same topology table. When configuring OSPF with multiple areas, you've got to remember that there must be an area 0 and that this is typically considered the backbone area. Areas also play a role in establishing a hierarchical network organization—something that really enhances the scalability of OSPF!

**Broadcast (multi-access)**   *Broadcast (multi-access) networks* such as Ethernet allow multiple devices to connect to or access the same network, enabling a *broadcast* ability in which a single packet is delivered to all nodes on the network. In OSPF, a DR and BDR must be elected for each broadcast multi-access network.

**Nonbroadcast multi-access**   *Nonbroadcast multi-access (NBMA)* networks are networks such as Frame Relay, X.25, and Asynchronous Transfer Mode (ATM). These types of networks allow for multi-access without broadcast ability like Ethernet. NBMA networks require special OSPF configuration to function properly.

**Point-to-point**    *Point-to-point* refers to a type of network topology made up of a direct connection between two routers that provides a single communication path. The point-to-point connection can be physical—for example, a serial cable that directly connects two routers—or logical, where two routers thousands of miles apart are connected by a circuit in a Frame Relay network. Either way, point-to-point configurations eliminate the need for DRs or BDRs.

**Point-to-multipoint**    *Point-to-multipoint* refers to a type of network topology made up of a series of connections between a single interface on one router and multiple destination routers. All interfaces on all routers share the point-to-multipoint connection and belong to the same network. Point-to-multipoint networks can be further classified according to whether they support broadcasts or not. This is important because it defines the kind of OSPF configurations you can deploy.

All of these terms play a critical role when you're trying to understand how OSPF actually works, so again, make sure you're familiar with each of them. Having these terms down will enable you to confidently place them in their proper context as we progress on our journey through the rest of this chapter!

## OSPF Operation

Fully equipped with your newly acquired knowledge of the terms and technologies we just covered, it's now time to delve into how OSPF discovers, propagates, and ultimately chooses routes. Once you know how OSPF achieves these tasks, you'll understand how OSPF operates internally really well.

OSPF operation is basically divided into these three categories:

- Neighbor and adjacency initialization
- LSA flooding
- SPF tree calculation

The beginning neighbor/adjacency formation stage is a very big part of OSPF operation. When OSPF is initialized on a router, the router allocates memory for it, as well as for the maintenance of both neighbor and topology tables. Once the router determines which interfaces have been configured for OSPF, it will then check to see if they're active and begin sending Hello packets.

**FIGURE 9.2**    The Hello protocol

Hello? ⟶
224.0.0.5

The Hello protocol is used to discover neighbors, establish adjacencies, and maintain relationships with other OSPF routers. Hello packets are periodically sent out of each enabled OSPF interface and in environments that support multicast.

The address used for this is 224.0.0.5, and the frequency with which Hello packets are sent out depends upon the network type and topology. Broadcast and point-to-point networks send Hellos every 10 seconds, whereas non-broadcast and point-to-multipoint networks send them every 30 seconds.

## LSA Flooding

*LSA flooding* is the method OSPF uses to share routing information. Via LSU packets, LSA information containing link-state data is shared with all OSPF routers within an area. The network topology is created from the LSA updates, and flooding is used so that all OSPF routers have the same topology map to make SPF calculations with.

Efficient flooding is achieved through the use of a reserved multicast address: 224.0.0.5 (AllSPFRouters). LSA updates, which indicate that something in the topology has changed, are handled a bit differently. The network type determines the multicast address used for sending updates. Table 9.2 contains the multicast addresses associated with LSA flooding. Point-to-multipoint networks use the adjacent router's unicast IP address.

**TABLE 9.2**   LSA update multicast addresses

| Network Type | Multicast Address | Description |
| --- | --- | --- |
| Point-to-point | 224.0.0.5 | AllSPFRouters |
| Broadcast | 224.0.0.6 | AllDRouters |
| Point-to-multipoint | NA | NA |

Once the LSA updates have been flooded throughout the network, each recipient must acknowledge that the flooded update has been received. It's also important for recipients to validate the LSA update.

## SPF Tree Calculation

Within an area, each router calculates the best/shortest path to every network in that same area. This calculation is based upon the information collected in the topology database and an algorithm called shortest path first (SPF). Picture each router in an area constructing a tree—much like a family tree—where the router is the root and all other networks are arranged along the branches and leaves. This is the shortest path tree used by the router to insert OSPF routes into the routing table.

It's important to understand that this tree contains only networks that exist in the same area as the router itself does. If a router has interfaces in multiple areas, then separate trees will be constructed for each area. One of the key criteria considered during the route selection process of the SPF algorithm is the metric or cost of each potential path to a network. But this SPF calculation doesn't apply to routes from other areas.

### OSPF Metrics

OSPF uses a metric referred to as *cost*. A cost is associated with every outgoing interface included in an SPF tree. The cost of the entire path is the sum of the costs of the outgoing interfaces along the path. Because cost is an arbitrary value as defined in RFC 2338, Cisco had to implement its own method of calculating the cost for each OSPF-enabled interface. Cisco uses a simple equation of $10^8/bandwidth$, where *bandwidth* is the configured bandwidth for the interface. Using this rule, a 100 Mbps Fast Ethernet interface would have a default OSPF cost of 1 and a 1,000 Mbps Ethernet interface would have a cost of 1.

Important to note is that this value can be overridden with the `ip ospf cost` command. The cost is manipulated by changing the value to a number within the range of 1 to 65,535. Because the cost is assigned to each link, the value must be changed on the specific interface you want to change the cost on.

Cisco bases link cost on bandwidth. Other vendors may use other metrics to calculate a given link's cost. When connecting links between routers from different vendors, you'll probably have to adjust the cost to match another vendor's router because both routers must assign the same cost to the link for OSPF to work properly.

# Configuring OSPF

Configuring basic OSPF isn't as simple as configuring RIP and EIGRP, and it can get really complex once the many options that are allowed within OSPF are factored in. But that's okay because you really only need to focus on basic, single-area OSPF configuration at this point. Coming up, I'll show you how to configure single-area OSPF.

The two factors that are foundational to OSPF configuration are enabling OSPF and configuring OSPF areas.

## Enabling OSPF

The easiest and also least scalable way to configure OSPF is to just use a single area. Doing this requires a minimum of two commands.

The first command used to activate the OSPF routing process is as follows:

```
Router(config)#router ospf ?
<1-65535> Process ID
```

A value in the range from 1 to 65,535 identifies the OSPF process ID. It's a unique number on this router that groups a series of OSPF configuration commands under a specific running process. Different OSPF routers don't have to use the same process ID to communicate. It's a purely local value that doesn't mean a lot, but you still need to remember that it cannot start at 0; it has to start at a minimum of 1.

You can have more than one OSPF process running simultaneously on the same router if you want, but this isn't the same as running multi-area OSPF. The second process will maintain an entirely separate copy of its topology table and manage its communications independently of the first one and you use it when you want OSPF to connect multiple ASs together. Also, because the Cisco exam objectives only cover single-area OSPF with each router running a single OSPF process, that's what we'll focus on in this book.

The OSPF process ID is needed to identify a unique instance of an OSPF database and is locally significant.

## Configuring OSPF Areas

After identifying the OSPF process, you need to identify the interfaces that you want to activate OSPF communications on as well as the area in which each resides. This will also configure the networks you're going to advertise to others. OSPF uses wildcards in the configuration, which are also used in the access list configurations that we'll cover in Chapter 12, "Security."

Here's an example of a basic OSPF configuration for you, showing our second minimum command needed, the network command:

```
Router#config t
Router(config)#router ospf 1
Router(config-router)#network 10.0.0.0 0.255.255.255 area ?
  <0-4294967295>   OSPF area ID as a decimal value
  A.B.C.D          OSPF area ID in IP address format
Router(config-router)#network 10.0.0.0 0.255.255.255 area 0
```

The areas can be any number from 0 to 4.2 billion. Don't get these numbers confused with the process ID, which ranges from 1 to 65,535.

Remember, the OSPF process ID number is irrelevant. It can be the same on every router on the network, or it can be different—doesn't matter. It's locally significant and just enables the OSPF routing on the router.

The arguments of the network command are the network number (10.0.0.0) and the wildcard mask (0.255.255.255). The combination of these two numbers identifies the interfaces that OSPF will operate on and will also be included in its OSPF LSA advertisements. Based on my sample configuration, OSPF will use this command to find any interface on the router configured in the 10.0.0.0 network and will place any interface it finds into area 0. Notice that you can create about 4.2 billion areas! In reality, a router wouldn't let you create that many, but you can certainly name them using the numbers up to 4.2 billion. You can also label an area using an IP address format.

Let me stop here a minute to give you a quick explanation of wildcards: A 0 octet in the wildcard mask indicates that the corresponding octet in the network must match exactly. On the other hand, a 255 indicates that you don't care what the corresponding octet is in the network number. A network and wildcard mask combination of 1.1.1.1 0.0.0.0 would match an interface configured exactly with 1.1.1.1 only, and nothing else. This is really useful if you want to activate OSPF on a specific interface in a very clear and simple way. If you insist on matching a range of networks, the network and wildcard mask combination of 1.1.0.0 0.0.255.255 would match any interface in the range of 1.1.0.0 to 1.1.255.255. Because of this, it's simpler and safer to stick to using wildcard masks of 0.0.0.0 and identify each OSPF interface individually. Once configured, they'll function exactly the same—one way is really isn't better than the other.

The final argument is the area number. It indicates the area to which the interfaces identified in the network and wildcard mask portion belong. Remember that OSPF routers will become neighbors only if their interfaces share a network that's configured to belong to the same area number. The format of the area number is either a decimal value from the range 1 to 4,294,967,295 or a value represented in standard dotted-decimal notation. For example, area 0.0.0.0 is a legitimate area and is identical to area 0.

## Wildcard Example

Before getting down to configuring our network, let's take a quick peek at a more complex OSPF network configuration to find out what our OSPF network statements would be if we were using subnets and wildcards.

In this scenario, you have a router with these four subnets connected to four different interfaces:

- 192.168.10.64/28
- 192.168.10.80/28
- 192.168.10.96/28
- 192.168.10.8/30

All interfaces need to be in area 0, so it seems to me the easiest configuration would look like this:

```
Test#config t
Test(config)#router ospf 1
Test(config-router)#network 192.168.10.0 0.0.0.255 area 0
```

Okay—I'll admit that preceding example is actually pretty simple, but easy isn't always best—especially when dealing with OSPF! So even though this is an easy-button way to configure OSPF, it doesn't make good use of its capabilities and what fun is that? Worse yet, the objectives aren't very likely to present something this simple for you! So let's create a separate network statement for each interface using the subnet numbers and wildcards. Doing that would look something like this:

```
Test#config t
Test(config)#router ospf 1
Test(config-router)#network 192.168.10.64 0.0.0.15 area 0
Test(config-router)#network 192.168.10.80 0.0.0.15 area 0
Test(config-router)#network 192.168.10.96 0.0.0.15 area 0
Test(config-router)#network 192.168.10.8 0.0.0.3 area 0
```

Wow, now that's a different looking config! Truthfully, OSPF would work exactly the same way as it would with the easy configuration I showed you first—but unlike the easy configuration, this one covers the objectives!

And although this looks a bit complicated, trust me, it really isn't. All you need for clarity is to fully understand your block sizes! Just remember that when configuring wildcards, they're always one less than the block size. A /28 is a block size of 16, so we would add our network statement using the subnet number and then add a wildcard of 15 in the interesting octet. For the /30, which is a block size of 4, we would go with a wildcard of 3. Once you practice this a few times, it gets really easy. And do practice because we'll deal with them again when we get to access lists later on!

Let's use Figure 9.3 as an example and configure that network with OSPF using wildcards to make sure you have a solid grip on this. The figure shows a three-router network with the IP addresses of each interface.

**FIGURE 9.3**   Sample OSPF wildcard configuration

The very first thing you need to be able to do is to look at each interface and determine the subnet that the addresses are in. Hold on, I know what you're thinking: "Why don't I just use the exact IP addresses of the interface with the 0.0.0.0 wildcard?" Well, you can, but we're paying attention to Cisco exam objectives here, not just what's easiest, remember?

The IP addresses for each interface are shown in the figure. The Lab_A router has two directly connected subnets: 192.168.10.64/29 and 10.255.255.80/30. Here's the OSPF configuration using wildcards:

```
Lab_A#config t
Lab_A(config)#router ospf 1
Lab_A(config-router)#network 192.168.10.64 0.0.0.7 area 0
Lab_A(config-router)#network 10.255.255.80 0.0.0.3 area 0
```

The Lab_A router is using a /29, or 255.255.255.248, mask on the Fa0/0 interface. This is a block size of 8, which is a wildcard of 7. The G0/0 interface is a mask of 255.255.255.252—block size of 4, with a wildcard of 3. Notice that I typed in the network number, not the interface number. You can't configure OSPF this way if you can't look at the IP address and slash notation and then figure out the subnet, mask, and wildcard, can you? So don't take your exam until you can do this.

Here are other two configurations to help you practice:

```
Lab_B#config t
Lab_B(config)#router ospf 1
Lab_B(config-router)#network 192.168.10.48 0.0.0.7 area 0
Lab_B(config-router)#network 10.255.255.80 0.0.0.3 area 0
Lab_B(config-router)#network 10.255.255.8 0.0.0.3 area 0


Lab_C#config t
Lab_C(config)#router ospf 1
Lab_C(config-router)#network 192.168.10.16 0.0.0.7 area 0
Lab_C(config-router)#network 10.255.255.8 0.0.0.3 area 0
```

As I mentioned with the Lab_A configuration, you've got to be able to determine the subnet, mask, and wildcard just by looking at the IP address and mask of an interface. If you can't do that, you won't be able to configure OSPF using wildcards as I just demonstrated. So go over this until you're really comfortable with it!

## Configuring Our Network with OSPF

Okay—now we get to have some fun! Let's configure our internetwork with OSPF using just area 0. OSPF has an administrative distance of 110, but let's remove RIP while we're at it because I don't want you to get in the habit of having RIP running on your network.

There's a bunch of different ways to configure OSPF, and as I said, the simplest and easiest is to use the wildcard mask 0.0.0.0. But I want to demonstrate that we can configure each router differently with OSPF and still come up with the exact same result. This is one reason why OSPF is more fun and challenging than other routing protocols—it gives us all a lot more ways to screw things up, which automatically provides a trouble-shooting opportunity! We'll use our network as shown in Figure 9.4 to configure OSPF and by the way, notice I added a new router!

**FIGURE 9.4**   Our new network layout

## Corp

Here's the Corp router's configuration:

```
Corp#sh ip int brief
Interface        IP-Address     OK? Method Status                     Protocol
FastEthernet0/0  10.10.10.1     YES manual up                         up
Serial0/0        172.16.10.1    YES manual up                         up
FastEthernet0/1  unassigned     YES unset  administratively down down
Serial0/1        172.16.10.5    YES manual up                         up
Corp#config t
Corp(config)#no router rip
Corp(config)#router ospf 132
Corp(config-router)#network 10.10.10.1 0.0.0.0 area 0
Corp(config-router)#network 172.16.10.1 0.0.0.0 area 0
Corp(config-router)#network 172.16.10.5 0.0.0.0 area 0
```

Alright—it looks like we have a few things to talk about here. First, I removed RIP and then added OSPF. Why did I use OSPF 132? It really doesn't matter—the number is irrelevant. I guess it just felt good to use 132. But notice that I started with the show ip int brief command, just like when I was configuring RIP. I did this because it's always important to verify exactly what you are directly connected to. Doing this really helps prevent typos!

The network commands are pretty straightforward. I typed in the IP address of each interface and used the wildcard mask of 0.0.0.0, which means that the IP address must precisely match each octet. This is actually one of those times where easier is better, so just do this:

```
Corp(config)#router ospf 132
Corp(config-router)#network 172.16.10.0 0.0.0.255 area 0
```

Nice—there's only one line instead of two for the 172.16.10.0 network! I really want you to understand that OSPF will work the same here no matter which way you configure the network statement. Now, let's move on to SF. To simplify things, we're going to use our same sample configuration.

## SF

The SF router has two directly connected networks. I'll use the IP addresses on each interface to configure this router.

```
SF#sh ip int brief
Interface     IP-Address      OK? Method Status                 Protocol
FastEthernet0/0  192.168.10.1    YES manual up                      up
FastEthernet0/1  unassigned      YES unset  administratively down down
Serial0/0/0      172.16.10.2     YES manual up                      up
Serial0/0/1      unassigned      YES unset  administratively down down
SF#config t
SF(config)#no router rip
SF(config)#router ospf 300
SF(config-router)#network 192.168.10.1 0.0.0.0 area 0
SF(config-router)#network 172.16.10.2 0.0.0.0 area 0
*Apr 30 00:25:43.810: %OSPF-5-ADJCHG: Process 300, Nbr 172.16.10.5 on Serial0/0/0
from LOADING to FULL, Loading Done
```

Here, all I did was to first disable RIP, turn on OSPF routing process 300, and then I added my two directly connected networks. Now let's move on to LA!

## LA

We're going to give some attention to the LA router that's directly connected to two networks:

```
LA#sh ip int brief
Interface     IP-Address      OK? Method Status                 Protocol
```

```
FastEthernet0/0 192.168.20.1    YES manual up                          up
FastEthernet0/1 unassigned      YES unset  administratively down down
Serial0/0/0     unassigned      YES unset  administratively down down
Serial0/0/1     172.16.10.6     YES manual up                          up
LA#config t
LA(config)#router ospf 100
LA(config-router)#network 192.168.20.0 0.0.0.255 area 0
LA(config-router)#network 172.16.0.0 0.0.255.255 area 0
*Apr 30 00:56:37.090: %OSPF-5-ADJCHG: Process 100, Nbr 172.16.10.5 on Serial0/0/1
from LOADING to FULL, Loading Done
```

Remember that when you're configuring dynamic routing, using the show ip int brief command first will make it all so much easier!

And don't forget, I can use any process ID I want, as long as it's a value from 1 to 65,535, because it doesn't matter if all routers use the same process ID. Also, notice that I used different wildcards in this example. Doing this works really well too.

Okay, I want you to think about something for a second before we move onto more advanced OSPF topics: What if the Fa0/1 interface of the LA router was connected to a link that we didn't want, or need to have on in order to have OSPF working, as shown in Figure 9.5?

**FIGURE 9.5**    Adding a non-OSPF network to LA router

You've seen this before because I demonstrated this already back in Chapter 8, in the RIP section. We can use the same command that we did under that routing process here as well! Take a look:

```
LA(config)#router ospf 100
LA(config-router)#passive-interface fastEthernet 0/1
```

Even though this is pretty simple, you've really got to be careful before you configure this command on your router! I added this command as an example on interface Fa0/1, which happens to be an interface we're not using in this network because I want OSPF to work on my other router's interfaces.

Now it's time to configure our Corp router to advertise a default route to the SF and LA routers because doing so will make our lives a lot easier. Instead of having to configure all our routers with a default route, we'll only configure one router and then advertise that this router is the one that holds the default route—elegant!

In Figure 9.4, keep in mind that, for now, the corporate router is connected to the Internet off of Fa0/0. We'll create a default route toward this imaginary Internet and then tell the other routers that this is the route they'll use to get to the Internet. Here is the configuration:

```
Corp#config t
Corp(config)#ip route 0.0.0.0 0.0.0.0 Fa0/0
Corp(config)#router ospf 1
Corp(config-router)#default-information originate
```

Now, let's check and see if our other routers have received this default route from the Corp router:

```
SF#show ip route
[output cut]
E1 - OSPF external type 1, E2 - OSPF external type 2
[output cut]
O*E2 0.0.0.0/0 [110/1] via 172.16.10.1, 00:01:54, Serial0/0/0
SF#
```

Sure enough—the last line in the SF router shows that it received the advertisement from the Corp router regarding the fact that the corporate router is the one holding the default route out of the AS.

But hold on a second! I need to configure our new router into my lab to create the example network we'll use from here on. Here's the configuration of the new router that I connected to the same network that the Corp router is connected to via the Fa0/0 interface:

```
Router#config t
Router(config)#hostname Boulder
Boulder(config)#int f0/0
Boulder(config-if)#ip address 10.10.10.2 255.255.255.0
Boulder(config-if)#no shut
*Apr  6 18:01:38.007: %LINEPROTO-5-UPDOWN: Line protocol on Interface
FastEthernet0/0, changed state to up
Boulder(config-if)#router ospf 2
Boulder(config-router)#network 10.0.0.0 0.255.255.255 area 0
*Apr  6 18:03:27.267: %OSPF-5-ADJCHG: Process 2, Nbr 223.255.255.254 on
FastEthernet0/0 from LOADING to FULL, Loading Done
```

This is all good, but I need to make sure that you don't follow my example to a tee because here, I just quickly brought a router up without setting my passwords first. I can get away with this only because I am in a nonproduction network, so don't do this in the real world where security is key!

Anyway, now that I have my new router nicely connected with a basic configuration, we're going to move on to cover loopback interfaces, how to set the router ID (RID) used with OSPF, and finally, how to verify OSPF.

# OSPF and Loopback Interfaces

It's really vital to configure loopback interfaces when using OSPF. In fact, Cisco suggests using them whenever you configure OSPF on a router for stability purposes.

*Loopback interfaces* are logical interfaces, which means they're virtual, software-only interfaces, not actual, physical router interfaces. A big reason we use loopback interfaces with OSPF configurations is because they ensure that an interface is always active and available for OSPF processes.

Loopback interfaces also come in very handy for diagnostic purposes as well as for OSPF configuration. Understand that if you don't configure a loopback interface on a router, the highest active IP address on a router will become that router's RID during bootup! Figure 9.6 illustrates how routers know each other by their router ID.

**FIGURE 9.6**   OSPF router ID (RID)

The RID is not only used to advertise routes, it's also used to elect the designated router (DR) and the backup designated router (BDR). These designated routers create adjacencies when a new router comes up and exchanges LSAs to build topological databases.

By default, OSPF uses the highest IP address on any active interface at the moment OSPF starts up to determine the RID of the router. But this behavior can be overridden via a logical interface. Remember—the highest IP address of any logical interface will always become a router's RID!

Now it's time to show you how to configure these logical loopback interfaces and how to verify them, as well as verify RIDs.

## Configuring Loopback Interfaces

Configuring loopback interfaces rocks mostly because it's the easiest part of OSPF configuration, and we all need a break about now—right? So hang on—we're in the home stretch!

First, let's see what the RID is on the Corp router with the show ip ospf command:

```
Corp#sh ip ospf
 Routing Process "ospf 1" with ID 172.16.10.5
[output cut]
```

Okay—we can see that the RID is 172.16.10.5—the Serial0/0 interface of the router. So let's configure a loopback interface using a completely different IP addressing scheme:

```
Corp(config)#int loopback 0
*Mar 22 01:23:14.206: %LINEPROTO-5-UPDOWN: Line protocol on Interface
   Loopback0, changed state to up
Corp(config-if)#ip address 172.31.1.1 255.255.255.255
```

The IP scheme really doesn't matter here, but each one being in a separate subnet does! By using the /32 mask, we can use any IP address we want as long as the addresses are never the same on any two routers.

Let's configure the other routers now:

```
SF#config t
SF(config)#int loopback 0
*Mar 22 01:25:11.206: %LINEPROTO-5-UPDOWN: Line protocol on Interface
   Loopback0, changed state to up
SF(config-if)#ip address 172.31.1.2 255.255.255.255
```

Here's the configuration of the loopback interface on LA:

```
LA#config t
LA(config)#int loopback 0
*Mar 22 02:21:59.686: %LINEPROTO-5-UPDOWN: Line protocol on Interface
   Loopback0, changed state to up
LA(config-if)#ip address 172.31.1.3 255.255.255.255
```

I'm pretty sure you're wondering what the IP address mask of 255.255.255.255 (/32) means and why we don't just use 255.255.255.0 instead. While it's true that either mask works, the /32 mask is called a host mask and works fine for loopback interfaces. It also allows us to save subnets. Notice how I was able to use 172.31.1.1, .2, .3, and .4? If I didn't use the /32, I'd have to use a separate subnet for each and every router—not good!

One important question to answer before we move on is did we actually change the RIDs of our router by setting the loopback interfaces? Let's find out by taking a look at the Corp's RID:

```
Corp#sh ip ospf
 Routing Process "ospf 1" with ID 172.16.10.5
```

Okay—what happened here? You would think that because we set logical interfaces, the IP addresses under them would automatically become the RID of the router, right? Well, sort of, but only if you do one of two things: either reboot the router or delete OSPF and re-create the database on your router. Neither is all that great an option, so try to remember to create your logical interfaces before you start OSPF routing. That way, the loopback interface would always become your RID straight away!

With all this in mind, I'm going with rebooting the Corp router because it's the easier of the two options I have right now.

Now let's look and see what our RID is:

```
Corp#sh ip ospf
 Routing Process "ospf 1" with ID 172.31.1.1
```

Okay, that did the trick! The Corp router now has a new RID, so I guess I'll just go ahead and reboot all my routers to get their RIDs reset to our logical addresses. But should I really do that?

Maybe not because there is *one* other way. What do you think about adding a new RID for the router right under the router ospf *process-id* command instead? Sounds good, so I'd say let's give that a shot! Here's an example of doing that on the Corp router:

```
Corp#config t
Corp(config)#router ospf 1
Corp(config-router)#router-id 223.255.255.254
Reload or use "clear ip ospf process" command, for this to take effect
Corp(config-router)#do clear ip ospf process
Reset ALL OSPF processes? [no]: yes
*Jan 16 14:20:36.906: %OSPF-5-ADJCHG: Process 1, Nbr 192.168.20.1
on Serial0/1 from FULL to DOWN, Neighbor Down: Interface down
or detached
*Jan 16 14:20:36.906: %OSPF-5-ADJCHG: Process 1, Nbr 192.168.10.1
on Serial0/0 from FULL to DOWN, Neighbor Down: Interface down
or detached
*Jan 16 14:20:36.982: %OSPF-5-ADJCHG: Process 1, Nbr 192.168.20.1
```

```
on Serial0/1 from LOADING to FULL, Loading Done
*Jan 16 14:20:36.982: %OSPF-5-ADJCHG: Process 1, Nbr 192.168.10.1
on Serial0/0 from LOADING to FULL, Loading Done
Corp(config-router)#do sh ip ospf
 Routing Process "ospf 1" with ID 223.255.255.254
```

Now look at that—it worked! We changed the RID without reloading the router! But wait—remember, we set a logical loopback interface earlier. Does that mean the loopback interface will win over the router-id command? Well, we can see our answer... A loopback interface will *not* override the router-id command, and we don't have to reboot the router to make it take effect as the RID!

So this process follows this hierarchy:

1. Highest active interface by default.

2. Highest logical interface overrides a physical interface.

3. The router-id overrides the interface and loopback interface.

The only thing left now is to decide whether you want to advertise the loopback interfaces under OSPF. There are pros and cons to using an address that won't be advertised versus using an address that will be. Using an unadvertised address saves on real IP address space, but the address won't appear in the OSPF table, which means you can't ping it.

So basically, what you're faced with here is a choice that equals a trade-off between the ease of debugging the network and conservation of address space—what to do? A really tight strategy is to use a private IP address scheme as I did. Do this and all will be well!

Now that we've configured all the routers with OSPF, what's next? Miller time? Nope—not yet. It's that verification thing again. We still have to make sure that OSPF is really working, and that's exactly what we're going to do next.

# Verifying OSPF Configuration

There are several ways to verify proper OSPF configuration and operation, so next, I'm going to demonstrate the various OSPF show commands you need to know in order to achieve this. We're going to start by taking a quick look at the routing table of the Corp router.

First, let's issue a show ip route command on the Corp router:

```
O    192.168.10.0/24 [110/65] via 172.16.10.2, 1d17h, Serial0/0
     172.131.0.0/32 is subnetted, 1 subnets
     172.131.0.0/32 is subnetted, 1 subnets
C        172.131.1.1 is directly connected, Loopback0
     172.16.0.0/30 is subnetted, 4 subnets
C        172.16.10.4 is directly connected, Serial0/1
L        172.16.10.5/32 is directly connected, Serial0/1
```

```
C        172.16.10.0 is directly connected, Serial0/0
L        172.16.10.1/32 is directly connected, Serial0/0
O    192.168.20.0/24 [110/65] via 172.16.10.6, 1d17h, Serial0/1
     10.0.0.0/24 is subnetted, 2 subnets
C        10.10.10.0 is directly connected, FastEthernet0/0
L        10.10.10.1/32 is directly connected, FastEthernet0/0
```

The Corp router shows only two dynamic routes for the internetwork, with the O representing OSPF internal routes. The Cs are clearly our directly connected networks, and our two remote networks are showing up too—nice! Notice the 110/65, which is our administrative distance/metric.

Now that's a really sweet-looking OSPF routing table! It's important to make it easier to troubleshoot and fix an OSPF network, which is why I always use the show ip int brief command when configuring my routing protocols. It's very easy to make little mistakes with OSPF, so keep your eyes on the details!

It's time to show you all the OSPF verification commands that you need in your toolbox for now.

## The *show ip ospf* Command

The show ip ospf command is what you'll need to display OSPF information for one or all OSPF processes running on the router. Information contained therein includes the router ID, area information, SPF statistics, and LSA timer information. Let's check out the output from the Corp router:

```
Corp#sh ip ospf
 Routing Process "ospf 1" with ID 223.255.255.254
 Start time: 00:08:41.724, Time elapsed: 2d16h
 Supports only single TOS(TOS0) routes
 Supports opaque LSA
 Supports Link-local Signaling (LLS)
 Supports area transit capability
 Router is not originating router-LSAs with maximum metric
 Initial SPF schedule delay 5000 msecs
 Minimum hold time between two consecutive SPFs 10000 msecs
 Maximum wait time between two consecutive SPFs 10000 msecs
 Incremental-SPF disabled
 Minimum LSA interval 5 secs
 Minimum LSA arrival 1000 msecs
 LSA group pacing timer 240 secs
 Interface flood pacing timer 33 msecs
 Retransmission pacing timer 66 msecs
 Number of external LSA 0. Checksum Sum 0x000000
```

```
Number of opaque AS LSA 0. Checksum Sum 0x000000
Number of DCbitless external and opaque AS LSA 0
Number of DoNotAge external and opaque AS LSA 0
Number of areas in this router is 1. 1 normal 0 stub 0 nssa
Number of areas transit capable is 0
External flood list length 0
IETF NSF helper support enabled
Cisco NSF helper support enabled
    Area BACKBONE(0)
        Number of interfaces in this area is 3
        Area has no authentication
        SPF algorithm last executed 00:11:08.760 ago
        SPF algorithm executed 5 times
        Area ranges are
        Number of LSA 6. Checksum Sum 0x03B054
        Number of opaque link LSA 0. Checksum Sum 0x000000
        Number of DCbitless LSA 0
        Number of indication LSA 0
        Number of DoNotAge LSA 0
        Flood list length 0
```

Notice the router ID (RID) of 223.255.255.254, which is the highest IP address configured on the router. Hopefully, you also noticed that I set the RID of the corporate router to the highest available IP address available with IPv4.

## The *show ip ospf database* Command

Using the show ip ospf database command will give you information about the number of routers in the internetwork (AS) plus the neighboring router's ID—the topology database I mentioned earlier. Unlike the show ip eigrp topology command, this command reveals the OSPF routers, but not each and every link in the AS like EIGRP does.

The output is broken down by area. Here's a sample output, again from Corp:

```
Corp#sh ip ospf database


              OSPF Router with ID (223.255.255.254) (Process ID 1)
Router Link States (Area 0)


Link ID         ADV Router      Age      Seq#       Checksum Link count
10.10.10.2      10.10.10.2      966      0x80000001 0x007162 1
```

```
172.31.1.4       172.31.1.4       885        0x80000002 0x00D27E 1
192.168.10.1     192.168.10.1     886        0x8000007A 0x00BC95 3
192.168.20.1     192.168.20.1     1133       0x8000007A 0x00E348 3
223.255.255.254 223.255.255.254 925         0x8000004D 0x000B90 5


                    Net Link States (Area 0)


Link ID          ADV Router       Age        Seq#       Checksum
10.10.10.1       223.255.255.254 884        0x80000002 0x008CFE
```

You can see all the routers and the RID of each router—the highest IP address on each of them. For example, the Link ID and ADV Router of my new Boulder router shows up twice: once with the directly connected IP address (10.10.10.2) and as the RID that I set under the OSPF process (172.31.1.4).

The router output shows the link ID—remember that an interface is also a link—and the RID of the router on that link under the ADV router, or advertising router.

## The *show ip ospf interface* Command

The show ip ospf interface command reveals all interface-related OSPF information. Data is displayed about OSPF information for all OSPF-enabled interfaces or for specified interfaces. I'll highlight some of the more important factors for you. Check it out:

```
Corp#sh ip ospf int f0/0
FastEthernet0/0 is up, line protocol is up
  Internet Address 10.10.10.1/24, Area 0
  Process ID 1, Router ID 223.255.255.254, Network Type BROADCAST, Cost: 1
  Transmit Delay is 1 sec, State DR, Priority 1
  Designated Router (ID) 223.255.255.254, Interface address 10.10.10.1
  Backup Designated router (ID) 172.31.1.4, Interface address 10.10.10.2
  Timer intervals configured, Hello 10, Dead 40, Wait 40, Retransmit 5
    oob-resync timeout 40
    Hello due in 00:00:08
  Supports Link-local Signaling (LLS)
  Cisco NSF helper support enabled
  IETF NSF helper support enabled
  Index 3/3, flood queue length 0
  Next 0x0(0)/0x0(0)
  Last flood scan length is 1, maximum is 1
```

```
Last flood scan time is 0 msec, maximum is 0 msec
Neighbor Count is 1, Adjacent neighbor count is 1
  Adjacent with neighbor 172.31.1.  Suppress hello for 0 neighbor(s)
```

Okay—so this command has given us the following information:

- Interface IP address
- Area assignment
- Process ID
- Router ID
- Network type
- Cost
- Priority
- DR/BDR election information (if applicable)
- Hello and Dead timer intervals
- Adjacent neighbor information

The reason I used the show ip ospf interface f0/0 command is because I knew that there would be a designated router elected on the FastEthernet broadcast multi-access network between our Corp and Boulder routers. The information that I highlighted is all very important, so make sure you've noted it! A good question to ask you here is what are the Hello and Dead timers set to by default?

Type in the show ip ospf interface command and receive this response:

```
Corp#sh ip ospf int f0/0
%OSPF: OSPF not enabled on FastEthernet0/0
```

This error occurs when OSPF is enabled on the router, but not the interface. When this happens, you need to check your network statements because it means that the interface you're trying to verify is not in your OSPF process!

## The *show ip ospf neighbor* Command

The show ip ospf neighbor command is super-useful because it summarizes the pertinent OSPF information regarding neighbors and the adjacency state. If a DR or BDR exists, that information will also be displayed. Here's a sample:

```
Corp#sh ip ospf neighbor
```

```
Neighbor ID     Pri   State      Dead Time   Address        Interface
172.31.1.4       1    FULL/BDR   00:00:34    10.10.10.2     FastEthernet0/0
192.168.20.1     0    FULL/  -   00:00:31    172.16.10.6    Serial0/1
192.168.10.1     0    FULL/  -   00:00:32    172.16.10.2    Serial0/0
```

🌐 **Real World Scenario**

**An Admin Connects Two Disparate Routers Together with OSPF and the Link Between them Never Comes Up**

Quite a few years ago, an admin called me in a panic because he couldn't get OSPF working between two routers, one of which was an older router that they needed to use while they were waiting for their new router to be shipped to them.

OSPF can be used in a multi-vendor network so he was confused as to why this wasn't working. He turned on RIP and it worked so he was super confused with why OSPF was not creating adjacencies. I had him use the show ip ospf interface command to look at the link between the two routers and sure enough, the hello and dead timers didn't match. I had him configure the mismatched parameters so they would match, but it still wouldn't create an adjacency. Looking more closely at the show ip ospf interface command, I noticed the cost did not match! Cisco calculated the bandwidth differently than the other vendor. Once I had him configure both as the same value, the link came up! Always remember, just because OSPF can be used in a multi-vendor network, does not mean it will work out of the box!

This is a critical command to understand because it's extremely useful in production networks. Let's take a look at the Boulder router output:

```
Boulder>sh ip ospf neighbor


Neighbor ID      Pri   State     Dead Time   Address      Interface
223.255.255.254  1     FULL/DR   00:00:31    10.10.10.1   FastEthernet0/0
```

Okay—here we can see that since there's an Ethernet link (broadcast multi-access) on the link between the Boulder and the Corp router, there's going to be an election to determine who will be the designated router (DR) and who will be the backup designated router (BDR). We can see that the Corp became the designated router, and it won because it had the highest IP address on the network—the highest RID.

Now the reason that the Corp connections to SF and LA don't have a DR or BDR listed in the output is that by default, elections don't happen on point-to-point links and they show FULL/ - . But we can still determine that the Corp router is fully adjacent to all three routers from its output.

## The *show ip protocols* Command

The show ip protocols command is also highly useful, whether you're running OSPF, EIGRP, RIP, BGP, IS-IS, or any other routing protocol that can be configured on your router. It provides an excellent overview of the actual operation of all currently running protocols! Check out the output from the Corp router:

```
Corp#sh ip protocols
Routing Protocol is "ospf 1"
  Outgoing update filter list for all interfaces is not set
  Incoming update filter list for all interfaces is not set
  Router ID 223.255.255.254
  Number of areas in this router is 1. 1 normal 0 stub 0 nssa
  Maximum path: 4
  Routing for Networks:
    10.10.10.1 0.0.0.0 area 0
    172.16.10.1 0.0.0.0 area 0
    172.16.10.5 0.0.0.0 area 0
 Reference bandwidth unit is 100 mbps
  Routing Information Sources:
    Gateway         Distance      Last Update
    192.168.10.1        110       00:21:53
    192.168.20.1        110       00:21:53
  Distance: (default is 110) Distance: (default is 110)
```

From looking at this output, you can determine the OSPF process ID, OSPF router ID, type of OSPF area, networks and areas configured for OSPF, and the OSPF router IDs of neighbors—that's a lot. It's super-efficient!

# Summary

This chapter gave you a great deal of information about OSPF. It's really difficult to include everything about OSPF because so much of it falls outside the scope of this chapter and book, but I've given you a few tips here and there, so you're good to go—as long as you make sure you've got what I presented to you dialed in, that is!

I talked about a lot of OSPF topics, including terminology, operations, and configuration as well as verification and monitoring.

Each of these topics encompasses quite a bit of information—the terminology section just scratched the surface of OSPF. But you've got the goods you really need for your studies. Finally, I gave you a tight survey of commands highly useful for observing the operation of OSPF so you can verify that things are moving along as they should. So eat it all up, and you're set!

# Exam Essentials

**Compare OSPF and RIPv1.**    OSPF is a link-state protocol that supports VLSM and classless routing; RIPv1 is a distance-vector protocol that does not support VLSM and supports only classful routing.

**Know how OSPF routers become neighbors and/or adjacent.**    OSPF routers become neighbors when each router sees the other's Hello packets.

**Be able to configure single-area OSPF.**    A minimal single-area configuration involves only two commands: router ospf *process-id* and network *x.x.x.x y.y.y.y area Z*.

**Be able to verify the operation of OSPF.**    There are many show commands that provide useful details on OSPF, and it is useful to be completely familiar with the output of each: show ip ospf, show ip ospf database, show ip ospf interface, show ip ospf neighbor, and show ip protocols.

# Written Lab 9

The answers to this lab can be found in Appendix A, "Answers to Written Labs."

1. Write the command that will enable the OSPF process 101 on a router.

2. Write the command that will display details of all OSPF routing processes enabled on a router.

3. Write the command that will display interface-specific OSPF information.

4. Write the command that will display all OSPF neighbors.

5. Write the command that will display all different OSPF route types that are currently known by the router.

# Hands-on Labs

In this section, you will use the following network and add OSPF routing.

The first lab (Lab 9.1) requires you to configure three routers for OSPF and then view the configuration. Note that the labs in this chapter were written to be used with real equipment—but they can be used with any router simulator. You can replace the WAN links with Ethernet links if you want to.

The labs in this chapter are as follows:

Lab 9.1: Enabling the OSPF Process

Lab 9.2: Configuring OSPF Interfaces

Lab 9.3: Verifying OSPF Operation

Table 9.5 shows our IP addresses for each router (each interface uses a /24 mask).

**TABLE 9.5**   Our IP addresses

| Router | Interface | IP address |
|--------|-----------|------------|
| Lab_A | Fa0/0 | 172.16.10.1 |
| Lab_A | S0/0 | 172.16.20.1 |
| Lab_B | S0/2 | 172.16.20.2 |
| Lab_B | S0/1 | 172.16.30.1 |
| Lab_C | S0/0 | 172.16.30.2 |
| Lab_C | Fa0/0 | 172.16.40.1 |

# Hands-on Lab 9.1: Enabling the OSPF Process

This is the first mandatory step in OSPF configuration.

1. Enable OSPF process 100 on Lab_A:

```
Lab_A#conf t
Enter configuration commands, one per line.
  End with CNTL/Z.
Lab_A (config)#router ospf 100
Lab_A (config-router)#^Z
```

2. Enable OSPF process 101 on Lab_B:

```
Lab_B#conf t
Enter configuration commands, one per line.
  End with CNTL/Z.
Lab_B (config)#router ospf 101
Lab_B (config-router)#^Z
```

3. Enable OSPF process 102 on Lab_C:

```
Lab_C#conf t
Enter configuration commands, one per line.
  End with CNTL/Z.
Lab_C (config)#router ospf 102
Lab_C (config-router)#^Z
```

# Hands-on Lab 9.2: Configuring OSPF Interfaces

The second mandatory step in OSPF is adding your network statements.

1. Configure the LAN and the network between Lab_A and Lab_B. Assign it to area 0.

```
Lab_A#conf t
Enter configuration commands, one per line.
  End with CNTL/Z.
Lab_A (config)#router ospf 100
Lab_A (config-router)#network 172.16.10.1 0.0.0.0 area 0
Lab_A (config-router)#network 172.16.20.1 0.0.0.0 area 0
Lab_A (config-router)#^Z
Lab_A #
```

2. Configure the networks on the Lab_B router. Assign them to area 0.

```
Lab_B#conf t
Enter configuration commands, one per line.
  End with CNTL/Z.
Lab_B(config)#router ospf 101
Lab_B(config-router)#network 172.16.20.2 0.0.0.0 area 0
Lab_B(config-router)#network 172.16.30.1 0.0.0.0 area 0
Lab_B(config-router)#^Z
Lab_B #
```

3. Configure the networks on the Lab_C router. Assign them to area 0.

```
Lab_C#conf t
Enter configuration commands, one per line.
  End with CNTL/Z.
Lab_C(config)#router ospf 102
Lab_C(config-router)#network 172.16.30.2 0.0.0.0 area 0
Lab_C(config-router)#network 172.16.40.1 0.0.0.0 area 0
Lab_C(config-router)#^Z
Lab_C#
```

# Hands-on Lab 9.3: Verifying OSPF Operation

You need to be able to verify what you configure.

1. Execute a show ip ospf neighbors command from the Lab_A router and view the results.

   Lab_A#**sho ip ospf neig**

2. Execute a show ip route command to verify that all other routers are learning all routes.

   Lab_A#**sho ip route**

3. Execute a show ip protocols command to verify OSPF information.

   Lab_A#**sho ip protocols**

4. Execute a show ip OSPF command to verify your RID.

   Lab_A#**sho ip ospf**

5. Execute a show ip ospf interface f0/0 command to verify your timers.

   Lab_A#**sho ip ospf int f0/0**

# Review Questions

The following questions are designed to test your understanding of this chapter's material. For more information on how to get additional questions, please see this book's introduction.

The answers to these questions can be found in Appendix B, "Answers to Chapter Review Questions."

1. There are three possible routes for a router to reach a destination network. The first route is from OSPF with a metric of 782. The second route is from RIPv2 with a metric of 4. The third is from EIGRP with a composite metric of 20514560. Which route will be installed by the router in its routing table?

   **A.** RIPv2

   **B.** EIGRP

   **C.** OSPF

   **D.** All three

2. In the accompanying diagram, which of the routers must be ABRs? (Choose all that apply.)

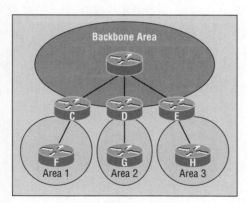

   **A.** C

   **B.** D

   **C.** E

   **D.** F

   **E.** G

   **F.** H

3. Which of the following describe the process identifier that is used to run OSPF on a router? (Choose two.)

   A. It is locally significant.

   B. It is globally significant.

   C. It is needed to identify a unique instance of an OSPF database.

   D. It is an optional parameter required only if multiple OSPF processes are running on the router.

   E. All routes in the same OSPF area must have the same process ID if they are to exchange routing information.

4. All of the following must match for two OSPF routers to become neighbors except which?

   A. Area ID

   B. Router ID

   C. Stub area flag

   D. Authentication password if using one

5. In the diagram, by default what will be the router ID of Lab_B?

   A. 10.255.255.82

   B. 10.255.255.9

   C. 192.168.10.49

   D. 10.255.255.81

6. You get a call from a network administrator who tells you that he typed the following into his router:

```
Router(config)#router ospf 1
Router(config-router)#network 10.0.0.0 255.0.0.0 area 0
```

He tells you he still can't see any routes in the routing table. What configuration error did the administrator make?

  **A.** The wildcard mask is incorrect.

  **B.** The OSPF area is wrong.

  **C.** The OSPF process ID is incorrect.

  **D.** The AS configuration is wrong.

7. Which of the following statements is true with regard to the output shown?

```
Corp#sh ip ospf neighbor
Neighbor ID     Pri   State      Dead Time   Address        Interface
172.31.1.4       1    FULL/BDR   00:00:34    10.10.10.2     FastEthernet0/0
192.168.20.1     0    FULL/ -    00:00:31    172.16.10.6    Serial0/1
192.168.10.1     0    FULL/ -    00:00:32    172.16.10.2    Serial0/0
```

  **A.** There is no DR on the link to 192.168.20.1.

  **B.** The Corp router is the BDR on the link to 172.31.1.4.

  **C.** The Corp router is the DR on the link to 192.168.20.1.

  **D.** The link to 192.168.10.1 is Active.

8. What is the administrative distance of OSPF?

  **A.** 90

  **B.** 100

  **C.** 120

  **D.** 110

9. In OSPF, Hellos are sent to what IP address?

  **A.** 224.0.0.5

  **B.** 224.0.0.9

  **C.** 224.0.0.10

  **D.** 224.0.0.1

**10.** What command generated the following output?

```
172.31.1.4       1    FULL/BDR    00:00:34    10.10.10.2    FastEthernet0/0
192.168.20.1     0    FULL/  -    00:00:31    172.16.10.6   Serial0/1
192.168.10.1     0    FULL/  -    00:00:32    172.16.10.2   Serial0/0
```

**A.** show ip ospf neighbor

**B.** show ip ospf database

**C.** show ip route

**D.** show ip ospf interface

**11.** Updates addressed to 224.0.0.6 are destined for which type of OSPF router?

**A.** DR

**B.** ASBR

**C.** ABR

**D.** All OSPF routers

**12.** For some reason, you cannot establish an adjacency relationship on a common Ethernet link between two routers. Looking at this output, what is the cause of the problem?

```
RouterA#
Ethernet0/0 is up, line protocol is up
  Internet Address 172.16.1.2/16, Area 0
  Process ID 2, Router ID 172.126.1.2, Network Type BROADCAST, Cost: 10
  Transmit Delay is 1 sec, State DR, Priority 1
  Designated Router (ID) 172.16.1.2, interface address 172.16.1.1
  No backup designated router on this network
  Timer intervals configured, Hello 5, Dead 20, Wait 20, Retransmit 5


RouterB#
Ethernet0/0 is up, line protocol is up
  Internet Address 172.16.1.1/16, Area 0
  Process ID 2, Router ID 172.126.1.1, Network Type BROADCAST, Cost: 10
  Transmit Delay is 1 sec, State DR, Priority 1
  Designated Router (ID) 172.16.1.1, interface address 172.16.1.2
  No backup designated router on this network
  Timer intervals configured, Hello 10, Dead 40, Wait 40, Retransmit 5
```

A. The OSPF area is not configured properly.

B. The priority on RouterA should be set higher.

C. The cost on RouterA should be set higher.

D. The Hello and Dead timers are not configured properly.

E. A backup designated router needs to be added to the network.

F. The OSPF process ID numbers must match.

**13.** In the work area match each OSPF term (by line) to its definition.

| | |
|---|---|
| Designated router | contains only the best routes |
| Topological database | elected on broadcast networks |
| Hello protocol | contains all routes learned |
| Routing table | provides dynamic neighbor discovery |

**14.** Type the command that will disable OSPF on the Fa0/1 interface under the routing process. Write only the command and not the prompt.

**15.** Which two of the following commands will place network 10.2.3.0/24 into area 0? (Choose two.)

A. `router eigrp 10`

B. `router ospf 10`

C. `router rip`

D. `network 10.0.0.0`

E. `network 10.2.3.0 255.255.255.0 area 0`

F. `network 10.2.3.0 0.0.0.255 area0`

G. `network 10.2.3.0 0.0.0.255 area 0`

16. Given the following output, which statement or statements can be determined to be true? (Choose all that apply.)

RouterA2# **show ip ospf neighbor**

```
Neighbor ID Pri State Dead Time Address Interface
192.168.23.2 1 FULL/BDR 00:00:29 10.24.4.2 FastEthernet1/0
192.168.45.2 2 FULL/BDR 00:00:24 10.1.0.5 FastEthernet0/0
192.168.85.1 1 FULL/- 00:00:33 10.6.4.10 Serial0/1
192.168.90.3 1 FULL/DR 00:00:32 10.5.5.2 FastEthernet0/1
192.168.67.3 1 FULL/DR 00:00:20 10.4.9.20 FastEthernet0/2
192.168.90.1 1 FULL/BDR 00:00:23 10.5.5.4 FastEthernet0/1
<<output omitted>>
```

   A. The DR for the network connected to Fa0/0 has an interface priority higher than 2.
   B. This router (A2) is the BDR for subnet 10.1.0.0.
   C. The DR for the network connected to Fa0/1 has a router ID of 10.5.5.2.
   D. The DR for the serial subnet is 192.168.85.1.

17. What are three reasons for creating OSPF in a hierarchical design? (Choose three.)
   A. To decrease routing overhead
   B. To speed up convergence
   C. To confine network instability to single areas of the network
   D. To make configuring OSPF easier

**18.** Type the command that produced the following output. Write only the command and not the prompt.

```
FastEthernet0/0 is up, line protocol is up
  Internet Address 10.10.10.1/24, Area 0
  Process ID 1, Router ID 223.255.255.254, Network Type BROADCAST, Cost: 1
Transmit Delay is 1 sec, State DR, Priority 1
  Designated Router (ID) 223.255.255.254, Interface address 10.10.10.1
Backup Designated router (ID) 172.31.1.4, Interface address 10.10.10.2
Timer intervals configured, Hello 10, Dead 40, Wait 40, Retransmit 5
    oob-resync timeout 40
    Hello due in 00:00:08
  Supports Link-local Signaling (LLS)
  Cisco NSF helper support enabled
  IETF NSF helper support enabled
  Index 3/3, flood queue length 0
  Next 0x0(0)/0x0(0)
  Last flood scan length is 1, maximum is 1
  Last flood scan time is 0 msec, maximum is 0 msec
  Neighbor Count is 1, Adjacent neighbor count is 1
    Adjacent with neighbor 172.31.1.  Suppress hello for 0 neighbor(s)
```

**19.** A(n) _____is an OSPF data packet containing link-state and routing information that are shared among OSPF routers.

   **A.** LSA

   **B.** TSA

   **C.** Hello

   **D.** SPF

**20.** If routers in a single area are configured with the same priority value, what value does a router use for the OSPF router ID in the absence of a loopback interface?

   **A.** The lowest IP address of any physical interface

   **B.** The highest IP address of any physical interface

   **C.** The lowest IP address of any logical interface

   **D.** The highest IP address of any logical interface

# Chapter

# 10

# Layer 2 Switching

## THE FOLLOWING ICND1 EXAM TOPICS ARE COVERED IN THIS CHAPTER:

✓ **LAN Switching Technologies**

- Identify basic switching concepts and the operation of Cisco switches.
  - Collision Domains
  - Broadcast Domains
  - Types of switching
  - CAM Table
- Configure and verify initial switch configuration including remote access management.
  - Cisco IOS commands to perform basic switch setup
- Verify network status and switch operation using basic utilities such as Ping, Telnet and SSH.

✓ **Network Device Security**

- Configure and verify Switch Port Security features such as:
  - Sticky MAC
  - MAC address limitation
  - Static/dynamic
  - Violation modes
  - Err-disable
  - Shutdown
  - Protect restrict
  - Shutdown unused ports
  - Err-disable recovery

When people at Cisco discuss switching in regards to the Cisco exam objectives, they're talking about layer 2 switching unless they say otherwise. Layer 2 switching is the process of using the hardware address of devices on a LAN to segment a network. Since you've got the basic idea of how that works nailed down by now, we're going to dive deeper into the particulars of layer 2 switching to ensure that your concept of how it works is solid and complete.

You already know that we rely on switching to break up large collision domains into smaller ones and that a collision domain is a network segment with two or more devices sharing the same bandwidth. A hub network is a typical example of this type of technology. But since each port on a switch is actually its own collision domain, we were able to create a much better Ethernet LAN network by simply replacing our hubs with switches!

Switches truly have changed the way networks are designed and implemented. If a pure switched design is properly implemented, it absolutely will result in a clean, cost-effective, and resilient internetwork. In this chapter, we'll survey and compare how networks were designed before and after switching technologies were introduced.

I'll be using three switches to begin our configuration of a switched network, and we'll actually continue with their configurations in Chapter 11, "VLANs and Inter-VLAN Routing."

To find up-to-the-minute updates for this chapter, please see www.lammle.com/forum or the book's web page at www.sybex.com.

# Switching Services

Unlike old bridges, which used software to create and manage a Content Addressable Memory (CAM) filter table, our new, fast switches use application-specific integrated circuits (ASICs) to build and maintain their MAC filter tables. But it's still okay to think of a layer 2 switch as a multiport bridge because their basic reason for being is the same: to break up collision domains.

Layer 2 switches and bridges are faster than routers because they don't take up time looking at the Network layer header information. Instead, they look at the frame's hardware addresses before deciding to either forward, flood, or drop the frame.

Unlike hubs, switches create private, dedicated collision domains and provide independent bandwidth exclusive on each port.

Here's a list of four important advantages we gain when using Layer 2 switching:

- Hardware-based bridging (ASICs)
- Wire speed
- Low latency
- Low cost

A big reason layer 2 switching is so efficient is that no modification to the data packet takes place. The device only reads the frame encapsulating the packet, which makes the switching process considerably faster and less error-prone than routing processes are.

And if you use layer 2 switching for both workgroup connectivity and network segmentation (breaking up collision domains), you can create more network segments than you can with traditional routed networks. Plus, layer 2 switching increases bandwidth for each user because, again, each connection, or interface into the switch, is its own, self-contained collision domain.

# Three Switch Functions at Layer 2

There are three distinct functions of layer 2 switching that are vital for you to remember: *address learning*, *forward/filter decisions*, and *loop avoidance*.

**Address learning**   Layer 2 switches remember the source hardware address of each frame received on an interface and enter this information into a MAC database called a forward/filter table.

**Forward/filter decisions**   When a frame is received on an interface, the switch looks at the destination hardware address, then chooses the appropriate exit interface for it in the MAC database. This way, the frame is only forwarded out of the correct destination port.

**Loop avoidance**   If multiple connections between switches are created for redundancy purposes, network loops can occur. Spanning Tree Protocol (STP) is used to prevent network loops while still permitting redundancy.

Next, I'm going to talk about address learning and forward/filtering decisions. Loop avoidance is beyond the scope of the objectives being covered in this chapter.

## Address Learning

When a switch is first powered on, the MAC forward/filter table (CAM) is empty, as shown in Figure 10.1.

When a device transmits and an interface receives a frame, the switch places the frame's source address in the MAC forward/filter table, allowing it to refer to the precise interface the sending device is located on. The switch then has no choice but to flood the network with this frame out of every port except the source port because it has no idea where the destination device is actually located.

If a device answers this flooded frame and sends a frame back, then the switch will take the source address from that frame and place that MAC address in its database as well, associating this address with the interface that received the frame. Because the switch now has both of the relevant MAC addresses in its filtering table, the two devices can now make a point-to-point connection. The switch doesn't need to flood the frame as it did the first time because now the frames can and will only be forwarded between these two devices. This is exactly why layer 2 switches are so superior to hubs. In a hub network, all frames are forwarded out all ports every time—no matter what. Figure 10.2 shows the processes involved in building a MAC database.

**FIGURE 10.1**    Empty forward/filter table on a switch

**FIGURE 10.2**    How switches learn hosts' locations

In this figure, you can see four hosts attached to a switch. When the switch is powered on, it has nothing in its MAC address forward/filter table, just as in Figure 10.1. But when the hosts start communicating, the switch places the source hardware address of each frame into the table along with the port that the frame's source address corresponds to.

Let me give you an example of how a forward/filter table is populated using Figure 10.2:

1. Host A sends a frame to Host B. Host A's MAC address is 0000.8c01.000A; Host B's MAC address is 0000.8c01.000B.

2. The switch receives the frame on the Fa0/0 interface and places the source address in the MAC address table.

**3.** Since the destination address isn't in the MAC database, the frame is forwarded out all interfaces except the source port.

**4.** Host B receives the frame and responds to Host A. The switch receives this frame on interface Fa0/1 and places the source hardware address in the MAC database.

**5.** Host A and Host B can now make a point-to-point connection and only these specific devices will receive the frames. Hosts C and D won't see the frames, nor will their MAC addresses be found in the database because they haven't sent a frame to the switch yet.

If Host A and Host B don't communicate to the switch again within a certain time period, the switch will flush their entries from the database to keep it as current as possible.

## Forward/Filter Decisions

When a frame arrives at a switch interface, the destination hardware address is compared to the forward/filter MAC database. If the destination hardware address is known and listed in the database, the frame is only sent out of the appropriate exit interface. The switch won't transmit the frame out any interface except for the destination interface, which preserves bandwidth on the other network segments. This process is called *frame filtering.*

But if the destination hardware address isn't listed in the MAC database, then the frame will be flooded out all active interfaces except the interface it was received on. If a device answers the flooded frame, the MAC database is then updated with the device's location—its correct interface.

If a host or server sends a broadcast on the LAN, by default, the switch will flood the frame out all active ports except the source port. Remember, the switch creates smaller collision domains, but it's always still one large broadcast domain by default.

In Figure 10.3, Host A sends a data frame to Host D. What do you think the switch will do when it receives the frame from Host A?

**FIGURE 10.3**   Forward/filter table

| VLAN | Mac Address | Ports |
|------|-------------|-------|
| 1 | 0005.dccb.d74b | Fa0/4 |
| 1 | 000a.f467.9e80 | Fa0/5 |
| 1 | 000a.f467.9e8b | Fa0/6 |

Let's examine Figure 10.4 to find the answer.

Since Host A's MAC address is not in the forward/filter table, the switch will add the source address and port to the MAC address table, then forward the frame to Host D. It's really important to remember that the source MAC is always checked first to make sure it's in the CAM table. After that, if Host D's MAC address wasn't found in the forward/filter table, the switch would've flooded the frame out all ports except for port Fa0/3 because that's the specific port the frame was received on.

**FIGURE 10.4**   Forward/filter table answer

Now let's take a look at the output that results from using a show mac address-table command:

```
Switch#sh mac address-table
Vlan    Mac Address     Type        Ports
----    -----------     --------    -----
   1    0005.dccb.d74b  DYNAMIC     Fa0/1
   1    000a.f467.9e80  DYNAMIC     Fa0/3
   1    000a.f467.9e8b  DYNAMIC     Fa0/4
   1    000a.f467.9e8c  DYNAMIC     Fa0/3
   1    0010.7b7f.c2b0  DYNAMIC     Fa0/3
   1    0030.80dc.460b  DYNAMIC     Fa0/3
   1    0030.9492.a5dd  DYNAMIC     Fa0/1
   1    00d0.58ad.05f4  DYNAMIC     Fa0/1
```

But let's say the preceding switch received a frame with the following MAC addresses:

Source MAC: **0005.dccb.d74b**

Destination MAC: **000a.f467.9e8c**

How will the switch handle this frame? The right answer is that the destination MAC address will be found in the MAC address table and the frame will only be forwarded out Fa0/3. Never forget that if the destination MAC address isn't found in the forward/filter table, the frame will be forwarded out all of the switch's ports except for the one on which it was originally received in an attempt to locate the destination device. Now that you can see the MAC address table and how switches add host addresses to the forward filter table, how do think we can secure it from unauthorized users?

## Port Security

It's usually not a good thing to have your switches available for anyone to just plug into and play around with. I mean, we worry about wireless security, so why wouldn't we demand switch security just as much, if not more?

But just how do we actually prevent someone from simply plugging a host into one of our switch ports—or worse, adding a hub, switch, or access point into the Ethernet jack in their office? By default, MAC addresses will just dynamically appear in your MAC forward/filter database and you can stop them in their tracks by using port security!

Figure 10.5 shows two hosts connected to the single switch port Fa0/3 via either a hub or access point (AP).

**FIGURE 10.5**    "Port security" on a switch port restricts port access by MAC address.

Port Fa0/3 is configured to observe and allow only certain MAC addresses to associate with the specific port, so in this example, Host A is denied access, but Host B is allowed to associate with the port.

By using port security, you can limit the number of MAC addresses that can be assigned dynamically to a port, set static MAC addresses, and—here's my favorite part—set penalties for users who abuse your policy! Personally, I like to have the port shut down when the security policy is violated. Making abusers bring me a memo from their boss explaining why they violated the security policy brings with it a certain poetic justice, which is nice. And I'll also require something like that before I'll enable their port again. Things like this really seem to help people remember to behave!

This is all good, but you still need to balance your particular security needs with the time that implementing and managing them will realistically require. If you have tons of time on your hands, then go ahead and seriously lock your network down vault-tight! If you're busy like the rest of us, I'm here to reassure you that there are ways to secure things nicely without being totally overwhelmed with a massive amount of administrative overhead. First, and painlessly, always remember to shut down unused ports or assign them to an unused VLAN. All ports are enabled by default, so you need to make sure there's no access to unused switch ports!

Here are your options for configuring port security:

```
Switch#config t
Switch(config)#int f0/1
Switch(config-if)#switchport mode access
Switch(config-if)#switchport port-security
Switch(config-if)#switchport port-security ?
  aging          Port-security aging commands
  mac-address    Secure mac address
  maximum        Max secure addresses
  violation      Security violation mode
  <cr>
```

Most Cisco switches ship with their ports in desirable mode, which means that those ports will desire to trunk when sensing that another switch has just been connected. So first, we need to change the port out from desirable mode and make it an access port instead. If we don't do that, we won't be able to configure port security on it at all! Once that's out of the way, we can move on using our port-security commands, never forgetting that we must enable port security on the interface. Notice that I did this after I made the port an access port!

The preceding output clearly illustrates that the switchport port-security command can be used with four options. You can use the switchport port-security mac-address *mac-address* command to assign individual MAC addresses to each switch port, but be warned because if you go with that option, you had better have boatloads of time on your hands!

If you want to set up a switch port to allow only one host per port and make sure the port will shut down if this rule is violated, use the following commands like this:

```
Switch(config-if)#switchport port-security maximum 1
Switch(config-if)#switchport port-security violation shutdown
```

These commands really are probably the most popular because they prevent random users from connecting to a specific switch or access point that's in their office. The maximum setting is 1, which is the port security default that's immediately set on a port when it's enabled. Sounds okay, but the drawback to this is that it only allows a single MAC address to be used on the port, so if anyone, including you, tries to add another host on that segment, the switch port will immediately shut down. And when that happens, you have to manually go into the switch and re-enable the port by cycling it with a shutdown and then a no shutdown command.

Probably one of my favorite commands is the sticky command and not just because it's got a cool name. It also makes very cool things happen! You can find this command under the mac-address command:

```
Switch(config-if)#switchport port-security mac-address sticky
Switch(config-if)#switchport port-security maximum 2
Switch(config-if)#switchport port-security violation shutdown
```

Basically, with the sticky command you can provide static MAC address security without having to type in absolutely everyone's MAC address on the network. I like things that save me time like that!

In the preceding example, the first two MAC addresses coming into the port "stick" to it as static addresses and will be placed in the running-config, but when a third address tried to connect, the port would shut down immediately.

Let me show you one more example. Figure 10.6 displays a host in a company lobby that needs to be secured against the Ethernet cable used by anyone other than a single authorized individual.

**FIGURE 10.6**   Protecting a PC in a lobby

What can you do to ensure that only the MAC address of the lobby PC is allowed by switch port Fa0/1?

The solution is pretty straightforward because in this case, the defaults for port security will work well. All I have left to do is add a static MAC entry:

```
Switch(config-if)#switchport port-security
Switch(config-if)#switchport port-security violation restrict
Switch(config-if)#switchport port-security mac-address aa.bb.cc.dd.ee.ff
```

To protect the lobby PC, we would set the maximum allowed MAC addresses to 1 and the violation to restrict so the port didn't get shut down every time someone tried to use the Ethernet cable (which would be constantly). By using violation restrict, the unauthorized frames would just be dropped. But did you notice that I enabled port-security and then set a static MAC address? Remember that as soon as you enable port-security on a port, it defaults to violation shutdown and a maximum of 1. So all I needed to do was change the violation mode and add the static MAC address and our business requirement is solidly met!

I'll be going over port security again in the configuration examples later in this chapter.

---

 **Real World Scenario**

**Lobby PC Always Being Disconnected Becomes a Security Risk**

At a large Fortune 50 company in San Jose, CA, there was a PC in the lobby that held the company directory. With no security guard present in the lobby, the Ethernet cable connecting the PC was free game to all vendors, contractors, and visitors waiting in the lobby.

Port security to the rescue! By enabling port security on the port with the `switchport port-security` command, the switch port connecting to the PC was automatically secured with the defaults of allowing only one MAC address to associate to the port and violation shutdown. However, the port was always going into err-shutdown mode whenever anyone tried to use the Ethernet port. By changing the violation mode to restrict and setting a static MAC address for the port with the `switchport port-security mac-address` *mac-address* command, only the Lobby PC was able to connect and communicate on the network! Problem solved!

---

## Loop Avoidance

Redundant links between switches are important to have in place because they help prevent nasty network failures in the event that one link stops working.

But while it's true that redundant links can be extremely helpful, they can also cause more problems than they solve! This is because frames can be flooded down all redundant links simultaneously, creating network loops as well as other evils. Here's a list of some of the ugliest problems that can occur:

- If no loop avoidance schemes are put in place, the switches will flood broadcasts endlessly throughout the internetwork. This is sometimes referred to as a *broadcast storm*. Most of the time, they're referred to in very unprintable ways! Figure 10.7 illustrates how a broadcast can be propagated throughout the network. Observe how a frame is continually being flooded through the internetwork's physical network media.

- A device can receive multiple copies of the same frame because that frame can arrive from different segments at the same time. Figure 10.8 demonstrates how a whole bunch of frames can arrive from multiple segments simultaneously. The server in the figure sends a unicast frame to Router C. Because it's a unicast frame, Switch A forwards the frame and Switch B provides the same service—it forwards the unicast. This is bad because it means that Router C receives that unicast frame twice, causing additional overhead on the network.

- You may have thought of this one: The MAC address filter table could be totally confused about the source device's location because the switch can receive the frame from more than one link. Worse, the bewildered switch could get so caught up in constantly updating the MAC filter table with source hardware address locations that it will fail to forward a frame! This is called thrashing the MAC table.

- One of the most vile events is when multiple loops propagate throughout a network. Loops can occur within other loops, and if a broadcast storm were to occur simultaneously, the network wouldn't be able to perform frame switching—period!

**FIGURE 10.7**    Broadcast storm

**FIGURE 10.8**    Multiple frame copies

All of these problems spell disaster or close and are all evil situations that must be avoided or fixed somehow. That's where the Spanning Tree Protocol comes into play. It was actually developed to solve each and every one of the problems I just told you about!

Now that I explained the issues that can occur when you have redundant links, or when you have links that are improperly implemented, I'm sure you understand how vital it is to prevent them. However, the best solutions are beyond the scope of this chapter and among the territory covered in the more advanced Cisco exam objectives. For now, let's focus on configuring some switching!

# Configuring Catalyst Switches

Cisco Catalyst switches come in many flavors; some run 10 Mbps, while others can speed all the way up to 10 Gbps switched ports with a combination of twisted-pair and fiber. These newer switches, like the 2960s and 3560s, also have more intelligence, so they can give you data fast—mixed media services, too!

With that in mind, it's time to show you how to start up and configure a Cisco Catalyst switch using the command-line interface (CLI). After you get the basic commands down in this chapter, I'll show you how to configure virtual LANs (VLANs) plus Inter-Switch Link (ISL), and 802.1q trunking in the next one.

Here's a list of the basic tasks we'll be covering next:

- Administrative functions
- Configuring the IP address and subnet mask
- Setting the IP default gateway
- Setting port security
- Testing and verifying the network

> You can learn all about the Cisco family of Catalyst switches at
> www.cisco.com/en/US/products/hw/switches/index.html.

## Catalyst Switch Configuration

But before we actually get into configuring one of the Catalyst switches, I've got to fill you in regarding the boot process of these switches, just as I did with the routers in Chapter 7, "Managing a Cisco Internetwork." Figure 10.9 shows a typical Cisco Catalyst switch and I need to tell you about the different interfaces and features of this device.

The first thing I want to point out is that the console port for the Catalyst switches are typically located on the back of the switch. Yet, on a smaller switch like the 3560 shown in the figure, the console is right in the front to make it easier to use. (The eight-port 2960 looks exactly the same.) If the POST completes successfully, the system LED turns green, but if the POST fails, it will turn amber. And seeing that amber glow is an ominous thing—typically fatal. So you may just want to keep a spare switch around—especially in case it's a production switch that's croaked! The bottom button is used to show you which lights are providing Power over Ethernet (PoE). You can see this by pressing the Mode button. The PoE is a very nice feature of these switches. It allows me to power my access point and phone by just connecting them into the switch with an Ethernet cable—sweet.

**FIGURE 10.9**    A Cisco Catalyst switch

Just as we did with the routers we configured in Chapter 8, "IP Routing," and Chapter 9, "Open Shortest Path First (OSPF)," we'll use a diagram and switch setup to configure in this chapter as well as in Chapter 11. Figure 10.10 shows the switched network we'll be working on.

**FIGURE 10.10**    Our switched network

I'm going to use three 3560 switches, which I also used for demonstration in Chapter 6, "Cisco's Internetworking Operating System (IOS)," and Chapter 7. You can use any layer 2 switches for this chapter to follow the configuration, but when we get to Chapter 11, you'll need at least one router as well as a layer 3 switch, like my 3560.

Now if we connect our switches to each other, as shown in Figure 10.10, remember that first we'll need a crossover cable between the switches. My 3560 switches autodetect the connection type, so I was able to use straight-through cables. But not all switches autodetect the cable type. Different switches have different needs and abilities, so just keep this in mind when connecting your various switches together. Make a note that in the Cisco exam objectives, switches never autodetect!

When you first connect the switch ports to each other, the link lights are amber and then turn green indicating normal operation. What you're actually watching is spanning-tree converging, and this process takes around 50 seconds with no extensions enabled. But if you connect into a switch port and the switch port LED is alternating green and amber, it means the port is experiencing errors. If this happens, check the host NIC or the cabling, possibly even the duplex settings on the port to make sure they match the host setting.

## Do We Need to Put an IP Address on a Switch?

Absolutely not! Switches have all ports enabled and ready to rock. Take the switch out of the box, plug it in, and the switch starts learning MAC addresses in the CAM. So why would I need an IP address since switches are providing layer 2 services? Because you still need it for in-band management purposes! Telnet, SSH, SNMP, etc. all need an IP address in order to communicate with the switch through the network (in-band). Remember, since all ports are enabled by default, you need to shut down unused ports or assign them to an unused VLAN.

So where do we put this management IP address the switch needs for management purposes? On what is predictably called the management VLAN interface—a routed interface on every Cisco switch and called interface VLAN 1. This management interface can be changed, and Cisco recommends that you do change this to a different management interface for security purposes. No worries—I'll demonstrate how to do this in Chapter 11.

Let's configure our switches now so you can watch how I configure the management interfaces on each switch.

## S1

We're going to begin our configuration by connecting into each switch and setting the administrative functions. We'll also assign an IP address to each switch, but as I said, doing that isn't really necessary to make our network function. The only reason we're going to do that is so we can manage/administer it remotely, via Telnet for example. Let's use a simple IP scheme like 192.168.10.16/28. This mask should be familiar to you! Check out the following output:

```
Switch>en
Switch#config t
Switch(config)#hostname S1
S1(config)#enable secret todd
S1(config)#int f0/15
S1(config-if)#description 1st connection to S3
S1(config-if)#int f0/16
S1(config-if)#description 2nd connection to S3
S1(config-if)#int f0/17
S1(config-if)#description 1st connection to S2
```

```
S1(config-if)#int f0/18
S1(config-if)#description 2nd connection to S2
S1(config-if)#int f0/8
S1(config-if)#desc Connection to IVR
S1(config-if)#line con 0
S1(config-line)#password console
S1(config-line)#login
S1(config-line)#line vty 0 15
S1(config-line)#password telnet
S1(config-line)#login
S1(config-line)#int vlan 1
S1(config-if)#ip address 192.168.10.17 255.255.255.240
S1(config-if)#no shut
S1(config-if)#exit
S1(config)#banner motd #this is my S1 switch#
S1(config)#exit
S1#copy run start
Destination filename [startup-config]? [enter]
Building configuration...
[OK]
S1#
```

The first thing to notice about this is that there's no IP address configured on the switch's physical interfaces. Since all ports on a switch are enabled by default, there's not really a whole lot to configure! The IP address is configured under a logical interface, called a management domain or VLAN. You can use the default VLAN 1 to manage a switched network just as we're doing here, or you can opt to use a different VLAN for management.

The rest of the configuration is basically the same as the process you go through for router configuration. So remember... no IP addresses on physical switch interfaces, no routing protocols, and so on. We're performing layer 2 switching at this point, not routing! Also, make a note to self that there is no AUX port on Cisco switches.

## S2

Here is the S2 configuration:

```
Switch#config t
Switch(config)#hostname S2
S2(config)#enable secret todd
S2(config)#int f0/1
S2(config-if)#desc 1st connection to S1
S2(config-if)#int f0/2
S2(config-if)#desc 2nd connection to s2
```

```
S2(config-if)#int f0/5
S2(config-if)#desc 1st connection to S3
S2(config-if)#int f0/6
S2(config-if)#desc 2nd connection to s3
S2(config-if)#line con 0
S2(config-line)#password console
S2(config-line)#login
S2(config-line)#line vty 0 15
S2(config-line)#password telnet
S2(config-line)#login
S2(config-line)#int vlan 1
S2(config-if)#ip address 192.168.10.18 255.255.255.240
S2(config)#exit
S2#copy run start
Destination filename [startup-config]?[enter]
Building configuration...
[OK]
S2#
```

We should now be able to ping from S2 to S1. Let's try it:

```
S2#ping 192.168.10.17


Type escape sequence to abort.
Sending 5, 100-byte ICMP Echos to 192.168.10.17, timeout is 2 seconds:
.!!!!
Success rate is 80 percent (4/5), round-trip min/avg/max = 1/1/1 ms
S2#
```

Okay—now why did I get only four pings to work instead of five? The first period [.] is a timeout, but the exclamation point [!] is a success.

It's a good question, and here's your answer: the first ping didn't work because of the time that ARP takes to resolve the IP address to its corresponding hardware MAC address.

## S3

Check out the S3 switch configuration:

```
Switch>en
Switch#config t
SW-3(config)#hostname S3
S3(config)#enable secret todd
S3(config)#int f0/1
S3(config-if)#desc 1st connection to S1
```

```
S3(config-if)#int f0/2
S3(config-if)#desc 2nd connection to S1
S3(config-if)#int f0/5
S3(config-if)#desc 1st connection to S2
S3(config-if)#int f0/6
S3(config-if)#desc 2nd connection to S2
S3(config-if)#line con 0
S3(config-line)#password console
S3(config-line)#login
S3(config-line)#line vty 0 15
S3(config-line)#password telnet
S3(config-line)#login
S3(config-line)#int vlan 1
S3(config-if)#ip address 192.168.10.19 255.255.255.240
S3(config-if)#no shut
S3(config-if)#banner motd #This is the S3 switch#
S3(config)#exit
S3#copy run start
Destination filename [startup-config]?[enter]
Building configuration...
[OK]
S3#
```

Now let's ping to S1 and S2 from the S3 switch and see what happens:

```
S3#ping 192.168.10.17
Type escape sequence to abort.
Sending 5, 100-byte ICMP Echos to 192.168.10.17, timeout is 2 seconds:
.!!!!
Success rate is 80 percent (4/5), round-trip min/avg/max = 1/3/9 ms
S3#ping 192.168.10.18
Type escape sequence to abort.
Sending 5, 100-byte ICMP Echos to 192.168.10.18, timeout is 2 seconds:
.!!!!
Success rate is 80 percent (4/5), round-trip min/avg/max = 1/3/9 ms
S3#sh ip arp
Protocol  Address          Age (min)  Hardware Addr   Type   Interface
Internet  192.168.10.17           0   001c.575e.c8c0  ARPA   Vlan1
Internet  192.168.10.18           0   b414.89d9.18c0  ARPA   Vlan1
Internet  192.168.10.19           -   ecc8.8202.82c0  ARPA   Vlan1
S3#
```

In the output of the show ip arp command, the dash (-) in the minutes column means that it is the physical interface of the device.

Now, before we move on to verifying the switch configurations, there's one more command you need to know about, even though we don't really need it in our current network because we don't have a router involved. It's the ip default-gateway command. If you want to manage your switches from outside your LAN, you must set a default gateway on the switches just as you would with a host, and you do this from global config. Here's an example where we introduce our router with an IP address using the last IP address in our subnet range:

```
S3#config t
S3(config)#ip default-gateway 192.168.10.30
```

Now that we have all three switches basically configured, let's have some fun with them!

## Port Security

A secured switch port can associate anywhere from 1 to 8,192 MAC addresses, but the 3560s I am using can support only 6,144, which seems like way more than enough to me. You can choose to allow the switch to learn these values dynamically, or you can set static addresses for each port using the switchport port-security mac-address *mac-address* command.

So let's set port security on our S3 switch now. Ports Fa0/3 and Fa0/4 will have only one device connected in our lab. By using port security, we're assured that no other device can connect once our hosts in ports Fa0/3 and in Fa0/4 are connected. Here's how to easily do that with just a couple commands:

```
S3#config t
S3(config)#int range f0/3-4
S3(config-if-range)#switchport mode access
S3(config-if-range)#switchport port-security
S3(config-if-range)#do show port-security int f0/3
Port Security              : Enabled
Port Status                : Secure-down
Violation Mode             : Shutdown
Aging Time                 : 0 mins
Aging Type                 : Absolute
SecureStatic Address Aging : Disabled
Maximum MAC Addresses      : 1
Total MAC Addresses        : 0
Configured MAC Addresses   : 0
Sticky MAC Addresses       : 0
Last Source Address:Vlan   : 0000.0000.0000:0
Security Violation Count   : 0
```

The first command sets the mode of the ports to "access" ports. These ports must be access or trunk ports to enable port security. By using the command switchport port-security on the interface, I've enabled port security with a maximum MAC address of 1 and violation of shutdown. These are the defaults, and you can see them in the highlighted output of the show port-security int f0/3 command in the preceding code.

Port security is enabled, as displayed on the first line, but the second line shows Secure-down because I haven't connected my hosts into the ports yet. Once I do, the status will show Secure-up and would become Secure-shutdown if a violation occurs.

I've just got to point out this all-so-important fact one more time: It's very important to remember that you can set parameters for port security but it won't work until you enable port security at the interface level. Notice the output for port F0/6:

```
S3#config t
S3(config)#int range f0/6
S3(config-if-range)#switchport mode access
S3(config-if-range)#switchport port-security violation restrict
S3(config-if-range)#do show port-security int f0/6
Port Security              : Disabled
Port Status                : Secure-up
Violation Mode             : restrict
[output cut]
```

Port Fa0/6 has been configured with a violation of shutdown, but the first line shows that port security has not been enabled on the port yet. Remember, you must use this command at interface level to enable port security on a port:

```
S3(config-if-range)#switchport port-security
```

There are two other modes you can use instead of just shutting down the port. The restrict and protect modes mean that another host can connect up to the maximum MAC addresses allowed, but after the maximum has been met, all frames will just be dropped and the port won't be shut down. Additionally, both the restrict mode and shutdown violation modes alert you via SNMP that a violation has occurred on a port. You can then call the abuser and tell them they're so busted—you can see them, you know what they did, and they're in serious trouble!

If you've configured ports with the violation shutdown command, then the ports will look like this when a violation occurs:

```
S3#sh port-security int f0/3
Port Security              : Enabled
Port Status                : Secure-shutdown
Violation Mode             : Shutdown
Aging Time                 : 0 mins
Aging Type                 : Absolute
SecureStatic Address Aging : Disabled
```

```
Maximum MAC Addresses      : 1
Total MAC Addresses        : 2
Configured MAC Addresses   : 0
Sticky MAC Addresses       : 0
Last Source Address:Vlan   : 0013:0ca69:00bb3:00ba8:1
Security Violation Count   : 1
```

Here you can see that the port is in Secure-shutdown mode and the light for the port would be amber. To enable the port again, you'd need to do the following:

```
S3(config-if)#shutdown
S3(config-if)#no shutdown
```

Let's verify our switch configurations before we move onto VLANs in the next chapter. Beware that even though some switches will show err-disabled instead of Secure-shutdown as my switch shows, there is no difference between the two.

## Verifying Cisco Catalyst Switches

The first thing I like to do with any router or switch is to run through the configurations with a show running-config command. Why? Because doing this gives me a really great overview of each device. But it is time consuming, and showing you all the configs would take up way too many pages in this book. Besides, we can instead run other commands that will still stock us up with really good information.

For example, to verify the IP address set on a switch, we can use the show interface command. Here's the output:

```
S3#sh int vlan 1
Vlan1 is up, line protocol is up
  Hardware is EtherSVI, address is ecc8.8202.82c0 (bia ecc8.8202.82c0)
  Internet address is 192.168.10.19/28
  MTU 1500 bytes, BW 1000000 Kbit/sec, DLY 10 usec,
     reliability 255/255, txload 1/255, rxload 1/255
  Encapsulation ARPA, loopback not set
[output cut]
```

The above output shows the interface is in up/up status. Remember to always check this interface, either with this command or the show ip interface brief command. Lots of people tend to forget that this interface is shutdown by default.

 Never forget that IP addresses aren't needed on a switch for it to operate. The only reason we would set an IP address, mask, and default gateway is for management purposes.

### show mac address-table

I'm sure you remember being shown this command earlier in the chapter. Using it displays the forward filter table, also called a content addressable memory (CAM) table. Here's the output from the S1 switch:

```
S3#sh mac address-table
        Mac Address Table
-------------------------------------------


Vlan    Mac Address       Type        Ports
----    -----------       --------    -----
All     0100.0ccc.cccc    STATIC      CPU
[output cut]
  1     000e.83b2.e34b    DYNAMIC     Fa0/1
  1     0011.1191.556f    DYNAMIC     Fa0/1
  1     0011.3206.25cb    DYNAMIC     Fa0/1
  1     001a.2f55.c9e8    DYNAMIC     Fa0/1
  1     001a.4d55.2f7e    DYNAMIC     Fa0/1
  1     001c.575e.c891    DYNAMIC     Fa0/1
  1     b414.89d9.1886    DYNAMIC     Fa0/5
  1     b414.89d9.1887    DYNAMIC     Fa0/6
```

The switches use things called base MAC addresses, which are assigned to the CPU. The first one listed is the base mac address of the switch. From the preceding output, you can see that we have six MAC addresses dynamically assigned to Fa0/1, meaning that port Fa0/1 is connected to another switch. Ports Fa0/5 and Fa0/6 only have one MAC address assigned, and all ports are assigned to VLAN 1.

Let's take a look at the S2 switch CAM and see what we can find out.

```
S2#sh mac address-table
        Mac Address Table
-------------------------------------------


Vlan    Mac Address       Type        Ports
----    -----------       --------    -----
All     0100.0ccc.cccc    STATIC      CPU
[output cut
  1     000e.83b2.e34b    DYNAMIC     Fa0/5
  1     0011.1191.556f    DYNAMIC     Fa0/5
  1     0011.3206.25cb    DYNAMIC     Fa0/5
  1     001a.4d55.2f7e    DYNAMIC     Fa0/5
```

```
   1     581f.aaff.86b8    DYNAMIC    Fa0/5
   1     ecc8.8202.8286    DYNAMIC    Fa0/5
   1     ecc8.8202.82c0    DYNAMIC    Fa0/5
Total Mac Addresses for this criterion: 27
S2#
```

This output tells us that we have seven MAC addresses assigned to Fa0/5, which is our connection to S3. But where's port 6? Since port 6 is a redundant link to S3, STP placed Fa0/6 into blocking mode.

## Assigning Static MAC Addresses

You can set a static MAC address in the MAC address table, but like setting static MAC port security without the sticky command, it's a ton of work. Just in case you want to do it, here's how it's done:

```
S3(config)#mac address-table ?
  aging-time    Set MAC address table entry maximum age
  learning      Enable MAC table learning feature
  move          Move keyword
  notification  Enable/Disable MAC Notification on the switch
  static        static keyword


S3(config)#mac address-table static aaaa.bbbb.ccc vlan 1 int fa0/7
S3(config)#do show mac address-table
         Mac Address Table
-------------------------------------------


Vlan    Mac Address      Type       Ports
----    -----------      --------   -----
 All    0100.0ccc.cccc   STATIC     CPU
[output cut]
   1    000e.83b2.e34b   DYNAMIC    Fa0/1
   1    0011.1191.556f   DYNAMIC    Fa0/1
   1    0011.3206.25cb   DYNAMIC    Fa0/1
   1    001a.4d55.2f7e   DYNAMIC    Fa0/1
   1    001b.d40a.0538   DYNAMIC    Fa0/1
   1    001c.575e.c891   DYNAMIC    Fa0/1
   1    aaaa.bbbb.0ccc   STATIC     Fa0/7
[output cut]
Total Mac Addresses for this criterion: 59
```

As shown on the left side of the output, you can see that a static MAC address has now been assigned permanently to interface Fa0/7 and that it's also been assigned to VLAN 1 only.

Now admit it—this chapter had a lot of great information, and you really did learn a lot and, well, maybe even had a little fun along the way too! You've now configured and verified all switches and set port security. That means you're now ready to learn all about virtual LANs! I'm going to save all our switch configurations so we'll be able to start right from here in Chapter 11.

# Summary

In this chapter, I talked about the differences between switches and bridges and how they both work at layer 2. They create MAC address forward/filter tables in order to make decisions on whether to forward or flood a frame.

I also covered some problems that can occur if you have multiple links between bridges (switches).

Finally, I covered detailed configuration of Cisco's Catalyst switches, including verifying the configuration.

# Exam Essentials

**Remember the three switch functions.** Address learning, forward/filter decisions, and loop avoidance are the functions of a switch.

**Remember the command** show mac address-table. The command show mac address-table will show you the forward/filter table used on the LAN switch.

**Understand the reason for port security.** Port security restricts access to a switch based on MAC addresses.

**Know the command to enable port security.** To enable port security on a port, you must first make sure the port is an access port and then use the switchport port-security command at interface level. You can set the port security parameters before or after enabling port security.

**Know the commands to verify port security.** To verify port security, use the show port-security, show port-security interface interface, and show running-config commands.

# Written Lab 10

The answers to this lab can be found in Appendix A, "Answers to Written Labs."
Write the answers to the following questions:

1. What command will show you the forward/filter table?

2. If a destination MAC address is not in the forward/filter table, what will the switch do with the frame?

3. What are the three switch functions at layer 2?

4. If a frame is received on a switch port and the source MAC address is not in the forward/filter table, what will the switch do?

5. What are the default modes for a switch port configured with port security?

# Hands-on Labs

In this section, you will use the following switched network to configure your switching labs. You can use any Cisco switches to do this lab, as well as LammleSim IOS version. They do not need to be multilayer switches, just layer 2 switches.

The first lab (Lab 10.1) requires you to configure three switches, and then you will verify them in Lab 10.2.

The labs in this chapter are as follows:

Hands-on Lab 10.1: Configuring Layer 2 Switches

Hands-on Lab 10.2 Verifying Layer 2 Switches

Hands-on Lab 10.3: Configuring Port Security

# Lab 10.1: Configuring Layer 2 Switches

In this lab, you will configure the three switches in the graphic:

1. Connect to the S1 switch and configure the following, not in any particular order:

   - Hostname
   - Banner
   - Interface description
   - Passwords
   - IP address, subnet mask, default gateway

```
Switch>en
Switch#config t
Switch(config)#hostname S1
S1(config)#enable secret todd
S1(config)#int f0/15
S1(config-if)#description 1st connection to S3
S1(config-if)#int f0/16
S1(config-if)#description 2nd connection to S3
S1(config-if)#int f0/17
S1(config-if)#description 1st connection to S2
S1(config-if)#int f0/18
S1(config-if)#description 2nd connection to S2
S1(config-if)#int f0/8
S1(config-if)#desc Connection to IVR
S1(config-if)#line con 0
S1(config-line)#password console
S1(config-line)#login
S1(config-line)#line vty 0 15
S1(config-line)#password telnet
S1(config-line)#login
S1(config-line)#int vlan 1
S1(config-if)#ip address 192.168.10.17 255.255.255.240
S1(config-if)#no shut
S1(config-if)#exit
S1(config)#banner motd #this is my S1 switch#
S1(config)#exit
S1#copy run start
Destination filename [startup-config]? [enter]
Building configuration...
```

2. Connect to the S2 switch and configure all the settings you used in step 1. Do not forget to use a different IP address on the switch.

3. Connect to the S3 switch and configure all the settings you used in step 1 and 2. Do not forget to use a different IP address on the switch.

## Lab 10.2: Verifying Layer 2 Switches

Once you configure a device, you must be able to verify it.

1. Connect to each switch and verify the management interface.

```
S1#sh interface vlan 1
```

2. Connect to each switch and verify the CAM.

```
S1#sh mac address-table
```

3. Verify your configurations with the following commands:

```
S1#sh running-config
S1#sh ip int brief
```

## Lab 10.3: Configuring Port Security

Port security is a big Cisco objective. Do not skip this lab!

1. Connect to your S3 switch.

2. Configure port Fa0/3 with port security.

```
S3#config t
S(config)#int fa0/3
S3(config-if#Switchport mode access
S3(config-if#switchport port-security
```

3. Check your default setting for port security.

```
S3#show port-security int f0/3
```

4. Change the settings to have a maximum of two MAC addresses that can associate to interface Fa0/3.

```
S3#config t
S(config)#int fa0/3
S3(config-if#switchport port-security maximum 2
```

**5.** Change the violation mode to restrict.

```
S3#config t
S(config)#int fa0/3
S3(config-if#switchport port-security violation restrict
```

**6.** Verify your configuration with the following commands:

```
S3#show port-security
S3#show port-security int fa0/3
S3#show running-config
```

# Review Questions

The following questions are designed to test your understanding of this chapter's material. For more information on how to get additional questions, please see this book's introduction.

The answers to these questions can be found in Appendix B, "Answers to Chapter Review Questions."

1. Which of the following statements is *not* true with regard to layer 2 switching?

   **A.** Layer 2 switches and bridges are faster than routers because they don't take up time looking at the Data Link layer header information.

   **B.** Layer 2 switches and bridges look at the frame's hardware addresses before deciding to either forward, flood, or drop the frame.

   **C.** Switches create private, dedicated collision domains and provide independent bandwidth on each port.

   **D.** Switches use application-specific integrated circuits (ASICs) to build and maintain their MAC filter tables.

2. Type the command that generated the last entry in the MAC address table shown. Type the command only, without the prompt.

```
Mac Address Table
-------------------------------------------
```

| Vlan | Mac Address | Type | Ports |
| ---- | ----------- | -------- | ----- |
| All  | 0100.0ccc.cccc | STATIC | CPU |
| [output cut] | | | |
| 1 | 000e.83b2.e34b | DYNAMIC | Fa0/1 |
| 1 | 0011.1191.556f | DYNAMIC | Fa0/1 |
| 1 | 0011.3206.25cb | DYNAMIC | Fa0/1 |
| 1 | 001a.4d55.2f7e | DYNAMIC | Fa0/1 |
| 1 | 001b.d40a.0538 | DYNAMIC | Fa0/1 |
| 1 | 001c.575e.c891 | DYNAMIC | Fa0/1 |
| 1 | aaaa.bbbb.0ccc | STATIC | Fa0/7 |

**3.** In the diagram shown, what will the switch do if a frame with a destination MAC address of 000a.f467.63b1 is received on Fa0/4? (Choose all that apply.)

```
Switch# show mac address-table
 VLAN     Mac Address      Ports
   1      0005.dccb.d74b   Fa0/4
   1      000a.f467.9e80   Fa0/5
   1      000a.f467.9e8b   Fa0/6
```

**A.** Drop the frame.

**B.** Send the frame out of Fa0/3.

**C.** Send the frame out of Fa0/4.

**D.** Send the frame out of Fa0/5.

**E.** Send the frame out of Fa0/6.

**4.** Write the command that generated the following output.

```
        Mac Address Table
-------------------------------------------

Vlan    Mac Address     Type        Ports
----    -----------     --------    -----
All     0100.0ccc.cccc  STATIC      CPU
[output cut]
  1     000e.83b2.e34b  DYNAMIC     Fa0/1
  1     0011.1191.556f  DYNAMIC     Fa0/1
  1     0011.3206.25cb  DYNAMIC     Fa0/1
  1     001a.2f55.c9e8  DYNAMIC     Fa0/1
  1     001a.4d55.2f7e  DYNAMIC     Fa0/1
  1     001c.575e.c891  DYNAMIC     Fa0/1
  1     b414.89d9.1886  DYNAMIC     Fa0/5
  1     b414.89d9.1887  DYNAMIC     Fa0/6
```

5. In the work area draw the functions of a switch from the list on the left to the right.

| | |
|---|---|
| Address learning | Target 1 |
| Packet forwarding | Target 2 |
| Layer three security | Target 3 |
| Forward/filter decisions | |
| Loop avoidance | |

6. What statement(s) is/are true about the output shown below? (Choose all that apply.)

```
S3#sh port-security int f0/3
Port Security              : Enabled
Port Status                : Secure-shutdown
Violation Mode             : Shutdown
Aging Time                 : 0 mins
Aging Type                 : Absolute
SecureStatic Address Aging : Disabled
Maximum MAC Addresses      : 1
Total MAC Addresses        : 2
Configured MAC Addresses   : 0
Sticky MAC Addresses       : 0
Last Source Address:Vlan   : 0013:0ca69:00bb3:00ba8:1
Security Violation Count   : 1
```

   A. The port light for F0/3 will be amber in color.

   B. The F0/3 port is forwarding frames.

   C. This problem will resolve itself in a few minutes.

   D. This port requires the shutdown command to function.

7. Write the command that would limit the number of MAC addresses allowed on a port to 2. Write only the command and not the prompt.

**8.** Which of the following commands in the configuration, is a prerequisite for the other commands to function?

```
S3#config t
S(config)#int fa0/3
S3(config-if#switchport port-security
S3(config-if#switchport port-security maximum 3
S3(config-if#switchport port-security violation restrict
S3(config-if#Switchport mode-security aging time 10
```

  **A.** switchport mode-security aging time 10

  **B.** switchport port-security

  **C.** switchport port-security maximum 3

  **D.** switchport port-security violation restrict

**9.** Which if the following is *not* an issue addressed by STP?

  **A.** Broadcast storms

  **B.** Gateway redundancy

  **C.** A device receiving multiple copies of the same frame

  **D.** Constant updating of the MAC filter table

**10.** What issue that arises when redundancy exists between switches is shown in the figure?

  **A.** Broadcast storm

  **B.** Routing loop

  **C.** Port violation

  **D.** Loss of gateway

11. Which two of the following switch port violation modes will alert you via SNMP that a violation has occurred on a port?

    **A.** Restrict

    **B.** Protect

    **C.** Shutdown

    **D.** Err-disable

12. _____ is the loop avoidance mechanism used by switches.

13. Write the command that must be present on any switch that you need to manage from a different subnet.

14. On which interface have you configured an IP address for a switch?

    **A.** `int fa0/0`

    **B.** `int vty 0 15`

    **C.** `int vlan 1`

    **D.** `int s/0/0`

15. Which Cisco IOS command is used to verify the port security configuration of a switch port?

    **A.** `show interfaces port-security`

    **B.** `show port-security interface`

    **C.** `show ip interface`

    **D.** `show interfaces switchport`

16. Write the command that will save a dynamically learned MAC address in the running-configuration of a Cisco switch?

17. Which of the following methods will ensure that only one specific host can connect to port F0/3 on a switch? (Choose two. Each correct answer is a separate solution.)

    **A.** Configure port security on F0/3 to accept traffic other than that of the MAC address of the host.

    **B.** Configure the MAC address of the host as a static entry associated with port F0/3.

    **C.** Configure an inbound access control list on port F0/3 limiting traffic to the IP address of the host.

    **D.** Configure port security on F0/3 to accept traffic only from the MAC address of the host.

**18.** What will be the effect of executing the following command on port F0/1?

```
switch(config-if)# switchport port-security mac-address 00C0.35F0.8301
```

    **A.** The command configures an inbound access control list on port F0/1, limiting traffic to the IP address of the host.

    **B.** The command expressly prohibits the MAC address of 00c0.35F0.8301 as an allowed host on the switch port.

    **C.** The command encrypts all traffic on the port from the MAC address of 00c0.35F0.8301.

    **D.** The command statically defines the MAC address of 00c0.35F0.8301 as an allowed host on the switch port.

**19.** The conference room has a switch port available for use by the presenter during classes, and each presenter uses the same PC attached to the port. You would like to prevent other PCs from using that port. You have completely removed the former configuration in order to start anew. Which of the following steps is *not* required to prevent any other PCs from using that port?

    **A.** Enable port security.

    **B.** Assign the MAC address of the PC to the port.

    **C.** Make the port an access port.

    **D.** Make the port a trunk port.

**20.** Write the command required to disable the port if a security violation occurs. Write only the command and not the prompt.

# Chapter

# 11

# VLANs and InterVLAN Routing

## THE FOLLOWING ICND1 EXAM TOPICS ARE COVERED IN THIS CHAPTER:

✓ **LAN Switching Technologies**

- Describe how VLANs create logically separate networks and the need for routing between them.
  - Explain network segmentation and basic traffic management concepts
- Configure and verify VLANs
- Configure and verify trunking on Cisco switches
  - DTP
  - Auto negotiation

✓ **IP Routing Technologies**

- Configure and verify InterVLAN routing (Router on a stick)
  - Sub interfaces
  - Upstream routing
  - Encapsulation
- Configure SVI interfaces

✓ **Troubleshooting**

- Troubleshoot and Resolve VLAN problems
  - Identify that VLANs are configured
  - Port membership correct
  - IP address configured
- Troubleshoot and Resolve trunking problems on Cisco switches
  - Correct trunk states
  - Correct encapsulation configured
  - Correct VLANS allowed

I know I keep telling you this, but so you never forget it, here I go, one last time: By default, switches break up collision domains and routers break up broadcast domains. Okay, I feel better! Now we can move on.

In contrast to the networks of yesterday that were based on collapsed backbones, today's network design is characterized by a flatter architecture—thanks to switches. So now what? How do we break up broadcast domains in a pure switched internetwork? By creating virtual local area networks (VLANs). A VLAN is a logical grouping of network users and resources connected to administratively defined ports on a switch. When you create VLANs, you're given the ability to create smaller broadcast domains within a layer 2 switched internetwork by assigning different ports on the switch to service different subnetworks. A VLAN is treated like its own subnet or broadcast domain, meaning that frames broadcast onto the network are only switched between the ports logically grouped within the same VLAN.

So, does this mean we no longer need routers? Maybe yes; maybe no. It really depends on what your particular networking needs and goals are. By default, hosts in a specific VLAN can't communicate with hosts that are members of another VLAN, so if you want interVLAN communication, the answer is that you still need a router or Inter-VLAN Routing (IVR).

In this chapter, you're going to comprehensively learn exactly what a VLAN is and how VLAN memberships are used in a switched network. You'll also become well-versed in what a trunk link is and how to configure and verify them.

I'll finish this chapter by demonstrating how you can make inter-VLAN communication happen by introducing a router into a switched network. Of course, we'll configure our familiar switched network layout we used in the last chapter for creating VLANs and for implementing trunking and Inter-VLAN routing on a layer 3 switch by creating Switched Virtual Interfaces (SVIs).

**To find up-to-the-minute updates for this chapter, please see** www.lammle.com/forum or the book's web page at www.sybex.com.

# VLAN Basics

Figure 11.1 illustrates the flat network architecture that used to be so typical for layer 2 switched networks. With this configuration, every broadcast packet transmitted is seen by every device on the network regardless of whether the device needs to receive that data or not.

**FIGURE 11.1**   Flat network structure

Host A

By default, routers allow broadcasts to occur only within the originating network, while switches forward broadcasts to all segments. Oh, and by the way, the reason it's called a *flat network* is because it's one *broadcast domain*, not because the actual design is physically flat. In Figure 11.1 we see Host A sending out a broadcast and all ports on all switches forwarding it—all except the port that originally received it.

Now check out Figure 11.2. It pictures a switched network and shows Host A sending a frame with Host D as its destination. Clearly, the important factor here is that the frame is only forwarded out the port where Host D is located.

**FIGURE 11.2**   The benefit of a switched network

Host A          Host D

This is a huge improvement over the old hub networks, unless having one *collision domain* by default is what you really want for some reason!

Okay—you already know that the biggest benefit gained by having a layer 2 switched network is that it creates individual collision domain segments for each device plugged into each port on the switch. This scenario frees us from the old Ethernet density constraints and makes us able to build larger networks. But too often, each new advance comes with new issues. For instance, the more users and devices that populate and use a network, the more broadcasts and packets each switch must handle.

And there's another big issue—security! This one is real trouble because within the typical layer 2 switched internetwork, all users can see all devices by default. And you can't stop devices from broadcasting, plus you can't stop users from trying to respond to broadcasts. This means your security options are dismally limited to placing passwords on your servers and other devices.

But wait—there's hope if you create a *virtual LAN (VLAN)*! You can solve many of the problems associated with layer 2 switching with VLANs, as you'll soon see.

VLANs work like this: Figure 11.3 shows all hosts in this very small company connected to one switch, meaning all hosts will receive all frames, which is the default behavior of all switches.

**FIGURE 11.3**    One switch, one LAN: Before VLANs, there were no separations between hosts.

If we want to separate the host's data, we could either buy another switch or create virtual LANs, as shown in Figure 11.4.

**FIGURE 11.4**    One switch, two virtual LANs (*logical* separation between hosts): Still physically one switch, but this switch acts as many separate devices.

In Figure 11.4, I configured the switch to be two separate LANs, two subnets, two broadcast domains, two VLANs—they all mean the same thing—without buying another switch. We can do this 1,000 times on most Cisco switches, which saves thousands of dollars and more!

Notice that even though the separation is virtual and the hosts are all still connected to the same switch, the LANs can't send data to each other by default. This is because they are still separate networks, but no worries—we'll get into inter-VLAN communication later in this chapter.

Here's a short list of ways VLANs simplify network management:

- Network adds, moves, and changes are achieved with ease by just configuring a port into the appropriate VLAN.

- A group of users that need an unusually high level of security can be put into its own VLAN so that users outside of that VLAN can't communicate with it.

- As a logical grouping of users by function, VLANs can be considered independent from their physical or geographic locations.

- VLANs greatly enhance network security if implemented correctly.

- VLANs increase the number of broadcast domains while decreasing their size.

Coming up, we'll thoroughly explore the world of switching, and you learn exactly how and why switches provide us with much better network services than hubs can in our networks today.

## Broadcast Control

Broadcasts occur in every protocol, but how often they occur depends upon three things:

- The type of protocol

- The application(s) running on the internetwork

- How these services are used

Some older applications have been rewritten to reduce their bandwidth consumption, but there's a new generation of applications that are so bandwidth greedy they'll consume any and all they can find. These gluttons are the legion of multimedia applications that use both broadcasts and multicasts extensively. As if they weren't enough trouble, factors like faulty equipment, inadequate segmentation, and poorly designed firewalls can seriously compound the problems already caused by these broadcast-intensive applications. All of this has added a major new dimension to network design and presents a bunch of new challenges for an administrator. Positively making sure your network is properly segmented so you can quickly isolate a single segment's problems to prevent them from propagating throughout your entire internetwork is now imperative. And the most effective way to do that is through strategic switching and routing!

Since switches have become more affordable, most everyone has replaced their flat hub networks with pure switched network and VLAN environments. All devices within a VLAN are members of the same broadcast domain and receive all broadcasts relevant to it. By default, these broadcasts are filtered from all ports on a switch that aren't members of the same VLAN. This is great because you get all the benefits you would with a switched design without getting hit with all the problems you'd have if all your users were in the same broadcast domain—sweet!

## Security

But there's always a catch, right? Time to get back to those security issues. A flat internetwork's security used to be tackled by connecting hubs and switches together with routers. So it was basically the router's job to maintain security. This arrangement was pretty ineffective for several reasons. First, anyone connecting to the physical network could access the network resources located on that particular physical LAN. Second, all anyone had to do to observe any and all traffic traversing that network was to simply plug a network analyzer into the hub. And similar to that last, scary, fact, users could easily join a workgroup by just plugging their workstations into the existing hub. That's about as secure as a barrel of honey in a bear enclosure!

But that's exactly what makes VLANs so cool. If you build them and create multiple broadcast groups, you can still have total control over each port and user! So the days when anyone could just plug their workstations into any switch port and gain access to network resources are history because now you get to control each port and any resources it can access.

And that's not even all—VLANs can be created in harmony with a specific user's need for the network resources. Plus, switches can be configured to inform a network management station about unauthorized access to those vital network resources. And if you need inter-VLAN communication, you can implement restrictions on a router to make sure this all happens securely. You can also place restrictions on hardware addresses, protocols, and applications. *Now* we're talking security—our honey barrel is now sealed tightly, made of solid titanium and wrapped in razor wire!

## Flexibility and Scalability

If you've been paying attention so far, you know that layer 2 switches only read frames for filtering because they don't look at the Network layer protocol. You also know that by default, switches forward broadcasts to all ports. But if you create and implement VLANs, you're essentially creating smaller broadcast domains at layer 2.

As a result, broadcasts sent out from a node in one VLAN won't be forwarded to ports configured to belong to a different VLAN. But if we assign switch ports or users to VLAN groups on a switch or on a group of connected switches, we gain the flexibility to exclusively add only the users we want to let into that broadcast domain regardless of their physical location. This setup can also work to block broadcast storms caused by a faulty network interface card (NIC) as well as prevent an intermediate device from propagating broadcast storms throughout the entire internetwork. Those evils can still happen on the VLAN where the problem originated, but the disease will be fully contained in that one ailing VLAN!

Another advantage is that when a VLAN gets too big, you can simply create more VLANs to keep the broadcasts from consuming too much bandwidth. The fewer users in a VLAN, the fewer users affected by broadcasts. This is all good, but you seriously need to keep network services in mind and understand how the users connect to these services when creating a VLAN. A good strategy is to try to keep all services, except for the email and Internet access that everyone needs, local to all users whenever possible.

# Identifying VLANs

Switch ports are layer 2–only interfaces that are associated with a physical port that can belong to only one VLAN if it's an access port or all VLANs if it's a trunk port.

Switches are definitely pretty busy devices. As myriad frames are switched throughout the network, switches have to be able to keep track of all of them, plus understand what to do with them depending on their associated hardware addresses. And remember—frames are handled differently according to the type of link they're traversing.

There are two different types of ports in a switched environment. Let's take a look at the first type in Figure 11.5.

**FIGURE 11.5**   Access ports

Notice there are access ports for each host and an access port between switches—one for each VLAN.

**Access ports**   An *access port* belongs to and carries the traffic of only one VLAN. Traffic is both received and sent in native formats with no VLAN information (tagging) whatsoever. Anything arriving on an access port is simply assumed to belong to the VLAN assigned to the port. Because an access port doesn't look at the source address, tagged traffic—a frame with added VLAN information—can be correctly forwarded and received only on trunk ports.

With an access link, this can be referred to as the *configured VLAN* of the port. Any device attached to an *access link* is unaware of a VLAN membership—the device just assumes it's part of some broadcast domain. But it doesn't have the big picture, so it doesn't understand the physical network topology at all.

Another good bit of information to know is that switches remove any VLAN information from the frame before it's forwarded out to an access-link device. Remember that access-link devices can't communicate with devices outside their VLAN unless the packet is routed. Also, you can only create a switch port to be either an access port or a trunk port—not both. So you've got to choose one or the other and know that if you make it an access port, that port can be assigned to one VLAN only. In Figure 11.5, only the hosts in the Sales VLAN can talk to other hosts in the same VLAN. This is the same with Admin VLAN, and they can both communicate to hosts on the other switch because of an access link for each VLAN config- ured between switches.

**Voice access ports**  Not to confuse you, but all that I just said about the fact that an access port can be assigned to only one VLAN is really only sort of true. Nowadays, most switches will allow you to add a second VLAN to an access port on a switch port for your voice traffic, called the voice VLAN. The voice VLAN used to be called the aux- iliary VLAN, which allowed it to be overlaid on top of the data VLAN, enabling both types of traffic to travel through the same port. Even though this is technically considered to be a different type of link, it's still just an access port that can be configured for both data and voice VLANs. This allows you to connect both a phone and a PC device to one switch port but still have each device in a separate VLAN.

**Trunk ports**  Believe it or not, the term *trunk port* was inspired by the telephone system trunks, which carry multiple telephone conversations at a time. So it follows that trunk ports can similarly carry multiple VLANs at a time as well.

A *trunk link* is a 100, 1,000, or 10,000 Mbps point-to-point link between two switches, between a switch and router, or even between a switch and server, and it carries the traffic of multiple VLANs—from 1 to 4,094 VLANs at a time. But the amount is really only up to 1,001 unless you're going with something called extended VLANs.

Instead of an access link for each VLAN between switches, we'll create a trunk link demonstrated in Figure 11.6.

Trunking can be a real advantage because with it, you get to make a single port part of a whole bunch of different VLANs at the same time. This is a great feature because you can actually set ports up to have a server in two separate broadcast domains simultane- ously so your users won't have to cross a layer 3 device (router) to log in and access it. Another benefit to trunking comes into play when you're connecting switches. Trunk links can carry the frames of various VLANs across them, but by default, if the links between your switches aren't trunked, only information from the configured access VLAN will be switched across that link.

It's also good to know that all VLANs send information on a trunked link unless you clear each VLAN by hand, and no worries, I'll show you how to clear individual VLANs from a trunk in a bit.

Okay—it's finally time to tell you about frame tagging and the VLAN identification methods used in it across our trunk links.

**FIGURE 11.6**  VLANs can span across multiple switches by using trunk links, which carry traffic for multiple VLANs.

## Frame Tagging

As you now know, you can set up your VLANs to span more than one connected switch. You can see that going on in Figure 11.6, which depicts hosts from two VLANs spread across two switches. This flexible, power-packed capability is probably the main advantage to implementing VLANs, and we can do this with up to a thousand VLANs and thousands upon thousands of hosts!

All this can get kind of complicated—even for a switch—so there needs to be a way for each one to keep track of all the users and frames as they travel the switch fabric and VLANs. When I say, "switch fabric," I'm just referring to a group of switches that share the same VLAN information. And this just happens to be where *frame tagging* enters the scene. This frame identification method uniquely assigns a user-defined VLAN ID to each frame.

Here's how it works: Once within the switch fabric, each switch that the frame reaches must first identify the VLAN ID from the frame tag. It then finds out what to do with the frame by looking at the information in what's known as the filter table. If the frame reaches a switch that has another trunked link, the frame will be forwarded out of the trunk-link port.

Once the frame reaches an exit that's determined by the forward/filter table to be an access link matching the frame's VLAN ID, the switch will remove the VLAN identifier. This is so the destination device can receive the frames without being required to understand their VLAN identification information.

Another great thing about trunk ports is that they'll support tagged and untagged traffic simultaneously if you're using 802.1q trunking, which we will talk about next. The trunk port is assigned a default port VLAN ID (PVID) for a VLAN upon which all untagged traffic will travel. This VLAN is also called the native VLAN and is always VLAN 1 by default, but it can be changed to any VLAN number.

Similarly, any untagged or tagged traffic with a NULL (unassigned) VLAN ID is assumed to belong to the VLAN with the port default PVID. Again, this would be VLAN 1 by default. A packet with a VLAN ID equal to the outgoing port native VLAN is sent untagged and can communicate to only hosts or devices in that same VLAN. All other VLAN traffic has to be sent with a VLAN tag to communicate within a particular VLAN that corresponds with that tag.

## VLAN Identification Methods

VLAN identification is what switches use to keep track of all those frames as they're traversing a switch fabric. It's how switches identify which frames belong to which VLANs, and there's more than one trunking method.

### Inter-Switch Link (ISL)

*Inter-Switch Link (ISL)* is a way of explicitly tagging VLAN information onto an Ethernet frame. This tagging information allows VLANs to be multiplexed over a trunk link through an external encapsulation method. This allows the switch to identify the VLAN membership of a frame received over the trunked link.

By running ISL, you can interconnect multiple switches and still maintain VLAN information as traffic travels between switches on trunk links. ISL functions at layer 2 by encapsulating a data frame with a new header and by performing a new cyclic redundancy check (CRC).

Of note is that ISL is proprietary to Cisco switches and it's used for Fast Ethernet and Gigabit Ethernet links only. *ISL routing* is pretty versatile and can be used on a switch port, router interfaces, and server interface cards to trunk a server. Although some Cisco switches still support ISL frame tagging, Cisco is moving toward using only 802.1q.

### IEEE 802.1q

Created by the IEEE as a standard method of frame tagging, IEEE 802.1q actually inserts a field into the frame to identify the VLAN. If you're trunking between a Cisco switched link and a different brand of switch, you've got to use 802.1q for the trunk to work.

Unlike ISL, which encapsulates the frame with control information, 802.1q inserts an 802.1q field along with tag control information, as shown in Figure 11.7.

For the Cisco exam objectives, it's only the 12-bit VLAN ID that matters. This field identifies the VLAN and can be $2^{12}$, minus 2 for the 0 and 4,095 reserved VLANs, which means an 802.1q tagged frame can carry information for 4,094 VLANs.

It works like this: You first designate each port that's going to be a trunk with 802.1q encapsulation. The other ports must be assigned a specific VLAN ID in order for them to communicate. VLAN 1 is the default native VLAN, and when using 802.1q, all traffic for a native VLAN is untagged. The ports that populate the same trunk create a group with this native VLAN and each port gets tagged with an identification number reflecting that. Again the default is VLAN 1. The native VLAN allows the trunks to accept information that was received without any VLAN identification or frame tag.

**FIGURE 11.7** IEEE 802.1q encapsulation with and without the 802.1q tag

Most 2960 model switches only support the IEEE 802.1q trunking protocol, but the 3560 will support both the ISL and IEEE methods, which you'll see later in this chapter.

The basic purpose of ISL and 802.1q frame-tagging methods is to provide inter-switch VLAN communication. Remember that any ISL or 802.1q frame tagging is removed if a frame is forwarded out an access link—tagging is used internally and across trunk links only!

# Routing between VLANs

Hosts in a VLAN live in their own broadcast domain and can communicate freely. VLANs create network partitioning and traffic separation at layer 2 of the OSI, and as I said when I told you why we still need routers, if you want hosts or any other IP-addressable device to communicate between VLANs, you must have a layer 3 device to provide routing.

For this, you can use a router that has an interface for each VLAN or a router that supports ISL or 802.1q routing. The least expensive router that supports ISL or 802.1q routing is the 2600 series router. You'd have to buy that from a used-equipment reseller because they are end-of-life, or EOL. I'd recommend at least a 2800 as a bare minimum, but even that only supports 802.1q; Cisco is really moving away from ISL, so you probably should only be using 802.1q anyway. Some 2800s may support both ISL and 802.1q; I've just have never seen it supported.

Anyway, as shown in Figure 11.8, if you had two or three VLANs, you could get by with a router equipped with two or three FastEthernet connections. And 10Base-T is okay for home study purposes, and I mean only for your studies, but for anything else I'd highly recommend Gigabit interfaces for real power under the hood!

What we see in Figure 11.8 is that each router interface is plugged into an access link. This means that each of the routers' interface IP addresses would then become the default gateway address for each host in each respective VLAN.

**FIGURE 11.8**   Router connecting three VLANs together for inter-VLAN communication, one router interface for each VLAN

If you have more VLANs available than router interfaces, you can configure trunking on one FastEthernet interface or buy a layer 3 switch, like the Cisco 3560 or a higher-end switch like a 3750. You could even opt for a 6500 if you've got money to burn!

Instead of using a router interface for each VLAN, you can use one FastEthernet interface and run ISL or 802.1q trunking. Figure 11.9 shows how a FastEthernet interface on a router will look when configured with ISL or 802.1q trunking. This allows all VLANs to communicate through one interface. Cisco calls this a router on a stick (ROAS).

**FIGURE 11.9**   Router on a stick: Single router interface connecting all three VLANs together for inter-VLAN communication

I really want to point out that this creates a potential bottleneck, as well as a single point of failure, so your host/VLAN count is limited. To how many? Well, that depends on your traffic level. To really make things right, you'd be better off using a higher-end switch and routing on the backplane. But if you just happen to have a router sitting around, configuring this method is free, right?

Figure 11.10 shows how we would create a router on a stick using a router's physical interface by creating logical interfaces—one for each VLAN.

**FIGURE 11.10** A router creates logical interfaces.

GigabitEthernet 0/0.1
GigabitEthernet 0/0.2
GigabitEthernet 0/0.3
GigabitEthernet 0/0

Here we see one physical interface divided into multiple subinterfaces, with one subnet assigned per VLAN, each subinterface being the default gateway address for each VLAN/subnet. An encapsulation identifier must be assigned to each subinterface to define the VLAN ID of that subinterface. In the next section where I'll configure VLANs and inter-VLAN routing, I'll configure our switched network with a router on a stick and demonstrate this configuration for you.

But wait, there's still one more way to go about routing! Instead of using an external router interface for each VLAN, or an external router on a stick, we can configure logical interfaces on the backplane of the layer 3 switch; this is called inter-VLAN routing (IVR), and is configured with a switched virtual interface (SVI). Figure 11.11 shows how hosts see these virtual interfaces.

**FIGURE 11.11** With IVR, routing runs on the backplane of the switch, and it appears to the hosts that a router is present.

VLAN 10    I'm Virtual!    VLAN 20

VLAN 10   VLAN 20

3560

In Figure 11.11, it appears there's a router present, but there is no physical router present as there was when we used router on a stick. The IVR process takes little effort and is easy to implement, which makes it very cool! Plus, it's a lot more efficient for inter-VLAN routing than an external router is. To implement IVR on a multilayer switch, we just need to create logical interfaces in the switch configuration for each VLAN. We'll configure this method in a minute, but first let's take our existing switched network from Chapter 10, "Layer 2

Switching," and add some VLANs, then configure VLAN memberships and trunk links between our switches.

# Configuring VLANs

Now this may come as a surprise to you, but configuring VLANs is actually pretty easy. It's just that figuring out which users you want in each VLAN is not, and doing that can eat up a lot of your time! But once you've decided on the number of VLANs you want to create and established which users you want belonging to each one, it's time to bring your first VLAN into the world.

To configure VLANs on a Cisco Catalyst switch, use the global config vlan command. In the following example, I'm going to demonstrate how to configure VLANs on the S1 switch by creating three VLANs for three different departments—again, remember that VLAN 1 is the native and management VLAN by default:

```
S1(config)#vlan ?
  WORD        ISL VLAN IDs 1-4094
  access-map  Create vlan access-map or enter vlan access-map command mode
  dot1q       dot1q parameters
  filter      Apply a VLAN Map
  group       Create a vlan group
  internal    internal VLAN
S1(config)#vlan 2
S1(config-vlan)#name Sales
S1(config-vlan)#vlan 3
S1(config-vlan)#name Marketing
S1(config-vlan)#vlan 4
S1(config-vlan)#name Accounting
S1(config-vlan)#^Z
S1#
```

In this output, you can see that you can create VLANs from 1 to 4094. But this is only mostly true. As I said, VLANs can really only be created up to 1001, and you can't use, change, rename, or delete VLANs 1 or 1002 through 1005 because they're reserved. The VLAN numbers above 1005 are called extended VLANs and won't be saved in the database unless your switch is set to what is called VLAN Trunk Protocol (VTP) transparent mode. You won't see these VLAN numbers used too often in production. Here's an example of me attempting to set my S1 switch to VLAN 4000 when my switch is set to VTP server mode (the default VTP mode):

```
S1#config t
S1(config)#vlan 4000
S1(config-vlan)#^Z
```

```
% Failed to create VLANs 4000
Extended VLAN(s) not allowed in current VTP mode.
%Failed to commit extended VLAN(s) changes.
```

After you create the VLANs that you want, you can use the show vlan command to check them out. But notice that, by default, all ports on the switch are in VLAN 1. To change the VLAN associated with a port, you need to go to each interface and specifically tell it which VLAN to be a part of.

Remember that a created VLAN is unused until it is assigned to a switch port or ports and that all ports are always assigned in VLAN 1 unless set otherwise.

Once the VLANs are created, verify your configuration with the show vlan command (sh vlan for short):

```
S1#sh vlan


VLAN Name                             Status    Ports
---- -------------------------------- --------- -------------------------------
1    default                          active    Fa0/1, Fa0/2, Fa0/3, Fa0/4
                                                Fa0/5, Fa0/6, Fa0/7, Fa0/8
                                                Fa0/9, Fa0/10, Fa0/11, Fa0/12
                                                Fa0/13, Fa0/14, Fa0/19, Fa0/20
                                                Fa0/21, Fa0/22, Fa0/23, Gi0/1
                                                Gi0/2
2    Sales                            active
3    Marketing                        active
4    Accounting                       active
[output cut]
```

This may seem repetitive, but it's important, and I want you to remember it: You can't change, delete, or rename VLAN 1 because it's the default VLAN and you just can't change that—period. It's also the native VLAN of all switches by default, and Cisco recommends that you use it as your management VLAN. If you're worried about security issues, then change it! Basically, any ports that aren't specifically assigned to a different VLAN will be sent down to the native VLAN—VLAN 1.

In the preceding S1 output, you can see that ports Fa0/1 through Fa0/14, Fa0/19 through 23, and Gi0/1 and Gi02 uplinks are all in VLAN 1. But where are ports 15 through 18? First, understand that the command show vlan only displays access ports, so now that you know what you're looking at with the show vlan command, where do you think ports Fa15–18 are? That's right! They are trunked ports. Cisco switches run a proprietary protocol called *Dynamic Trunk Protocol (DTP)*, and if there is a compatible switch connected, they will

start trunking automatically, which is precisely where my four ports are. You have to use the
`show interfaces trunk` command to see your trunked ports like this:

```
S1# show interfaces trunk
Port        Mode          Encapsulation  Status      Native vlan
Fa0/15      desirable     n-isl          trunking    1
Fa0/16      desirable     n-isl          trunking    1
Fa0/17      desirable     n-isl          trunking    1
Fa0/18      desirable     n-isl          trunking    1


Port        Vlans allowed on trunk
Fa0/15      1-4094
Fa0/16      1-4094
Fa0/17      1-4094
Fa0/18      1-4094


[output cut]
```

This output reveals that the VLANs from 1 to 4094 are allowed across the trunk by
default. Another helpful command, which is also part of the Cisco exam objectives, is the
`show interfaces interface switchport` command:

```
S1#sh interfaces fastEthernet 0/15 switchport
Name: Fa0/15
Switchport: Enabled
Administrative Mode: dynamic desirable
Operational Mode: trunk
Administrative Trunking Encapsulation: negotiate
Operational Trunking Encapsulation: isl
Negotiation of Trunking: On
Access Mode VLAN: 1 (default)
Trunking Native Mode VLAN: 1 (default)
Administrative Native VLAN tagging: enabled
Voice VLAN: none
[output cut]
```

The highlighted output shows us the administrative mode of `dynamic desirable`, that the
port is a trunk port, and that DTP was used to negotiate the frame tagging method of ISL. It
also predictably shows that the native VLAN is the default of 1.

Now that we can see the VLANs created, we can assign switch ports to specific ones.
Each port can be part of only one VLAN, with the exception of voice access ports. Using
trunking, you can make a port available to traffic from all VLANs. I'll cover that next.

## Assigning Switch Ports to VLANs

You configure a port to belong to a VLAN by assigning a membership mode that specifies the kind of traffic the port carries plus the number of VLANs it can belong to. You can also configure each port on a switch to be in a specific VLAN (access port) by using the interface switchport command. You can even configure multiple ports at the same time with the interface range command.

In the next example, I'll configure interface Fa0/3 to VLAN 3. This is the connection from the S3 switch to the host device:

```
S3#config t
S3(config)#int fa0/3
S3(config-if)#switchport ?
  access        Set access mode characteristics of the interface
  autostate     Include or exclude this port from vlan link up calculation
  backup        Set backup for the interface
  block         Disable forwarding of unknown uni/multi cast addresses
  host          Set port host
  mode          Set trunking mode of the interface
  nonegotiate   Device will not engage in negotiation protocol on this
                interface
  port-security Security related command
  priority      Set appliance 802.1p priority
  private-vlan  Set the private VLAN configuration
  protected     Configure an interface to be a protected port
  trunk         Set trunking characteristics of the interface
  voice         Voice appliance attributes  voice
```

Well now, what do we have here? There's some new stuff showing up in our output now. We can see various commands—some that I've already covered, but no worries because I'm going to cover the access, mode, nonegotiate, and trunk commands very soon. Let's start with setting an access port on S1, which is probably the most widely used type of port you'll find on production switches that have VLANs configured:

```
S3(config-if)#switchport mode ?
  access        Set trunking mode to ACCESS unconditionally
  dot1q-tunnel  set trunking mode to TUNNEL unconditionally
  dynamic       Set trunking mode to dynamically negotiate access or trunk mode
  private-vlan  Set private-vlan mode
  trunk         Set trunking mode to TRUNK unconditionally


S3(config-if)#switchport mode access
S3(config-if)#switchport access vlan 3
```

By starting with the `switchport mode access` command, you're telling the switch that this is a nontrunking layer 2 port. You can then assign a VLAN to the port with the `switchport access` command. Remember, you can choose many ports to configure simultaneously with the `interface range` command.

Let's take a look at our VLANs now:

```
S3#show vlan
VLAN Name                        Status    Ports
---- -------------------------- --------- ------------------------------
1    default                     active    Fa0/4, Fa0/5, Fa0/6, Fa0/7
                                           Fa0/8, Fa0/9, Fa0/10, Fa0/11,
                                           Fa0/12, Fa0/13, Fa0/14, Fa0/19,
                                           Fa0/20, Fa0/21, Fa0/22, Fa0/23,
                                           Gi0/1 ,Gi0/2


2    Sales                       active
3    Marketing                   active    Fa0/3
```

Notice that port Fa0/3 is now a member of VLAN 3. But, can you tell me where ports 1 and 2 are? And why aren't they showing up in the output of show vlan? That's right, because they are trunk ports!

We can also see this with the show interfaces interface switchport command:

```
S3#sh int fa0/3 switchport
Name: Fa0/3
Switchport: Enabled
Administrative Mode: static access
Operational Mode: static access
Administrative Trunking Encapsulation: negotiate
Negotiation of Trunking: Off
Access Mode VLAN: 3 (Marketing)
```

The highlighted output shows that Fa0/3 is an access port and a member of VLAN 3 (Marketing).

That's it. Well, sort of. If you plugged devices into each VLAN port, they can only talk to other devices in the same VLAN. But as soon as you learn a bit more about trunking, we're going to enable inter-VLAN communication!

## Configuring Trunk Ports

The 2960 switch only runs the IEEE 802.1q encapsulation method. To configure trunking on a FastEthernet port, use the interface command `switchport mode trunk`. It's a tad different on the 3560 switch.

The following switch output shows the trunk configuration on interfaces Fa0/15–18 as set to trunk:

```
S1(config)#int range f0/15-18
S1(config-if-range)#switchport trunk encapsulation dot1q
S1(config-if-range)#switchport mode trunk
```

If you have a switch that only runs the 802.1q encapsulation method, then you wouldn't use the encapsulation command as I did in the preceding output. Let's check out our trunk ports now:

```
S1(config-if-range)#do sh int f0/15 swi
Name: Fa0/15
Switchport: Enabled
Administrative Mode: trunk
Operational Mode: trunk
Administrative Trunking Encapsulation: dot1q
Operational Trunking Encapsulation: dot1q
Negotiation of Trunking: On
Access Mode VLAN: 1 (default)
Trunking Native Mode VLAN: 1 (default)
Administrative Native VLAN tagging: enabled
Voice VLAN: none
```

Notice that port Fa0/15 is a trunk and running 802.1q. Let's take another look:

```
S1(config-if-range)#do sh int trunk

Port        Mode           Encapsulation   Status      Native vlan
Fa0/15      on             802.1q          trunking    1
Fa0/16      on             802.1q          trunking    1
Fa0/17      on             802.1q          trunking    1
Fa0/18      on             802.1q          trunking    1

Port        Vlans allowed on trunk
Fa0/15      1-4094
Fa0/16      1-4094
Fa0/17      1-4094
Fa0/18      1-4094
```

Take note of the fact that ports 15–18 are now in the trunk mode of on and the encapsulation is now 802.1q instead of the negotiated ISL. Here's a description of the different options available when configuring a switch interface:

**switchport mode access**   I discussed this in the previous section, but this puts the interface (access port) into permanent nontrunking mode and negotiates to convert the link into a nontrunk link. The interface becomes a nontrunk interface regardless of whether the neighboring interface is a trunk interface. The port would be a dedicated layer 2 access port.

**switchport mode dynamic auto** This mode makes the interface able to convert the link to a trunk link. The interface becomes a trunk interface if the neighboring interface is set to trunk or desirable mode. The default is dynamic auto on a lot of Cisco switches, but that default trunk method is changing to dynamic desirable on most new models.

**switchport mode dynamic desirable** This one makes the interface actively attempt to convert the link to a trunk link. The interface becomes a trunk interface if the neighboring interface is set to trunk, desirable, or auto mode. I used to see this mode as the default on some switches, but not any longer. This is now the default switch port mode for all Ethernet interfaces on all new Cisco switches.

**switchport mode trunk** Puts the interface into permanent trunking mode and negotiates to convert the neighboring link into a trunk link. The interface becomes a trunk interface even if the neighboring interface isn't a trunk interface.

**switchport nonegotiate** Prevents the interface from generating DTP frames. You can use this command only when the interface switchport mode is access or trunk. You must manually configure the neighboring interface as a trunk interface to establish a trunk link.

> Dynamic Trunking Protocol (DTP) is used for negotiating trunking on a link between two devices as well as negotiating the encapsulation type of either 802.1q or ISL. I use the nonegotiate command when I want dedicated trunk ports; no questions asked.

To disable trunking on an interface, use the switchport mode access command, which sets the port back to a dedicated layer 2 access switch port.

## Defining the Allowed VLANs on a Trunk

As I've mentioned, trunk ports send and receive information from all VLANs by default, and if a frame is untagged, it's sent to the management VLAN. Understand that this applies to the extended range VLANs too.

But we can remove VLANs from the allowed list to prevent traffic from certain VLANs from traversing a trunked link. I'll show you how you'd do that, but first let me again demonstrate that all VLANs are allowed across the trunk link by default:

```
S1#sh int trunk
[output cut]

Port       Vlans allowed on trunk
Fa0/15     1-4094
Fa0/16     1-4094
Fa0/17     1-4094
Fa0/18     1-4094
```

```
S1(config)#int f0/15
S1(config-if)#switchport trunk allowed vlan 4,6,12,15
S1(config-if)#do show int trunk
[output cut]

Port       Vlans allowed on trunk
Fa0/15     4,6,12,15
Fa0/16     1-4094
Fa0/17     1-4094
Fa0/18     1-4094
```

The preceding command affected the trunk link configured on S1 port F0/15, causing it to drop all traffic sent and received for VLANs 4, 6, 12, and 15. You can try to remove VLAN 1 on a trunk link, but it will still send and receive management like CDP, DTP, and VTP, so what's the point?

To remove a range of VLANs, just use the hyphen:

```
S1(config-if)#switchport trunk allowed vlan remove 4-8
```

If by chance someone has removed some VLANs from a trunk link and you want to set the trunk back to default, just use this command:

```
S1(config-if)#switchport trunk allowed vlan all
```

Next, I want to show you how to configure a native VLAN for a trunk before we start routing between VLANs.

## Changing or Modifying the Trunk Native VLAN

You can change the trunk port native VLAN from VLAN 1, which many people do for security reasons. To change the native VLAN, use the following command:

```
S1(config)#int f0/15
S1(config-if)#switchport trunk native vlan ?
  <1-4094>  VLAN ID of the native VLAN when this port is in trunking mode


S1(config-if)#switchport trunk native vlan 4
1w6d: %CDP-4-NATIVE_VLAN_MISMATCH: Native VLAN mismatch discovered on
FastEthernet0/15 (4), with S3 FastEthernet0/1 (1).
```

So we've changed our native VLAN on our trunk link to 4, and by using the show running-config command, I can see the configuration under the trunk link:

```
S1#sh run int f0/15
Building configuration...
```

```
Current configuration : 202 bytes
!
interface FastEthernet0/15
 description 1st connection to S3
 switchport trunk encapsulation dot1q
 switchport trunk native vlan 4
 switchport trunk allowed vlan 4,6,12,15
 switchport mode trunk
end
```

```
S1#!
```

Oops—wait a minute! You didn't think it would be this easy and would just start work-ing, did you? Of course not! Here's the rub: If all switches don't have the same native VLAN configured on the given trunk links, then we'll start to receive this error, which happened immediately after I entered the command:

```
1w6d: %CDP-4-NATIVE_VLAN_MISMATCH: Native VLAN mismatch discovered
on FastEthernet0/15 (4), with S3 FastEthernet0/1 (1).
```

Actually, this is a good, noncryptic error, so either we can go to the other end of our trunk link(s) and change the native VLAN or we set the native VLAN back to the default to fix it. Here's how we'd do that:

```
S1(config-if)#no switchport trunk native vlan
1w6d: %SPANTREE-2-UNBLOCK_CONSIST_PORT: Unblocking FastEthernet0/15
on VLAN0004. Port consistency restored.
```

Now our trunk link is using the default VLAN 1 as the native VLAN. Just remember that all switches on a given trunk must use the same native VLAN or you'll have some serious management problems. These issues won't affect user data, just management traffic between switches. Now, let's mix it up by connecting a router into our switched network and configure inter-VLAN communication.

## Configuring Inter-VLAN Routing

By default, only hosts that are members of the same VLAN can communicate. To change this and allow inter-VLAN communication, you need a router or a layer 3 switch. I'm going to start with the router approach.

To support ISL or 802.1q routing on a FastEthernet interface, the router's interface is divided into logical interfaces—one for each VLAN—as was shown in Figure 11.10. These are called *subinterfaces*. From a FastEthernet or Gigabit interface, you can set the interface to trunk with the encapsulation command:

```
ISR#config t
ISR(config)#int f0/0.1
```

```
ISR(config-subif)#encapsulation ?
  dot1Q  IEEE 802.1Q Virtual LAN
ISR(config-subif)#encapsulation dot1Q ?
  <1-4094>  IEEE 802.1Q VLAN ID
```

Notice that my 2811 router (named ISR) only supports 802.1q. We'd need an older-model router to run the ISL encapsulation, but why bother?

The subinterface number is only locally significant, so it doesn't matter which subinterface numbers are configured on the router. Most of the time, I'll configure a subinterface with the same number as the VLAN I want to route. It's easy to remember that way since the subinterface number is used only for administrative purposes.

It's really important that you understand that each VLAN is actually a separate subnet. True, I know—they don't *have* to be. But it really is a good idea to configure your VLANs as separate subnets, so just do that. Before we move on, I want to define *upstream routing*. This is a term used to define the router on a stick. This router will provide inter-VLAN routing, but it can also be used to forward traffic upstream from the switched network to other parts of the corporate network or Internet.

Now, I need to make sure you're fully prepared to configure inter-VLAN routing as well as determine the IP addresses of hosts connected in a switched VLAN environment. And as always, it's also a good idea to be able to fix any problems that may arise. To set you up for success, let me give you few examples.

First, start by looking at Figure 11.12 and read the router and switch configuration within it. By this point in the book, you should be able to determine the IP address, masks, and default gateways of each of the hosts in the VLANs.

**FIGURE 11.12**   Configuring inter-VLAN example 1

The next step is to figure out which subnets are being used. By looking at the router configuration in the figure, you can see that we're using 192.168.1.64/26 with VLAN 2, 192.168.1.128/27, and VLAN 10.

By looking at the switch configuration, you can see that ports 2 and 3 are in VLAN 2 and port 4 is in VLAN 10. This means that Host A and Host B are in VLAN 2, and Host C is in VLAN 10.

But wait—what's that IP address doing there under the physical interface? Can we even do that? Sure we can! If we place an IP address under the physical interface, the result is that frames sent from the IP address would be untagged. So what VLAN would those frames be a member of? By default, they would belong to VLAN 1, our management VLAN. This means the address 192.168.10.1/24 is my native VLAN IP address for this switch.

Here's what the hosts' IP addresses should be:

**Host A:** 192.168.1.66, 255.255.255.192, default gateway 192.168.1.65

**Host B:** 192.168.1.67, 255.255.255.192, default gateway 192.168.1.65

**Host C:** 192.168.1.130, 255.255.255.224, default gateway 192.168.1.129

The hosts could be any address in the range—I just chose the first available IP address after the default gateway address. That wasn't so hard, was it?

Now, again using Figure 11.12, let's go through the commands necessary to configure switch port 1 so it will establish a link with the router and provide inter-VLAN communication using the IEEE version for encapsulation. Keep in mind that the commands can vary slightly depending on what type of switch you're dealing with.

For a 2960 switch, use the following:

```
2960#config t
2960(config)#interface fa0/1
2960(config-if)#switchport mode trunk
```

That's it! As you already know, the 2960 switch can only run the 802.1q encapsulation, so there's no need to specify it. You can't anyway. For a 3560, it's basically the same, but because it can run ISL and 802.1q, you have to specify the trunking encapsulation protocol you're going to use.

 Remember that when you create a trunked link, all VLANs are allowed to pass data by default.

Let's take a look at Figure 11.13 and see what we can determine. This figure shows three VLANs, with two hosts in each of them. The router in Figure 11.13 is connected to the Fa0/1 switch port, and VLAN 4 is configured on port F0/6.

When looking at this diagram, keep in mind that these three factors are what Cisco expects you to know:

- The router is connected to the switch using subinterfaces.

- The switch port connecting to the router is a trunk port.

- The switch ports connecting to the clients and the hub are access ports, not trunk ports.

**FIGURE 11.13** Inter-VLAN example 2

The configuration of the switch would look something like this:

```
2960#config t
2960(config)#int f0/1
2960(config-if)#switchport mode trunk
2960(config-if)#int f0/2
2960(config-if)#switchport access vlan 2
2960(config-if)#int f0/3
2960(config-if)#switchport access vlan 2
2960(config-if)#int f0/4
2960(config-if)#switchport access vlan 3
2960(config-if)#int f0/5
2960(config-if)#switchport access vlan 3
2960(config-if)#int f0/6
2960(config-if)#switchport access vlan 4
```

Before we configure the router, we need to design our logical network:

VLAN 1: 192.168.10.0/28

VLAN 2: 192.168.10.16/28

VLAN 3: 192.168.10.32/28

VLAN 4: 192.168.10.48/28

The configuration of the router would then look like this:

```
ISR#config t
ISR(config)#int fa0/0
```

```
ISR(config-if)#ip address 192.168.10.1 255.255.255.240
ISR(config-if)#no shutdown
ISR(config-if)#int f0/0.2
ISR(config-subif)#encapsulation dot1q 2
ISR(config-subif)#ip address 192.168.10.17 255.255.255.240
ISR(config-subif)#int f0/0.3
ISR(config-subif)#encapsulation dot1q 3
ISR(config-subif)#ip address 192.168.10.33 255.255.255.240
ISR(config-subif)#int f0/0.4
ISR(config-subif)#encapsulation dot1q 4
ISR(config-subif)#ip address 192.168.10.49 255.255.255.240
```

Notice I didn't tag VLAN 1. Even though I could have created a subinterface and tagged VLAN 1, it's not necessary with 802.1q because untagged frames are members of the native VLAN.

The hosts in each VLAN would be assigned an address from their subnet range, and the default gateway would be the IP address assigned to the router's subinterface in that VLAN.

Now, let's take a look at another figure and see if you can determine the switch and router configurations without looking at the answer—no cheating! Figure 11.14 shows a router connected to a 2960 switch with two VLANs. One host in each VLAN is assigned an IP address. What would your router and switch configurations be based on these IP addresses?

**FIGURE 11.14**    Inter-VLAN example 3

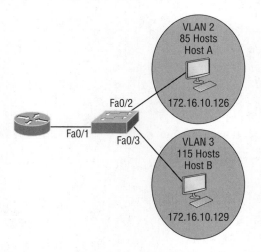

Okay—since the hosts don't list a subnet mask, you have to look for the number of hosts used in each VLAN to figure out the block size. VLAN 2 has 85 hosts and VLAN 3 has 115 hosts. Each of these will fit in a block size of 128, which is a /25 mask, or 255.255.255.128.

You should know by now that the subnets are 0 and 128; the 0 subnet (VLAN 2) has a host range of 1–126, and the 128 subnet (VLAN 3) has a range of 129–254. You can almost be fooled since Host A has an IP address of 126, which makes it *almost* seem that Host A and B are in the same subnet. But they're not, and you're way too smart by now to be fooled by this one!

Here is the switch configuration:

```
2960#config t
2960(config)#int f0/1
2960(config-if)#switchport mode trunk
2960(config-if)#int f0/2
2960(config-if)#switchport access vlan 2
2960(config-if)#int f0/3
2960(config-if)#switchport access vlan 3
```

Here is the router configuration:

```
ISR#config t
ISR(config)#int f0/0
ISR(config-if)#ip address 192.168.10.1 255.255.255.0
ISR(config-if)#no shutdown
ISR(config-if)#int f0/0.2
ISR(config-subif)#encapsulation dot1q 2
ISR(config-subif)#ip address 172.16.10.1 255.255.255.128
ISR(config-subif)#int f0/0.3
ISR(config-subif)#encapsulation dot1q 3
ISR(config-subif)#ip address 172.16.10.254 255.255.255.128
```

I used the first address in the host range for VLAN 2 and the last address in the range for VLAN 3, but any address in the range would work. You would just have to configure the host's default gateway to whatever you make the router's address. Also, I used a different subnet for my physical interface, which is my management VLAN router's address.

Now, before we go on to the next example, I need to make sure you know how to set the IP address on the switch. Since VLAN 1 is typically the administrative VLAN, we'll use an IP address from out of that pool of addresses. Here's how to set the IP address of the switch (not nagging, but you really should already know this!):

```
2960#config t
2960(config)#int vlan 1
2960(config-if)#ip address 192.168.10.2 255.255.255.0
2960(config-if)#no shutdown
2960(config-if)#exit
2960(config)#ip default-gateway 192.168.10.1
```

Yes, you have to execute a no shutdown on the VLAN interface and set the ip default-gateway address to the router.

One more example, and then we'll move on to IVR using a multilayer switch—another important subject that you definitely don't want to miss! In Figure 11.15 there are two VLANs, plus the management VLAN 1. By looking at the router configuration: What's the IP address, subnet mask, and default gateway of Host A? Use the last IP address in the range for Host A's address.

If you really look carefully at the router configuration (the hostname in this configuration is just Router), there's a simple and quick answer. All subnets are using a /28, which is a 255.255.255.240 mask. This is a block size of 16. The router's address for VLAN 2 is in subnet 128. The next subnet is 144, so the broadcast address of VLAN 2 is 143 and the valid host range is 129–142. So the host address would be this:

**IP address:** 192.168.10.142

**Mask:** 255.255.255.240

**Default gateway:** 192.168.10.129

**FIGURE 11.15**    Inter-VLAN example 4

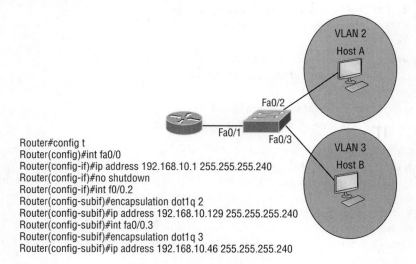

```
Router#config t
Router(config)#int fa0/0
Router(config-if)#ip address 192.168.10.1 255.255.255.240
Router(config-if)#no shutdown
Router(config-if)#int f0/0.2
Router(config-subif)#encapsulation dot1q 2
Router(config-subif)#ip address 192.168.10.129 255.255.255.240
Router(config-subif)#int fa0/0.3
Router(config-subif)#encapsulation dot1q 3
Router(config-subif)#ip address 192.168.10.46 255.255.255.240
```

This section was probably the hardest part of this entire book, and I honestly created the simplest configuration you can possibly get away with using to help you through it!

I'll use Figure 11.16 to demonstrate configuring inter-VLAN routing (IVR) with a multilayer switch, which is often referred to as a switched virtual interface (SVI). I'm going to use the same network that I used to discuss a multilayer switch back in Figure 11.11, and I'll use this IP address scheme: 192.168.x.0/24, where x represents the VLAN subnet. In my example this will be the same as the VLAN number.

**FIGURE 11.16**   Inter-VLAN routing with a multilayer switch

The hosts are already configured with the IP address, subnet mask, and default gateway address using the first address in the range. Now I just need to configure the routing on the switch, which is pretty simple actually:

```
S1(config)#ip routing
S1(config)#int vlan 10
S1(config-if)#ip address 192.168.10.1 255.255.255.0
S1(config-if)#int vlan 20
S1(config-if)#ip address 192.168.20.1 255.255.255.0
```

And that's it! Enable IP routing and create one logical interface for each VLAN using the interface vlan number command and voilà! You've now accomplished making inter-VLAN routing work on the backplane of the switch!

# Summary

In this chapter, I introduced you to the world of virtual LANs and described how Cisco switches can use them. We talked about how VLANs break up broadcast domains in a switched internetwork—a very important, necessary thing because layer 2 switches only break up collision domains, and by default, all switches make up one large broadcast domain. I also described access links to you, and we went over how trunked VLANs work across a FastEthernet or faster link.

Trunking is a crucial technology to understand really well when you're dealing with a network populated by multiple switches that are running several VLANs.

You were also presented with some key troubleshooting and configuration examples for access and trunk ports, configuring trunking options, and a huge section on IVR.

# Exam Essentials

**Understand the term** *frame tagging.* *Frame tagging* refers to VLAN identification; this is what switches use to keep track of all those frames as they're traversing a switch fabric. It's how switches identify which frames belong to which VLANs.

**Understand the 802.1q VLAN identification method.**    This is a nonproprietary IEEE method of frame tagging. If you're trunking between a Cisco switched-link and a different brand of switch, you have to use 802.1q for the trunk to work.

**Remember how to set a trunk port on a 2960 switch.**    To set a port to trunking on a 2960, use the switchport mode trunk command.

**Remember to check a switch port's VLAN assignment when plugging in a new host.**    If you plug a new host into a switch, then you must verify the VLAN membership of that port. If the membership is different than what is needed for that host, the host will not be able to reach the needed network services, such as a workgroup server or printer.

**Remember how to create a Cisco router on a stick to provide inter-VLAN communication.** You can use a Cisco FastEthernet or Gigabit Ethernet interface to provide inter-VLAN routing. The switch port connected to the router must be a trunk port; then you must create virtual interfaces (subinterfaces) on the router port for each VLAN connecting to it. The hosts in each VLAN will use this subinterface address as their default gateway address.

**Remember how to provide inter-VLAN routing with a layer 3 switch.**    You can use a layer 3 (multilayer) switch to provide IVR just as with a router on a stick, but using a layer 3 switch is more efficient and faster. First you start the routing process with the command ip routing, then create a virtual interface for each VLAN using the command interface vlan vlan, and then apply the IP address for that VLAN under that logical interface.

# Written Lab 11

The answers to these labs can be found in Appendix A, "Answers to Written Labs."
   In this section, write the answers to the following questions:

1. True/False: To provide IVR with a layer 3 switch, you place an IP address on each interface of the switch.

2. What protocol will stop loops in a layer 2 switched network?

3. VLANs break up _____ domains.

4. Switches, by default, only break up _____ domains.

5. If you have a switch that provides both ISL and 802.1q frame tagging, what command under the trunk interface will make the trunk use 802.1q?

6. What does trunking provide?

7. What is frame tagging?

8. True/False: The 802.1q encapsulation is removed from the frame if the frame is forwarded out an access link.

9. What type of link on a switch is a member of only one VLAN?

10. You want to change from the default of VLAN 1 to VLAN 4 for untagged traffic. What command will you use?

# Hands-on Labs

In these labs, you will use three switches and a router. To perform the last lab, you'll need a layer 3 switch.

   Lab 11.1: Configuring and Verifying VLANs

   Lab 11.2: Configuring and Verifying Trunk Links

   Lab 11.3: Configuring Router on a Stick Routing

   Lab 11.4: Configuring IVR with a Layer 3 Switch

In these labs, I'll use the following layout:

## Hands-on Lab 11.1: Configuring and Verifying VLANs

This lab will have you configure VLANs from global configuration mode, and then verify the VLANs.

1. Configure two VLANs on each switch, VLAN 10 and VLAN 20.

```
S1(config)#vlan 10
S1(config-vlan)#vlan 20


S2(config)#vlan 10
S2(config-vlan)#vlan 20


S3(config)#vlan 10
S3(config-vlan)#vlan 20
```

2. Use the show vlan and show vlan brief command to verify your VLANs. Notice that all interfaces are in VLAN 1 by default

```
S1#sh vlan
S1#sh vlan brief
```

# Hands-on Lab 11.2: Configuring and Verifying Trunk Links

This lab will have you configure trunk links and then verify them.

**1.** Connect to each switch and configure trunking on all switch links. If you are using a switch that supports both 802.1q and ISL frame tagging, then use the encapsulation command; if not, then skip that command.

```
S1#config t
S1(config)#interface fa0/15
S1(config-if)#switchport trunk encapsulation ?
  dot1q  Interface uses only 802.1q trunking encapsulation when trunking
  isl    Interface uses only ISL trunking encapsulation when trunking
  negotiate   Device will negotiate trunking encapsulation with peer on
interface
```

Again, if you typed the above and received an error, then your switch does not support both encapsulation methods:

```
S1 (config-if)#switchport trunk encapsulation dot1q
S1 (config-if)#switchport mode trunk
S1 (config-if)#interface fa0/16
S1 (config-if)#switchport trunk encapsulation dot1q
S1 (config-if)#switchport mode trunk
S1 (config-if)#interface fa0/17
S1 (config-if)#switchport trunk encapsulation dot1q
S1 (config-if)#switchport mode trunk
S1 (config-f)#interface fa0/18
S1 (config-if)#switchport trunk encapsulation dot1q
S1 (config-if)#switchport mode trunk
```

**2.** Configure the trunk links on your other switches.

**3.** On each switch, verify your trunk ports with the show interface trunk command:

```
S1#show interface trunk
```

**4.** Verify the switchport configuration with the following:

```
S1#show interface interface switchport
```

The second *interface* in the command is a variable, such as Fa0/15.

## Hands-on Lab 11.3: Configuring Router on a Stick Routing

In this lab, you'll use the router connected to port F0/8 of switch S1 to configure ROAS.

1. Configure the F0/0 of the router with two subinterfaces to provide inter-VLAN routing using 802.1q encapsulation. Use 172.16.10.0/24 for your management VLAN, 10.10.10.0/24 for VLAN 10, and 20.20.20.0/24 for VLAN 20.

```
Router#config t
Router (config)#int f0/0
Router (config-if)#ip address 172.16.10.1 255.255.255.0
Router (config-if)#interface f0/0.10
Router (config-subif)#encapsulation dot1q 10
Router (config-subif)#ip address 10.10.10.1 255.255.255.0
Router (config-subif)#interface f0/0.20
Router (config-subif)#encapsulation dot1q 20
Router (config-subif)#ip address 20.20.20.1 255.255.255.0
```

2. Verify the configuration with the show running-config command.
3. Configure trunking on interface F0/8 of the S1 switch connecting to your router.
4. Verify that your VLANs are still configured on your switches with the sh vlan command.
5. Configure your hosts to be in VLAN 10 and VLAN 20 with the switchport access vlan x command.
6. Ping from your PC to the router's subinterface configured for your VLAN.
7. Ping from your PC to your PC in the other VLAN. You are now routing through the router!

## Hands-on Lab 11.4: Configuring IVR with a Layer 3 Switch

In this lab, you will disable the router and use the S1 switch to provide inter VLAN routing by creating SVI's.

1. Connect to the S1 switch and make interface F0/8 an access port, which will make the router stop providing inter-VLAN routing.
2. Enable IP routing on the S1 switch.

```
S1(config)#ip routing
```

3. Create two new interfaces on the S1 switch to provide IVR.

```
S1(config)#interface vlan 10
S1(config-if)#ip address 10.10.10.1 255.255.255.0
S1(config-if)#interface vlan 20
S1(config-if)#ip address 20.20.20.1 255.255.255.0
```

4. Clear the ARP cache on the switch and hosts.

   S1#**clear arp**

5. Ping from your PC to the router's subinterface configured for your VLAN.

6. Ping from your PC to your PC in the other VLAN. You are now routing through the S1 switch!

# Review Questions

 The following questions are designed to test your understanding of this chapter's material. For more information on how to get additional questions, please see this book's introduction.

The answers to these questions can be found in Appendix B, "Answers to Chapter Review Questions."

1. Which of the following statements is true with regard to VLANs?

    **A.** VLANs greatly reduce network security.

    **B.** VLANs increase the number of collision domains while decreasing their size.

    **C.** VLANs decrease the number of broadcast domains while decreasing their size.

    **D.** Network adds, moves, and changes are achieved with ease by just configuring a port into the appropriate VLAN.

2. Write the command that must be present for this layer 3 switch to provide inter-VLAN routing between the two VLANs created with these commands:

```
S1(config)#int vlan 10
S1(config-if)#ip address 192.168.10.1 255.255.255.0
S1(config-if)#int vlan 20
S1(config-if)#ip address 192.168.20.1 255.255.255.0
```

**3.** In the diagram, how must the port on each end of the line be configured to carry traffic between the two hosts in the Sales VLAN?

 **A.** Access port

 **B.** 10 GB

 **C.** Trunk

 **D.** Spanning

**4.** What is the only type of *second* VLAN of which an access port can be a member?

 **A.** Secondary

 **B.** Voice

 **C.** Primary

 **D.** Trunk

**5.** In the following configuration, what command is missing in the creation of the VLAN interface?

```
2960#config t
2960(config)#int vlan 1
2960(config-if)#ip address 192.168.10.2 255.255.255.0
2960(config-if)#exit
2960(config)#ip default-gateway 192.168.10.1
```

   **A.** no shutdown under int vlan 1

   **B.** encapsulation dot1q 1 under int vlan 1

   **C.** switchport access vlan 1

   **D.** passive-interface

**6.** Which of the following statements is true with regard to ISL and 802.1q?

   **A.** 802.1q encapsulates the frame with control information; ISL inserts an ISL field along with tag control information.

   **B.** 802.1q is Cisco proprietary.

   **C.** ISL encapsulates the frame with control information; 802.1q inserts an 802.1q field along with tag control information.

   **D.** ISL is a standard.

**7.** What concept is depicted in the diagram?

Gi0/0

   **A.** Multiprotocol routing

   **B.** Passive interface

   **C.** Gateway redundancy

   **D.** Router on a stick

**8.** Write the command that places an interface into VLAN 2. Write only the command and not the prompt.

**9.** Write the command that generated the following output:

```
VLAN Name                              Status    Ports
---- ------------------------------   ---------  ------------------------
1    default                          active    Fa0/1, Fa0/2, Fa0/3, Fa0/4
                                                Fa0/5, Fa0/6, Fa0/7, Fa0/8
                                              Fa0/9, Fa0/10, Fa0/11, Fa0/12
                                             Fa0/13, Fa0/14, Fa0/19, Fa0/20
                                             Fa0/21, Fa0/22, Fa0/23, Gi0/1
                                                Gi0/2

2    Sales                            active
3    Marketing                        active
4    Accounting                       active
[output cut]
```

**10.** In the configuration and diagram shown, what command is missing to enable inter-VLAN routing between VLAN 2 and VLAN 3?

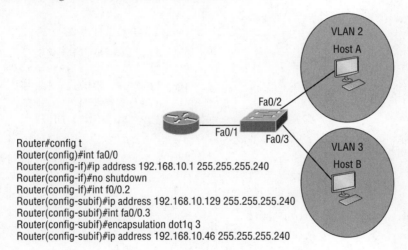

```
Router#config t
Router(config)#int fa0/0
Router(config-if)#ip address 192.168.10.1 255.255.255.240
Router(config-if)#no shutdown
Router(config-if)#int f0/0.2
Router(config-subif)#ip address 192.168.10.129 255.255.255.240
Router(config-subif)#int fa0/0.3
Router(config-subif)#encapsulation dot1q 3
Router(config-subif)#ip address 192.168.10.46 255.255.255.240
```

**A.** encapsulation dot1q 3 under int f0/0.2

**B.** encapsulation dot1q 2 under int f0/0.2

**C.** no shutdown under int f0/0.2

**D.** no shutdown under int f0/0.3

11. Based on the configuration shown below, what statement is true?

```
S1(config)#ip routing
S1(config)#int vlan 10
S1(config-if)#ip address 192.168.10.1 255.255.255.0
S1(config-if)#int vlan 20
S1(config-if)#ip address 192.168.20.1 255.255.255.0
```

  A. This is a multilayer switch.

  B. The two VLANs are in the same subnet.

  C. Encapsulation must be configured.

  D. VLAN 10 is the management VLAN.

12. What is true of the output shown below?

```
S1#sh vlan
```

```
VLAN Name                     Status    Ports
---- ------------------------ --------- ------------------------------
1    default                  active    Fa0/1, Fa0/2, Fa0/3, Fa0/4
                                        Fa0/5, Fa0/6, Fa0/7, Fa0/8
                                        Fa0/9, Fa0/10, Fa0/11, Fa0/12
                                        Fa0/13, Fa0/14, Fa0/19, Fa0/20,
                                        Fa0/22, Fa0/23, Gi0/1, Gi0/2
2    Sales                    active
3    Marketing                          Fa0/21
4    Accounting               active
[output cut]
```

  A. Interface F0/15 is a trunk port.

  B. Interface F0/17 is an access port.

  C. Interface F0/21 is a trunk port.

  D. VLAN 1 was populated manually.

13. 802.1q untagged frames are members of the _____ VLAN.

  A. Auxiliary

  B. Voice

  C. Native

  D. Private

**14.** Write the command that generated the following output. Write only the command and not the prompt:

```
Name: Fa0/15
Switchport: Enabled
Administrative Mode: dynamic desirable
Operational Mode: trunk
Administrative Trunking Encapsulation: negotiate
Operational Trunking Encapsulation: isl
Negotiation of Trunking: On
Access Mode VLAN: 1 (default)
Trunking Native Mode VLAN: 1 (default)
Administrative Native VLAN tagging: enabled
Voice VLAN: none
[output cut]
```

**15.** Which statement is true regarding virtual local area networks (VLANs)?

    **A.** VLANs are location dependent.

    **B.** VLANs are limited to a single switch.

    **C.** VLANs may be subnets of major networks.

    **D.** VLANs define collision domains.

**16.** In the diagram, what should be the default gateway address of Host B?

    **A.** 192.168.10.1

    **B.** 192.168.1.65

    **C.** 192.168.1.129

    **D.** 192.168.1.2

**17.** What is the purpose of frame tagging in virtual LAN (VLAN) configurations?

   **A.** Inter-VLAN routing

   **B.** Encryption of network packets

   **C.** Frame identification over trunk links

   **D.** Frame identification over access links

**18.** Write the command to create VLAN 2 on a layer 2 switch. Write only the command and not the prompt.

**19.** Which statement is true regarding 802.1q frame tagging?

   **A.** 802.1q adds a 26-byte trailer and 4-byte header.

   **B.** 802.1q uses a native VLAN.

   **C.** The original Ethernet frame is not modified.

   **D.** 802.1q only works with Cisco switches.

**20.** Write the command that prevents an interface from generating DTP frames. Write only the command and not the prompt.

# Chapter

# 12

# Security

THE FOLLOWING ICND1 EXAM TOPICS
ARE COVERED IN THIS CHAPTER:

✓ **IP Services**

- Describe the types, features, and applications of ACLs
    - Standard
        - Sequence numbers
        - Editing
    - Extended
    - Named
    - Numbered
    - Log option
- Configure and verify ACLs in a network environment
    - Named
    - Numbered
    - Log option

✓ **Network Device Security**

- Configure and verify ACLs to filter network traffic
- Configure and verify ACLs to limit telnet and SSH access to the router

✓ **Troubleshooting**

- Troubleshoot and Resolve ACL issues
    - Statistics
    - Permitted networks
    - Direction
        - Interface

If you're a sys admin, it's my guess that shielding sensitive, critical data, as well as your network's resources, from every possible evil exploit is a top priority of yours, right? Good to know you're on the right page because Cisco has some really effective security solutions to equip you with the tools you'll need to make this happen in a very real way!

The first power tool I'm going to hand you is known as the access control list (ACL). Being able to execute an ACL proficiently is an integral part of Cisco's security solution, so I'm going to begin by showing you how to create and implement simple ACLs. From there, I'll move to demonstrating more advanced ACLs and describe how to implement them strategically to provide serious armor for an internetwork in today's challenging, high-risk environment.

In Appendix C, "Disabling and Configuring Network Services," I'll show you how to mitigate most security-oriented network threats. Make sure you don't skip this appendix because it is chock full of great security information, and the information it contains is part of the Cisco exam objectives as well!

The proper use and configuration of access lists is a vital part of router configuration because access lists are such versatile networking accessories. Contributing mightily to the efficiency and operation of your network, access lists give network managers a huge amount of control over traffic flow throughout the enterprise. With access lists, we can gather basic statistics on packet flow and security policies can be implemented. These dynamic tools also enable us to protect sensitive devices from the dangers of unauthorized access.

In this chapter, we'll cover ACLs for TCP/IP as well as explore effective ways available to us for testing and monitoring how well applied access lists are functioning. We'll begin now by discussing key security measures deployed using hardware devices and VLANs and then I'll introduce you to ACLs.

To find up-to-the-minute updates for this chapter, please see www.lammle.com/forum or the book's web page at www.sybex.com.

# Perimeter, Firewall, and Internal Routers

You see this a lot—typically, in medium to large enterprise networks—the various strategies for security are based on some mix of internal and perimeter routers plus firewall devices. Internal routers provide additional security by screening traffic to various parts of the protected corporate network, and they achieve this using access lists. You can see where each of these types of devices would be found in Figure 12.1.

**FIGURE 12.1**    A typical secured network

I'll use the terms *trusted network* and *untrusted network* throughout this chapter, as well as in Chapter 13, "Network Address Translation (NAT)," so it's important that you can see where they're found in a typical secured network. The demilitarized zone (DMZ) can be global (real) Internet addresses or private addresses, depending on how you configure your firewall, but this is typically where you'll find the HTTP, DNS, email, and other Internet-type corporate servers.

As you now know, instead of using routers, we can create VLANs with switches on the inside trusted network. Multilayer switches containing their own security features can sometimes replace internal (LAN) routers to provide higher performance in VLAN architectures.

Let's look at some ways of protecting the internetwork using access lists.

# Introduction to Access Lists

An *access list* is essentially a list of conditions that categorize packets, and they really come in handy when you need to exercise control over network traffic. An ACL would be your tool of choice for decision making in these situations.

One of the most common and easiest-to-understand uses of access lists is to filter unwanted packets when implementing security policies. For example, you can set them up to make very specific decisions about regulating traffic patterns so that they'll allow only certain hosts to access web resources on the Internet while restricting others. With the right combination of access lists, network managers arm themselves with the power to enforce nearly any security policy they can invent.

Creating access lists is really a lot like programming a series of if-then statements—if a given condition is met, then a given action is taken. If the specific condition isn't met, nothing happens and the next statement is evaluated. Access-list statements are basically packet filters that packets are compared against, categorized by, and acted upon accordingly. Once the lists are built, they can be applied to either inbound or outbound traffic on any interface. Applying an access list causes the router to analyze every packet crossing that interface in the specified direction and take the appropriate action.

There are three important rules that a packet follows when it's being compared with an access list:

- The packet is always compared with each line of the access list in sequential order—it will always start with the first line of the access list, move on to line 2, then line 3, and so on.

- The packet is compared with lines of the access list only until a match is made. Once it matches the condition on a line of the access list, the packet is acted upon and no further comparisons take place.

- There is an implicit "deny" at the end of each access list—this means that if a packet doesn't match the condition on any of the lines in the access list, the packet will be discarded.

Each of these rules has some powerful implications when filtering IP packets with access lists, so keep in mind that creating effective access lists definitely takes some practice.

There are two main types of access lists:

**Standard access lists**    These ACLs use only the source IP address in an IP packet as the condition test. All decisions are made based on the source IP address. This means that standard access lists basically permit or deny an entire suite of protocols. They don't distinguish between any of the many types of IP traffic such as Web, Telnet, UDP, and so on.

**Extended access lists**    Extended access lists can evaluate many of the other fields in the layer 3 and layer 4 headers of an IP packet. They can evaluate source and destination IP addresses, the Protocol field in the Network layer header, and the port number at the Transport layer header. This gives extended access lists the ability to make much more granular decisions when controlling traffic.

**Named access lists**    Hey, wait a minute—I said there were only two types of access lists but listed three! Well, technically there really are only two since *named access lists* are either standard or extended and not actually a distinct type. I'm just distinguishing them because they're created and referred to differently than standard and extended access lists are, but they're still functionally the same.

    **We'll cover these types of access lists in more depth later in the chapter.**

Once you create an access list, it's not really going to do anything until you apply it. Yes, they're there on the router, but they're inactive until you tell that router what to do with them.

To use an access list as a packet filter, you need to apply it to an interface on the router where you want the traffic filtered. And you've got to specify which direction of traffic you want the access list applied to. There's a good reason for this—you may want different controls in place for traffic leaving your enterprise destined for the Internet than you'd want for traffic coming into your enterprise from the Internet. So, by specifying the direction of traffic, you can and must use different access lists for inbound and outbound traffic on a single interface:

**Inbound access lists**    When an access list is applied to inbound packets on an interface, those packets are processed through the access list before being routed to the outbound interface. Any packets that are denied won't be routed because they're discarded before the routing process is invoked.

**Outbound access lists**    When an access list is applied to outbound packets on an interface, packets are routed to the outbound interface and then processed through the access list before being queued.

There are some general access-list guidelines that you should keep in mind when creating and implementing access lists on a router:

- You can assign only one access list per interface per protocol per direction. This means that when applying IP access lists, you can have only one inbound access list and one outbound access list per interface.

 When you consider the implications of the implicit deny at the end of any access list, it makes sense that you can't have multiple access lists applied on the same interface in the same direction for the same protocol. That's because any packets that don't match some condition in the first access list would be denied and there wouldn't be any packets left over to compare against a second access list!

- Organize your access lists so that the more specific tests are at the top.
- Anytime a new entry is added to the access list, it will be placed at the bottom of the list, which is why I highly recommend using a text editor for access lists.
- You can't remove one line from an access list. If you try to do this, you will remove the entire list. This is why it's best to copy the access list to a text editor before trying to edit the list. The only exception is when you're using named access lists.

 You can edit, add, or delete a single line from a named access list. I'll show you how shortly.

- Unless your access list ends with a `permit any` command, all packets will be discarded if they do not meet any of the list's tests. This means every list should have at least one `permit` statement or it will deny all traffic.
- Create access lists and then apply them to an interface. Any access list applied to an interface without access-list test statements present will not filter traffic.

- Access lists are designed to filter traffic going through the router. They will not filter traffic that has originated from the router.

- Place IP standard access lists as close to the destination as possible. This is the reason we don't really want to use standard access lists in our networks. You can't put a standard access list close to the source host or network because you can only filter based on source address and all destinations would be affected as a result.

- Place IP extended access lists as close to the source as possible. Since extended access lists can filter on very specific addresses and protocols, you don't want your traffic to traverse the entire network just to be denied. By placing this list as close to the source address as possible, you can filter traffic before it uses up precious bandwidth.

Before I move on to demonstrate how to configure basic and extended ACLs, let's talk about how they can be used to mitigate the security threats I mentioned earlier.

## Mitigating Security Issues with ACLs

The most common attack is a denial of service (DoS) attack. Although ACLs can help with a DoS, you really need an intrusion detection system (IDS) and intrusion prevention system (IPS) to help prevent these common attacks. Cisco sells the Adaptive Security Appliance (ASA), which has IDS/IPS modules, but lots of other companies sell IDS/IPS products too.

Here's a list of the many security threats you can mitigate with ACLs:

- IP address spoofing, inbound

- IP address spoofing, outbound

- Denial of service (DoS) TCP SYN attacks, blocking external attacks

- DoS TCP SYN attacks, using TCP Intercept

- DoS smurf attacks

- Denying/filtering ICMP messages, inbound

- Denying/Filtering ICMP messages, outbound

- Denying/Filtering Traceroute

 This is not an "introduction to security" book, so you may have to research some of the preceding terms if you don't understand them.

It's generally a bad idea to allow into a private network any external IP packets that contain the source address of any internal hosts or networks—just don't do it!

Here's a list of rules to live by when configuring ACLs from the Internet to your production network to mitigate security problems:

- Deny any source addresses from your internal networks.

- Deny any local host addresses (127.0.0.0/8).

- Deny any reserved private addresses (RFC 1918).

- Deny any addresses in the IP multicast address range (224.0.0.0/4).

None of these source addresses should be ever be allowed to enter your internetwork. Okay, now finally, let's get our hands dirty and configure some basic and advanced access lists!

# Standard Access Lists

Standard IP access lists filter network traffic by examining the source IP address in a packet. You create a *standard IP access list* by using the access-list numbers 1–99 or in the expanded range of 1300–1999 because the type of ACL is generally differentiated using a number. Based on the number used when the access list is created, the router knows which type of syntax to expect as the list is entered. By using numbers 1–99 or 1300–1999, you're telling the router that you want to create a standard IP access list, so the router will expect syntax specifying only the source IP address in the test lines.

The following output displays a good example of the many access-list number ranges that you can use to filter traffic on your network. The IOS version delimits the protocols you can specify access for:

```
Corp(config)#access-list ?
  <1-99>            IP standard access list
  <100-199>         IP extended access list
  <1000-1099>       IPX SAP access list
  <1100-1199>       Extended 48-bit MAC address access list
  <1200-1299>       IPX summary address access list
  <1300-1999>       IP standard access list (expanded range)
  <200-299>         Protocol type-code access list
  <2000-2699>       IP extended access list (expanded range)
  <300-399>         DECnet access list
  <600-699>         Appletalk access list
  <700-799>         48-bit MAC address access list
  <800-899>         IPX standard access list
  <900-999>         IPX extended access list
  dynamic-extended  Extend the dynamic ACL absolute timer
  rate-limit        Simple rate-limit specific access list
```

Wow—there certainly are lot of old protocols listed in that output! IPX, AppleTalk, or DECnet would no longer be used in any of today's networks. Let's take a look at the syntax used when creating a standard IP access list:

```
Corp(config)#access-list 10 ?
  deny    Specify packets to reject
  permit  Specify packets to forward
  remark  Access list entry comment
```

As I said, by using the access-list numbers 1–99 or 1300–1999, you're telling the router that you want to create a standard IP access list, which means you can only filter on source IP address.

Once you've chosen the access-list number, you need to decide whether you're creating a permit or deny statement. I'm going to create a deny statement now:

```
Corp(config)#access-list 10 deny ?
  Hostname or A.B.C.D  Address to match
  any                  Any source host
  host                 A single host address
```

The next step is more detailed because there are three options available in it:

1. The first option is the any parameter is used to permit or deny any source host or network.

2. The second choice is to use an IP address to specify either a single host or a range of them.

3. The last option is to use the host command to specify a specific host only.

The any command is pretty obvious—any source address matches the statement, so every packet compared against this line will match. The host command is relatively simple too, as you can see here:

```
Corp(config)#access-list 10 deny host ?
  Hostname or A.B.C.D  Host address
Corp(config)#access-list 10 deny host 172.16.30.2
```

This tells the list to deny any packets from host 172.16.30.2. The default parameter is host. In other words, if you type **access-list 10 deny 172.16.30.2**, the router assumes you mean host 172.16.30.2 and that's exactly how it will show in your running-config.

But there's another way to specify either a particular host or a range of hosts, and it's known as wildcard masking. In fact, to specify any range of hosts, you must use wildcard masking in the access list.

So exactly what is wildcard masking? Coming up, I'm going to show you using a standard access list example. I'll also guide you through how to control access to a virtual terminal. We'll be using the same wildcard masks we used in the Configuring OSPF section of Chapter 9, "Open Shortest Path First (OSPF)."

## Wildcard Masking

Wildcards are used with access lists to specify an individual host, a network, or a specific range of a network or networks. The block sizes you learned about earlier used to specify a range of addresses are key to understanding wildcards.

Let me pause here for a quick review of block sizes before we go any further. I'm sure you remember that the different block sizes available are 64, 32, 16, 8, and 4. When you need to specify a range of addresses, you choose the next-largest block size for your needs. So if you need to specify 34 networks, you need a block size of 64. If you want to specify 18 hosts, you need a block size of 32. If you specify only 2 networks, then go with a block size of 4.

Wildcards are used with the host or network address to tell the router a range of available addresses to filter. To specify a host, the address would look like this:

```
172.16.30.5 0.0.0.0
```

The four zeros represent each octet of the address. Whenever a zero is present, it indicates that octet in the address must match the corresponding reference octet exactly. To specify that an octet can be any value, use the value 255. Here's an example of how a /24 subnet is specified with a wildcard mask:

```
172.16.30.0 0.0.0.255
```

This tells the router to match up the first three octets exactly, but the fourth octet can be any value.

Okay—that was the easy part. But what if you want to specify only a small range of subnets? This is where block sizes come in. You have to specify the range of values in a block size, so you can't choose to specify 20 networks. You can only specify the exact amount that the block size value allows. This means that the range would have to be either 16 or 32, but not 20.

Let's say that you want to block access to the part of the network that ranges from 172.16.8.0 through 172.16.15.0. To do that, you would go with a block size of 8, your network number would be 172.16.8.0, and the wildcard would be 0.0.7.255. The 7.255 equals the value the router will use to determine the block size. So together, the network number and the wildcard tell the router to begin at 172.16.8.0 and go up a block size of eight addresses to network 172.16.15.0.

This really is easier than it looks! I could certainly go through the binary math for you, but no one needs that kind of pain because all you have to do is remember that the wildcard is always one number less than the block size. So, in our example, the wildcard would be 7 since our block size is 8. If you used a block size of 16, the wildcard would be 15. Easy, right?

Just to make you've got this, we'll go through some examples that will definitely help you nail it down. The following example tells the router to match the first three octets exactly but that the fourth octet can be anything:

```
Corp(config)#access-list 10 deny 172.16.10.0 0.0.0.255
```

The next example tells the router to match the first two octets and that the last two octets can be any value:

```
Corp(config)#access-list 10 deny 172.16.0.0 0.0.255.255
```

Now, try to figure out this next line:

```
Corp(config)#access-list 10 deny 172.16.16.0 0.0.3.255
```

This configuration tells the router to start at network 172.16.16.0 and use a block size of 4. The range would then be 172.16.16.0 through 172.16.19.255, and by the way, the Cisco objectives seem to really like this one!

Okay, let's keep practicing. What about this next one?

```
Corp(config)#access-list 10 deny 172.16.16.0 0.0.7.255
```

This example reveals an access list starting at 172.16.16.0 going up a block size of 8 to 172.16.23.255.

Let's keep at it... What do you think the range of this one is?

```
Corp(config)#access-list 10 deny 172.16.32.0 0.0.15.255
```

This one begins at network 172.16.32.0 and goes up a block size of 16 to 172.16.47.255.

You're almost done practicing! After a couple more, we'll configure some real ACLs.

```
Corp(config)#access-list 10 deny 172.16.64.0 0.0.63.255
```

This example starts at network 172.16.64.0 and goes up a block size of 64 to 172.16.127.255.

What about this last example?

```
Corp(config)#access-list 10 deny 192.168.160.0 0.0.31.255
```

This one shows us that it begins at network 192.168.160.0 and goes up a block size of 32 to 192.168.191.255.

Here are two more things to keep in mind when working with block sizes and wildcards:

- Each block size must start at 0 or a multiple of the block size. For example, you can't say that you want a block size of 8 and then start at 12. You must use 0–7, 8–15, 16–23, etc. For a block size of 32, the ranges are 0–31, 32–63, 64–95, etc.

- The command any is the same thing as writing out the wildcard 0.0.0.0 255.255.255.255.

Wildcard masking is a crucial skill to master when creating IP access lists, and it's used identically when creating standard and extended IP access lists.

## Standard Access List Example

In this section, you'll learn how to use a standard access list to stop specific users from gaining access to the Finance department LAN.

In Figure 12.2, a router has three LAN connections and one WAN connection to the Internet. Users on the Sales LAN should not have access to the Finance LAN, but they should be able to access the Internet and the marketing department files. The Marketing LAN needs to access the Finance LAN for application services.

**FIGURE 12.2**    IP access list example with three LANs and a WAN connection

We can see that the following standard IP access list is configured on the router:

```
Lab_A#config t
Lab_A(config)#access-list 10 deny 172.16.40.0 0.0.0.255
Lab_A(config)#access-list 10 permit any
```

It's very important to remember that the any command is the same thing as saying the following using wildcard masking:

```
Lab_A(config)#access-list 10 permit 0.0.0.0 255.255.255.255
```

Since the wildcard mask says that none of the octets are to be evaluated, every address matches the test condition, so this is functionally doing the same as using the any keyword.

At this point, the access list is configured to deny source addresses from the Sales LAN to the Finance LAN and to allow everyone else. But remember, no action will be taken until the access list is applied on an interface in a specific direction!

But where should this access list be placed? If you place it as an incoming access list on Fa0/0, you might as well shut down the FastEthernet interface because all of the Sales LAN devices will be denied access to all networks attached to the router. The best place to apply this access list is on the Fa0/1 interface as an outbound list:

```
Lab_A(config)#int fa0/1
Lab_A(config-if)#ip access-group 10 out
```

Doing this completely stops traffic from 172.16.40.0 from getting out FastEthernet0/1. It has no effect on the hosts from the Sales LAN accessing the Marketing LAN and the Internet because traffic to those destinations doesn't go through interface Fa0/1. Any packet trying to exit out Fa0/1 will have to go through the access list first. If there were an inbound list placed on F0/0, then any packet trying to enter interface F0/0 would have to go through the access list before being routed to an exit interface.

Now, let's take a look at another standard access list example. Figure 12.3 shows an internetwork of two routers with four LANs.

**FIGURE 12.3**  IP standard access list example 2

Now we're going to stop the Accounting users from accessing the Human Resources server attached to the Lab_B router but allow all other users access to that LAN using a standard ACL. What kind of standard access list would we need to create and where would we place it to achieve our goals?

The real answer is that we should to use an extended access list and place it closest to the source! But this question specifies using a standard access list, and as a rule, standard ACLs are placed closest to the destination. In this example, Ethernet 0 is the outbound interface on the Lab_B router and here's the access list that should be placed on it:

```
Lab_B#config t
Lab_B(config)#access-list 10 deny 192.168.10.128 0.0.0.31
Lab_B(config)#access-list 10 permit any
Lab_B(config)#interface Ethernet 0
Lab_B(config-if)#ip access-group 10 out
```

Keep in mind that to be able to answer this question correctly, you really need to understand subnetting, wildcard masks, and how to configure and implement ACLs. The accounting subnet is the 192.168.10.128/27, which is a 255.255.255.224, with a block size of 32 in the fourth octet.

With all this in mind and before we move on to restricting Telnet access on a router, let's take a look at one more standard access list example. This one is going to require some thought. In Figure 12.4, you have a router with four LAN connections and one WAN connection to the Internet.

**FIGURE 12.4**    IP standard access list example 3

172.16.92.10/21

E3  S0

EO

E2

E1

172.16.144.17/19                172.16.198.94/18

172.16.50.173/20

Okay—you need to write an access list that will stop access from each of the four LANs shown in the diagram to the Internet. Each of the LANs reveals a single host's IP address, which you need to use to determine the subnet and wildcards of each LAN to configure the access list.

Here is an example of what your answer should look like, beginning with the network on E0 and working through to E3:

```
Router(config)#access-list 1 deny 172.16.128.0 0.0.31.255
Router(config)#access-list 1 deny 172.16.48.0 0.0.15.255
Router(config)#access-list 1 deny 172.16.192.0 0.0.63.255
Router(config)#access-list 1 deny 172.16.88.0 0.0.7.255
Router(config)#access-list 1 permit any
Router(config)#interface serial 0
Router(config-if)#ip access-group 1 out
```

Sure, you could have done this with one line:

```
Router(config)#access-list 1 deny 172.16.0.0 0.0.255.255
```

But what fun is that?

And remember the reasons for creating this list. If you actually applied this ACL on the router, you'd effectively shut down access to the Internet, so why even have an Internet connection? I included this exercise so you can practice how to use block sizes with access lists, which is vital for succeeding when you take the Cisco exam!

## Controlling VTY (Telnet/SSH) Access

Trying to stop users from telnetting or trying to SSH to a router is really challenging because any active interface on a router is fair game for VTY/SSH access. Creating an extended IP ACL that limits access to every IP address on the router may sound like a solution, but if you did that, you'd have to apply it inbound on every interface, which really wouldn't scale well if you happen to have dozens, even hundreds, of interfaces, now would it? And think of all the latency dragging down your network as a result of each and every router checking every packet just in case the packet was trying to access your VTY lines—horrible!

Don't give up—there's always a solution! And in this case, a much better one, which employs a standard IP access list to control access to the VTY lines themselves.

Why does this work so well? Because when you apply an access list to the VTY lines, you don't need to specify the protocol since access to the VTY already implies terminal access via the Telnet or SSH protocols. You also don't need to specify a destination address because it really doesn't matter which interface address the user used as a target for the Telnet session. All you really need control of is where the user is coming from, which is betrayed by their source IP address.

You need to do these two things to make this happen:

1. Create a standard IP access list that permits only the host or hosts you want to be able to telnet into the routers.

2. Apply the access list to the VTY line with the access-class in command.

Here, I'm allowing only host 172.16.10.3 to telnet into a router:

```
Lab_A(config)#access-list 50 permit host 172.16.10.3
Lab_A(config)#line vty 0 4
Lab_A(config-line)#access-class 50 in
```

Because of the implied deny any at the end of the list, the ACL stops any host from telnetting into the router except the host 172.16.10.3, regardless of the individual IP address on the router being used as a target. It's a good idea to include an admin subnet address as the source instead of a single host, but the reason I demonstrated this was to show you how to create security on your VTY lines without adding latency to your router.

---

### Real World Scenario

**Should You Secure Your VTY Lines on a Router?**

You're monitoring your network and notice that someone has telnetted into your core router by using the show users command. You use the disconnect command and they're disconnected from the router, but you notice that they're right back in there a few minutes later. You consider putting an ACL on the router interfaces, but you don't want to add latency on each interface since your router is already pushing a lot of packets. At this point, you think about putting an access list on the VTY lines themselves, but not having done this before, you're not sure if this is a safe alternative to putting an ACL on each interface. Would placing an ACL on the VTY lines be a good idea for this network?

Yes—absolutely! And the access-class command covered in this chapter is the way to do it. Why? Because it doesn't use an access list that just sits on an interface looking at every packet, resulting in unnecessary overhead and latency.

When you put the access-class in command on the VTY lines, only packets trying to telnet into the router will be checked and compared, providing easy-to-configure yet solid security for your router!

---

Just a reminder—Cisco recommends using Secure Shell (SSH) instead of Telnet on the VTY lines of a router, as we covered in Chapter 6, "Cisco's Internetworking Operating System (IOS)," so review that chapter if you need a refresher on SSH and how to configure it on your routers and switches.

## Extended Access Lists

Let's go back to the standard IP access list example where you had to block all access from the Sales LAN to the finance department and add a new requirement. You now must allow Sales to gain access to a certain server on the Finance LAN but not to other network services for security reasons. What's the solution? Applying a standard IP access list won't allow users to get to one network service but not another because a standard ACL won't allow you to make decisions based on both source and destination addresses. It makes decisions based only on source address, so we need another way to achieve our new goal—but what is it?

Using an *extended access list* will save the day because extended ACLs allow us to specify source and destination addresses as well as the protocol and port number that identify the upper-layer protocol or application. An extended ACL is just what we need to affectively allow users access to a physical LAN while denying them access to specific hosts—even specific services on those hosts!

We're going to take a look at the commands we have in our arsenal, but first, you need to know that you must use the extended access-list range from 100 to 199. The 2000–2699 range is also available for extended IP access lists.

After choosing a number in the extended range, you need to decide what type of list entry to make. For this example, I'm going with a deny list entry:

```
Corp(config)#access-list 110 ?
  deny     Specify packets to reject
  dynamic  Specify a DYNAMIC list of PERMITs or DENYs
  permit   Specify packets to forward
  remark   Access list entry comment
```

And once you've settled on the type of ACL, you then need to select a protocol field entry:

```
Corp(config)#access-list 110 deny ?
  <0-255>  An IP protocol number
  ahp      Authentication Header Protocol
  eigrp    Cisco's EIGRP routing protocol
  esp      Encapsulation Security Payload
  gre      Cisco's GRE tunneling
  icmp     Internet Control Message Protocol
  igmp     Internet Gateway Message Protocol
  ip       Any Internet Protocol
  ipinip   IP in IP tunneling
  nos      KA9Q NOS compatible IP over IP tunneling
  ospf     OSPF routing protocol
  pcp      Payload Compression Protocol
  pim      Protocol Independent Multicast
  tcp      Transmission Control Protocol
  udp      User Datagram Protocol
```

If you want to filter by Application layer protocol, you have to choose the appropriate layer 4 transport protocol after the permit or deny statement. For example, to filter Telnet or FTP, choose TCP since both Telnet and FTP use TCP at the Transport layer. Selecting IP wouldn't allow you to specify a particular application protocol later and only filter based on source and destination addresses.

So now, let's filter an Application layer protocol that uses TCP by selecting TCP as the protocol and indicating the specific destination TCP port at the end of the line. Next, we'll be prompted for the source IP address of the host or network and we'll choose the any command to allow any source address:

```
Corp(config)#access-list 110 deny tcp ?
  A.B.C.D  Source address
  any      Any source host
  host     A single source host
```

After we've selected the source address, we can then choose the specific destination address:

```
Corp(config)#access-list 110 deny tcp any ?
  A.B.C.D  Destination address
  any      Any destination host
  eq       Match only packets on a given port number
  gt       Match only packets with a greater port number
  host     A single destination host
  lt       Match only packets with a lower port number
  neq      Match only packets not on a given port number
  range    Match only packets in the range of port numbers
```

In this output, you can see that any source IP address that has a destination IP address of 172.16.30.2 has been denied:

```
Corp(config)#access-list 110 deny tcp any host 172.16.30.2 ?
  ack          Match on the ACK bit
  dscp         Match packets with given dscp value
  eq           Match only packets on a given port number
  established  Match established connections
  fin          Match on the FIN bit
  fragments    Check non-initial fragments
  gt           Match only packets with a greater port number
  log          Log matches against this entry
  log-input    Log matches against this entry, including input interface
  lt           Match only packets with a lower port number
  neq          Match only packets not on a given port number
  precedence   Match packets with given precedence value
  psh          Match on the PSH bit
  range        Match only packets in the range of port numbers
  rst          Match on the RST bit
  syn          Match on the SYN bit
```

```
time-range    Specify a time-range
tos           Match packets with given TOS value
urg           Match on the URG bit
<cr>
```

And once we have the destination host addresses in place, we just need to specify the type of service to deny using the equal to command, entered as eq. The following help screen reveals the options available now. You can choose a port number or use the application name:

```
Corp(config)#access-list 110 deny tcp any host 172.16.30.2 eq ?
  <0-65535>    Port number
  bgp          Border Gateway Protocol (179)
  chargen      Character generator (19)
  cmd          Remote commands (rcmd, 514)
  daytime      Daytime (13)
  discard      Discard (9)
  domain       Domain Name Service (53)
  drip         Dynamic Routing Information Protocol (3949)
  echo         Echo (7)
  exec         Exec (rsh, 512)
  finger       Finger (79)
  ftp          File Transfer Protocol (21)
  ftp-data     FTP data connections (20)
  gopher       Gopher (70)
  hostname     NIC hostname server (101)
  ident        Ident Protocol (113)
  irc          Internet Relay Chat (194)
  klogin       Kerberos login (543)
  kshell       Kerberos shell (544)
  login        Login (rlogin, 513)
  lpd          Printer service (515)
  nntp         Network News Transport Protocol (119)
  pim-auto-rp  PIM Auto-RP (496)
  pop2         Post Office Protocol v2 (109)
  pop3         Post Office Protocol v3 (110)
  smtp         Simple Mail Transport Protocol (25)
  sunrpc       Sun Remote Procedure Call (111)
  syslog       Syslog (514)
  tacacs       TAC Access Control System (49)
  talk         Talk (517)
  telnet       Telnet (23)
  time         Time (37)
```

```
uucp          Unix-to-Unix Copy Program (540)
whois         Nicname (43)
www           World Wide Web (HTTP, 80)
```

Okay—now let's block Telnet (port 23) to host 172.16.30.2 only. If the users want to use FTP, fine—that's allowed. The log command is used to log messages every time the access list entry is hit. This can be an extremely cool way to monitor inappropriate access attempts, but be careful because in a large network, this command can overload your console's screen with messages!

Here's our result:

```
Corp(config)#access-list 110 deny tcp any host 172.16.30.2 eq 23 log
```

This line says to deny any source host trying to telnet to destination host 172.16.30.2. Keep in mind that the next line is an implicit deny by default. If you apply this access list to an interface, you might as well just shut the interface down because by default, there's an implicit deny all at the end of every access list. So we've got to follow up the access list with the following command:

```
Corp(config)#access-list 110 permit ip any any
```

The IP in this line is important because it will permit the IP stack. If TCP was used instead of IP in this line, then UDP, etc. would all be denied. Remember, the 0.0.0.0 255.255.255.255 is the same command as any, so the command could also look like this:

```
Corp(config)#access-list 110 permit ip 0.0.0.0 255.255.255.255
0.0.0.0 255.255.255.255
```

But if you did this, when you looked at the running-config, the commands would be replaced with the any any. I like efficiency so I'll just use the any command because it requires less typing.

As always, once our access list is created, we must apply it to an interface with the same command used for the IP standard list:

```
Corp(config-if)#ip access-group 110 in
```

Or this:

```
Corp(config-if)#ip access-group 110 out
```

Next, we'll check out some examples of how to use an extended access list.

## Extended Access List Example 1

For our first scenario, we'll use Figure 12.5. What do we need to do to deny access to a host at 172.16.50.5 on the finance department LAN for both Telnet and FTP services? All other services on this and all other hosts are acceptable for the sales and marketing departments to access.

**FIGURE 12.5** Extended ACL example 1

Here's the ACL we must create:

```
Lab_A#config t
Lab_A(config)#access-list 110 deny tcp any host 172.16.50.5 eq 21
Lab_A(config)#access-list 110 deny tcp any host 172.16.50.5 eq 23
Lab_A(config)#access-list 110 permit ip any any
```

The access-list 110 tells the router we're creating an extended IP ACL. The tcp is the protocol field in the Network layer header. If the list doesn't say tcp here, you cannot filter by TCP port numbers 21 and 23 as shown in the example. Remember that these values indicate FTP and Telnet, which both use TCP for connection-oriented services. The any command is the source, which means any source IP address, and the host is the destination IP address. This ACL says that all IP traffic will be permitted from any host except FTP and Telnet to host 172.16.50.5 from any source.

Remember that instead of the host 172.16.50.5 command when we created the extended access list, we could have entered 172.16.50.5 0.0.0.0. There would be no difference in the result other than the router would change the command to host 172.16.50.5 in the running-config.

After the list is created, it must be applied to the FastEthernet 0/1 interface outbound because we want to block all traffic from getting to host 172.16.50.5 and performing FTP and Telnet. If this list was created to block access only from the Sales LAN to host 172.16.50.5, then we'd have put this list closer to the source, or on FastEthernet 0/0. In that situation, we'd apply the list to inbound traffic. This highlights the fact that you really need to analyze each situation carefully before creating and applying ACLs!

Okay—now let's go ahead and apply the list to interface Fa0/1 to block all outside FTP and Telnet access to the host 172.16.50.5:

```
Lab_A(config)#int fa0/1
Lab_A(config-if)#ip access-group 110 out
```

## Extended Access List Example 2

We're going to use Figure 12.4 again, which has four LANs and a serial connection. We need to prevent Telnet access to the networks attached to the E1 and E2 interfaces.

The configuration on the router would look something like this, although the answer can vary:

```
Router(config)#access-list 110 deny tcp any 172.16.48.0 0.0.15.255
eq 23
Router(config)#access-list 110 deny tcp any 172.16.192.0 0.0.63.255
eq 23
Router(config)#access-list 110 permit ip any any
Router(config)#interface Ethernet 1
Router(config-if)#ip access-group 110 out
Router(config-if)#interface Ethernet 2
Router(config-if)#ip access-group 110 out
```

Here are the key factors to understand from this list:

- First, you need to verify that the number range is correct for the type of access list you are creating. In this example, it's extended, so the range must be 100–199.

- Second, you must verify that the protocol field matches the upper-layer process or application, which in this case, is TCP port 23 (Telnet).

The protocol parameter must be TCP since Telnet uses TCP. If it were TFTP instead, then the protocol parameter would have to be UDP because TFTP uses UDP at the Transport layer

- Third, verify that the destination port number matches the application you're filtering for. In this case, port 23 matches Telnet, which is correct, but know that you can also type **telnet** at the end of the line instead of 23.

- Finally, the test statement permit ip any any is important to have there at the end of the list because it means to enable all packets other than Telnet packets destined for the LANs connected to Ethernet 1 and Ethernet 2.

# Extended Access List Example 3

I want to guide you through one more extended ACL example before we move on to named ACLs. Figure 12.6 displays the network we're going to use for this last scenario.

**FIGURE 12.6** Extended ACL example 3

In this example, we're going to allow HTTP access to the Finance server from source Host B only. All other traffic will be permitted. We need to be able to configure this in only three test statements, and then we'll need to add the interface configuration.

Let's take what we've learned and knock this one out:

```
Lab_A#config t
Lab_A(config)#access-list 110 permit tcp host 192.168.177.2 host 172.22.89.26 eq 80
Lab_A(config)#access-list 110 deny tcp any host 172.22.89.26 eq 80
Lab_A(config)#access-list 110 permit ip any any
```

This is really pretty simple! First we need to permit Host B HTTP access to the Finance server. But since all other traffic must be allowed, we must detail who cannot HTTP to the Finance server, so the second test statement is there to deny anyone else from using HTTP on the Finance server. Finally, now that Host B can HTTP to the Finance server and everyone else can't, we'll permit all other traffic with our third test statement.

Okay, not so bad—this just takes a little thought! But wait—we're not done yet because we still need to apply this to an interface. Since extended access lists are typically applied closest to the source, we should simply place this inbound on F0/0, right? Well, this is one time we're not going to follow the rules. Our challenge required us to allow only HTTP traffic to the Finance server from Host B. If we apply the ACL inbound on Fa0/0, then the branch office would be able to access the Finance server and perform HTTP. So in this example, we need to place the ACL closest to the destination:

```
Lab_A(config)#interface fastethernet 0/1
Lab_A(config-if)#ip access-group 110 out
```

Perfect! Now let's get into how to create ACLs using names.

## Named ACLs

As I said earlier, *named* access lists are just another way to create standard and extended access lists. In medium to large enterprises, managing ACLs can become a real hassle over time! A handy way to make things easier is to copy the access list to a text editor, edit the list, then paste the new list back into the router, which works pretty well if it weren't for the "pack rat" mentality. It's really common to think things like, "What if I find a problem with the new list and need to back out of the change?" This and other factors cause people to hoard unapplied ACLs, and over time, they can seriously build up on a router, leading to more questions, like, "What were these ACLs for? Are they important? Do I need them?" All good questions, and named access lists are the answer to this problem!

And of course, this kind of thing can also apply to access lists that are up and running. Let's say you come into an existing network and are looking at access lists on a router. Suppose you find an access list 177, which happens to be an extended access list that's a whopping 93 lines long. This leads to more of the same bunch of questions and can even lead to needless existential despair! Instead, wouldn't it be a whole lot easier to identify an access with a name like "FinanceLAN" rather than one mysteriously dubbed "177"?

To our collective relief, named access lists allow us to use names for creating and applying either standard or extended access lists. There's really nothing new or different about these ACLs aside from being readily identifiable in a way that makes sense to humans, but there are some subtle changes to the syntax. So let's re-create the standard access list we created earlier for our test network in Figure 12.2 using a named access list:

```
Lab_A#config t
Lab_A(config)# ip access-list ?
  extended     Extended Access List
  log-update   Control access list log updates
  logging      Control access list logging
  resequence   Resequence Access List
  standard     Standard Access List
```

Notice that I started by typing **ip access-list**, not **access-list**. Doing this allows me to enter a named access list. Next, I'll need to specify it as a standard access list:

```
Lab_A(config)#ip access-list standard ?
  <1-99>       Standard IP access-list number
```

```
<1300-1999>  Standard IP access-list number (expanded range)
WORD         Access-list name
```

```
Lab_A(config)#ip access-list standard BlockSales
Lab_A(config-std-nacl)#
```

I've specified a standard access list, then added the name, BlockSales. I definitely could've used a number for a standard access list, but instead, I chose to use a nice, clear descriptive name. And notice that after entering the name, I hit Enter and the router prompt changed. This confirms that I'm now in named access list configuration mode and that I'm entering the named access list:

```
Lab_A(config-std-nacl)#?
Standard Access List configuration commands:
  default  Set a command to its defaults
  deny     Specify packets to reject
  exit     Exit from access-list configuration mode
  no       Negate a command or set its defaults
  permit   Specify packets to forward
```

```
Lab_A(config-std-nacl)#deny 172.16.40.0 0.0.0.255
Lab_A(config-std-nacl)#permit any
Lab_A(config-std-nacl)#exit
Lab_A(config)#^Z
Lab_A#
```

Okay—so I've entered the access list and then exited configuration mode. Next, I'll take a look at the running configuration to verify that the access list is indeed in the router:

```
Lab_A#sh running-config | begin ip access
ip access-list standard BlockSales
 deny   172.16.40.0 0.0.0.255
 permit any
!
```

And there it is: the BlockSales access list has truly been created and is in the running-config of the router. Next, I'll need to apply the access list to the correct interface:

```
Lab_A#config t
Lab_A(config)#int fa0/1
Lab_A(config-if)#ip access-group BlockSales out
```

Clear skies! At this point, we've re-created the work done earlier using a named access list. But let's take our IP extended example, shown in Figure 12.6, and redo that list using a named ACL instead as well.

Same business requirements: Allow HTTP access to the Finance server from source Host B only. All other traffic is permitted.

```
Lab_A#config t
Lab_A(config)#ip access-list extended 110
Lab_A(config-ext-nacl)#permit tcp host 192.168.177.2 host 172.22.89.26 eq 80
Lab_A(config-ext-nacl)#deny tcp any host 172.22.89.26 eq 80
Lab_A(config-ext-nacl)#permit ip any any
Lab_A(config-ext-nacl)#int fa0/1
Lab_A(config-if)#ip access-group 110 out
```

Okay—true—I named the extended list with a number, but sometimes it's okay to do that! I'm guessing that named ACLs don't seem all that exciting or different to you, do they? Maybe not in this configuration, except that I don't need to start every line with access-list 110, which is nice. But where named ACLs really shine is that they allow us to insert, delete, or edit a single line. That isn't just nice, it's wonderful! Numbered ACLs just can't compare with that, and I'll demonstrate this in a minute.

## Remarks

The remark keyword is really important because it arms you with the ability to include comments—remarks—regarding the entries you've made in both your IP standard and extended ACLs. Remarks are very cool because they efficiently increase your ability to examine and understand your ACLs to superhero level! Without them, you'd be caught in a quagmire of potentially meaningless numbers without anything to help you recall what all those numbers mean.

Even though you have the option of placing your remarks either before or after a permit or deny statement, I totally recommend that you choose to position them consistently so you don't get confused about which remark is relevant to a specific permit or deny statement.

To get this going for both standard and extended ACLs, just use the access-list *access-list number* remark *remark* global configuration command like this:

```
R2#config t
R2(config)#access-list 110 remark Permit Bob from Sales Only To Finance
R2(config)#access-list 110 permit ip host 172.16.40.1 172.16.50.0 0.0.0.255
R2(config)#access-list 110 deny ip 172.16.40.0 0.0.0.255 172.16.50.0 0.0.0.255
R2(config)#ip access-list extended No_Telnet
R2(config-ext-nacl)#remark Deny all of Sales from Telnetting to Marketing
R2(config-ext-nacl)#deny tcp 172.16.40.0 0.0.0.255 172.16.60.0 0.0.0.255 eq 23
R2(config-ext-nacl)#permit ip any any
R2(config-ext-nacl)#do show run
[output cut]
!
ip access-list extended No_Telnet
```

```
remark Stop all of Sales from Telnetting to Marketing
deny    tcp 172.16.40.0 0.0.0.255 172.16.60.0 0.0.0.255 eq telnet
permit ip any any
!
access-list 110 remark Permit Bob from Sales Only To Finance
access-list 110 permit ip host 172.16.40.1 172.16.50.0 0.0.0.255
access-list 110 deny    ip 172.16.40.0 0.0.0.255 172.16.50.0 0.0.0.255
access-list 110 permit ip any any
!
```

Sweet—I was able to add a remark to both an extended list and a named access list. Keep in mind that you cannot see these remarks in the output of the show access-list command, which we'll cover next because they only show up in the running-config.

Speaking of ACLs, I still need to show you how to monitor and verify them. This is an important topic, so pay attention!

# Monitoring Access Lists

It's always good to be able to verify a router's configuration. Table 12.1 lists the commands that we can use to achieve that.

**TABLE 12.1**  Commands used to verify access-list configuration

| Command | Effect |
| --- | --- |
| show access-list | Displays all access lists and their parameters configured on the router. Also shows statistics about how many times the line either permitted or denied a packet. This command does not show you which interface the list is applied on. |
| show access-list 110 | Reveals only the parameters for access list 110. Again, this command will not reveal the specific interface the list is set on. |
| show ip access-list | Shows only the IP access lists configured on the router. |
| show ip interface | Displays which interfaces have access lists set on them. |
| show running-config | Shows the access lists and the specific interfaces that have ACLs applied on them. |

We've already used the show running-config command to verify that a named access list was in the router, so now let's take a look at the output from some of the other commands.

The show access-list command will list all ACLs on the router, whether they're applied to an interface or not:

```
Lab_A#show access-list
Standard IP access list 10
    10 deny    172.16.40.0, wildcard bits 0.0.0.255
    20 permit any
Standard IP access list BlockSales
    10 deny    172.16.40.0, wildcard bits 0.0.0.255
    20 permit any
Extended IP access list 110
    10 deny tcp any host 172.16.30.5 eq ftp
    20 deny tcp any host 172.16.30.5 eq telnet
    30 permit ip any any
    40 permit tcp host 192.168.177.2 host 172.22.89.26 eq www
    50 deny tcp any host 172.22.89.26 eq www
Lab_A#
```

First, notice that access list 10 as well as both of our named access lists appear on this list—remember, my extended named ACL was named 110! Second, notice that even though I entered actual numbers for TCP ports in access list 110, the show command gives us the protocol names rather than TCP ports for serious clarity.

But wait! The best part is those numbers on the left side: 10, 20, 30, etc. Those are called sequence numbers, and they allow us to edit our named ACL. Here's an example where I added a line into the named extended ACL 110:

```
Lab_A (config)#ip access-list extended 110
Lab_A (config-ext-nacl)#21 deny udp any host 172.16.30.5 eq 69
Lab_A#show access-list
[output cut]
Extended IP access list 110
    10 deny tcp any host 172.16.30.5 eq ftp
    20 deny tcp any host 172.16.30.5 eq telnet
    21 deny udp any host 172.16.30.5 eq tftp
    30 permit ip any any
    40 permit tcp host 192.168.177.2 host 172.22.89.26 eq www
    50 deny tcp any host 172.22.89.26 eq www
```

You can see that I added line 21. I could have deleted a line or edited an existing line as well—very nice!

Here's the output of the show ip interface command:

```
Lab_A#show ip interface fa0/1
FastEthernet0/1 is up, line protocol is up
  Internet address is 172.16.30.1/24
  Broadcast address is 255.255.255.255
  Address determined by non-volatile memory
  MTU is 1500 bytes
  Helper address is not set
  Directed broadcast forwarding is disabled
  Outgoing access list is 110
  Inbound access list is not set
  Proxy ARP is enabled
  Security level is default
  Split horizon is enabled
[output cut]
```

Be sure to notice the bold line indicating that the outgoing list on this interface is 110, yet the inbound access list isn't set. What happened to BlockSales? I had configured that outbound on Fa0/1! That's true, I did, but I configured my extended named ACL 110 and applied it to Fa0/1 as well. You can't have two lists on the same interface, in the same direction, so what happened here is that my last configuration overwrote the BlockSales configuration.

And as I've already mentioned, you can use the show running-config command to see any and all access lists.

# Summary

In this chapter you learned how to configure standard access lists to properly filter IP traffic. You discovered what a standard access list is and how to apply it to a Cisco router to add security to your network. You also learned how to configure extended access lists to further filter IP traffic. We also covered the key differences between standard and extended access lists as well as how to apply them to Cisco routers.

Moving on, you found out how to configure named access lists and apply them to interfaces on the router and learned that named access lists offer the huge advantage of being easily identifiable and, therefore, a whole lot easier to manage than mysterious access lists that are simply referred to by obscure numbers.

Appendix C, "Disabling and Configuring Network Services," which takes off from this chapter, had a fun section in it: turning off default services. I've always found performing this administration task fun, and the auto secure command can help us configure basic, much-needed security on our routers.

The chapter wrapped up by showing you how to monitor and verify selected access-list configurations on a router.

# Exam Essentials

**Remember the standard and extended IP access-list number ranges.**   The number ranges you can use to configure a standard IP access list are 1–99 and 1300–1999. The number ranges for an extended IP access list are 100–199 and 2000–2699.

**Understand the term** *implicit deny*.   At the end of every access list is an *implicit deny*. What this means is that if a packet does not match any of the lines in the access list, it will be discarded. Also, if you have nothing but deny statements in your list, the list will not permit any packets.

**Understand the standard IP access-list configuration command.**   To configure a standard IP access list, use the access-list numbers 1–99 or 1300–1999 in global configuration mode. Choose permit or deny, then choose the source IP address you want to filter on using one of the three techniques covered in this chapter.

**Understand the extended IP access-list configuration command.**   To configure an extended IP access list, use the access-list numbers 100–199 or 2000–2699 in global configuration mode. Choose permit or deny, the Network layer protocol field, the source IP address you want to filter on, the destination address you want to filter on, and finally, the Transport layer port number if TCP or UDP has been specified as the protocol.

**Remember the command to verify an access list on a router interface.**   To see whether an access list is set on an interface and in which direction it is filtering, use the show ip interface command. This command will not show you the contents of the access list, merely which access lists are applied on the interface.

**Remember the command to verify the access-list configuration.**   To see the configured access lists on your router, use the show access-list command. This command will not show you which interfaces have an access list set.

# Written Lab 12

The answers to this lab can be found in Appendix A, "Answers to Written Labs."

In this section, write the answers to the following questions:

1. What command would you use to configure a standard IP access list to prevent all machines on network 172.16.0.0/16 from accessing your Ethernet network?

2. What command would you use to apply the access list you created in question 1 to an Ethernet interface outbound?

3. What command(s) would you use to create an access list that denies host 192.168.15.5 access to an Ethernet network?

4. Which command verifies that you've entered the access list correctly?

5. What two tools can help notify and prevent DoS attacks?

6. What command(s) would you use to create an extended access list that stops host 172.16.10.1 from telnetting to host 172.16.30.5?

7. What command would you use to set an access list on a VTY line?

8. Write the same standard IP access list you wrote in question 1 but this time as a named access list.

9. Write the command to apply the named access list you created in question 8 to an Ethernet interface outbound.

10. Which command verifies the placement and direction of an access list?

# Hands-on Labs

In this section, you will complete two labs. To complete these labs, you will need at least three routers. You can easily perform these labs with the Cisco Packet Tracer program. If you are studying to take your Cisco exam, you really need to do these labs!

Lab 12.1: Standard IP Access Lists

Lab 12.2: Extended IP Access Lists

All of the labs will use the following diagram for configuring the routers.

## Hands-on Lab 12.1: Standard IP Access Lists

In this lab, you will allow only packets from a single host on the SF LAN to enter the LA LAN.

1. Go to LA router and enter global configuration mode by typing **config t**.

2. From global configuration mode, type **access-list ?** to get a list of all the different access lists available.

3. Choose an access-list number that will allow you to create an IP standard access list. This is a number between 1 and 99 or 1300 and 1399.

4. Choose to permit host 192.168.10.2, which is the host address:

   ```
   LA(config)#access-list 10 permit 192.168.20.2 ?
     A.B.C.D  Wildcard bits
     <cr>
   ```

   To specify only host 192.168.20.2, use the wildcards 0.0.0.0:

   ```
   LA(config)#access-list 10 permit 192.168.20.2
     0.0.0.0
   ```

5. Now that the access list is created, you must apply it to an interface to make it work:

   ```
   LA(config)#int f0/0
   Lab_A(config-if)#ip access-group 10 out
   ```

6. Verify your access list with the following commands:

```
LA#sh access-list
Standard IP access list 10
    permit 172.16.30.2
LA#sh run
[output cut]
interface FastEthernet0/0
 ip address 192.168.20.1 255.255.255.0
 ip access-group 10 out
```

7. Test your access list by pinging from 192.168.10.2 to 192.168.20.2.

8. If you have another host on the LA LAN, ping that address, which should fail if your ACL is working.

## Hands-on Lab 12.2: Extended IP Access Lists

In this lab, you will use an extended IP access list to stop host 192.168.10.2 from creating a Telnet session to router LA (172.16.10.6). However, the host still should be able to ping the LA router. IP extended lists should be placed close to the source, so add the extended list on router SF. Pay attention to the log command used in Step 6. It is a Cisco objective!

1. Remove any access lists on SF and add an extended list to SF.

2. Choose a number to create an extended IP list. The IP extended lists use 100–199 or 2000–2699.

3. Use a deny statement. (You'll add a permit statement in step 7 to allow other traffic to still work.)

```
SF(config)#access-list 110 deny ?
  <0-255>  An IP protocol number
  ahp      Authentication Header Protocol
  eigrp    Cisco's EIGRP routing protocol
  esp      Encapsulation Security Payload
  gre      Cisco's GRE tunneling
  icmp     Internet Control Message Protocol
  igmp     Internet Gateway Message Protocol
  igrp     Cisco's IGRP routing protocol
  ip       Any Internet Protocol
  ipinip   IP in IP tunneling
  nos      KA9Q NOS compatible IP over IP tunneling
  ospf     OSPF routing protocol
  pcp      Payload Compression Protocol
```

```
tcp      Transmission Control Protocol
udp      User Datagram Protocol
```

**4.** Since you are going to deny Telnet, you must choose TCP as a Transport layer protocol:

```
SF(config)#access-list 110 deny tcp ?
A.B.C.D  Source address
any      Any source host
host     A single source host
```

**5.** Add the source IP address you want to filter on, then add the destination host IP address. Use the host command instead of wildcard bits.

```
SF(config)#access-list 110 deny tcp host
192.168.10.2 host 172.16.10.6 ?
ack          Match on the ACK bit
eq           Match only packets on a given port
             number
established  Match established connections
fin          Match on the FIN bit
fragments    Check fragments
gt           Match only packets with a greater
             port number
log          Log matches against this entry
log-input    Log matches against this entry,
             including input interface
lt           Match only packets with a lower port
             number
neq          Match only packets not on a given
             port number
precedence   Match packets with given precedence
             value
psh          Match on the PSH bit
range        Match only packets in the range of
             port numbers
rst          Match on the RST bit
syn          Match on the SYN bit
tos          Match packets with given TOS value
urg          Match on the URG bit
<cr>
```

6. At this point, you can add the eq telnet command to filter host 192.168.10.2 from telnetting to 172.16.10.6. The log command can also be used at the end of the command so that whenever the access-list line is hit, a log will be generated on the console.

```
SF(config)#access-list 110 deny tcp host
   192.168.10.2 host 172.16.10.6 eq telnet log
```

7. It is important to add this line next to create a permit statement. (Remember that 0.0.0.0 255.255.255.255 is the same as the any command.)

```
SF(config)#access-list 110 permit ip any 0.0.0.0
   255.255.255.255
```

You must create a permit statement; if you just add a deny statement, nothing will be permitted at all. Please see the sections earlier in this chapter for more detailed information on the deny any command implied at the end of every ACL.

8. Apply the access list to the FastEthernet0/0 on SF to stop the Telnet traffic as soon as it hits the first router interface.

```
SF(config)#int f0/0
SF(config-if)#ip access-group 110 in
SF(config-if)#^Z
```

9. Try telnetting from host 192.168.10.2 to LA using the destination IP address of 172.16.10.6. This should fail, but the ping command should work.

10. On the console of SF, because of the log command, the output should appear as follows:

```
01:11:48: %SEC-6-IPACCESSLOGP: list 110 denied tcp
   192.168.10.2(1030) -> 172.16.10.6(23), 1 packet
01:13:04: %SEC-6-IPACCESSLOGP: list 110 denied tcp
   192.168.10.2(1030) -> 172.16.10.6(23), 3 packets
```

# Review Questions

 The following questions are designed to test your understanding of this chapter's material. For more information on how to get additional questions, please see this book's introduction.

The answers to these questions can be found in Appendix B, "Answers to Chapter Review Questions."

1. Which of the following statements is false when a packet is being compared to an access list?

   **A.** It's always compared with each line of the access list in sequential order.

   **B.** Once the packet matches the condition on a line of the access list, the packet is acted upon and no further comparisons take place.

   **C.** There is an implicit "deny" at the end of each access list.

   **D.** Until all lines have been analyzed, the comparison is not over.

2. You need to create an access list that will prevent hosts in the network range of 192.168.160.0 to 192.168.191.0. Which of the following lists will you use?

   **A.** `access-list 10 deny 192.168.160.0 255.255.224.0`

   **B.** `access-list 10 deny 192.168.160.0 0.0.191.255`

   **C.** `access-list 10 deny 192.168.160.0 0.0.31.255`

   **D.** `access-list 10 deny 192.168.0.0 0.0.31.255`

3. You have created a named access list called Blocksales. Which of the following is a valid command for applying this to packets trying to enter interface Fa0/0 of your router?

   **A.** `(config)#ip access-group 110 in`

   **B.** `(config-if)#ip access-group 110 in`

   **C.** `(config-if)#ip access-group Blocksales in`

   **D.** `(config-if)#Blocksales ip access-list in`

4. Which access list statement will permit all HTTP sessions to network 192.168.144.0/24 containing web servers?

   **A.** `access-list 110 permit tcp 192.168.144.0 0.0.0.255 any eq 80`

   **B.** `access-list 110 permit tcp any 192.168.144.0 0.0.0.255 eq 80`

   **C.** `access-list 110 permit tcp 192.168.144.0 0.0.0.255 192.168.144.0 0.0.0.255 any eq 80`

   **D.** `access-list 110 permit udp any 192.168.144.0 eq 80`

**5.** Which of the following access lists will allow only HTTP traffic into network 196.15.7.0?

**A.** `access-list 100 permit tcp any 196.15.7.0 0.0.0.255 eq www`

**B.** `access-list 10 deny tcp any 196.15.7.0 eq www`

**C.** `access-list 100 permit 196.15.7.0 0.0.0.255 eq www`

**D.** `access-list 110 permit ip any 196.15.7.0 0.0.0.255`

**E.** `access-list 110 permit www 196.15.7.0 0.0.0.255`

**6.** What router command allows you to determine whether an IP access list is enabled on a particular interface?

**A.** `show ip port`

**B.** `show access-lists`

**C.** `show ip interface`

**D.** `show access-lists interface`

**7.** In the work area, connect the `show` command to its function on the right.

| | |
|---|---|
| show access-list | Shows only the parameters for the access list 110. This command does not show you the interface the list is set on. |
| show access-list 110 | Shows only the IP access lists configured on the router. |
| show ip access-list | Shows which interfaces have access lists set. |
| show ip interface | Displays all access lists and their parameters configured on the router. This command does not show you which interface the list is set on. |

**8.** If you wanted to deny all Telnet connections to only network 192.168.10.0, which command could you use?

**A.** `access-list 100 deny tcp 192.168.10.0 255.255.255.0 eq telnet`

**B.** `access-list 100 deny tcp 192.168.10.0 0.255.255.255 eq telnet`

**C.** `access-list 100 deny tcp any 192.168.10.0 0.0.0.255 eq 23`

**D.** `access-list 100 deny 192.168.10.0 0.0.0.255 any eq 23`

**9.** If you wanted to deny FTP access from network 200.200.10.0 to network 200.199.11.0 but allow everything else, which of the following command strings is valid?

**A.** `access-list 110 deny 200.200.10.0 to network 200.199.11.0 eq ftp`

`access-list 111 permit ip any 0.0.0.0 255.255.255.255`

**B.** `access-list 1 deny ftp 200.200.10.0 200.199.11.0 any any`

**C.** `access-list 100 deny tcp 200.200.10.0 0.0.0.255 200.199.11.0 0.0.0.255 eq ftp`

**D.** `access-list 198 deny tcp 200.200.10.0 0.0.0.255 200.199.11.0 0.0.0.255 eq ftp`

`access-list 198 permit ip any 0.0.0.0 255.255.255.255`

**10.** You want to create an extended access list that denies the subnet of the following host: 172.16.50.172/20. Which of the following would you start your list with?

**A.** `access-list 110 deny ip 172.16.48.0 255.255.240.0 any`

**B.** `access-list 110 udp deny 172.16.0.0 0.0.255.255 ip any`

**C.** `access-list 110 deny tcp 172.16.64.0 0.0.31.255 any eq 80`

**D.** `access-list 110 deny ip 172.16.48.0 0.0.15.255 any`

**11.** Which of the following is the wildcard (inverse) version of a /27 mask?

**A.** 0.0.0.7

**B.** 0.0.0.31

**C.** 0.0.0.27

**D.** 0.0.31.255

**12.** You want to create an extended access list that denies the subnet of the following host: 172.16.198.94/19. Which of the following would you start your list with?

**A.** `access-list 110 deny ip 172.16.192.0 0.0.31.255 any`

**B.** `access-list 110 deny ip 172.16.0.0 0.0.255.255 any`

**C.** `access-list 10 deny ip 172.16.172.0 0.0.31.255 any`

**D.** `access-list 110 deny ip 172.16.188.0 0.0.15.255 any`

**13.** The following access list has been applied to an interface on a router:

`access-list 101 deny tcp 199.111.16.32 0.0.0.31 host 199.168.5.60`

Which of the following IP addresses will be blocked because of this single rule in the list? (Choose all that apply.)

**A.** 199.111.16.67

**B.** 199.111.16.38

**C.** 199.111.16.65

**D.** 199.111.16.54.14

**14.** Which of the following commands connects access list 110 inbound to interface Ethernet0?

**A.** Router(config)#`ip access-group 110 in`

**B.** Router(config)#`ip access-list 110 in`

**C.** Router(config-if)#`ip access-group 110 in`

**D.** Router(config-if)#`ip access-list 110 in`

**15.** What is the effect of this single-line access list?

```
access-list 110 deny ip 172.16.10.0 0.0.0.255 host 1.1.1.1
```

**A.** Denies only the computer at 172.16.10

**B.** Denies all traffic

**C.** Denies the subnet 172.16.10.0/26

**D.** Denies the subnet 172.16.10.0/25

**16.** You configure the following access list. What will the result of this access list be?

```
access-list 110 deny tcp 10.1.1.128 0.0.0.63 any eq smtp
access-list 110 deny tcp any any eq 23
int ethernet 0
ip access-group 110 out
```

**A.** Email and Telnet will be allowed out E0.

**B.** Email and Telnet will be allowed in E0.

**C.** Everything but email and Telnet will be allowed out E0.

**D.** No IP traffic will be allowed out E0.

**17.** Which of the following series of commands will restrict Telnet access to the router?

**A.** Lab_A(config)#`access-list 10 permit 172.16.1.1`

Lab_A(config)#`line con 0`

Lab_A(config-line)#`ip access-group 10 in`

**B.** Lab_A(config)#`access-list 10 permit 172.16.1.1`

Lab_A(config)#`line vty 0 4`

Lab_A(config-line)#`access-class 10 out`

**C.** Lab_A(config)#`access-list 10 permit 172.16.1.1`

Lab_A(config)#`line vty 0 4`

Lab_A(config-line)#`access-class 10 in`

**D.** Lab_A(config)#`access-list 10 permit 172.16.1.1`

Lab_A(config)#`line vty 0 4`

Lab_A(config-line)#`ip access-group 10 in`

**18.** Which of the following is true regarding access lists applied to an interface?

   **A.** You can place as many access lists as you want on any interface until you run out of memory.

   **B.** You can apply only one access list on any interface.

   **C.** One access list may be configured, per direction, for each layer 3 protocol configured on an interface.

   **D.** You can apply two access lists to any interface.

**19.** What is the most common attack on a network today?

   **A.** Lock picking

   **B.** Naggle

   **C.** DoS

   **D.** auto secure

**20.** You need to stop DoS attacks in real time and have a log of anyone who has tried to attack your network. What should you do your network?

   **A.** Add more routers.

   **B.** Use the auto secure command.

   **C.** Implement IDS/IPS.

   **D.** Configure Naggle.

# Chapter

# 13

# Network Address Translation (NAT)

## THE FOLLOWING ICND1 EXAM TOPICS ARE COVERED IN THIS CHAPTER:

✓ **Operation of IP Data Networks**

- Predict the data flow between two hosts across a network

✓ **IP Services**

- Identify the basic operation of NAT
  - Purpose
  - Pool
  - Static
  - one-to-one
  - Overloading
  - Source addressing
  - One-way NAT
- Configure and verify NAT for given network requirements

In this chapter, we're going to dig into Network Address Translation (NAT), Dynamic NAT, and Port Address Translation (PAT), also known as NAT Overload. Of course, I'll demonstrate all the NAT commands. I also provided some fantastic hands-on labs for you to configure at the end of this chapter, so be sure not to miss those!

It's important to understand the Cisco objectives for this chapter. They are very straight-forward: you have hosts on your inside Corporate network using RFC 1918 addresses and you need to allow those hosts access to the Internet by configuring NAT translations. With that objective in mind, that will be my direction with this chapter.

Because we'll be using ACLs in our NAT configurations, it's important that you're really comfortable with the skills you learned in the previous chapter before proceeding with this one.

**To find up-to-the-minute updates for this chapter, please see www.lammle.com/forum or the book's web page at www.sybex.com.**

# When Do We Use NAT?

*Network Address Translation (NAT)* is similar to Classless Inter-Domain Routing (CIDR) in that the original intention for NAT was to slow the depletion of available IP address space by allowing multiple private IP addresses to be represented by a much smaller number of public IP addresses.

Since then, it's been discovered that NAT is also a useful tool for network migrations and mergers, server load sharing, and creating "virtual servers." So in this chapter, I'm going to describe the basics of NAT functionality and the terminology common to NAT.

Because NAT really decreases the overwhelming amount of public IP addresses required in a networking environment, it comes in really handy when two companies that have dupli-cate internal addressing schemes merge. NAT is also a great tool to use when an organization changes its Internet service provider (ISP) but the networking manager needs to avoid the hassle of changing the internal address scheme.

Here's a list of situations when NAT can be especially helpful:

- When you need to connect to the Internet and your hosts don't have globally unique IP addresses

- When you've changed to a new ISP that requires you to renumber your network
- When you need to merge two intranets with duplicate addresses

You typically use NAT on a border router. For example, in Figure 13.1, NAT is used on the Corporate router connected to the Internet.

**FIGURE 13.1** Where to configure NAT

Now you may be thinking, "NAT's totally cool and I just gotta have it!" But don't get too excited yet because there are some serious snags related to using NAT that you need to understand first. Don't get me wrong—it can truly be a lifesaver sometimes, but NAT has a bit of a dark side you need to know about too. For the pros and cons linked to using NAT, check out Table 13.1.

**TABLE 13.1** Advantages and disadvantages of implementing NAT

| Advantages | Disadvantages |
|---|---|
| Conserves legally registered addresses. | Translation results in switching path delays. |
| Remedies address overlap events. | Causes loss of end-to-end IP traceability |
| Increases flexibility when connecting to the Internet. | Certain applications will not function with NAT enabled |
| Eliminates address renumbering as a network evolves. | |

The most obvious advantage associated with NAT is that it allows you to conserve your legally registered address scheme. But a version of it known as PAT is also why we've only just recently run out of IPv4 addresses. Without NAT/PAT, we'd have run out of IPv4 addresses more than a decade ago!

# Types of Network Address Translation

In this section, I'm going to go over the three types of NATs with you:

**Static NAT**    This type of NAT is designed to allow one-to-one mapping between local and global addresses. Keep in mind that the static version requires you to have one real Internet IP address for every host on your network.

**Dynamic NAT**    This version gives you the ability to map an unregistered IP address to a registered IP address from out of a pool of registered IP addresses. You don't have to statically configure your router to map each inside address to an individual outside address as you would using static NAT, but you do have to have enough real, bona fide IP addresses for everyone who's going to be sending packets to and receiving them from the Internet at the same time.

**Overloading**    This is the most popular type of NAT configuration. Understand that overloading really is a form of dynamic NAT that maps multiple unregistered IP addresses to a single registered IP address (many-to-one) by using different source ports. Now, why is this so special? Well, because it's also known as *Port Address Translation (PAT)*, which is also commonly referred to as NAT Overload. Using PAT allows you to permit thousands of users to connect to the Internet using only one real global IP address—pretty slick, right? Seriously, NAT Overload is the real reason we haven't run out of valid IP addresses on the Internet. Really—I'm not joking!

I'll show you how to configure all three types of NAT throughout this chapter and at the end of this chapter with the hands-on labs.

# NAT Names

The names we use to describe the addresses used with NAT are fairly straightforward. Addresses used after NAT translations are called *global addresses*. These are usually the public addresses used on the Internet, which you don't need if you aren't going on the Internet.

*Local addresses* are the ones we use before NAT translation. This means that the inside local address is actually the private address of the sending host that's attempting to get to the Internet. The outside local address would typically be the router interface connected to your ISP and is also usually a public address used as the packet begins its journey.

After translation, the inside local address is then called the *inside global address* and the outside global address then becomes the address of the destination host. Check out Table 13.2, which lists all this terminology and offers a clear picture of the various names used with NAT. Keep in mind that these terms and their definitions can vary somewhat based on implementation. The table shows how they're used according to the Cisco exam objectives.

**TABLE 13.2**   NAT terms

| Names | Meaning |
| --- | --- |
| Inside local | Source host inside address before translation—typically an RFC 1918 address. |
| Outside local | Address from which source host is known on the Internet. This is usually the address of the router interface connected to ISP—the actual Internet address. |
| Inside global | Source host address used after translation to get onto the Internet. This is also the actual Internet address. |
| Outside global | Address of outside destination host and, again, the real Internet address. |

# How NAT Works

Okay, it's time to look at how this whole NAT thing works. I'm going to start by using Figure 13.2 to describe basic NAT translation.

In this figure, we can see host 10.1.1.1 sending an Internet-bound packet to the border router configured with NAT. The router identifies the source IP address as an inside local IP address destined for an outside network, translates the source IP address in the packet, and documents the translation in the NAT table.

The packet is sent to the outside interface with the new translated source address. The external host returns the packet to the destination host and the NAT router translates the inside global IP address back to the inside local IP address using the NAT table. This is as simple as it gets!

Let's take a look at a more complex configuration using overloading, also referred to as PAT. I'll use Figure 13.3 to demonstrate how PAT works by having an inside host HTTP to a server on the Internet.

**FIGURE 13.2**    Basic NAT translation

NAT Table

| Inside Local IP Addresses | Inside Global IP Addresses |
|---------------------------|----------------------------|
| 10.1.1.3                  | 170.168.2.4                |
| 10.1.1.2                  | 170.168.2.3                |
| 10.1.1.1                  | 170.168.2.2                |

**FIGURE 13.3**    NAT overloading example (PAT)

NAT Table

| Inside Local IP Addresses | Inside Global IP Addresses |
|---------------------------|----------------------------|
| 10.1.1.3:1024             | 170.168.2.1:1024           |
| 10.1.1.2:1025             | 170.168.2.1:1025           |
| 10.1.1.1:1026             | 170.168.2.1:1026           |

With PAT, all inside hosts get translated to one single IP address, hence the term *overloading*. Again, the reason we've just run out of available global IP addresses on the Internet is because of overloading (PAT).

Take a look at the NAT table in Figure 13.3 again. In addition to the inside local IP address and inside global IP address, we now have port numbers. These port numbers help the router identify which host should receive the return traffic. The router uses the source port number from each host to differentiate the traffic from each of them. Notice the packet has a destination port number of 80 when it leaves the router, and the HTTP server sends back the data with a destination port number of 1026, in this example. This allows the NAT translation router to differentiate between hosts in the NAT table and then translate the destination IP address back to the inside local address.

Port numbers are used at the Transport layer to identify the local host in this example. If we had to use real global IP addresses to identify the source hosts, that's called *static NAT* and we would run out of addresses. PAT allows us to use the Transport layer to identify the hosts, which in turn allows us to theoretically use up to about 65,000 hosts with only one real IP address!

## Static NAT Configuration

Let's take a look at a simple example of a basic static NAT configuration:

```
ip nat inside source static 10.1.1.1 170.46.2.2
!
interface Ethernet0
 ip address 10.1.1.10 255.255.255.0
 ip nat inside
!
interface Serial0
 ip address 170.46.2.1 255.255.255.0
 ip nat outside
!
```

In the preceding router output, the ip nat inside source command identifies which IP addresses will be translated. In this configuration example, the ip nat inside source command configures a static translation between the inside local IP address 10.1.1.1 to the outside global IP address 170.46.2.2.

Scrolling farther down in the configuration, we find an ip nat command under each interface. The ip nat inside command identifies that interface as the inside interface. The ip nat outside command identifies that interface as the outside interface. When you look back at the ip nat inside source command, you can see that the command is referencing the inside interface as the source or starting point of the translation. You could also use the command like this: ip nat outside source. This option indicates the interface that you designated as the outside interface should become the source or starting point for the translation.

## Dynamic NAT Configuration

Basically, dynamic NAT really means we have a pool of addresses that we'll use to provide real IP addresses to a group of users on the inside. Because we don't use port numbers, we must have real IP addresses for every user who's trying to get outside the local network simultaneously.

Here is a sample output of a dynamic NAT configuration:

```
ip nat pool todd 170.168.2.3 170.168.2.254
    netmask 255.255.255.0
ip nat inside source list 1 pool todd
!
interface Ethernet0
 ip address 10.1.1.10 255.255.255.0
 ip nat inside
!
interface Serial0
 ip address 170.168.2.1 255.255.255.0
 ip nat outside
!
access-list 1 permit 10.1.1.0 0.0.0.255
!
```

The ip nat inside source list 1 pool todd command tells the router to translate IP addresses that match access-list 1 to an address found in the IP NAT pool named todd. Here the ACL isn't there to filter traffic for security reasons by permitting or denying traffic. In this case, it's there to select or designate what we often call interesting traffic. When interesting traffic has been matched with the access list, it's pulled into the NAT process to be translated. This is actually a common use for access lists, which aren't always just stuck with the dull job of just blocking traffic at an interface!

The command ip nat pool todd 170.168.2.3 192.168.2.254 netmask 255.255.255.0 creates a pool of addresses that will be distributed to the specific hosts that require global addresses. When troubleshooting NAT for the Cisco objectives, always check this pool to confirm that there are enough addresses in it to provide translation for all the inside hosts. Last, check to make sure the pool names match exactly on both lines, remembering that they are case sensitive; if they don't, the pool won't work!

## PAT (Overloading) Configuration

This last example shows how to configure inside global address overloading. This is the typical form of NAT that we would use today. It's actually now rare to use static or dynamic NAT unless it is for something like statically mapping a server, for example.

Here is a sample output of a PAT configuration:

```
ip nat pool globalnet 170.168.2.1 170.168.2.1 netmask 255.255.255.0
ip nat inside source list 1 pool globalnet overload
!
interface Ethernet0/0
 ip address 10.1.1.10 255.255.255.0
 ip nat inside
!
interface Serial0/0
 ip address 170.168.2.1 255.255.255.0
 ip nat outside
!
access-list 1 permit 10.1.1.0 0.0.0.255
```

The nice thing about PAT is that these are the only differences between this configuration and the previous dynamic NAT configuration:

- Our pool of addresses has shrunk to only one IP address.
- We included the overload keyword at the end of our ip nat inside source command.

A really key factor to see in the example is that the one IP address that's in the pool for us to use is the IP address of the outside interface. This is perfect if you are configuring NAT Overload for yourself at home or for a small office that only has one IP address from your ISP. You could, however, use an additional address such as 170.168.2.2 if you had that address available to you as well, and doing that could prove very helpful in a very large implementation where you've got such an abundance of simultaneously active internal users that you need to have more than one overloaded IP address on the outside!

## Simple Verification of NAT

Okay—as always, once you've chosen and configured the type of NAT you're going to run, which is typically PAT, you must be able to verify your configuration.

To see basic IP address translation information, use the following command:

Router#**show ip nat translations**

When looking at the IP NAT translations, you may see many translations from the same host to the corresponding host at the destination. Understand that this is typical when there are many connections to the same server.

You can also verify your NAT configuration via the debug ip nat command. This output will show the sending address, the translation, and the destination address on each debug line:

Router#**debug ip nat**

But wait—how do you clear your NAT entries from the translation table? Just use the `clear ip nat translation` command, and if you want to clear all entries from the NAT table, just use an asterisk (*) at the end of the command.

# Testing and Troubleshooting NAT

Cisco's NAT gives you some serious power—and it does so without much effort, because the configurations are really pretty simple. But we all know nothing's perfect, so in case something goes wrong, you can figure out some of the more common culprits by running through this list of potential causes:

- Check the dynamic pools. Are they composed of the right scope of addresses?
- Check to see if any dynamic pools overlap.
- Check to see if the addresses used for static mapping and those in the dynamic pools overlap.
- Ensure that your access lists specify the correct addresses for translation.
- Make sure there aren't any addresses left out that need to be there, and ensure that none are included that shouldn't be.
- Check to make sure you've got both the inside and outside interfaces delimited properly.

A key thing to keep in mind is that one of the most common problems with a new NAT configuration often isn't specific to NAT at all—it usually involves a routing blooper. So, because you're changing a source or destination address in a packet, make sure your router still knows what to do with the new address after the translation!

The first command you should typically use is the `show ip nat translations` command:

```
Router#show ip nat trans
Pro    Inside global    Inside local    Outside local    Outside global
---    192.2.2.1        10.1.1.1        ---              ---
---    192.2.2.2        10.1.1.2        ---              ---
```

After checking out this output, can you tell me if the configuration on the router is static or dynamic NAT? The answer is yes, either static or dynamic NAT is configured because there's a one-to-one translation from the inside local to the inside global. Basically, by looking at the output, you can't tell if it's static or dynamic per se; but you absolutely can tell that you're not using PAT because there are no port numbers.

Let's take a look at another output:

```
Router#sh ip nat trans
Pro Inside global      Inside local      Outside local      Outside global
tcp 170.168.2.1:11003  10.1.1.1:11003    172.40.2.2:23      172.40.2.2:23
tcp 170.168.2.1:1067   10.1.1.1:1067     172.40.2.3:23      172.40.2.3:23
```

Okay, you can easily see that the above output is using NAT Overload (PAT). The protocol in this output is TCP, and the inside global address is the same for both entries.

Supposedly the sky's the limit regarding the number of mappings the NAT table can hold. But this is reality, so things like memory and CPU, or even the boundaries set in place by the scope of available addresses or ports, can cause limitations on the actual number of entries. Consider that each NAT mapping devours about 160 bytes of memory. And sometimes the amount of entries must be limited for the sake of performance or because of policy restrictions, but this doesn't happen very often. In situations like these, just go to the `ip nat translation max-entries` command for help.

Another handy command for troubleshooting is `show ip nat statistics`. Deploying this gives you a summary of the NAT configuration, and it will count the number of active translation types too. Also counted are hits to an existing mapping as well any misses, with the latter causing an attempt to create a mapping. This command will also reveal expired translations. If you want to: check into dynamic pools, their types, the total available addresses, how many addresses have been allocated and how many have failed, plus the number of translations that have occurred, just use the `pool` keyword.

Here is an example of the basic NAT debugging command:

```
Router#debug ip nat
NAT: s=10.1.1.1->192.168.2.1, d=172.16.2.2 [0]
NAT: s=172.16.2.2, d=192.168.2.1->10.1.1.1 [0]
NAT: s=10.1.1.1->192.168.2.1, d=172.16.2.2 [1]
NAT: s=10.1.1.1->192.168.2.1, d=172.16.2.2 [2]
NAT: s=10.1.1.1->192.168.2.1, d=172.16.2.2 [3]
NAT*: s=172.16.2.2, d=192.168.2.1->10.1.1.1 [1]
```

Notice the last line in the output and how the NAT at the beginning of the line has an asterisk (*). This means the packet was translated and fast-switched to the destination. What's fast-switched? Well in brief, fast-switching has gone by several aliases such as cache-based switching and this nicely descriptive name, "route one switch many." The fast-switching process is used on Cisco routers to create a cache of layer 3 routing information to be accessed at layer 2 so packets can be forwarded quickly through a router without the routing table having to be parsed for every packet. As packets are packet switched (looked up in the routing table), this information is stored in the cache for later use if needed for faster routing processing.

Okay, let's get back to verifying NAT. Did you know you can manually clear dynamic NAT entries from the NAT table? You can, and doing this can come in seriously handy if you need to get rid of a specific rotten entry without sitting around waiting for the timeout to expire! A manual clear is also really useful when you want to clear the whole NAT table to reconfigure a pool of addresses.

You also need to know that the Cisco IOS software just won't allow you to change or delete an address pool if any of that pool's addresses are mapped in the NAT table. The `clear ip nat translations` command clears entries—you can indicate a single entry via the global and local address and through TCP and UDP translations, including ports, or you can just type in an asterisk (*) to wipe out the entire table. But know that if you do that, only dynamic entries will be cleared because this command won't remove static entries.

Oh, and there's more—any outside device's packet destination address that happens to be responding to any inside device is known as the inside global (IG) address. This means that the initial mapping has to be held in the NAT table so that all packets arriving from a specific connection get translated consistently. Holding entries in the NAT table also cuts down on repeated translation operations happening each time the same inside machine sends packets to the same outside destinations on a regular basis.

Let me clarify: when an entry is placed into the NAT table the first time, a timer begins ticking and its duration is known as the translation timeout. Each time a packet for a given entry translates through the router, the timer gets reset. If the timer expires, the entry will be unceremoniously removed from the NAT table and the dynamically assigned address will then be returned to the pool. Cisco's default translation timeout is 86,400 seconds (24 hours), but you can change that with the ip nat translation timeout command.

Before we move on to the configuration section and actually use the commands I just talked about, let's go through a couple of NAT examples and see if you can figure out the best configuration to go with. To start, look at Figure 13.4 and ask yourself two things: Where would you implement NAT in this design? What type of NAT would you configure?

**FIGURE 13.4**   NAT example

In Figure 13.4, the NAT configuration would be placed on the corporate router, just as I demonstrated with Figure 13.1, and the configuration would be dynamic NAT with overload (PAT). In this next NAT example, what type of NAT is being used?

```
ip nat pool todd-nat 170.168.10.10 170.168.10.20 netmask 255.255.255.0
ip nat inside source list 1 pool todd-nat
```

The preceding command uses dynamic NAT without PAT. The pool in the command gives the answer away as dynamic, plus there's more than one address in the pool and there is no overload command at the end of our ip nat inside source command. This means we are not using PAT!

In the next NAT example, refer to Figure 13.5 and see if you can come up with the configuration needed.

**FIGURE 13.5**   Another NAT example

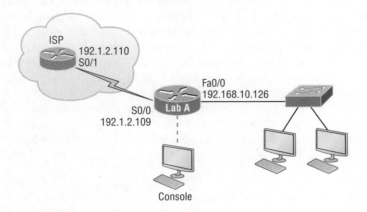

Figure 13.5 shows a border router that needs to be configured with NAT and allow the use of six public IP addresses to the inside locals, 192.1.2.109 through 192.1.2.114. However, on the inside network, you have 62 hosts that use the private addresses of 192.168.10.65 through 192.168.10.126. What would your NAT configuration be on the border router?

Actually, two different answers would both work here, but the following would be my first choice based on the exam objectives:

```
ip nat pool Todd 192.1.2.109 192.1.2.109 netmask 255.255.255.248
access-list 1 permit 192.168.10.64 0.0.0.63
ip nat inside source list 1 pool Todd overload
```

The command ip nat pool Todd 192.1.2.109 192.1.2.109 netmask 255.255.255.248 sets the pool name as Todd and creates a dynamic pool of only one address using NAT address 192.1.2.109. Instead of the netmask command, you can use the prefix-length 29 statement. Just in case you're wondering, you cannot do this on router interfaces as well!

The second answer would get you the exact same result of having only 192.1.2.109 as your inside global, but you can type this in and it will also work: ip nat pool Todd

192.1.2.109 192.1.2.114 netmask 255.255.255.248. But this option really is a waste because the second through sixth addresses would only be used if there was a conflict with a TCP port number. You would use something like what I've shown in this example if you literally had about ten thousand hosts with one Internet connection! You would need it to help with the TCP-Reset issue when two hosts are trying to use the same source port number and get a negative acknowledgment (NAK). But in our example, we've only got up to 62 hosts connecting to the Internet at the same time, so having more than one inside global gets us nothing!

If you're fuzzy on the second line where the access list is set in the NAT configuration, do a quick review of Chapter 12, "Security." But this isn't difficult to grasp because it's easy to see in this access-list line that it's just the *network number* and *wildcard* used with that command. I always say, "Every question is a subnet question," and this one is no exception. The inside locals in this example were 192.168.10.65–126, which is a block of 64, or a 255.255.255.192 mask. As I've said in pretty much every chapter, you really need to be able to subnet quickly!

The command ip nat inside source list 1 pool Todd overload sets the dynamic pool to use PAT by using the overload command.

And be sure to add the ip nat inside and ip nat outside statements on the appropriate interfaces.

> If you're planning on testing for any Cisco exam, configure the hands-on labs at the end of this chapter until you're really comfortable with doing that!

Okay, one more example, and then you are off to the written lab, hands-on labs, and review questions.

The network in Figure 13.6 is already configured with IP addresses as shown in the figure, and there is only one configured host. However, you need to add 25 more hosts to the LAN. Now, all 26 hosts must be able to get to the Internet at the same time.

**FIGURE 13.6** Last NAT example

By looking at the configured network, use only the following inside addresses to configure NAT on the Corp router to allow all hosts to reach the Internet:

- Inside globals: 198.18.41.129 through 198.18.41.134
- Inside locals: 192.168.76.65 through 192.168.76.94

This one is a bit more challenging because all we have to help us figure out the configuration is the inside globals and the inside locals. But even meagerly armed with these crumbs of information, plus the IP addresses of the router interfaces shown in the figure, we can still configure this correctly.

To do that, we must first determine what our block sizes are so we can get our subnet mask for our NAT pool. This will also equip us to configure the wildcard for the access list.

You should easily be able to see that the block size of the inside globals is 8 and the block size of the inside locals is 32. Know that it's critical not to stumble on this foundational information!

Okay, so we can configure NAT now that we have our block sizes:

```
ip nat pool Corp 198.18.41.129 198.18.41.134 netmask 255.255.255.248
ip nat inside source list 1 pool Corp overload
access-list 1 permit 192.168.76.64 0.0.0.31
```

Since we had a block of only 8 for our pool, we had to use the overload command to make sure all 26 hosts can get to the Internet at the same time.

There is one other simple way to configure NAT, and I use this command at my home office to connect to my ISP. One command line and it's done! Here it is:

```
ip nat inside source list 1 int s0/0/0 overload
```

I can't say enough how much I love efficiency, and being able to achieve something cool using one measly line always makes me happy! My one little powerfully elegant line essentially says, "Use my outside local as my inside global and overload it." Nice! Of course, I still had to create ACL 1 and add the inside and outside interface commands to the configuration, but this is a really nice, fast way to configure NAT if you don't have a pool of addresses to use.

# Summary

Now this really was a fun chapter. Come on—admit it! You learned a lot about Network Address Translation (NAT) and how it's configured as static and dynamic as well as with Port Address Translation (PAT), also called NAT Overload.

I also described how each flavor of NAT is used in a network as well as how each type is configured.

We finished up by going through some verification and troubleshooting commands. Now don't forget to practice all the wonderfully helpful labs until you've got them nailed down tight!

# Exam Essentials

**Understand the term** *NAT.* This may come as news to you, because I didn't—okay, failed to—mention it earlier, but NAT has a few nicknames. In the industry, it's referred to as network masquerading, IP-masquerading, and (for those who are besieged with OCD and compelled to spell everything out) Network Address Translation. Whatever you want to dub it, basically, they all refer to the process of rewriting the source/destination addresses of IP packets when they go through a router or firewall. Just focus on the process that's occurring and your understanding of it (i.e., the important part) and you're on it for sure!

**Remember the three methods of NAT.** The three methods are static, dynamic, and overloading; the latter is also called PAT.

**Understand static NAT.** This type of NAT is designed to allow one-to-one mapping between local and global addresses.

**Understand dynamic NAT.** This version gives you the ability to map a range of unregistered IP addresses to a registered IP address from out of a pool of registered IP addresses.

**Understand overloading.** Overloading really is a form of dynamic NAT that maps multiple unregistered IP addresses to a single registered IP address (many-to-one) by using different ports. It's also known as *PAT.*

# Written Lab 13

The answers to this lab can be found in Appendix A, "Answers to Written Labs."

In this section, write the answers to the following questions:

1. What type of address translation can use only one address to allow thousands of hosts to be translated globally?

2. What command can you use to show the NAT translations as they occur on your router?

3. What command will show you the translation table?

4. What command will clear all your NAT entries from the translation table?

5. An inside local is before or after translation?

6. An inside global is before or after translation?

7. Which command can be used for troubleshooting and displays a summary of the NAT configuration as well as counts of active translation types and hits to an existing mapping?

8. What commands must be used on your router interfaces before NAT will translate addresses?

9. In the following output, what type of NAT is being used?

   ```
   ip nat pool todd-nat 170.168.10.10 170.168.10.20 netmask 255.255.255.0
   ```

10. Instead of the netmask command, you can use the _____ statement.

# Hands-on Labs

I am going to use some basic routers for these labs, but really, almost any Cisco router will work. Also, you can use the LammleSim IOS version to run through all the labs in this (and every) chapter in this book.

Here is a list of the labs in this chapter:

   Lab 13.1: Preparing for NAT

   Lab 13.2: Configuring Dynamic NAT

   Lab 13.3: Configuring PAT

I am going to use the network shown in the following diagram for our hands-on labs. I highly recommend you connect up some routers and run through these labs. You will configure NAT on router Lab_A to translate the private IP address of 192.168.10.0 to a public address of 171.16.10.0.

Table 13.3 shows the commands we will use and the purpose of each command.

**TABLE 13.3** Command summary for NAT/PAT hands-on labs

| Command | Purpose |
| --- | --- |
| ip nat inside source list *acl* pool *name* | Translates IPs that match the ACL to the pool |
| ip nat inside source static *inside_addr* *outside_addr* | Statically maps an inside local address to an outside global address |
| ip nat pool *name* | Creates an address pool |
| ip nat inside | Sets an interface to be an inside interface |
| ip nat outside | Sets an interface to be an outside interface |
| show ip nat translations | Shows current NAT translations |

# Lab 13.1: Preparing for NAT

In this lab, you'll set up your routers with IP addresses and RIP routing.

**1.** Configure the routers with the IP addresses listed in the table below:

| Router | Interface | IP Address |
| --- | --- | --- |
| ISP | S0 | 171.16.10.1/24 |
| Lab_A | S0/2 | 171.16.10.2/24 |
| Lab_A | S0/0 | 192.168.20.1/24 |
| Lab_B | S0 | 192.168.20.2/24 |
| Lab_B | E0 | 192.168.30.1/24 |
| Lab_C | E0 | 192.168.30.2/24 |

After you configure IP addresses on the routers, you should be able to ping from router to router, but since we do not have a routing protocol running until the next step, you can verify only from one router to another but not through the network until RIP is set up. You can use any routing protocol you wish; I am just using RIP for simplicity's sake to get this up and running.

2. On Lab_A, configure RIP routing, set a passive interface, and configure the default network.

```
Lab_A#config t
Lab_A(config)#router rip
Lab_A(config-router)#network 192.168.20.0
Lab_A(config-router)#network 171.16.0.0
Lab_A(config-router)#passive-interface s0/2
Lab_A(config-router)#exit
Lab_A(config)#ip default-network 171.16.10.1
```

The passive-interface command stops RIP updates from being sent to the ISP and the ip default-network command advertises a default network to the other routers so they know how to get to the Internet.

3. On Lab_B, configure RIP routing:

```
Lab_B#config t
Lab_B(config)#router rip
Lab_B(config-router)#network 192.168.30.0
Lab_B(config-router)#network 192.168.20.0
```

4. On Lab_C, configure RIP routing:

```
Lab_C#config t
Lab_C(config)#router rip
Lab_C(config-router)#network 192.168.30.0
```

5. On the ISP router, configure a default route to the corporate network:

```
ISP#config t
ISP(config)#ip route 0.0.0.0 0.0.0.0 s0
```

6. Configure the ISP router so you can telnet into the router without being prompted for a password:

```
ISP#config t
ISP(config)#line vty 0 4
ISP(config-line)#no login
```

7. Verify that you can ping from the ISP router to the Lab_C router and from the Lab_C router to the ISP router. If you cannot, troubleshoot your network.

# Lab 13.2: Configuring Dynamic NAT

In this lab, you'll configure dynamic NAT on the Lab_A router.

1. Create a pool of addresses called GlobalNet on the Lab_A router. The pool should contain a range of addresses of 171.16.10.50 through 171.16.10.55.

```
Lab_A(config)#ip nat pool GlobalNet 171.16.10.50 171.16.10.55
net 255.255.255.0
```

2. Create access list 1. This list permits traffic from the 192.168.20.0 and 192.168.30.0 network to be translated.

```
Lab_A(config)#access-list 1 permit 192.168.20.0 0.0.0.255
Lab_A(config)#access-list 1 permit 192.168.30.0 0.0.0.255
```

3. Map the access list to the pool that was created.

```
Lab_A(config)#ip nat inside source list 1 pool GlobalNet
```

4. Configure serial 0/0 as an inside NAT interface.

```
Lab_A(config)#int s0/0
Lab_A(config-if)#ip nat inside
```

5. Configure serial 0/2 as an outside NAT interface.

```
Lab_A(config-if)#int s0/2
Lab_A(config-if)#ip nat outside
```

6. Move the console connection to the Lab_C router. Log in to the Lab_C router. Telnet from the Lab_C router to the ISP router.

```
Lab_C#telnet 171.16.10.1
```

7. Move the console connection to the Lab_B router. Log in to the Lab_B router. Telnet from the Lab_B router to the ISP router.

```
Lab_B#telnet 171.16.10.1
```

8. Execute the command **show users** from the ISP router. (This shows who is accessing the VTY lines.)

```
ISP#show users
```

   a. What does it show as your source IP address?_____
   b. What is your real source IP address?_____

The show users output should look something like this:

```
ISP>sh users
    Line        User        Host(s)              Idle        Location
   0 con 0                   idle                00:03:32
   2 vty 0                   idle                00:01:33 171.16.10.50
 * 3 vty 1                   idle                00:00:09 171.16.10.51
   Interface  User        Mode                 Idle Peer Address
ISP>
```

Notice that there is a one-to-one translation. This means you must have a real IP address for every host that wants to get to the Internet, which is not typically possible.

**9.** Leave the session open on the ISP router and connect to Lab_A. (Use **Ctrl+Shift+6**, let go, and then press **X**.)

**10.** Log in to your Lab_A router and view your current translations by entering the show ip nat translations command. You should see something like this:

```
Lab_A#sh ip nat translations
Pro Inside global      Inside local      Outside local      Outside global
--- 171.16.10.50       192.168.30.2      ---                ---
--- 171.16.10.51       192.168.20.2      ---                ---
Lab_A#
```

**11.** If you turn on debug ip nat on the Lab_A router and then ping through the router, you will see the actual NAT process take place, which will look something like this:

```
00:32:47: NAT*: s=192.168.30.2->171.16.10.50, d=171.16.10.1 [5]
00:32:47: NAT*: s=171.16.10.1, d=171.16.10.50->192.168.30.2
```

# Lab 13.3: Configuring PAT

In this lab, you'll configure PAT on the Lab_A router. We will use PAT because we don't want a one-to-one translation, which uses just one IP address for every user on the network.

**1.** On the Lab_A router, delete the translation table and remove the dynamic NAT pool.

```
Lab_A#clear ip nat translations *
Lab_A#config t
Lab_A(config)#no ip nat pool GlobalNet 171.16.10.50
171.16.10.55 netmask 255.255.255.0
Lab_A(config)#no ip nat inside source list 1 pool GlobalNet
```

2. On the Lab_A router, create a NAT pool with one address called Lammle. The pool should contain a single address, 171.16.10.100. Enter the following command:

```
Lab_A#config t
Lab_A(config)#ip nat pool Lammle 171.16.10.100 171.16.10.100
net 255.255.255.0
```

3. Create access list 2. It should permit networks 192.168.20.0 and 192.168.30.0 to be translated.

```
Lab_A(config)#access-list 2 permit 192.168.20.0 0.0.0.255
Lab_A(config)#access-list 2 permit 192.168.30.0 0.0.0.255
```

4. Map access list 2 to the new pool, allowing PAT to occur by using the overload command.

```
Lab_A(config)#ip nat inside source list 2 pool Lammle overload
```

5. Log in to the Lab_C router and telnet to the ISP router; also, log in to the Lab_B router and telnet to the ISP router.

6. From the ISP router, use the show users command. The output should look like this:

```
ISP>sh users
    Line       User      Host(s)          Idle      Location
*   0 con 0              idle             00:00:00
    2 vty 0              idle             00:00:39 171.16.10.100
    4 vty 2              idle             00:00:37 171.16.10.100


    Interface  User      Mode             Idle Peer Address


ISP>
```

7. From the Lab_A router, use the show ip nat translations command.

```
Lab_A#sh ip nat translations
Pro Inside global  Inside local  Outside local Outside global
tcp 171.16.10.100:11001 192.168.20.2:11001 171.16.10.1:23   171.16.10.1:23
tcp 171.16.10.100:11002 192.168.30.2:11002 171.16.10.1:23   171.16.10.1:23
```

**8.** Also make sure the debug ip nat command is on for the Lab_A router. If you ping from the Lab_C router to the ISP router, the output will look like this:

```
01:12:36: NAT: s=192.168.30.2->171.16.10.100, d=171.16.10.1 [35]
01:12:36: NAT*: s=171.16.10.1, d=171.16.10.100->192.168.30.2 [35]
01:12:36: NAT*: s=192.168.30.2->171.16.10.100, d=171.16.10.1 [36]
01:12:36: NAT*: s=171.16.10.1, d=171.16.10.100->192.168.30.2 [36]
01:12:36: NAT*: s=192.168.30.2->171.16.10.100, d=171.16.10.1 [37]
01:12:36: NAT*: s=171.16.10.1, d=171.16.10.100->192.168.30.2 [37]
01:12:36: NAT*: s=192.168.30.2->171.16.10.100, d=171.16.10.1 [38]
01:12:36: NAT*: s=171.16.10.1, d=171.16.10.100->192.168.30.2 [38]
01:12:37: NAT*: s=192.168.30.2->171.16.10.100, d=171.16.10.1 [39]
01:12:37: NAT*: s=171.16.10.1, d=171.16.10.100->192.168.30.2 [39]
```

# Review Questions

 The following questions are designed to test your understanding of this chapter's material. For more information on how to get additional questions, please see this book's introduction.

The answers to these questions can be found in Appendix B, "Answers to Chapter Review Questions."

1. Which of the following are disadvantages of using NAT? (Choose three.)
    A. Translation introduces switching path delays.
    B. NAT conserves legally registered addresses.
    C. NAT causes loss of end-to-end IP traceability.
    D. NAT increases flexibility when connecting to the Internet.
    E. Certain applications will not function with NAT enabled.
    F. NAT reduces address overlap occurrence.

2. Which of the following are advantages of using NAT? (Choose three.)
    A. Translation introduces switching path delays.
    B. NAT conserves legally registered addresses.
    C. NAT causes loss of end-to-end IP traceability.
    D. NAT increases flexibility when connecting to the Internet.
    E. Certain applications will not function with NAT enabled.
    F. NAT remedies address overlap occurrence.

3. Which command will allow you to see real-time translations on your router?
    A. show ip nat translations
    B. show ip nat statistics
    C. debug ip nat
    D. clear ip nat translations *

4. Which command will show you all the translations active on your router?
    A. show ip nat translations
    B. show ip nat statistics
    C. debug ip nat
    D. clear ip nat translations *

**5.** Which command will clear all the translations active on your router?

   **A.** `show ip nat translations`

   **B.** `show ip nat statistics`

   **C.** `debug ip nat`

   **D.** `clear ip nat translations *`

**6.** Which command will show you the summary of the NAT configuration?

   **A.** `show ip nat translations`

   **B.** `show ip nat statistics`

   **C.** `debug ip nat`

   **D.** `clear ip nat translations *`

**7.** Which command will create a dynamic pool named Todd that will provide you with 30 global addresses?

   **A.** `ip nat pool Todd 171.16.10.65 171.16.10.94 net 255.255.255.240`

   **B.** `ip nat pool Todd 171.16.10.65 171.16.10.94 net 255.255.255.224`

   **C.** `ip nat pool Todd 171.16.10.65 171.16.10.94 net 255.255.255.224`

   **D.** `ip nat pool Todd 171.16.10.1 171.16.10.254 net 255.255.255.0`

**8.** Which of the following are methods of NAT? (Choose three.)

   **A.** Static

   **B.** IP NAT pool

   **C.** Dynamic

   **D.** NAT double-translation

   **E.** Overload

**9.** When creating a pool of global addresses, which of the following can be used instead of the netmask command?

   **A.** / (slash notation)

   **B.** `prefix-length`

   **C.** `no mask`

   **D.** `block-size`

**10.** Which of the following would be a good starting point for troubleshooting if your router is not translating?

   **A.** Reboot

   **B.** Call Cisco

   **C.** Check your interfaces for the correct configuration

   **D.** Run the `debug all` command

11. Which of the following would be good reasons to run NAT? (Choose three.)

    A. You need to connect to the Internet and your hosts don't have globally unique IP addresses.

    B. You change to a new ISP that requires you to renumber your network.

    C. You don't want any hosts connecting to the Internet.

    D. You require two intranets with duplicate addresses to merge.

12. Which of the following is considered to be the inside host's address after translation?

    A. Inside local

    B. Outside local

    C. Inside global

    D. Outside global

13. Which of the following is considered to be the inside host's address before translation?

    A. Inside local

    B. Outside local

    C. Inside global

    D. Outside global

14. By looking at the following output, which of the following commands would allow dynamic translations?

```
Router#show ip nat trans
Pro    Inside global    Inside local    Outside local Outside global
---    1.1.128.1        10.1.1.1        ---           ---
---    1.1.130.178      10.1.1.2        ---           ---
---    1.1.129.174      10.1.1.10       ---           ---
---    1.1.130.101      10.1.1.89       ---           ---
---    1.1.134.169      10.1.1.100      ---           ---
---    1.1.135.174      10.1.1.200      ---           ---
```

    A. ip nat inside source pool todd 1.1.128.1 1.1.135.254 prefix-length 19

    B. ip nat pool todd 1.1.128.1 1.1.135.254 prefix-length 19

    C. ip nat pool todd 1.1.128.1 1.1.135.254 prefix-length 18

    D. ip nat pool todd 1.1.128.1 1.1.135.254 prefix-length 21

**15.** Your inside locals are not being translated to the inside global addresses. Which of the following commands will show you if your inside globals are allowed to use the NAT pool?

```
ip nat pool Corp 198.18.41.129 198.18.41.134 netmask 255.255.255.248
ip nat inside source list 100 int pool Corp overload
```

   **A.** debug ip nat

   **B.** show access-list

   **C.** show ip nat translation

   **D.** show ip nat statistics

**16.** Which command would you place on the interface of a private network?

   **A.** ip nat inside

   **B.** ip nat outside

   **C.** ip outside global

   **D.** ip inside local

**17.** Which command would you place on an interface connected to the Internet?

   **A.** ip nat inside

   **B.** ip nat outside

   **C.** ip outside global

   **D.** ip inside local

**18.** Port Address Translation is also called what?

   **A.** NAT Fast

   **B.** NAT Static

   **C.** NAT Overload

   **D.** Overloading Static

**19.** What does the asterisk (*) represent in the following output?

```
NAT*: s=172.16.2.2, d=192.168.2.1->10.1.1.1 [1]
```

   **A.** The packet was destined for a local interface on the router.

   **B.** The packet was translated and fast-switched to the destination.

   **C.** The packet attempted to be translated but failed.

   **D.** The packet was translated but there was no response from the remote host.

**20.** Which of the following needs to be added to the configuration to enable PAT?

```
ip nat pool Corp 198.18.41.129 198.18.41.134 netmask 255.255.255.248
access-list 1 permit 192.168.76.64 0.0.0.31
```

**A.** ip nat pool inside overload

**B.** ip nat inside source list 1 pool Corp overload

**C.** ip nat pool outside overload

**D.** ip nat pool Corp 198.41.129 net 255.255.255.0 overload

# Chapter

# 14

# Internet Protocol Version 6 (IPv6)

## THE FOLLOWING ICND1 EXAM TOPICS ARE COVERED IN THIS CHAPTER:

✓ **IP addressing (IPv4 / IPv6)**

- Identify the appropriate IPv6 addressing scheme to satisfy addressing requirements in a LAN/WAN environment

- Describe the technological requirements for running IPv6 in conjunction with IPv4 such as dual stack

- Describe IPv6 addresses

  - Global unicast

  - Multicast

  - Link local

  - Unique local

  - EUI 64

  - Autoconfiguration

✓ **IP Routing Technologies**

- Configure and verify OSPF (single area)

  - Configure OSPFv3

We've covered a lot of ground in this book, and though the journey has been tough at times, it's been well worth it! But our networking expedition isn't quite over yet because we still have the vastly important frontier of IPv6 to explore. There's still some expansive territory to cover with this sweeping new subject, so gear up and get ready to discover all you need to know about IPv6. Understanding IPv6 is vital now, so you'll be much better equipped and prepared to meet today's real-world networking challenges as well as to ace the exam. This final chapter is packed and brimming with all the IPv6 information you'll need to complete your Cisco exam trek successfully, so get psyched—we're in the home stretch!

I probably don't need to say this, but I will anyway because I really want to go the distance and do everything I can to ensure that you arrive and achieve... You absolutely must have a solid hold on IPv4 by now, but if you're still not confident with it, or feel you could use a refresher, just page back to the chapters on TCP/IP and subnetting. And if you're not crystal clear on the address problems inherent to IPv4, you really need to review Chapter 13, "Network Address Translation (NAT)", before we decamp for this chapter's IPv6 summit push!

People refer to IPv6 as "the next-generation Internet protocol," and it was originally created as the solution to IPv4's inevitable and impending address-exhaustion crisis. Though you've probably heard a thing or two about IPv6 already, it has been improved even further in the quest to bring us the flexibility, efficiency, capability, and optimized functionality that can affectively meet our world's seemingly insatiable thirst for ever-evolving technologies and increasing access. The capacity of its predecessor, IPv4, pales wan and ghostly in comparison, which is why IPv4 is destined to fade into history completely, making way for IPv6 and the future.

The IPv6 header and address structure has been completely overhauled, and many of the features that were basically just afterthoughts and addendums in IPv4 are now included as full-blown standards in IPv6. It's power-packed, well equipped with robust and elegant features, poised and prepared to manage the mind-blowing demands of the Internet to come!

After an introduction like that, I understand if you're a little apprehensive, but I promise—really—to make this chapter and its VIP topic pretty painless for you. In fact, you might even find yourself actually enjoying it—I definitely did! Because IPv6 is so complex, while still being so elegant, innovative, and powerful, it fascinates me like some weird combination of a sleek, new Aston Martin and a riveting futuristic novel. Hopefully you'll experience this chapter as an awesome ride and enjoy reading it as much as I did writing it!

To find up-to-the-minute updates for this chapter, please see www.lammle.com/forum or the book's web page at www.sybex.com.

# Why Do We Need IPv6?

Well, the short answer is because we need to communicate and our current system isn't really cutting it anymore. It's kind of like the Pony Express trying to compete with airmail! Consider how much time and effort we've been investing for years while we scratch our heads to resourcefully come up with slick new ways to conserve bandwidth and IP addresses. Sure, variable length subnet masks (VLSMs) are wonderful and cool, but they're really just another invention to help us cope while we desperately struggle to overcome the worsening address drought.

I'm not exaggerating, at all, about how dire things are getting, because it's simply reality. The number of people and devices that connect to networks increases dramatically each and every day, which is not a bad thing. We're just finding new and exciting ways to communicate to more people, more often, which is good thing. And it's not likely to go away or even decrease in the littlest bit, because communicating and making connections are, in fact, basic human needs—they're in our very nature. But with our numbers increasing along with the rising tide of people joining the communications party increasing as well, the forecast for our current system isn't exactly clear skies and smooth sailing. IPv4, upon which our ability to do all this connecting and communicating is presently dependent, is quickly running out of addresses for us to use.

IPv4 has only about 4.3 billion addresses available—in theory—and we know that we don't even get to use most of those! Sure, the use of Classless Inter-Domain Routing (CIDR) and Network Address Translation (NAT) has helped to extend the inevitable dearth of addresses, but we will still run out of them, and it's going to happen within a few years. China is barely online, and we know there's a huge population of people and corporations there that surely want to be. There are myriad reports that give us all kinds of numbers, but all you really need to think about to realize that I'm not just being an alarmist is this: there are about 7 billion people in the world today, and it's estimated that only just over 10 percent of that population is currently connected to the Internet—wow!

That statistic is basically screaming at us the ugly truth that based on IPv4's capacity, every person can't even have a computer, let alone all the other IP devices we use with them! I have more than one computer, and it's pretty likely that you do too, and I'm not even including phones, laptops, game consoles, fax machines, routers, switches, and a mother lode of other devices we use every day into the mix! So I think I've made it pretty clear that we've got to do something before we run out of addresses and lose the ability to connect with each other as we know it. And that "something" just happens to be implementing IPv6.

# The Benefits and Uses of IPv6

So what's so fabulous about IPv6? Is it really the answer to our coming dilemma? Is it really worth it to upgrade from IPv4? All good questions—you may even think of a few more. Of course, there's going to be that group of people with the time-tested "resistance to change syndrome," but don't listen to them. If we had done that years ago, we'd still be waiting weeks, even months for our mail to arrive via horseback. Instead, just know that the answer is a resounding *yes*, it is really the answer, and it is worth the upgrade! Not only does IPv6 give us lots of addresses ($3.4 \times 10^{38}$ = definitely enough), there are tons of other features built into this version that make it well worth the cost, time, and effort required to migrate to it.

Today's networks, as well as the Internet, have a ton of unforeseen requirements that simply weren't even considerations when IPv4 was created. We've tried to compensate with a collection of add-ons that can actually make implementing them more difficult than they would be if they were required by a standard. By default, IPv6 has improved upon and included many of those features as standard and mandatory. One of these sweet new standards is IPsec—a feature that provides end-to-end security.

But it's the efficiency features that are really going to rock the house! For starters, the headers in an IPv6 packet have half the fields, and they are aligned to 64 bits, which gives us some seriously souped-up processing speed. Compared to IPv4, lookups happen at light speed! Most of the information that used to be bound into the IPv4 header was taken out, and now you can choose to put it, or parts of it, back into the header in the form of optional extension headers that follow the basic header fields.

And of course there's that whole new universe of addresses—the $3.4 \times 10^{38}$ I just mentioned—but where did we get them? Did some genie just suddenly arrive and make them magically appear? That huge proliferation of addresses had to come from somewhere! Well it just so happens that IPv6 gives us a substantially larger address space, meaning the address itself is a whole lot bigger—four times bigger as a matter of fact! An IPv6 address is actually 128 bits in length, and no worries—I'm going to break down the address piece by piece and show you exactly what it looks like coming up in the section, "IPv6 Addressing and Expressions." For now, let me just say that all that additional room permits more levels of hierarchy inside the address space and a more flexible addressing architecture. It also makes routing much more efficient and scalable because the addresses can be aggregated a lot more effectively. And IPv6 also allows multiple addresses for hosts and networks. This is especially important for enterprises veritably drooling for enhanced access and availability. Plus, the new version of IP now includes an expanded use of multicast communication—one device sending to many hosts or to a select group—that joins in to seriously boost efficiency on networks because communications will be more specific.

IPv4 uses broadcasts quite prolifically, causing a bunch of problems, the worst of which is of course the dreaded broadcast storm. This is that uncontrolled deluge of forwarded broadcast traffic that can bring an entire network to its knees and devour every last bit of bandwidth! Another nasty thing about broadcast traffic is that it interrupts each and every device on the network. When a broadcast is sent out, every machine has to stop what it's doing and respond to the traffic whether the broadcast is relevant to it or not.

But smile assuredly, everyone. There's no such thing as a broadcast in IPv6 because it uses multicast traffic instead. And there are two other types of communications as well: unicast, which is the same as it is in IPv4, and a new type called *anycast*. Anycast communication allows the same address to be placed on more than one device so that when traffic is sent to the device service addressed in this way, it's routed to the nearest host that shares the same address. And this is just the beginning—we'll get into the various types of communication later in the section called, "Address Types."

# IPv6 Addressing and Expressions

Just as understanding how IP addresses are structured and used is critical with IPv4 addressing, it's also vital when it comes to IPv6. You've already read about the fact that at 128 bits, an IPv6 address is much larger than an IPv4 address. Because of this, as well as the new ways the addresses can be used, you've probably guessed that IPv6 will be more complicated to manage. But no worries! As I said, I'll break down the basics and show you what the address looks like and how you can write it as well as many of its common uses. It's going to be a little weird at first, but before you know it, you'll have it nailed!

So let's take a look at Figure 14.1, which has a sample IPv6 address broken down into sections.

**FIGURE 14.1**   IPv6 address example

As you can clearly see, the address is definitely much larger. But what else is different? Well, first, notice that it has eight groups of numbers instead of four and also that those groups are separated by colons instead of periods. And hey, wait a second... there are letters in that address! Yep, the address is expressed in hexadecimal just like a MAC address is, so you could say this address has eight 16-bit hexadecimal colon-delimited blocks. That's already quite a mouthful, and you probably haven't even tried to say the address out loud yet!

One other thing I want to point out is an important thing to keep in mind for when you set up your test network to actually experiment with IPv6 (because I know you're going to want to do that). When you use a web browser to make an HTTP connection to an IPv6 device, you have to type the address into the browser with brackets around the literal address. Why? Well, a colon is already being used by the browser for specifying a port number, so basically, if you don't enclose the address in brackets, the browser will have no way to identify the information.

Here's an example of how this looks:

```
http://[2001:0db8:3c4d:0012:0000:0000:1234:56ab]/default.html
```

Now obviously if you can, you would rather use names to specify a destination (like www.lammle.com), but even though it's definitely going to be a pain in the rear, we just have to accept the fact that sometimes we have to bite the bullet and type in the address number. So it should be pretty clear that DNS is going to remain extremely important when implementing IPv6.

 There are four hexadecimal characters (16 bits) in each IPv6 field, separated by colons.

## Shortened Expression

The good news is there are a few tricks to help rescue us when writing these monster addresses. For one thing, you can actually leave out parts of the address to abbreviate it, but to get away with doing that you have to follow a couple of rules. First, you can drop any leading zeros in each of the individual blocks. After you do that, the sample address from earlier would then look like this:

2001:db8:3c4d:12:0:0:1234:56ab

Okay, that's a definite improvement—at least we don't have to write all of those extra zeros! But what about whole blocks that don't have anything in them except zeros? Well, we can kind of lose those too—at least some of them. Again referring to our sample address, we can remove the two consecutive blocks of zeros by replacing them with a doubled colon, like this:

2001:db8:3c4d:12::1234:56ab

Cool—we replaced the blocks of all zeros with a doubled colon. The rule you have to follow to get away with this is that you can replace only one contiguous block of such zeros in an address. So if my address has four blocks of zeros and each of them were separated, I just don't get to replace them all because I can replace only one contiguous block with a doubled colon. Check out this example:

2001:0000:0000:0012:0000:0000:1234:56ab

And just know that you *can't* do this:

2001::12::1234:56ab

Instead, the best you can do is this:

2001::12:0:0:1234:56ab

The reason the preceding example is our best shot is that if we remove two sets of zeros, the device looking at the address will have no way of knowing where the zeros go back in.

Basically, the router would look at the incorrect address and say, "Well, do I place two blocks into the first set of doubled colons and two into the second set, or do I place three blocks into the first set and one block into the second set?" And on and on it would go because the information the router needs just isn't there.

## Address Types

We're all familiar with IPv4's unicast, broadcast, and multicast addresses that basically define who or at least how many other devices we're talking to. But as I mentioned, IPv6 modifies that trio and introduces the anycast. Broadcasts, as we know them, have been eliminated in IPv6 because of their cumbersome inefficiency and basic tendency to drive us insane!

So let's find out what each of these types of IPv6 addressing and communication methods do for us:

**Unicast**    Packets addressed to a unicast address are delivered to a single interface. For load balancing, multiple interfaces across several devices can use the same address, but we'll call that an anycast address. There are a few different types of unicast addresses, but we don't need to get further into that here.

**Global unicast addresses (2000::/3)**    These are your typical publicly routable addresses and they're the same as in IPv4. Global addresses start at 2000::/3. Figure 14.2 shows how a unicast address breaks down. The ISP can provide you with a minimum /48 network ID, which in turn provides you 16-bits to create a unique 64-bit router interface address. The last 64-bits are the unique host ID.

**FIGURE 14.2**    IPv6 global unicast addresses

**Link-local addresses (FE80::/10)**    These are like the Automatic Private IP Address (APIPA) addresses that Microsoft uses to automatically provide addresses in IPv4 in that they're not meant to be routed. In IPv6 they start with FE80::/10, as shown in Figure 14.3. Think of these addresses as handy tools that give you the ability to throw a temporary LAN together for meetings or create a small LAN that's not going to be routed but still needs to share and access files and services locally.

**FIGURE 14.3**     IPv6 link local FE80::/10: The first 10 bits define the address type.

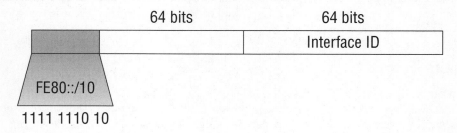

**Unique local addresses (FC00::/7)**   These addresses are also intended for nonrouting purposes over the Internet, but they are nearly globally unique, so it's unlikely you'll ever have one of them overlap. Unique local addresses were designed to replace site-local addresses, so they basically do almost exactly what IPv4 private addresses do: allow communication throughout a site while being routable to multiple local networks. Site-local addresses were deprecated as of September 2004.

**Multicast (FF00::/8)**   Again, as in IPv4, packets addressed to a multicast address are delivered to all interfaces tuned into the multicast address. Sometimes people call them "one-to-many" addresses. It's really easy to spot a multicast address in IPv6 because they always start with *FF*. We'll get deeper into multicast operation coming up in, "How IPv6 Works in an Internetwork."

**Anycast**   Like multicast addresses, an anycast address identifies multiple interfaces on multiple devices. But there's a big difference: the anycast packet is delivered to only one device—actually, to the closest one it finds defined in terms of routing distance. And again, this address is special because you can apply a single address to more than one host. These are referred to as "one-to-nearest" addresses. Anycast addresses are typically only configured on routers, never hosts, and a source address could never be an anycast address. Of note is that the IETF did reserve the top 128 addresses for each /64 for use with anycast addresses.

You're probably wondering if there are any special, reserved addresses in IPv6 because you know they're there in IPv4. Well there are—plenty of them! Let's go over those now.

## Special Addresses

I'm going to list some of the addresses and address ranges (in Table 14.1) that you should definitely make sure to remember because you'll eventually use them. They're all special or reserved for a specific use, but unlike IPv4, IPv6 gives us a galaxy of addresses, so reserving a few here and there doesn't hurt at all!

**TABLE 14.1**  Special IPv6 addresses

| Address | Meaning |
| --- | --- |
| 0:0:0:0:0:0:0:0 | Equals ::. This is the equivalent of IPv4's 0.0.0.0 and is typically the source address of a host before the host receives an IP address when you're using DHCP-driven stateful configuration. |
| 0:0:0:0:0:0:0:1 | Equals ::1. The equivalent of 127.0.0.1 in IPv4. |
| 0:0:0:0:0:0:192.168.100.1 | This is how an IPv4 address would be written in a mixed IPv6/IPv4 network environment. |
| 2000::/3 | The global unicast address range. |
| FC00::/7 | The unique local unicast range. |
| FE80::/10 | The link-local unicast range. |
| FF00::/8 | The multicast range. |
| 3FFF:FFFF::/32 | Reserved for examples and documentation. |
| 2001:0DB8::/32 | Also reserved for examples and documentation. |
| 2002::/16 | Used with 6-to-4 tunneling, which is an IPv4-to-IPv6 transition system. The structure allows IPv6 packets to be transmitted over an IPv4 network without the need to configure explicit tunnels. |

When you run IPv4 and IPv6 on a router, you have what is called "dual-stack."

Let me show you how IPv6 actually works in an internetwork. We all know how IPv4 works, so let's see what's new!

# How IPv6 Works in an Internetwork

It's time to explore the finer points of IPv6. A great place to start is by showing you how to address a host and what gives it the ability to find other hosts and resources on a network.

I'll also demonstrate a device's ability to automatically address itself—something called stateless autoconfiguration—plus another type of autoconfiguration known as stateful.

Keep in mind that stateful autoconfiguration uses a DHCP server in a very similar way to how it's used in an IPv4 configuration. I'll also show you how Internet Control Message Protocol (ICMP) and multicasting works for us in an IPv6 network environment.

## Manual Address Assignment

In order to enable IPv6 on a router, you have to use the ipv6 unicast-routing global configuration command:

```
Corp(config)#ipv6 unicast-routing
```

By default, IPv6 traffic forwarding is disabled, so using this command enables it. Also, as you've probably guessed, IPv6 isn't enabled by default on any interfaces either, so we have to go to each interface individually and enable it.

There are a few different ways to do this, but a really easy way is to just add an address to the interface. You use the interface configuration command ipv6 address <ipv6prefix>/<prefix-length> [eui-64]to get this done.

Here's an example:

```
Corp(config-if)#ipv6 address 2001:db8:3c4d:1:0260:d6FF.FE73:1987/64
```

You can specify the entire 128-bit global IPv6 address as I just demonstrated with the preceding command, or you can use the EUI-64 option. Remember, the EUI-64 (extended unique identifier) format allows the device to use its MAC address and pad it to make the interface ID. Check it out:

```
Corp(config-if)#ipv6 address 2001:db8:3c4d:1::/64 eui-64
```

As an alternative to typing in an IPv6 address on a router, you can enable the interface instead to permit the application of an automatic link-local address.

To configure a router so that it uses only link-local addresses, use the ipv6 enable interface configuration command:

```
Corp(config-if)#ipv6 enable
```

Remember, if you have only a link-local address, you will be able to communicate only on that local subnet.

## Stateless Autoconfiguration (EUI-64)

Autoconfiguration is an especially useful solution because it allows devices on a network to address themselves with a link-local unicast address as well as with a global unicast address. This process happens through first learning the prefix information from the router and then appending the device's own interface address as the interface ID. But where does it get that interface ID? Well, you know every device on an Ethernet network has a physical MAC address, which is exactly what's used for the interface ID. But since the interface ID in an IPv6 address is 64 bits in length and a MAC address is only 48 bits, where do the extra 16 bits come from? The MAC address is padded in the middle with the extra bits—it's padded with FFFE.

For example, let's say I have a device with a MAC address that looks like this: 0060:d673:1987. After it's been padded, it would look like this: 0260:d6FF:FE73:1987. Figure 14.4 illustrates what an EUI-64 address looks like.

**FIGURE 14.4**  EUI-64 interface ID assignment

So where did that 2 in the beginning of the address come from? Another good question. You see that part of the process of padding, called modified EUI-64 format, changes a bit to specify if the address is locally unique or globally unique. And the bit that gets changed is the 7th bit in the address.

The reason for modifying the U/L bit is that, when using manually assigned addresses on an interface, it means you can simply assign the address 2001:db8:1:9::1/64 instead of the much longer 2001:db8:1:9:0200::1/64. Also, if you are going to manually assign a link-local address, you can assign the short address fe80::1 instead of the long fe80::0200:0:0:1 or fe80:0:0:0:0200::1. So, even though at first glance it seems the IETF made this harder for you to simply understand IPv6 addressing by flipping the 7th bit, in reality this made addressing much simpler. Also, since most people don't typically override the burned-in address, the U/L bit is a 0, which means that you'll see this inverted to a 1 most of the time. But because you're studying the Cisco exam objectives, you'll need to look at inverting it both ways.

Here are a few examples:

- MAC address 0090:2716:fd0f
- IPv6 EUI-64 address: 2001:0db8:0:1:0290:27ff:fe16:fd0f

That one was easy! Too easy for the Cisco exam, so let's do another:

- MAC address aa12:bcbc:1234
- IPv6 EUI-64 address: 2001:0db8:0:1:a812:bcff:febc:1234

10101010 represents the first 8 bits of the MAC address (aa), which when inverting the 7th bit becomes 10101000. The answer becomes A8. I can't tell you how important this is for you to understand, so bear with me and work through a couple more!

- MAC address 0c0c:dede:1234
- IPv6 EUI-64 address: 2001:0db8:0:1:0e0c:deff:fede:1234

0c is 00001100 in the first 8 bits of the MAC address, which then becomes 00001110 when flipping the 7th bit. The answer is then 0e. Let's practice one more:

- MAC address 0b34:ba12:1234
- IPv6 EUI-64 address: 2001:0db8:0:1:0934:baff:fe12:1234

0b in binary is 00001011, the first 8 bits of the MAC address, which then becomes 00001001. The answer is 09.

 Pay extra-special attention to this EUI-64 address assignment and be able to convert the 7th bit based on the EUI-64 rules! Written Lab 14.2 will help you practice this.

To perform autoconfiguration, a host goes through a basic two-step process:

1. First, the host needs the prefix information, similar to the network portion of an IPv4 address, to configure its interface, so it sends a router solicitation (RS) request for it. This RS is then sent out as a multicast to all routers (FF02::2). The actual information being sent is a type of ICMP message, and like everything in networking, this ICMP message has a number that identifies it. The RS message is ICMP type 133.

2. The router answers back with the required prefix information via a router advertisement (RA). An RA message also happens to be a multicast packet that's sent to the all-nodes multicast address (FF02::1) and is ICMP type 134. RA messages are sent on a periodic basis, but the host sends the RS for an immediate response so it doesn't have to wait until the next scheduled RA to get what it needs.

These two steps are shown in Figure 14.5.

**FIGURE 14.5**   Two steps to IPv6 autoconfiguration

Step 1: Host sends RS message FF02::2 ICMP type 133

Step 2: Router sends RA message FF02::1 ICMP type 134

Host receives the RA and included prefix, allowing it to autoconfigure its interface.

By the way, this type of autoconfiguration is also known as stateless autoconfiguration because it doesn't contact or connect to and receive any further information from the other device. We'll get to stateful configuration when we talk about DHCPv6 next.

But before we do that, first take a look at Figure 14.6. In this figure, the Branch router needs to be configured, but I just don't feel like typing in an IPv6 address on the interface connecting to the Corp router. I also don't feel like typing in any routing commands, but I need more than a link-local address on that interface, so I'm going to have to do something! So basically, I want to have the Branch router work with IPv6 on the internetwork with the least amount of effort from me. Let's see if I can get away with that.

**FIGURE 14.6**   IPv6 autoconfiguration example

Ah ha—there is an easy way! I love IPv6 because it allows me to be relatively lazy when dealing with some parts of my network, yet it still works really well. By using the command `ipv6 address autoconfig`, the interface will listen for RAs and then, via the EUI-64 format, it will assign itself a global address—sweet!

Okay, this is all really great, but you're hopefully wondering what that `default` is doing there at the end of the command. If so, good catch! It happens to be a wonderful, optional part of the command that smoothly delivers a default route received from the Corp router, which will be automatically injected it into my routing table and set as the default route—so easy!

## DHCPv6 (Stateful)

DHCPv6 works pretty much the same way DHCP does in v4, with the obvious difference that it supports IPv6's new addressing scheme. And it might come as a surprise, but there are a couple of other options that DHCP still provides for us that autoconfiguration doesn't. And no, I'm not kidding— in autoconfiguration, there's absolutely no mention of DNS servers, domain names, or many of the other options that DHCP has always generously provided for us via IPv4. This is a big reason that the odds favor DHCP's continued use into the future in IPv6 at least partially—maybe even most of the time!

Upon booting up in IPv4, a client sends out a DHCP discover message looking for a server to give it the information it needs. But remember, in IPv6, the RS and RA process happens first, so if there's a DHCPv6 server on the network, the RA that comes back to the client will tell it if DHCP is available for use. If a router isn't found, the client will respond by sending out a DHCP solicit message, which is actually a multicast message addressed with a destination of ff02::1:2 that calls out, "All DHCP agents, both servers and relays."

It's good to know that there's some support for DHCPv6 in the Cisco IOS even though it's limited. This rather miserly support is reserved for stateless DHCP servers and tells us it doesn't offer any address management of the pool or the options available for configuring that address pool other than the DNS, domain name, default gateway, and SIP servers.

This means that you're definitely going to need another server around to supply and dispense all the additional, required information—maybe to even manage the address assignment, if needed!

## IPv6 Header

An IPv4 header is 20 bytes long, so since an IPv6 address is four times the size of IPv6 at 128 bits, then its header must then be 80 bytes long, right? That makes sense and is totally intuitive, but it's also completely wrong! When IPv6 designers devised the header, they created fewer, streamlined fields that would also result in a faster routed protocol at the same time. Let's take a look at the streamlined IPv6 header using Figure 14.7.

**FIGURE 14.7** IPv6 header

The basic IPv6 header contains eight fields, making it only twice as large as an IP header at 40 bytes. Let's zoom in on these fields:

**Version** This 4-bit field contains the number 6, instead of the number 4 as in IPv4.

**Traffic Class** This 8-bit field is like the Type of Service (ToS) field in IPv4.

**Flow Label** This new field, which is 24 bits long, is used to mark packets and traffic flows. A flow is a sequence of packets from a single source to a single destination host, an anycast or multicast address. The field enables efficient IPv6 flow classification.

**Payload Length** IPv4 had a total length field delimiting the length of the packet. IPv6's payload length describes the length of the payload only.

**Next Header**   Since there are optional extension headers with IPv6, this field defines the next header to be read. This is in contrast to IPv4, which demands static headers with each packet.

**Hop Limit**   This field specifies the maximum number of hops that an IPv6 packet can traverse.

**Source Address**   This field of 16 bytes or 128 bits identifies the source of the packet.

**Destination Address**   This field of 16 bytes or 128 bits identifies the destination of the packet.

There are also some optional extension headers following these eight fields, which carry other Network layer information. These header lengths are not a fixed number—they're of variable size.

It's time to move on to talk about another IPv4 familiar face and find out how a certain very important, built-in protocol has evolved in IPv6.

## ICMPv6

IPv4 used the ICMP workhorse for lots of tasks, including error messages like destination unreachable and troubleshooting functions like Ping and Traceroute. ICMPv6 still does those things for us, but unlike its predecessor, the v6 flavor isn't implemented as a separate layer 3 protocol. Instead, it's an integrated part of IPv6 and is carried after the basic IPv6 header information as an extension header. And ICMPv6 gives us another really cool feature—by default, it prevents IPv6 from doing any fragmentation through an ICMPv6 process called path MTU discovery. Figure 14.8 shows how ICMPv6 has evolved to become part of the IPv6 packet itself.

**FIGURE 14.8**   ICMPv6

The ICMPv6 packet is identified by the value 58 in the Next Header field, located inside the ICMPv6 packet. The Type field identifies the particular kind of ICMP message that's being carried, and the Code field further details the specifics of the message. The Data field contains the ICMPv6 payload.

And this is how it works: the source node of a connection sends a packet that's equal to the MTU size of its local link's MTU. As this packet traverses the path toward its destination, any link that has an MTU smaller than the size of the current packet will force the intermediate router to send a "packet too big" message back to the source machine. This message tells the source node what the maximum size the restrictive link will allow and asks the source to send a new scaled-down packet that can pass through. This process will continue until the destination is finally reached, with the source node now sporting the new path's MTU. So now, when the rest of the data packets are transmitted, they'll be protected from fragmentation.

ICMPv6 is used for router solicitation and advertisement, for neighbor solicitation and advertisement (i.e., finding the MAC data addresses for IPv6 neighbors), and for redirecting the host to the best router (default gateway).

## Neighbor Discovery (NDP)

ICMPv6 also takes over the task of finding the address of other devices on the local link. The Address Resolution Protocol is used to perform this function for IPv4, but that's been renamed neighbor discovery (ND) in ICMPv6. This process is now achieved via a multicast address called the solicited node address because all hosts join this multicast group upon connecting to the network.

Neighbor discovery enables these functions:

- Determining the MAC address of neighbors
- Router solicitation (RS) FF02::2
- Router advertisements (RA) FF02::1
- Neighbor solicitation (NS)
- Neighbor advertisement (NA)
- Duplicate address detection (DAD)

The part of the IPv6 address designated by the 24 bits farthest to the right is added to the end of the multicast address FF02:0:0:0:0:1:FF/104. When this address is queried, the corresponding host will send back its layer 2 address. Devices can find and keep track of other neighbor devices on the network in pretty much the same way. When I talked about RA and RS messages earlier and told you that they use multicast traffic to request and send address information, that too is actually a function of ICMPv6—specifically, neighbor discovery.

In IPv4, the protocol IGMP was used to allow a host device to tell its local router that it was joining a multicast group and would like to receive the traffic for that group. This IGMP function has been replaced by ICMPv6, and the process has been renamed multicast listener discovery.

With IPv4, our hosts could have only one default gateway configured, and if that router went down we had to either fix the router, change the default gateway, or run some type of virtual default gateway with other protocols created as a solution for this inadequacy in IPv4. Figure 14.9 shows how IPv6 devices find their default gateways using neighbor discovery.

**FIGURE 14.9**   Router solicitation (RS) and router advertisement (RA)

IPv6 hosts send a router solicitation (RS) onto their data link asking for all routers to respond, and they use the multicast address FF02::2 to achieve this. Routers on the same link respond with a unicast to the requesting host, or with a router advertisement (RA) using FF02::1.

But that's not all! Hosts also can send solicitations and advertisements between themselves using a neighbor solicitation (NS) and neighbor advertisement (NA), as shown in Figure 14.10. Remember that RA and RS gather or provide information about routers, and NS and NA gather information about hosts. Remember that a "neighbor" is a host on the same data link or VLAN.

**FIGURE 14.10**   Neighbor solicitation (NS) and neighbor advertisement (NA)

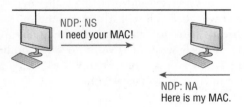

So what do you think are the odds that two hosts will assign themselves the same random IPv6 address? Personally, I think you could probably win the lotto every day for a year and still not come close to the odds against two hosts on the same data link duplicating an IPv6 address! Still, to make sure this doesn't ever happen, duplicate address detection (DAD) was created, which isn't an actual protocol, but a function of the NS/NA messages. Figure 14.11 shows how a host sends an NDP NS when it receives or creates an IPv6 address.

When hosts make up or receive an IPv6 address, they send three DADs out via NDP NS asking if anyone has this same address. The odds are unlikely that this will ever happen, but they ask anyway.

**FIGURE 14.11**    Duplicate address detection (DAD)

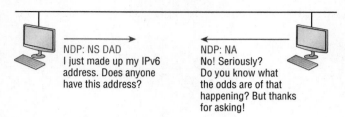

# IPv6 Routing Protocols

All of the routing protocols we've already discussed have been tweaked and upgraded for use in IPv6 networks, so it figures that many of the functions and configurations that you've already learned will be used in almost the same way as they are now. Knowing that broadcasts have been eliminated in IPv6, it's safe to conclude that any protocols relying entirely on broadcast traffic will go the way of the dodo. But unlike with the dodo, it'll be really nice to say goodbye to these bandwidth-hogging, performance-annihilating little gremlins!

The routing protocols we'll still use in IPv6 have been renovated and given new names. Even though this chapter's focus is on the Cisco exam objectives, which cover only static routing and OSPFv3, I want to discuss a few of the more important ones too.

First on the list is the IPv6 RIPng (next generation). Those of you who've been in IT for a while know that RIP has worked pretty well for us on smaller networks. This happens to be the very reason it didn't get whacked and will still be around in IPv6. And we still have EIGRPv6 because EIGRP already had protocol-dependent modules and all we had to do was add a new one to it to fit in nicely with the IPv6 protocol. Rounding out our group of protocol survivors is OSPFv3—that's not a typo, it really is v3! OSPF for IPv4 was actually v2, so when it got its upgrade to IPv6, it became OSPFv3.

## Static Routing with IPv6

Okay, now don't let the heading of this section scare you into looking on Monster.com for some job that has nothing to do with networking! I know that static routing has always run a chill up our collective spines because it's cumbersome, difficult, and really easy to screw up. And I won't lie to you—it's certainly not any easier with IPv6's longer addresses, but you can do it!

Okay—we know that to make static routing work, whether in IP or IPv6, you need these three tools:

- An accurate, up-to-date network map of your entire internetwork
- Next-hop address and exit interface for each neighbor connection
- All the remote subnet IDs

Of course, we don't need to have any of these for dynamic routing, which is why we mostly use dynamic routing. It's just so awesome to have the routing protocol do all that work for us by finding all the remote subnets and automatically placing them into the routing table!

Figure 14.12 shows a really good example of how to use static routing with IPv6. It really doesn't have to be that hard, but just as with IPv4, you absolutely need an accurate network map to make static routing work!

**FIGURE 14.12**   IPv6 static and default routing

So here's what I did: First, I created a static route on the Corp router to the remote network 2001:1234:4321:1::/64 using the next hop address. I could've just as easily used the Corp router's exit interface. Next, I just set up a default route for the Branch router with ::/0 and the Branch exit interface of Gi0/0—not so bad!

## OSPFv3

The new version of OSPF continues with the trend of routing protocols being quite similar to their IPv4 versions. For instance, the foundation of OSPF remains the same—it's still a link-state routing protocol that divides an entire internetwork or AS into areas, creating a hierarchy. And just trust me on this one—be really thankful that multi-area OSPF is beyond the scope for the Cisco objectives covered in this chapter!

Anyway, in OSPF version 2, the router ID (RID) is determined by either the highest IP addresses assigned to the router or one you manually assigned. In version 3, you assign the RID and area ID, which are both still 32-bit values but aren't found via the IP address anymore because an IPv6 address is 128 bits. Changes in how these values are assigned, plus the removal of the IP address information from OSPF packet headers, make the new version of OSPF flexible enough to be used over almost any Network layer protocol—sweet!

Adjacencies and next-hop attributes now use link-local addresses. OSPFv3 still uses multicast traffic to send its updates and acknowledgments, with the addresses FF02::5 for OSPF routers and FF02::6 for OSPF-designated routers. These new addresses are the replacements for 224.0.0.5 and 224.0.0.6, respectively.

Other, less-flexible IPv4 protocols just can't compete with OSPFv2's ability to assign specific networks and interfaces into the OSPF process, but these are still configured during router configuration. In OSPFv3, the interfaces and therefore the networks attached to them are simply configured directly on the interface in interface configuration mode instead.

Here's a sample of how the OSPFv3 configuration will look, starting with the optional configuration of the RID in global configuration mode:

```
Router1(config)#ipv6 router osfp 10
Router1(config-rtr)#router-id 1.1.1.1
```

You get to execute some configurations from router configuration mode, like summarization and redistribution, but we don't even need to configure OSPFv3 from this prompt if we configure OSPFv3 from the interface!

This is because if we go with the interface configuration option, the router configuration process is added automatically. The interface configuration looks like this:

```
Router1(config-if)#ipv6 ospf 10 area 0
```

So, if we just go to each interface and assign a process ID and area—shazam, we're done!

Let' configure static, default, and OSPFv3 routing on our internetwork. It's actually pretty painless, and there's still a lot for you to learn about OSPFv3!

# Configuring IPv6 on Our Internetwork

We're going to continue working on the same internetwork we've been configuring throughout this book, as shown in Figure 14.13. Let's add IPv6 to the Corp, SF, and LA routers by using a simple subnet scheme of 11, 12, 13, 14, and 15. After that, we'll add the OSPFv3 routing protocol. Notice in Figure 14.13 how the subnet numbers are the same on each end of the WAN links. Keep in mind that we'll finish this chapter by running through some verification commands.

As usual, I'll start with the Corp router:

```
Corp#config t
Corp(config)#ipv6 unicast-routing
Corp(config)#int f0/0
Corp(config-if)#ipv6 address 2001:db8:3c4d:11::/64 eui-64
Corp(config-if)#int s0/0
Corp(config-if)#ipv6 address 2001:db8:3c4d:12::/64 eui-64
Corp(config-if)#int s0/1
Corp(config-if)#ipv6 address 2001:db8:3c4d:13::/64 eui-64
Corp(config-if)#^Z
Corp#copy run start
```

```
Destination filename [startup-config]?[enter]
Building configuration...
[OK]
```

**FIGURE 14.13**  Our internetwork

Pretty simple! In the above configuration, I only changed the subnet address for each interface slightly. Let's take a look at the routing table now:

```
Corp(config-if)#do sho ipv6 route
C    2001:DB8:3C4D:11::/64 [0/0]
     via ::, FastEthernet0/0
L    2001:DB8:3C4D:11:20D:BDFF:FE3B:D80/128 [0/0]
     via ::, FastEthernet0/0
C    2001:DB8:3C4D:12::/64 [0/0]
     via ::, Serial0/0
L    2001:DB8:3C4D:12:20D:BDFF:FE3B:D80/128 [0/0]
     via ::, Serial0/0
C    2001:DB8:3C4D:13::/64 [0/0]
     via ::, Serial0/1
L    2001:DB8:3C4D:13:20D:BDFF:FE3B:D80/128 [0/0]
     via ::, Serial0/1
L    FE80::/10 [0/0]
     via ::, Null0
L    FF00::/8 [0/0]
     via ::, Null0
Corp(config-if)#
```

Alright, but what's up with those two addresses for each interface? One shows C for connected, one shows L. The connected address indicates the IPv6 address I configured on each interface and the L is the link-local that's been automatically assigned. Notice in the link-local address that the FF:FE is inserted into the address to create the EUI-64 address.

Let's configure the SF router now:

```
SF#config t
SF(config)#ipv6 unicast-routing
SF(config)#int s0/0/0
SF(config-if)#ipv6 address 2001:db8:3c4d:12::/64
% 2001:DB8:3C4D:12::/64 should not be configured on Serial0/0/0, a subnet router
anycast
SF(config-if)#ipv6 address 2001:db8:3c4d:12::/64 eui-64
SF(config-if)#int fa0/0
SF(config-if)#ipv6 address 2001:db8:3c4d:14::/64 eui-64
SF(config-if)#^Z
SF#show ipv6 route
C   2001:DB8:3C4D:12::/64 [0/0]
     via ::, Serial0/0/0
L   2001:DB8:3C4D:12::/128 [0/0]
     via ::, Serial0/0/0
L   2001:DB8:3C4D:12:21A:2FFF:FEE7:4398/128 [0/0]
     via ::, Serial0/0/0
C   2001:DB8:3C4D:14::/64 [0/0]
     via ::, FastEthernet0/0
L   2001:DB8:3C4D:14:21A:2FFF:FEE7:4398/128 [0/0]
     via ::, FastEthernet0/0
L   FE80::/10 [0/0]
     via ::, Null0
L   FF00::/8 [0/0]
     via ::, Null0
```

Did you notice that I used the exact IPv6 subnet addresses on each side of the serial link? Good... but wait—what's with that anycast error I received when trying to configure the interfaces on the SF router? I didn't meant to create that error; it happened because I forgot to add the eui-64 at the end of the address. Still, what's behind that error? An anycast address is a host address of all 0s, meaning the last 64 bits are all off, but by typing in /64 without the eui-64, I was telling the interface that the unique identifier would be nothing but zero's, and that's not allowed!

Let's configure the LA router now, and then add OSPFv3:

```
SF#config t
SF(config)#ipv6 unicast-routing
```

```
SF(config)#int s0/0/1
SF(config-if)#ipv6 address 2001:db8:3c4d:13::/64 eui-64
SF(config-if)#int f0/0
SF(config-if)#ipv6 address 2001:db8:3c4d:15::/64 eui-64
SF(config-if)#do show ipv6 route
C   2001:DB8:3C4D:13::/64 [0/0]
      via ::, Serial0/0/1
L   2001:DB8:3C4D:13:21A:6CFF:FEA1:1F48/128 [0/0]
      via ::, Serial0/0/1
C   2001:DB8:3C4D:15::/64 [0/0]
      via ::, FastEthernet0/0
L   2001:DB8:3C4D:15:21A:6CFF:FEA1:1F48/128 [0/0]
      via ::, FastEthernet0/0
L   FE80::/10 [0/0]
      via ::, Null0
L   FF00::/8 [0/0]
      via ::, Null0
```

This looks good, but I want you to notice that I used the exact same IPv6 subnet addresses on each side of the links from the Corp router to the SF router as well as from the Corp to the LA router. Now let's start adding OSPFv3!

# Configuring Routing on Our Internetwork

We're going to begin with default routing and then deal with OSPFv3. I'll start at the Corp router and add simple static routes. Check it out:

```
Corp(config)#ipv6 route 2001:db8:3c4d:14::/64  2001:DB8:3C4D:12:21A:2FFF:
FEE7:4398 150
Corp(config)#ipv6 route 2001:DB8:3C4D:15::/64 s0/1 150
Corp(config)#do sho ipv6 route static
[output cut]
S   2001:DB8:3C4D:14::/64 [150/0]
      via 2001:DB8:3C4D:12:21A:2FFF:FEE7:4398
```

Okay—I agree that first static route line was pretty long because I used the next-hop address, but notice that I used the exit interface on the second entry. But it still wasn't really all that hard to create the longer static route entry. I just went to the SF router, used the command show ipv6 int brief, and then copied and pasted the interface address used for the next hop. You'll get used to IPv6 addresses (You'll get used to doing a lot of copy/paste moves!).

Okay, now since I put an AD of 150 on the static routes, once I configure OSPF they'll be replaced with an OSPF injected route. Let's go to the SF and LA routers and put a single entry in each router to get to remote subnet 11.

```
SF(config)#ipv6 route 2001:db8:3c4d:11::/64 s0/0/0 150
```

That's it! I'm going to head over to LA and put a default route on that router now:

```
LA(config)#ipv6 route ::/0 s0/0/1
```

Let's take a peek at the Corp router's routing table and see if our static routes are in there.

```
Corp#sh ipv6 route static
[output cut]
S    2001:DB8:3C4D:14::/64 [150/0]
     via 2001:DB8:3C4D:12:21A:2FFF:FEE7:4398
S    2001:DB8:3C4D:15::/64 [150/0]
     via ::, Serial0/1
```

Voilà! I can see both of my static routes in the routing table, so IPv6 can now route to those networks. But we're not done because we still need to test our network! First I'm going to go to the SF router and get the IPv6 address of the Fa0/0 interface:

```
SF#sh ipv6 int brief
FastEthernet0/0               [up/up]
    FE80::21A:2FFF:FEE7:4398
    2001:DB8:3C4D:14:21A:2FFF:FEE7:4398
FastEthernet0/1               [administratively down/down]
Serial0/0/0                   [up/up]
    FE80::21A:2FFF:FEE7:4398
    2001:DB8:3C4D:12:21A:2FFF:FEE7:4398
```

Next, I'm going to go back to the Corporate router and ping that remote interface by copying and pasting in the address. No sense doing all that typing when copy/paste works great!

```
Corp#ping ipv6 2001:DB8:3C4D:14:21A:2FFF:FEE7:4398
Type escape sequence to abort.
Sending 5, 100-byte ICMP Echos to 2001:DB8:3C4D:14:21A:2FFF:FEE7:4398, timeout is
2 seconds:
!!!!!
Success rate is 100 percent (5/5), round-trip min/avg/max = 0/0/0 ms
Corp#
```

We can see that static route worked, so next, I'll go get the IPv6 address of the LA router and ping that remote interface as well:

```
LA#sh ipv6 int brief
FastEthernet0/0            [up/up]
    FE80::21A:6CFF:FEA1:1F48
    2001:DB8:3C4D:15:21A:6CFF:FEA1:1F48
Serial0/0/1               [up/up]
    FE80::21A:6CFF:FEA1:1F48
    2001:DB8:3C4D:13:21A:6CFF:FEA1:1F48
```

It's time to head over to Corp and ping LA:

```
Corp#ping ipv6 2001:DB8:3C4D:15:21A:6CFF:FEA1:1F48
Type escape sequence to abort.
Sending 5, 100-byte ICMP Echos to 2001:DB8:3C4D:15:21A:6CFF:FEA1:1F48, timeout is
2 seconds:
!!!!!
Success rate is 100 percent (5/5), round-trip min/avg/max = 4/4/4 ms
Corp#
```

Static routing really isn't so bad with IPv6! I'm not saying I'd like to do this in a ginormous network—no way—I wouldn't want to opt for doing that with IPv4 either! But you can see that it can be done. Also, notice how easy it was to ping an IPv6 address. Copy/paste really is your friend!

Okay, since I created my static and default routes with an AD of 150, I can see that the OSPF routes have replaced the static ones in the routing table by turning on OSPF. All we have to do in order to enable OSPF on the internetwork is to individually deal with each interface we want to run OSPF on.

Here's the Corp configuration:

```
Corp(config)#int f0/0
Corp(config-if)#ipv6 ospf 1 area 0
Corp(config-if)#int s0/0
Corp(config-if)#ipv6 ospf 1 area 0
Corp(config-if)#int s0/1
Corp(config-if)#ipv6 ospf 1 area 0
```

This is actually much easier than it is with IPv4! Let's configure the other two routers now:

```
SF(config)#int f0/0
SF(config-if)#ipv6 ospf 1 area 0
SF(config-if)#int s0/0/0
SF(config-if)#ipv6 ospf 1 area 0
```

```
*May 10 23:06:10.432: %OSPFv3-5-ADJCHG: Process 1, Nbr 172.131.1.1
on Serial0/0/0 from LOADING to FULL, Loading Done
```

Sweet! SF has become adjacent to the Corp router. One interesting output is that the 32-bit address RID is being used in the OSPFv3 adjacent change.

```
LA#config t
LA(config)#int fa0/0
LA(config-if)#ipv6 ospf 1 area 0
LA(config-if)#int s0/0/1
LA(config-if)#ipv6 ospf 1 area 0
*May 10 23:42:56.865: %OSPFv3-5-ADJCHG: Process 1, Nbr 172.31.1.2
on FastEthernet0/0 from LOADING to FULL, Loading Done
*May 10 23:42:57.197: %OSPFv3-5-ADJCHG: Process 1, Nbr 172.131.1.1
on Serial0/0/1 from LOADING to FULL, Loading Done
```

Presto—again, our adjacency popped up. This is great! Without even verifying our network, it appears that our internetwork is up and running. But, we still have to verify!

Before we do that, remember that fourth router I used back in Chapter 9, "Open Shortest Path First (OSPF)," to demonstrate the OSPF configuration and verification? I want to use it again here. I named that router Boulder, and here is its simple configuration, because having another router on the backbone area will really make a difference in our verification commands:

```
Boulder#config t
Boulder(config)#int f0/0
Boulder(config-if)#ipv6 address autoconfig default
Boulder(config-if)#ipv6 ospf 1 area 0
*Apr 15 00:21:18.986: %OSPFv3-5-ADJCHG: Process 1, Nbr 172.131.1.1 on
FastEthernet0/0 from LOADING to FULL, Loading Done
```

I couldn't even remember the IPv4 address that I assigned to the router's Fa0/0 interface, but it doesn't matter because I just configured this router without adding even a single address! And yet there it is—up and working! Yea IPv6! Since I had the Corp router configured, I just told the Boulder router to autoconfigure the interface, then added Fa0/0 into OSPF area 0.

## Verifying OSPFv3

Because verification is always important, I'll run through the commands needed to verify OSPFv3. I'll start with the show ipv6 route command:

```
Corp#sh ipv6 route ospf
[output cut]
O    2001:DB8:3C4D:14::/64 [110/65]
```

```
        via FE80::21A:2FFF:FEE7:4398, Serial0/0
O   2001:DB8:3C4D:15::/64 [110/65]
        via FE80::21A:6CFF:FEA1:1F48, Serial0/1
Corp#
```

Perfect! I see both remote subnets 15 and 16 off the SF and LA routers, and the static routes are no longer in the routing table because they had a higher AD. Let's take a look at what the show ipv6 protocols command reveals:

```
Corp#show ipv6 protocols
IPv6 Routing Protocol is "connected"
IPv6 Routing Protocol is "static"
IPv6 Routing Protocol is "ospf 1"
  Interfaces (Area 0):
    Serial0/1
    Serial0/0
    FastEthernet0/0
  Redistribution:
  None
```

This is an interesting command for sure, and it shows us the interfaces running the OSPF process, but it's very useful if you have multiple routing protocols buzzing around. A command for checking your RID is also a compelling prospect, so let's see what doing that reveals:

```
Corp#sh ipv6 ospf
Routing Process "ospfv3 1" with ID 223.255.255.254
SPF schedule delay 5 secs, Hold time between two SPFs 10 secs
Minimum LSA interval 5 secs. Minimum LSA arrival 1 secs
LSA group pacing timer 240 secs
Interface flood pacing timer 33 msecs
Retransmission pacing timer 66 msecs
Number of external LSA 0. Checksum Sum 0x000000
Number of areas in this router is 1. 1 normal 0 stub 0 nssa
Reference bandwidth unit is 100 mbps
    Area BACKBONE(0) (Inactive)
        Number of interfaces in this area is 1
        SPF algorithm executed 1 times
        Number of LSA 3. Checksum Sum 0x019C58
        Number of DCbitless LSA 0
        Number of indication LSA 0
        Number of DoNotAge LSA 0
        Flood list length 0 --More--
```

The first line shows the process number and the router ID. Did you happen to notice that it's the same RID we set for our IPv4 OSPF RID back in Chapter 9? Let's change the RID under the OSPF process ID in the global configuration and see what happens:

```
Corp#config t
Corp(config)#ipv6 router ospf 1
Corp(config-rtr)#router-id 1.1.1.1
Reload or use "clear ip ospf process" command, for this to take effect
Corp(config-rtr)#do clear ip ospf process
Reset ALL OSPF processes? [no]: yes
```

Even though this is the first time I've used global configuration mode to configure options for OSPF, it's working just fine. Let's check our RID now:

```
Corp(config-router)#do sh ipv6 ospf
Routing Process "ospfv3 1" with ID 1.1.1.1
 SPF schedule delay 5 secs, Hold time between two SPFs 10 secs
 Minimum LSA interval 5 secs. Minimum LSA arrival 1 secs
 LSA group pacing timer 240 secs
[output cut]
```

Let's check on the Corp router's OSPF neighbors with the show ipv6 ospf neighbor command:

```
Corp#sh ipv6 ospf neighbor
Neighbor ID     Pri   State        Dead Time    Interface ID     Interface
192.168.20.1     1    FULL/  -     00:00:33     7                  Serial0/1
172.31.1.2       1    FULL/  -     00:00:33     6                  Serial0/0
10.10.10.2       1    FULL/BDR     00:00:39     4              FastEthernet0/0
Corp#
```

I know it is weird to look at the output of an IPv6 command and see IPv4 addresses, because the listed neighbor ID is clearly the RID of our neighbors. Actually, I'm really glad the IETF used a 32-bit address for the RID. Did we really need more 128-bit addresses hanging around our networks to confuse us even more?

And of course, no verification would be complete without the show ipv6 interfaces command:

```
Corp#sh ipv6 int
FastEthernet0/0 is up, line protocol is up
  IPv6 is enabled, link-local address is FE80::20D:BDFF:FE3B:D80
  No Virtual link-local address(es):
  Global unicast address(es):
    2001:DB8:3C4D:11:20D:BDFF:FE3B:D80, subnet is 2001:DB8:3C4D:11::/64 [EUI]
  Joined group address(es):
    FF02::1
```

```
      FF02::2
      FF02::5
      FF02::6
      FF02::1:FF3B:D80
    MTU is 1500 bytes
    ICMP error messages limited to one every 100 milliseconds
    ICMP redirects are enabled
    ICMP unreachables are sent
    ND DAD is enabled, number of DAD attempts: 1
    ND reachable time is 30000 milliseconds
    ND advertised reachable time is 0 milliseconds
    ND advertised retransmit interval is 0 milliseconds
    ND router advertisements are sent every 200 seconds
    ND router advertisements live for 1800 seconds
    ND advertised default router preference is Medium
    Hosts use stateless autoconfig for addresses.
  Serial0/0 is up, line protocol is up
    IPv6 is enabled, link-local address is FE80::20D:BDFF:FE3B:D80
    No Virtual link-local address(es):
    Global unicast address(es):
      2001:DB8:3C4D:12:20D:BDFF:FE3B:D80, subnet is 2001:DB8:3C4D:12::/64 [EUI]
    Joined group address(es):
  [output cut]
```

This output reveals the interface IPv6 address, and even the subnet address is listed in there. Now let's use one of my favorite commands:

```
Corp#sh ipv6 int brief
FastEthernet0/0          [up/up]
    FE80::20D:BDFF:FE3B:D80
    2001:DB8:3C4D:11:20D:BDFF:FE3B:D80
Serial0/0                [up/up]
    FE80::20D:BDFF:FE3B:D80
    2001:DB8:3C4D:12:20D:BDFF:FE3B:D80
FastEthernet0/1          [administratively down/down]
    unassigned
Serial0/1                [up/up]
    FE80::20D:BDFF:FE3B:D80
    2001:DB8:3C4D:13:20D:BDFF:FE3B:D80
Loopback0                [up/up]
    unassigned
Corp#
```

What a nice output! All our interfaces are up/up and we can see the link-local and assigned global address.

But we still need to execute our debugging commands, and I'm going to use two of them: the debug ipv6 ospf packet and debug ipv6 ospf hello. By the way, these are the same commands I used with IPv4:

```
Corp#debug ipv6 ospf packet
OSPFv3 packet debugging is on
*Jan 26 14:49:40.738: OSPFv3: rcv. v:3 t:1 l:40 rid:10.10.10.2
     aid:0.0.0.0 chk:AFF9 inst:0 from FastEthernet0/0
*Jan 26 14:49:43.982: OSPFv3: rcv. v:3 t:1 l:40 rid:172.31.1.2
     aid:0.0.0.0 chk:2E42 inst:0 from Serial0/0
*Jan 26 14:49:44.306: OSPFv3: rcv. v:3 t:1 l:40 rid:192.168.20.1
     aid:0.0.0.0 chk:EE4E inst:0 from Serial0/1
*Jan 26 14:49:50.738: OSPFv3: rcv. v:3 t:1 l:40 rid:10.10.10.2
     aid:0.0.0.0 chk:AFF9 inst:0 from FastEthernet0/0
*Jan 26 14:49:53.982: OSPFv3: rcv. v:3 t:1 l:40 rid:172.31.1.2
     aid:0.0.0.0 chk:2E42 inst:0 from Serial0/0
*Jan 26 14:49:54.306: OSPFv3: rcv. v:3 t:1 l:40 rid:192.168.20.1
     aid:0.0.0.0 chk:EE4E inst:0 from Serial0/1
Corp#un all
All possible debugging has been turned off
Corp#debug ipv6 ospf hello
OSPFv3 hello events debugging is on
*Jan 26 14:50:10.738: OSPFv3: Rcv hello from 10.10.10.2 area 0
 from FastEthernet0/0 FE80::20D:BDFF:FE3B:C20 interface ID 4
*Jan 26 14:50:10.738: OSPFv3: End of hello processing
*Jan 26 14:50:13.982: OSPFv3: Rcv hello from 172.31.1.2 area 0
 from Serial0/0 FE80::21A:2FFF:FEE7:4398 interface ID 6
*Jan 26 14:50:13.982: OSPFv3: End of hello processing
*Jan 26 14:50:14.306: OSPFv3: Rcv hello from 192.168.20.1 area 0
 from Serial0/1 FE80::21A:6CFF:FEA1:1F48 interface ID 7
*Jan 26 14:50:14.310: OSPFv3: End of hello processing
*Jan 26 14:50:20.738: OSPFv3: Rcv hello from 10.10.10.2 area 0
 from FastEthernet0/0 FE80::20D:BDFF:FE3B:C20 interface ID 4
*Jan 26 14:50:20.738: OSPFv3: End of hello processing
*Jan 26 14:50:23.982: OSPFv3: Rcv hello from 172.31.1.2 area 0
 from Serial0/0 FE80::21A:2FFF:FEE7:4398 interface ID 6
*Jan 26 14:50:23.982: OSPFv3: End of hello processing
*Jan 26 14:50:24.310: OSPFv3: Rcv hello from 192.168.20.1 area 0
 from Serial0/1 FE80::21A:6CFF:FEA1:1F48 interface ID 7
*Jan 26 14:50:24.310: OSPFv3: End of hello processing
```

Holy output! That pretty much gives us the big picture! I hope you found this chapter as rewarding as I did. The best thing you can do to learn IPv6 is to get some routers and just go at it. Don't give up because it's seriously worth your time!

# Summary

This last chapter introduced you to some very key IPv6 structural elements as well as how to make IPv6 work within a Cisco internetwork. You now know that even when covering and configuring IPv6 basics, there's still a great deal to understand—and we just scratched the surface! But you're still well equipped with all you need to meet the Cisco exam objectives.

You learned the vital reasons why we need IPv6 and the benefits associated with it. I covered IPv6 addressing and the importance of using the shortened expressions. As I covered addressing with IPv6, I also showed you the different address types, plus the special addresses reserved in IPv6.

IPv6 will mostly be deployed automatically, meaning hosts will employ autoconfiguration. I demonstrated how IPv6 utilizes autoconfiguration and how it comes into play when configuring a Cisco router. You also learned that in IPv6, we can and still should use a DHCP server to the router to provide options to hosts just as we've been doing for years with IPv4—not necessarily IPv6 addresses, but other mission-critical options like providing a DNS server address.

From there, I discussed the evolution of some more integral and familiar protocols like ICMP and OSPF. They've been upgraded to work in the IPv6 environment, but these networking workhorses are still vital and relevant to operations, and I detailed how ICMP works with IPv6, followed by how to configure OSPFv3. I wrapped up this pivotal chapter by demonstrating key methods to use when verifying that all is running correctly in your IPv6 network. So take some time and work through all the essential study material, especially the written labs, to ensure that you meet your networking goals!

# Exam Essentials

**Understand why we need IPv6.**   Without IPv6, the world would be depleted of IP addresses.

**Understand link-local.**   Link-local is like an IPv4 private IP address, but it can't be routed at all, not even in your organization.

**Understand unique local.**   This, like link-local, is like a private IP address in IPv4 and cannot be routed to the Internet. However, the difference between link-local and unique local is that unique local can be routed within your organization or company.

**Remember IPv6 addressing.**   IPv6 addressing is not like IPv4 addressing. IPv6 addressing has much more address space, is 128 bits long, and represented in hexadecimal, unlike IPv4, which is only 32 bits long and represented in decimal.

**Understand and be able to read a EUI-64 address with the 7th bit inverted.**   Hosts can use autoconfiguration to obtain an IPv6 address, and one of those ways is through what is called EUI-64. This takes the unique MAC address of a host and inserts FF:FE in the middle of the address to change a 48-bit MAC address to a 64-bit interface ID. In addition to inserting the 16-bits into the interface ID, the 7th bit of the first byte is inverted, typically from a 0 to a 1. Practice this with Written Lab 14.2.

# Written Labs

The answers to these labs can be found in Appendix A, "Answers to Written Labs."

## Written Lab 14.1

In this section, write the answers to the following IPv6 questions:

1. Which type of packet is addressed and delivered to only a single interface?
2. Which type of address is used just like a regular public routable address in IPv4?
3. Which type of address is not meant to be routed?
4. Which type of address is not meant to be routed to the Internet but is still globally unique?
5. Which type of address is meant to be delivered to multiple interfaces?
6. Which type of address identifies multiple interfaces, but packets are delivered only to the first address it finds?
7. Which routing protocol uses multicast address FF02::5?
8. IPv4 had a loopback address of 127.0.0.1. What is the IPv6 loopback address?
9. What does a link-local address always start with?
10. What does a unique local unicast range start with?

## Written Lab 14.2

In this section, you will practice inverting the 7th bit of a EUI-64 address. Use the prefix 2001:db8:1:1/64 for each address.

1. Convert the following MAC address into a EUI-64 address: 0b0c:abcd:1234.
2. Convert the following MAC address into a EUI-64 address: 060c:32f1:a4d2.
3. Convert the following MAC address into a EUI-64 address: 10bc:abcd:1234.
4. Convert the following MAC address into a EUI-64 address: 0d01:3a2f:1234.
5. Convert the following MAC address into a EUI-64 address: 0a0c.abac.caba.

# Hands-on Labs

You'll need at least three routers to complete these labs, five would be better, but if you are using the LammleSim IOS version, then these lab layouts are preconfigured for you. This section will have you configure the following labs:

Lab 14.1: Manual and Stateful Autoconfiguration

Lab 14.2: Static and Default Routing

Lab 14.3: OSPFv3

Here is our network:

## Hands-on Lab 14.1: Manual and Stateful Autoconfiguration

In this lab, you will configure the C router with manual IPv6 addresses on the Fa0/0 and Fa0/1 interfaces and then configure the other routers to automatically assign themselves an IPv6 address.

1. Log in to the C router and configure IPv6 addresses on each interface based on the subnets (1 and 2) shown in the graphic.

```
C(config)#ipv6 unicast-routing
C(config)#int fa0/0
C(config-if)#ipv6 address 2001:db8:3c4d:1::1/64
C(config-if)#int fa0/1
C(config-if)#ipv6 address 2001:db8:3c4d:2::1/64
```

2. Verify the interfaces with the show ipv6 route connected and sho ipv6 int brief commands.

```
C(config-if)#do show ipv6 route connected
[output cut]
C   2001:DB8:3C4D:1::/64 [0/0]
     via ::, FastEthernet0/0
C   2001:DB8:3C4D:2::/64 [0/0]
     via ::, FastEthernet0/0
```

```
C(config-if)#sh ipv6 int brief
FastEthernet0/0            [up/up]
    FE80::20D:BDFF:FE3B:D80
    2001:DB8:3C4D:1::1
FastEthernet0/1            [up/up]
    FE80::20D:BDFF:FE3B:D81
    2001:DB8:3C4D:2::1
Loopback0                  [up/up]
    Unassigned
```

3. Go to your other routers and configure the Fa0/0 on each router to autoconfigure an IPv6 address.

```
A(config)#ipv6 unicast-routing
A(config)#int f0/0
A(config-if)#ipv6 address autoconfig
A(config-if)#no shut


B(config)#ipv6 unicast-routing
B(config)#int fa0/0
B(config-if)#ipv6 address autoconfig
B(config-if)#no shut


D(config)#ipv6 unicast-routing
D(config)#int fa0/0
D(config-if)#ipv6 address autoconfig
D(config-if)#no shut


E(config)#ipv6 unicast-routing
E(config)#int fa0/0
E(config-if)#ipv6 address autoconfig
E(config-if)#no shut
```

4. Verify that your routers received an IPv6 address.

```
A#sh ipv6 int brief
FastEthernet0/0            [up/up]
    FE80::20D:BDFF:FE3B:C20
    2001:DB8:3C4D:1:20D:BDFF:FE3B:C20
```

Continue to verify your addresses on all your other routers.

# Hands-on Lab 14.2: Static and Default Routing

Router C is directly connected to both subnets, so no routing of any type needs to be configured. However, all the other routers are connected to only one subnet, so at least one route needs to be configured on each router.

**1.** On the A router, configure a static route to the 2001:db8:3c4d:2::/64 subnet.

```
A(config)#ipv6 route 2001:db8:3c4d:2::/64 fa0/0
```

**2.** On the B router, configure a default route.

```
B(config)#ipv6 route ::/0 fa0/0
```

**3.** On the D router, create a static route to the remote subnet.

```
D(config)#ipv6 route 2001:db8:3c4d:1::/64 fa0/0
```

**4.** On the E router, create a static route to the remote subnet.

```
E(config)#ipv6 route 2001:db8:3c4d:1::/64 fa0/0
```

**5.** Verify your configurations with a show running-config and show ipv6 route.

**6.** Ping from router D to router A. First, you need to get router A's IPv6 address with a show ipv6 int brief command. Here is an example:

```
A#sh ipv6 int brief
FastEthernet0/0           [up/up]
    FE80::20D:BDFF:FE3B:C20
    2001:DB8:3C4D:1:20D:BDFF:FE3B:C20
```

**7.** Now go to router D and ping the IPv6 address from router A:

```
D#ping ipv6 2001:DB8:3C4D:1:20D:BDFF:FE3B:C20
Type escape sequence to abort.
Sending 5, 100-byte ICMP Echos to 2001:DB8:3C4D:1:20D:BDFF:FE3B:C20, timeout
is 2 seconds:
!!!!!
Success rate is 100 percent (5/5), round-trip min/avg/max = 0/2/4 ms
```

Our static and default routing is working. Now let's add OSPFv3.

# Hands-on Lab 14.3: OSPFv3

In this lab, you'll add OSPFv3 to your routers.

**1.** Before you start configuring OSPF, you need to remove any static and default routing you have configured on your routers.

```
A(config)#no ipv6 route 2001:db8:3c4d:2::/64 fa0/0
B(config)#no ipv6 route ::/0 fa0/0
D(config)#no ipv6 route 2001:db8:3c4d:1::/64 fa0/0
E(config)#no ipv6 route 2001:db8:3c4d:1::/64 fa0/0
```

**2.** Go to each router and configure each interface with IPv6 OSPFv3. If you don't have IPv4 configured on your routers, you'll need to create a RID at global configuration mode.

```
A(config)#ipv6 router ospf 1
A(config-rtr)#router-id 1.1.1.1
A(config-rtr)#int f0/0
A(config-if)#ipv6 ospf 1 area 0


B(config)#ipv6 router ospf 1
B(config-rtr)#router-id 2.2.2.2
B(config-rtr)#int f0/0
B(config-if)#ipv6 ospf 1 area 0


C(config)#ipv6 router ospf 1
C(config-rtr)#router-id 3.3.3.3
C(config-rtr)#int f0/0
C(config-if)#ipv6 ospf 1 area 0
C(config-if)#int fa0/1
C(config-if)#ipv6 ospf 1 area 0


D(config)#ipv6 router ospf 1
D(config-rtr)#router-id 4.4.4.4
D(config-rtr)#int f0/0
D(config-if)#ipv6 ospf 1 area 0


E(config)#ipv6 router ospf 1
E(config-rtr)#router-id 5.5.5.5
E(config-rtr)#int f0/0
E(config-if)#ipv6 ospf 1 area 0
```

3. From each router, use the following commands to verify your network.

   A#**sh ipv6 route**

   A#**sh ipv6 route ospf**

   A#**sh ipv6 int fa0/0**

   A#**sh ipv6 neighbor**

4. From each router, ping the other routers. First, you need to get the address of each interface.

   A#**sh ipv6 int brief**

   B#**sh ipv6 int brief**

   C#**sh ipv6 int brief**

   D#**sh ipv6 int brief**

   E#**sh ipv6 int brief**

5. Using the addresses you learned in step 4, ping to the neighbor routers, as in this example:

   A#**ping ipv6 2001:DB8:3C4D:1:20D:BDFF:FE3B:C20**

# Review Questions

The answers to these questions can be found in Appendix B, "Answers to Chapter Review Questions."

1. Which of the following is true when describing a global unicast address?

   A. Packets addressed to a unicast address are delivered to a single interface.

   B. These are your typical publicly routable addresses, just like a regular publicly routable address in IPv4.

   C. These are like private addresses in IPv4 in that they are not meant to be routed over the Internet.

   D. These addresses are meant for nonrouting purposes, but they are almost globally unique, so it is unlikely they will have an address overlap.

2. Which of the following is true when describing a unicast address?

   A. Packets addressed to a unicast address are delivered to a single interface.

   B. These are your typical publicly routable addresses, just like a regular publicly routable address in IPv4.

   C. These are like private addresses in IPv4 in that they are not meant to be routed.

   D. These addresses are meant for nonrouting purposes, but they are almost globally unique, so it is unlikely they will have an address overlap.

3. Which of the following is true when describing a link-local address?

   A. Packets addressed to a broadcast address are delivered to a single interface.

   B. These are your typical publicly routable addresses, just like a regular publicly routable address in IPv4.

   C. These are like private addresses in IPv4 in that they are not meant to be routed over the Internet.

   D. These addresses are meant for nonrouting purposes, but they are almost globally unique, so it is unlikely they will have an address overlap.

4. Which of the following is true when describing a unique local address?

   **A.** Packets addressed to a unique local address are delivered to a single interface.

   **B.** These are your typical publicly routable addresses, just like a regular publicly routable address in IPv4.

   **C.** These are like private addresses in IPv4 in that they are not meant to be routed.

   **D.** These addresses are not meant for Internet routing purposes, but they are unique, so it is unlikely they will have an address overlap.

5. Which of the following is true when describing a multicast address?

   **A.** Packets addressed to a multicast address are delivered to a single interface.

   **B.** Packets are delivered to all interfaces identified with the address. This is also called a one-to-many address.

   **C.** A multicast address identifies multiple interfaces and is delivered to only one address. This address can also be called one-to-one-of-many.

   **D.** These addresses are meant for nonrouting purposes, but they are almost globally unique, so it is unlikely they will have an address overlap.

6. Which of the following is true when describing an anycast address?

   **A.** Packets addressed to an anycast address are delivered to a single interface.

   **B.** Packets are delivered to all interfaces identified by the address. This is also called a one-to-many address.

   **C.** This address identifies multiple interfaces and the anycast packet is only delivered to one device. This address can also be called one-to-one-of-many.

   **D.** These addresses are meant for nonrouting purposes, but they are almost globally unique, so it is unlikely they will have an address overlap.

7. You want to ping the loopback address of your IPv6 local host. What will you type?

   **A.** `ping 127.0.0.1`

   **B.** `ping 0.0.0.0`

   **C.** `ping ::1`

   **D.** `trace 0.0.::1`

8. What two multicast addresses does OSPFv3 use? (Choose two.)

   **A.** FF02::A

   **B.** FF02::9

   **C.** FF02::5

   **D.** FF02::6

**9.** An IPv6 hostname Host A is trying to connect to a web page on a remote server. Which of the following is true? (Choose two.)

**A.** A RA would be used by R1 to communicate its layer 2 MAC address to Host A.

**B.** OSPFv2 is used for the routers to share IPv6 routes.

**C.** IPv6 uses a two-part addressing scheme, similar to the way IPv4 uses a network and host portion of an IPv4 address.

**D.** Host A would send the server's link-local address to the router.

**10.** A host sends a router solicitation (RS) on the data link. What destination address is sent with this request?

**A.** FF02::A

**B.** FF02::9

**C.** FF02::2

**D.** FF02::1

**E.** FF02::5

**11.** IPv6 unicast routing is running on the Corp router. Which of the following addresses would show up with the show ipv6 int brief command?

```
Corp#sh int f0/0
FastEthernet0/0 is up, line protocol is up
  Hardware is AmdFE, address is 000d.bd3b.0d80 (bia 000d.bd3b.0d80)
[output cut]
```

**A.** FF02::3c3d:0d:bdff:fe3b:0d80

**B.** FE80::3c3d:2d:bdff:fe3b:0d80

**C.** FE80::3c3d:0d:bdff:fe3b:0d80

**D.** FE80::3c3d:2d:ffbd:3bfe:0d80

**12.** A host sends a type of NDP message providing the MAC address that was requested. Which type of NDP was sent?

   **A.** NA

   **B.** RS

   **C.** RA

   **D.** NS

**13.** To enable OSPFv3, which of the following would you use?

   **A.** `Router(config-if)#ipv6 ospf 10 area 0.0.0.0`

   **B.** `Router(config-if)#ipv6 router rip 1`

   **C.** `Router(config)#ipv6 router eigrp 10`

   **D.** `Router(config-rtr)#no shutdown`

   **E.** `Router(config-if)#ospf ipv6 10 area 0`

**14.** Which of the following statements about IPv6 addresses are true? (Choose two.)

   **A.** Leading zeros are required.

   **B.** Two colons (::) are used to represent successive hexadecimal fields of zeros.

   **C.** Two colons (::) are used to separate fields.

   **D.** A single interface will have multiple IPv6 addresses of different types.

**15.** What two statements about IPv4 and IPv6 addresses are true? (Choose two.)

   **A.** An IPv6 address is 32 bits long, represented in hexadecimal.

   **B.** An IPv6 address is 128 bits long, represented in decimal.

   **C.** An IPv4 address is 32 bits long, represented in decimal.

   **D.** An IPv6 address is 128 bits long, represented in hexadecimal.

**16.** Which of the following descriptions about IPv6 is correct?

   **A.** Addresses are not hierarchical and are assigned at random.

   **B.** Broadcasts have been eliminated and replaced with multicasts.

   **C.** There are 2.7 billion addresses.

   **D.** An interface can only be configured with one IPv6 address.

**17.** How many bits are in an IPv6 address field?

   **A.** 24

   **B.** 4

   **C.** 3

   **D.** 16

   **E.** 32

   **F.** 128

**18.** Which of the following correctly describe characteristics of IPv6 unicast addressing? (Choose two.)

   **A.** Global addresses start with 2000::/3.

   **B.** Link-local addresses start with FF00::/10.

   **C.** Link-local addresses start with FE00:/12.

   **D.** There is only one loopback address and it is ::1.

**19.** Which of the following statements are true of IPv6 address representation? (Choose two.)

   **A.** The first 64 bits represent the dynamically created interface ID.

   **B.** A single interface may be assigned multiple IPv6 addresses of any type.

   **C.** Every IPv6 interface contains at least one loopback address.

   **D.** Leading zeroes in an IPv6 16-bit hexadecimal field are mandatory.

**20.** Which of the following is true regarding OSPFv3? (Choose three.)

   **A.** Uses a wildcard to define interfaces

   **B.** Uses a network command under global configuration mode

   **C.** Uses a 32-bit router ID

   **D.** Uses link-state advertisements

   **E.** Uses an interface command to enable OSPF on an interface

# Appendix

# A

# Answers to Written Labs

# Chapter 1: Internetworking

## Written Lab 1.1: OSI Questions

1. The Application layer is responsible for finding the network resources broadcast from a server and adding flow control and error control (if the application developer chooses).

2. The Physical layer takes frames from the Data Link layer and encodes the 1s and 0s into a digital signal for transmission on the network medium.

3. The Network layer provides routing through an internetwork and logical addressing.

4. The Presentation layer makes sure that data is in a readable format for the Application layer.

5. The Session layer sets up, maintains, and terminates sessions between applications.

6. PDUs at the Data Link layer are called frames and provide physical addressing plus other options to place packets on the network medium.

7. The Transport layer uses virtual circuits to create a reliable connection between two hosts.

8. The Network layer provides logical addressing, typically IP addressing and routing.

9. The Physical layer is responsible for the electrical and mechanical connections between devices.

10. The Data Link layer is responsible for the framing of data packets.

11. The Session layer creates sessions between different hosts' applications.

12. The Data Link layer frames packets received from the Network layer.

13. The Transport layer segments user data.

14. The Network layer creates packets out of segments handed down from the Transport layer.

**15.** The Physical layer is responsible for transporting 1s and 0s (bits) in a digital signal.

**16.** Segments, packets, frames, bits

**17.** Transport

**18.** Data Link

**19.** Network

**20.** 48 bits (6 bytes) expressed as a hexadecimal number

# Written Lab 1.2: Defining the OSI Layers and Devices

| Description | Device or OSI Layer |
| --- | --- |
| This device sends and receives information about the Network layer. | Router |
| This layer creates a virtual circuit before transmitting between two end stations. | Transport |
| This device uses hardware addresses to filter a network. | Bridge or switch |
| Ethernet is defined at these layers. | Data Link and Physical |
| This layer supports flow control, sequencing, and acknowledgments. | Transport |
| This device can measure the distance to a remote network. | Router |
| Logical addressing is used at this layer. | Network |
| Hardware addresses are defined at this layer. | Data Link (MAC sublayer) |
| This device creates one big collision domain and one large broadcast domain. | Hub |
| This device creates many smaller collision domains, but the network is still one large broadcast domain. | Switch or bridge |
| This device can never run full-duplex. | Hub |
| This device breaks up collision domains and broadcast domains. | Router |

# Written Lab 1.3: Identifying Collision and Broadcast Domains

**A.** Hub: One collision domain, one broadcast domain

**B.** Bridge: Two collision domains, one broadcast domain

**C.** Switch: Four collision domains, one broadcast domain

**D.** Router: Three collision domains, three broadcast domains

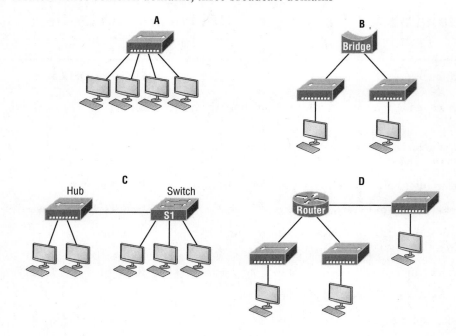

# Chapter 2: Ethernet Networking and Data Encapsulation

## Written Lab 2.1: Binary/Decimal/Hexadecimal Conversion

**1.**

| Decimal | 128 | 64 | 32 | 16 | 8 | 4 | 2 | 1 | Binary |
|---|---|---|---|---|---|---|---|---|---|
| 192 | 1 | 1 | 0 | 0 | 0 | 0 | 0 | 0 | 11000000 |
| 168 | 1 | 0 | 1 | 0 | 1 | 0 | 0 | 0 | 10101000 |
| 10 | 0 | 0 | 0 | 0 | 1 | 0 | 1 | 0 | 00001010 |
| 15 | 0 | 0 | 0 | 0 | 1 | 1 | 1 | 1 | 00001111 |

| Decimal | 128 | 64 | 32 | 16 | 8 | 4 | 2 | 1 | Binary |
|---|---|---|---|---|---|---|---|---|---|
| 172 | 1 | 0 | 1 | 0 | 1 | 1 | 0 | 0 | 10101100 |
| 16 | 0 | 0 | 0 | 1 | 0 | 0 | 0 | 0 | 00010000 |
| 20 | 0 | 0 | 0 | 1 | 0 | 1 | 0 | 0 | 00010100 |
| 55 | 0 | 0 | 1 | 1 | 0 | 1 | 1 | 1 | 00110111 |

| Decimal | 128 | 64 | 32 | 16 | 8 | 4 | 2 | 1 | Binary |
|---|---|---|---|---|---|---|---|---|---|
| 10 | 0 | 0 | 0 | 0 | 1 | 0 | 1 | 0 | 00001010 |
| 11 | 0 | 0 | 0 | 0 | 1 | 0 | 1 | 1 | 00001011 |
| 12 | 0 | 0 | 0 | 0 | 1 | 1 | 0 | 0 | 00001100 |
| 99 | 0 | 1 | 1 | 0 | 0 | 0 | 1 | 1 | 01100011 |

**2.**

| Binary | 128 | 64 | 32 | 16 | 8 | 4 | 2 | 1 | Decimal |
|--------|-----|----|----|----|---|---|---|---|---------|
| 11001100 | 1 | 1 | 0 | 0 | 1 | 1 | 0 | 0 | 204 |
| 00110011 | 0 | 0 | 1 | 1 | 0 | 0 | 1 | 1 | 51 |
| 10101010 | 1 | 0 | 1 | 0 | 1 | 0 | 1 | 0 | 170 |
| 01010101 | 0 | 1 | 0 | 1 | 0 | 1 | 0 | 1 | 85 |

| Binary | 128 | 64 | 32 | 16 | 8 | 4 | 2 | 1 | Decimal |
|--------|-----|----|----|----|---|---|---|---|---------|
| 11000110 | 1 | 1 | 0 | 0 | 0 | 1 | 1 | 0 | 198 |
| 11010011 | 1 | 1 | 0 | 1 | 0 | 0 | 1 | 1 | 211 |
| 00111001 | 0 | 0 | 1 | 1 | 1 | 0 | 0 | 1 | 57 |
| 11010001 | 1 | 1 | 0 | 1 | 0 | 0 | 0 | 1 | 209 |

| Binary | 128 | 64 | 32 | 16 | 8 | 4 | 2 | 1 | Decimal |
|--------|-----|----|----|----|---|---|---|---|---------|
| 10000100 | 1 | 0 | 0 | 0 | 0 | 1 | 0 | 0 | 132 |
| 11010010 | 1 | 1 | 0 | 1 | 0 | 0 | 1 | 0 | 210 |
| 10111000 | 1 | 0 | 1 | 1 | 1 | 0 | 0 | 0 | 184 |
| 10100110 | 1 | 0 | 1 | 0 | 0 | 1 | 1 | 0 | 166 |

**3.**

| Binary | 128 | 64 | 32 | 16 | 8 | 4 | 2 | 1 | Hexadecimal |
|--------|-----|----|----|----|---|---|---|---|-------------|
| 11011000 | 1 | 1 | 0 | 1 | 1 | 0 | 0 | 0 | D8 |
| 00011011 | 0 | 0 | 0 | 1 | 1 | 0 | 1 | 1 | 1B |
| 00111101 | 0 | 0 | 1 | 1 | 1 | 1 | 0 | 1 | 3D |
| 01110110 | 0 | 1 | 1 | 1 | 0 | 1 | 1 | 0 | 76 |

| Binary | 128 | 6 | 32 | 16 | 8 | 4 | 2 | 1 | Hexadecimal |
|---|---|---|---|---|---|---|---|---|---|
| 11001010 | 1 | 1 | 0 | 0 | 1 | 0 | 1 | 0 | CA |
| 11110101 | 1 | 1 | 1 | 1 | 0 | 1 | 0 | 1 | F5 |
| 10000011 | 1 | 0 | 0 | 0 | 0 | 0 | 1 | 1 | 83 |
| 11101011 | 1 | 1 | 1 | 0 | 1 | 0 | 1 | 1 | EB |

| Binary | 128 | 64 | 32 | 16 | 8 | 4 | 2 | 1 | Hexadecimal |
|---|---|---|---|---|---|---|---|---|---|
| 10000100 | 1 | 0 | 0 | 0 | 0 | 1 | 0 | 0 | 84 |
| 11010010 | 1 | 1 | 0 | 1 | 0 | 0 | 1 | 0 | D2 |
| 01000011 | 0 | 1 | 0 | 0 | 0 | 0 | 1 | 1 | 43 |
| 10110011 | 1 | 0 | 1 | 1 | 0 | 0 | 1 | 1 | B3 |

## Written Lab 2.2: CSMA/CD Operations

When a collision occurs on an Ethernet LAN, the following happens:

1. A jam signal informs all devices that a collision occurred.
2. The collision invokes a random back-off algorithm.
3. Each device on the Ethernet segment stops transmitting for a short time until the timers expire.
4. All hosts have equal priority to transmit after the timers have expired.

## Written Lab 2.3: Cabling

1. Crossover
2. Straight-through
3. Crossover
4. Crossover
5. Straight-through
6. Crossover
7. Crossover
8. Rolled

## Written Lab 2.4: Encapsulation

At a transmitting device, the data encapsulation method works like this:

1. User information is converted to data for transmission on the network.

2. Data is converted to segments, and a reliable connection is set up between the transmitting and receiving hosts.

3. Segments are converted to packets or datagrams, and a logical address is placed in the header so each packet can be routed through an internetwork.

4. Packets or datagrams are converted to frames for transmission on the local network. Hardware (Ethernet) addresses are used to uniquely identify hosts on a local network segment.

5. Frames are converted to bits, and a digital encoding and clocking scheme is used.

# Chapter 3: Introduction to TCP/IP

## Written Lab 3.1: TCP/IP

1. 192 through 223, 110*xxxxx*

2. Host-to-host

3. 1 through 126

4. Loopback or diagnostics

5. Turn all host bits off.

6. Turn all host bits on.

7. 10.0.0.0 through 10.255.255.255

8. 172.16.0.0 through 172.31.255.255

9. 192.168.0.0 through 192.168.255.255

10. 0 through 9 and *A*, *B*, *C*, *D*, *E*, and *F*

## Written Lab 3.2: Mapping Applications to the DoD Model

1. Internet

2. Process/Application

3. Process/Application

4. Process/Application

5. Process/Application

6. Internet
7. Process/Application
8. Host-to-host
9. Process/Application
10. Host-to-host
11. Process/Application
12. Internet
13. Internet
14. Internet
15. Process/Application
16. Process/Application
17. Process/Application

# Chapter 4: Easy Subnetting

## Written Lab 4.1: Written Subnet Practice #1

1. 192.168.100.25/30. A /30 is 255.255.255.252. The valid subnet is 192.168.100.24, broadcast is 192.168.100.27, and valid hosts are 192.168.100.25 and 26.

2. 192.168.100.37/28. A /28 is 255.255.255.240. The fourth octet is a block size of 16. Just count by 16s until you pass 37. 0, 16, 32, 48. The host is in the 32 subnet, with a broadcast address of 47. Valid hosts 33–46.

3. A /27 is 255.255.255.224. The fourth octet is a block size of 32. Count by 32s until you pass the host address of 66. 0, 32, 64, 96. The host is in the 64 subnet, and the broadcast address is 95. Valid host range is 65–94.

4. 192.168.100.17/29. A /29 is 255.255.255.248. The fourth octet is a block size of 8. 0, 8, 16, 24. The host is in the 16 subnet, broadcast of 23. Valid hosts 17–22.

5. 192.168.100.99/26. A /26 is 255.255.255.192. The fourth octet has a block size of 64. 0, 64, 128. The host is in the 64 subnet, broadcast of 127. Valid hosts 65–126.

6. 192.168.100.99/25. A /25 is 255.255.255.128. The fourth octet is a block size of 128. 0, 128. The host is in the 0 subnet, broadcast of 127. Valid hosts 1–126.

7. A default Class B is 255.255.0.0. A Class B 255.255.255.0 mask is 256 subnets, each with 254 hosts. We need fewer subnets. If we used 255.255.240.0, this provides 16 subnets. Let's add one more subnet bit. 255.255.248.0. This is 5 bits of subnetting, which provides 32 subnets. This is our best answer, a /21.

8. A /29 is 255.255.255.248. This is a block size of 8 in the fourth octet. 0, 8, 16. The host is in the 8 subnet, broadcast is 15.

9. A /29 is 255.255.255.248, which is 5 subnet bits and 3 host bits. This is only 6 hosts per subnet.

10. A /23 is 255.255.254.0. The third octet is a block size of 2. 0, 2, 4. The subnet is in the 16.2.0 subnet; the broadcast address is 16.3.255.

# Written Lab 4.2: Written Subnet Practice #2

**Written Lab 4.3:** Written Subnet Practice #3

| Classful Address | Subnet Mask | Number of Hosts per Subnet ($2^x - 2$) |
| --- | --- | --- |
| /16 | 255.255.0.0 | 65,534 |
| /17 | 255.255.128.0 | 32,766 |
| /18 | 255.255.192.0 | 16,382 |
| /19 | 255.255.224.0 | 8,190 |
| /20 | 255.255.240.0 | 4,094 |
| /21 | 255.255.248.0 | 2,046 |
| /22 | 255.255.252.0 | 1,022 |
| /23 | 255.255.254.0 | 510 |
| /24 | 255.255.255.0 | 254 |
| /25 | 255.255.255.128 | 126 |
| /26 | 255.255.255.192 | 62 |
| /27 | 255.255.255.224 | 30 |
| /28 | 255.255.255.240 | 14 |
| /29 | 255.255.255.248 | 6 |
| /30 | 255.255.255.252 | 2 |

## Written Lab 4.3: Written Subnet Practice #3

| Decimal IP Address | Address Class | Number of Subnet and Host Bits | Number of Subnets ($2x$) | Number of Hosts ($2x - 2$) |
|---|---|---|---|---|
| 10.25.66.154/23 | A | 15/9 | 32,768 | 510 |
| 172.31.254.12/24 | B | 8/8 | 256 | 254 |
| 192.168.20.123/28 | C | 4/4 | 16 | 14 |
| 63.24.89.21/18 | A | 10/14 | 1,024 | 16,382 |
| 128.1.1.254/20 | B | 4/12 | 16 | 4,094 |
| 208.100.54.209/30 | C | 6/2 | 64 | 2 |

# Chapter 5: VLSMs, Summarization and Troubleshooting TCP/IP

1. 192.168.0.0/20
2. 172.144.0.0 255.240.0.0
3. 192.168.32.0 255.255.224.0
4. 192.168.96.0 255.255.240.0
5. 66.66.0.0 255.255.240.0
6. 192.168.0.0/25
7. 172.16.1.0 255.255.248.0
8. 192.168.128.0 255.255.192.0
9. 53.60.96.0 255.255.224.0
10. 172.16.0.0 255.255.192.0

# Chapter 6: Cisco's Internetworking Operating System (IOS)

## Written Lab 6

1. Router(config)#**clock rate 1000000**
2. Switch#**config t**
   switch config)# **line vty 0 15**
   switch(config-line)# **no login**
3. Switch#**config t**
   Switch(config)# **int f0/1**
   Switch(config-if)# **no shutdown**
4. Switch#**erase startup-config**
5. Switch#**config t**
   Switch(config)# **line console 0**
   Switch(config)# **password todd**
   Switch(config)# **login**
6. Switch#**config t**
   Switch(config)# **enable secret cisco**
7. Router#**show controllers serial 0/2**
8. Switch#**show terminal**
9. Switch#**reload**
10. Switch#**config t**
    Switch(config)#**hostname Sales**

# Chapter 7: Managing a Cisco Internetwork

## Written Lab 7.1: IOS Management

1. copy start run
2. show cdp neighbor detail or show cdp entry *
3. show cdp neighbor

**4.** Ctrl+Shift+6, then X

**5.** show sessions

**6.** Either copy tftp run or copy start run

**7.** NTP

**8.** ip helper-address

**9.** ntp server *ip_address* version 4

**10.** show ntp status

## Written Lab 7.2: Router Memory

**1.** Flash memory

**2.** ROM

**3.** NVRAM

**4.** ROM

**5.** RAM

**6.** RAM

**7.** ROM

**8.** ROM

**9.** RAM

**10.** RAM

# Chapter 8: IP Routing

**1.** router(config)#**ip route 172.16.10.0 255.255.255.0 172.16.20.1 150**

**2.** It will use the gateway interface MAC at L2 and the actual destination IP at L3.

**3.** router(config)#**ip route 0.0.0.0 0.0.0.0 172.16.40.1**

**4.** Stub network

**5.** Router#**show ip route**

**6.** Exit interface

**7.** False. The MAC address would be the router interface, not the remote host.

**8.** True

**9.** router(config)#**router rip**

router(config-router)#**passive-interface S1**

**10.** True

# Chapter 9: Open Shortest Path First (OSPF)

1. `router ospf 101`
2. `show ip ospf`
3. `show ip ospf interface`
4. `show ip ospf neighbor`
5. `show ip route ospf`

# Chapter 10: Layer 2 Switching

1. `show mac address-table`
2. Flood the frame out all ports except the port on which it was received
3. Address learning, forward/filter decisions, and loop avoidance
4. It will add the source MAC address in the forward/filter table and associate it with the port on which the frame was received.
5. Maximum 1, violation shutdown

# Chapter 11: VLANs and InterVLAN Routing

1. False! You do not provide an IP address under any physical port.
2. STP
3. Broadcast
4. Collision
5. `switchport trunk encapsulation dot1q`
6. Trunking allows you to make a single port part of multiple VLANs at the same time.
7. Frame identification (frame tagging) uniquely assigns a user-defined ID to each frame. This is sometimes referred to as a VLAN ID or color.
8. True
9. Access link
10. `switchport trunk native vlan 4`

# Chapter 12: Security

1. access-list 10 deny 172.16.0.0 0.0.255.255
    access-list 10 permit any
2. ip access-group 10 out
3. access-list 10 deny host 192.168.15.5
    access-list 10 permit any
4. show access-lists
5. IDS, IPS
6. access-list 110 deny tcp host
    172.16.10.1 host  172.16.30.5 eq 23
    access-list 110 permit ip any any
7. line vty 0 4
    access-class 110 in
8. ip access-list standard No172Net
    deny 172.16.0.0 0.0.255.255
    permit any
9. ip access-group No172Net out
10. show ip interfaces

# Chapter 13: Network Address Translation

1. Port Address Translation (PAT), also called NAT Overload
2. debug ip nat
3. show ip nat translations
4. clear ip nat translations *
5. Before
6. After
7. show ip nat statistics
8. The ip nat inside and ip nat outside commands
9. Dynamic NAT
10. prefix-length

# Chapter 14: Internet Protocol Version 6 (IPv6)

## Written Lab 14.1

1. Unicast
2. Global unicast
3. Link-local
4. Unique local (used to be called site-local)
5. Multicast
6. Anycast
7. OSPFv3
8. ::1
9. FE80::/10
10. FC00:: /7

## Written Lab 14.2

1. 2001:db8:1:1:090c:abff:fecd:1234
2. 2001:db8:1:1: 040c:32ff:fef1:a4d2
3. 2001:db8:1:1:12:abff:fecd:1234
4. 2001:db8:1:1:0f01:3aff:fe2f:1234
5. 2001:db8:1:1:080c:abff:feac:caba

# Appendix B

# Answers to Review Questions

# Chapter 1: Internetworking

1. A. The device shown is a hub and hubs place all ports in the same broadcast domain and the same collision domain.

2. B. The contents of a protocol data unit (PDU) depend on the PDU as they are created in a specific order and their contents are based on that order. A packet will contain IP addresses but not MAC addresses as MAC addresses are not present until the PDU becomes a frame.

3. C. You should select a router to connect the two groups. When computers are in different subnets, as these two groups are, you will require a device that can make decisions based on IP addresses. Routers operate at layer 3 of the Open Systems Interconnect (OSI) model and make data-forwarding decisions based on layer 3 networking information, which are IP addresses. They create routing tables that guide them in forwarding traffic out of the proper interface to the proper subnet.

4. C. Replacing the hub with a switch would reduce collisions and retransmissions which would have the most impact on reducing congestion.

5. Answer:

| Layer | Description |
|---|---|
| Transport | Bits |
| Data Link | Segment |
| Physical | Packet |
| Network | Frame |

The given layers of the OSI model use the PDUs shown in the above diagram.

6. C. The diagram depicts the three steps taken to create a TCP connection.

7. B. You should use a switch to accomplish the task in this scenario. A switch is used to provide dedicated bandwidth to each node by eliminating the possibility of collisions on the switch port where the node resides. Switches work at layer 2 in the Open System Interconnection (OSI) model and perform the function of separating collision domains.

**8.**

| | |
|---|---|
| Transport | End-to-end connection |
| Physical | Conversion to bits |
| Data Link | Framing |
| Network | Routing |

The listed layers of the OSI model have the functions shown in the diagram above.

**9.** D. Reliable data delivery ensures the integrity of a stream of data sent from one machine to the other through a fully functional data link. It guarantees that the data won't be duplicated or lost. This is achieved through something called positive acknowledgment with retransmission—a technique that requires a receiving machine to communicate with the transmitting source by sending an acknowledgment message, based on the window size, back to the sender when it receives data.

**10.** B. Protocols used to support data traffic are called routed protocols and some key examples of them include IP and IPv6.

**11.** B. Data translation and code formatting occur on the Presentation layer of the OSI model.

**12.** C. The IEEE Ethernet Data Link layer has two sublayers, the Media Access Control (MAC) and the Logical Link Control (LLC).

**13.** B. Windows are used to control the amount of outstanding, unacknowledged data segments. In the diagram, a windows size of three has been agreed upon by the stations.

**14.** A. Hubs operate on the Physical Layer as they have no intelligence and send all traffic in all directions.

**15.** C. While it is true that the OSI model's primary purpose is to allow different vendors' networks to interoperate, there is no requirement that any vendor follows the model.

**16.** B. Routers by default do NOT forward broadcasts.

**17.** C. Switches create separate collision domains within a single broadcast domain. Routers provide a separate broadcast domain for each interface.

**18.** B. The all-hub network at the bottom is one collision domain; the bridge network on top equals three collision domains. Add in the switch network of five collision domains—one for each switch port—and you get a total of nine.

**19.** A. The top three layers define how the applications within the end stations will communicate with each other as well as with users.

**20.** A. The following network devices operate at all seven layers of the OSI model: network management stations (NMSs), gateways (not default gateways), servers and network hosts.

# Chapter 2: Ethernet Networking and Data Encapsulation

1. D. The organizationally unique identifier (OUI) is assigned by the IEEE to an organization composed of 24 bits, or 3 bytes, which in turn assigns a globally administered address also comprised of 24 bits, or 3 bytes, that's supposedly unique to each and every adapter it manufactures.

2. A. Back-off on an Ethernet network is the retransmission delay that's enforced when a collision occurs. When that happens, a host will only resume transmission after the forced time delay has expired. Keep in mind that after the backoff has elapsed, all stations have equal priority to transmit data.

3. A. When using a hub all ports are in the same collision domain which will introduce collisions as shown between devices connected to the same hub.

4. B. FCS is a field at the end of the frame that's used to store the cyclic redundancy check (CRC) answer. The CRC is a mathematical algorithm that's run when each frame is built based on the data in the frame. When a receiving host receives the frame and runs the CRC, the answer should be the same. If not, the frame is discarded, assuming errors have occurred.

5. B. Ethernet networking uses a protocol called Carrier Sense Multiple Access with Collision Detection (CSMA/CD), which helps devices share the bandwidth evenly, while preventing two devices from transmitting simultaneously on the same network medium

6. D. Hubs are not capable of providing a full-duplex connection.

7. D. The cable shown is a straight-through cable which is used between dissimilar devices.

8. B, C. The high-order bit is the Individual/Group (I/G) bit. When it has a value of 0, we can assume that the address is the MAC address of a device and that it may well appear in the source portion of the MAC header. When it's a 1, we can assume that the address represents either a broadcast or multicast address in Ethernet.

9. B. In creating the gigabit crossover cable, you'd still cross 1 to 3 and 2 to 6, but you would add 4 to 7 and 5 to 8.

10. D. When you set up the connection, use these settings:
    - Bits per sec: 9600
    - Data bits: 8
    - Parity: none
    - Stop bits: 1
    - Flow control: none

11. D. When set to 0, this bit represents a globally administered address, as by the IEEE, but when it's a 1, it represents a locally governed and administered address.

12. B. You can use a rolled Ethernet cable to connect a host EIA-TIA 232 interface to a router console serial communication (COM) port.

13. B. The collision will invoke a back-off algorithm on all systems, not just the ones involve in the collision.

14. A. There are no collisions in full-duplex mode.

15. B. The connection between the two switches requires a crossover and the connection from the hosts to the switches required a straight through.

16. The given cable types are matched with their standards in the diagram below.

| | |
|---|---|
| IEEE 802.3u | 100Base-Tx |
| IEEE 802.3 | 10Base-T |
| IEEE 802.3ab | 1000Base-T |
| IEEE 802.3z | 1000Base-SX |

The given cable types are matched with their standards in the diagram above.

17. B. Although rolled cable isn't used to connect any Ethernet connections together, you can use a rolled Ethernet cable to connect a host EIA-TIA 232 interface to a router console serial communication (COM) port.

18. B. If you're using TCP, the virtual circuit is defined by the source and destination port number plus the source and destination IP address and called a *socket*.

19. A. The hex value 1C is converted as 28 in decimal.

20. A. Fiber optic cables are the only ones that have a core surrounded by a material called cladding.

# Chapter 3: Introduction to TCP/IP

1. C. If a DHCP conflict is detected, either by the server sending a ping and getting a response or by a host using a gratuitous ARP (arp'ing for its own IP address and seeing if a host responds), then the server will hold that address and not use it again until it is fixed by an administrator.

2. B. Secure Shell (SSH) protocol sets up a secure session that's similar to Telnet over a standard TCP/IP connection and is employed for doing things like logging into systems, running programs on remote systems, and moving files from one system to another.

**3.** C. A host uses something called a gratuitous ARP to help avoid a possible duplicate address. The DHCP client sends an ARP broadcast out on the local LAN or VLAN using its newly assigned address to solve conflicts before they occur.

**4.** B. Address Resolution Protocol (ARP) is used to find the hardware address from a known IP address.

**5.** A, C, D. The listed answers are from the OSI model and the question asked about the TCP/IP protocol stack (DoD model). Yes, it is normal for the objectives to have this type of question. However, let's just look for what is wrong. First, the Session layer is not in the TCP/IP model; neither are the Data Link and Physical layers. This leaves us with the Transport layer (Host-to-host in the DoD model), Internet layer (Network layer in the OSI), and Application layer (Application/Process in the DoD). Remember, the CCENT objectives can list the layers as OSI layers or DoD layer at any time, regardless of what the question is asking.

**6.** C. A Class C network address has only 8 bits for defining hosts: $2^8 - 2 = 256$.

**7.** A, B. A client that sends out a DHCP Discover message in order to receive an IP address sends out a broadcast at both layer 2 and layer 3. The layer 2 broadcast is all *F*s in hex, or *FF:FF:FF:FF:FF:FF*. The layer 3 broadcast is 255.255.255.255, which means any networks and all hosts. DHCP is connectionless, which means it uses User Datagram Protocol (UDP) at the Transport layer, also called the Host-to-host layer.

**8.** B. Although Telnet does use TCP and IP (TCP/IP), the question specifically asks about layer 4, and IP works at layer 3. Telnet uses TCP at layer 4.

**9.** RFC 1918 These addresses can be used on a private network, but they're not routable through the Internet.

**10.** B, D, E. SMTP, FTP, and HTTP use TCP.

**11.** C. Class C addresses devote 24 bits to the network portion and 8 bits to the host portion.

**12.** C. The range of multicast addresses starts with 224.0.0.0 and goes through 239.255.255.255.

**13.** C. First, you should know easily that only TCP and UDP work at the Transport layer, so now you have a 50/50 shot. However, since the header has sequencing, acknowledgment, and window numbers, the answer can only be TCP.

**14.** A. Both FTP and Telnet use TCP at the Transport layer; however, they both are Application layer protocols, so the Application layer is the best answer for this question.

**15.** C. The four layers of the DoD model are Application/Process, Host-to-Host, Internet, and Network Access. The Internet layer is equivalent to the Network layer of the OSI model.

**16.** C, E. The Class A private address range is 10.0.0.0 through 10.255.255.255. The Class B private address range is 172.16.0.0 through 172.31.255.255, and the Class C private address range is 192.168.0.0 through 192.168.255.255.

**17.** B. The four layers of the TCP/IP stack (also called the DoD model) are Application/Process, Host-to-host, Internet, and Network Access. The Host-to-host layer is equivalent to the Transport layer of the OSI model.

**18.** B, C. ICMP is used for diagnostics and destination unreachable messages. ICMP is encapsulated within IP datagrams, and because it is used for diagnostics, it will provide hosts with information about network problems.

**19.** C. The range of a Class B network address is 128–191. This makes our binary range 10xxxxxx.

**20.**

| | |
|---|---|
| DHCPOffer | TargetB |
| DHCPDiscover | TargetA |
| DHCPAck | TargetD |
| DHCPRequest | TargetC |

The steps are as shown in the answer diagram.

# Chapter 4: Easy Subnetting

**1.** D. A /27 (255.255.255.224) is 3 bits on and 5 bits off. This provides 8 subnets, each with 30 hosts. Does it matter if this mask is used with a Class A, B, or C network address? Not at all. The number of host bits would never change.

**2.** D. A 240 mask is 4 subnet bits and provides 16 subnets, each with 14 hosts. We need more subnets, so let's add subnet bits. One more subnet bit would be a 248 mask. This provides 5 subnet bits (32 subnets) with 3 host bits (6 hosts per subnet). This is the best answer.

**3.** C. This is a pretty simple question. A /28 is 255.255.255.240, which means that our block size is 16 in the fourth octet. 0, 16, 32, 48, 64, 80, etc. The host is in the 64 subnet.

**4.** F. A CIDR address of /19 is 255.255.224.0. This is a Class B address, so that is only 3 subnet bits, but it provides 13 host bits, or 8 subnets, each with 8,190 hosts.

**5.** B,D The mask 255.255.254.0 (/23) used with a Class A address means that there are 15 subnet bits and 9 host bits. The block size in the third octet is 2 (256 – 254). So this makes the subnets in the interesting octet 0, 2, 4, 6, etc., all the way to 254. The host 10.16.3.65 is in the 2.0 subnet. The next subnet is 4.0, so the broadcast address for the 2.0 subnet is 3.255. The valid host addresses are 2.1 through 3.254.

**6.** D. A /30, regardless of the class of address, has a 252 in the fourth octet. This means we have a block size of 4 and our subnets are 0, 4, 8, 12, 16, etc. Address 14 is obviously in the 12 subnet.

**7.** D. A point-to-point link uses only two hosts. A /30, or 255.255.255.252, mask provides two hosts per subnet.

**8.** C. A /21 is 255.255.248.0, which means we have a block size of 8 in the third octet, so we just count by 8 until we reach 66. The subnet in this question is 64.0. The next subnet is 72.0, so the broadcast address of the 64 subnet is 71.255.

**9.** A. A /29 (255.255.255.248), regardless of the class of address, has only 3 host bits. Six hosts are the maximum number of hosts on this LAN, including the router interface.

**10.** C. A /29 is 255.255.255.248, which is a block size of 8 in the fourth octet. The subnets are 0, 8, 16, 24, 32, 40, etc. 192.168.19.24 is the 24 subnet, and since 32 is the next subnet, the broadcast address for the 24 subnet is 31. 192.168.19.26 is the only correct answer.

**11.** A. A /29 (255.255.255.248) has a block size of 8 in the fourth octet. This means the subnets are 0, 8, 16, 24, etc. 10 is in the 8 subnet. The next subnet is 16, so 15 is the broadcast address.

**12.** B. You need 5 subnets, each with at least 16 hosts. The mask 255.255.255.240 provides 16 subnets with 14 hosts—this will not work. The mask 255.255.255.224 provides 8 subnets, each with 30 hosts. This is the best answer.

**13.** C. First, you cannot answer this question if you can't subnet. The 192.168.10.62 with a mask of 255.255.255.192 is a block size of 64 in the fourth octet. The host 192.168.10.62 is in the zero subnet, and the error occurred because `ip subnet-zero` is not enabled on the router.

**14.** A. A /25 mask is 255.255.255.128. Used with a Class B network, the third and fourth octets are used for subnetting with a total of 9 subnet bits, 8 bits in the third octet and 1 bit in the fourth octet. Since there is only 1 bit in the fourth octet, the bit is either off or on—which is a value of 0 or 128. The host in the question is in the 0 subnet, which has a broadcast address of 127 since 112.128 is the next subnet.

**15.**  A. A /28 is a 255.255.255.240 mask. Let's count to the ninth subnet (we need to find the broadcast address of the eighth subnet, so we need to count to the ninth subnet). Starting at 16 (remember, the question stated that we will not use subnet zero, so we start at 16, not 0), 16, 32, 48, 64, 80, 96, 112, 128, 144 etc.. The eighth subnet is 128 and the next subnet is 144, so our broadcast address of the 128 subnet is 143. This makes the host range 129–142. 142 is the last valid host.

**16.**  C. A /28 is a 255.255.255.240 mask. The first subnet is 16 (remember that the question stated not to use subnet zero) and the next subnet is 32, so our broadcast address is 31. This makes our host range 17–30. 30 is the last valid host.

**17.**  E. A Class C subnet mask of 255.255.255.224 is 3 bits on and 5 bits off (11100000) and provides 8 subnets, each with 30 hosts. However, if the command ip subnet-zero is not used, then only 6 subnets would be available for use.

**18.**  E. A Class B network ID with a /22 mask is 255.255.252.0, with a block size of 4 in the third octet. The network address in the question is in subnet 172.16.16.0 with a broadcast address of 172.16.19.255. Only option E has the correct subnet mask listed, and 172.16.18.255 is a valid host.

**19.**  D,E The router's IP address on the E0 interface is 172.16.2.1/23, which is 255.255.254.0. This makes the third octet a block size of 2. The router's interface is in the 2.0 subnet, and the broadcast address is 3.255 because the next subnet is 4.0. The valid host range is 2.1 through 3.254. The router is using the first valid host address in the range.

**20.**  C. To test the local stack on your host, ping the loopback interface of 127.0.0.1.

# Chapter 5: VLSMs, Summarization, and Troubleshooting TCP/IP

**1.**  D. A point-to-point link uses only two hosts. A /30, or 255.255.255.252, mask provides two hosts per subnet.

**2.**  C. Using a /28 mask, there are 4 bits available for hosts. Two to the fourth power minus 2 = 14.

**3.**  D. For 6 hosts we need to leave 3 bits in the host portion since 2 to the third power = 8 and 8 less 2 is 6.With 3 bits for the host portion, that leaves 29 bits for the mask or /29.

**4.**  C. To use VLSM, the routing protocols in use possess the capability to transmit subnet mask information.

5. D. In a question like this, you need to look for an interesting octet where you can combine networks. In this example, the third octet has all our subnets so we just need to find our block size now. If we used a block of 8 starting at 172.16.0.0/19, then we cover 172.16.0.0 through 172.16.7.255. However, if we used 172.16.0.0/20, then we'd cover a block of 16 which would be from 172.16.0.0 through 172.16.15.255, which is the best answer.

6. C. The IP address of the station and the gateway are not in the same network. Since the address of the gateway is correct on the station, it is *most likely* the IP address of the station is incorrect.

7. B. With an incorrect gateway, Host A will not be able to communicate with the router or beyond the router but will be able to communicate within the subnet.

8. A. Pinging the remote computer would fail if any of the other tests fail.

9. C. When a ping to the local host IP address fails, you can assume the NIC is not functional.

10. C, D. If a ping to the local host succeeds, you can rule out IP stack or NIC failure.

11. E. A /29 mask yields only 6 addresses, so none of the networks could use it.

12. A. The most likely problem if you can ping a computer by IP address but not by name is a failure of DNS.

13. D. When you issue the ping command, you are using the ICMP protocol.

14. B. The traceroute command displays the networks traversed on a path to a network destination.

15. C. The ping command tests connectivity to another station. The full command is shown below.

```
C:\>ping 172.16.10.2
Pinging 172.16.10.2 with 32 bytes of data:
Reply from 172.16.10.2: bytes=32 time<1ms TTL=128
Reply from 172.16.10.2: bytes=32 time<1ms TTL=128
Reply from 172.16.10.2: bytes=32 time<1ms TTL=128
Reply from 172.16.10.2: bytes=32 time<1ms TTL=128
Ping statistics for 172.16.10.2:
    Packets: Sent = 4, Received = 4, Lost = 0 (0% loss),
Approximate round trip times in milli-seconds:
    Minimum = 0ms, Maximum = 0ms, Average = 0ms
```

**16.**

| | |
|---|---|
| traceroute | Displays the list of routers on a path to a network destination |
| arp -a | Displays IP-to-MAC-address mappings on a Windows PC |
| show ip arp | Displays the ARP table on a Cisco router |
| ipconfig /all | Shows you the PC network configuration |

The command uses the functions described in the answer table.

**17.** C. The interesting octet in this example is the second octet, and it is a block size of four starting at 10.0.0.0. By using a 255.252.0.0 mask, we are telling the summary to use a block size of four in the 2nd octet. This will cover 10.0.0.0 through 10.3.255.255. This is the best answer.

**18.** A. The command that displays the ARP table on a Cisco router is show ip arp.

**19.** C. The /all switch must be added to the ipconfig command on a PC to verify DNS configuration.

**20.** C. If you start at 192.168.128.0 and go through 192.168.159.0, you can see this is a block of 32 in the third octet. Since the network address is always the first one in the range, the summary address is 192.168.128.0. What mask provides a block of 32 in the third octet? The answer is 255.255.224.0, or /19.

# Chapter 6: Cisco's Internetworking Operating System (IOS)

**1.** D. Typically we'd see the input errors and CRC statistics increase with a duplex error, but it could be another Physical layer issue such as the cable might be receiving excessive interference or the network interface cards might have a failure. Typically you can tell if it is interference when the CRC and input errors output grow but the collision counters do not, which is the case with this question.

**2.** C. Once the IOS is loaded and up and running, the startup-config will be copied from NVRAM into RAM and from then on, referred to as the running-config.

**3.** C, D. To configure SSH on your router, you need to set the username command, the ip domain-name, login local, and the transport input ssh under the VTY lines and the crypto key command. However, SSH version 2 is suggested but not required.

**4.** C. The show controllers serial 0/0 command will show you whether either a DTE or DCE cable is connected to the interface. If it is a DCE connection, you need to add clocking with the clock rate command.

**5.**

| Mode | Definition |
|------|------------|
| User EXEC mode | Commands that affect the entire system |
| Privileged EXEC mode | Commands that affect interfaces/processes only |
| Global configuration mode | Interactive configuration dialog |
| Specific configuration modes | Provides access to all other router commands |
| Setup mode | Limited to basic monitoring commands |

User exec mode is limited to basic monitoring commands; privileged exec mode provides access to all other router commands. Specific configuration modes include the commands that affect a specific interface or process, while global configuration mode allows commands that affect the entire system. Setup mode is where you access the interactive configuration dialog.

**6.** B. We can see that the bandwidth is 100000 Kbit, which is 100,000,000. Kbit means to add three zeros, which is 100 Mbits per second, or FastEthernet.

**7.** B. From global configuration mode, use the line vty 0 4 command to set all five default VTY lines. However, you would typically always set all lines, not just the defaults.

**8.** C. The enable secret password is case sensitive, so the second option is wrong. To set the enable secret password, use the enable secret *password* command from global configuration mode. This password is automatically encrypted.

**9.** C. The typical banner is a message of the day (MOTD) and is set by using the global configuration mode command banner MOTD.

**10.** C. The prompts offered as options indicate the following modes:

Switch(config)# is global configuration mode.

Switch> is user mode.

Switch# is privileged mode.

Switch(config-if)# is interface configuration mode.

**11.** D. To copy the running-config to NVRAM so that it will be used if the router is restarted, use the copy running-config startup-config command in privileged mode (copy run start for short).

**12.** D. To allow a VTY (Telnet) session into your router, you must set the VTY password. Option C is wrong because it is setting the password on the wrong router. Notice that you have to set the password before you set the login command. Remember, Cisco may have you set the password before the login command.

**13.** D. The erase `startup-config` command erases the contents of NVRAM and will put you in setup mode if the switch is restarted. Option E is wrong because you must type in the full command!

**14.** B. If an interface is shut down, the `show interface` command will show the interface as administratively down. (It is possible that no cable is attached, but you can't tell that from this message.)

**15.** C. With the `show interfaces` command, you can view the configurable parameters, get statistics for the interfaces on the switch, check for input and CRC errors, and verify if the interfaces are shut down.

**16.** C. If you delete the startup-config and reload the switch, the device will automatically enter setup mode. You can also type **setup** from privileged mode at any time.

**17.** D. You can view the interface statistics from user mode, but the command is `show interface fastethernet 0/0`.

**18.** B. The `% ambiguous command` error means that there is more than one possible show command that starts with *r*. Use a question mark to find the correct command.

**19.** B, D. The commands `show interfaces` and `show ip interface` will show you the layer 1 and 2 status and the IP addresses of your router's interfaces.

**20.** A. If you see that a serial interface and the protocol are both down, then you have a Physical layer problem. If you see `serial1 is up, line protocol is down`, then you are not receiving (Data Link) keepalives from the remote end.

# Chapter 7: Managing a Cisco Internetwork

**1.** B. The IEEE created a new standardized discovery protocol called 802.1AB for Station and Media Access Control Connectivity Discovery. We'll just call it Link Layer Discovery Protocol (LLDP).

**2.** C. The `show processes` (or `show processes cpu`) is a good tool for determining a given router's CPU utilization. When it is high, it is not a good time to execute a debug command.

**3.** B. The command `traceroute` (trace for short), which can be issued from user mode or privileged mode, is used to find the path a packet takes through an internetwork and will also show you where the packet stops because of an error on a router.

**4.** C. Since the configuration looks correct, you probably didn't screw up the copy job. However, when you perform a copy from a network host to a router, the interfaces are automatically shut down and need to be manually enabled with the *no shutdown* command.

**5.** D. Specifying the address of the DHCP server allows the router to relay broadcast traffic destined for a DHCP server to that server.

**6.** C. Before you start to configure the router, you should erase the NVRAM with the erase startup-config command and then reload the router using the reload command.

**7.** C. This command can be run on both routers and switches and it displays detailed information about each device connected to the device you're running the command on, including the IP address.

**8.** C. The Port ID column describes the interfaces on the remote device end of the connection.

**9.** C. This command can be run on both routers and switches, and it displays detailed information about each device connected to the device you're running the command on, including the IP address.

**10.** C. If you save a configuration and reload the router and it comes up either in setup mode or as a blank configuration, chances are you have the configuration register setting incorrect.

**11.** D. To keep open one or more Telnet sessions, use the Ctrl+Shift+6 and then X keystroke combination.

**12.** B, D. The best answers, the ones you need to remember, are that either an access control list is filtering the Telnet session or the VTY password is not set on the remote device.

**13.** A, D. The show hosts command provides information on temporary DNS entries and permanent name-to-address mappings created using the ip host command.

**14.** A, B, D. The tracert command is a Windows command and will not work on a router or switch! IOS uses the traceroute command.

**15.** D. Since the question never mentioned anything about a suspended session, you can assume that the Telnet session is still open, and you would just type **exit** to close the session.

**16.** C. To see console messages through your Telnet session, you must enter the terminal monitor command.

**17.** terminal monitor When you telnet into a remote device, you will not see console messages by default. For example, you will not see debugging output. To allow console messages to be sent to your Telnet session, use the terminal monitor command.

**18.** E. Although option A is certainly the "best" answer, unfortunately option E will work just fine and your boss would probably prefer you to use the show cdp neighbors detail command.

**19.** D. To enable a device to be an NTP client, use the `ntp server` *IP_address* `version` `version` command at global configuration mode. That's all there is to it! Assuming your NTP server is working of course.

**20.** B, D. You can verify your NTP client with the `show ntp status` and `show ntp associations` commands.

# Chapter 8: IP Routing

**1.** `show ip route` The `ip route` command is used to display the routing table of a router.

**2.** B. In the new 15 IOS code, Cisco defines a different route called a local route. Each has a /32 prefix defining a route just for the one address.

**3.** A, B. Although option D almost seems right, it is not; the mask is the mask used on the remote network, not the source network. Since there is no number at the end of the static route, it is using the default administrative distance of 1.

**4.** C, F. The switches are not used as either a default gateway or other destination. Switches have nothing to do with routing. It is very important to remember that the destination MAC address will always be the router's interface. The destination address of a frame, from HostA, will be the MAC address of the Fa0/0 interface of RouterA. The destination address of a packet will be the IP address of the network interface card (NIC) of the HTTPS server. The destination port number in the segment header will have a value of 443 (HTTPS).

**5.** B. This mapping was learned dynamically which means it was learned through ARP.

**6.** B. Hybrid protocols use aspects of both distance vector and link state—for example, EIGRP. Although be advised that Cisco typically just calls EIGRP an advanced distance vector routing protocol. Do not be mislead by the way the question is worded. Yes, I know that MAC addresses are not in a packet. You must read the question for understanding of what they are really asking.

**7.** A. Since the destination MAC address is different at each hop, it must keep changing. The IP address which is used for the routing process does not.

**8.** B, E. Classful routing means that all hosts in the internetwork use the same mask and that only default masks are in use. Classless routing means that you can use variable length subnet masks (VLSMs).

**9.** B, C. The distance-vector routing protocol sends its complete routing table out of all active interfaces at periodic time intervals. Link-state routing protocols send updates containing the state of their own links to all routers in the internetwork.

**10.** C. This is how most people see routers, and certainly they could do this type of plain ol' packet switching in 1990 when Cisco released their very first router and traffic was seriously slow, but not in today's networks! This process involves looking up every destination in the routing table and finding the exit interface for every packet.

**11.** A, C. The S* shows that this is a candidate for default route and that it was configured manually.

**12.** B. RIP has an administrative distance (AD) of 120, while EIGRP has an administrative distance of 90, so the router will discard any route with a higher AD than 90 to that same network.

**13.** D. Recovery from a lost route requires manual intervention by a human to replace the lost route.

**14.** A. RIPv1 and RIPv2 only use the lowest hop count to determine the best path to a remote network.

**15.** A. Since the routing table shows no route to the 192.168.22.0 network, the router will discard the packet and send an ICMP destination unreachable message out of interface FastEthernet 0/0, which is the source LAN from which the packet originated.

**16.** C. Static routes have an administrative distance of 1 by default. Unless you change this, a static route will always be used over any other dynamically learned route. EIGRP has an administrative distance of 90, and RIP has an administrative distance of 120, by default.

**17.** C. BGP is the only EGP listed.

**18.** D. Recovery from a lost route requires manual intervention by a human to replace the lost route. The advantages are less overhead on the router and network, as well as more security.

**19.** C. The `show ip interface brief` command displays a concise summary of the interfaces.

**20.** B. The 150 at the end changes the default administrative distance (AD) of 1 to 150.

# Chapter 9: Open Shortest Path First (OSPF)

**1.** B. Only the EIGRP routes will be placed in the routing table because it has the lowest administrative distance (AD), and that is always used before metrics.

**2.** A, B, C. Any router that is member of two areas must be an area border router or ABR.

**3.** A, C. The process ID for OSPF on a router is only locally significant and you can use the same number on each router, or each router can have a different number—it just doesn't matter. The numbers you can use are from 1 to 65,535. Don't get this confused with area numbers, which can be from 0 to 4.2 billion.

**4.** B. The router ID (RID) is an IP address used to identify the router. It need not and should not match.

**5.** C. The router ID (RID) is an IP address used to identify the router. Cisco chooses the router ID by using the highest IP address of all configured loopback interfaces. If no loopback interfaces are configured with addresses, OSPF will choose the highest IP address of all active physical interfaces.

**6.** A. The administrator typed in the wrong wildcard mask configuration. The wildcard should have been 0.0.0.255 or even 0.255.255.255.

**7.** A. A dash (-) in the State column indicates no DR election, because they are not required on a point-to-point link such as a serial connection.

**8.** D. By default the administrative distance of OSPF is 110.

**9.** A. Hello packets are addressed to multicast address 224.0.0.5.

**10.** A. The show ip ospf neighbor command displays all interface-related neighbor information. This output shows the DR and BDR (unless your router is the DR or BDR), the RID of all directly connected neighbors and the IP address and name of the directly connected interface.

**11.** A. 224.0.0.6 is used on broadcast networks to reach the DR and BDR.

**12.** D. The Hello and Dead timers must be set the same on two routers on the same link or they will not form an adjacency (relationship). The default timers for OSPF are 10 seconds for the Hello timer and 40 seconds for the Dead timer.

**13.**

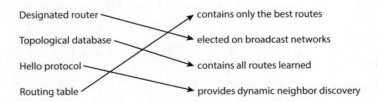

A designated router is elected on broadcast networks. Each OSPF router maintains an identical database describing the AS topology. A Hello protocol provides dynamic neighbor discovery. A routing table contains only the best routes.

14. `passive-interface fastEthernet 0/1` The command `passive-interface fastEthernet 0/1` will disable OSPF on the specified interface only.

15. B, G. To enable OSPF, you must first start OSPF using a process ID. The number is irrelevant; just choose a number from 1 to 65,535 and you're good to go. After you start the OSPF process, you must configure interfaces on which to activate OSPF using the network command with wildcards and specification of an area. Option F is wrong because there must be a space after the parameter area and before you list the area number.

16. A. The default OSPF interface priority is 1, and the highest interface priority determines the designated router (DR) for a subnet. The output indicates that the router with a router ID of 192.168.45.2 is currently the backup designated router (BDR) for the segment, which indicates that another router became the DR. It can be then be assumed that the DR router has an interface priority higher than 2. (The router serving the DR function is not present in the truncated sample output.)

17. A, B, C. OSPF is created in a hierarchical design, not a flat design like RIP. This decreases routing overhead, speeds up convergence, and confines network instability to a single area of the network.

18. `show ip ospf interface` The `show ip ospf interface` command displays all interface-related OSPF information. Data is displayed about OSPF information for all OSPF-enabled interfaces or for specified interfaces.

19. A. LSA packets are used to update and maintain the topological database.

20. B. At the moment of OSPF process startup, the highest IP address on any active interface will be the router ID (RID) of the router. If you have a loopback interface configured (logical interface), then that will override the interface IP address and become the RID of the router automatically.

# Chapter 10: Layer 2 Switching

1. A. Layer 2 switches and bridges are faster than routers because they don't take up time looking at the Network Layer header information. They do make use of the Data Link layer information.

2. `mac address-table static aaaa.bbbb.cccc vlan 1 int fa0/7` You can set a static MAC address in the MAC address table and when done it will appear as a static entry in the table.

3. B, D, E. Since the MAC address is not present in the table, it will send the frame out of all ports in the same VLAN with the exception of the port on which it was received.

4. `show mac address-table` This command displays the forward filter table, also called a content addressable memory (CAM) table.

5.

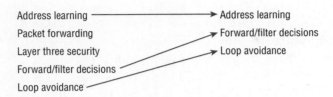

   The three functions are address learning, forward/filter decisions, and loop avoidance.

6. A, D. In the above output, you can see that the port is in Secure-shutdown mode and the light for the port would be amber. To enable the port again you'd need to do the following:

   S3(config-if)#**shutdown**
   S3(config-if)#**no shutdown**

7. `switchport port-security maximum 2` The maximum setting of 2 means only two MAC addresses can be used on that port; if the user tries to add another host on that segment, the switch port will take the action specified. In the port-security violation command.

8. B. The `switchport port-security` command enables port security, which is a prerequisite for the other commands to function.

9. B. Gateway redundancy is not an issue addressed by STP.

10. A. If no loop avoidance schemes are put in place, the switches will flood broadcasts endlessly throughout the internetwork. This is sometimes referred to as a broadcast storm.

11. B, C. Shutdown and protect mode will alert you via SNMP that a violation has occurred on a port.

12. Spanning tree protocol (STP) STP is a switching loop avoidance scheme use by switches.

13. `ip default-gateway` If you want to manage your switches from outside your LAN, you need to set a default gateway on the switches, just as you would with a host.

14. C. The IP address is configured under a logical interface, called a management domain or VLAN 1.

**15.** B. The show port-security interface command displays the current port security and status of a switch port, as in this sample output:

```
Switch# show port-security interface fastethernet0/1
Port Security: Enabled
Port status: SecureUp
Violation mode: Shutdown
Maximum MAC Addresses: 2
Total MAC Addresses: 2
Configured MAC Addresses: 2
Aging Time: 30 mins
Aging Type: Inactivity
SecureStatic address aging: Enabled
Security Violation count: 0
```

**16.** switchport port-security mac-address sticky Issuing the switchport port-security mac-address sticky command will allow a switch to save a dynamically learned MAC address in the running-configuration of the switch, which prevents the administrator from having to document or configure specific MAC addresses.

**17.** B, D. To limit connections to a specific host, you should configure the MAC address of the host as a static entry associated with the port, although be aware that this host can still connect to any other port, but no other port can connect to f0/3, in this example. Another solution would be to configure port security to accept traffic only from the MAC address of the host. By default, an unlimited number of MAC addresses can be learned on a single switch port, whether it is configured as an access port or a trunk port. Switch ports can be secured by defining one or more specific MAC addresses that should be allowed to connect and by defining violation policies (such as disabling the port) to be enacted if additional hosts try to gain a connection.

**18.** D. The command statically defines the MAC address of 00c0.35F0.8301 as an allowed host on the switch port. By default, an unlimited number of MAC addresses can be learned on a single switch port, whether it is configured as an access port or a trunk port. Switch ports can be secured by defining one or more specific MAC addresses that should be allowed to connect and violation policies (such as disabling the port) if additional hosts try to gain a connection.

**19.** D. You would not make the port a trunk. In this example, this switchport is a member of one VLAN. However, you can configure port security on a trunk port, but again, not valid for this question.

**20.** switchport port-security violation shutdown This command is used to set the reaction of the switch to a port violation of shutdown.

# Chapter 11: VLANs and InterVLAN Routing

1.  D. Here's a list of ways VLANs simplify network management:
    - Network adds, moves, and changes are achieved with ease by just configuring a port into the appropriate VLAN.
    - A group of users that need an unusually high level of security can be put into its own VLAN so that users outside of the VLAN can't communicate with them.
    - As a logical grouping of users by function, VLANs can be considered independent from their physical or geographic locations.
    - VLANs greatly enhance network security if implemented correctly.
    - VLANs increase the number of broadcast domains while decreasing their size.

2.  `ip routing` Routing must be enabled on the layer 3 switch.

3.  C. VLANs can span across multiple switches by using trunk links, which carry traffic for multiple VLANs.

4.  B. While in all other cases access ports can be a member of only one VLAN, most switches will allow you to add a second VLAN to an access port on a switch port for your voice traffic; it's called the voice VLAN. The voice VLAN used to be called the auxiliary VLAN, which allowed it to be overlaid on top of the data VLAN, enabling both types of traffic through the same port.

5.  A. Yes, you have to do a `no shutdown` on the VLAN interface.

6.  C. Unlike ISL which encapsulates the frame with control information, 802.1q inserts an 802.1q field along with tag control information.

7.  D. Instead of using a router interface for each VLAN, you can use one FastEthernet interface and run ISL or 802.1q trunking. This allows all VLANs to communicate through one interface. Cisco calls this a "router on a stick."

8.  `switchport access vlan 2` This command is executed under the interface (switch port) that is being placed in the VLAN.

9.  `show vlan` After you create the VLANs that you want, you can use the `show vlan` command to check them out.

10. B. The encapsulation command specifying the VLAN for the subinterface must be present under both subinterfaces.

11. A. With a multilayer switch, enable IP routing and create one logical interface for each VLAN using the `interface vlan number` command and you're now doing inter-VLAN routing on the backplane of the switch!

12. A. Ports Fa0/15–18 are not present in any VLANs. They are trunk ports.

13. C. Untagged frames are members of the native VLAN, which by default is VLAN 1.

14. `sh interfaces fastEthernet 0/15 switchport` This `show interfaces` *interface* `switchport` command shows us the administrative mode of dynamic desirable and that the port is a trunk port, DTP was used to negotiate the frame tagging method of ISL, and the native VLAN is the default of 1.

15. C. VLANs are *not* location dependent and can span to multiple switches using trunk links. Moreover, they can be subnets of major networks.

16. B. The host's default gateway should be set to the IP address of the subinterface that is associated with the VLAN of which the host is a member, in this case VLAN 2.

17. C. Frame tagging is used when VLAN traffic travels over a trunk link. Trunk links carry frames for multiple VLANs. Therefore, frame tags are used for identification of frames from different VLANs.

18. `vlan 2` To configure VLANs on a Cisco Catalyst switch, use the global config `vlan` command.

19. B. 802.1q uses the native VLAN.

20. `switchport nonegotiate` You can use this command only when the interface switchport mode is access or trunk. You must manually configure the neighboring interface as a trunk interface to establish a trunk link.

# Chapter 12: Security

1. D. It's compared with lines of the access list only until a match is made. Once the packet matches the condition on a line of the access list, the packet is acted upon and no further comparisons take place.

2. C. The range of 192.168.160.0 to 192.168.191.0 is a block size of 32. The network address is 192.168.160.0 and the mask would be 255.255.224.0, which for an access list must be a wildcard format of 0.0.31.255. The 31 is used for a block size of 32. The wildcard is always one less than the block size.

3. C. Using a named access list just replaces the number used when applying the list to the router's interface. `ip access-group Blocksales in` is correct.

4. B. The list must specify TCP as the Transport layer protocol and use a correct wild-card mask (in this case 0.0.0.255), and it must specify the destination port (80). It also should specify all as the set of computers allowed to have this access.

5. A. The first thing to check in a question like this is the access-list number. Right away, you can see that the second option is wrong because it is using a standard IP access-list number. The second thing to check is the protocol. If you are filtering by upper-layer protocol, then you must be using either UDP or TCP; this eliminates the fourth option. The third and last answers have the wrong syntax.

6. C. Of the available choices, only the show ip interface command will tell you which interfaces have access lists applied. show access-lists will not show you which interfaces have an access list applied.

7.

The command show access-list displays all access lists and their parameters configured on the router; it does not show you which interface the list is set on. show access-list 110 shows only the parameters for the access list 110 and, again, does not tell you which interface the list is set on. show ip access-list reveals only the IP access lists configured on the router. Finally, show ip interface shows which interfaces have access lists set.

The functions of each command are as shown in the solution graphic.

8. C. The extended access list ranges are 100–199 and 2000–2699, so the access-list number of 100 is valid. Telnet uses TCP, so the protocol TCP is valid. Now you just need to look for the source and destination address. Only the third option has the correct sequence of parameters. Option B may work, but the question specifically states "only" to network 192.168.10.0, and the wildcard in option B is too broad.

9. D. Extended IP access lists use numbers 100–199 and 2000–2699 and filter based on source and destination IP address, protocol number, and port number. The last option is correct because of the second line that specifies permit ip any any. (I used 0.0.0.0 255.255.255.255, which is the same as the any option.) The third option does not have this, so it would deny access but not allow everything else.

**10.** D. First, you must know that a /20 is 255.255.240.0, which is a block size of 16 in the third octet. Counting by 16s, this makes our subnet 48 in the third octet, and the wildcard for the third octet would be 15 since the wildcard is always one less than the block size.

**11.** B. To find the wildcard (inverse) version of this mask, the zero and one bits are simply reversed as follows:

11111111.11111111.11111111.11100000 (27 one bits, or /27)

00000000.00000000.00000000.00011111 (wildcard/inverse mask)

**12.** A. First, you must know that a /19 is 255.255.224.0, which is a block size of 32 in the third octet. Counting by 32s, this makes our subnet 192 in the third octet, and the wildcard for the third octet would be 31 since the wildcard is always one less than the block size.

**13.** B. The scope of an access list is determined by the wildcard mask and the network address to which it is applied. For example, in this case the starting point of the list of addresses affected by the mask is the network ID 192.111.16.32. The wildcard mask is 0.0.0.31. Adding the value of the last octet in the mask to the network address (32 + 31 = 63) tells you where the effects of the access list ends, which is 192.111.16.63. Therefore, all addresses in the range 192.111.16.32–192.111.16.63 will be denied by this list.

**14.** C. To place an access list on an interface, use the `ip access-group` command in interface configuration mode.

**15.** B. With no permit statement, the ACL will deny all traffic.

**16.** D. If you add an access list to an interface and you do not have at least one permit statement, then you will affectively shut down the interface because of the implicit deny any at the end of every list.

**17.** C. Telnet access to the router is restricted by using either a standard or extended IP access list inbound on the VTY lines of the router. The command `access-class` is used to apply the access list to the VTY lines.

**18.** C. A Cisco router has rules regarding the placement of access lists on a router interface. You can place one access list per direction for each layer 3 protocol configured on an interface.

**19.** C. The most common attack on a network today is a denial of service (DoS) because they are the easiest attack to achieve.

**20.** C. Implementing intrusion detection services and intrusion prevention services will help notify you and stop attacks in real time.

# Chapter 13: Network Address Translation

1. A, C, E. NAT is not perfect and can cause some issues in some networks, but most networks work just fine. NAT can cause delays and troubleshooting problems, and some applications just won't work.

2. B, D, F. NAT is not perfect, but there are some advantages. It conserves global addresses, which allow us to add millions of hosts to the Internet without "real" IP addresses. This provides flexibility in our corporate networks. NAT can also allow you to use the same subnet more than once in the same network without overlapping networks.

3. C. The command debug ip nat will show you in real time the translations occurring on your router.

4. A. The command show ip nat translations will show you the translation table containing all the active NAT entries.

5. D. The command clear ip nat translations * will clear all the active NAT entries in your translation table.

6. B. The show ip nat statistics command displays a summary of the NAT configuration as well as counts of active translation types, hits to an existing mapping, misses (causing an attempt to create a mapping), and expired translations.

7. B. The command ip nat pool *name* creates the pool that hosts can use to get onto the global Internet. What makes option B correct is that the range 171.16.10.65 through 171.16.10.94 includes 30 hosts, but the mask has to match 30 hosts as well, and that mask is 255.255.255.224. Option C is wrong because there is a lowercase t in the pool name. Pool names are case sensitive.

8. A, C, E. You can configure NAT three ways on a Cisco router: static, dynamic, and NAT Overload (PAT).

9. B. Instead of the netmask command, you can use the prefix-length *length* statement.

10. C. In order for NAT to provide translation services, you must have ip nat inside and ip nat outside configured on your router's interfaces.

11. A, B, D. The most popular use of NAT is if you want to connect to the Internet and you don't want hosts to have global (real) IP addresses, but options B and D are correct as well.

12. C. An inside global address is considered to be the IP address of the host on the private network after translation.

13. A. An inside local address is considered to be the IP address of the host on the private network before translation.

14. D. What we need to figure out for this question is only the inside global pool. Basically we start at 1.1.128.1 and end at 1.1.135.174; our block size is 8 in the third octet, or /21. Always look for your block size and the interesting octet and you can find your answer every time.

15. B. Once you create your pool, the command ip nat inside source must be used to say which inside locals are allowed to use the pool. In this question we need to see if access-list 100 is configured correctly, if at all, so show access-list is the best answer.

16. A. You must configure your interfaces before NAT will provide any translations. On the inside network interfaces, you would use the command ip nat inside. On the outside network interfaces, you will use the command ip nat outside.

17. B. You must configure your interfaces before NAT will provide any translations. On the inside networks you would use the command ip nat inside. On the outside network interfaces, you will use the command ip nat outside.

18. C. Another term for Port Address Translation is NAT Overload because that is the keyword used to enable port address translation.

19. B. Fast-switching is used on Cisco routers to create a type of route cache in order to quickly forward packets through a router without having to parse the routing table for every packet. As packets are processed-switched (looked up in the routing table), this information is stored in the cache for later use if needed for faster routing processing.

20. B. Once you create a pool for the inside locals to use to get out to the global Internet, you must configure the command to allow them access to the pool. The ip nat inside source list number pool-name overload command has the correct sequence for this question.

# Chapter 14: Internet Protocol Version 6 (IPv6)

1. B. Unlike unicast addresses, global unicast addresses are meant to be routed.

2. A. Packets addressed to a unicast address are delivered to a single interface. For load balancing, multiple interfaces can use the same address.

3. C. Link-local addresses are meant for throwing together a temporary LAN for meetings or a small LAN that is not going to be routed but needs to share and access files and services locally.

**4.** D. These addresses are meant for nonrouting purposes like link-local, but they are almost globally unique, so it is unlikely they will have an address overlap. Unique local addresses were designed as a replacement for site-local addresses.

**5.** B. Packets addressed to a multicast address are delivered to all interfaces identified with the multicast address, the same as in IPv4. It is also called a one-to-many address. You can always tell a multicast address in IPv6 because multicast addresses always start with FF.

**6.** C. Anycast addresses identify multiple interfaces, which is somewhat similar to multicast addresses; however, the big difference is that the anycast packet is only delivered to one address, the first one it finds defined in the terms of routing distance. This address can also be called one-to-one-of-many, or one-to-nearest.

**7.** C. The loopback address with IPv4 is 127.0.0.1. With IPv6, that address is ::1.

**8.** C, D. Adjacencies and next-hop attributes now use link-local addresses, and OSPFv3 still uses multicast traffic to send its updates and acknowledgments with the addresses FF02::5 for OSPF routers and FF02::6 for OSPF designated routers. These are the replacements for 224.0.0.5 and 224.0.0.6, respectively.

**9.** A, C. Host A would send an RS to R1, which would respond with an RA, if the host hasn't already learned this information previously. The host now has the default gateway information it needs to send packets to a remote network. IPv6, like IPv4, has both a network portion and host portion in the IPv6 packet.

**10.** C. A router solicitation is sent out using the all-routers multicast address of FF02::2. The router can send a router advertisement to all hosts using the FF02::1 multicast address.

**11.** B. This can be a hard question if you don't remember to invert the 7th bit! Always look for the 7th bit when studying for the Cisco exams. The EUI-64 autoconfiguration inserts an FF:FE in the middle of the 48-bit MAC address to create a unique IPv6 address.

**12.** A. The NDP neighbor advertisement (NA) contains the MAC address. A neighbor solicitation (NS) was initially sent asking for the MAC address.

**13.** A. To enable OSPFv3, you enable the protocol at the interface level as with RIPng. The command string is `ipv6 ospf` *process-id* `area` *area-id*.

**14.** B, D. To shorten the written length of an IPv6 address, successive fields of zeros may be replaced by double colons. In trying to shorten the address further, leading zeros may also be removed. Just as with IPv4, a single device's interface can have more than one address; with IPv6 there are more types of addresses and the same rule applies. There can be link-local, global unicast, multicast, and anycast addresses all assigned to the same interface.

**15.** C, D. IPv4 addresses are 32 bits long and are represented in decimal format. IPv6 addresses are 128 bits long and represented in hexadecimal format.

**16.** B. There are no broadcasts with IPv6. Unicast, multicast, anycast, global, and link-local unicast are used.

**17.** D. There are 16 bits (four hex characters) in an IPv6 field.

**18.** A, D. Global addresses start with 2000::/3, link-locals start with FE80::/10, loopback is ::1, and unspecified is just two colons (::). Each interface will have a loopback address automatically configured.

**19.** B, C. If you verify your IP configuration on your host, you'll see that you have multiple IPv6 addresses, including a loopback address. The last 64 bits represent the dynamically created interface ID, and leading zeros are not mandatory in a 16-bit IPv6 field.

**20.** C, D, E. OSPFv2 does not use the network command under global configuration mode, nor does it use wildcard masks as IPv4 does. However, they can both use the interface command to configure OSPF, use a 32-bit RID, and both use LSAs.

# Appendix C

# Disabling and Configuring Network Services

By default, the Cisco IOS runs some services that are unnecessary to its normal operation, and if you don't disable them, they can be easy targets for denial-of-service (DoS) attacks and break-in attempts.

DoS attacks are the most common attacks because they are the easiest to perform. Using software and/or hardware tools such as an intrusion detection system (IDS) and intrusion prevention system (IPS) can both warn and stop these simple, but harmful, attacks. However, if we can't implement IDS/IPS, there are some basic commands we can use on our router to make them more safe. Keep in mind, though, that nothing will make you completely safe in today's networks.

Let's take a look at the basic services we should disable on our routers.

# Blocking SNMP Packets

The Cisco IOS default configurations permit remote access from any source, so unless you're either way too trusting or insane, it should be totally obvious to you that those configurations need a bit of attention. You've got to restrict them. If you don't, the router will be a pretty easy target for an attacker who wants to log in to it. This is where access lists come into the game—they can really protect you.

If you place the following command on the serial0/0 interface of the perimeter router, it'll stop any SNMP packets from entering the router or the DMZ. (You'd also need to have a permit command along with this list to really make it work, but this is just an example.)

```
Lab_B(config)#access-list 110 deny udp any any eq snmp
Lab_B(config)#interface s0/0
Lab_B(config-if)#access-group 110 in
```

# Disabling Echo

In case you don't know this already, small services are servers (daemons) running in the router that are quite useful for diagnostics. And here we go again—by default, the Cisco router has a series of diagnostic ports enabled for certain UDP and TCP services, including echo, chargen, and discard.

When a host attaches to those ports, a small amount of CPU is consumed to service these requests. All a single attacking device needs to do is send a whole slew of requests with different, random, phony source IP addresses to overwhelm the router, making it slow down or even fail. You can use the no version of these commands to stop a chargen attack:

```
Lab_B(config)#no service tcp-small-servers
Lab_B(config)#no service udp-small-servers
```

Finger is a utility program designed to allow users of Unix hosts on the Internet to get information about each other:

```
Lab_B(config)#no service finger
```

This matters because the finger command can be used to find information about all users on the network and/or the router. It's also why you should disable it. The finger command is the remote equivalent to issuing the show users command on the router.

Here are the TCP small services:

**Echo**   Echoes back whatever you type. Type the command *telnet x.x.x.x echo ?* to see the options.

**Chargen**   Generates a stream of ASCII data. Type the command *telnet x.x.x.x chargen ?* to see the options.

**Discard**   Throws away whatever you type. Type the command *telnet x.x.x.x discard ?* to see the options.

**Daytime**   Returns the system date and time, if correct. It is correct if you are running NTP or have set the date and time manually from the EXEC level. Type the command *telnet x.x.x.x daytime ?* to see the options.

The UDP small services are as follows:

**Echo**   Echoes the payload of the datagram you send.

**Discard**   Silently pitches the datagram you send.

**Chargen**   Pitches the datagram you send and responds with a 72-character string of ASCII characters terminated with a CR+LF.

# Turning off BootP and Auto-Config

Again, by default, the Cisco router also offers BootP service as well as remote auto-configuration. To disable these functions on your Cisco router, use the following commands:

```
Lab_B(config)#no ip boot server
Lab_B(config)#no service config
```

# Disabling the HTTP Interface

The `ip http server` command may be useful for configuring and monitoring the router, but the cleartext nature of HTTP can obviously be a security risk. To disable the HTTP process on your router, use the following command:

```
Lab_B(config)#no ip http server
```

To enable an HTTP server on a router for AAA, use the global configuration command `ip http server`.

# Disabling IP Source Routing

The IP header source-route option allows the source IP host to set a packet's route through the IP network. With IP source routing enabled, packets containing the source-route option are forwarded to the router addresses specified in the header. Use the following command to disable any processing of packets with source-routing header options:

```
Lab_B(config)#no ip source-route
```

# Disabling Proxy ARP

Proxy ARP is the technique in which one host—usually a router—answers ARP requests intended for another machine. By "faking" its identity, the router accepts responsibility for getting those packets to the "real" destination. Proxy ARP can help machines on a subnet reach remote subnets without configuring routing or a default gateway. The following command disables proxy ARP:

```
Lab_B(config)#interface fa0/0
Lab_B(config-if)#no ip proxy-arp
```

Apply this command to all your router's LAN interfaces.

# Disabling Redirect Messages

ICMP redirect messages are used by routers to notify hosts on the data link that a better route is available for a particular destination. To disable the redirect messages so bad people can't draw out your network topology with this information, use the following command:

```
Lab_B(config)#interface s0/0
Lab_B(config-if)#no ip redirects
```

Apply this command to all your router's interfaces. However, just understand that if this is configured, legitimate user traffic may end up taking a suboptimal route. Use caution when disabling this command.

# Disabling the Generation of ICMP Unreachable Messages

The no ip unreachables command prevents the perimeter router from divulging topology information by telling external hosts which subnets are not configured. This command is used on a router's interface that is connected to an outside network:

```
Lab_B(config)#interface s0/0
Lab_B(config-if)#no ip unreachables
```

Again, apply this to all the interfaces of your router that connect to the outside world.

# Disabling Multicast Route Caching

The multicast route cache lists multicast routing cache entries. These packets can be read, and so they create a security problem. To disable the multicast route caching, use the following command:

```
Lab_B(config)#interface s0/0
Lab_B(config-if)#no ip mroute-cache
```

Apply this command to all the interfaces of the router. However, use caution when disabling this command because it may slow legitimate multicast traffic.

# Disabling the Maintenance Operation Protocol (MOP)

The Maintenance Operation Protocol (MOP) works at the Data Link and Network layers in the DECnet protocol suite and is used for utility services like uploading and downloading system software, remote testing, and problem diagnosis. So, who uses DECnet? Anyone with their hands up? I didn't think so. To disable this service, use the following command:

```
Lab_B(config)#interface s0/0
Lab_B(config-if)#no mop enabled
```

Apply this command to all the interfaces of the router.

# Turning Off the X.25 PAD Service

Packet assembler/disassembler (PAD) connects asynchronous devices like terminals and computers to public/private X.25 networks. Since every computer in the world is pretty much IP savvy, and X.25 has gone the way of the dodo bird, there is no reason to leave this service running. Use the following command to disable the PAD service:

```
Lab_B(config)#no service pad
```

# Enabling the Nagle TCP Congestion Algorithm

The Nagle TCP congestion algorithm is useful for small packet congestion, but if you're using a higher setting than the default MTU of 1,500 bytes, it can create an above-average traffic load. To enable this service, use the following command:

```
Lab_B(config)#service nagle
```

It is important to understand that the Nagle congestion service can break X Window connections to an X server, so don't use it if you're using X Window.

# Logging Every Event

Used as a syslog server, the Cisco ACS server can log events for you to verify. Use the logging trap debugging or logging trap *level* command and the logging *ip_address* command to turn this feature on:

```
Lab_B(config)#logging trap debugging
Lab_B(config)#logging 192.168.254.251
Lab_B(config)#exit
```

```
Lab_B#sh logging
Syslog logging: enabled (0 messages dropped, 0 flushes, 0 overruns)
    Console logging: level debugging, 15 messages logged
    Monitor logging: level debugging, 0 messages logged
    Buffer logging: disabled
    Trap logging: level debugging, 19 message lines logged
        Logging to 192.168.254.251, 1 message lines logged
```

The show logging command provides you with statistics of the logging configuration on the router.

# Disabling Cisco Discovery Protocol

Cisco Discovery Protocol (CDP) does just that—it's a Cisco proprietary protocol that discovers directly connected Cisco devices on the network. But because it's a Data Link layer protocol, it can't find Cisco devices on the other side of a router. Plus, by default, Cisco switches don't forward CDP packets, so you can't see Cisco devices attached to any other port on a switch.

When you are bringing up your network for the first time, CDP can be a really helpful protocol for verifying it. But since you're going to be thorough and document your network, you don't need the CDP after that. And because CDP does discover Cisco routers and switches on your network, you should disable it. You do that in global configuration mode, which turns off CDP completely for your router or switch:

```
Lab_B(config)#no cdp run
```

Or, you can turn off CDP on each individual interface using the following command:

```
Lab_B(config-if)#no cdp enable
```

# Disabling the Default Forwarded UDP Protocols

When you use the ip helper-address command as follows on an interface, your router will forward UDP broadcasts to the listed server or servers:

```
Lab_B(config)#interface f0/0
Lab_B(config-if)#ip helper-address 192.168.254.251
```

You would generally use the ip helper-address command when you want to forward DHCP client requests to a DHCP server. The problem is that not only does this forward port 67 (BootP server request), it forwards seven other ports by default as well. To disable the unused ports, use the following commands:

```
Lab_B(config)#no ip forward-protocol udp 69
Lab_B(config)#no ip forward-protocol udp 53
Lab_B(config)#no ip forward-protocol udp 37
Lab_B(config)#no ip forward-protocol udp 137
Lab_B(config)#no ip forward-protocol udp 138
Lab_B(config)#no ip forward-protocol udp 68
Lab_B(config)#no ip forward-protocol udp 49
```

Now, only the BOOTP server request (67) will be forwarded to the DHCP server. If you want to forward a certain port—say, TACACS+, for example—use the following command:

```
Lab_B(config)#ip forward-protocol udp 49
```

# Cisco's *Auto Secure*

Okay, so ACLs seem like a lot of work and so does turning off all those services I just discussed. But you do want to secure your router with ACLs, especially on your interface connected to the Internet. However, you are just not sure what the best approach should be, or maybe you just don't want to miss happy hour with your buddies because you're creating ACLs and turning off default services all night long.

Either way, Cisco has a solution that is a good start, and it's darn easy to implement. The command is called auto secure, and you just run it from privileged mode as shown:

```
R1#auto secure
              --- AutoSecure Configuration ---


*** AutoSecure configuration enhances the security of
the router, but it will not make it absolutely resistant
to all security attacks ***


AutoSecure will modify the configuration of your device.
All configuration changes will be shown. For a detailed
explanation of how the configuration changes enhance
security and any possible side effects, please refer to Cisco.com
for Autosecure documentation.
At any prompt you may enter '?' for help.
Use ctrl-c to abort this session at any prompt.
```

```
Gathering information about the router for AutoSecure
Is this router connected to internet? [no]: yes
Enter the number of interfaces facing the internet [1]: [enter]
Interface              IP-Address      OK? Method Status                  Protocol
FastEthernet0/0        10.10.10.1      YES NVRAM  up                      up
Serial0/0              1.1.1.1         YES NVRAM  down                    down
FastEthernet0/1        unassigned      YES NVRAM  administratively down   down
Serial0/1              unassigned      YES NVRAM  administratively down   down
Enter the interface name that is facing the internet: serial0/0


Securing Management plane services...


Disabling service finger
Disabling service pad
Disabling udp & tcp small servers
Enabling service password encryption
Enabling service tcp-keepalives-in
Enabling service tcp-keepalives-out
Disabling the cdp protocol


Disabling the bootp server
Disabling the http server
Disabling the finger service
Disabling source routing
Disabling gratuitous arp


Here is a sample Security Banner to be shown
at every access to device. Modify it to suit your
enterprise requirements.


Authorized Access only
  This system is the property of So-&-So-Enterprise.
  UNAUTHORIZED ACCESS TO THIS DEVICE IS PROHIBITED.
  You must have explicit permission to access this
  device. All activities performed on this device
  are logged. Any violations of access policy will result
  in disciplinary action.
```

```
Enter the security banner {Put the banner between
k and k, where k is any character}:
#
If you are not part of the www.globalnettc.com domain, disconnect now!
#
Enable secret is either not configured or
 is the same as enable password
Enter the new enable secret: [password not shown]
% Password too short - must be at least 6 characters. Password configuration
failed
Enter the new enable secret: [password not shown]
Confirm the enable secret : [password not shown]
Enter the new enable password: [password not shown]
Confirm the enable password: [password not shown]
Configuration of local user database
Enter the username: Todd
Enter the password: [password not shown]
Confirm the password: [password not shown]
Configuring AAA local authentication
Configuring Console, Aux and VTY lines for
local authentication, exec-timeout, and transport
Securing device against Login Attacks
Configure the following parameters
Blocking Period when Login Attack detected: ?
% A decimal number between 1 and 32767.
Blocking Period when Login Attack detected: 100
Maximum Login failures with the device: 5
Maximum time period for crossing the failed login attempts: 10
Configure SSH server? [yes]: [enter to take default of yes]
Enter the domain-name: lammle.com
Configuring interface specific AutoSecure services
Disabling the following ip services on all interfaces:


 no ip redirects
 no ip proxy-arp
 no ip unreachables
 no ip directed-broadcast
 no ip mask-reply
Disabling mop on Ethernet interfaces
```

```
Securing Forwarding plane services...


Enabling CEF (This might impact the memory requirements for your platform)
Enabling unicast rpf on all interfaces connected
to internet


Configure CBAC Firewall feature? [yes/no]:
Configure CBAC Firewall feature? [yes/no]: no
Tcp intercept feature is used prevent tcp syn attack
on the servers in the network. Create autosec_tcp_intercept_list
to form the list of servers to which the tcp traffic is to
be observed


Enable tcp intercept feature? [yes/no]: yes
```

And that's it—all the services I mentioned earlier are disabled, plus some! By saving the configuration that the auto secure command created, you can then take a look at your running-config to see your new configuration. It's a long one!

Although it is tempting to run out to happy hour right now, you still need to verify your security and add your internal access-list configurations to your intranet.

# Appendix D

# About the Additional Study Tools

## IN THIS APPENDIX:

✓ Additional study tools

✓ System requirements

✓ Using the study tools

✓ Troubleshooting

# Additional Study Tools

The following sections are arranged by category and summarize the software and other goodies you'll find on the book's companion website. If you need help with installing the items, refer to the installation instructions in the section, "Using the Study Tools" later in this appendix.

 The additional study tools can be found at www.sybex.com/go/ccentsg. Here, you will get instructions on how to download the files to your hard drive. Bonus lab material is available from the author at www.lammle.com/forum.

## Test Engine

The files contain a test engine, which includes the Assessment Test, all of the chapter review questions located in the book, and bonus exams.

## Electronic Flashcards

These handy electronic flashcards are just what they sound like. One side contains a question, and the other side shows the answer.

## Videos

Author Todd Lammle has provided approximately 60 minutes of companion videos to walk through some of the more difficult concepts of the book.

## Network Simulator

Readers can get access to the LammleSim IOS Version simulator, which can be used to perform all of the hands-on labs in the book.

## PDF of Glossary of Terms

We have included an electronic version of the glossary in PDF format. You can view the electronic version of the glossary with Adobe Reader.

# System Requirements

Make sure your computer meets the minimum system requirements shown in the following list. If your computer doesn't match up to most of these requirements, you may have problems using the software and files. For the latest and greatest information, please refer to the ReadMe file located in the downloads.

- A PC running Windows XP or newer
- An Internet connection

# Using the Study Tools

To install the items, follow these steps:

1. Download the Zip file to your hard drive, and unzip to an appropriate location. Instructions on where to download this file can be found here: www.sybex.com/go/ccentsg.

2. Click the Start.exe file to open up the study tools file.

3. Read the license agreement, and then click the Accept button if you want to use the study tools.

The main interface appears. The interface allows you to access the content with just one or two clicks.

Check back to www.sybex.com/go/ccentsg regularly to find updates to the study tools. Also, bonus lab material is available from the author's website. Information on how to obtain this information can be found at www.lammle.com/forum.

# Troubleshooting

Wiley has attempted to provide programs that work on most computers with the minimum system requirements. Alas, your computer may differ, and some programs may not work properly for some reason.

The two likeliest problems are that you don't have enough memory (RAM) for the programs you want to use or you have other programs running that are affecting installation or running of a program. If you get an error message such as "Not enough memory" or "Setup cannot continue," try one or more of the following suggestions and then try using the software again:

**Turn off any antivirus software running on your computer.** Installation programs sometimes mimic virus activity and may make your computer incorrectly believe that it's being infected by a virus.

**Close all running programs.** The more programs you have running, the less memory is available to other programs. Installation programs typically update files and programs, so if you keep other programs running, installation may not work properly.

**Have your local computer store add more RAM to your computer.** This is, admittedly, a drastic and somewhat expensive step. However, adding more memory can really help the speed of your computer and allow more programs to run at the same time.

## Customer Care

If you have trouble with the book's companion study tools, please call the Wiley Product Technical Support phone number at (800) 762-2974, or contact them at http://sybex.custhelp.com/.

# Index

**Note to the reader:** Throughout this index boldfaced page numbers indicate primary discussions of a topic. Italicized page numbers indicate illustrations.

# S

## T

# W

# X

# Y